Popes, Monks and Crusaders

Popes, Monks and Crusaders

H.E.J. COWDREY

THE HAMBLEDON PRESS

Published by The Hambledon Press
35 Gloucester Avenue, London NW1 7AX
1984

ISBN 0 907628 34 6

History Series Volume 27

British Library Cataloguing in Publication Data

Cowdrey, H. E. J.
    Popes, monks and crusaders. — (History series; 27)
    1. Church history — primitive and early church,
    ca. 30-600   2. Church history — Middle Ages,
    600-1500
    I. Title II. Series
    270 BR160

Printed and bound in Great Britain by
Robert Hartnoll Ltd., Bodmin, Cornwall

This book contains 368 pages.

CONTENTS

ACKNOWLEDGEMENTS

The articles collected here were originally published in the following places and are reprinted by the kind permission of the original publishers.

I   *The Journal of Theological Studies*, XX (1969).

II   *Studia Patristica*, XI (1972).

III   *Journal of Religious History*, XI (1981).

IV   *History*, LI (1966).

V   *Transactions of the Royal Historical Society*,
            5th Series, 18 (1968).

VI   *The English Historical Review*, LXXXIII (1968).

VII   *Past and Present*, 46 (1970). World Copyright:
            The Past and Present Society, Corpus Christi College,
            Oxford, England.

VIII   *Viator*, 12 (1981).

IX   *Studi Gregoriani*, IX (1972).

X   *Outremer: Studies in the History of the Crusading
            Kingdom of Jerusalem Presented to Joshua Prawer*
            (Jerusalem, 1982).

XI   *The Journal of Theological Studies*, XXIV (1973).

XII   *The English Historical Review*, XCII (1977).

XIII   *The Holy War*, ed. Thomas Patrick Murphy
            (Columbus, Ohio, 1976).

XIV   *The International History Review*, I (1979).

XV   *Revue Bénédictine*, LXXXIII (1973).

XVI   *History*, LV (1970).

XVII   *History*, LVII (1972).

XVIII   *Bulletin of the Institute of Historical Research*,
            LIV (1981).

PREFACE

Such unity as these studies may possess comes from my principal concern as an historian, which is with the reform movements in the Western Church during the later eleventh century and with such developments as the First Crusade that resulted from them and especially from the revival of the papacy itself. More specifically they are by-products of my study and teaching of the three popes, Gregory VII, Victor III, and Urban II, who reigned between 1073 and 1099, of the two great monastic centres of Cluny and Montecassino, and of the emergence of the Crusading movement. All these subjects must be studied against the background of the society and politics of the transition from Marc Bloch's first to his second feudal age. They also lead the historian back to times like the later Roman Empire and the Carolingian Age, of which eleventh-century figures were keenly if not always authentically aware. But an historian's concern is not to be defined only, or principally, in terms of periods and topics. At a deeper level it arises from preoccupations that are personal to himself. Three things above all have fascinated me, in particular, during my working career. First, there is the spectacle of power — how men gain, use, and forfeit it, and what impact it has upon them and those whom they influence. The second is the springs of conflict within and between human societies, and especially the encounter of and interaction between contrasting cultures. And thirdly, there is the investigation of human beings at every social level as they explore the limits of human aspiration as they are set at any given time. Few periods of human history offer more than does the late eleventh century to anyone with such fascinations, and few offer more by way of insight into the human condition which is also a legitimate quest for an historian. These studies, *quantulacumque*, owe any significance that they may have to these underlying concerns.

When I wrote Chapter XII, I was unaware of G. Scalia's excellent study 'Il carme pisano sull'impresa contro i Saraceni del 1087', in *Studi di filologia romanza offerti a Silvio Pellegrino* (Padua, 1971), 565-625. I approached the *Carmen* from a very different angle, and in particular was concerned with its relation to the First Crusade.

Among many debts I acknowledge two with especial gratitude. The first is to the learned but anonymous readers who commented upon many of these studies for the journals or other places of their first publication, often to my great benefit. Secondly I am most obliged to Mr. Martin Sheppard for his kindness in publishing this book and for his helpful and genial advice at every stage.

St. Edmund Hall   H.E.J.C.
Oxford

I

THE DISSEMINATION OF ST. AUGUSTINE'S DOCTRINE OF HOLY ORDERS DURING THE LATE PATRISTIC AGE

IN his anti-Donatist writings, Augustine argued with force and clarity against the contention that, whereas a baptism which was duly conferred outside the Church held good if the recipient were reconciled to it, an ordination which was so conferred was null and void, and must be repeated before a clerk might administer the sacraments in the Church. Augustine insisted that, in the case of holy orders no less than of baptism, the unworthiness of the minister in no way detracted from the validity of the sacraments. It made no difference to this validity whether the unworthiness were that of a sinful minister who acted within the Church, or that of a schismatic who was separated from it. The sacraments were the same, wherever they were. As Augustine himself made these points,

. . . nulla ostenditur causa, cur ille, qui ipsum baptismum amittere non potest, ius dandi possit amittere. Utrumque enim sacramentum est et quadam consecratione utrumque homini datur, illud, cum baptizatur, istud, cum ordinatur, ideoque in catholica utrumque non licet iterari. Nam si quando ex ipsa parte venientes etiam praepositi bono pacis correcto schismatis errore suscepti sunt, etiamsi visum est opus esse ut eadem officia gererent quae gerebant, non sunt rursus ordinati, sed sicut baptismus in eis ita ordinatio mansit integra, quia in praecisione fuerat vitium quod unitatis pace correctum est, non in sacramentis, quae ubicumque sunt ipsa sunt.[1]

During the twelfth and thirteenth centuries, the doctrine of holy orders which Augustine expressed in such passages as this, became firmly accepted as the foundation of western thought and practice. But the seven centuries which intervened saw a long history of reordinations, and an underlying uncertainty about the validity of sacraments, and especially of ordinations, that were administered outside the Church.[2] Even Gratian, in his *Decretum* (*c.* 1140–1), took account of a current thesis, that 'potestas dandi baptismum et ius consecrandi dominicum

---

[1] *Contra epistolam Parmeniani*, ii. 13. 28, ed. M. Petschenig, *Corpus scriptorum ecclesiasticorum Latinorum* (= *C.S.E.L.*), li. 79.

[2] For comprehensive studies, see L. Saltet, *Les Réordinations: Étude sur le sacrement de l'ordre* (Paris, 1907) (= Saltet); É. Amann, 'Réordinations', *Dictionnaire de théologie catholique*, xiii (Paris, 1936), cols. 2385–431; A. Schebler, *Die Reordinationen in der 'altkatholischen' Kirche* (Bonn, 1936) (= Schebler).

corpus et largiendi sacros ordines plurimum inter se differunt.'[1] This thesis directly contradicted the principle upon which Augustine expressly based his teaching that they were altogether similar. The centuries-long delay before the west fully understood and appropriated Augustine's teaching, and the frequent occurrence of ecclesiastical dealings which were incompatible with it, create a presumption that, during the later Patristic age, his arguments and conclusions did not become firmly embedded in the dogmatic and canonical outlook of the west. It is the purpose of this study to suggest that this was, in fact, the case. On the one hand, Augustine did not present his teaching about holy orders in such a way that it commanded lasting attention either inside or outside Africa. On the other hand, the two centuries after he wrote his anti-Donatist works were marked by the setting, in the Latin west, of numerous precedents, which caused the practice of the early Middle Ages to run contrary to his teaching.

I. THE TEACHING OF ST. AUGUSTINE

That Augustine's teaching about holy orders should not have found speedy acceptance in the west was partly owing to its own characteristics, as they were determined by its context in African thought and Church history. It was also prevented from attracting notice by the remarkably inconspicuous way in which Augustine himself presented it within the whole *corpus* of his works.

So far as its context in African thought is concerned, it is, indeed, true that as regards the validity of sacraments that were administered outside the Church, Augustine stands in sharp enough contrast to his great predecessor in treating of the Church and sacraments, Cyprian (Bishop of Carthage, 249–57). Cyprian allowed to such sacraments none of the recognition that Augustine was to accord them. He taught that Christ gave the sacraments to the Church, which was alone the vehicle upon earth of the Holy Spirit. Whoever abandoned the Church, or was abandoned by it, wholly lacked the Spirit and had no part in the dispensation of God's grace. All the sacraments, including baptism, that he seemed to administer were utterly empty. They were nothing more than counterfeits. Those who, having received them, later entered the Church, must be treated as if they had never been conferred.[2] On this point, Augustine's difference from Cyprian was certainly complete.

---

[1] *Decretum*, secunda pars, c.i., q.i, c. 97, *Corpus iuris canonici*, ed. A. Friedberg, i (Leipzig, 1879), p. 395.

[2] For a summary of Cyprian's teaching see, e.g., J. H. Bernard, 'The Cyprianic Doctrine of the Ministry', in *Essays on the Early History of the Church and Ministry*, ed. H. B. Swete (2nd edn., London, 1921), pp. 215–62.

Yet if Augustine's full teaching about the Church and sacraments, of which it was no more than a detail, be considered as part of the development of African doctrine, he introduced into it no radically new pattern of thought concerning these wider matters. What he taught was not a contradiction of Cyprian's position, so much as a decisive stage in its gradual revision. In his doctrine of the Church, in particular, Augustine owed a large debt to Cyprian; and his characteristic differences from him regarding the sacraments were already foreshadowed by earlier African writers in the Donatist controversy. Cyprian, as it is important to remember, not only left a doctrinal legacy to the Donatists, who, for the most part, hardened his position; but also to their Catholic opponents, who, in accepting it, sought to temper its rigour. The Catholics were prompted to temper it, partly by western councils which, following the prevailing European outlook, legislated in a sense contrary to Cyprian regarding baptism;[1] and partly by the writings of two Africans, one of whom was himself a Donatist, although not a typical one. These two Africans in general thought with Cyprian; but they also sought to provide a dogmatic justification for such departures from him as were made in practice; and so they pointed the way to Augustine.

The earlier of them, Optatus, Bishop of Milev, in his *Contra Parmenianum Donatistam* (366/7), anticipated him by asserting that the sacraments were holy in themselves, not through those who administered them. The human ministers of the sacraments were the agents who brought them to others, not the masters to whom they belonged.[2] Optatus wrote about the sacraments as if in general; but he applied his principles only to baptism: he contended that Catholic and Donatist baptisms were equally valid; but he drew no parallel between baptism and holy orders. However, he made a clear dogmatic advance upon the strict Cyprianic position, that all sacraments dispensed outside the Church were, of necessity, utterly null. Soon afterwards, Tyconius, a Donatist whose powers of mind so greatly impressed Augustine,[3] seems to have argued in a similar way. So far as his thought can be recovered, he distinguished, as did Optatus before and Augustine after, between the moral quality of a minister and the acts that he performed in the name and power of God. He allowed that, within the Church, unworthy ministers could confer not only baptisms, but also holy orders.[4] He also

---

[1] e.g. Arles (314). For western views at the time of Cyprian, see Saltet, pp. 18–34; Schebler, pp. 25–36.

[2] 'Videatis omnes, qui baptizant, operarios esse, non dominos, et sacramenta per se esse sancta, non per homines': v. 4, ed. C. Ziwsa, *C.S.E.L.* xxvi. 127.

[3] *Contra epist. Parm.* i. 1. L, *C.S.E.L.* li. 19.

[4] See *Beati in Apocalypsin libri duodecim*, ed. H. A. Sanders (Rome, 1930),

recognized as valid the baptisms of heretics outside the Church; but he stopped short of Augustine by expressing no opinion about their orders.[1]

It was this line of argument, opened up by Optatus and Tyconius in their revision of Cyprian, that Augustine developed with greater insight and power, but with relatively little change of substance. He did not so far move out of line with the existing thought and practice of Africa and Europe as to throw down a radical challenge to them. As the foundation of his thought, he continued Cyprian's teaching about the Church as the exclusive vehicle of the Holy Spirit. But he also took account of later modifications of it. His achievement was to sum up and to build upon the experience of Churchmen since Cyprian's day with fidelity to the past, and yet with an underlying fullness of dogmatic outlook that was altogether his own.

Regarded in the context of African thought, Augustine's general teaching about the sacraments, like his teaching about the Church, was not novel. As the only part of it which was, in substance, strikingly new, his teaching about holy orders was most inconspicuously presented and very incompletely argued. Discussion of it was restricted to a very few passages in his anti-Donatist writings.[2] Even in them, Augustine followed the accepted form of current debate by establishing all possible substantive points with reference primarily to baptism, not to holy orders themselves.[3]

Thus, if their contents be analysed, Augustine insisted in general terms, no less than did Cyprian and the Donatists, that the ministers of Christ should be men of personal holiness. But the holiness of the

---

pp. 25, 336–7, 492. Tyconius wrote *c.* 380, and his teachings were extensively preserved by the late eighth-century Spanish monk, Beatus of Liebana.

[1] Ibid. pp. 67–8.

[2] Augustine's most extensive treatment of holy orders is *Contra epist. Parm.* ii. 13. 28–14. 32, *C.S.E.L.* li. 79–86, written *c.* 400. See also *De baptismo* i. 1. 2, *C.S.E.L.* li. 146, written 400–1; *Epistolae*, lxi. 2, ed. A. Goldbacher, *C.S.E.L.* xxxiv. 223–4, xciii. 11. 46, 488–9; *Ep.* clxxxv. 44–6, ed. Goldbacher, *C.S.E.L.* lvii. 38–40; *Sermo ad Caesareensis ecclesiae plebem*, ii, J. P. Migne, *Patrologia Latina* (= *P.L.*) xliii. 691–2. Some anti-Donatist writings of Augustine are known to have been lost. His teaching is particularly well discussed by F. Hofmann, *Der Kirchenbegriff des hl. Augustins* (Munich, 1933), and N. M. Haring, 'St. Augustine's Use of the Word *Character*', *Mediaeval Studies*, xiv (1952), pp. 79–97.

[3] C. H. Turner well observed that 'the sacrament of Baptism was still, at the beginning of the fifth century as much as in the middle of the third, the pivot of African controversy. Holy Orders hardly come into the immediate purview of St. Augustine more directly than into that of St. Cyprian': 'Apostolic Succession', in *Essays on the Early History of the Church and Ministry*, p. 181. Augustine himself habitually referred to ordination as 'ius dandi [baptismum]', and did not discuss it under its more general aspects.

Church did not depend, as it was the Donatist error to make it depend, upon the lives of holy men. Holiness was the mark of the whole communion of saints gathered about Jesus Christ, the great high priest and the one mediator, who was its sole source. If the holiness of human lives was entirely derived from Christ's holiness, so was that of the sacraments. The holiest of ministers could add nothing to them by virtue of his holiness; but, equally, a wicked minister could take nothing away from them by reason of his sins. Augustine applied this principle without hesitation to schismatic ministers who acted outside the Church, as well as to wicked ones who acted within it. In either case, the fault was, at root, the same: it was a want of charity, of which the unworthy minister inside the Church gave evidence by his sinfulness; and the schismatic outside it by his departure from the unity of the Spirit and the bond of peace. The sacraments, as the work of Christ, were never touched by the uncharity of the minister. Thus, for example, a baptism outside the Church was a baptism into Christ, not into, say, Donatus; it held good when hands of reconciliation were laid upon a returning schismatic.

In all this, Augustine spoke with baptism primarily in view; and the validity of schismatic baptisms had for long been allowed in Europe, and increasingly in Africa. So far as the more controversial matter of ordination outside the Church was concerned, he was content to assume that there was a parity of argument with baptism. He nowhere sought to prove the soundness of his assumption. All that he did was to take the novel step of casting the burden of proof upon those who would deny it. It was enough that baptism and orders were sacraments; both were conferred by a consecration; therefore, neither of them might be repeated. As there was no question of rebaptizing a lay convert from schism, so there was none of reordaining a clerk. In either case, one thing was necessary—the conferring of the Holy Spirit by the laying on of hands in reconciliation. As Augustine elsewhere made the point, outside the Church, a man might validly receive the *sacramentum*: the external ministerial act that God's work in Christ guaranteed; only inside it could he have the *res* (*effectus, virtus*) *sacramenti*: the spiritual benefit that accrued when the recipient was received into the unity of the Church.[1]

The distinction was Augustine's own; but it safeguarded the generally held belief, which Cyprian had so strongly insisted upon, that the Holy Spirit was exclusively given in the Catholic Church. It is a further reminder of how limited was Augustine's divergence from the line of

[1] e.g. *Tractatus in Johannem*, xxvi. 11, ed. R. Willems, *Corpus Christianorum*, xxxvi. 265.

earlier African writers, beginning with Cyprian, in his general doctrine of the Church and sacraments. His writings were most likely to attract notice in the many aspects of them that tended to confirm current thought and practice. The few, briefly expressed and inconspicuous elements of novelty that they embodied, such as the teaching about holy orders, were only likely to be taken up if and when there was currently an active discussion of some special need that served to focus attention on them.

Even in Africa, there is no evidence to suggest that the practical importance of Augustine's discussion of holy orders was more than transient. For a short time it was, indeed, considerable; for, when Augustine returned to Africa, the Catholic offer to the Donatists of *receptio cum ordinibus*, which had first been made under Constantine,[1] quickly became a very live issue. The *Contra epistolam Parmeniani*, in which Augustine's principal discussion of holy orders appeared, was written *c*. 400. Parmenian had died some ten years earlier, and the Donatist Church had since found no comparable figure to succeed him as its leader. On the Catholic side, however, Aurelius (*c*. 391–*c*. 427) had emerged as an active occupant of the see of Carthage. In 391, Augustine was himself ordained presbyter at Hippo; henceforth, together with Aurelius, he took a vigorous lead in Church affairs. In particular, he took part in the councils that met frequently after 393. One of their preoccupations was with the problem of whether the shortage of Catholic clergy might be made good by admitting converted Donatist priests to their ranks. The legislative work of these councils has been preserved in the *Codex canonum ecclesiae Africanae*,[2] of which canon 68, associated with the council of Carthage (401), dealt with the reconciliation of Donatist clergy. In this canon, the greatest care was taken to show deference to those Catholics, particularly at Milan and Rome (*in transmarinis partibus*), who held that former Donatist clergy should never be allowed to officiate in the Catholic Church. But it left a loophole for them to do so,[3] and a number of Donatist clergy were thereafter admitted to the exercise of their orders in the African Church.[4]

[1] See e.g. W. H. C. Frend, *The Donatist Church* (Oxford, 1952), pp. 148–9.

[2] See especially F. L. Cross, 'History and Fiction in the African Canons', *J.T.S.*, N.S. xii (1961), pp. 227–47.

[3] 'Non eis obsit quod contra honores eorum, quamvis salus nulla interclusa sit, in transmarino consilio statutum est; id est, ut ordinati in parte Donati, si ad catholicam correcti transire voluerint, non suscipiantur in honoribus suis secundum transmarinum consilium: sed exceptis his, per quos catholicae unitati consulitur': *apud* Dionysius Exiguus, *Codex canonum ecclesiasticorum, P.L.* lxvii. 204, cf. *P.L.* xi. 1197–9.

[4] See Frend, *The Donatist Church*, p. 252.

It was to assist this result that Augustine put forward his doctrine of holy orders; and it helped to resolve a current and local problem. But, in the long run, it was not decisive for events, even in Africa. On the contrary, the Vandal invasion seems to have put a complete stop to its influence. For when, a little more than a century later, in 535, a council met at Carthage to consider what should be done about Arian clergy who had been ordained during the intervening period of Vandal domination, the question was discussed as though Augustine had never written about holy orders. The Africans vied with the Romans in their rigour towards the Arians. Neither group of Catholics showed any trace of Augustine's generous desire for comprehension or of his dogmatic approach when he had dealt with the question of Donatist orders.[1]

Nor does Augustine's doctrine of orders seem to have made headway outside Africa. There is remarkably little evidence for the circulation in the west of the anti-Donatist writings in which the brief discussions of it are contained, and the topic was not referred to in current compendia of his teaching.[2] In the matter of holy orders as in wider respects, Augustine stood alone in achieving a synthesis of the spiritual and the institutional aspects of the Church, which was uniquely informed by his own generous vision of the grace of God at work. Alike in his arguing forcibly for the admission of convert clerks to the exercise of their orders, in his seeking to justify their admission upon the basis of assumptions of a dogmatic character, and in his willingness to go to the limit in relaxing the requirements of the Church's discipline,[3] Augustine stood apart from the generality of Latin Churchmen, in Europe as in Africa. The normal western outlook was determined by other, and often contrary, considerations.

II. SOME HINDRANCES TO THE SPREAD OF ST. AUGUSTINE'S TEACHING

Quite apart from the fact that the character and presentation of Augustine's teaching about holy orders rendered it unlikely to find a wide, clear, and permanent hearing, a number of formidable hindrances to the reception of such teaching by the western Church in general

[1] See below, pp. 468–9. Augustine had never expressly considered any ordinations save those of the Donatists.

[2] See the evidence given in H. E. J. Cowdrey, 'Pope Anastasius II and St. Augustine's Doctrine of Holy Orders', to be published in the *Proceedings of the Fifth International Conference on Patristic Studies, Oxford, 1967*. For a longer-term view, see N. M. Haring, 'The Augustinian axiom: *Nulli sacramenti iniuria facienda est*', *Mediaeval Studies*, xvi (1954), pp. 89–90. *See below*, Chapter II.

[3] *Ep.* clxxxv, see above.

were presented by the Church's own discipline and dogmatic pre-suppositions. Four of these hindrances which were of especial importance may next be considered.

(i) *The discipline of the penitential system*

When he pleaded, on grounds of dogma and charity, for a readiness to admit converted Donatist clergy to the exercise of their orders in the Church, Augustine knew that to do so would involve a relaxation of the rigour of Church discipline;[1] and, in 401, the Council of Carthage recognized that its rulings diverged from what was customary 'in trans-marinis partibus'. At Rome, the disabilities that were imposed upon schismatics or heretics who came into the Church, were such as by themselves to rule out, in all normal circumstances, the admission of convert clergy to the exercise of holy orders. The very fact of having belonged to a sect deserved penance, and to have done penance was in itself a bar to the clerical office. Clerks who had been ordained outside the Church might have only lay status within it; laymen who came into the Church might not thereafter be ordained. Hence, the specifically dogmatic issues that attended reordination remained insufficiently clarified throughout the later Patristic age, because the discipline of the Church normally precluded them from arising.[2]

No one stated the position regarding clergy who were ordained outside the Church more clearly and more rigorously than did Augustine's contemporary, Pope Innocent I (402–17). In 414, he prohibited the accession to the Catholic clergy of certain Illyrian clerks who had been ordained outside the Church by the heretical Bonosus of Naissus. He argued that men who were ordained by heretics had, as it were, sustained a head wound by the laying on of their hands. The wound required medicine for its healing. Even when health was restored, a scar was left, which lastingly marred the cleanness that was requisite in those who held office in the Church.[3] Wherever the remedy of penance had

---

[1] Ibid.

[2] The disciplinary rule was at least as old as Cyprian: *Ep.* lxxii. 2, ed. W. Hartel, *C.S.E.L.* iii, pt. 2, p. 777; cf. Turner, in *Early History of the Church and Ministry*, pp. 162–4. There is a history of exceptions to the rule, extending back to Cyprian's day; but in no case does the issue of reordinations seem to have arisen.

[3] 'Ventum est igitur ad tertiam quaestionem . . .: cum nos dicamus, ab haereticis ordinatos, vulneratum per illam manus impositionem habere caput. Et ubi vulnus infixum est, medicina adhibenda est, ut possit recipere sanitatem. Quae sanitas post vulnus secuta, sine cicatrice esse non poterit: atque ubi poenitentiae remedium necessarium est, illic ordinationis honorem locum habere non posse. Nam si, ut legitur, quod tetigerit immundus, immundum erit: quomodo id ei tribuetur, quod munditia ac puritas consuevit accipere?' *Ep.* xvii. 7, *P.L.* xx. 530.

once been called for, there was, according to the logic of this argument, no possibility of admittance to sacred functions, whether by way of reordination or not.

With the course of time, the rapid expansion of the Church promoted an increasing relaxation of the penitential rules. But, particularly in the second half of the fifth century, Innocent's thesis continued to provide the popes with a powerful line of argument against the organized Christological heretics of the east. For example, in 490, Pope Felix III (483–92) wrote of the Monophysite Bishop Peter Mongus of Alexandria, in respect of his possible reconciliation to the Church, that 'si de legitima fuisset curatione sanatus, ad indulgentiam suscipi deberet, non ad sacerdotii dignitatem: qui a damnatis atque haereticis institutus, catholicis plebibus nulla posset ratione praeponi'.[1] Roman thought was dominated by a sense of the canonical impropriety of the setting in authority over Catholic peoples of anyone who had been ordained by heretics; and, during the later Patristic age, it never overcame it.

The tendency of the western penitential system, and of the canonical criteria that were associated with it, was thus to keep in the background the kind of dogmatic issues that, in his dealings with the Donatists, Augustine openly and clearly faced. Only in the most exceptional circumstances could they arise, or could there be even the possibility that a solution might be sought upon such lines as he proposed.

(ii) *The western tendency to distinguish between baptism and other sacraments*

When Augustine considered the problem of holy orders, he had in mind the doctrinally orthodox Donatists. In so far as Latin Christians had earlier moved towards a similar position with regard to baptism, they, too, had not done so with grave doctrinal heretics in mind.[2] When, however, they came face-to-face with Arians[3] and other major heretics, they tended, in dealing with their sacraments, to take a line that differed from Augustine's in a highly significant way. They were never able to take the crucial step of drawing a parallel between baptism

---

[1] *Ep.* 14. 3, *Epistolae Romanorum pontificum genuinae*, ed. A. Thiel, i (Braunsberg, 1868) (= Thiel), 268. For reiterations of this principle, see *Epp.* 1. 9, p. 228; 2. 4, p. 235; 8. 2–3, p. 248; 9, p. 250; 15. 3, p. 272; 17. 2, p. 276; also Gelasius I, *Ep.* 1. 5–9, pp. 289–92.

[2] Thus, in Cyprian's time, Pope Stephen I had accepted baptisms which were performed outside the Catholic Church: see, e.g., the discussion in Saltet, pp. 18–21.

[3] i.e. with the Arians in organized communities. In the different circumstances of Milan, Ambrose accepted the ordinations of his Arian predecessor Auxentius: *The Sixth Book of the Select Letters of Severus, Patriarch of Antioch*, ed. E. W. Brooks, ii, pt. 2 (London, 1904), p. 304.

and holy orders; rather, so far as sacraments outside the Church were concerned, they distinguished between the sacraments which did and did not depend for their validity upon the conferring of the Holy Spirit. This was a consequence of the general opinion, which the west always fully shared with Cyprian, that the Holy Spirit could only be given within the Catholic Church. By the fifth century, western Church-men accepted the validity of baptisms which were conferred outside the Church for the special reason that the heretics, as well as the Catho-lics, baptized in the name of the Holy Trinity; they had no doubt that to rebaptize would be an intolerable denial of its power.[1] But they saw no such clear criterion of validity in the case of the other sacraments, which were, therefore, unlike baptism: the salient point about them was the negative one, that, outside the Church, they did not confer the gift of the Holy Spirit. This gift came only with the reconciliation of the baptized person to the Church. Its medium was a laying on of hands, which was not, as a rule, distinguished from confirmation. So far as holy orders were concerned, a parity of argument with confirmation on *a fortiori* grounds was inevitable: if the Holy Spirit could not be given outside the Church in the sacrament of confirmation, how much more could he not be given in the sacrament of holy orders?[2] Following this line of thought, it was conceivable that a reordination might take place, but not a rebaptism; since baptism was, and ordination was not, con-ferred in the name of the Trinity.[3]

Once more, the letters of Pope Innocent I well illustrate the point. In 414, he wrote to Bishop Alexander of Antioch about the sacraments of the Arians of his city, whom Alexander proposed to admit to the exercise of their orders in the Church. Innocent readily conceded that their baptism was valid (*ratum*); their laity might, therefore, be received by way of penance and the laying on of hands. But their orders gave rise to the gravest doubts: if the sect of the Arians lacked the Holy Spirit, how, Innocent asked, could their profane priests possibly be worthy (*dignos*) of the offices of God?[4] In the case of the Arians, Innocent

[1] For a statement of this view, which was for long of the greatest importance in the west see, e.g., Gennadius, *Liber ecclesiasticarum dogmatum*, xxi, ed. C. H. Turner, *J.T.S.* vii (1905–6), pp. 93–4. This fifth-century tract was commonly ascribed, in the Middle Ages, to Augustine, an ascription which itself illustrates how far the west was from appreciating the true character of Augustine's teaching.

[2] See the discussion of this point by Turner, in *Early History of the Church and Ministry*, pp. 164–9.

[3] Augustine himself spoke of the especial power of the Name in baptism, but drew no conclusions from it regarding the other sacraments: cf. G. W. H. Lampe, *The Seal of the Spirit* (London, 1951), p. 288.

[4] *Ep.* xxiv. 4, *P.L.* xx. 549–51. The adjective *dignos* is significant, for Innocent

envisaged no such self-evident comparability of holy orders with
baptism, as Augustine had been content to assume in his anti-Donatist
writings; instead, he did not even present a clear and confident formu-
lation of the issue.

The difference between Augustine's position and the general western
point of view was the more marked, because, while it was common
ground that the Holy Spirit was only given in the Church, the laying
on of hands, by means of which heretics and schismatics were reconciled to the Church, was differently understood. For Augustine, such
a reconciliation was something quite distinct from confirmation: its
essence was the saying of prayer over a person, and it could be repeated.[1]
Western sources of the fifth and sixth centuries were unaware of such
a distinction; they equated the laying on of hands upon heretics with
the confirmation of Catholics.[2] Augustine had an unusually generous
room for manœuvre when he assimilated ordination outside the Church
to baptism; for his laying on of hands could be deemed to quicken with
the gift of the Holy Spirit any of the sacraments which had been conferred outside the Church. The greater rigidity of the western outlook
made it hard for it to borrow his ideas, or to develop its own practice
in a comparable way to that which he recommended. In this particular
as more generally, the west had its own dogmatic presuppositions about
the sacraments, which were not easily compatible with Augustine's.

(iii) *Western deference to conciliar rulings*

A further hindrance to the possible spread of Augustine's teaching
about holy orders was presented by the prestige with which fifth- and
sixth-century churchmen invested the rulings of ecclesiastical councils,
and especially those of Nicaea (325). Where councils had spoken in
matters of dogma and discipline, they were to be followed; where they
were silent, matters were liable to remain in doubt. This was not least
true of the attitude of the popes. Those who, like Felix III and Gelasius I
(492–6), were the most concerned to assert their authority, were also the
most insistent that this authority should be guided by conciliar decisions. As they saw it, it was a principal function of the Apostolic See

appears, in effect, to have changed the character of his argument; whereas he
began with dogmatic principles, he concluded by making a disciplinary suggestion. Having made the traditional points, with which Augustine would have
agreed, that Arian clergy could not confer the 'plenitudo Spiritus' either in
baptism or in ordination, he then failed to argue, as Augustine would have
argued, that there was a parallel between them. Instead, he took refuge in the
disciplinary rule, that clerks should not be admitted to the *honores* of the Church.

[1] *De baptismo*, iii. 16. 21, *C.S.E.L.* li. 212–13; v. 23. 33, *C.S.E.L.* li. 289–90.
[2] See Saltet, pp. 22–8.

to be the *executrix* of the great councils.[1] The popes must uphold not only their dogmatic statements but also their canons; and the scope of their own activity was in no small measure determined by what the councils had laid down.

In the matter of ordinations, conciliar rulings were fragmentary, haphazard, and ambiguous. Regarding the orders of Arians, Nestorians, and Eutychians, the Councils of Nicaea, Ephesus and Chalcedon had said nothing. The canons of Nicaea, however, did offer some guidance in the case of the Novatianists and the Paulianists.[2] Of the latter, who were followers of Paul of Samosata, it said that all converts to the Catholic Church must be rebaptized. This was tantamount to treating them as converts from paganism; therefore, if they were of blameless life, they might be ordained after their Catholic baptism.[3] The ruling about the Novatianists was wholly ambiguous, and its proper interpretation was no clearer in the later Patristic age than it has been to modern scholars. Baptism was not mentioned; but, so far as clerks were concerned, the canon provided that, after hands had been laid on them, they might remain among the clergy. The significance of this laying on of hands is wholly uncertain. It may have been in reconciliation. If so, Novatianist orders were recognized, and the effect of the canon was to permit the waiving, in their case, of the disciplinary rule debarring those who had done penance from joining the Catholic clergy. Alternatively, the laying on of hands may have been an ordination;

---

[1] e.g. Felix III, *Ep.* 17. 2, Thiel, p. 275; Gelasius I, *Ep.* 26. 9, Thiel, p. 405, cf. p. 418. Pope Pelagius I thought similarly of his obligation to the Council of Constantinople (553): *Ep.* 19, *Pelagii I papae epistulae quae supersunt* (556–561), ed. P. M. Gassó and C. M. Batlle (Montserrat, 1956) (= Gassó and Batlle), pp. 55–61; *Ep.* 59. 7–9, pp. 157–8.

[2] The Council of Nicaea also considered the orders of the Meletians; but, because their schism was merely a local one in Egypt, no reference was made to them in the canons. From the Council's letter to the Church of Alexandria, preserved in Socrates, *Historia ecclesiastica*, i. 9, ed. W. Bright (Oxford, 1878), p. 20, it is known that the Meletian bishops were allowed to keep their orders in the Church if they were "μυστικωτέρᾳ χειροτονίᾳ βεβαιωθέντας". This would seem to have required their reordination by a Catholic rite. The ruling, however, had no influence in the west until Carolingian times; then, Hincmar of Rheims invoked it, apparently in support of reordination: Schebler, pp. 183–4.

[3] Canon xix, J. D. Mansi, *Conciliorum nova et amplissima collectio* (= Mansi), ii. 676–7. The Paulianists were Trinitarian heretics. Their baptisms were condemned because, although they used a verbally correct formula, they did not believe rightly about it: Athanasius, *Oratio II contra Arianos*, 43, J. P. Migne, *Patrologia Graeca* (= *P.G.*) xxvi. 237. The erroneous view was later current in the west, that it was because their formula was itself incorrect: Augustine, *De haeresibus*, xliv, *P.L.* xlii. 34; Innocent I, *Ep.* xvii. 10, *P.L.* xx. 533.

this would imply that Novatianist orders were deemed to be null and void, and that reordination was requisite. What matters in the present context is that the canonists of the west for long often took the canon in the latter sense, as enjoining reordination.[1]

Thus, in the precedents set by the councils, the west lacked sufficient guidance. So far as it went, such guidance as there was appeared to point to, rather than to prohibit, reordination; it, therefore, ran counter to the direction of Augustine's thought.

(iv) *The increasing concern of the west with jurisdiction*

A further hindrance to the spread of Augustinian ideas was the ever-increasing tendency, in the western Church, to speak of the Church and its ministry, far more systematically than Augustine ever did, in categories drawn from the secular order. The dignities, constitution, and jurisdiction of the Church were expressed in a symbolism, vocabulary, and conceptual framework which were derived from it.[2] For example, the ministerial hierarchy was commonly, and increasingly, spoken of as a structure of *honores*.[3] The term *honor* was used of an ecclesiastical office in its totality, as something which was one and indivisible.[4] In the context of the increasing presumption that ordinations which were conferred outside the Church were void because they did not confer the Holy Spirit, it reinforced the tendency to take an all-or-nothing view of holy orders. If they were void, they were so absolutely, with no such qualification as Augustine made between the *sacramentum* and the *res sacramenti*. Thus, for example, Pope Innocent I's rulings about Bishop Bonosus of Naissus expressed the view that, if a bishop lost the *honor* of the episcopate, nothing whatsoever was left to him that he might exercise himself or transmit to others.[5]

---

[1] Canon viii, Mansi, ii. 672. For the later interpretation of the canon, see Turner, in *Early History of the Church and Ministry*, pp. 176–7, 208–10; Schebler, pp. 47–51. It is significant that, in Turner's note on the Latin versions of the Nicene canons (p. 209), the African text, against all others, renders "χειροθετουμένους αὐτοὺς μένειν οὕτως ἐν τῷ κλήρῳ" 'inpositis manibus reconciliationis': this tends to confirm that there was a difference between African and other western approaches.

[2] There was, in fact, an interchange between Church and Empire in these matters over many centuries. For a general discussion, see P. E. Schramm, 'Sacerdotium und Regnum im Austausch ihrer Vorrechte', *Studi Gregoriani*, ed. G. B. Borino, ii (Rome, 1947), pp. 403–57, esp. 407–11.

[3] The usage was beginning as early as Tertullian, *De exhortatione castitatis*, 7, ed. A. Kroymann, *C.S.E.L.* lxx. 138.

[4] Augustine himself used the term *honor* in discussing holy orders, but infrequently.

[5] 'Sed e contra asseritur, eum qui honorem amisit, honorem dare non posse:

While Latin writers were using the term *honor* in this way, they were also beginning to borrow and to use of the sacraments the terms *ratus* and *irritus*. As Innocent I's letter to Alexander of Antioch about Arian sacraments makes clear, *ratus* might be used to express the validity that Arian baptisms certainly had, because they were conferred in the name of the Trinity; by contrast with other sacraments, in which it did not seem possible to place a similar confidence.[1] As such terminology became current, it helped to harden, both in language and in substance, the condemnation of sacraments administered outside the Church, which the popes, in particular, felt increasingly called upon to make.

This usage had its complement in a wider tendency to regard the problems that arose in connection with the Church and sacraments from the point of view of the canonist and the legislator, rather than of the theologian, and to think about them upon a model drawn from the political order of society. This tendency gained impetus in the aftermath of the Council of Chalcedon (451). This aftermath raised, in a clear and acute form, the problems concerning the competing jurisdictions of pope and emperor, which were to remain critical for European history into the high Middle Ages,[2] and which led to the two jurisdictions being increasingly discussed in common terms. The letters of Pope Leo I (440–61) well illustrate the genesis of the two considerations about the rival jurisdictions which were to underlie papal pronouncements and policies in the late fifth century, and which coloured the contemporary attitude to the problem of holy orders. On the one hand, jurisdiction in the Church had its source in St. Peter and his vicar, not in the emperor: thus, Leo rebutted the Emperor Leo I's suggestion that another council might be held to supplement the work of Chalcedon; he insisted that it was the prerogative of the Apostolic See to defend the conciliar decrees.[3] Yet, on the other hand, he also proclaimed

nec illum aliquid accepisse, quia nihil in dante erat, quod ille posset accipere. Acquiescimus, et verum est. Certe quia quod non habuit dare non potuit, damnationem utique quam habuit, per pravam manus impositionem dedit: et qui comparticeps factus est damnationis, quomodo debeat honorem accipere, invenire non possum.' *Ep.* xvii. 7, *P.L.* xx. 530–1.

[1] See above, p. 457, n. 4. For Augustine's similar use of *ratus* in connection with baptism, see *De bapt.* v. 21. 29, *C.S.E.L.* li. 287; *Contra litteras Petiliani*, iii. 32. 37, ed. M. Petschenig, *C.S.E.L.* lii. 192; *Contra Cresconium*, iii. 12. 15, *C.S.E.L.* lii. 422.

[2] See especially A. Michel, 'Der Kampf um das politische oder petrinische Prinzip der Kirchenführung', in *Das Konzil von Chalkedon, Geschichte und Gegenwart*, ed. A. Grillmeier and H. Bacht, ii (Würzburg, 1953) (= Grillmeier–Bacht), pp. 491–562, and *Die Kaisermacht in der Ostkirche (843–1204)* (Darmstadt, 1959).

[3] *Epp.* clvi. 1–2, *P.L.* liv. 1127–9; clvii. 3, *P.L.* liv. 1133; clxii. 1, *P.L.* liv. 1143–4.

that, together with the pope, the emperor had a special responsibility for the orthodox faith and good order of the Church: he was the custodian in all the world of the peace established by Chalcedon, and he should actively bring to bear his own authority and jurisdiction to curb its adversaries.[1] Leo's letters indicate a delicate balance of papal and imperial authority, which might easily become distorted or upset. It was quickly subjected to a prolonged and searching test.

After 457, the victory at Alexandria of Timothy Aelurus led to the establishment there of an organized Monophysite Church. The popes not only themselves condemned it, but they also appealed to the emperors to exercise their jurisdiction in defence of the Chalcedonian faith.[2] They especially sought their collaboration to dispose of Timothy Aelurus and his successor, Peter Mongus, and those who supposed themselves to have been ordained by them. In 477, Pope Simplicius (468–83) enlisted the aid of the Emperor Zeno (474–91);[3] the early letters of his successor, Felix III, provide striking evidence of how Zeno had then responded by, amongst other things, using his own imperial jurisdiction to declare null and void (*irritas*) the ordinations of the Alexandrian Monophysites.[4]

Such events, and Felix's letters about them, show how fully the question of holy orders was now being dealt with in terms of office and jurisdiction; and how far, therefore, the west was moving from the dogmatic approach of Augustine. The question of orders was becoming part of the wider issue of papal as against imperial prerogatives. Zeno's annulling of Alexandrian sacraments by imperial fiat demonstrates how far Leo's delicate balance between these prerogatives was being upset. A speedy disenchantment with Zeno after the publication of his *Henoticon* (482) led Popes Felix and Gelasius I to restore and confirm Leo's position, by asserting that St. Peter's jurisdiction, not the emperor's, was properly the deciding factor in Church affairs.[5] The

[1] *Epp.* cxlviii, *P.L.* liv. 1117–18; clvi. 3, *P.L.* liv. 1129–30; clxiv. 1, *P.L.* liv. 1148–9.

[2] For an account of events, see that by G. Bardy in P. de Labriolle, G. Bardy, L. Brehier, and G. de Plinval, *De la mort de Théodose à l'élection de Grégoire le Grand* (Paris, 1948), pp. 271–97. [3] *Ep.* 7. 3, Thiel, pp. 190–1.

[4] 'Simul etiam, quibus Petri, quem illicite se Alexandrinae ecclesiae iniecisse perhibuit, ac Timothei haeretici iam defuncti ordinationes vel ea, quae de secreto per domos dicebatur actitare, [Zeno] cassavit': *Ep.* 2. 4, Thiel, pp. 234–5; again, 'Petrum conversatum cum haereticis et parricidae illi Timotheo cohaerentem, a profanis, quia nec ab aliis talis fieri poterat, Alexandrinae ecclesiae episcopum, quantum sibi existimaverat, ordinatum, acceptissima Deo praeceptione [Zeno] deiecerat . . . Haec [i.e. the imperial *auctoritas*] deinde illicitas ordinationes eius vel Timothei, utpote haereticorum, irritas fecit, atque eos, quantum extra ecclesiam fuerint, iudicavit': *Ep.* 4. 1, Thiel, pp. 240–1.

[5] Felix III, *Ep.* 8. 5, Thiel, pp. 249–50.

condemnation of Peter Mongus was still upheld, but by papal authority.[1]
Gelasius, in particular, insisted that it was the prerogative of popes,
rather than emperors, to deal with the problems of heresy in all their
aspects.[2]

The question of holy orders and their validity was thus made part
and parcel of controversies of a political and legal character about who
exercised ultimate jurisdiction over the Church; and discussion of it took
place in the appropriate categories. It was not, and did not become, a
matter which fifth-century writers primarily expressed in dogmatic terms.
In the copious papal literature that directly or indirectly related to it, the
problem of heretical orders became more and more an aspect of the controversy about the respective jurisdictions of *sacerdotium* and *regnum*. This
controversy became the overmastering concern of the later fifth-century
popes. It provided a most unfertile soil for the principles of dogma, rather
than of jurisdiction, that Augustine had propounded for settling the
problem of holy orders which were conferred outside the Church.

III. THE PAPACY AND THE VALIDITY OF ORDERS

In the light of these serious hindrances that were presented to the
dissemination of Augustine's doctrine of holy orders, the question may
well be asked whether Saltet was, indeed, justified in claiming that, after
Augustine's lifetime, the western Church really thought as he had
thought in the matter of holy orders.[3] Indeed, it becomes reasonable to
ask whether Augustine's distinctive arguments did, in fact, enter into
circulation at all; and, if so, how fully they were apprehended. They
were, after all, not so presented as to render it likely that they would
command a hearing to the north of the Mediterranean; and they did
not provide a natural solution to current problems as churchmen there
saw them. It is, therefore, worth looking again at the attitude of the
papacy to the orders of the principal fifth- and sixth-century heretical
and schismatic groups, to examine how far Augustine's doctrine was,
in fact, known and followed; and what kind of precedents the popes of
these crucial centuries handed down to the later canonical tradition of
the western Church.

[1] Felix III, *Ep.* 9, Thiel, p. 250.
[2] e.g. *Epp.* 1. 10, Thiel, pp. 292–3; 12. 2–3, pp. 350–2; *Tractatus*, ii. 8,
p. 528; iv. 11–3, pp. 567–70.
[3] 'L'Église romaine pensait comme saint Augustin. Au v{e} siècle, sa doctrine,
sur cette question, se trouve exprimée dans des textes qui ne présentent aucune
réelle difficulté. Mais, par un fâcheux concours de circonstances, ils ont été
mal compris dans la suite': Saltet, p. 68, cf. p. 59; see Turner's doubts about
this judgement in *Early History of the Church and Ministry*, p. 174, n. 2; cf.
pp. 145–6.

(i) *The Bonosan heresy*

The otherwise obscure Bonosan heresy is of cardinal importance as providing evidence for the attitude of Pope Innocent I, and as having occasioned the text which, above all others, determined the early medieval outlook.[1] During the last decade of the fourth century, Bonosus, Bishop of Naissus in Illyria, became notorious as the head of an organized sect, in which he propagated teachings which certainly included a denial of the perpetual virginity of the Mother of Christ and an assertion that she bore other sons than Jesus.[2] Proceedings against him began at the Council of Capua (391),[3] which was unable to reach agreement about his heresy. It set up a commission of bishops, under Bishop Anysius of Thessalonica, to investigate further. There is no direct evidence about their findings. But it is clear from Innocent's letters that they condemned and deposed Bonosus and proscribed his heresy; and that, both before and after Bonosus was condemned, he carried out ordinations. It was with the problems which these two groups of ordinations presented that Innocent was especially concerned.

His concern was the more active because Illyria had lately become a papal vicariate.[4] Western discipline impinged upon a region whose outlook was differently formed, so that it had, perhaps, something in common with eastern points of view. In the east, the very fact of adhering to certain separatist groups which professed any of a wide range of false doctrines, was believed to result in the loss of the Holy Spirit; it was, therefore, often held that clerks ordained in heresy must be reordained when they were reconciled to the Church.[5] From the more legalistic viewpoint of Rome, Innocent, on the other hand, had no

[1] For fuller discussions of Bonosus, see Saltet, pp. 68–70; Schebler, pp. 79–92; G. Bardy, 'Bonosus', *Dictionnaire d'histoire et de géographie ecclésiastiques*, ix (Paris, 1937), 1096–7.

[2] See the proceedings of the Council of Capua: Mansi, iii. 685.

[3] Ibid. The Council also issued a firm prohibition of re-baptisms, re-ordinations, and the translation of bishops. It is not clear from which point of view reordinations were forbidden—whether of dogma or of discipline. In favour of the former, it may be said that the canon seems to draw a parallel between baptism and ordination; and that Ambrose, who accepted Arian clergy at Milan without reordaining them, was familiar with the proceedings of the Council: *Ep.* lvi, *P.L.* xvi. 1170–2. Yet the difficulties of this interpretation are formidable. It is doubtful whether one council could have quickly and decisively settled so open a question as the dogmatic issue of reordinations; and, if a settlement were attempted, it could hardly have failed either to generate controversy or to serve as a precedent later on. It did neither of these things. The prohibition was almost certainly disciplinary. See Schebler's discussion, pp. 36–7.

[4] See J.-R. Palanque, G. Bardy, and P. de Labriolle, *De la paix constantinienne à la mort de Théodose* (Paris, 1947), p. 244.

[5] See Saltet, pp. 39–58; Schebler, pp. 38–41.

doubt that, unless and until Bonosus had been formally condemned by the due exercise of ecclesiastical jurisdiction, the ordinations that he performed were valid. In a letter which has been lost, he affirmed that clerks whom Bonosus had ordained before he was condemned but who had abandoned his heresy, might be admitted to the exercise of their orders in the Church.[1] The Illyrians were reluctant to do as Innocent directed. Marcian, the orthodox Bishop of Naissus, and others would only so far obey as to let Bonosan clergy keep their churches; unless they were reordained, they would not enter into communion with them. So, in 409, Innocent sent a further letter, in which he repeated that clerks whom Bonosus had ordained while he was uncondemned should be received into the Catholic Church and allowed to minister in it without their being reordained.[2]

By the time of Innocent's next letter, written in 414, the graver question had also arisen of the second category of Bonosan clerks: those whom Bonosus had ordained after the episcopal condemnation of his heresy. Innocent was compelled to indicate his attitude to reordinations of such clerks, in both their disciplinary and their dogmatic aspects. From the disciplinary angle of a Roman churchman, the position was clear, and Innocent stated it uncompromisingly at the beginning and at the end of his discussion. Bonosus' condemnation had put him and his associates in heresy outside the Catholic Church. It rendered clerks whom he later ordained, and who returned to the Church, liable to a penance that for ever disqualified them from the exercise of holy orders.[3] On the dogmatic issue, he was no less forthright. He set forth plainly the case that, at about the same time, he advanced more tentatively with regard to the Arians of Antioch. Those who were ordained by heretics received nothing from them, because their ordainers had nothing that they might give. The Bonosans had lost the gift of the Holy Spirit; what they had lost, they could not give; therefore, their orders were absolutely void.[4] So far as dogmatic considerations went, Innocent

---

[1] See *Ep.* xvi, *P.L.* xx. 519.

[2] *Ep.* xvi, *P.L.* xx. 519–21. In this letter, Innocent seems to have been troubled, not only because a clerk of Bonosus' party, named Rusticius, had been reordained priest; but because he had used his reordination as a means of avoiding penance for grave sin: 'Et non levi impedimento fit, dum aut illi dolent, huiusmodi hominem in ecclesia retineri, aut ille sic peccari in alios arbitretur, quemadmodum in se agnoscit esse peccatum.' It is doubtful whether the 'peccatum' in this difficult sentence was the reordination itself: see O. Vighetti, 'I sacramenti della penitenza e dell'ordine nella dottrina di S. Innocenzo I', *Miscellanea Francescana*, lii (1952), pp. 104–12; cf. Saltet, p. 70. It is more likely to have been the kind of grave moral offence that is discussed by Innocent in *Ep.* xvii. 12, *P.L.* xx. 534–5; for there seems to be no other case of a reordination being described as a 'peccatum'.

[3] *Ep.* xvii. 8, 11, *P.L.* xx. 531, 533–4.　　　　[4] *Ep.* xvii. 7, *P.L.* xx. 530–1.

showed that, after the formal condemnation of the Bonosan heresy, he and the Illyrian bishops were at one in thinking that Bonosan clerks who returned to the Church were possible subjects for reordination.

However, he found further strong reasons for condemning the reordinations that had occurred in Illyria on grounds of discipline. He laid especial emphasis upon two things. First, he showed himself to have been particularly shocked by the remarkable contention of the Illyrians, that ordination was, as it were, a second baptism; so that, when the Bonosan clerks received the gift of the Holy Spirit in their reordination, the effect was, like that of baptism, to wipe out all past sins and to render penance otiose. Innocent would have nothing of what he regarded as an evasion of penitential discipline. He insisted upon the Roman rule, that heretical clergy might only be admitted to lay communion, and then by way of penance.[1]

Moreover, Anysius and his fellow bishops had always justified their sanctioning of the reordination of Bonosan clergy, by an appeal to the Nicene canon about the Novatianists.[2] They pleaded that they hoped thus to win clerks from the Bonosan party and to avoid scandal. Innocent tacitly accepted the Illyrians' reading of the Nicene canon as a sanction for reordination;[3] but he argued that it was an exceptional ruling. Normally, 'the old rules handed down from the apostles and from apostolic men' to the Roman Church must be observed;[4] there could be no general relaxation of the Church's discipline.[5] Innocent was above all else insistent upon this point: persons ordained, or even wishing to be ordained, by Bonosus after his condemnation deserved penance; as a consequence, they were eligible only for lay status in the Church.[6]

Thus, the events of the Catholic reaction against the Bonosan heresy in the vicariate of Illyria prompted Innocent to make it clear that he could, without dogmatic difficulty, envisage the possibility of reordination. His letters contain no suggestion that he knew of Augustine's teachings about holy orders, much less that he took serious account of

[1] *Ep.* xvii. 8, *P.L.* xx. 531. For a similar idea, that the profession (*ordinatio*) of a monk was a second baptism, cf. the canons of Theodore of Tarsus, 2. 3. 3, *Die Canones Theodori Cantuarensis und ihre Ueberlieferungsformen*, ed. P. W. Finsterwalder (Weimar, 1929), p. 315; where eastern influence is also likely.

[2] *Ep.* xvii. 9, *P.L.* 531–2.

[3] The Latin phrase used by the Illyrians was 'ordinati reciperentur'. This clearly referred to canon viii of Nicaea: ὥστε χειροθετουμένους αὐτοὺς μένειν οὕτως ἐν τῷ κλήρῳ. For its interpretation see Schebler, p. 85, n. 17; Turner, in *Early History of the Church and Ministry*, pp. 208–10.

[4] *Ep.* xvii. 8–9, *P.L.* xx. 531–2.   [5] *Ep.* xvii. 10, *P.L.* 532–3.

[6] *Ep.* xvii. 11, *P.L.* xx. 533–4.

them. They demonstrate very clearly how, in all ordinary circumstances, Roman insistence upon the rigour of the penitential system was such as to preclude the question of reordination from arising; on the rare occasions when it did arise, the doctrine that the Holy Spirit was not possessed or given outside the Church pointed to the nullity of holy orders which were conferred by formally condemned heretics.

To the early Middle Ages, Innocent's letter of 414 provided the most decisive of all warrants for the practice of reordination. Innocent's assessment of the nullity of Bonosus' ordinations after he was condemned had exceptionally widespread currency,[1] and the dominant line of interpretation was, quite justifiably, to understand it in a way that ran counter to Augustine's teaching with regard to the Donatists.[2]

(ii) *Arianism*

During Augustine's own lifetime, western opinion about Arian ordinations perceptibly hardened; and this tendency was maintained during the later Patristic age. The Trinitarian heresy of Arius had for long usually been regarded as the gravest of all the heresies. But three new factors now came in. First, the Arians suffered in western eyes because they were increasingly identified with the barbarian invaders of the Empire, and a political and racial grievance against them embittered the dogmatic issue. Secondly, the term 'Arian' became much less fluid in meaning than it had been, and was more rigorously applied to clearly Trinitarian heretics. Thirdly, during the fourth century, the west had not dealt with Arians who were organized in separate Churches apart from the Catholics; they had been mixed with them in the same community. Arian bishops ordained within the structure of the Catholic Church, and difficulties did not arise about the recognition of their orders.[3] Early in the fifth century, however, the problem arose of Arian bodies, which were formally organized over against the Church; it might well be that, because the Holy Spirit could not be conferred apart from the Church, the ordinations of such bodies were null and void. In this form, the problem of Arian orders was novel, and no clear guidance was to be had from Nicaea or elsewhere.[4] But the presumption was against their validity.

[1] In what became known as the Decretal *Ventum est*, i.e. the consecutive portions of *Ep.* xvii. 7, *P.L.* xx. 530–1, cited above, p. 455, n. 3 and p. 460, n. 5.   [2] See Schebler, pp. 90–1.

[3] Cf. Ambrose's attitude, above, p. 456, n. 3.

[4] I cannot follow Schebler when he holds that Pope Julius I (341–52) regarded Arian orders as null: p. 72. Schebler had in mind his condemnation of Pistus, whom the Arian Secundus intruded into the see of Alexandria during the exile of Athanasius, which is referred to by Athanasius, *Apologia contra*

Such was the purport of Pope Innocent I's letter of 414 to Bishop Alexander of Antioch.[1] Alexander proposed to admit the clergy of an organized Arian body to the exercise of their orders in the Catholic Church. He sought Innocent's approval, which the pope withheld. In justification, he appealed to the traditional dogmatic principle, that outside the Church there could be no gift of the Holy Spirit. When the Arian leaders cut themselves off from the Catholic faith, they lost the perfection of the Spirit, which they had received. Arian baptism was, indeed, still valid (*ratum*), since it was conferred in the name of the Trinity. However, Arian laity could only receive the gift of the Spirit when they were reconciled to the Church by the laying on of hands in penance. If heretics could not confer the Spirit in baptism, Innocent argued, it was surely the case that they could not do so in ordination.

A remarkable feature of Innocent's discussion is its tentative character, and especially the note of questioning upon which it ends. Earlier in his letter, Innocent said that he was 'pondering the authority of the Council of Nicaea, which showed the mind of all the bishops throughout the whole world'. Nicaea had not pronounced upon Arian sacraments, although the Council of Arles had said with authority that heretical baptisms were valid. Finding no clear fourth-century precedent, Innocent did not go so far as to say that Arian ordinations were null (*irritae*). He merely suggested that, as Arian laity were *imperfecti* because they lacked the Holy Spirit, so their priests were *profani*, or lacking in the gifts of the ministry. In this uncertainty of mind, then, Innocent once again gave no hint of an acquaintance with Augustine's doctrine of orders. He showed no awareness that any such exact parallel between baptism and orders might, perhaps, be drawn, as Augustine had propounded with dogmatic clarity and had persuaded the African Church to implement in the case of the Donatists.[2]

As time went on, the western attitude to Arian ordinations moved further away from an Augustinian standpoint, not nearer towards one. It is from Augustine's Africa that the next evidence comes, more than a century later. After the expulsion of the Vandals, the African bishops

Arianos, 19, 24–5, *P.G.* xxv, 280, 288–9. The terms used (κατάστασις, καθίστημι) suggest that the pope's objection was to the impropriety of intruding an Arian, because a man instituted by heretics ought not to rule over Catholic peoples. This need not have implied the nullity of his orders.

[1] *Ep.* xxiv. 4, *P.L.* xx. 549–51.

[2] Cf. Schebler's judicious comment: 'Seine Verordnung will keine dogmatische Entscheidung sein, sondern eine das praktische Verhalten ordnende Disziplinarmaßregel, die gewiß auf dogmatischem Fundament basiert, aber keineswegs beabsichtigt, eine bisher ungeklärte Frage authoritativ und endgültig zu entscheiden', p. 75.

met at Carthage in order to consider how they might sweep away the vestiges of their domination. The Vandals had been Arians. In 535 there took place an exchange of views about Arian ordinations between the bishops who assembled at Carthage and Pope Agapetus I. The bishops expressed their desire to restore the best custom of former times after a century of affliction. They said that their reading of the Nicene canons had led to a debate regarding how Arian priests should be received into the Church—whether in their orders, or merely to lay communion. They found themselves of one mind in their hostility to Arian orders, and they went so far as to deprecate the ordination of anyone whom the Arians had baptized. Agapetus entirely concurred in this opinion. He argued on grounds of discipline: he said that it was the traditional usage of his see that Arian clerks should not be allowed to exercise their orders in the Church. As so often in Roman decisions, the demand of the penitential system made irrelevant the kind of dogmatic issues that had exercised the mind of Augustine. But neither the pope nor the bishops showed any trace either of the generous desire for comprehension or of the distinctive dogmatic approach that Augustine had shown in his dealings with the Donatists.[1]

In the Africa of 535, the Arian Vandals and their native associates were, no doubt, an inconsiderable minority. The Arians of Spain and Gaul were not so easily to be brushed aside. Councils which were held there had to take a different line from that of Carthage, if only because of the larger Arian population. But in Europe as in Africa, there is no trace of the influence of Augustine's kind of argument. The reordination of Arian clergy appears to have become a widespread practice: Arians were not, as in Africa, excluded from the Catholic clergy altogether; but, in order to join it, they must be ordained anew by Catholic rites. Thus, when the victories of Clovis and the Catholic Franks were followed, in 511, by a Council at Orleans, it was laid down that, if heretical clerks of otherwise good character came into the Church, they were to be received with imposition of hands; while churches were to be reconsecrated according to the Catholic order.[2] That the imposition of hands was, indeed, ordination, and not simply reconciliation, was made clear in the reiteration of the rule by the Council of Saragossa (592). All Arian ordinations and consecrations of churches were deemed to be null; convert clergy were explicitly to be reordained by Catholic rites.[3]

Concerning Arian ordinations, then, western opinion in the later

[1] For the correspondence, see *Collectio Avellana*, 85–6, ed. O. Guenther, *C.S.E.L.* xxxv. 328–32.
[2] Canon x, Mansi, viii. 353.   [3] Canons i, iii, Mansi, x. 471–2.

Patristic age was consistently hostile. Sometimes the rules of the penitential system sufficed to exclude Arians from the Catholic clergy. If they did not, and dogmatic considerations arose, men harked back with renewed confidence to the old pre-Augustinian thesis that the Holy Spirit was only given in the Church and that the sacraments, other than baptism, were invalid when conferred outside it. When it was expedient to admit Arians to Catholic orders, the practice, so far as it emerges, was to reordain them. There is nothing to suggest that Augustine's arguments or conclusions were ever brought into the picture. So far as the early medieval future was concerned, Innocent I's letter to Alexander of Antioch, in particular, survived as yet another precedent which tended to retain the mind of the west in non-Augustinian ways of thought.

(iii) *Christological heresies of the later fifth century*

The most considerable body of evidence relating to the problem of holy orders in the later Patristic age emerges from the Christological disputes which followed the Council of Chalcedon.[1] These disputes were a principal concern of the popes during the second half of the fifth century.

The first pope to be involved was Leo I. He became preoccupied with events at Alexandria and with their repercussions at Constantinople, after the death, in 457, of the Emperor Marcian, under whose orthodox protection the Council of Chalcedon had been held. With the advent of his successor, Leo I (457–74), the Monophysites' hopes revived. Their leader at Alexandria, Timothy Aelurus, was ordained bishop; the Chalcedonian Patriarch, Proterius, was savagely murdered; and the other Chalcedonian bishops were driven out. Timothy Aelurus summoned a council which anathematized Pope Leo and Patriarch Anatolius of Constantinople. By reason of these events, the Alexandrian Church itself fell into heresy. At Constantinople, on the other hand, it was only a small but vocal band of individuals that echoed Timothy Aelurus, in opposition to the patriarch whom he had anathematized; they did so from within a Church which itself remained corporately orthodox.

---

[1] For fuller discussions, see especially E. Caspar, *Geschichte des Papsttums*, i (Tübingen, 1930), pp. 547–59; ii (Tübingen, 1933), pp. 15–88; E. Schwartz, *Publizistische Sammlungen zum Acacianischen Schisma* (Abh. d. Bayer. Akad. d. Wiss., phil.-hist. Abt., N.F. 10, Munich, 1934); Bardy, *De la mort de Théodose à l'élection de Grégoire le Grand*, pp. 271–307; J. Haller, *Das Papsttum. Idee und Wirklichkeit*, i (2nd edn., Darmstadt, 1950), pp. 196–236; and the essays by F. Hofmann, 'Der Kampf der Päpste um Konzil und Dogma von Chalkedon von Leo dem Grossen bis Hormisdas (451–519)', and R. Haacke, 'Die kaiserliche Politik in den Auseinandersetzung um Chalkedon (451–553)', Grillmeier–Bacht, pp. 13–177.

In his reaction to the crisis of 457, Pope Leo I took precise account of these contrasting situations. When he wrote to Patriarch Anatolius of Constantinople about a clerk of his Church who followed Timothy Aelurus, his argument was that it was vain to resist groups which, like the Alexandrians, were outside the Church, if such individuals as this clerk, who were inside it, could with impunity wound their fellow Christians.[1] But with regard to the Monophysites of Alexandria Leo took a similar view to that which Innocent I had taken of the Arians of Antioch, although a more forthright one. He elsewhere made it clear that he maintained the normal distinction between baptism and the other sacraments.[2] Writing to the Emperor Leo I, he stigmatized Timothy Aelurus and his followers as being disqualified by their heresy and by their violent ways from belonging to the priesthood and from bearing even the name of Christian.[3] Presumably making a tacit exception in favour of baptism, Leo declared that all the sacraments had withdrawn themselves from a Church which had been made captive by a band of robbers. Rhetorical though the letter was, Leo appears to have followed the familiar line, that the sacraments of gravely heretical sects, apart from baptism, were utterly null.[4] The argument was no less non-Augustinian, both in language and in substance, than the letters of Innocent I had been.[5]

Leo's assessment of the sacraments of the Alexandrian Monophysites was maintained by subsequent popes, who did this the more readily because of the eventual succession at Alexandria of rival Chalcedonian shadow-patriarchs in Timothy Salofaciolus (460–82) and John Talaia

---

[1] *Ep.* clv. 2, *P.L.* liv. 1126–7.   [2] *Ep.* clix. 7, *P.L.* liv. 1138–9.

[3] '. . . cum sive impietatem erroris aspicias, sive opus perpetrati furoris attendas, non solum ad sacerdotii honorem admitti nequeant, sed ab ipso Christiano nomine mereantur abscindi': *Ep.* clvi. 3, *P.L.* liv. 1130.

[4] 'Nonne perspicuum est, quibus pietas vestra succurrere, et quibus debeat obviare; ne Alexandrina ecclesia, quae semper fuit domus orationis, spelunca nunc sit latronum? Manifestum quippe est, per crudelissimam insanissimamque saevitiam, omne illic coelestium sacramentorum lumen exstinctum. Intercepta est sacrificii oblatio, defecit chrismatis sanctificatio, et parricidalibus manibus impiorum omnia se subtraxere mysteria': *Ep.* clvi. 5, *P.L.* liv. 1131. Cf. Turner, in *Early History of the Church and Ministry*, pp. 167–8.

[5] It is sometimes asserted that Leo I's letter of 446 to the bishops of Mauretania (*Ep.* xii. 6, *P.L.* liv. 662) embodied a conscious following of Augustine's doctrine of orders: see, e.g. J. Tixeront, *Histoire des dogmes* (8th edn., Paris, 1928), iii, p. 416. It approved the reception into full status in the Church of the Novatianist bishop of Salicene and his flock, and also of a Donatist bishop named Maximus. The problem with regard to the latter was not, however, his Donatism, but his episcopal ordination while he was a layman (*ex laico*). Leo gives no hint of a conscious following of Augustine, and this very fragmentary evidence cannot gainsay the clear conclusions which are to be drawn from his dealings with Alexandria.

(482–*c.* 95). Thus, Pope Simplicius maintained the nullity of Timothy Aelurus' sacraments.[1] In 477, when Peter Mongus succeeded at Alexandria, his complicity in Timothy Aelurus' deeds and his irregular ordination as bishop added new fuel to the fire of Roman condemnation of the organized heresy there.[2] It was then that Simplicius so remarkably called upon the Emperor Zeno to add his sentence to the pope's, in order that the nullity of Alexandrian ordinations might be placed beyond question.[3]

But then changing relations between the popes and the emperors altered matters. In the middle years of the fifth century, the invasion of Italy had disposed the popes to look deferentially to Constantinople. The stability of barbarian rule under Odoacer and Theodoric, however, left them, in the last quarter of the century, with a new freedom to advance the claim that papal authority was superior to imperial power. It was Zeno's intervention in eastern Church affairs that provoked such an advance, and pointed the way to the Gelasian thesis. In 482, in an endeavour to unite the Christians of the east whom Chalcedon had so bitterly divided, he published his *Henoticon*. Like Pope Leo I, the popes would countenance nothing that might be construed as a revision of Chalcedon; and Felix III, Gelasius I,[4] and Anastasius II (496–8) were all moved vigorously to champion papal prerogatives against imperial ones.

So far as holy orders are concerned, the popes maintained their existing position with regard to Alexandria, with some shift in the balance of their arguments. The dogmatic argument, that the sacraments, other than baptism, were not possessed by organized heretics outside the Church, fell from prominence. The popes preferred to insist upon the rights of John Talaia by propounding the disciplinary argument, that those ordained by heretics ought not to rule over Catholic peoples.[5] But no new point of view emerged. At no time did the popes give a hint that they thought about the sacraments of the Alexandrian Monophysites with Augustine's doctrine in mind.

---

[1] *Epp.* 3. 2–3, Thiel, pp. 180–1; 6. 4, pp. 188–9; 7. 2–3, pp. 190–1.

[2] Like Timothy Aelurus, Peter Mongus was ordained by fewer than the correct number of bishops. There were differing stories. One had it that Peter was ordained by only two bishops, his associates in false belief: Evagrius, *Ecclesiastical History*, iii. 20, ed. J. Bidez and L. Parmentier (London, 1898), p. 118. At Rome, it was thought that there was only one bishop: Felix III, *Ep.* 8. 3, Thiel, p. 248. But the real charge against Timothy and Peter alike was not the breach of the Nicene rule, but that their sacramental acts took place outside the Church and in organized schismatic opposition to it: e.g. Felix III, *Ep.* 4. 1, Thiel, pp. 240–1.   [3] See above, p. 462.

[4] Gelasius was for some years before he became pope the *dictator*, who composed his predecessor's letters.   [5] See the references above, p. 456, n. 1.

As regards Constantinople, there broke out, in 484, the Acacian
Schism, which henceforth occupied the centre of the stage, and which
lasted until 519. The popes saw it in terms which were broadly similar
to those of Pope Leo I's letter to Patriarch Anatolius.[1] It was more
grave, however, because of the breach of communion between Rome
and Constantinople, and because of the anathematization of Patriarch
Acacius himself, who had been Zeno's chief adviser in preparing the
Henoticon. But, as in the earlier instance, papal dealings were with an
individual partisan of heretics, in a Church whose collective orthodoxy
was not impugned. There was never at Constantinople, as there was
at Alexandria, a succession of rival patriarchs; and the orthodox of the
east did not sever communion with it. Acacius was the head of no
separatist group of heretics, organized outside the unity of the Church.
Thus, whereas the popes called into question Acacius' personal actions
and associations and condemned him in the severest terms, they had
no grounds for casting doubt upon his sacraments.[2]

They made this clear when individuals concerned in the Acacian
Schism sought reconciliation with Rome. The first case occurred in
490. Felix III ruled that those whom Acacius had ordained or baptized
might, if they were Catholic in belief, be received in full status.[3]
Gelasius I reiterated this ruling,[4] as did Anastasius II.[5] The last of
these popes also gave some statement of his reasons. He was insistent
that according to the custom of the Catholic Church, no one whom
Acacius had canonically baptized or ordained in any way shared his
penalty. When the sacraments were conferred by evil men, the grace
that they conveyed was in no way compromised.[6]

For the first time in the papal sources of the fifth century, Anastasius
undoubtedly here enunciated an Augustinian principle; and he turned
to Augustine for support.[7] He demonstrated beyond reasonable doubt
his reliance upon Augustine's discussion of holy orders in the second

[1] See above, p. 471.

[2] See Turner's remarks, *Early History of the Church and Ministry*, p. 175 and
notes. It is particularly significant that Gelasius I drew a distinction between
Acacius, as only the 'communicator' of Eutyches, and Peter Mongus, as his
'sectator', or separatist adherent: *Tractatus* ii. 5, Thiel, p. 526; cf. *Ep.* 3. 7–11,
pp. 316–18.   [3] *Ep.* 14. 5, Thiel, p. 269.

[4] *Ep.* 3. 6, Thiel, pp. 315–16.

[5] *Ep.* 1. 8–9, Thiel, pp. 620–3.

[6] 'Nam secundum ecclesiae catholicae consuetudinem . . . nullum de his,
vel quos baptizavit Acacius vel quos sacerdotes sive levitas secundum canones
ordinavit, ulla eos ex nomine Acacii portio laesionis attingat, quo forsitan per
iniquum tradita sacramenta gratia minus firma videatur': *Ep.* 1. 8–9, Thiel,
pp. 620–3.

[7] For a fuller discussion, and for references for the points made in this paragraph, see Cowdrey, cited above.

book of the *Contra epistolam Parmeniani*.[1] Yet, in doing so, he altogether avoided making use of or transmitting the really distinctive elements in Augustine's teaching. He cautiously drew upon his arguments only in so far as they related to the non-controversial case of baptism. He made no reference to Augustine's crucial insistence that there was a parity of argument between baptism and holy orders. In the circumstances of Acacius' case, it was not necessary for him to do so; for, as Anastasius saw Acacius' canonical position, it was that of a single sinful minister, led astray by his own pride, who acted within a Church that was corporately orthodox. He was not the head of an organized body outside the Church, like the Donatists or the Monophysites of Alexandria. Augustine's characteristic arguments did not, therefore, apply. It was thus a very much diluted Augustinianism that Anastasius expressed; and even it was not current at Rome for long. Anastasius' death heralded a reaction against his mild and relatively eirenic attitude towards Constantinople. His successors were not concerned to offer easy terms of reconciliation to its clergy, and an end was put to the kind of discussion that he had engaged in. With it, the appeal to Augustine, even in the limited form in which Anastasius made it, quickly lapsed.

This use of Augustine's doctrine of orders was thus much qualified and very short-lived, and was made by only one of the popes. The facts do not justify the supposition that it was well known to, and increasingly understood by, all of them. It was, so far as can be seen, never considered in relation to the organized heresy of Alexandria. With regard to Constantinople, it was only drawn upon in a situation which did not call for its full application, and then so incompletely and temporarily as to have had little, if any, result in reshaping the western outlook, at the time or later. Instead, papal dealings with the problems that Chalcedon left as its aftermath were recorded in a copious Latin literature, which pointed to the nullity of heretical ordinations, and which was widely drawn upon by the early medieval canonical tradition. It was invested with the authority of such popes as Leo I, Felix III, and Gelasius I; and it left the writings and the ideas of Augustine out of the picture, save in a case that was not strictly relevant.

(iv) *The schism of the Three Chapters*

It was part of the later fifth-century popes' achievement that, especially in their dealings during the Acacian Schism, they asserted the superiority of the papal authority to the imperial power; and that, as a rider, they vindicated a practice regarding holy orders, which made

[1] This is the last certain reference to the treatise until the early tenth century.

the conditions of their exercise a matter for ecclesiastical, not political, authority to determine. Despite the continuing priority of canonical considerations, the sixth century saw an attempt to express in dogmatic terms the conception of the Church and ministry to which this upholding of papal authority had given rise. Indecisive though it was in itself, the partial appeal that Anastasius II made to Augustine foreshadowed a desire by the papacy to look to the Latin Fathers for a dogmatic framework in which to set the current canonical view of the Church and its ministry. The sixth century saw an appeal to them which had no real parallel in the fifth. But it was not only, or even primarily, to Augustine that an appeal was made. Augustine himself had built upon the work of Cyprian; and, no doubt in view of his emphasis upon the prerogatives of the Apostolic See, it was to Cyprian that the sixth-century popes particularly turned.[1]

The growth of papal interest in Cyprian, and especially in the *De catholicae ecclesiae unitate*, is one of the most striking dogmatic developments of the century.[2] Such fifth-century popes as Innocent I, Leo I, and Gelasius I show little, if any, evidence of direct acquaintance with him. But Pelagius I (556–61), who wrote with some frequency in his letters about the doctrine of the Church, appealed to him as the source *par excellence* of teaching in face of schism. In spite of his regard for Augustine, it is more than doubtful whether Pelagius owed any debt to the *Contra epistolam Parmeniani*, or to any of Augustine's express discussions of holy orders. He seems to have been altogether unaware of any differences between the two Fathers in matters relating to the Church and ministry. He cited them as though they were in basic agreement; and it was Cyprian, rather than Augustine, whom he chiefly followed. He usually called upon Augustine only to confirm the views that he took from Cyprian.[3]

---

[1] Pelagius I, *Ep.* 24. 17, Gassó and Batlle, p. 77; cf. *Ep.* 39. 4, p. 112.

[2] This development was noticed by Schebler (esp. pp. 113–18), but he reacted too strongly against the thesis of R. Sohm, *Das altkatholische Kirchenrecht und das Dekret Gratians* (Leipzig, 1918) to give it sufficient recognition. For some comments on the post sixth-century reading of Cyprian, see P. R. L. Brown, 'Approaches to the Religious Crisis of the Third Century A.D.', *E.H.R.* lxxxiii (1968), pp. 556–8.

[3] Pelagius' debt to Cyprian and Augustine may be summarized as follows: He three times quoted or paraphrased Cyprian when discussing the Church, and proceeded to confirm or amplify his teaching by an appeal to Augustine. (i) *Ep.* 19. 5–18, Gassó and Batlle, pp. 56–9: Cyprian, *Ep.* lxxi, 3, *C.S.E.L.* iii, pt. 2, 773; Augustine, *De anima et eius origine*, iii. 15. 23, ed. C. F. Urba and J. Zycha, *C.S.E.L.* lx. 378, *Enarrationes in psalmis*, lxxii. 16, *P.L.* xxxvi. 758, *Retractationes*, prol., ed. P. Knoell, *C.S.E.L.* xxxvi. 7–8. (ii) *Ep.* 24. 17–18, p. 77: Cyprian, *De cath. eccl. unit.* 4, *C.S.E.L.* iii, pt. 1, 212–13, is paraphrased and supported by an unidentifiable quotation from Augustine. (iii) *Ep.* 35.

This renewed study of Cyprian was important for the sixth century,[1] and, indeed, for the early Middle Ages, because it ushered in a harder and more inflexible doctrine of the Church and sacraments than Augustine would have inspired; because it focused attention only upon such passages of Augustine as broadly confirmed the sixth-century reading of Cyprian; and because it, therefore, continued to obscure Augustine's distinctive contribution to the doctrine of holy orders. There was no question of old-fashioned Cyprianic ideas of the Church and ministry yielding ground before the inexorable advance of new Augustinian ones. The ideas of both Fathers were disseminated jointly, for they had much in common. But it was Cyprianic ideas, rather than Augustinian, that tended to control their common growth. If Cyprian was so modified as to allow for western developments since the Council of Arles, Augustine was so selectively read that his points of difference from Cyprian were little regarded.

The letters of Pelagius I, which most fully attest these developments, do so in connection with another crisis which followed in the aftermath of Chalcedon. In 544, the Emperor Justinian published his Edict in Three Chapters, in which he condemned certain tenets of the Antiochene school of Christology, as they had been expressed by Theodore of Mopsuestia, Theodoret of Cyrus, and Ibas of Edessa. Although Justinian protested that his edict in no way challenged the authority of Chalcedon, he excited western fears that his appeasement of the Monophysites was, in fact, placing it in jeopardy. In 553 he procured the succession to the papacy of Pelagius I, who, after some hesitation, had declared himself the emperor's supporter.[2] But the bishops of Italy

4–10, pp. 98–9: a summary of Cyprianic teaching, which includes an apparent reference to Augustine, is followed by two other unidentifiable references to him.

In the fragmentary *Ep.* 39, pp. 111–12, which is particularly important for Pelagius' doctrine of the Church and ministry, he refers to Cyprian only: cf. *De cath. eccl. unit.* 4, *C.S.E.L.* iii, pt. 1, 212–13.

Citations of Augustine, either verbal or substantial, appear by themselves as follows: *Ep.* 52. 12, p. 138: *Ep.* cxxxviii. 2. 14, *C.S.E.L.* xliv. 140, *Encheiridion*, lxxii, *P.L.* xl. 266; *Ep.* 35. 2, p. 97: *Sermones*, ccl. 2, *P.L.* xxxviii. 1165. Pelagius also cited unknown works of, or ascribed to, Augustine in *Epp.* 10. 3, pp. 32–3; 24. 14, pp. 77–8; 52. 8, p. 137. He made no certain references to the *Contra epist. Parm.*; the one which Gassó and Batlle suggest in *Ep.* 35. 7, p. 98, is very doubtful indeed.

It is further worthy of note that the description of bishops in organized schism from the Church as 'pseudoepiscopi' is Cyprianic: *Epp.* lv. 24, *C.S.E.L.* iii, pt. 2, 642; lix. 9, p. 676. For Pelagius' usage, see below, p. 478.

[1] Cf. Pope Pelagius II (579–80): see *Gregorii I Registrum*, ii, ed. L. M. Hartmann, Appendix ii, 2, 3, *Monumenta Germaniae Historica, Epistolae* (= *M.G.H. Epp.*) ii. 447–8, 466–7.

[2] For an account of these events, see, e.g. de Labriolle, etc. *De la mort de Théodose à l'élection de Grégoire le Grand*, pp. 467–80.

were hostile to Justinian. At Rome, only two bishops could be found to consecrate Pelagius;[1] while, led by the bishops of Milan and Aquileia, the North Italian bishops refused communion with him.

The schism of Aquileia, which grew out of this refusal, took definite shape in 557, upon the death of Bishop Macedonius of Aquileia. His successor, Paulinus, was consecrated at Milan by its bishop, Auxanus.[2] Pelagius condemned this action in the strongest possible terms, saying that the immediate circumstances of the ceremony were a defiance of legitimate right and canonical custom. Moreover, because it was performed in schism, it was, in truth, not a case of ordination but of destruction; it was not a consecration, but, rather, an execration.[3]

Was such language merely rhetorical exaggeration, or did Pelagius really maintain that sacraments which were administered within the schism were null? The case for the latter view is strong. Pelagius was careful to follow fifth-century precedent by declaring that the schism of Aquileia was an organized one, which was constituted apart from the vital unity of the Church.[4] He made this the basis of a categorical assertion that sacraments which were administered in such an organized schism were mere desecrations.[5] Here, particularly, he expressed himself in uncompromisingly Cyprianic language, and cited Augustine only to support Cyprian. Furthermore, he diverged sharply from Augustine by making a contrast between the sacraments of evil ministers inside the Church and those of schismatics outside it: in the interests of unity, the vices of evil ministers inside might be tolerated when they could not be amended; but schismatics were barren branches, fit only to be burned.[6] Following upon his Cyprianic language, the contrast

[1] *Liber Pontificalis*, ed. L. Duchesne, i (Paris, 1886), pp. 303–4.

[2] See F. Savio, *Gli antichi vescovi d'Italia: La Lombardia*, i (Florence, 1913), pp. 234–9; F. Bonnard, 'Auxane', *Dictionnaire d'histoire et de géographie ecclésiastiques*, v (Paris, 1930), col. 932.

[3] *Ep.* 24, Gassó and Batlle, pp. 73–8.

[4] *Ep.* 24. 2, Gassó and Batlle, p. 74.

[5] 'Si enim ipsum consecrationis nomen rationabili ac vivaci intellectu discutimus, is qui cum in universali consecrari detractat ecclesia, consecratus dici vel esse nulla poterit ratione. Consecrare enim est simul sacrare. Sed ab ecclesiae visceribus divisus et ab apostolicis sedibus separatus dissecrat potius iste, non consecrat. Iure ergo execratus tantum non consecratus poterit dici, quem simul secum sacrare in unitate coniunctis membris non agnoscit ecclesia': *Ep.* 24. 8–10, Gassó and Batlle, pp. 75–6; cf. *Ep.* 74, pp. 187–8.

[6] 'Ecce agnovisti unam esse ecclesiam, et eam in radice sedis apostolicae constitutam extingui non posse. Noli catholicam semper mentem aliqua schismaticorum communione polluere. Unum Christi corpus, unam constat esse ecclesiam. Divisum ab universitate altare, veritatem Christi corporis non potest consecrare. Toleranda sunt in compage corporis positorum etiam illa nonnumquam vitia, quae unitati interdum parcentes resecare non possumus. Quia et evangelicum agricolam minus afferentem fructum palmitem, si tamen in vite

is a clear indication that Pelagius did not follow Augustine and that his condemnation of schismatic sacraments was absolute.

Pelagius' adherence to the fifth-century distinction between sacraments which were, and which were not, administered in an organized schism is further made clear by certain other letters about the schism of Aquileia. When he rebuked a certain patrician, named Valerian, for asking the central figure of the schism, Paulinus of Aquileia, to admit another patrician to communion, he made a significant contrast between the bishops of Milan and Aquileia. He referred to Auxanus of Milan as 'episcopus': his only offence was that of an individual who had ordained Paulinus in improper circumstances. Paulinus, however, was 'pseudoepiscopus'; for it was from him that the schism stemmed.[1] Again, Pelagius elsewhere appears to have distinguished between a bishop who was only on the verge of schism, and a pseudo-bishop who had forfeited his episcopal office by identifying himself with organized schism outside the Church. He had dealings, which are illustrated by three of his letters, with Bishop Paulinus of Fossombrone, who became an adherent of the schism of Aquileia. In his first letter, the pope treated him as an erring individual within the Church, whom he urged to repent and to be fully reconciled to the Church of Christ; he was, accordingly, spoken of as 'episcopus'.[2] Pelagius next described in serious terms the consequences of the settled schism into which he was falling.[3] Finally, the fact of Paulinus' committed adherence to the schism was confirmed by his contumacy; he was no longer an 'episcopus' but a 'pseudoepiscopus'.[4] For Pelagius, there was clearly a critical distinction between not being, and then being, an adherent of a schismatic group organized apart from the Church; in the latter case, Pelagius used language which pointed to the nullity of the sacraments.

In seeking to defend the compatibility of Pelagius' letters with Augustine's teaching, both Saltet[5] and Schebler[6] made much of another letter about the reconciliation to the Catholic Church of a priest whose sacraments he declared to have been acceptable and at one with his own: 'eadem siquidem fides in symbolis, eadem forma in baptismatis

maneat, purgare posse noster salvator edocuit. Abscissum autem a vite palmitem nisi igni ad comburendum aptum esse non posse, eiusdem caelestis magistri veritate didicimus. Noli ergo eorum qui igni apti sunt non consecrationibus sed execrationibus consentire, nec existimes illos vel esse vel dici ecclesiam posse': *Ep.* 24. 13–16, Gassó and Batlle, pp. 76–7; cf. *Ep.* 35. 5–14, pp. 98–100. The passage quoted provides a particularly instructive contrast with Augustine, *Ep.* clxxxv. 44, *C.S.E.L.* lvii. 38–9.

[1] *Ep.* 59, Gassó and Batlle, pp. 155–8; cf. also *Ep.* 53. 10, Gassó and Batlle, p. 142.   [2] *Ep.* 35. 15–17, Gassó and Batlle, pp. 100–1.

[3] *Ep.* 60, Gassó and Batlle, pp. 159–61.

[4] *Epp.* 69–71, Gassó and Batlle, pp. 178–82.   [5] p. 83.   [6] pp. 117–18.

sacramento, eadem in dominici corporis consecratione mysteria'.[1] But there is no evidence to suggest either that the clerk in question was ordained in schism, or that he was more deeply committed to it than was Paulinus of Fossombrone when Pelagius wrote the first of his three letters to him. The pope knew of no graver charge against him than that of temporary and individual separation from the Church. His case is to be contrasted with organized and confirmed schismatics, whose episcopal office and authority were forfeit:[2] because they were utterly apart from the unity of the Church, their sacrifices were merely sacrileges. Of them, unlike isolated individuals, it could be said that they lacked the Holy Spirit, and that, where the Holy Spirit did not dwell, there could be no sacrifice and no Body of Christ.[3]

Pelagius' letters afford no suggestion that the strength of his language against schismatic ordinations should not be taken to mean what it says. He followed the precedent of his fifth-century predecessors, and he added his own confirmation of it by reviving the language and the ideas of Cyprian. He invoked Augustine only to confirm this position, and he showed no awareness of elements in Augustine's teaching which had a very different tendency. His letters added to the later Patristic legacy to the medieval West of texts which told against its adopting a truly Augustinian standpoint about holy orders.

(v) *Pope Gregory I*

The extremely adverse judgement of Pelagius I upon schismatic orders was somewhat mitigated by Pelagius II;[4] but it was left to Gregory I (590–604), in one of his letters, to clarify the question of reordination in what was tantamount to an Augustinian way. In a letter of 592 to Bishop John of Ravenna, he scouted the opinion which was then current in North Italy, that a man who had once been ordained might subsequently be ordained again. He corrected it by drawing an explicit parallel between baptism and ordination, and by stating that in neither case might a sacrament be repeated.[5] Gregory here in effect enunciated the cardinal principle of Augustine's doctrine.

---

[1] *Ep.* 38, Gassó and Batlle, pp. 109–10.
[2] *Ep.* 74, Gassó and Batlle, pp. 187–8.
[3] *Ep.* 35, Gassó and Batlle, pp. 96–101.
[4] See above, p. 476, n. 1.
[5] 'Illud autem quod dicitis, ut is qui ordinatus est iterum ordinetur, valde ridiculum est et ab ingenii vestri consideratione extraneum, nisi forte quod exemplum ad medium deducitur, de quo et ille iudicandus est, qui tale aliquid fecisse perhibetur. Absit enim a fraternitate vestra sic sapere. Sicut enim baptizatus semel baptizari iterum non debet, ita qui consecratus est semel in eodem ordine iterum non valet consecrari. Sed si quis cum levi forsitan culpa ad sacerdotium venit, pro culpa penitentia indici debet et tamen ordo servari':

Yet it was an isolated case, and its limitations must be appreciated. It is by no means clear that Gregory invariably applied this principle.[1] Nor did he expressly or tacitly appeal to the authority of Augustine in his letter to John of Ravenna; and his writings yield no evidence that he was acquainted with the *Contra epistolam Parmeniani*. In the general course of western developments, the fact of Gregory's having once drawn a parallel between baptism and ordination had little effect; the theory and the practice of Rome for centuries to come was to show that he made no radical or lasting change in the customary Roman outlook.

CONCLUSION

It was Saltet's opinion that, during the fifth and sixth centuries, Augustine's doctrine of orders was familiar to the popes. According to him, their apparently unequivocal language, from Innocent I to Pelagius I, about the nullity of sacraments conferred outside the unity of the Church, was certainly unguarded. But, in all cases, it was to be read in the light of Augustine's distinction between the *sacramentum* and the *res sacramenti*. Augustine himself taught that, although sacraments administered outside the Church were valid, they were wholly devoid of the Holy Spirit. The popes expressed themselves so strongly, partly because the papal chancery clung to out-dated formulas; but partly, too, because they laid all their emphasis upon what was just one side of Augustine's teaching—the spiritual deadness of schismatic sacraments. In doing so, they must be understood to have safeguarded tacitly, as Augustine did expressly, the validity of the rites themselves. So far as the substance of their teaching was concerned, they professed the same principles as did Augustine.[2]

It must be conceded that such a view is, strictly, not open to absolute disproof. But it rests upon nothing more solid than the silence of sources which admittedly lacked the dogmatic sophistication of Augustine's writings. These sources provide no positive evidence that the Latin West, in general, drew any distinction that was comparable with Augustine's between the *sacramentum* and the *res sacramenti*. By something of a *tour de force*, Augustine's distinction can be read into the evidence; but it cannot be shown to be required by it. Nor does

Registrum, ii. 45, *M.G.H. Epp.* i. 145. Gregory thus insisted upon the old Roman practice that, as a matter of penitential discipline, clerks in a state of grave sin might only be admitted to lay communion.

[1] Thus, in dealing with Arians, Gregory never gave an explicit ruling about their orders. But he required Arian churches to be reconsecrated, at a time when the Council of Saragossa was associating such a requirement with the reordination of Arian clergy: *Reg.* iii. 19, *M.G.H Epp.* i. 177; *Dialogi*, iii. 30, *P.L.* lxxvii. 288-9.   [2] See Saltet, pp. 68, 76, 82-3, 388.

Pelagius I's disregard of Augustine's teaching that the sacraments of
a schismatic outside the Church and of a sinful minister inside it are
strictly comparable, tell in favour of his familiarity with Augustine's
teaching about holy orders.

On the contrary, it is far more likely that the Latin West knew little
about this teaching, and that it normally thought and legislated on
quite different lines. Augustine so presented his teaching that it was
unlikely to gain wide currency or to make a profound impact. The only
clear evidence that the West so much as knew of it—Pope Anastasius II's
letter about Acacian orders—did not go to the heart of the problem,
nor did it involve what was truly original in Augustine. Whenever the
issue of orders conferred outside the Church was really at stake, the
West seems to have adhered to a pre-Augustinian position, by which
a distinction was made between baptism and the other sacraments, and
which afforded no clear grounds for maintaining the validity of the
latter, when they were administered outside the Church. In the fifth
century, moreover, western attitudes to holy orders were increasingly
coloured by considerations of a canonical, rather than of a dogmatic,
character. In so far as a dogmatic approach to the problem evolved in
the sixth century, its conclusions were drawn, not from Augustine's
most characteristic discussions, but from a combination of Cyprian's
ideas with Augustine's, in a way which represented a kind of highest
common factor between them. The possibility of reordination was
never decisively condemned nor excluded.

The disappearance of Arianism from the West, the remarkable freedom of the West from heretical movements during the early Middle
Ages, and the poverty of its dogmatic thought, were not conducive to
new developments of a significant kind. For centuries, the West drew
upon the letters of Innocent I with regard to the Bonosans and the
Arians, of the popes from Leo I to Anastasius II with regard to the
aftermath of Chalcedon, and of Pelagius I with regard to the schism of
Aquileia, to justify the reordinations of clergy which from time to time
took place. Its use of this material was often crude and unperceptive;
but to use it in favour of reordinations was, in itself, by no means an
unfair way of applying it. It was not until the time of the *ius novum* and
of high medieval discussion from Peter Lombard and Master Roland to
Raymond of Peñafort, that Augustine's doctrine of holy orders became
without doubt the generally accepted doctrine of the Latin West.[1]

[1] I hope to illustrate the medieval development in future studies. I am
greatly indebted to the Revd. Dr. S. L. Greenslade for his kindness in commenting on a draft of this paper.

II

POPE ANASTASIUS II AND ST. AUGUSTINE'S DOCTRINE OF HOLY ORDERS

St. Augustine contended with vigour for the validity of holy orders which were conferred outside the unity of the church by a bishop who had himself been duly ordained. Yet it is well known that his position in this matter was by no means fully understood and followed in the western church up to the scholastic period of the twelfth and thirteenth centuries[1]. Hence, the long history of re-ordinations; and hence, too, Gratian, in his *Decretum* (*c.* 1140—41), could still bear witness to the currency of an opinion which was incompatible with it: that the powers of baptizing and of conferring orders are fundamentally different[2]. The long history of divergence upon this point from the great doctor of the west calls for explanation.

In seeking to provide it, the nature of St. Augustine's teaching must be borne in mind. In the anti-Donatist writings, which contain practically all his references to the doctrine of holy orders, his sacramental theology was worked out with the single case of baptism at the centre of the picture[3]. With it in view, he argued that the sacraments are what they are by Christ's promise and grace alone. Inside the church, unworthy ministers do not harm them, any more than worthy ones add to them; outside the church, schismatic and even heretical ministers do not harm them, either. So long as they are rightly administered, the sacraments are the same wherever they are; there is no breach of their holiness. When he turned to consider orders, St. Augustine simply insisted that, by a parity of argument, what is true of baptism is also true of them. If a clerk comes into the church from schism, his ordination holds good just as does his baptism. In the one case as in the other, the fault lies in the human perversity by which he has been cut off from the charity of unity; it is fully made good, when he enters the catholic church, by the laying on of hands in reconciliation. St. Augustine was content to assume this full comparability of baptism and orders; he never

---

[1] See esp. the studies of reordinations by L. Saltet, Les Réordinations. Étude sur le sacrement de l'ordre, Paris 1907, and A. Schebler, Die Reordinationen in der 'altkatholischen' Kirche, Bonn 1936.

[2] *Potestas dandi baptismum et ius consecrandi dominicum corpus et largiendi sacros ordines plurimum inter se differunt*: Decretum, secunda pars, c. 1, q. 1, c. 97, Corpus iuris canonici, ed. A. Friedberg, I, Leipzig 1879, p. 395.

[3] See esp. the remarks of C. H. Turner, Apostolic Succession, in: Early History of the Church and Ministry, ed. H. B. Swete, 2nd edn. London 1921, 181.

expressly justified it on grounds of dogma. For him, the burden of proof rests with those who would argue otherwise[1].

Several reasons why St. Augustine's teaching did not clearly impress itself upon the west during the centuries which divided St. Augustine from Gratian can readily be stated. St. Augustine discussed holy orders only very briefly and occasionally. His only at all extensive treatment was in the second book of the *Contra epistolam Parmeniani;* in addition, there are just a few allusions in the other anti-Donatist works which survive[2]. Thus, even had the early medieval world been familiar with the whole Augustinian *corpus*, the doctrine of orders occupies only a tiny and secondary place in it, being overshadowed by baptism. But the evidence for the distribution of St. Augustine's works, so far as it has been studied, yields very few references indeed to manuscripts of the *Contra epistolam Parmeniani*. It seems to have been something of a rarity; so that St. Augustine's teaching about orders was, in any case, seldom available for study at first hand[3]. In addition the compendia of his teaching which circulated widely, like those of St. Prosper Tiro of Aquitaine and Eugippius, include no material on the subject of orders which might have kept the Augustinian view alive[4]. It is not, therefore, surprising that, from the letters of Pope Anastasius II (496–98)[5] right up to the *Infensor et defensor* of the Roman writer Auxilius (c. 911)[6] there should nowhere, at Rome or elsewhere, have been an assured reference to, or citation of, the *Contra epistolam Parmeniani* regarding holy orders; or that what was really distinctive in St. Augustine's teaching about orders should

---

[1] See esp. Contra epistolam Parmeniani 2, 13, 28–2, 14, 32 (CSEL 51, pp. 79–86).

[2] Loc. cit., cp. Epistolae, XCLIII 46 (CSEL 34, pp. 488–89), CLXXXV 44–46 (CSEL 57, pp. 38–40); De baptismo 1, 1, 2 (CSEL 51, p. 146): Sermo ad Caesareenis ecclesiae plebem, II (PL 43, col. 52). Several anti-Donatist works are known to have been lost.

[3] The distribution in the early middle ages of the Contra epistolam Parmeniani deserves a full enquiry. The lists printed by E. A. Lowe, The Oldest Extant Manuscripts of St. Augustine, in: Miscellanea Agostiniana, II, Rome, 1931, 235–251, do not refer to it. It does not appear in Bede's library as reconstructed by M. L. W. Laistner, The Intellectual Heritage of the Early Middle Ages, New York 1957, 145–49, nor is it referred to in M. R. James, The Ancient Libraries of Canterbury and Dover, Cambridge 1903. It was catalogued in 1093 in the library of the monastery of Pomposa: G. Mercati, Il catalogo della biblioteca di Pomposa, in: Studi e documenti di storia e diritto. 17, 1896, 143–77. G. Becker, Catalogi bibliothecarum antiqui, Bonn 1885, prints the catalogues of 136 medieval libraries, but (apart from Pomposa) only cites three MSS: at Bec (pp. 199, 258); Prüfening (p. 211); and Naumburg (p. 272). In Mittelalterliche Bibliothekskataloge Deutschlands und der Schweiz, ed. P. Lehmann, München 1918–1962, it is only recorded at the Charterhouse of Salvatorsberg (II, pp. 293, 535, 540) and at Michelsberg, Bamberg (III, p. 355)

[4] For St. Prosper Tiro's Liber sententiarum ex operibus sancti Augustini delibatarum, written c. 450, widely known in the middle ages and often held to be by St. Augustine himself, see PL 51, cols 427–96; for Eugippius († c. 533), Excerpta ex operibus sancti Augustini, see CSEL 9, pp. 5–1149.

[5] Ep. I: Epistolae Romanorum pontificum genuinae, ed. A. Thiel, I, Braunsberg 1868, pp. 615–23.

[6] Inf. et def. III (PL 129, cols. 1079–80); cp. De ordinationibus a Formoso papa factis XXI (PL 129, col. 1067).

have attracted little, if any, notice[1]. These reasons for the slowness of the west fully to grasp his teaching concern matters of fact, rather than of interpretation. I should like to add another, and perhaps more controversial, reason. It is that the fifth-century popes from Innocent I (401–17) to Anastasius II, some of whom, at least, knew the *Contra epistolam Parmeniani*, did not, on the evidence of their surviving writings, fully transmit St. Augustine's teaching as contained in it. I hope, in the future, to demonstrate this as part of a discussion of re-ordinations; I should like, now, to illustrate it from a letter of Anastasius II.

Anastasius had to deal with the Acacian schism (484–519) between Rome and Constantinople, which was occasioned by the Emperor Zeno's *Henoticon* (482)[2]. Acacius, the patriarch of Constantinople, was Zeno's adviser. The Papacy would countenance no such revision of Chalcedon as the *Henoticon* proposed; therefore, in 484, Pope Felix III (483–92) excommunicated and deposed Acacius, and severed communion between Rome and Constantinople[3]. The Roman view of Acacius's consequent situation must be carefully defined. Before and after his death in 489, the popes saw in him someone who, although he had fallen foul of the Eutychian heresy, had done so as an individual[4]. The collective orthodoxy of his church was not impugned; nor was there at Constantinople, by contrast with Alexandria, a succession of rival patriarchs. In Roman eyes, then, Acacius was an individual associate of heretics; he was not the head of an antagonistic body organized right outside the church. Thus, by traditional western standards, there was no real doubt that his sacraments were valid[5]. The Acacian schism did not call for the full application of the principles which St. Augustine had drawn up with the independently organized Donatist church in mind.

So, when individuals who had been baptized or ordained by Acacius sought to be reconciled with Rome, Popes Felix III[6], Gelasius I (492–96)[7] and Anastasius II[8] all ruled that, as long as they were catholic in belief, they might be received into the church in full status. In his first letter,

---

[1] In their edition of the letters of Pope Pelagius I (556–61), Gassó and Batlle find one possible reference, but it is not a clear one, and there are no traces in these letters of St. Augustine's distinctive teachings about orders: Pelagii I papae epistulae quae supersunt (556–661), ed. P. M. Gassó and C. M. Batlle, Montserrat 1956, p. 98.

[2] For the schism, see G. Bardy, De la Mort de Théodose à l'élection de Grégoire le Grand, in: Histoire de l'église, ed. A. Fliche and V. Martin, IV, Paris 1948, 289–308.

[3] Epp. VI–VII, Epist. Rom. pont., ed. Thiel, I, pp. 243–47.

[4] Gelasius I, in particular, drew a distinction between Peter Mongus, the head of the schism at Alexandria, who was the *sectator*, or separatist adherent, of Eutyches, and Acacius, who was merely a *communicator* with him: Tractatus II 5, op. cit., p. 526; cp. Tract. III 7–9, pp. 316–17.

[5] Cp. the comments of C. H. Turner, Apostolic Succession, in: Early History of the Church and Ministry, p. 175.

[6] Ep. XIV 5, Epist. Rom. pont., ed. Thiel, p. 269.

[7] Ep. III 6, pp. 315–16.

[8] Ep. I 8–9, pp. 620–23.

Anastasius, in particular, gave his reasons; and, as far as they go, his debt to St. Augustine is evident. He insisted that, according to the custom of the catholic church, no one whom Acacius had canonically baptized or ordained in any way shared his penalty; for, when sacraments are conferred by evil men, the grace which God gives through them is not compromised. Anastasius claimed St. Augustine's authority for declaring that baptism administered by a sinful man conveys grace to the recipient unimpaired; that what is done in the sacraments is wholly the result of God's working; and that what matters is not who or what manner of man preaches, but the Christ who is preached. Anastasius supported these Augustinian statements by quoting three biblical texts, all of which St. Augustine used in the *Contra epistolam Parmeniani*[1]; and his debt to it is virtually certain[2].

Yet the limitations of his transmission of St. Augustine's teaching are also apparent. For Anastasius, Acacius's offences were those of an individual[3]; they were, at root, the outcome of his own pride[4]. Anastasius drew upon St. Augustine only to justify his recognition of the sacraments of a single sinful minister, who had not acted in an organized body which stood outside and in opposition to the church. He had, therefore, no need to explore the real peculiarities of St. Augustine's thought. In fact, he sidestepped them; for, once he had passed from delivering his verdict upon Acacius's sacraments to explaining it, he confined himself exclusively to baptism and made no further reference whatsoever to orders. He studiously avoided making any allusion to the parallel which St. Augustine drew so clearly with baptism. Anastasius's reasoned account of his dealings with the Acacian schism made no reference at all to the really novel elements in St. Augustine's teaching about orders. There was no cause for it to do so.

Even this very restricted use of St. Augustine's teaching was short-lived, for Anastasius's conciliatory policy towards Constantinople was short-lived. During his brief reign, a faction at Rome opposed it; and his sudden and untimely death was interpreted as a divine condemnation of his mildness. There followed a disputed election in which Laurentius, who would have continued his policy, was defeated and Symmachus (498–514), who was hostile to Constantinople, became pope[5]. Thereafter, no more is heard of eirenic discussions at Rome of Acacian sacraments; and, so far as the doctrine of holy orders is concerned, no further reference to St. Augustine's teaching recurs there for more than four hundred years.

Thus, while he was almost certainly familiar with the discussion of orders in the *Contra epistolam Parmeniani*, Anastasius did nothing to transmit

---

[1] Luke 3, 16 in Con. ep. Parm. II 10, 22 (CSEL 51, p. 71) and 2, 10, 23 (p. 73); Matt. 23, 2–3 in II 9, 19 (p. 64); I Cor. 3, 6–7 in II 14, 32 (p. 84).

[2] Esp. to 2, 11 (pp. 73–76).

[3] Ep. I 1, p. 616.

[4] Ep. I, 8–9, pp. 621–23.

[5] Le Liber Pontificalis, ed. L. Duchesne, I, Paris 1886, pp. XLIII–XLIV, 258–60.

St. Augustine's full teaching that holy orders conferred outside the church must be regarded in the same way as baptism. That, like the other popes of the later patristic age, he did not do so, helps to explain why the early medieval west, whose canonical discipline was largely guided by such papal pronouncements, should have been slow to grasp what is most distinctive in St. Augustine's doctrine of orders.

III

BEDE AND THE 'ENGLISH PEOPLE'

I

Since 1896, when Charles Plummer published his edition of Bede's *Ecclesiastical History,* successive generations of scholars have shed light upon Bede as a historian and have drawn upon his *History* as a source for the settlement and conversion of the Anglo-Saxons up to 731, when the work was completed.[1] With their studies in mind, the purpose of this paper is a simple and limited one. It is to investigate, on the basis of the *History* considered in itself and as a literary whole, Bede's distinctive contribution by its means to the formation of the English people as a self-conscious unity. It would be misguided to look in the *Ecclesiastical History* for a plot or theme which is systematically worked out in its five books. Yet its full title, the *Historia gentis Anglorum ecclesiastica,*[2] announces not only a subject but also a purpose. The purpose seems to emerge, perhaps more clearly than has

---

1. The principal editions of the *Ecclesiastical History* are C. Plummer (ed.), *Venerabilis Baedae Opera Historica,* 2 vols, Oxford 1896, and B. Colgrave and R. A. B. Mynors (eds), *Bede's Ecclesiastical History of the English People,* Oxford 1969. Unless otherwise indicated, references in the present article are to the latter edition; translations are my own. The modern studies that have most notably influenced this article are: A. Hamilton Thompson (ed.), *Bede, his Life, Times and Writings,* Oxford 1932; C. G. Starr (ed.), *The Intellectual Heritage of the Early Middle Ages: Selected Essays by M. L. W. Laistner,* New York 1966; J. Campbell, 'Bede', in T. A. Dorey (ed.) *Latin Historians,* London 1966, pp. 159-90; R. W. Southern, 'Bede', in *Medieval Humanism and Other Studies,* Oxford 1970, pp. 1-8; J. M. Wallace-Hadrill, *Early Germanic Kingship in England and on the Continent,* Oxford 1971, and *Early Medieval History,* Oxford 1975; H. Mayr-Harting, *The Coming of Christianity to Anglo-Saxon England,* London 1972; G. Bonner (ed.), *Famulus Christi: Essays in Commemoration of the Thirteenth Centenary of the Birth of the Venerable Bede,* London 1976; J. N. Stephens, 'Bede's Ecclesiastical History', *History,* Vol. 62, 1977, pp. 1-14; and successive Jarrow Lectures, especially B. Colgrave, *The Venerable Bede and his Times,* 1958, P. Hunter Blair, *Bede's Ecclesiastical History of the English Nation and its Importance To-day,* 1959, D. Whitelock, *After Bede,* 1960, P. Meyvaert, *Bede and Gregory the Great,* 1964, R. A. Markus, *Bede and the Tradition of Ecclesiastical Historiography,* 1975, H. Mayr-Harting, *The Venerable Bede, The Rule of St. Benedict, and Social Class,* 1976, P. Wormald, 'Bede, "Beowulf" and the Conversion of the Anglo-Saxon Aristocracy', in R. T. Farrell (ed.) *Bede and Anglo-Saxon England.* British Archaeological Reports, Vol. 46, Oxford 1978, pp. 32-95 came to my notice only after this paper was completed; it offers a brilliant view of the contribution of secular poetry to the making of the English people.
2. As given in Bede's *Praefatio* (p. 2).

---

* This paper was originally read to Dr R. B. Mitchell's graduate seminar for students for the degree of Bachelor of Philosophy in Old English Literature and Anglo-Saxon Society at St Edmund Hall, Oxford. I am grateful to members of the seminar for the points raised in discussion. The paper also owes a great deal to the criticisms and suggestions of Dr Mitchell and of Dr Henry Mayr-Harting. Errors of fact and judgement remain wholly my own responsibility.

been appreciated, in and through Bede's way of presenting the interplay of the languages and peoples which were to be found in Britain. He wrote as if to meet a need. For the Germanic peoples who had settled in Britain during the three hundred years and more before Bede wrote had not been swift to achieve a common and positive identity as a *gens Anglorum*. They did, indeed, share a fund of religion, language, culture and customs. Yet recent study, in particular of early kingship in western Europe, has tended to emphasize how recent and how shifting many of their institutions were, and how little the gods and the human leaders with whom the invaders came served to provide them with social and political cohesion. After the migration, however, the adopting of the Christian God brought with it a legacy from Roman government and law-making. Thus it was by legislation, undertaken as Bede said of Kentish law *iuxta exempla Romanorum*,[3] that kings established their image as masters of their peoples, consolidating their authority as rulers in peace no less than in war.[4] By his historical writing Bede seems to have sought to supplement such a legislative filling out of royal authority by communicating not only to kings but also to the settled English people as a whole a more deeply rooted sense of its unity and identity. He wrote as if to elicit and to nourish a self-awareness which in religious terms was Christian and Roman, but which was also strong enough politically to guarantee temporal stability and prosperity.[5]

Bede gives a hint of his purpose and of his way of pursuing it in definitions of the subject-matter of his work that come near its end: it is 'an ecclesiastical history of Britain, and especially of the English people' *(historia ecclesiastica Brittaniarum, et maxime gentis Anglorum)*, and again, 'an ecclesiastical history of our island and people' *(historia ecclesiastica nostrae insulae ac gentis)*.[6] These formulations are strictly correct; for in a critically important sentence that Bede himself composed in his very first chapter where so much is borrowed, he was quick to announce that in his *History* he would not be concerned with one people alone, but with the interplay of a number of peoples living in what was, topographically, Britain *(Brittania)*:

> Haec in praesenti iuxta numerum librorum quibus lex divina scripta est, quinque gentium linguis unam eandemque summae veritatis et verae sublimitatis scientiam scrutatur et confitetur, Anglorum videlicet Brettonum Scottorum Pictorum et Latinorum, quae meditatione scripturarum ceteris omnibus est facta communis.
>
> Just as the law of God [i.e. the Pentateuch] is written in five books, so at the present time Britain searches out and confesses the self-same

3. ii, 5 (p. 150).
4. See esp. I. N. Wood, 'Kings, Kingdoms and Consent', and P. Wormald, *'Lex scripta* and *Verbum regis*: Legislation and Germanic Kingship, from Euric to Cnut', in P. H. Sawyer and I. N. Wood (eds), *Early Medieval Kingship*, Leeds 1977, pp. 6-29, 105-38.
5. Cf. Southern, *Medieval Humanism*, p. 5.
6. v, 24 (pp. 566, 570).

knowledge of the highest truth and the true excellency in the languages of five peoples: the English, the British, the Irish, the Picts, and the Latins; the last of these languages has been made common to all by the study of the scriptures.[7]

Four languages were those of peoples in an ethnic sense: the English, Bede's own people which was to be the principal subject of his history; the British, the original inhabitants of the land who had conquered it from the south; the Irish *(Scotti),* who came later from Ireland but remained the Irish whether they were to be found in Ireland, Scotland, or England in modern terms; and the Picts, who had settled in the northernmost parts of Britain. The fifth, that of the Latins, was the language not of a secular people but of the catholic church as the people of God; it had become the common property of the peoples of Britain in an ethnic sense because it was the language of scriptural study.

As it develops, the *Ecclesiastical History* exhibits the interaction of the four peoples—English, British, Irish and Pictish—who dwelt in Britain, and especially the degrees by which they established and harmonized their identities upon the principle of unity supplied by the *lingua Latinorum.* By this Bede meant *Latinitas,* the catholic Christianity of the Latin language: centred upon obedience to the apostolic see of Rome but above all its patrons St Peter and St Paul; informed by the work of the four Latin doctors St Jerome, St Ambrose, St Augustine of Hippo, and especially St Gregory the Great;[8] and through them resting foursquare upon the Latin tradition of scriptural study *(meditatio scripturarum).* It must be remembered how central scriptural study was to Bede's own work. There is, indeed, no cause to question Laistner's judgement that the *Ecclesiastical History* 'by universal consent is the supreme example of Bede's genius',[9] or that it is the culmination of his life's activity—a valedictory and deeply-felt testament to the English people. But the list of Bede's works up to 731 which he placed at its conclusion is a reminder that his historical works were but a small part of a vast scholarly output.[10] He dwelt upon his scriptural and theological works: Plummer was right to observe that 'the greater number of Bede's works and those to which he himself no doubt assigned the greatest value are theological in character'.[11] By such works above all Bede aspired to form the mind of the English people according to the principle of Christian unity that

---

7. i, 1 (p. 16). Dr Mayr-Harting suggests to me that Bede's division of the *Ecclesiastical History* into five books may be explained by the Pentateuchal symbolism of this passage. It may be no coincidence that, as the Pentateuch ends with Moses' Pisgah view of the promised land, so the *Ecclesiastical History* ends with Bede's survey of the 'whole state of Britain': Deut. xxxiv; v, 23 (pp. 556-60). As in the five books of Moses Israel had become a people subject to Mosaic law, so in the five books of Bede's work the English became a people subject to the law of catholic Christianity.
8. For Bede and Gregory, see ii, 1 (pp. 122-34).
9. Starr (ed.), *Intellectual Heritage,* p. 99.
10. v, 24 (pp. 566-70).
11. *Opera historica,* Vol. I, p. xlvii.

the *lingua Latinorum* represented. In his *Ecclesiastical History* he was at pains to show how, under the hand of Providence, this principle had begun to take effect, and to promote its continuing effectiveness.

There are three respects in which the *Ecclesiastical History* accordingly seems calculated to exhibit the English people as a nation, and as a Christian nation. First, Bede represented the English people, in terms that were probably clearer than any it had itself hitherto formulated or, indeed, than its past history altogether warranted, as a self-aware ethnic unity comprehending all the Germanic elements which had settled in Britain, as he thought since the mid-fifth century. Secondly, he so handled the paschal question and related issues that divided Christians in Britain as to indicate that the place and identity of the English people there were largely determined by the manner of their debate and resolution. Thirdly, Bede's didactic purpose in writing his *History* was particularly directed towards certain key groups in English society—notably the kings, and the monks and bishops—by whose instruction he hoped to secure both the Christian order and the political vitality of the English people. These three topics will be discussed in turn, and an attempt will be made to assess the effectiveness with which Bede in each case promoted English nationhood.

II

How, then, and with what success did Bede attempt to make the English more aware of themselves and of their destiny as a *gens Anglorum*? A principal means seems to have been by tracing the interaction of the peoples who spoke the first four of his five *linguae*: the English, British, Irish and Picts. In this context, after firmly establishing the Roman background Bede lost little time in showing how positive a vocation the English people had in God's designs relatively to the other peoples of Britain. When the British under Vortigern summoned the *gens Saxonum* from across the sea to defend them against the other two peoples, the Irish and the Picts, Bede saw already the hidden hand of Providence: 'It was clearly by God's will that this took place, so that evil might befall such wicked men [as the British], just as the outcome so clearly showed.'[12] As soon as they had settled in Britain, the *Anglorum sive Saxonum gens*[13] stood out by contrast with the reprobate British as 'the people whom God foreknew'.[14] Even the pagan King Aethelfrith of the Northumbrians began to assert the dominion of the *gens Anglorum* over the British and the Irish, 'so that he might be compared with Saul who was once king of the Israelite people, save only that he was ignorant of the true religion'.[15] Bede thereafter traced the growth of the English in nationhood, by God's providence, under the Christian kings in the succession of royal overlords whom the

12. i, 14 (p. 48); cf. i, 15 (p. 52).
13. i, 15 (p. 50).
14. i, 22 (p. 68); cf. Pope Gregory I's letter, i, 31 (p. 108).
15. i, 34 (p. 116).

Anglo-Saxon Chronicle (but not Bede) called Bretwaldas.[16] Thus, for Bede, Aethelbert of Kent had an *imperium* over all England south of the Humber; his conversion followed, and his exemplary attitude to Christian evangelization made it possible for Augustine of Canterbury to become archbishop of the *gens Anglorum*.[17] Under the Christianized Northumbrians Edwin, Oswald and Oswiu the English people prospered yet more widely. It was Edwin who first, 'Like no other of the English before him, held under his sway all the bounds of Britain, where there were provinces of either English or British'; the increase of his earthly power foreshadowed the conversion to Christianity that duly followed.[18] Soon afterwards, through the instruction of Bishop Aidan, God raised up Oswald. Under him the English people achieved still greater heights: 'Oswald received from the one God . . . greater earthly realms than any of his forebears; there came under his sway all the nations and provinces of Britain, divided as they are among the four languages of the British, the Picts, the Irish and the English'.[19] The providential growth in power and unity of the *gens Anglorum* culminated in the arch-episcopal authority of Theodore of Tarsus, archbishop of Canterbury from 668 to 690, 'first among the archbishops to whom all the English church would give obedience'. 'Never', Bede wrote, 'had there been such happy times since the English first came to Britain. For having very brave Christian kings, they were a terror to all the barbarian nations; all men's desires were set on the joys of the heavenly kingdom, of which they had lately heard; while all who wished for instruction in sacred studies had teachers ready to hand.'[20] Half a century later, when Bede drafted his final chapter in which he reviewed 'the whole state of Britain at the present time', he let his readers see that the gilt was wearing a little thin. Kings were not quite as they once were. There had been under Ceolwulf (king of Northumbria 729-37/8) so many and such great commotions and adversities that Bede did not know what their outcome would be. And yet, that having been said, Bede could conclude that the times were made favourable by peace and serenity. For the English people retained the pre-eminence that it had won over the other three people of Britain—the Picts, the Irish, and the British.[21]

Bede thus began to set forth the identity of the English people by indicating how in the long run it rose to hegemony over its neighbours in Britain. The repeated harking back to his description of the peoples of Britain in his very first chapter suggests that he did so deliberately. Furthermore, he emphasized the identity of the English people more intensively by the moral judgements that he passed upon the other

16. ii, 5 (pp. 148-50); cf. *Anglo-Saxon Chronicle, a.* 829, in D. Whitelock (ed.), *English Historical Documents, c. 500-1042*, London 1955, p. 171.
17. i, 25-7 (pp. 75-8).
18. ii, 9 (p. 162).
19. iii, 6 (p. 230).
20. iv, 2 (pp. 332-4); cf. v, 8 (p. 474).
21. v, 23 (pp. 556-60).

peoples of the island when he reviewed 'the whole state of Britain' in his final chapter. So far as the Picts and the Irish are concerned, Bede thought it necessary to notice only the state of peace and harmony with the English to which they had by 731 been reduced.

> The Pictish nation now has a treaty of peace with the English people, and rejoices to have a share with the church universal in catholic peace and truth. The Irish who live in Britain are content with their borders, and they practise no plots or treachery against the English people.[22]

Both nations knew their place in the rightful pattern of peoples, and they kept it. Not so the British. From first to last in the *Ecclesiastical History* they were rebellious and antagonistic, both to the English people and to the providence of God; and Bede never lost sight of this. As long ago as the days of Vortigern 'they cast off Christ's easy yoke and bowed their necks to drunkenness, hatred, strife, contention, envyings and other crimes of that sort'.[23] Bede represented the fires that the still-heathen English, when they came, kindled against the British as God's righteous vengeance upon British wickedness.[24] Worse was to follow. 'On top of all the unspeakable crimes that Gildas, their own historian, sets forth in doleful words', wrote Bede, 'they added this: they never preached the word of faith to the Saxon or English people who inhabited Britain with them.'[25] All this was a bad start from which the British in Bede's eyes never recovered. In dealings with St Augustine of Canterbury they refused to mend their ways when a healing miracle performed upon a blind man of English race showed that they should do so.[26] When the pagan King Aethelfrith of Northumbria slaughtered the British-Christian monks of Bangor, Bede saw the fulfilment of Augustine's prophecy made when British bishops— not surprisingly since Augustine did not rise to greet them—refused to talk with him: 'namely, that those heretics *(perfidi)* would also feel the vengeance of temporal death, because they had spurned the counsels of eternal salvation that they were offered'.[27] Again, in the 630s Caedwalla, the British-Christian king of Gwynedd, was for Bede in worse case than his ally Penda, the pagan king of the Mercians. Penda was a heathen who knew no better; Caedwalla was a barbarian who did. 'He meant to obliterate the whole English race from the confines of Britain', said Bede; 'nor did he have any respect for the Christian religion. . . . Indeed, to this very day it is the British custom to account the faith and religion of the English as nothing, and to have no more communion with them than with the pagans'.[28] Thus whereas in Bede's 'whole state of Britain' summary the beneficient and obedient

---

22. v, 23 (p. 560); cf. iv, 26 (p. 426). For Bede and the Picts, see D. P. Kirby, 'Bede and the Pictish Church', *The Innes Review*, Vol. 24, 1973, pp. 6-25.
23. i, 14 (p. 48).
24. i, 15 (p. 52).
25. i, 22 (p. 68).
26. ii, 2 (pp. 134-6).
27. ii, 2 (pp. 138-42); cf. ii, 4 (p. 146).
28. ii, 20 (pp. 202-4).

Picts and Irish had a good write-up, the British fared badly: obdurate sinners to the end, their will to do evil was deservedly frustrated by division and subjection.

> Although, for the most part, the British resist the English people through their inbred hatred, and the good order of the whole catholic church by their incorrect Easter and their wicked customs, they are opposed by the forces of God and man alike. So they can have their desire in neither of their objects. For although they are partly under their own rule, they are also partly under that of the English.[29]

Throughout the *Ecclesiastical History* the British people was uniformly presented in such sombre terms by reason of its wickedness. In the pattern of the inhabitants of Britain it served as a foil which made the identity of the English people which it resisted stand out in high relief.

How far was Bede's sustained contrast between the English and the three other peoples well conceived to give the Germanic settlers in Britain a more positive identity as a *gens Anglorum* than they had felt before? To the modern observer, and perhaps also to contemporaries, its weaknesses are considerable. More, perhaps, than his tripartite division of the Germanic invaders into Saxons, Angles and Jutes,[30] the scheme of four people was rather the product of a neat, systematizing mind than a description of things as they were. Earlier sources, such as the papal responses and letters in the *Ecclesiastical History,* or the *Life of Gregory the Great* by a monk of Whitby, or Eddius' *Life of Wilfrid,* occasionally but clearly show that the English were already aware of themselves collectively as *Angli* before Bede wrote.[31] There were grounds for such an awareness; differences of dialect amongst them were not great, and archaeological evidence points to a fairly homogeneous culture. Thus, the English probably had other, less artificial reasons than Bede disclosed for feeling themselves to be a self-conscious *gens Anglorum.* At the same time he seems through over-simplification to have exaggerated their political unity. The seventh century saw not only the hegemony of Bede's three Northumbrian overlords but also the competing aspirations of all three marcher kingdoms—of Wessex and Mercia along with Northumbria. Bede said

---

29. v, 23 (p. 560). Bede's attitude to the British is well discussed by L. W. Barnard, 'Bede and Eusebius as Church Historians', in Bonner (ed.), *Famulus Christi,* pp. 106-24, esp. pp. 116-8. It is very hard to account for Bede's deep and sustained hostility to them. He formulates no clear reasons; but much is probably to be explained by a scholar's reaction to the Pelagian heresy (i, 10, 17, 21 (pp. 38, 54-6, 64); ii, 19 (pp. 200-2); v, 21 (p. 544)); and by a Northumbrian's to Caedwalla's ravaging of Northumbria *quasi tyrannus saeviens:* ii, 20 (pp. 202-4); iii, 1 (pp. 212-4); and his alliance with King Penda of Mercia, for which and for much else relating to Mercian history see H. P. R. Finberg, 'Mercians and Welsh', in *Lucerna,* London 1964, pp. 66-82.
30. i, 15 (p. 500); but for a favourable assessment of Bede's evidence on this matter, see J. N. L. Myres, 'The Angles, the Saxons, and the Jutes', *Proceedings of the British Academy,* Vol. 56, 1970, pp. 145-74.
31. i, 27 (p. 84); i, 32 (p. 110); Plummer (ed.), *Baedae Opera Historica,* Vol. II, p. 390; B. Colgrave (ed.), *The Life of Bishop Wilfrid by Eddius Stephanus,* Cambridge 1927, p. 14.

little about the first two and especially Mercia, giving an inadequate account of Wulfhere in the seventh century just as he ignored King Aethelbald in the eighth. The *gens Anglorum* had less political cohesion than he indicated; clarity was purchased at a price. Again, Bede overdrew the contrast between the predestined English and the reprobate British. From evidence in Nennius and elsewhere that historians are increasingly prepared to heed, it may be that the British, despite Bede's silence about them, had their place. with the Irish and the Romans in bringing about the conversion of Northumbria. There may have been political and dynastic links between the Northumbrian and British kingdoms of which Bede gave no inkling.[32] It has also become increasingly apparent that in Northumbria as elsewhere there was no hard division between British and English. A large proportion of the Bernician population, in particular, was of British stock. Caedmon, whom Bede himself made famous, had a British name; if of British descent he may well have been more exceptional for his poetry than for his piety.[33] Bede himself told how a Briton carried with him miracle-working dust from the spot where Oswald died.[34] In practice, then, the peoples mixed and even merged. The artificiality of Bede's scheme of peoples, in respect of English feelings about nationhood as well as of the hard facts of history, could scarcely escape men's notice. It could not but weaken the force of his exposition of how the English found their identity as a people.

If Bede's attempt to show how the English were a people was weak in its broad outlines, it was nevertheless strong in its particular details. Thanks largely to his scheme of peoples which turned upon the providential role of the English, Bede presented the succession of bishops in sees and of kings in kingdoms not piecemeal but as aspects of the development of a single, English people. Levison pointed out how, especially in the third book of the *Ecclesiastical History,* Bede's synchronous presentation of events in Northumbria, Wessex and Kent, in East Anglia and among the Middle Angles, in Essex and in Mercia, created a vivid awareness of the unity and .interdependence of the English church and so by implication of the English nation.[35] Bede's skilful depiction of the speed of the English conversion and of the Anglicization of the episcopate heightened the effect. As it has been succinctly put, 'In 630 there was only one kingdom [Kent] in which [Christianity] was established at all firmly. By 660 it was established for good in all but one [Sussex]. . . . Until 644 there was no English bishop. By 678 there was only one who was not English, Theodore himself'.[36] Bede's literary models, notably Rufinus' Latin translation of Eusebius' *Ecclesiastical History,* also led him to stress the coherence

---

32. J. Campbell, 'Bede', in Dorey (ed.), *Latin Historians,* pp. 181-2.
33. iv, 24 (pp. 414-20).
34. iii, 10 (p. 244).
35. W. Levison, 'Bede as Historian', in Thompson (ed.), *Bede, his Life, Times and Writings,* p. 143.

of developments in Britain, and so the identity of the English people.[37] Eusebius traced the succession of bishops in a church that grew within the unitary Roman Empire. The church had its golden age under Constantine, whose victories and triumphs were the sequel to his conversion. It was but a small step for Bede to use the catalogues of kings, as well as the succession-lists of bishops, to show how conversion, ecclesiastical order, and the military victories of Christian kings created in the English people the unity and prosperity which marked the happy times under Theodore of Tarsus.

It was Bede's building up of this detailed picture within his too-artificial scheme of the interaction of the four peoples, rather than that scheme itself, which offered the English a new sense of their identity as a people stronger than anything discernible before he expressed it for them.

III

This new sense was further developed by Bede's handling of the paschal controversy and other differences between Celtic and Latin Christians; for in his eyes these controversies, too, helped the formation of the English people. A consideration of them brings in the fifth of the languages of Britain: the *lingua Latinorum* which was the language of the Catholic church in its doctrine, discipline, and worship, and which according to Bede should bind the four other languages in such a unity of race and obedience as the Pentateuch prefigured.[38]

The matters at issue, which appear in the *Ecclesiastical History* with wearisome iteration, are in their essentials simple to state.[39] With respect to the paschal controversy, both the Celtic and the Latin churches agreed that Easter should be kept on a Sunday; they also agreed that it should fall in the third week of the first lunar month of the year counting from the vernal equinox. But there was disagreement about what constituted the third week: the Latins held that it ran from the fifteenth day of the month until the twenty-first, while the Celts insisted that it ran from the fourteenth to the twentieth. There was further disagreement about the way to determine when this week should fall. It was necessary to adopt a correct cycle for reconciling the solar and lunar year: the Celts persisted with an old, eighty-four year cycle; whereas the Latins in due course adopted one of nineteen years. The second critical point of difference was the shape of the clerical tonsure: the Latins tonsured the crown of the head in a circle; while the Celts, it would seem, tonsured in a semi-circle from ear to ear.

36. Campbell, 'Bede', in Dorey (ed.), *Latin Historians*, p. 173.
37. Barnard, 'Bede and Eusebius', in Bonner (ed.), *Famulus Christi*, pp. 106-24.
38. i, 1 (p. 16), discussed above.
39. See especially Plummer's 'Excursus on the Paschal Controversy and Tonsure', in *Baedae Opera Historica*, Vol. II, pp. 348-54.

In modern eyes these are trivial issues. But Bede repeatedly made it clear that for him as for his contemporaries they carried deep and grave implications, and that upon their resolution depended the unity, peace and harmony of the church. They raised questions of authority and jurisdiction: correct paschal observance was enjoined by the apostolic see of Rome; a deliberate refusal of it amounted to a with-holding of the obedience that was due from all Christians to St Peter and to the pope as his vicar, and to an obdurate neglecting of the canonical custom of catholic bishops the world over.[40] Above all there were the dogmatic implications explored in the long letter from Abbot Ceolfrith of Jarrow to Nechtan, king of the Picts, which Bede cited in the fifth book of the *Ecclesiastical History*.[41] The letter originated in Bede's own monastery. Whether he took part in its drafting is de-batable, but his full citation demonstrates his approval of its contents.[42] Ceolfrith argued that incorrect usages regarding Easter and the tonsure proved complicity in two of the deadliest of ancient heresies. Thus to keep Easter on the fourteenth day was to allow that the paschal full moon might fall before the vernal equinox. But this equinox was when the sun as the source of light demonstrated Christ's victory over death by shining for longer than the moon which is the lesser light. To keep Easter in advance of this visible token of Christ's victory over death which was the source of all grace, was tantamount to saying that men might be saved by their own wills antecedently to God's grace. Those who held such an opinion were Pelagians—victims of the treacherous poison of Pelagius the Briton,[43] and so adherents of a British heresy from of old.[44] In a similar way the Celtic, ear-to-ear tonsure was no passing and insignificant fashion: it was the characteristic sign of Simon Magus. By Bede's time Simon Magus was thought of not only as the first simoniac who had tried to buy from St Peter the ability to confer the Holy Spirit,[45] but also as Peter's deadly foe throughout his ministry at Antioch and Rome.[46] It was the badge of such a heresiarch that the Celts, by their tonsure, were wearing.[47] Seen in this light, Celtic obser-vances, especially as maintained by the stiff-necked British, struck at the very heart of the Christian religion. As Bede saw matters their correction was a cardinal theme in the effective Christianization of the peoples of Britain. Only if all were guided away from them to unity in a single, Latin observance would the designs of Providence be ful-filled.

40. ii, 19 (pp. 198-200); iii, 25 (p. 306).
41. v, 21 (pp. 532-52).
42. For the question of authorship, see the differing views expressed in Bonner (ed.), *Famulus Christi*, pp. 24, 107, 214, 286.
43. i, 10 (p. 38).
44. i, 17 (p. 54); i, 21 (p. 64); v, 21 (p. 544).
45. Acts viii, 18-24.
46. Simon was so displayed in the *Pseudo-Clementine Recognitions* which Bede knew: Laistner, *Intellectual Heritage*, p. 148.
47. v, 21 (p. 548).

In Bede's scheme the English people in no small measure found itself by striving for such a unity; it was his concern in the *Ecclesiastical History* to keep this fact in the forefront of its mind. Bede interwove this theme of the paschal controversy and its implications for making the *lingua Latinorum* the common property of the peoples of Britain, with his record of how the English people found its identity by inter-acting politically with the other three peoples. When, in earliest times, the British wickedly refused to have anything to do with the conversion of the pagan English, it was a sign of God's purpose that the English people should be the means whereby the Christianity and culture of the Latins became the unifying force amongst the peoples of Britain.[48] The Latin Christianity which the English began to adopt in 597 was from the beginning outward-looking. Augustine's successor as arch-bishop, Laurence, set the pattern of the future by not merely taking charge of the new church gathered from the English, but by seeking also to bestow his pastoral care on the other inhabitants of Britain and Ireland; and he did so with an especial eye to securing the correct paschal observance and so fostering unity.[49]

The English role in vindicating Roman Christianity and making it the basis of religious and political unity throughout Britain runs like a thread through the third and fifth books of the *Ecclesiastical History*. In Book Three, following the withdrawal of Paulinus, the reconversion of Northumbria by Aidan and monks of the Celtic observance led, in the longest and most important chapter of the Book, to the synod of Whitby (664).[50] It is almost certain that Bede there invested the synod with a larger and more entirely religious significance than it in reality possessed.[51] King Oswiu definitively committed himself and his king-dom to Roman usages; he decided the issue, not on the rights and wrongs of paschal observance, but on the need to consult his eternal salvation by obeying St Peter's commands in all things.[52] Bede was not behindhand in underlining the consequences of so momentous a decision for the internal unity and for the external mission of the English. He described how Oswiu, though educated by the Irish, clearly realized that the Roman church was catholic and apostolic. With the consent of the whole church of the English people, he and King Egbert of Kent together dispatched Wigheard to Rome for consecration as archbishop so that he, in his turn, might consecrate catholic bishops for the English churches through the whole of Britain.[53] Wigheard died, but the pope sent Théodore of Tarsus; with him began the happy time when everywhere those who wished for wholesome instruction had

---

48. i, 22-3, discussed above.
49. ii, 4 (pp. 144-6).
50. iii, 25 (pp. 294-308).
51. Cf. the failure of the *Anglo-Saxon Chronicle* to allude directly to it: *a.* 664, in Whitelock (ed.), *English Historical Documents*, p. 153; and the recapitulation of his *Ecclesiastical History* by Bede, v, 24 (p. 564).
52. iii, 25 (p. 306).
53. iii, 29 (p. 318).

teachers ready to hand.[54] The church in Britain became a model of
right belief and right order;[55] the *lingua Latinorum* had become uni-
versally current among the English people and the foundation of its
unity.

In his fifth book Bede goes on to tell how the other three peoples—
the Irish, the Picts and even a few of the British—were brought into
the catholic belief and order that the English had embraced. And it
all happened by the instrumentality of the English people who spread
the *lingua Latinorum* throughout Britain and indeed Ireland as well,
save only where the obdurate British refused to hear. First Adamnan,
abbot of the Celtic stronghold of Iona, visited an English court, that
of the Northumbrian King Aldfrith, in whose province he stayed for
some time to see the canonical rites of the church:

> He was diligently exhorted by many who were better instructed than he,
> living as he did with but a very few followers in a remote corner of the
> world, that he should not venture to live contrary to the universal custom
> of the church in respect of keeping Easter and of other ordinances. He
> so changed his mind that he most gladly preferred to his own and his
> followers' usage the things that he saw and heard in the English churches.
> For he was a good and wise man, and excellently instructed in the
> knowledge of the scriptures.[56]

When Adamnan's own monks at Iona as yet refused to follow his good
example, he sailed to Northern Ireland (the south having adopted
Roman usages in the early 630s) and converted the Irish there.[57] The
conversion of the Picts followed by the agency of another Englishman—
this time Bede's own abbot, Ceolfrith of Jarrow, whose letter to the
Pictish King Nechtan Bede so prominently cited.[58] It led up to the
culminating triumph, when the monks of Aidan's Iona itself at last
came round. Again, the agent was an English monk: Egbert, who in
the last books of the *Ecclesiastical History* held an especial place in
Bede's esteem.[59] No reader alive to the way things develop in Bede's
History can miss the climax and fulfilment that gather in Book Five,
as in Egbert the long work of the English people came to fruition.
Egbert was prepared for his task at Iona (716-29) by the appearance
of a brother-monk of Boisil, the sometime prior of Melrose, with the
commission: 'He [Egbert] must go to Columba's monasteries; for their
ploughs are cutting a crooked furrow, and he must recall them to a
straight.'[60] Bede never penned a more majestic paragraph, or one that
drew together more of the strands of his *History,* than when he told

54. iv, 2 (p. 334).
55. iv, 18 (pp. 388-90).
56. v, 15 (p. 506).
57. Ibid.
58. See above.
59. iii, 4 (p. 224); iii, 27 (pp. 312-4); iv, 3 (p. 344); iv, 26 (p. 428); v, 9 (pp. 474-
80); v, 22 (pp. 552-6); v, 24 (p. 566). See esp. Kirby, 'Bede and the Pictish Church'
The Innes Review, Vol. 24, 1973, pp. 18-19, 24.
60. v, 9 (pp. 476-8).

how the Englishman Egbert ended his life at Iona on—of all days—
Easter Day 729, after he had celebrated mass for its monks according
to the catholic order:

> The monks of Iona accepted catholic rules of Christian order through
> Egbert's teaching some eighty years after they themselves had sent Bishop
> Aidan to preach to the English people. Egbert the man of God remained
> thirteen years upon their island, which he consecrated to Christ by
> causing to shine there anew the grace of ecclesiastical fellowship and
> peace. In 729, when Easter Day fell on 24 April [and so three days
> later than was ever possible under the Celtic computation], after cele-
> brating mass in memory of the Lord's resurrection, he passed to the Lord
> upon that very day. So he began the joyful celebration of the greatest
> of Christian festivals with the monks whom he had converted to the
> grace of unity, and he ended it with the Lord and the apostles and the
> whole company of heaven; verily, he entered upon that keeping of it
> which knows no end. It was a truly wonderful dispensation of God's
> providence that this venerable man should not only pass from this world
> to the Father at Eastertide, but that he should do so when Easter was
> being celebrated on a day when it had never before been celebrated in
> those parts. Thus the monks rejoiced to know the true and catholic time
> of Easter; and they were glad to enjoy the patronage of the father through
> whom they had been set right, as he passed to the presence of the Lord.
> As for Egbert, he was thankful to have lived long enough to see his
> hearers observe and keep with him an Easter Day that previously they
> had always avoided. So the most reverend father, in the assurance of
> their conversion, rejoiced to see the day of the Lord; he saw it, and was
> glad.[61]

For Bede, writing but two years later, it remained only to declare
the whole state of Britain at the present time. He could now show
that, save for the ever-disobedient majority of the British, the peoples
which lived in Britain had come to catholic unity under the guidance
of the English people. They shared the peace and truth of the church
universal.[62] Under the Providence that guided the church the English
had found nationhood by realizing their destiny to spread, throughout
the island of Britain and beyond, the catholic, Roman and Petrine way
of life which the *lingua Latinorum* expressed.

As a means of underlining the identity of the English people, Bede's
tracing of its achievement in resolving the paschal controversy and in
disseminating Latin Christianity had, again, points of weakness and
of strength. It was very much a churchman's view, and its appeal to
the lay world was, no doubt, limited. Moreover, even for churchmen
the very completeness of the Roman triumph which culminated in 729
with Egbert's Easter mass at Iona must have meant that, for the future,
the paschal controversy began to look as dead and archaic as yester-
day's ecclesiastical wrangles always tend quickly to look. Yet Bede's

61. v, 22 (p. 554); cf. John viii, 56.
62. v, 23 (p. 560).

picture of the English people which was schooled in the *lingua Latinorum* and also triumphantly disseminated it amongst other peoples had this strength to shape the future: it was underpinned by the whole of Bede's own erudition, not only or mainly in his *Ecclesiastical History* but also in his scientific and theological work. It was he, and he uniquely, who exploited such resources as the library brought from Italy to Jarrow by Benedict Biscop.[63] In so far as future generations of the English were learned, they were so as Bede's pupils. As they made his learning their own, they could scarcely fail to share his conviction, as expressed in the *Ecclesiastical History,* that they had come to be a people above all by first learning and then teaching catholic ways.

IV

Bede's handling of the history of the paschal question itself contained a didactic element: Christians have a duty to obey the apostolic see and its rulings, and to promote unity within and among Christian peoples. But he also had a more directly didactic purpose, through which he aimed at building up the English people, and especially key elements of it, with an eye to its national well-being in the present and future. It thus constitutes a third means by which Bede sought to help the formation of the English people.

Bede stated his didactic purpose to King Ceolwulf as follows:

> History sometimes tells good things of good men, so that the attentive hearer is moved to follow what is good; or else it sometimes relates bad deeds of evil men, whereby the devout and godly hearer or reader is no less enkindled to avoid what is harmful and wicked, and himself follow the more earnestly whatever he recognizes to be good and well-pleasing to God.[64]

He accordingly devoted much care to the edification of individuals and, through them, to the collective welfare and morale of the English people. His ways of doing this call for comment. He tended to praise explicitly and at length the good examples that he would have people follow, whereas he condemned only implicitly, or with the greatest economy of words, the bad examples that he would have people shun. His churchmen illustrate the point. Apart from the paschal aberrations which were, in his case, pardonable because he had no chance of being correctly instructed, or perhaps because he lived under duress, Aidan was a model monk.[65] Bede therefore related of him several stories of miracles by which God who judges the heart made plain what his merits were.[66] He also accorded Aidan a moving obituary, extolling

---

63. For Bede's library see Laistner, *Intellectual Heritage,* pp. 117-49; also R. W. Southern's remarks in *Medieval Humanism,* pp. 4-7.
64. *Praefatio* (p. 2); cf. ii, 1 (p. 128); iii, 17 (pp. 264-6).
65. iii, 17 (pp. 264-6).
66. iii, 15 (p. 260); for the purpose of miracle stories, cf. ii, 1 (p. 128).

the virtues in which monks of all generations should follow him.[67] Wilfrid, however, stands in a certain contrast. Despite the zeal for the Roman cause and for spreading the faith which made him a *reverentissimus vir,* and especially despite his conversion of the South Saxons, Bede clearly had reservations about him.[68] He was eloquently silent about aspects of his career which were common knowledge or which were recorded in Eddius' *Life,* such as his wealth and retinue like a lay nobleman's, the triumphalism of his episcopal ordination, or his disturbed relations with Theodore of Tarsus.[69] Again, Bede told no miracle story exclusively of Wilfrid himself though Eddius offered him many which seem at least as well authenticated as his own 'ut fertur' stories; and when Wilfrid died Bede simply devoted a long chapter to telling the facts of his forty-five years as a bishop.[70] From this chapter the reader forms an impression of his zeal. Yet Wilfrid received no such obituary as Aidan's, expressly extolling his virtues; Bede merely cited his somewhat stylized epitaph at Ripon.[71] Bede's many-sided reserve leaves the reader with the impression that there was much about Wilfrid for good men not to copy, which qualified the things that they should copy.

The same applies to kings. Bede held up his exemplary kings for imitation by speaking of them at length. Oswald, *christianissimus rex,* 'a man beloved of God', was the subject of many miracle stories, and above all of the anecdote of how he sent out to the poor his silver dish and the royal dainties set upon it.[72] Here was a model of royal *pietas*—of godly charity and kindness—for other kings to copy. Oswine of Deira was Bede's exemplar of his other royal virtue *par excellence: humilitas.* He exhibited it in his obedience to Aidan as bishop; so he received an obituary in which this virtue was expressly applauded, with an illustrative anecdote.[73] But despite his role at the synod of Whitby, Oswiu of Bernicia was not a model king: he had ordered Oswine's murder.[74] His death in 670 received but a brief notice, the only favourable comment being that by this time he was minded to die at Rome.[75] If very good kings like Oswald were a source of blessing to their whole people and extended its power,[76] the worst kings of all were apostates, like Eadbald of Kent, Osric of Deira, Eanfrith of Bernicia and Cenwealh of Wessex.[77] Their renunciation of Christianity swiftly and inexorably spelt temporal disaster for them-

67. iii, 17 (p. 266).
68. iv, 2, 13-16 (pp. 334, 370-84). But cf. the views expressed in Bonner (ed.), *Famulus Christi,* pp. 31-3, 380.
69. Colgrave (ed.), *The Life of Bishop Wilfrid by Eddius Stephanus,* pp. 26, 48-50, 86-90, 136-7.
70. v, 19 (pp. 516-30).
71. v, 19 (pp. 528-30).
72. iii, 6 (p. 230).
73. iii, 14 (pp. 256-8).
74. Ibid.
75. iv, 5 (p. 348).
76. See above.
77. ii, 5 (p. 150); iii, 1 (pp. 212-4); iii, 7 (p. 232).

selves or their people for so long as they persisted in it. Bede wasted
no words upon them: thus, the two Northumbrians died *impia manu
sed iusta ultione;* to register his point there was no need to say more.

At least, that was one reason for Bede's reserve. Another, no doubt,
was that as a profoundly Christian man, and in accordance with the
sixth chapter of the Rule of St Benedict, Bede shrank from adversely
judging and condemning others: it is generous and good to praise; but
it is presumptuous, even wrong, to blame. But above all it has been
pointed out how, throughout his writings, Bede felt a duty of discretion
or reticence when denouncing evil in high places, whether in priests or
kings, lest he undermine their offices or public authority in general.[78]
When it is appreciated, Bede's reticence conveys much about what he
thought was morally amiss in the English people, and about how he
wished to build it up both spiritually and politically. An example of
Bede's reticence has already been noticed in Bede's final 'whole state
of Britain' summary: Bede there hinted at his anxiety regarding the
kings of his day, saying that Ceolwulf's reign had seen such commotions
and setbacks that no one knew what to say of them or what would be
the outcome.[79] He referred to the monasteries in a comparable way:

> In these favourable times of peace and serenity, many of the North-
> umbrian people, noble and common alike, have laid aside their arms and
> received the tonsure, preferring that they and their children should take
> monastic vows rather than practise the art of war. What the outcome
> will be, only a future generation will see.[80]

The magnitude of Bede's reticence in such passages is clear only
through the accident of the composition and survival of his letter of
734 to his sometime pupil Bishop (later Archbishop) Egbert of York.[81]
Bede committed himself to writing because he chanced to be unable
through sickness and a missed meeting to talk privately with Egbert
as he had hoped. Bede who three years ago had written so triumphantly
in the fifth book of his *Ecclesiastical History* about the state of Britain
and so reticently about the failings of kings and monks, now spelt out
how deeply he was troubled by rooted evils: 'de calamitate qua nostra
gens laborat'.[82] He dwelt upon the fewness of the bishops and their
lack of pastoral zeal, upon the sloth and secularization of the monasteries, upon the consequent attrition of the lay powers 'who defend
our people from the barbarians',[83] and much else. Such anxieties lay
behind Bede's reticence in the *Ecclesiastical History,* and they explain
the emphasis that he placed upon the need of the English people for
edification. He sought to promote its unity and well-being by appealing

78. Campbell, 'Bede', in Dorey (ed.), *Latin Historians,* p. 177.
79. v, 23 (p. 558); see above.
80. v, 23 (p. 560).
81. Plummer (ed.), *Baedae Opera Historica,* Vol. I, pp. 405-23; Eng. trans. in Whitelock (ed.), *English Historical Documents,* no. 170, pp. 735-45.
82. Plummer (ed.), *Baedae Opera Historica,* Vol. I, p. 412.
83. Ibid., Vol. I, p. 414.

to its leaders. He knew that a healthy society needed both kings and clergy who performed the proper duties of their respective orders. They were the key men, to whom he sought especially to provide examples for imitation in order that they might sustain the English people in the providential course that its past history marked out for it.

Bede's exemplars of kingship fall into several categories,[84] the most relevant of which for his didacticism comprised those who, in their lifetime of active rule, exhibited such virtues as *pietas* (Oswald) and *humilitas* (Oswine). These were not the cardinal virtues of Germanic society in its heroic age. Dr Wallace-Hadrill offers a reminder that Bede's biblical erudition determined his thought: 'The kingship that mattered to him was a historical institution, originating in Israel, not in the forests of Germany.'[85] Bede, in fact, sought to make the *lingua Latinorum* that of his English hearers. His kingship was rooted in the Vulgate Old Testament, and especially in Saul and David as rulers of the people of Israel. For example, with Bede's reticence in mind the reader cannot fail to notice how the lessons of Samuel and Saul—the admonishing priest and the king who lacked the *humilitas* to obey— stood behind Bede's depiction of royal weakness after Ecgfrith's defeat by the Picts at Nechtansmere in 685. Ecgfrith was defeated because he did not heed the advice of the holy father Egbert or of Bishop Cuthbert, who counselled him not to attack, respectively, the Irish— 'a harmless race and one always most friendly to the English nation'—and the Picts, towards whom Bede was also well disposed.[86] Nechtansmere was a just punishment for the sins of the royal house. It stood as a warning to future kings which was the more pointed because Bede showed how from that time 'the hope and strength of the English kingdom began "to ebb and fall away" '.[87]

As regards bishops and monks Bede's letter to Egbert of York lifted the veil of his reticence much further. Long parts of it are, in effect, a sustained commentary on the *segnitia nostri temporis* to which Bede discreetly alluded in the *Ecclesiastical History*.[88] In the light of Bede's strictures upon monks in his letter to Bishop Egbert, one grasps at once the point of Bede's extended depictions of exemplary monk-bishops. John of Hexham, Cuthbert and above all Aidan, placarded the virtues of pastoral zeal, simplicity of life, devotion to prayer and scriptural meditation, refusal to offer any save the most essential hospitality to the wealthy or to receive their gifts and endowments, and the like: these were the virtues that Bede deemed it essential to teach the clergy and monks of his day.[89] The didactic reason likewise emerges for the three powerful chapters of Book Five, in which Bede warned against the perils of laxity by Dryhthelm's vision, against delay

84. See Wallace-Hadrill, *Early Germanic Kingship*, pp. 85-91.
85. Ibid., p. 78.
86. iv, 26 (pp. 426-8).
87. iv, 26 (p. 428); the words quoted are from Virgil, *Aeneid* ii, 169.
88. iii, 5 (p. 226); iii, 26 (p. 310).
89. v, 2-6 (pp. 456-68); iv, 27-32 (pp. 430-49); iii, 5, 15-17 (pp. 226-7, 260-6).

in performing penance by the fate of a Mercian layman, and against an impenitent death by the damnation of an unnamed monk. 'This story', wrote Bede of the last of these, 'spread far and wide, prompting many to perform penance for their offences without delay. Would that from now onwards the reading of my words might have a like effect'.[90] When Bede's message is fully taken, Book Five is not less notable for the urgency of its recall to the standards of Aidan and Cuthbert than for its triumphant joy at the fulfilment of God's purposes in Britain by the agency of the English people. Only by dint of continual renewal according to the best standards of religion could that people secure its identity, character and well-being.

How well calculated was Bede's didactic purpose to renew the institutional and moral quality of kingship upon an Old Testament model, and the pastoral zeal and manner of life of bishops and monks upon the model of the seventh-century heroes of the conversion, and by these means to confirm the English in the high vocation that had above all made them a people? The considerable appeal to churchmen of Bede's didacticism is perhaps most apparent in connection with the Anglo-Saxon missions to the continent during the eighth century.[91] It was probably more acceptable to kings than might have been expected. Bede showed, not unpersuasively in such a case as Edwin of Northumbria, that whereas the pagan gods had helped the English kings but little, when kings were converted they might reign *gloriosissime*.[92] Bede's expectation that Christian kings would be brave and a terror to all the barbarian nations affirmed what was strongest in their traditional role.[93] If he confirmed their old role in war, he added a new one in peace. He himself suggests that there was not all that much kingly tradition for the invaders to bring from the woods of Germany. The Old Saxons, for example, had no kings but only viceroys *(satrapae)* with temporary power for the duration of a war.[94] It is, moreover, instructive to compare Bede's royal virtues of *pietas* and *humilitas* with Isidore of Seville's *iustitia* and *pietas*.[95] Even in Bede's day kingship—at least as he knew it in Northumbria—was still too unformed for Bede to exhibit it as discharging the royal function of upholding justice. Kings had not as yet created a clear image of their peacetime authority, nor were sufficient means at hand to bind themselves and their dynasties firmly to their peoples.[96] It was to supply these deficiencies that Bede urged kings to learn with *humilitas* the precepts of churchmen. When kingship was so rudimentary, kings

90. v, 12-14 (pp. 488-504).
91. For the circulation of the *Ecclesiastical History* in France and Germany, see Colgrave and Mynors (eds), *Bede's Ecclesiastical History*, pp. lxi-lxix.
92. ii, 20 (p. 202).
93. iv, 2 (p. 334).
94. v, 10 (pp. 480-2).
95. W. M. Lindsay (ed.), *Isidori Hispalensis episcopi Etymologiarum sive originum libri xx*, 2 vols, Oxford 1911, not paginated.
96. See Wormald, '*Lex scripta* and *Verbum regis*', in Sawyer and Wood (eds), *Early Medieval Kingship*, pp. 105-38.

stood only to gain by filling out their office through Old Testament examples and teachings, and by heeding a church that spoke the *lingua Latinorum* with its overtones of Roman legal and political authority. As Dr Wallace-Hadrill has put it, the *Ecclesiastical History* 'was, in effect, a mirror of princes of unexampled power'.[97] When Bede commended *humilitas* to kings it opened the gateway to *iustitia,* both as a kingly quality and as a quality that kings transmitted to their people. Abbot Ceolfrith made that clear to the Pictish King Nechtan: Christians, he said, trusted that 'the more powerful men were in this world, the more they would strive to hear the commands of the Judge of all and to have his commands obeyed by those committed to them as well through their example as by their authority'.[98] In this way Bede's refashioning of kingship in the light of Israelite precedents from the Vulgate gave it a new scope and sanction. It bound the English kings and people together, in peace no less than in war, upon a biblical model. To kings it brought authority and to their subjects a new solidarity with them in a shared obedience to God's commands as the church transmitted them through the *lingua Latinorum.*

V

The foregoing analysis of certain features of the *Ecclesiastical History* represents an attempt to grasp how the concept and the character of the English people presented themselves to Bede's mind. The consistency and force of his depiction, and his urgent didactic purpose, suggest that he wished to communicate his understanding widely to his English hearers. How far he succeeded in doing so is a different matter: it can be studied only by tracing the influence of the *Ecclesiastical History* (so far as it can be separated from Bede's legacy in general) in later Anglo-Saxon history.[99] The available evidence is slight, and mainly concerns the copying and circulation of the *Ecclesiastical History;* only very seldom can its direct impact be observed. The evidence may be divided into three periods: from Bede's death in 735 until the Danish invasions; the age of Alfred and his immediate successors; and from Dunstan's reforms until the Norman Conquest.

For the first period, the material has largely been assembled by Professor Whitelock.[100] Bede himself began the dissemination of the *Ecclesiastical History,* which he dedicated to King Ceolwulf of Northumbria; he sent it to Ceolwulf 'for copying and fuller study as time allows' *(ad transcribendum ac plenius ex tempore meditandum),*[101] and

---

97.   Wallace-Hadrill, *Early Germanic Kingship,* p. 151.
98.   v, 21 (p. 534). Ceolfrith here foreshadows the picture of kingship given in canons 11-12 of the synod of Chelsea (787): A. W. Haddan and W. Stubbs (eds), *Councils and Ecclesiastical Documents Relating to Great Britain and Ireland,* 3 vols, Oxford 1869-71, Vol. III, pp. 452-3.
99.   I leave aside the large question of Bede's influence on the continent, through the Anglo-Saxon missions and otherwise.
100.   Whitelock, *After Bede,* Jarrow Lecture, 1960.
101.   *Praefatio* (p. 3).

to Albinus at Canterbury to be copied there.[102] The Danish invasions, amongst other causes, must have led to the loss of much evidence for its fortunes. But seven manuscripts survive as a whole or in part which were copied in England,[103] and continental manuscripts establish the earlier existence of others now lost.[104] The *Ecclesiastical History,* then, was certainly copied. Moreover in the Moore manuscript, and at greater length in a group of continental manuscripts that must depend upon work done in eighth-century Northumbria, the annals at the end of Book Five were continued. Occasionally the *Ecclesiastical History* appears in use. A letter of Alcuin written *c.*793 to King Offa of Mercia shows that Offa had a copy;[105] Alcuin himself knew it while he was at York and he used it extensively in his *Versus de patribus regibus et sanctis Euboricensis ecclesiae.*[106] In 773 a Northumbrian abbot named Eanwulf who wrote to Charlemagne a letter commending royal *pietas* appears to have adapted from it a letter of Pope Gregory the Great to King Aethelberht of Kent.[107] A letter of Pope Paul I to Archbishop Egbert of York and his brother, King Eadberht, to be dated 757/8, suggests that Bede's advice about the suppression of spurious monasteries was being put into effect; but how far this was under the inspiration of the *Ecclesiastical History* as well as of the letter to Egbert does not emerge.[108] Although the pope viewed Eadberht's actions with misgivings, Alcuin looked back to the brothers' rule as something of a golden age of the Northumbrian church.[109] The evidence makes it clear that the *Ecclesiastical History* was copied during this period, and used by kings, bishops and monks.

Alfred's reign was a time of vernacular translations; no Latin manuscript establishes that the *Ecclesiastical History* was copied in Latin during or soon after it. But the Old English translation was made,

102. Plummer (ed.), *Baedae Opera Historica,* Vol. I, p. 3.
103. For a list of manuscripts, see Colgrave and Mynors (eds), *Bede's Ecclesiastical History of the English People,* pp. xlii-lxx. The seven here relevant are: of the *c*-text, Kassel, Landesbibliothek 4″ MS. theol. 2, late-eighth century, Northumbrian; London, British Library, Cotton Tiberius C. II, late-eighth century, southern England; of the *m*-text, Cambridge, University Library, Kk. 5. 16 (the Moore manuscript), written in Northumbria in or soon after 737; Leningrad, Public Library, Lat. Q. v. I. 18, probably copied at Wearmouth or Jarrow not later than 747; British Library, Cotton Tiberius A. XIV, since the Cottonian fire of 1731 a charred remnant but of mid-eighth century Northumbrian provenance. Also fragments in New York, Pierpont Morgan Library, M. 826, late-eighth century; and Bloomington (Ind.), Lilley Library, MS. Ricketts 177, eighth-century, probably English.
104. E.g., Wolfenbüttel, Herzog-August Bibliothek, Weissenburg 34; Namur, Public Library, Fonds de la Ville, 11.
105. W. Levison, *England and the Continent in the Eighth Century,* Oxford 1946, pp. 245-6.
106. Ibid., p. 245; E. Dümmler (ed.), *Monumenta Germaniae Historica, Poetae Latini Medii Aevi,* Vol. I, Berlin 1880, pp. 169-206.
107. P. Jaffé (ed.), *Monumenta Moguntina,* no. 118, Bibliotheca Rerum Germanicarum, Vol. 3, Berlin 1866, pp. 283-4; cf. *Historia ecclesiastica* i, 32 (pp. 110-12).
108. Haddan and Stubbs (eds), *Councils and Ecclesiastical Documents,* Vol. III, pp. 394-5; Eng. trans., in Whitelock (ed.), *English Historical Documents,* no. 184, pp. 764-5.
109. *Versus de sanctis Euboricensis ecclesiae,* 1276-86, in Dümmler, *M.G.H., Poetae Latini Medii Aevi,* Vol. I, pp. 197-8.

presumably in part for a lay audience.[110] Aelfric of Eynsham later ascribed a translation to Alfred,[111] and it is likely but not demonstrable that it was among the books that Alfred considered 'most necessary for all men to know'.[112] This period also probably saw a translation into Old Irish; parts of what has been described as 'a very free and often abbreviated' version survive.[113] The compilers of the Anglo-Saxon Chronicle used the *Ecclesiastical History,* especially the recapitulation at the end. This evidence is not extensive, but it is clear that the *Ecclesiastical History* made its contribution to the learning of Alfred's reign.

Its impact during and after the age of Dunstan must, again, mainly be judged from what little is known of the copying and circulation of manuscripts. As regards the Latin text, there are three full texts of early-eleventh century date and two fragments.[114] There are also extracts designed to record the lives of particular holy men—Oswald, Birinus and Dryhthelm;[115] these serve to establish that the *Ecclesiastical History* continued to be valued as a didactic and hagiographical source. The Old English version, too, continued to be copied, the five principal versions show how widely.[116] The inference which may be drawn, that the *Ecclesiastical History* was used for the edification of the laity, is strengthened by Aelfric's use of both the Latin and the Old English versions in his vernacular *Lives of the Saints* where he used Bede's stories of Aethelthryth and Oswald;[117] and in his (also vernacular) *De doctrina apostolica* he referred to the didactic material of Book Five, caps. 13-14.[118] In Latin Wulfstan's *Life of St. Aethelwold* also drew on Bede's account of Aethelthryth.[119] In another genre Wulfstan's letter of protest about the conferring of the *pallium,* written c.1000,

110. The fragments in British Library, Cotton Domitian A. IX, fo. 10, may be from an early copy. See T. Miller (ed.), *The Old English Version of Bede's Ecclesiastical History of the English People,* Early English Text Society, Vols 95-6, 110-1, London 1890-1, Vol. I, pp. xx, xxxiii, lix.

111. B. Thorpe (ed.), *The Homilies of the Anglo-Saxon Church,* 2 vols, London 1844-6, Vol. II, pp. 116-8. The reference comes at the beginning of Aelfric's homily on St Gregory the Great, which Aelfric composed 'because [the translation of Bede's *Historia Anglorum* (*sic*)] is not yet known to you all, although it is turned into English'.

112. H. Sweet (ed.), *King Alfred's West-Saxon Version of Gregory's Pastoral Care,* Vol. I, EETS, Vol. 45, London 1871, p. 6. But cf. n. 126.

113. In Oxford, Bodleian Library, Laud misc. 610; see Colgrave and Mynors (eds), *Bede's Ecclesiastical History of the English People,* p. xlvi.

114. The texts are: Oxford, Bodleian Library, Hatton 43 (4106), provenance unknown; Cambridge, Trinity College, R. 7. 5; Winchester, Cathedral Library, MS. 1. The fragments occur in London, British Library, Egerton 3278, and Cambridge, Corpus Christi College, 270.

115. Oxford, Bodleian Library, Digby 175 and 39; London, Lambeth Palace Library, 173.

116. Oxford, Bodleian Library, Tanner 10, from some such smaller house as Thorney; London, British Library, Cotton Otho B. XI, perhaps Winchester; Cambridge, Corpus Christi College, 41, southern origin, ?Exeter; Oxford, Corpus Christi College, 279, southern or Anglian; Cambridge, University Library, Kk. 3. 18, Worcester. The last may be later than 1066.

117. W. W. Skeat (ed.), *Aelfric's Lives of Saints,* EETS, Vols 76, 82, 94, 114, London 1881-1900, Vol. 1, pp. 433-40, no. 20; Vol. II, pp. 124-43, no. 26.

118. J. C. Pope (ed.), *Homilies of Aelfric, a Supplementary Collection,* EETS, Vols 259-60, London 1967-8, Vol. II, pp. 613-37, esp. pp. 629-34.

119. iv, 19, in M. Winterbottom (ed.), *Three Lives of English Saints,* Toronto 1972, pp. 47-8.

drew extensively upon historical material from Bede's first two books.[120] After Wulfstan II became bishop of Worcester in 1062 his first dedication of a church was to Bede, whom Wulfstan's biographer described as *literature princeps de gente Anglorum*.[121] Through William of Malmesbury, interest in the *Ecclesiastical History* was to become greater during and after Norman times, when its study and inspiration formed a large part of the Anglo-Saxon response to the Norman Conquest. But up to 1066 it was clearly much copied in Latin and in the vernacular, and used by teachers who wished to edify as by bishops in search of historical precedents.

So how considerable was its influence between Bede's death and the Norman Conquest after which its study became so critical for the subject English? There is need for a careful balance. It would be easy to exaggerate, for before the Conquest many factors may have told against it. Bede's conception of the English people as expressed in his over-neat schematization of the four people that inhabited Britain was artificial. His sense that it had a providential mission to give Britain a quasi-Pentateuchal unity by disseminating the *lingua Latinorum* of scriptural erudition and catholic order probably represented too much the personal vision of an altogether exceptional man for it to command general acceptance, especially amongst the laity. In some minds at least, the ravages and settlement of the Danes may have made Bede's depiction of English hegemony, and especially the optimism, qualified though it was, of his 'whole state of Britain' survey, seem contrived and outmoded if not plainly misleading. When the Anglo-Saxons began to recover under the Wessex kings, Bede's Northumbrian bias may have told against him; the vernacular Anglo-Saxon Chronicle perhaps counted for more than did the vernacular Bede. It may be doubted whether they found quite the cohesion with which Bede sought to invest the English people, either in their internal self-awareness or in their outward political unity. So much depended on practical matters like well-safeguarded rights of succession amongst the kings and the firm annexation of conquered lands. Kings, moreover, were a source of unity through a judicial power that was more an exercise of secular lordship than of Bede's kingly *humilitas* or the Latin-inspired *iustitia* to which it pointed.[122] So far as the monastic order is concerned, as monasteries grew in public consequence as centres of intercession for those outside the cloister in life and in death—a role which in Bede's day was still a restricted one[123]—Bede's insistence that monks should

120. Haddan and Stubbs, *Councils and Ecclesiastical Documents*, Vol. III, pp. 559-61. For the date see Levison, *England and the Continent in the Eighth Century*, pp. 241-8.
121. R. R. Darlington (ed.), *The Vita Wulfstani of William of Malmesbury* i, 14, Camden, third series, Vol. 40, London 1928, p. 20.
122. For assessments, see esp. H. R. Loyn, 'The King and the Structure of Society in Late Anglo-Saxon England', *History*, Vol. 42, 1957, pp. 87-100; and J. Le Patourel, 'The Norman Succession, 996-1135', *English Historical Review*, Vol. 86, 1971, pp. 225-50, at pp. 240-2.
123. For an indication of the extent and limitations, see Levison, *England and the Continent in the Eighth Century*, pp. 28, 101-3.

free themselves from the taint of avarice by whenever possible not accepting lands or possessions to build monasteries became out-dated.[124] Bede was no enemy of monastic endowment as such. But his appeals to the age of Aidan lost much of their relevance as monasteries assumed an ever-increasing duty of performing intercessions and alms which could be discharged only if large benefactions were allowed and, indeed, encouraged. People, in fact, came to look to monasteries for other benefits besides those which Bede had wished them to confer; while the relations of monks to kings' courts tended to follow the lines of Wilfrid rather than those of Bede.

Nevertheless it was Bede, and so far as can be determined he alone, who first gave strong and clear expression to what the Germanic settlers in Britain had, or might aspire to have, in common. That the homilist Aelfric of Eynsham should have referred to Bede's work *tout court* as the *Historia Anglorum* is indicative of its power to concentrate their descendants' thoughts about their nationhood.[125] The continuing tradition of copying and translating the *Ecclesiastical History* bears witness to the persistence of its appeal and the relevance of its message that the English were indeed a single and coherent entity. But, above all, by the wide range of the learning that Bede transmitted, the English were kept reminded that they did well to think of themselves as a people after the fashion that God willed the Old and the New Israel to be a people. In particular, Bede assigned to kings a function in their life that was largely founded on Old Testament models, and that in the early stages kings themselves needed to have defined on their behalf. In that sense, no Bede, no Alfred. The debt was not neglected. Nothing could be more in line with Bede's intention for the English kings and people than Alfred's disclosure of his own mind made, significantly, in his English preface to a work of Pope Gregory the Great. For the encouragement of his people Alfred there recalled

> what wise men there formerly were throughout England *(geond Angelcynn)*, both of sacred and secular orders; and how happy times thére were then throughout England; and how the kings who had power over the nation *(hæfdoṇ dæs folces)* in those days obeyed God and his ministers; and they preserved peace, morality and order at home, and at the same time enlarged their territory abroad; and how they prospered both with war and with wisdom. . . . Consider what punishments have come upon us on account of this world, because we neither loved wisdom ourselves nor allowed other men to obey it.[126]

Bede himself could not have stated more succinctly the lessons that he would wish the English people and its kings to draw from historical study.

124. iii, 26 (p. 310).
125. Thorpe (ed.), *Homilies of the Anglo-Saxon Church*, Vol. II, pp. 116-8.
126. Sweet (ed.), *King Alfred's West-Saxon Version of Gregory's Pastoral Care*, pp. 2-4,as corrected by R. B. Mitchell, 'Old English Syntactical Notes, ii', *Notes and Queries*, Vol. 208 (n.s. 10), No. 9, September 1963, p. 327. It is hard to think that Alfred did not have in mind such passages of the *Ecclesiastical History* as iv, 2 (pp. 332-4).

IV

ARCHBISHOP ARIBERT II OF MILAN

THE SEE OF MILAN is of especial interest for the historian of the Investiture Contest because a dispute about it was the immediate cause of the breach between Pope Gregory VII and the Emperor Henry IV. From the mid-1050s, when the weak and simoniacal Archbishop Guy (1045–1071) first met with the bitter opposition of the partly religious, partly social movement of the Patarenes, the course of events there is familiar. But the personalities and struggles of the previous generation, when Milan was already a theatre of conflict under the formidable Archbishop Aribert II (1018–1045),[1] are also of interest and importance. The confrontation of *sacerdotium* and *regnum* which became open in the 1070s was already, if as yet confusedly, being built up. The conflicting aspirations of thrusting social groups were working from within towards rapid social change, while political disorders and ecclesiastical abuses gave ample pretext for intervention from outside by both Empire and Papacy.

In 1018, Milan was a city of wealth and, in practice, independence. It commanded trade routes which ran from Germany through the Alpine passes down to central Italy and Rome, and from Burgundy across to Venice. It was the metropolis of an ecclesiastical province of eighteen dioceses which it was well situated to control, not only in spiritual but also in temporal matters. There was, in fact, little check upon the authority of the archbishop. The emperors of the early eleventh century did not have the means readily to intervene there. The

---

* This article is based on a paper read to the Anglo-American Conference of Historians in London on 9 July 1965.

[1] The principal Italian sources for Aribert are Arnulf, *Gesta Archiepiscoporum Mediolanensium*, ed. L. C. Bethmann and W. Wattenbach, Monumenta Germaniae Historica, Scriptorum (= M.G.H. SS.), viii. 1–31 and Landulf Senior, *Historia Mediolanensis*, ed. Bethmann and Wattenbach, M.G.H. SS., viii. 32–100. Aribert's relations with Conrad II were extensively recorded in German chronicles, of which the most important is Wipo, *Gesta Chuonradi II Imperatoris*, in *Wiponis Opera*, ed. H. Bresslau, Scriptores Rerum Germanicarum (= S.R.G.), 3rd edn. (Hanover, 1915), pp. 3–62. For a modern narrative with full references to sources, see the *Jahrbücher der Deutschen Geschichte* as relevant: *Jahrb. des Deut. Reichs unter Heinrich II*, iii, ed. S. Hirsch and H. Bresslau (Leipzig, 1875); *unter Konrad II*, ed. H. Bresslau (Leipzig, 1879–84); and *unter Heinrich III*, i, ed. E. Steindorff (Leipzig, 1874). For recent studies, see F. Savio, *Gli Antichi Vescovi d'Italia, i, La Lombardia* (Florence, 1913), pp. 386–410; C. Violante, *La Società Milanese nell'Età Precomunale* (Bari, 1953); M. Marzorati, 'Ariberto', *Dictionario Biografico degli Italiani*, iv (Rome, 1962), 144–51; and Y. Renouard, *Les Villes d'Italie de la Fin du Xe Siècle au Début du XIVe Siècle* (Paris, Les Cours de Sorbonne, 1961–3), fasc. xi, pp. 355–80. I have not been able to see E. Wunderlich, *Aribert von Mailand* (Halle, 1914). T. Schieffer, 'Heinrich II und Konrad II. Die Umprägung des Geschichtsbildes durch die Kirchenreform des 11 Jahrhunderts', *Deutsches Archiv* viii (1950–1), 384–437 is a fundamental background study which in my opinion reacts too strongly against the views which it is intended to revise, and does not give due weight to Italian affairs.

count of Milan was a mere shadow, and it was not feasible, as it was
elsewhere outside Lombardy, to appoint Germans to the bishoprics.
Unlike the patriarchs of Aquileia, the archbishops of Milan did not need
direct German support against such ecclesiastical rivals as the patriarchs
of Grado, or against such lay magnates as the dukes of Carinthia and
the marquises of Verona. They used the Germans, but they did not
depend upon them. The Germans were good to have in the background,
to keep lay society in salutary fear; but, like their suffragans, the archbishops of Milan were men of Lombardy, immersed in their own affairs
and pursuing their own ends. So the seeds of conflict between Milan and
the Empire were present, if ever an emperor should attempt to advance
his power in the Kingdom of Italy.[2]

It was not only between Milan and the emperor that conflict threatened; within Italy itself the traditions and claims of the see of Milan set
it at loggerheads with the other major sees, and might well give rise to
a clash with Rome. As their patron saint, the Milanese had their great
fourth-century bishop and doctor St. Ambrose: as the pope was the
vicar of St. Peter, so the archbishop of Milan was the vicar of St.
Ambrose and exercised his authority over the local church. The citizens
were proud of the Ambrosian liturgy and customs which were peculiar
to Milan. But its Ambrosian traditions had never secured for Milan the
precedence among the great churches of Italy to which its situation and
vitality seemed more and more to entitle it. The emperors had preferred
Ravenna: for example, in 811, when Charlemagne made a will, he gave
alms and largesse to the metropolises of Italy in the order Rome—
Ravenna—Milan;[3] and the Ravennese claimed that their first bishop,
St. Apollinaris, had been sent to them by St. Peter himself. But the
people of Aquileia, to which the popes gave precedence, capped this:
they maintained that the evangelist St. Mark had been sent there and
that (as the council of Mantua declared in 827) St. Peter in person had
appointed Hermagoras of Aquileia to be the *proton Italiae pontificem*.[4]
During the tenth century, both sees held to their claims;[5] and, by
reaction, the Milanese were already seeking to clear away the confusion and express the realities of power by propagating the title to
superiority of their own see. The *De situ civitatis Mediolani*,[6] a legendary

[2] For the above paragraph, see G. Schwartz, *Die Besetzung des Bistums Reichsitaliens* (Leipzig,
1913), especially pp. 5, 12. Schwartz estimated that under Henry II (1002–24) and Conrad II
(1024–39) one sixth of the Italian bishops whose origins are known were German, while under
Henry III (1039–56) the proportion rose to at least a quarter. But there were few German
bishops in the province of Milan, and none in the city.

[3] Einhard, *Vita Karoli Magni Imperatoris*, xxxiii, ed. L. Halphen (Paris, 1923), p. 96.

[4] J. D. Mansi, *Sacrorum Conciliorum Nova et Amplissima Collectio* (= Mansi), xiv. 497–8.

[5] In 963, for instance, Pope Leo VIII confirmed that Aquileia had precedence, after Rome,
among the churches of Italy: J. P. Migne, *Patrologia Latina* (= P.L.), cxxxiv. 991; in 983 it was
the archbishop of Ravenna who assisted the archbishop of Mainz at the coronation of Otto
III: W. Holtzmann, *Geschichte der Sächsischen Kaiserzeit*, 3rd edn. (Munich, 1955), p. 292.

[6] Ed. A. and G. Colombo, in L. A. Muratori, *Rerum Italicarum Scriptores*, new edn, i, pt. 2;
for the legend of St. Barnabas and St. Anatalon, see chs. i–ii (pp. 14–22). The editors argue
that the *De situ* was written in the eighth century by a contemporary of Paul the Deacon. The
ninth-century date proposed by Violante (*op. cit.*, pp. 240, n. 67) is to be preferred. The late
eleventh-century date favoured by Savio (*op. cit.*, pp. 6, 49–59) and others is improbable.

version of Milanese antiquity, went one better than the story of Herma-goras. As St. Peter was the first to teach at Rome, so (it was asserted) his brother-apostle St. Barnabas first established the faith at Milan. He chose one of his converts, St. Anatalon, to be bishop, and, in his death-bed testament, St. Anatalon, in no way differing from his master St. Barnabas, awarded to Milan a precedence next after Rome and a privilege and dignity over all churches whatsoever throughout North Italy.

In this way, for purposes of outside propaganda, the traditions of Milan were augmented. The legend of St. Anatalon reserved the primacy of Rome; indeed, there was good reason for laying a certain emphasis upon it, in order to provide a sanction for Milan's claims against those of its rival sees. But in different circumstances—if, for example, the papacy should ever lend its support to an emperor who attempted to bring Milan to heel—the controverting of the claims of Ravenna and Aquileia might serve as a precedent for controverting the claims of Rome. The process of tradition-making might be extended in support of the contention that the Ambrosian church ought not to be subject to Roman laws. In this way, given the pride and the jealous independence of the church of Milan, there were the makings of a conflict with Rome itself.

Furthermore, the internal structure and social basis of the church of Milan and the prevailing abuses within it gave rise to many possibili-ties of trouble. The archbishop was by custom elected from the *ordinarii* or *cardinales*, as the senior clergy of the cathedral were called, while the emperor merely approved whomever the Milanese elected.[7] Because the senior clergy were mostly drawn from the *capitanei*, the predominant group of Milanese society, the see was normally in safe hands. The *capitanei* were the more committed to the Milanese church because since 983 they had been enfeoffed with rich cathedral lands of which they enjoyed hereditary tenure.[8] Somewhat apart from this alliance of church and *capitanei* stood the *vavassores*, a group of lesser aristocracy who in 1018 had no hereditary claim to their fiefs. Their aspirations were a latent source of danger within Milanese society itself, and they were a potential ally for the external enemies of the archbishop.

Yet another source of menace in a century of reform was the Milanese customs, often dignified with the epithet 'Ambrosian', which certainly deserved the condemnation visited by more advanced reformers upon the 'heresies' of simony and nicolaitism. Simony was the buying and selling of orders and offices in the church. In his third will[9] Aribert II

---

[7] Arnulf, i. 3, M.G.H. SS., viii. 7.

[8] Arnulf, i. 10, M.G.H. SS., viii. 9.

[9] The texts of Aribert's four wills are printed as follows: (i) 1034: J. P. Puricelli, *Ambrosiae Mediolani Basilicae ac Monasterii Hodie Cistertiensis Singularis Descriptio*, ch. ccxxiv, pp. 168–70, in J. Graevius, *Thesaurus Antiquitatum et Historiarum Italiae* (Leyden, 1722), iv, pt. 2; (ii) 1042: A. Fumagalli, *Delle Anticità Langobardico-Milanesi* (Milan, 1792), diss. iii, p. 379; (iii) 1044: A. F. Frisi, *Memorie della Chiesa Monzese* (Monza, 1777), diss. iii, pp. 29–30; (iv) 1044: Puricelli, *op. cit.*, ch. ccxxv, p. 189.

expressly provided, in the case of a chapel which was left to the archbishops of Milan, that whenever a new priest was appointed, he was to pay sixpence to the archbishop: a grossly simoniacal provision.[10] Nicolaitism covered all deviations from celibacy. Marriage was open and acknowledged among the clergy of Milan;[11] the scope for marrying their daughters to well-beneficed clerks reinforced the bonds between the leading families and the church. This was all very shocking to more advanced reformers, and would soon begin to attract their censures.[12] But in 1018 it still bound together a proud, powerful and numerous church, which in practice, if not as yet in theory, was very much a law unto itself.

*   *   *

There were clearly great possibilities at Milan for an archbishop who had an instinct for action and dominion; but equally clearly such an archbishop might well be tempted to go too far for the good of his church and city. Aribert II was such a man. He continually augmented and safeguarded the already vast wealth of his church. He acquired monasteries for it: from the Emperor Henry II he gained the monastery of St. Filinus and St. Gratian near Milan, and from Conrad II the rich and important monastery of Nonantula. He set himself to improve the patrimony of the church. Too much of the church's wealth took the form of urban property, which in his day was not the most profitable form of wealth. He therefore acquired land, for preference outside the city; after the famine of 1033 and during the warfare of 1035 and later years he bought it up wherever he could, while prices were favourable. He also secured gifts of land and insisted on terms which forbade their future alienation by the church; the archives of Milan contain charters of Aribert's time granting land to the church and prohibiting alienation or subinfeudation on pain of return to the donor or his heirs. Aribert's own first will (of 1034) illustrates the same policy. In it are listed castles, chapels, houses and lands in twenty-six places which he left for the benefit of the cathedral, fourteen parish churches and seven monasteries. They were to provide income in money and kind for the clergy, and they were to be administered by specified clerks. No one might alienate or dispose of the property:

> I will and appoint [said Aribert] that no priest, deacon or subdeacon of the major order, and no abbot or abbess of the abbeys named, and no priest of the order of decumans of the aforesaid churches, and no pontiff of this holy

---

[10] In 1059, Cardinal Peter Damiani found that there was at Milan a well-known tariff of payments for promotion in holy orders: *Opuscula*, v (P.L. cxlv. 95).
[11] For clerical marriage at Milan, see Peter Damiani, *op. cit.* (P.L. cxlv. 95–6); Andrew of Strumi, *Vita Sancti Arialdi*, iv, ed. F. Baethgen, M.G.H. SS., xxx, pt. 2, 1051; cf. Anselm of Besate, *Rhetorimachia*, ii, 10, ed. K. Manitius, M.G.H., Quellen zur Geistesgeschichte des Mittelalters, ii (Weimar, 1958), 157–9.
[12] Guy of Arezzo, *Epistola ad Heribertum Archiepiscopum*, ed. F. Thaner, M.G.H., Libelli de Lite, i. 5–7, is an early attack on simony there.

see of the Milanese church, shall have licence regarding these buildings and lands to sell any or all of them, or to make a charter, or by any device to give them as a fief to anyone, or to invade them.

Aribert's policy was to accumulate land in the dead hand of the church. It must have been especially unpopular with the vavassours, hungry for land and hereditary right.

Aribert assembled wealth for himself and his family as well as for his church. The property of which he disposed in his four wills is evidence of this. He had a favourite nephew, Gerard, of whom little is known, though it seems that he was Aribert's agent-at-large in Lombardy; at least, during a long illness of the bishop of Cremona, Gerard made himself very unpopular there by his high-handed administration of the see on his uncle's behalf.[13] Gerard died before Aribert, but in his final will (of 1044), Aribert left land on a generous scale to his sons, who were to make an annual payment to the monks of St. Ambrose for prayers to be said for Aribert's soul. Characteristically, if Gerard's sons were to die without issue the lands were to pass to the monastery of St. Ambrose.

Aribert sought wealth, but still more he sought power. The chronicler Arnulf said that he 'devoted himself to his own business and to other people's; he was busy with many matters and skilful in great ones', and again, more directly, 'he lorded it too much and too selfishly over the city'.[14] Certainly he was active in the ecclesiastical affairs of the city and province, and in a mild way even a reformer. Like others of his time, he sought to restore the canonical life. After 1018, there appear clauses in lay donations to churches which made them conditional upon the leading of a common life, or at least the keeping of a common table, by the clerks. Aribert's wills of 1034 and 1042 sought to foster it amongst the cardinals and the other clergy of Milan. He also agreed to some direct steps against married clergy, although his motive was perhaps less reforming zeal than his usual concern to save church property from the danger of alienation, in this case to clerical families.[15] Here the work of the reformer ends. All too often Aribert was out simply to build up his own power. When Conrad II gave to Milan the abbey of Nonantula, Aribert secured for himself the right to nominate and invest its abbots. Control over bishoprics was even more to be desired. There was a precedent: in certain of their suffragan sees, Aribert's rivals, the arch-bishops of Ravenna and Aquileia, had the right to appoint and invest the bishops. Accordingly, when, in 1035, Aribert was given by Conrad II the see of Lodi, the terms of the gift included this right. He proceeded to abuse it. Uncanonically and without consulting the clergy of Lodi, he nominated a Milanese cardinal named Ambrose: a name which must

[13] M.G.H. Diplomatum (= DD), v, pt. 1, no. 29, pp. 37–9.
[14] '. . . ex quo praelatus est, suis et aliorum vacavit negotiis, pluribus intentus, grandia expertus . . .': Arnulf, ii. 1, M.G.H. SS., viii. 11; '. . . immoderate paululum dominabatur omnium, suum considerans non aliorum animum', *id.*, ii. 10, p. 14.
[15] At the council of Pavia (1022): Mansi, xix. 343–56.

have added insult to injury. Only after savage warfare did Aribert impose Ambrose on Lodi by sheer force of arms.

*   *   *

If Aribert was powerful in the ecclesiastical affairs of Lombardy, he was of the highest consequence in its political life as well. Soon after his death, it was said in a Charter of Henry III that he had the whole kingdom of Italy at his command.[16] When he stood at the height of his power, that was true enough; but, in fact, the story of his political fortunes has two parts. At first, he was necessary to the emperor, and therefore had the kingdom at his command; but afterwards, when his own strong actions had made him no longer necessary, he was an over-mighty subject, whom the emperor must strike down if it were possible.

From his accession in 1024 up to 1034, Conrad II needed Aribert and the bishops as a defence against the great lay families of the kingdom. In 1002, when Otto III died, these families had tried to secure the Italian crown for their own candidate, Ardoin of Ivrea, but he was eventually defeated by Henry II. The five main families in North Italy were the Aledramids, the Otbertines, and the houses of Turin, Tuscany and Spoleto. When, in 1024, Henry II died childless, all of them save the house of Tuscany were openly hostile to Conrad. They were supported by the citizens of Pavia, the ancient Lombard capital, who rose and destroyed the royal palace; thereby removing another obstacle to the authority of Milan and of its archbishop. But if the Italians were willing thus far to oppose Conrad, no one was prepared to court the fate of Ardoin by being nominated rival king of Italy. So they looked further afield: first to the Capetians, but with the usual caution of his line King Robert the Pious would not let a member of his family stand; then to Duke William V of Aquitaine, whose son provisionally became a candidate.[17]

Here was Aribert's chance to be useful to Conrad. Twice in twenty-five years the lay families had conspired to be rid of a German king. Conrad's need for allies against them was clear, and the bishops were the obvious choice. Their own traditional policy was to support the emperor in order to prevent the Italian kingdom from falling under the control of the lay families. So the Italian bishops rallied to Conrad and Aribert came forward as their leader. In 1025, at the Whitsun *Reichstag* in Constance, Aribert led the Italians who promised their loyalty. He declared that, when Conrad came to subdue Italy, he would himself receive him, publicly laud him as king and crown him without delay. Aribert had his reward: at Constance he was given his rights over the see of Lodi.

By the end of 1025 William of Aquitaine, who had prudently made the support of the bishops a condition of his intervention, withdrew his

---

[16] '. . . qui omne regnum Italicum ad suum disponebat nutum': see above, p. 5, n. 13.
[17] M. Bouquet, *Recueil des Historiens des Gaules et de la France*, x. 39, 483, 500-1.

son's candidature for the Italian crown. Aribert sent envoys round
Lombardy to rally support for Conrad, and, in 1026, Conrad made his
first Italian expedition. Aribert did what he had promised, once again
to his own advantage. He crowned Conrad king; because of Conrad's
anger at the revolt and contumacy of the Pavians, the ceremony, which
should have been performed at Pavia, took place at Milan. Another and
more tangible reward for Aribert was the abbey of Nonantula. Further,
Henry II's most able, zealous and trusted supporter among the Italian
bishops had been Leo of Vercelli, who suddenly died in 1026. Conrad
appointed Arderic, a cardinal of Milan, to succeed him as bishop, while
Aribert took Leo's place as the emperor's principal agent and supporter
in the kingdom.

In 1027, Conrad's imperial coronation at Rome witnessed a further
victory for Aribert. The Milanese version of the event survives in the
chronicle of Arnulf and in the so-called *Commemoratio superbiae Ravennatis
episcopi*.[18] It built upon the legend of St. Anatalon. In accordance with
the legend, Conrad himself repelled an attempt by the archbishop of
Ravenna to assert his own precedence by presenting the emperor to the
pope for consecration. Aribert of Milan himself was not at hand, but
Conrad insisted upon being presented by Arderic, the young Milanese
who had just become bishop of Vercelli. He thereby demonstrated the
precedence and the prerogatives of Milan: as the pope should crown the
emperor, so the archbishop of Milan should elect and crown the king of
Italy and present him to the pope to be made emperor. This (it was
claimed) was now expressly asserted by both Conrad and Pope John
XIX as against the archbishop of Ravenna.[19]

Arnulf's chronicle leaves no doubt of the pride and pleasure of the
Milanese at this exaltation of their see and in the bold policy of their
archbishop which led up to it. At last, it seemed, Milan had been given
its due. After the events of 1026–7 Aribert enjoyed a time of assured pre-
eminence in Lombardy; the kingdom indeed seemed to be at his command. Arnulf could well quote the words of scripture about Alexander
the Great: *siluit terra in conspectu eius*.[20]

Aribert's usefulness to Conrad and, therefore, his power reached their
high water mark at the time of Conrad's successful bid to secure the

[18] M.G.H. SS., viii. 12, n. 69.
[19] It should further be said that the precedence of Milan was by no means settled beyond
question in 1027. Only the Milanese version of events at the coronation survives, and it
clearly improves upon them. In the same year, Pope John XIX could call Aquileia 'caput et
metropolim super omnes Italiae ecclesias' (P.L. cxli. 1138); whereas in 1047 Pope Clement II
was perplexed when the archbishops of Milan,Ravenna and Aquileia squabbled about who
should sit in councils at the pope's right hand: after consulting the Roman clergy, he said it
should be Ravenna (P.L. cxlii. 581–2, Mansi, xix. 627–8). The Milanese kept to their claims,
(Landulf, iii. 4, M.G.H. SS., viii. 75) and found some support for them (e.g. Benzo of Alba,
Liber ad Heinricum, i. 9, M.G.H. SS., xi. 602); the imperialist Archbishop Tedald of Milan and
his papalist successor Anselm III both crowned kings in their cathedral. But in 1085 the
Antipope Clement III tried to settle a dispute between the three rival metropolises in favour
of his own former see of Ravenna (P.L. cxlviii. 828–30), and for this reason, no doubt, he lost
the favour of the imperialist party in Milan (Landulf, iii. 32, M.G.H. SS., viii. 99–100).
[20] I Macc. i. 3.

kingdom of Burgundy—the greatest single achievement of his reign. In 1032 King Rudolph of Burgundy died, leaving no direct heir to his crown. The claimants were Count Odo II of Champagne, who was Rudolph's nephew, and Conrad II, whose queen was Rudolph's niece and whose claim to succeed the late king had acknowledged. The campaign that finally decided the issue took place in 1034. Conrad planned a combined attack upon Odo in Burgundy: a German army coming down from Basle was to meet at Geneva an Italian army which had crossed the St. Bernard Pass, and together they were to invade the kingdom. The Italian army was organized and led by Aribert of Milan and Marquis Boniface of Tuscany, whom Arnulf called the *duo lumina regni*. Alarmed by the size of the two armies, Odo of Champagne fled without venturing upon a battle. Thus, thanks in no small measure to Aribert's marshalling of Italian support, Conrad was able to add the kingdom of Burgundy to the Empire.

The conquest of Burgundy seemed calculated to reinforce the well-tried alliance between the German emperor and the Italian bishops. From Aribert's standpoint, no doubt this was so. Conrad soon made it clear that he thought otherwise, and for good reasons. Whereas Leo of Vercelli had made himself unusually reliable in the service of the German emperors, Aribert was blatantly prepared to serve Conrad only so far as it suited his own interests. He wanted to avoid binding ties with the emperor, while consolidating his own power in the church and kingdom of Italy. Such an over-mighty subject was little to the liking of Conrad, and the addition of Burgundy to the Empire, a matter in which Aribert did Conrad an especial service, tended to make him superfluous.

The kingdom of Burgundy marched with Italy from the south-west of Germany right down to the Mediterranean. So long as it was independent of the Empire, the Italian lay magnates could look through it to France for support, as for example they did in 1024. With this help they could challenge German control in Italy and, above all, the German claim to the Italian crown. The remedy for the German emperors was an alliance with the bishops and the use of a Leo of Vercelli or an Aribert of Milan. But once Burgundy had become part of the Empire, and the western Alpine passes were more open to German control, the position was significantly changed. It was no longer so necessary for the emperor to rely on the bishops, who were too well entrenched in their ecclesiastical and local positions to be very devoted royal agents.

Conrad was an able ruler of secular and realist bent. In Germany he had already, during the revolt of Duke Ernest of Swabia, had good reason to value the loyalty of the lesser feudatories.[21] In Italy he started a policy of binding the lay feudal classes to himself and making them, rather than the bishops, the supporters of his power. There were good prospects for its success. The vavassours, in particular, were alienated from the bishops by such things as Aribert's insatiable appetite for lands

[21] Wipo, xx, S.R.G., pp. 39–40.

and wealth; they were open to just the approach that was binding the German feudatories to the emperor as the guardian of their rights. Conrad also began to look towards the great lay families, whose support was necessary if he was to exploit his acquisition of Burgundy. In 1034 Boniface of Canossa—head of the one great lay family that had not opposed Conrad's accession—stood beside Aribert as a *lumen regni*. Conrad had also successfully negotiated with his old enemy Count Humbert Whitehands of Turin in order that the Italian army might cross the Great St. Bernard Pass. At about this time marriages were arranged to link the houses of Tuscany and Turin and also the Otbertines with Germany. It was the start of a policy of recruiting lay support which was to be very successfully developed during the ensuing years.

Aribert, on the other hand, fell rapidly out of favour with Conrad, and at the same time his position in Milan became manifestly vulnerable. In 1035, the hostility of the vavassours came into the open: when the land of one of their number was confiscated, they rose in revolt. They were expelled from the city, but they found support in the country and at Lodi, where the imposition of Bishop Ambrose still rankled. A pitched battle between the vavassours and Aribert's forces at Campo Malo was indecisive; but since the vavassours went unpunished, the moral victory rested with them. Before the battle both Aribert and his opponents had appealed to Conrad. The appeal of the vavassours was peremptory: if the emperor would not give them justice, they would enforce the law on their own behalf. This drew from Conrad his famous retort: *Si Italia modo esurit legem, concedente Deo bene legibus hanc satiabo*. According to the German chronicler, Wipo, who tells the story, Aribert and his supporters also appealed to Conrad, but in confusion; and they awaited his intervention with alarm (*aegre*).[22]

The outcome of this twofold appeal was Conrad's second Italian expedition. He was prevented from reaching Milan until the early months of 1037. When he arrived, Aribert welcomed him in his cathedral with an eagerness that betrayed his anxiety. On the day after the welcome, a tumult broke out among the citizens which compelled Conrad to withdraw to Pavia. At the old capital which, when he was crowned, he had ignored in favour of Aribert's Milan, Conrad convened a general assembly of the Italian kingdom and offered justice to all who sought it. Aribert's Italian enemies were present in strength and made their accusations against him.[23] Conrad summoned the archbishop to judgement and ordered him to make restitution to all whom he had wronged.

Aribert flatly refused to obey the imperial command. Never before had a bishop so openly defied an emperor. Conrad ordered him to be imprisoned and committed him for custody to Patriarch Poppo of Aquileia and Duke Conrad of Carinthia. Aribert's predicament was

---

[22] Wipo, xxxiv, p. 54.

[23] According to Wipo (xxxv, p. 55), their spokesman was a count Hugh. If, as is likely, he was the count of Milan whose authority had been reduced to a shadow by the rise of Aribert, he was a member of the Otbertine house, which had once been hostile to Conrad.

an unenviable one. He was kept in prison at Piacenza, which lay outside his province, in the custody of a rival. Conrad, for whose favour he had looked, was now his bitter enemy and was recruiting more and more support among the ancient rivals of the bishops, the lay magnates. The vavassours, whose unaided resources had held Aribert off at Campo Malo, now, with Conrad's backing, had everything to hope for. Towns like Lodi remembered Aribert's wrongs. Conrad could count on plenty of Italian allies amongst laymen of all kinds.

Yet Aribert's fortunes revived dramatically. He managed after two months to escape from prison in the disguise of a monk and to reach Milan. Smarting at Conrad's insult to the Ambrosian see the populace rallied to him, and Aribert could confront Conrad on something like even terms. Whereas at Pavia Conrad seemed to have destroyed Aribert by a single blow, he was now committed to a protracted struggle in the fever-laden Italian summer. He branded Aribert as the enemy of himself and of the state, summoned fresh forces from Germany and, in May 1037, laid siege to Milan. Aribert meanwhile added to his own formidable local forces by enlisting the support of the other bishops. They responded readily, for they were alarmed by Conrad's favour towards the lay feudatories.

Events moved swiftly: Conrad wanted to finish with Aribert before the heat of summer. On Ascension Day (19 May) a fierce battle was fought outside Milan. Conrad's Italian supporters formed the left wing of his attack, and his standard was carried by Count Guy of Sezzé, an Aledramid: it is another example of a family which twelve years before had opposed Conrad now coming round to his support. The battle was indecisive and both sides withdrew to recover strength. But Milan had held off its assailants, and, although Conrad resumed the siege, he ventured upon no more battles. He was content to lay waste the surrounding countryside and, far more important, to conduct an experiment in binding lay society to him by feudal and legal means.

On Pentecost Eve (28 May) he promulgated his *Constitutio de feudis*,[24] which is usually said to have been issued in favour of the vavassours, whose support Conrad especially wanted. So far as it goes this statement is true enough. They were given their coveted claim to inherit their paternal fiefs; no knight who was the tenant of a bishop, abbot, marquis, count or any other might be deprived of his fief unless he were convicted of a grave fault by the law and by the judgement of his peers; and a structure of appeals was set up for the protection of tenants of land which gave them direct access to the emperor. This clearly met the vavassours' hunger for law. But Conrad saw clearly the danger of conceding too much to them. The law was drafted to please and unite all lay classes. That was the declared intention: it was designed (the preamble stated) 'to reconcile the hearts of the magnates and the knights so that they may always be found harmonious and may faithfully and con-

[24] M.G.H. DD. iv, no. 244, pp. 336–7.

stantly serve us and their lords with devotion'. There was a concession to please all when the emperor limited his right of *fodrum*. Conrad was trying to mobilize the whole of lay feudal society. In place of the old alliance of emperor and bishops against the lay feudatories, there was to be a new alliance of Conrad and the lay feudatories against Aribert and the bishops.[25]

As a tactical move against Aribert the *Constitutio de feudis* was well contrived. Yet on the day after it was published Conrad was cheated of his advantage. On Whit Sunday itself there happened a natural portent of a kind that medieval people understood as showing the judgement of God; plain for all to see, Aribert and not Conrad stood justified. As usually at Pentecost, Conrad solemnly wore his crown at mass, in a tiny church which was the only place to be found in the devastated countryside. During mass there suddenly broke from a cloudless sky a storm of fearful violence, which killed both men and horses in Conrad's camp and drove some men from their wits. It was a dire portent indeed that lightning should strike during the mass of Pentecost, and its effect was heightened since no part of the storm touched Milan or did damage outside Conrad's camp. No wonder some said that they saw St. Ambrose himself in the storm, watching over his city. This sign of divine displeasure lost Conrad the advantage that he had so lately won;[26] the contest was even once more.

Conrad prudently decided to disperse his army to cooler parts. Lest this should seem to be an admission of defeat he boldly pronounced by a fiat the deposition of Aribert from the see of Milan. To succeed him he named a cardinal of Milan and imperial chaplain with the appropriate name of Ambrose. The result was as might have been predicted: the Milanese destroyed Ambrose's property in the city and, for the most part, rallied to Aribert more zealously than ever. Aribert's reaction was also in character. If Conrad had declared that he was deposed from his see, Aribert would presume upon his newly-asserted claims in the kingdom of Italy to declare Conrad deposed from the crown, and he would find a successor to him as king whom he would sponsor for the Empire itself. Aribert's choice to be king of Italy was no other than Count Odo II of Champagne, who in 1034 had been Conrad's rival for the Burgundian crown. That Aribert had then been an agent of his defeat did not deter them from making common cause against Conrad now.

The advantage to Conrad of his recent acquisition of Burgundy and his cultivation of the lay families was soon clear. Cut off by the kingdom which he had helped Conrad to win, Aribert could do little to help Odo; in November 1037 Odo's attack on Conrad was defeated at Bar by Duke Godfrey, and Odo was killed. Aribert's envoys to Odo were captured on their return journey by Marchioness Bertha of Turin:

[25] Opportunist that he was, Conrad still looked with favour upon the exceptional bishop who opposed Aribert, like Hubert of Asti: M.G.H. DD., iv, no. 245, p. 338.

[26] The real impact of this portent was upon the camp of Conrad himself, where the *Constitutio de feudis* was published. It was the German, not the Italian, chroniclers who recorded it.

once again, a member of a family which in 1024 had opposed Conrad. She sent them in chains to the emperor, who, upon thus learning of Aribert's plans, was able to arrest and imprison, without a judgement, his leading accomplices at court—the bishops of Cremona, Vercelli and Piacenza. Aribert found that he could not oust Conrad from the Italian kingdom as easily as he had installed him.

Nevertheless, his local power at Milan was undiminished and his rival Ambrose was wholly unable to get possession of the see. For the moment Conrad did little further to effect the deposition of Aribert. He merely made a savage example of Parma which had independently risen against him on Christmas Day 1037, by slaughtering many of its citizens, burning the city and destroying most of its walls. In the spring of 1038 Conrad renewed his struggle with Milan. Pope Benedict IX, who was in the imperial camp, agreed to excommunicate Aribert and probably also to recognize Ambrose. The Milanese no more cared for papal sanctions than they did for imperial ones, and utterly disregarded their authority; it is from this support lent by a pope to a hostile emperor that there can be traced the most extravagant of all Milanese claims: that by Ambrosian custom the pope had no right to intervene in Milanese affairs.[27] Conrad's preoccupations in South Italy and a severe plague which fell upon his army in July and August made it impossible for him to deal with Milan in person. Before he returned to Germany, however, he ordered that Milan should be invested and the surrounding countryside harried every year until Aribert was compelled to submit.

In the summer of 1039, Conrad's Italian supporters obeyed by laying siege to Milan. As usual, Aribert's boldness and imagination did not fail him. Throughout the Ambrosian lands he proclaimed a general levy of all knights and peasantry who could bear arms and brought them to reinforce the citizens. To encourage them he contrived a kind of war-chariot or *carroccio*. According to Arnulf's description, a tall beam like the mast of a ship was erected upon a stout cart. It had a golden ball at the top, from which hung down two pennants of whitest stuff. Underneath was a cross upon which, with arms outstretched, the Saviour watched over the army; from it the Milanese might take comfort, whatever might be the fortunes of war. Thus originated the *carroccio* which, in the twelfth century, was to be the Palladium of the Milanese in yet direr strife against the Emperor. Aribert emerges as the first medieval figure to raise in arms an urban and local populace, drawn from all classes (as Arnulf expressed it) *a rustico usque ad militem, ab inope usque ad divitem*, and to deploy it for battle.[28] It was a significant prefiguration

---

[27] Thus, in 1059, when Peter Damiani came to Milan as a legate of the reformed papacy, he was nearly lynched by a populace which clamoured that the Ambrosian church ought not to be subject to Roman laws, and that the pope had no authority to judge or settle Milanese affairs. Peter answered by proclaiming the devotion to Rome of the earliest martyrs at Milan: Peter Damiani, *Opuscula*, v, P.L. cxlv. 90–2.

[28] 'Iubet . . . convenire ad urbem omnes Ambrosianae parochiae incolas armis instructos, a rustico usque ad militem, ab inope usque ad divitem, ut in tanta cohorte patriam tueretur ab hoste': Arnulf, ii. 16, M.G.H. SS., viii. 16.

of the commune. Aribert thus set the stage for what Arnulf called a *gravis inter urbem regnumque conflictus*. Led by its archbishop the city of Milan with its dependent countryside was under arms as a self-conscious unit, over against the Italian kingdom which Conrad had so lately sought to reconstruct on the basis of the lay feudatories both great and small.

Then came an anticlimax; battle was never joined. News reached Aribert's adversaries that Conrad had died far away in Utrecht, and they at once dispersed to their homes. For Aribert, this was a very mixed blessing. It was true that the threat to Milan was at an end and that in formal respects Aribert's bold defiance had brought him victory. Moreover, Conrad II's son and successor, Henry III, had an active sense of the reverence that was due to bishops by reason of their office. He had always quietly disapproved of his father's high-handed methods with Aribert and with his arbitrary imprisonment of the bishops of Cremona, Vercelli and Piacenza. In 1040 (after hearing and settling at Augsburg the complaints of the Italians against Aribert in his absence) Henry met Aribert at Ingelheim and took him into favour.[29] This rather qualified rehabilitation was, however, not at all to Aribert's real advantage. For one thing, Henry wanted no further royal coronation than he had had at Aachen in 1028; this left no opening for Aribert to be useful to Henry as he had once been useful to Conrad. Indeed, the title *rex Romanorum* which Henry used in 1040 indicated that he would centre his power in Italy not (like his feudally-minded father) upon Lombardy but (like Otto II and Otto III) upon a renovation of Roman and imperial ideas.[30] Again, by 1040 Aribert needed an adversary who was no less ruthless and resolute than himself—in fact, a Conrad—if he was to prosper and keep the loyalty of the city. Otherwise the social classes which he had awoken to self-consciousness, had organized militarily and had encouraged in a taste for violent excitement, might well turn against each other and against him. This was what happened: relieved of the salutary fear of an external foe, the Milanese gave themselves over to bitter civil wars which Henry III made abortive attempts to compose from a distance, and which Aribert did not have the means to put down on the spot.

The civil strife that now developed in Milan was marked by three important features. First, while it began with a private quarrel, it became in effect a class war between citizens and knights. The citizens, it must be remembered, were no mere rabble, but included merchants, notaries, moneyers, artisans, and the like, many of whom were men of substance. They were led by a certain Lanzo, whom Arnulf described as an *ingenuus civitatis miles*, and they had the better of the civil wars. At least as regards their social composition, the citizens whom Aribert had

[29] For Henry III's Italian policy, see C. Violante, 'La politica Italiana di Enrico III prima della sua discesa in Italia (1039–46)', *Rivista Storica Italiana* lxiv (1952), 157–76, 293–314.

[30] See P. E. Schramm, *Kaiser, Rom, Renovatio*, 2nd edn. (Darmstadt, 1957), pp. 226–9.

mobilized were already beginning to look very like the Patarenes of Hildebrandine times—the ultra-papalist enemies of all that Aribert stood for, who throve on violence, were at first financed by Nazarius the moneyer and were, in their heyday, led by the lay knight Erlembald.[31] Secondly, the vavassours made common cause with the *capitanei*, with whom Conrad had accorded them comparable rights. If not quite as Conrad had intended, the *Constitutio de feudis* won for him after his death the victory over Aribert that had eluded him during his life. Aribert was reduced to a state of hopeless dependence upon bands of lay feudatories whom he had no way of controlling. So, thirdly, in his declining years Aribert was more than anyone else the victim of the civil commotions. He had to leave the city in 1042 and flee to Monza; he was once more living outside Milan when two years later he fell mortally sick, although he was carried back there to die in 1045.

*   *   *

Aribert's own character and religion largely elude us: the pre-reforming figures of the early eleventh century do not reveal themselves to us as do a Peter Damiani, a Humbert or a Gregory VII. Clearly he was energetic, bold, acquisitive, a nepotist, a man who coveted power, hated restraint, tended to overplay his hand and did not shrink from bloodshed. He was jealous to guard and add to the rights of his patron St. Ambrose and to magnify his see by honouring the great figures of its past. He had some dogmatic competence, and, indeed, there was something about him of the reforming bishop of the imperial age.[32] His presence at Pavia in 1022 with Henry II, his real if limited action against nicolaitism, his fostering of the canonical life, his founding and enriching of monasteries, all provide evidence for this. Indeed, up to a certain point—but not beyond—there is a curious parallel between Aribert and Gregory VII himself: each was zealous for the saints of his see, and each had an indomitable will to power; each was willing to appeal to arms, and each looked for allies among the lower social strata; in either case there were mutual sentences of deposition with an emperor, and each of them suffered bitter ill-fortune and impotent exile in his latter years. But basically, Aribert and Gregory belonged to different and antagonistic worlds. If Aribert was something of a reformer, this was most evident under Henry II, when the vicar of Bray would have been a reformer, too. His true affinities were with the dying, residually classical culture of North Italy which is to be studied in tenth century writers like Gunzo or Liutprand of Cremona and still more in eleventh century ones like Anselm of Besate or Benzo of Alba.[33] Vain, self-

---

[31] For the leaders of the Patarenes, see esp. Andrew of Strumi, *Vita Sancti Arialdi*, M.G.H. SS., xxx, pt. 2, 1049-75.

[32] For this point, see Violante, *La Società Milanese nell'Età Precomunale*, pp. 233-45.

[33] Anselm of Besate, himself brought up at Milan and the nephew of Aribert's predecessor as archbishop, provides evidence in his *Rhetorimachia* of the intellectual, cultural and moral state of Milan in Aribert's day. It would not be unreasonable to see in him the intellectual counterpart to Aribert, the man of action.

opinionated, contentious, they yield glimpses of a world of low standards in religion and society alike—a world which the Gregorian reform deservedly swept away, leaving but little trace.

This brash, brittle, decadent Italy of Aribert, with its bogus traditions and its internecine feuds, was ripe for reform. Its ideas lacked conviction and its institutions were unstable; its society was rent by thrusting and conflicting classes. It is no wonder that the political power of Aribert melted like snow when his antagonist Conrad died. It was a personal *tour-de-force* and little more. Indeed, it was self-destructive, for the long-term result of the conflict between Aribert and Conrad was to assist to self-consciousness the very classes which were to provide allies for Gregory VII. The kind of people who had rallied to Aribert's *carroccio* would rally, too, to the *vexillum sancti Petri*.

V

THE PAPACY, THE PATARENES AND
THE CHURCH OF MILAN

BETWEEN 1046, when the Emperor Henry III reformed the papacy, and 1099, when Pope Urban II died, a very drastic change came over the loyalties of the church and city of Milan. In 1046, these loyalties were chiefly local; their centre was St Ambrose, the fourth-century bishop of Milan who was its patron saint. Apart from certain rather artificial purposes of propaganda in its long struggle for precedence over Ravenna and Aquileia, Milan did not actively look to the see of St Peter; nor was it, in practice, subject to Roman interference. Politically, it did, indeed, acknowledge an ultimate loyalty to the emperor; but this was because, so long as he ruled his kingdom of Italy from a distance, he was a safeguard for Milan's virtual autonomy in spiritual and temporal affairs. Milan had the appearance of a proud and self-sufficient metropolis, subject only to the ecclesiastical and civil rule of its own archbishop.[1] But, after 1056, its order and independence were rudely challenged when the Patarene movement gave rise to nineteen years of civil strife. The Patarenes sought help from Rome, where they found some ready and effective allies amongst the reformers. Milan, accordingly, reacted by showing itself actively hostile to the papacy; for a while, its citizens called upon the Emperor Henry IV to be active in vindicating his rights. Then, in 1075, the Patarenes suffered a sudden collapse and ceased to be an effective movement. Almost at once,

[1] For Milan before the middle of the eleventh century, see H. E. J. Cowdrey, 'Archbishop Aribert II of Milan', *History*, li (1966), pp. 1–15. For a concise narrative account of the Patarenes, see J. P. Whitney, *Hildebrandine Essays* (Cambridge, 1932), pp. 143–57; G. Meyer von Knonau, *Jahrbücher des deutschen Reiches unter Heinrich IV und Heinrich V* (Leipzig, 1890–1909), provides a fuller survey. For the Emperor Henry III's lack of concern with Italian affairs in the early years of his reign, see C. Violante, 'La politica Italiana di Enrico III prima della sua discesa in Italia (1039–46)', *Rivista storica Italiana*, lxiv (1952), pp. 157–76, 293–314. *See above*, Ch. IV.

the Milanese began to enlarge and entirely to redirect their loyalties: the claims of St Ambrose were made subject to those of St Peter and, amongst all classes, there developed an obedience to Rome and its demands. This transformation was already beginning to be evident at Canossa. Under Urban II, Milan was ruled by three archbishops who gained the support of most of their subjects when they embraced the cause of St Peter against the emperor. By 1099, the days were foreshadowed when Milan would be the ally of the papacy in its conflict with Barbarossa. So complete a reversal of front calls for explanation; in particular, the parts which the principal agencies of reform in eleventh-century Italy played in bringing it about need to be determined as clearly as the evidence will allow.

In the days of Archbishop Guy (1045–71), the reform which was being so generally promoted in Italy first came seriously to Milan in the violent form of the Patarene movement, which disrupted the city without making much real headway towards converting it. Milan's impatience of reform is only partly to be accounted for by the deep-rootedness there of the two 'heresies' against which the reformers were everywhere inveighing: simony (the buying and selling of orders and offices in the church) and nicolaitism (clerical marriage and concubinage).[1] More important, there was no foothold by which reform might establish itself gradually and renew the church from within. At Florence, for example, the reformed monasteries provided such a foothold; but the monasteries of Milan were identified with the order which the reformers assailed.[2] The defence of Ambrosian customs also served to build up resistance to reform. At Milan, as elsewhere in Italy, the cult of the urban patron reached its zenith in the eleventh century.[3] The hold of local traditions which had grown more elaborate with the centuries became stronger than ever;

---

[1] For the reformers' views of the Milanese church and clergy, see esp. Peter Damiani, *Opuscula*, v., [J. P. Migne,] *P[atrologia] L[atina]*, cxlv, cols 89–98; and Andrew of Strumi, *Vita sancti Arialdi*, 4, ed. F. Baethgen, *M[onumenta] G[ermaniae] H[istorica]*, *Scr[iptorum]*, xxx, p. 1051.

[2] *E.g.*, Andrew, 14, p. 1059; 16, p. 1060; and the appended letter of Syrus to Andrew, p. 1074; Arnulf, *Gesta archiepiscoporum Mediolanensium*, iii. 17, ed. L. C. Bethmann and W. Wattenbach, *M.G.H.*, *Scr.*, viii, p. 22.

[3] See H. C. Peyer, *Stadt und Stadtpatron im mittelalterlichen Italien* (Zürich, 1955), esp. pp. 25–45.

the more they grew, the more vulnerable to challenge they became, and the more jealously and nervously they were defended. To give but one example: for the Milanese, no local usage was more sacrosanct, or more symbolic of the city's independence, than the keeping of a three-day fast before Pentecost. Yet reformers could assail it, not only as being inappropriate (Christians should fast in the forty days of Lent but feast in the fifty days of Easter), but also as being un-Ambrosian (for a sermon ascribed to St Ambrose said expressly that such a fast was wrong).[1] It was because cherished 'Ambrosian' traditions were often vulnerable, quite as much as because many of them were ancient, that the Milanese stood so obstinately to their defence and set their faces against reform: if their traditions were challenged in any particular, who could say where the challenge might not end? The renewed activity of Rome confirmed this resistance to reform. For two centuries, Milan had not been made aware of Roman jurisdiction.[2] After 1046, when Roman councils increasingly settled the affairs of all the churches and popes sent their legates far and wide, the Milanese were provoked to rejoin that the Ambrosian church should not be subject to Roman laws and that the pope had no authority to settle its affairs.[3] They knew well enough that St Ambrose had thought otherwise.[4] But they were as much concerned to resist a challenge which came to them from outside as they were to scotch the reformers who threatened them from within.

In view of this defensiveness, those individuals at Milan who became persuaded of the need for reform could only promote it through a novel and radical association which would be like a foreign body in the city. In Archbishop Guy's days, the general

[1] For the fast, see Arnulf, iii. 17, p. 22; Landulf Senior, *Historia Mediolanensis*, iii. 30, ed. Bethmann and Wattenbach, *M.G.H.*, *Scr.*, viii, p. 95; Bonizo of Sutri, *Liber ad amicum*, vi, ed. E. Dümmler, *M.G.H.*, *L[ibelli] de l[ite imperatorum et pontificum]*, i, p. 596. For the Patarene leader Ariald's condemnation of it, for which he claimed the authority of St Ambrose, see Andrew, 17, pp. 1061–62.

[2] '... Mediolanensis ecclesia, quae fere per CC annos superbiae fastu a Romanae ecclesiae se subtraxerat dicione ...': Bonizo of Sutri, vi, pp. 590–91; *cf.* Arnulf, iii. 15, p. 21; see also P. F. Kehr, *Italia Pontificia*, vi, pt 1 (Berlin, 1913), esp. pp. 45–46, 110–11.

[3] During Peter Damiani's visit as legate in 1059: Peter Damiani, *Op.* v, *P.L.*, cxlv, col. 90; *cf.* the addition to Andrew, 20, p. 1064.

[4] *E.g.*, Arnulf, iii. 17, p. 22; v. 7, p. 30.

upsurge of reform in Italy joined with precocious social and economic developments at Milan itself to favour the emergence there of a radical and dissident movement like the Patarenes.[1] There had grown up sharp class divisions which it would be false to interpret in terms of a contrast between city and countryside, and, still less, between decaying feudal and rising urban classes. All the lay classes were building up both urban and rural interests; in an expanding economy, all were jostling to improve their positions. Thus, members of the highest class, the *capitanei*, used the church lands with which they were enfeoffed in 983 to develop a pre-eminence in the city and the countryside which they kept into the days of the commune.[2] Their inferiors, the vavassours, whom Conrad II had especially favoured in his *Constitutio de feudis* (1037),[3] were also prosperous. The *cives*—the moneyers, merchants, notaries and the like—were increasing in numbers as in urban and rural wealth.[4] Most people in these richer and rising classes identified themselves with the existing Ambrosian order. But, in the third quarter of the eleventh century, a minority of them did not. Instead, they foreshadowed the men and women of like background who, in the next century, turned away from worldly prosperity to movements like the Humiliati and the Waldenses, in which they sought a purer and more evangelical life of preaching and poverty than they found in the official church.[5] As yet, however, it was the corruption of a local church that was

[1] See the work of Violante, esp. *La società Milanese nell'età precomunale* (Bari, 1953); *La Pataria Milanese e la riforma ecclesiatica, i, Le premese* (Rome, 1955); 'I movimenti Patarini e la riforma ecclesiastica', *Annuario dell' Università cattolica del s. Cuore* (1955–57), pp. 209–23; 'L'età della riforma della chiesa in Italia (1002–1122), *Storia d'Italia*, ed. N. Valeri, i (2nd edn, Turin, 1966), pp. 69–276.

[2] Arnulf, i. 10, p. 9. The relative standing of the upper classes is indicated by the tariff of compositions prescribed by the papal legates of 1067 for breaches of the peace; a *capitaneus* was to pay twenty pounds, a vavassour ten, and a *negotiator* five: [J. D.] Mansi, [*Sacrorum*] *conc[iliorum nova et amplissima collectio*], xix, col. 948. Again, the first surviving list of consuls, dating from 1130, named ten *capitanei*, seven vavassours and five *cives*, and illustrates the persistence of this class structure: C. Manaresi, *Gli atti del comune di Milano fino dell'anno MCCXVI* (Milan, 1919), no. iii, pp. 6–8.

[3] *M.G.H., Diplomatum*, iv, no. 244, pp. 336–37.

[4] See R. S. Lopez, 'An Aristocracy of Money in the Early Middle Ages', *Speculum*, xxviii (1953), pp. 1–43.

[5] See H. Grundmann, *Religiöse Bewegungen im Mittelalter* (2nd edn, Hildesheim, 1961), esp. pp. 70–97, 487–524.

under attack, while the papacy was in the springtime of reform. The dissident minority at Milan could, therefore, embrace Rome as an ally. It could also look for support amongst the broad masses of the city and, no less, the countryside, whom the wars of Archbishop Aribert II (1018–45) had taught their power, and who cast covetous eyes on the wealth of the church and of the richer classes. It thus contributed to the armoury of Pope Gregory VII[1] a unique amalgamation of past and future: an ultra-papalist minority movement which, in respect of its militancy, harked back to the people-under-arms of Aribert's days; but which, in respect of its religious fervour, prematurely looked forward to the religious ferment of the twelfth century.

Such was the background to the Patarene attacks upon the Milanese church. Before all else, the Patarenes were a religious movement which pressed upon a hostile city establishment the arguments and demands of the most advanced reformers. Their leaders proclaimed that only clergy of pure and humble life were true ministers of Christ. As for the sacraments of the sinful majority, they were dead and idolatrous deceits which faithful Christians must shun. Their campaign began with an onslaught upon nicolaitism and with a demand that the clergy should return to an apostolic simplicity of life. The preaching of their first leader, Ariald, was recorded by his admiring disciple, Andrew of Strumi.[2] Before Christ came (he argued) men had lived in blindness and had worshipped idols. Christ brought light, and he left behind him followers who were to make it shine in all the world. Among the lettered, this was to be by the word of God; among the unlettered, it was to be by moral example. But the sinful Milanese clergy had relapsed into pre-Christian blindness, and so into that idolatry of wood and stones which the Old Testament writers condemned. Let the Milanese shun them and hear, instead, true teachers who followed Christ in poverty.[3] The hostile chronicler Arnulf represented Landulf, Ariald's colleague

[1] Of Gregory, it has justly been said that 'Misst man ihn an dem, was er gewollt hat, so war er wohl der kriegerischste Papst, der je auf Petri Stuhl gesessen hat': C. Erdmann, *Die Entstehung des Kreuzzugsgedankens* (Stuttgart, 1935), p. 161.

[2] For Andrew, see P. Lamma, 'Andrea da Parma', D[izionario] B[iografico degli] I[taliani] (Rome, 1960–), iii, pp. 110–12.

[3] Andrew, 4, pp. 1051–52.

in preaching, as warning the people more forcibly still: they were
blind men following blind leaders into the ditch; the sacraments
of sinful clergy were as dog's dung and their churches were as
cow-stalls.[1] The Patarenes, accordingly, organized a kind of lay
strike to coerce the clergy. Unless they were worthy, the faithful
were to boycott their churches.[2] Clerks were forced to sign an
undertaking to live chastely.[3] If they were impenitent, their
houses were spoiled; they were debarred from the altar; if they
tried to say mass, they were dragged away.[4]

In all this, the Patarenes did not seek to destroy the Ambrosian
church but to renew it.[5] Their ideal of a regenerated church is
revealed by Ariald's preaching when he began to attack simony
as well as nicolaitism. There were (he said) three orders in the
church: the preachers (*ordo predicatorum*), whose task was cease-
less exhortation; the continent (*ordo continentium*), whose task
was steadfast prayer; and the married (*ordo coniugatorum*), who
toiled with their hands and supported religion by their alms-
giving. Such was the pattern to which the church should conform.
But all who did not actively fight against simony incurred the
penalty of Simon Magus.[6] This effectively unchurched most of
the Milanese, so that the Patarenes were led to provide their own
separatist centres of true religion to which the faithful remnant
might resort. When a knight became persuaded that lay pro-
prietorship was wrong and put his church at Ariald's disposal,
Ariald installed in it clergy who would exercise a true ministry
of word and sacrament. In order that they might lead a common
life, he built for them a house, or *canonica*.[7] The church of St
Ambrose *ad Nemus* also became a centre of approved liturgical
usage.[8] The Patarenes tried to rally support at large by preaching,
public disputations and processions, and by providing the

[1] Arnulf, iii. 11, p. 19.

[2] Andrew, 10, p. 1057; Arnulf, iii. 13, p. 20.

[3] Arnulf, iii. 12, pp. 19–20.

[4] Andrew, 6, p. 1053; Arnulf, iii. 12, p. 20; Landulf Senior, iii. 10, pp. 80–81.

[5] They claimed the support of St Ambrose and the saints of the Milanese
church: Andrew, 10, p. 1056; 18, pp. 1062–63; 20, p. 1065; and they had a high
reverence for priesthood when exercised by worthy men: *ibid.*, 6, p. 1053.

[6] Andrew, 10, pp. 1056–57. For Simon Magus, see Acts viii. 9–24.

[7] Andrew, 11–12, pp. 1057–58; Bonizo of Sutri, vi, p. 595.

[8] Andrew, 17, p. 1061.

supreme witness of martyrdom.[1] Their zeal won them a large measure of support at Rome; particularly from Archdeacon Hildebrand and Cardinal Peter Damiani.[2]

Although these religious features predominated, the Patarenes were also a social movement. So far as numbers went, they found most of their support amongst the poorer populace of the city and countryside.[3] Yet the social analysis of the movement cannot proceed upon a simple class basis: Milanese society was too shifting and unsettled for this to be possible.[4] The Patarenes were socially eclectic; individual clergy and laity from every class adhered to them.[5] All their early leaders were disaffected members of the richer classes: Ariald sprang from a rural family of lesser knights[6] Landulf and his brother Erlembald were from the *capitanei*;[7] the *cives* were represented by the moneyer Nazarius who put his house and wealth at Ariald's disposal.[8] The Patarenes were also socially divisive, splitting every class asunder. Andrew himself said that

... one household was entirely faithful, and the next entirely

[1] Andrew, 18, pp. 1062–63; 19–20, pp. 1063–70.

[2] Arnulf, iii. 13, p. 20; iii. 17, p. 22; Andrew, 7, p. 1054; 19, p. 1063; *cf.* Peter Damiani, *Epp.* v, 14, 15, *P.L.*, cxliv, cols 367–69.

[3] Andrew, 10, pp. 1055–56. Arnulf despised the followers of the Patarenes as a 'turba civilis et agrestis': iii. 19, p. 23; iii. 20, p. 23; iii. 25, p. 25. For the emergence of a class of *rustici* who often gravitated, whether temporarily or permanently, to the cities, see Violante, 'L'età della riforma della chiesa in Italia', *Storia d'Italia*, i. pp. 80–84.

[4] For a Marxist interpretation of the Patarene movement as a class struggle of the urban and poorer classes against the feudal and richer ones, see E. Werner, *Pauperes Christi* (Leipzig, 1956), pp. 111–64. It is, however, against the evidence to suggest that Erlembald ever raised the lower classes 'fast vollständig' (p. 158); nor did the Patarenes ever altogether cease to find supporters among the knightly classes: see, *e.g.*, Gregory VII, *Registrum*, iii. 15, iv. 7, ed. E. Caspar, *M.G.H.*, *Epistolae selectae*, ii, pp. 276–77, 305; Landulf Senior, iii. 30, p. 97; Landulf of St Paul, *Historia Mediolanensis*, 57, ed. L. Bethmann and P. Jaffé, *M.G.H. Scr.*, xx, p. 45.

[5] For clerical support, see Andrew, 11, p. 1057; 19, p. 1063; 23, p. 1071.

[6] Andrew, 2, p. 1050; for Ariald, see C. D. Fonsega, 'Arialdo', *D.B.I.*, iv, pp. 135–39.

[7] Andrew, 8, p. 1054; Landulf Senior, iii. 14, p. 82. For Bishop Anselm I of Lucca (later Pope Alexander II), who sprang from the Milanese family of *capitanei* surnamed da Baggio, and for his relations with the Patarenes, see Violante, *La Pataria Milanese*, i, pp. 147–73, and 'Alessandro II', *D.B.I.*, ii, pp. 176–83.　　　　　[8] Andrew, 6, p. 1053.

faithless; in a third, the mother believed with one son, while the father disbelieved with another son. The whole city was thrown into disorder by this confusion and strife.[1]

The disarray was not least evident amongst the poor. According to Arnulf, the name 'Patarene' was first given sarcastically (*hyronice*) to Ariald's popular adherents by hostile members of their own class (*cetera vulgaritas*).[2] When need arose, the Patarenes and their adversaries could alike summon a crowd by sending couriers to sound bells and trumpets through the alleyways. Events turned on the fickle impulses of hostile mobs, not upon firmly-based class interests; oratory and the disbursement of money easily swayed popular loyalties from side to side.[3] Thus,

[1] Andrew, 10, p. 1057.

[2] Arnulf, iii. 13, p. 20. Most modern authorities have followed Giulini in linking the name 'Patarini' with the rag-pickers and dealers of the city: G. Giulini, *Memorie spettanti alla storia, al governo, ed alla discrizione . . . di Milano* (Milan, 1760), iv, p. 98; attention has also been drawn to a 'Via dei Pattari' which was named after the rag-pickers. On this interpretation, the name began in mockery of the lower-class social basis of the movement. It is, however, surprising that contemporary sources knew nothing of this derivation. Bonizo of Sutri, indeed, said that it was a term invented by the 'symoniaci' in mockery of the poverty of the Patarenes: 'eisque paupertatem improperantes, Paterinos, id est pannosos, vocabant'; yet, for him, their poverty was not social, but the spiritual poverty of those who, irrespective of class, were, like the apostles of Acts v. 41, counted worthy to suffer dishonour for the name of Jesus: Bonizo of Sutri, vi, pp. 591–92. Arnulf's ignorance of the origin of the word led him to invent a Greek derivation with less edifying overtones; it came from *pathos*, and 'pathos Graece Latine dicitur perturbatio': iv. 11, p. 28. Landulf Senior had no theory to offer, but he repeatedly linked the Patarenes with true or garbled forms of the Greek *cathari*: 'falsis catharis ordinem ipsum conturbantibus': Dedicatory Epistle, p. 36; 'Herlembaldus . . . suis cum chateris': iii. 29, p. 95; 'Herlembaldus cum suis omnibus cathedris': iii. 31, p. 98; *cf.* iii. 19, p. 88. Arnulf's search for a Greek etymology, together with Landulf Senior's tendentious attempts to link the Patarenes with Catharism (see also iii. 19, pp. 87–88; iii. 26, p. 93) may well indicate that the name 'Patarini' originated in the popular bandying about of half-understood religious terms imported from the Greek world: see E. Werner, 'παταρηνοί–Patarini: ein Beitrag zur Kirchen- und Sektengeschichte des 11 Jahrhunderts', *Von Mittelalter zur Neuzeit*, ed. H. Kretzschmar (Berlin, 1956), pp. 404–19; *Pauperes Christi*, pp. 138–44. Werner's suggestion that Catharist heresies contributed doctrines as well as a name to the Patarene movement is unconvincing.

[3] For the summoning of crowds both for and against the Patarenes, see Peter Damiani, *Op.* v, *P.L.*, cxlv, col. 90; Andrew, 23, pp. 1070–71; Landulf Senior, iii. 9, p. 80; iii. 18, p. 86.

the Patarene movement was highly unstable. At no time during its challenge did it firmly master the city, and it could never be sure of its popular support. The general revulsion from violence which followed the riots which it provoked on Whit Sunday, 1066, saw the nadir of its fortunes.[1] Moreover, it could not count upon Rome. Hildebrand, indeed, never failed it. But, more than once, when other counsels than his were uppermost, it suffered rebuffs: notably in 1059, after Pope Nicholas II had rehabilitated Archbishop Guy;[2] and in 1067, with the conciliatory legatine mission of Cardinals Mainard and John.[3] At times like these, when its following ebbed away, a modicum of statesmanship on the part of the archbishop and his supporters might have disarmed the Patarene challenge to the church of Milan.

It was not forthcoming. The opponents of the Patarenes were without resource to defend the existing order. This is well illustrated by the conservative chroniclers, Arnulf and Landulf Senior. In their very different ways, they reveal the predicament of men whom the Patarenes faced with a challenge that they could not effectively answer. Landulf Senior provides evidence for the much-harassed married clergy; he idealized the old, independent order which, for him, had finally died with Archbishop Aribert II. Taking refuge in a vanished past, he voiced the hopelessness of those lesser clergy who were about to be overwhelmed by what they felt to be the incongenial tides of reform and social progress.[4] Arnulf was a more subtle writer, with the outlook of the higher cathedral clergy and the *capitanei*, and so of a vigorously rising class.[5] He well knew that reform

[1] Landulf Senior, iii. 14, p. 82; Arnulf, iii. 20, p. 23.

[2] Arnulf, iii. 15, p. 21.

[3] Arnulf, iii. 21, p. 23; Mansi, *Conc.*, xix, cols 946–48.

[4] For Landulf, see the introduction to his chronicle in Landulf Senior, *Mediolanensis historiae libri quattuor*, ed. A. Cutolo, in *Rerum Italicarum scriptores*, ed. L. A. Muratori, new series, iv, pt 2 (1942), pp. iii–viii, xiv–xvi. He wrote in the early years of the twelfth century, but his attitude was formed during the events which he narrated.

[5] For Arnulf, see Violante, 'Arnolfo', *D.B.I.*, iv, pp. 281–82. His chronicle was written in three stages: (i) books i–iii, after the nomination of Archbishop Atto in 1072; (ii) book iv. 1–12, after the death of Erlembald; (iii) books iv. 13–v. end, after the election of Rudolf of Swabia in March 1077. His personal memory of events went back to the accession of Archbishop Aribert II in 1018: ii. 1, p. 11.

was called for,[1] and that, during his lifetime, the call had not been met: Milan was, therefore, vulnerable to the intervention of Rome.[2] But, if he half-admitted the disease of the Milanese church, the remedy which the Patarenes brought was worse. To him, they were impious and rigorist iconoclasts who scorned the laws of God and man, while they pandered to the appetites of people greedy for change.[3] Their aggressively lay character was an especial offence; it violated the right order of Christianity that lay mobs should be assembled to judge and coerce the clergy, and, still more, that a lay knight like Erlembald should lord it over the church:

> We do not resist you, O Roman lieges, [he protested when, as a crowning grievance, Erlembald found support at Rome] since our master St Ambrose says: I desire in all things to follow the church of Rome. We are one with you in faith; with you, we abjure all heresies. But it seems right to us that the law of the church should be taught by a doctor of the church, and not by an unskilled layman (*sed videtur nobis ratum, ut ius ecclesiasticum doctor exhibeat ecclesiasticus, non ydiota laycus*).[4]

As a consequence, Arnulf enlarged his hatred of the Patarenes' lawlessness to comprehend that of their allies at Rome.[5] Yet his insistence upon decency and order in the church[6] was not just a revulsion from the Patarenes: it reveals his own insecurity in face of the more general upsurge of reform in the late eleventh century. He was caught between the defence of a cherished but corrupt establishment which he saw no hope of setting right, and the demands of a reform which he knew was called for, but which

[1] Arnulf, iii. 10, p. 18; iii. 14, p. 21.

[2] Arnulf said that the exploits of Archbishop Aribert II were 'narranda, non iudicanda': ii. 1, p. 11; Archbishop Guy was 'idiotam et a rure venientem', and from his election 'omnia vertuntur in peius': iii. 2, p. 17. For the danger of Roman intervention, see iii. 15, p. 21. As Arnulf himself recorded, it was not the Patarenes but their adversaries who, despairing of Guy's ineffectiveness, first appealed to Rome: iii. 12, p. 20.

[3] For Arnulf's horror of the Patarenes' disregard for order, see esp. iii. 10, p. 19; iii. 12–13, pp. 19–20; iii. 17, p. 22.

[4] Arnulf, iii. 17, p. 22.

[5] See especially his comments on 'archidiaconus ille Hildebrandus': iii. 21, p. 23; iii. 25, p. 25; iv. 2, p. 26.

[6] Arnulf, iv. 12, pp. 28–29.

he abhorred in the drastic and violent guise of the Patarene movement. Like most of the Milanese, he turned his back upon it; nevertheless, he did so with a troubled conscience.

Matters became still worse for men like Arnulf, when, in 1066, the murder of Ariald provided the Patarenes with a martyr and left the layman Erlembald as their sole leader. Because the preaching and apostolic poverty of the clerks Ariald and Landulf had not won firm and continual support, Erlembald placed an even greater reliance than they had done upon coercion; under him, propaganda gave place to terror. Andrew of Strumi, to whom he was a familiar figure, said that he went about like a general (*quasi dux*), escorted by his retinue of knights and himself bearing arms. He was dressed outwardly in fine attire, although he wore a hermit's coarse cloth underneath; he flew from his lance the 'vexillum sancti Petri' which Pope Alexander II had given him to sanctify his warfare.[1] He recruited his retinue from young men of the feudal classes as well as from the people. They served him for payment, and were sworn to obey him;[2] however useful popular support might be, he treated it as an insufficient and secondary resource.[3] He sought to rule the city with a rod of iron:

> ... he was like a pope to judge the priests, [said Landulf Senior] and like a king to bruise the peoples. He now subdued the city by the sword and also by gold, and by many and diverse oaths; none of the nobles could withstand him.[4]

By such means, Erlembald revived the Patarenes; but he did so at the cost of marking them off more sharply than ever from the rest of the Milanese. He repressed, rather than overcame, the opposition which he stimulated, until it gathered the strength to break out and destroy him.

[1] Andrew, 15, pp. 1059–60; *cf.* Arnulf, iii. 17, p. 22, and Landulf Senior, iii. 14, pp. 82–83.

[2] Landulf Senior, iii. 15, p. 84; *cf.* iii. 14, p. 82.

[3] *E.g.*, in 1067, Erlembald is said to have summoned a host to recover the body of Ariald from Lake Maggiore in these terms: 'Discurrant itaque nuntii circumquaque velociter, qui omnes ad bella aptos nobiscum cum armis rusticosque huc venire hortentur cum plaustris, quatinus illi nobiscum pugnent, isti vero nostra arma et victus deportent': Andrew, 23, p. 1070. For Erlembald's skill as a mob orator, see Landulf Senior, iii. 14, p. 82.

[4] Landulf Senior, iii. 29, p. 95.

For a fresh look at the course of events will serve to suggest that this is what happened during the wider crisis of pope and emperor which Erlembald did much to precipitate, and which, as it developed, forced the Milanese to reconsider where their true loyalties lay. Erlembald worked in close collusion with Archdeacon Hildebrand, whose star rose at Rome in the last years of Pope Alexander II.[1] He provoked Henry IV by propagating the Patarene movement in other Lombard cities;[2] while, at Milan, he secretly made a plan that, when the aged Archbishop Guy died, the rights of the emperor should be ignored:[3] there should be a canonical election, subject to the consent of Rome. Archbishop Guy heard of this, and sought to forestall it by secretly resigning in favour of his sub-deacon, Godfrey, whom he dispatched to the emperor with his ring and staff for investiture. This secret, too, leaked out, and, when he returned from Germany, Godfrey found that the terrified archbishop had revoked his resignation.[4] Henry IV, however, stood by Godfrey, and, upon Guy's death in 1071, the Lombard bishops consecrated him at Novara.[5] In Arnulf's words, the Milanese were 'mindful of the ancient custom of Milan and of the honour of the emperor': they would have nothing to do with Erlembald's plan to hold a canonical election. He had committed himself to doing this by Epiphany, 1072; so, when that day came, he truculently acted alone. In the presence of a papal legate, he nominated as archbishop a young clerk named Atto. This provoked an uproar amongst the cathedral clergy and many of the laity, who later dragged Atto back into the cathedral from a banquet that Erlembald had arranged in the archbishop's palace and made him renounce the see for ever.[6] Hildebrand, on the other hand, upheld

[1] From his earliest days as archdeacon, Hildebrand had aspired to free the church from imperial control: see esp. his allocution at the Lent council of 1059 in A. Werminghoff, 'Die Beschlüsse des Aachener Concils im Jahre 816', *Neues Archiv [der Gesellschaft für ältere deutsche Geschichtskunde]*, xxvii (1901–2), pp. 669–75.

[2] Particularly in Piacenza and Cremona: Bonizo of Sutri, vi, pp. 596–98.

[3] For the emperor's right to approve the election of the archbishop of Milan, see Arnulf, i. 3, p. 7.

[4] Arnulf, iii. 21–23, pp. 23–24; Landulf Senior, iii. 18, p. 87; Bonizo of Sutri, vi, p. 598.

[5] Arnulf, iv. 3, p. 26; Landulf Senior, *loc. cit.*; Bonizo of Sutri, vi, pp. 599–600.

[6] Arnulf, iii. 25, p. 25.

him, and in 1073, when he became Pope Gregory VII, Atto joined him in Rome.[1] The result of Erlembald's brash and unsuccessful plans was, therefore, that, from the very outset of his pontificate, Gregory openly confronted Henry IV at Milan upon an issue that involved the conflicting claims of *sacerdotium* and *regnum*. Each was committed to a candidate for the see: the Patarenes depended upon the pope to help them promote the canonical succession of Atto; while the Ambrosian church looked to the emperor to vindicate his rights by assisting Godfrey. Once Milan was thus made the cockpit of pope and emperor, its apparent independence was at an end. For the moment at least, the Patarenes had thrown it back upon an active loyalty to the emperor.

Because Henry IV became preoccupied until the summer of 1075 with the Saxon rising, the crisis was slow to develop further. Henry's politic restraint deceived Gregory into hoping for an agreed settlement of Lombard affairs;[2] although, in Lent 1075, he went so far as to prohibit the investiture of bishops by Henry: a measure which, since it is only known from Milanese sources, seems to have had Lombardy particularly in view.[3] It was during this artificial pause, when there was no archbishop at all in the city, that Erlembald consolidated his armed dictatorship over church and city alike.[4] He was fortified by the full confidence and, probably, the financial support of Gregory VII, to whom, since he persecuted the simoniacal and married clergy with redoubled zeal, he was the 'strenuissimus Christi miles' who fought the warfare of God against the enemies of the church.[5] He treated as null the rites of the Lombard bishops: at Easter 1074, he

[1] Hildebrand ruled that the renunciation was invalid because made under duress: Arnulf, iv. 2, p. 26; *cf.* Greg. VII, *Reg.* ii. 30, p. 164. For Atto, see R. Abbondanza, 'Attone', *D.B.I.*, iv, pp. 564–65.

[2] Greg. VII, *Reg.*, i. 9, 11–12, 15, 19–21, 25–28, 29a, 43, 77, pp. 13–15, 17–20, 23–25, 31–35, 41–46, 47–49, 65–67, 109–11.

[3] Arnulf, iv. 7, p. 27; *cf.* Landulf Senior, iii. 31, p. 98.

[4] Arnulf, iv. 2, p. 26; Greg. VII, *Reg.*, i. 26–27, pp. 43–45. Erlembald also seems to have had the wealth of the see at his disposal: Arnulf, iii. 25, p. 25.

[5] At the same time, clergy were sent to Florence where John Gualbertus saw to their ordination; he also sent clerks of his own back to Milan, and dispatched Bishop Ralph of Todi to administer the sacraments in the city: Andrew of Strumi, *Vita sancti Ioannis Gualberti*, 78, ed. Baethgen, *M.G.H., Scr.*, xxx, p. 1100.

trampled underfoot the chrism that one of them had consecrated for the city and put off the Easter baptisms until he had procured some more. Arnulf complained that such deeds made the people more obedient to him, partly from simplicity, partly for money and partly because his crimes went unpunished. But he went on to record that Erlembald's party only seemed (*videretur*) to dominate the city,[1] thus implying that its ascendancy was, in fact, precarious and narrowly based. This is confirmed by no less a witness than Andrew of Strumi, who let slip that, in Erlembald's days, many people were left desolate of the sacraments;[2] and also by another Gregorian, Bonizo of Sutri, who credibly said that, at this time, Erlembald was on the defensive: 'crescebat cotidie numerus infidelium, et de die in diem numerus minuebatur Patarinorum'.[3] Moreover, Erlembald could neither coerce nor convince the cathedral clergy who, as the incident of the chrism proves, maintained contact with the Lombard bishops. Without them, he could not procure the canonical succession of an archbishop; so Atto remained at Rome, an unconsecrated and powerless exile. Most seriously of all, the *capitanei*, upon whom events at Milan most depended, hardened in their resistance to Erlembald.[4] It was they who took the lead in ridding the city of him.

Their chance came within a month of the investiture decree of 1075. A disastrous fire—the second in four years—swept through the city and destroyed the cathedral. To the Milanese, it was a divine punishment for the sins and excesses of the Patarenes. Erlembald rashly provoked them by trying once more to enforce his own Easter observances. A band of knights and others took an oath to uphold righteousness and the honour of St Ambrose by accepting the archbishop that the emperor gave them. They killed Erlembald, mutilated Liutprand, his low-born clerical aide who, at Eastertide, had usurped the place of the cathedral clergy, and put his supporters to rout. They sponsored a general thanksgiving in the church of St Ambrose, and a large concourse was absolved from the sin of adhering to the Patarenes.[5]

[1] Arnulf, iv. 6, p. 27.
[2] Andrew, *loc. cit.*; cf. 68, p. 1094.
[3] Bonizo of Sutri, vii, p. 604.
[4] According to Landulf Senior, Erlembald drove the *capitanei* from the city: iii. 30, p. 96.
[5] Arnulf, iv. 8–10, pp. 27–28; Landulf Senior, iii. 30, pp. 96–97; Bonizo of Sutri, vii, pp. 604–5. For Liutprand as Erlembald's aide, see Landulf Senior,

Many of the surviving Patarenes fled to other Lombard cities;[1] the rest receded into the twilight for nearly twenty years. At Rome, Gregory VII heard of these events with horror and dismay. He failed to grasp that the Patarene collapse was complete. He wrote a fervent letter of encouragement to Liutprand and for long looked in vain for the emergence of new knightly leaders after the likeness of Erlembald.[2] Preoccupied with his own religious principles of reform, he was always blind to the rootlessness of Erlembald's armed dictatorship.[3] Its collapse is the final proof that, at Milan, the Patarenes had never established reform upon a sure foundation. Perhaps, indeed, it was only by so violent a shock as they provided that reform could have found an entry into the proud city of St Ambrose. But their programme was too radical, their support was too narrow and their methods were too violent, for them ever to have firmly implanted it there. It must be concluded that, as allies of Gregory, they defeated the ends which he sponsored them to serve.

So, paradoxically, it was this putting to rout of Gregory's most favoured allies which opened the way for the steady progress of his cause in the Ambrosian church itself. Henry IV's own rashness also served actively to stimulate it; for, now that the Saxons were defeated and his hands were free, he dissipated the loyalty that the Milanese still showed towards him. When they invited him to settle the future of the see, he chose simply to disregard both the existing claimants, Godfrey and Atto; he nominated, instead, a young Milanese subdeacon of his chapel, named Tedald, who had served with him in the field against the

---

iii. 18, pp. 86–87. The mutilation was probably intended to disqualify him from exercising the priesthood: *cf.* Peter Crassus, *Defensio Heinrici IV regis*, 4, ed. L. de Heinemann, *M.G.H.*, *L. de L.*, i, p. 439.

[1] Bonizo of Sutri, vii, p. 605.

[2] Landulf of St Paul, 9, p. 24; Greg. VII, *Reg.* iii. 15, pp. 276–77, dated April 1076; iv. 7, p. 305, dated 31 October 1076. Erlembald's miracles were recalled at Gregory's Lent council of 1078: Berthold, *Annales*, *s.a.* 1077, *M.G.H.*, *Scr.*, v, pp. 305–6.

[3] For Gregory VII and the Patarenes, see Erdmann, *Die Entstehung des Kreuzzugsgedankens*, esp. pp. 127–30; *cf.* his well-grounded conclusion about Gregory: 'Gregor VII. rechnete nicht mit den Menschen, wie sie waren' (p. 210).

Saxons.[1] In the wider context of events, this led, during the early
months of 1076, to the mutual sentences of emperor and pope.
At Milan, it led, over the next ten years, to the virtual extinction
of support for the emperor. The two major chroniclers suggest
how it fell away. Landulf Senior indicates how Henry alienated
such people as the unreformed and unreformable clergy who
looked to the past. He makes it clear that, in spite of the considerable support that he must have enjoyed in the city, Tedald never
really established himself there. Only in 1081 did he have a brief
ascendancy when he crowned Henry king of Italy. But, in the
previous year, he had been at Brixen when Archbishop Wibert
of Ravenna was made antipope.[2] Because of Milan's long and
bitter rivalry with Ravenna, Henry's choice of Wibert was, in
any case, not calculated to please the Milanese; when Wibert was
installed at Rome (largely by Milanese arms), he ungratefully
used his papal dignity to assert Ravenna's superiority over Milan.[3]
This provides a plausible explanation for Landulf Senior's curt
dismissal of Wibert as 'out of his wits and rich in the devices of
the Greeks' (*dementum* [sic] *et Graecis facetiis affluentem*),[4] and
for his taking his story no further: he knew that, at Milan, disenchantment with an emperor who sponsored an antipope from
Ravenna had been final.

   In the mind of Arnulf, the nomination of Tedald as archbishop
also led to revulsion against the emperor; but it did so more
quickly, and with more positive results. Arnulf was gravely
offended that Henry should have disregarded the very existence

---

[1] The sources give differing details of the succession of Tedald. Landulf
Senior said that the Milanese sent four candidates to Henry, whom he rejected and named Tedald instead: iii. 32, p. 99. According to Bonizo of Sutri,
the Milanese *capitanei* elected Tedald at Henry's command, whereupon
Henry invested him: vii, pp. 605–6. Arnulf said nothing about Henry's
rejection of Milanese candidates, but only that he promoted Tedald 'proprio . . . indulgens arbitrio'. Arnulf also said nothing about an election,
although he did say that Tedald was received 'a clero et populo': v. 5, pp.
29–30. It seems clear that no one pressed the claims of Godfrey, although
Arnulf implied that he was still alive. For Gregory VII's reactions to the
nomination of Tedald, see *Reg.*, iii. 8–9, pp. 259–63.

[2] Landulf Senior, iii. 32, p. 99. According to Landulf, Henry first offered
the papacy to Tedald, who declined it. For the coronation *ordo* of 1081, see
Muratori, *Anecdota*, ii (Milan 1698), pp. 328–337.

[3] *Ep.* ii, *P.L.*, cxlviii, cols 828–30.

[4] Landulf Senior, iii. 32, p. 99.

of both Godfrey and Atto, and that Tedald should have been consecrated by the self-same Lombard bishops who had consecrated Godfrey at Novara. In his eyes, these actions of the emperor and his supporters offended against justice and right order as scandalously as had those of the Patarenes.

> In short [he protested] this archbishop [Tedald] was received by the clergy and by a people which was, as ever, avid for some new thing. The self-same bishops who had consecrated Godfrey now laid their hands upon him. A wonderful thing indeed, and unheard of in times past, that, when one bishop had been chosen for a city and another had been consecrated, yet a third should intrude himself.[1]

Worse still, Tedald's consecrators had been excommunicated. Arnulf felt compelled to place Tedald under St Ambrose's censure that whoever separates himself from Rome loses the name of catholic.[2] The Patarenes were no longer active in the city to frighten Arnulf into a hostile conservatism; therefore, under the shock of these events, the need for reform which he had always felt but never admitted could take possession of his mind. He abandoned his old solicitude for the emperor. By a conversion which he likened to that of St Paul on the road to Damascus, he turned, fully and conscientiously, to the Gregorian cause.[3] He was not alone in this, for he was one of a deputation of the upper clergy and laity of Milan who, early in 1077, went to Gregory at Canossa. Encouraged, no doubt, by the spectacle of the emperor's own submission, they sought absolution from Gregory for their resistance to Rome and to reform. Gregory seized his opportunity by sending to Milan the Cluniac Cardinal Gerald of Ostia and Bishop Anselm II of Lucca. (Anselm was himself a Milanese, of the family of da Baggio which had long been prominent among the *capitanei* on account of its zeal for reform.) They preached to the citizens, and then absolved and blessed all who would hear them.[4]

It was, no doubt, a small beginning of conversion to the

---

[1] Arnulf, v. 5, p. 30.
[2] Arnulf, v. 7, p. 30. According to Bonizo of Sutri, Tedald had himself been present at Godfrey's consecration: vi, p. 600.
[3] Arnulf, iv. 13, p. 29.   [4] Arnulf, v. 9, p. 31.

papal cause, and the career of Tedald had still to run its course; but it is undoubtedly the point from which future developments at Milan must be traced. By contrast with the excellent sources for the Patarene challenge and crisis, the evidence for Milanese history in the last two decades of the eleventh century is meagre and obscure. Yet it establishes that Milan now became open as never before to the winds of change which were blowing generally through the church, and that, on the whole, it found them congenial. Three interrelated agencies, in particular, between them claimed most of the Milanese for the papacy and reform. First, from 1081 until his death in 1086, Bishop Anselm II of Lucca was papal vicar in Lombardy, with oversight of all dioceses which had no resident Gregorian bishop. He was thus again in touch with Milan;[1] and the collection of canons which he compiled at this time promoted, on fully Gregorian lines, the authority of the pope in relation to the bishops and the temporal power.[2] Anselm, moreover, was a supporter of the Cluniacs, and, secondly, his vicariate saw the start of their widespread penetration of Lombardy. In 1081, the Milanese church of Santa Maria di Laveno was given to Cluny, and it was followed by the establishment in Lombardy of other Cluniac houses which helped to supply the lack of reformed monasteries in the Ambrosian church.[3] Throughout western Europe, the Cluniacs were encouraging both clergy and laity in zeal for reform; for example, by inducing laymen to surrender their possession of churches and tithes. At Milan, a charter of Archbishop Anselm III (1086–93) shows how the cathedral clergy and their lay associates, who had hitherto been prominent as the opponents of reform, were now experiencing the attractive power of Cluniac ideals. It states that the church of Santa Maria di Calvenzano had been held of the cathedral by three laymen who had also possessed certain tithes. Now, with their full agreement and with the approval of the cardinals of

[1] Bardo, *Vita Anselmi episcopi Lucensis*, 35, ed. R. Wilmans, *M.G.H., Scr.*, xii, p. 23.

[2] For Anselm, see Violante, 'Anselmo da Baggio', *D.B.I.*, iii, pp. 399–407.

[3] For the charter of Santa Maria di Laveno, see *Recueil des chartes de l'abbaye de Cluny*, ed. A. Bruel, iv (Paris, 1888), no. 3583, pp. 722–30; *cf.* the foundation of Santa Maria di Cantù, *ibid.*, no. 3612, pp. 773–74. For monastic reform at Milan, see P. Zerbi, 'Monasteri e riforma a Milano', *Aevum*, xxiv (1950), pp. 44–60, 166–78.

the cathedral, the archbishop delivered both church and tithes from lay hands and gave them to the monastery of Cluny.[1]

But, above all, it was the Cluniac Pope Urban II, 'more dangerous than Gregory VII because he was more diplomatic', who himself assiduously consolidated the papal cause at Milan and procured the victory of reform.[2] The evidence for Urban's success at Milan is very fragmentary; yet the considerations which disposed the city to make its peace with him can be inferred with fair probability, and they make the evidence intelligible enough. The first consideration seems to have been that, after its time of troubles, Milan was again experiencing the benefits of relative internal stability. Its upper-class families were successfully consolidating their economic position;[3] the earliest references to consuls and to 'boni homines', who sat as public witnesses in districts named after the gates of the city, herald the more orderly time of the commune.[4] These are signs that a new domestic order was emerging which, if it was to know tensions and con-flicts of its own, was settled enough after past upheavals. But, set in the midst of a torn and divided world, the Milanese needed

[1] Bruel, *op. cit.*, v (Paris, 1894), no. 3793, pp. 144–45. That this charter dates from the time of Archbishop Anselm III and not from that of Anselm IV is clear from the reference to Santa Maria di Calvenzano in Urban II's charter to Cluny of 1095: *P.L.*, cli, col. 412.

[2] The phrase is borrowed from Kehr. There is much truth—perhaps more than its author realized—in J. Haller's suggestion about Urban, 'Vielleicht war er im Grunde doch mehr Cluniazenser als Gregorianer': *Das Papsttum. Idee und Wirklichkeit*, ii (new edn, Darmstadt, 1962), p. 435. I hope to discuss the relation between Cluniacs and the Gregorian reform more fully in a forthcoming book.

[3] Violante, 'Les prêts sur gage foncier dans la vie économique et sociale de Milan au xie siècle', *Cahiers de civilisation mediévale*, v (1962), pp. 147–68, 437–59.

[4] Consuls were first referred to at Milan in 1081, when, according to the *Annales Pegavienses*, Henry IV was received 'a consulibus et primoribus civitatis': *M.G.H., Scr.*, xvi, p. 237; but, since the Annals were compiled *c.* 1150, this may be anachronistic. Firm evidence of their existence is pro-vided by a document of 1097, Archivio comunale di Cremona, codice Siccardi, 131, the relevant part of which is reproduced in *Storia di Milano*, ed. G. Treccani degli Alfieri, iii (Milan, 1954), p. 241. For the 'boni homines', see Giulini, *op. cit.*, iv, pp. 291, 298. It is now widely agreed that the Patar-enes did nothing to assist the coming of the commune: *e.g.*, E. Ennen, *Frühgeschichte der europäischen Stadt* (Bonn, 1953), pp. 279–80; Violante, *La Pataria Milanese e la riforma ecclesiastica*, i, pp. 191–92.

external protection. Since 1075, the emperor, who was traditionally their protector, had shown that little reliance could be placed upon him. The alternative was to seek peace with the pope: for, while he was near enough to be usefully appealed to, he was neither so near nor so powerful that he seemed likely to endanger Milan's burgeoning civic life. Secondly, Milan had based its loyalty to the emperor on the advantages which were to be gained from its situation on the routes running from Germany down into Italy. Its increasing detachment from the emperor put these advantages in jeopardy. Urban, however, was not slow to provide a means by which they might be resumed, when he built up an anti-imperial alliance of his partisans in north Italy and south Germany. Its linch-pin was Gregory VII's staunchest Italian adherent, Countess Matilda of Tuscany; the diplomatic marriage of 1089, which had Urban's full approval, between the forty-three-year-old countess and the seventeen-year-old Welf V, heir to Bavaria and Este, marked its inauguration.[1] Milan was critically situated between Tuscany and the Alpine passes, and so was of the utmost importance for the alliance; while, from its own side, it had every reason to welcome a place in the pope's schemes which would put it on the map again. Thirdly, its ancient jealousy of other cities may have impelled it towards Urban. Ravenna and Aquileia, its ecclesiastical rivals in north Italy, and Pavia, its rival in the kingdom, were either firmly in the imperial camp, or, at best, of wavering allegiance.[2] If Milan now turned to the pope and championed his cause in north Italy, it might hope to renew its own aspirations to precedence over them. If these political considerations pointed to a rapprochement with Rome, they were strongly reinforced by the lively religious appeal that the cause of reform now made to many of the Milanese. That the force of this appeal should not be under-estimated is clear from such evidence as the conversion of the chronicler Arnulf, the presence of the Milanese embassy at Canossa and the echo

---

[1] See K. Hampe, *Deutsche Kaisergeschichte* (10th edn, ed. F. Baethgen, Heidelberg, 1949), pp. 76–78; L. Simeoni, 'Il contributo della Contessa Matilde al papato nella lotta per le investiture', *Studi Gregoriani*, ed. G. B. Borino, i (1947), pp. 361–67. As Cardinal Odo of Ostia, Urban II had been legate in south Germany during Gregory VII's last winter: A. Becker, *Papst Urban II*, i (Stuttgart, 1964), pp. 62–77.

[2] For Aquileia and Pavia, see G. Schwartz, *Die Besetzung der Bistümer Reichsitaliens* (Leipzig and Berlin, 1913), pp. 24–35, 44–45.

which the aims of the Cluniacs found at the cathedral, the inner citadel of the old unreformed Ambrosian church.

From his own side, Urban cannot have been unaware of the strategic importance of Milan in his struggle against the emperor. His astute mind is likely to have appreciated that at least some of these considerations would dispose it to listen to his approaches. It is certain that his continual concern for Milan secured for him the alliance to which they pointed. So early as 1088, he wrote to press the claims of the Roman see and to recall St Ambrose's own warning that it is heretical to be separated from Rome.[1] He at once embarked upon his highly successful course of winning for the cause of St Peter the three archbishops who held office while he was pope.[2] He was fortunate in that the implacably imperialist Archbishop Tedald died on the self-same day as Gregory VII.[3] The new archbishop, Anselm III, also took office as an imperialist. He was invested by Henry IV and irregularly consecrated; so, in due course, a papal legate deposed him and he retired to a monastery. At this point, Urban personally intervened and recalled him; by a characteristic gesture, he relaxed one of Gregory VII's most rigid rules and followed tradition by sending the archbishop's pallium to Milan.[4] Anselm responded by henceforth serving the pope. Led by him, Milan took its place alongside Countess Matilda at the head of a first Lombard League which included Cremona, Piacenza and Lodi and was intended to last for twenty years. When the young King Conrad rebelled against his father, Henry IV, and came over to the pope, it was Anselm who crowned him at Milan. Milan and Urban both gained by these events: the city's pre-eminence in north Italy was asserted; while, when Anselm died, Bernold of Constance had good reason for eulogizing his services to the papacy: 'venerabilis Anselmus Mediolanensis archiepiscopus in causa sancti Petri studiosissimus . . . satis

[1] S. Loewenfeld, *Epistolae pontificum Romanorum selectae* (Leipzig, 1885), no. 122, p. 59.

[2] I discuss this policy more fully, and consider some further evidence, in an article on 'The Succession of the Archbishops of Milan in the Time of Pope Urban II', Chapter VI below.

[3] *Catalogus archiepiscoporum Mediolanensium*, ed. Bethmann and Wattenbach, *M.G.H.*, *Scr.*, viii, p. 104.

[4] L. Duchesne, *Le Liber Pontificalis*, ii (Paris, 1888), p. 293; P. Ewald, 'Die Papstbriefe der Brittischen Sammlung', nos 11–12, 33, *Neues Archiv*, v (1879), pp. 355–56, 362.

laudabilis fecit finem, magnumque merorem fidelibus sancti Petri dereliquit'.[1] His successors, Archbishops Arnulf III (1093–1097)[2] and Anselm IV (1097–1101),[3] were also established in their see under Urban's eye—the former of them by his direct intervention at the council of Piacenza. Both took their places in his anti-imperial alliance, and both imitated the zeal of Anselm III for the cause of St Peter in Lombardy. Anselm IV, moreover, died in Byzantium as he was returning with the Milanese contingent which he led when, in line with the most familiar of all Urban's initiatives, he took part in the crusade of 1101.[4]

Urban also took continual care to cultivate the archbishops' subjects of all classes and backgrounds, and so to broaden his support at Milan. For such newer and older reforming groups as the canons regular of St Ambrose[5] and the Patarene remnant under Liutprand,[6] he provided the security of papal privileges. He smoothed the path whereby Milanese clergy who had lapsed into the Wibertine schism might be reconciled to the church.[7] Such concessions as this and the politic favour which, 'necessitatem vehementissimam ecclesiae perpendentes',[8] he showed to

[1] For Anselm, see M. L. Marzorati, 'Anselmo da Rho', *D.B.I.*, iii, pp. 417–18. According to Landulf of St Paul, he was a kinsman of the knight who killed Erlembald and mutilated Liutprand: 66, p. 48. In addition to the references in the last note, the principal sources for Anselm are Landulf of St Paul, 3, p. 21; 13, p. 26; and Bernold, *Chronicon, s.a.* 1093, *M.G.H., Scr.*, v, pp. 456–57. The fact that a Swabian writer is a principal source for Milanese affairs is itself witness to the effectiveness of Urban's alliance of Germans and Italians.

[2] For Arnulf, the principal source is Bernold, *Chron., s.a.* 1095, p. 463.

[3] For Anselm IV, see Landulf of St Paul, 2–3, p. 21; see also Marzorati, 'Anselmo di Bovisio', *D.B.I.*, iii, pp. 409–10.

[4] See J. L. Cate, 'The Crusade of 1101', in *A History of the Crusades*, ed. K. M. Setton, i, *The First Hundred Years* (Philadelphia, 1958), esp. pp. 346–47, 352–53, 357.

[5] Giulini, *op. cit.*, iv, pp. 538–39. Urban also twice intervened to obtain for the canons of St Ambrose the undisturbed possession of oblations which were claimed by the monks of St Ambrose: see his letter of 1096 in *Acta pontificum Romanorum inedita*, ed. J. von Pflugk-Harttung, ii (Stuttgart, 1884), no. 196, p. 163.

[6] Landulf of St Paul, 11, p. 25.

[7] *Ep.* lxxiv, *P.L.*, cli, col. 358.

[8] Ewald, *art. cit.*, no. 33a, p. 362. Such phrases recur in Urban's dealings with Milan: 'necessitate cogente aecclesiae': *Lib. Pont.*, p. 293; 'prospectu utilitatis ecclesiae toleravimus': Ewald, *loc. cit.*; 'ecclesiae necessitate exigente': *ibid.*; 'pro utilitate ecclesiae': Ewald, *art. cit.*, no. 33b, p. 362.

Archbishop Anselm III, helped to win him support from penitent imperialists.[1] But his flexibility seems also to have gravely
offended the opposite wing of Milanese opinion—the rigorous
reformers who had survived the Patarene defeat of 1075, and
who were shocked by the easy terms which Urban now offered
to their former rivals.[2] Urban, therefore, made at least two
bold attempts to retrieve the Patarenes for his cause. On his
way from Piacenza to Clermont, he encouraged the head of the
Ambrosian church to heal the wounds of the past by beginning the local canonization of the Patarene saints. He stood at
Archbishop Arnulf III's side when Erlembald's remains were
translated to the monastery of St Dionysius, and honour was paid
to the 'miles Christi reverendus', now a saint, who had destroyed
the servants of Venus and Simon Magus.[3] After Clermont,
Urban again emphasized his concern for unity at Milan by re-
visiting the city and preaching on the theme 'quod minimus
clericulus de ecclesia Dei est maior quolibet rege mortali'. He
succeeded in winning over some of the Patarenes; for his sermon
inspired a group of them to undertake a vigorous campaign against
unworthy clergy, and, in 1097, it was they who promoted the
election of Archbishop Anselm IV.[4] Anselm repaid his debt to
them by placing the remains of Ariald near those of Erlembald;
thus (as a new inscription ran), 'the two *pugiles Christi* might be
venerated together by the famous people of Milan, of whose blood
they were born'.[5] In 1098, the same group assisted Anselm at the
reforming council of Milan whose decrees, which implemented
the demands of the Gregorian reform, are the final and conclusive
evidence that Milan was, indeed, converted to the aims of the
papacy. Simony was condemned and lay investiture was prohibited as Gregory VII had prohibited it in 1075. The poverty
of the clergy was commended and the alienation of church lands

[1] See the letter of the five Milanese clerks to Urban: Giulini, *op. cit.*, iv,
pp. 537–38.

[2] *E.g.*, Ewald, *art. cit.*, no. 33a, p. 362.

[3] Giulini, *op. cit.*, iv, p. 319; it is ironical that the monastery was founded
by Archbishop Aribert II. That Urban came to Milan in 1095 in order to
compose its religious differences is confirmed by the account of his ordination there of Bishop Humbald of Auxerre: *Bibliothèque historique de l'Yonne*,
ed. L. M. Duru, i (Auxerre, 1850), p. 402.

[4] Landulf of St Paul, 40, p. 37.

[5] Giulini, *op. cit.*, iv, p. 408; *cf.* Landulf Senior, iii. 30, p. 96.

was forbidden. The Wibertine bishops were anathematized and Tedald's ordinations were declared to be null. Ordinations performed by Anselm III before he was rehabilitated were submitted to the judgement of the pope, and the whole work of the council was done 'salva . . . in omnibus apostolica auctoritate'.[1]

To those who remembered the Ambrosian church of 1046, or even of 1075, these official acts of a local council presided over by the vicar of St Ambrose and generally accepted by his subjects must, indeed, have marked a new age. The Ambrosian church was now papalist. It had made peace with its own tumultuous past, even to the extent of allowing that the Patarene saints who had fought simony and nicolaitism under the banner of St Peter were, after all, of its own flesh and blood. Former imperialists and former Patarenes had alike accepted the authority of Rome. It seems that relatively few of the Milanese finally stood apart from Urban and from their archbishops. At one extreme, there was Landulf Senior and his like;[2] and, at the other, a bizarre Patarene faction under Liutprand, which, in the name of thorough reforming zeal, ineffectively resisted Urban's political plans and Milan's part in them.[3] Otherwise, the new direction that Milan's loyalties had begun to take after 1075 was fully confirmed. Reforming ideals had won the day and St Ambrose's injunction that his church must follow that of St Peter was obeyed.[4] Under Pope Urban II, Milan thus became the champion of the cause of St Peter in Lombardy.[5]

[1] Giulini, *op. cit.*, iv, pp. 539–42.
[2] Landulf Senior addressed his Dedicatory Epistle to an unnamed *archipresbyter* of the Ambrosian church: *M.G.H., Scr.*, viii, p. 36.
[3] Landulf of St Paul, 1–3, pp. 21–22.
[4] *Cf.* Schwartz, *op. cit.*, pp. 9–10.
[5] I am greatly indebted to Mr R. H. C. Davis for his comments on a draft of this paper.

THE SUCCESSION OF THE ARCHBISHOPS OF MILAN IN THE TIME OF POPE URBAN II

In close collaboration with Pope Urban II (1088–99), three arch-bishops of Milan achieved notable success in rallying their city to the cause of St. Peter against the Emperor Henry IV. Their names and the dates upon which they succeeded and died are certainly and precisely known from the *Catalogus archiepiscoporum Mediolan-ensium*, which, from 1075 to 1206, was kept up to date with the death of each archbishop. After the death on 25 May 1085 of the zealous imperialist Tedald, the three archbishops in question were as follows:

> Anselm III, succeeded 1 July 1086, died 4 December 1093;
> Arnulf III, succeeded 5 December 1093, died 24 September 1097;
> Anselm IV, succeeded 2 December 1097, died 30 September 1101.[1]

The circumstances in which each of these archbishops succeeded, however, raise problems of evidence and interpretation which have never been sufficiently clarified.

The first problem arises from the passage in the *Liber Pontificalis* which records Urban II's dealings with Milan:

Temporibus istius summi pontificis, A. Mediolanensis archiepiscopus, qui ab uno tantum catholico fuerat episcopo consecratus, assentientibus quidem aliis episcopis sed manum non imponentibus eo quod scismatici essent et a Romano antistite excommunicati, et quia post electionem canonicam a rege baculum sumpserat, per legatum sedis apostolicae sponte depositus est. Cumque mox mutato habitu in cenobio vixisset sanctissime, necessitate cogente aecclesiae, per domnum Urbanum papam ad episcopatum redire praeceptus est et compulsus, eique atque Romanae ecclesiae sacramentum pro more iuravit episcoporum. Cui post palleum subpliciter expetenti, a domno Urbano papa cum his verbis per Heri-mannum cardinalem presbiterum transmittitur: 'Palleum fraternitati tuae praeter consuetudinem Romanae aecclesiae, quae nulli hoc dignitatis genus nisi praesenti concedit, tuis litteris exorati ex apostolicae sedis benedictione transmittimus'.[2]

It is left wholly unclear to which of the three archbishops, all of whose names began with the letter A, the passage relates. Anselm IV

1. *Catalogus archiepiscoporum Mediolanensium,* ed. L. C. Bethmann and W. Wattenbach, M[onumenta] G[ermaniae] H[istorica], Scr[iptorum], viii. 104–5; cf. G. Schwartz, *Die Besetzung der Bistümer Reichsitaliens* (Leipzig and Berlin, 1913), pp. 83–85.
2. *Le Liber Pontificalis,* ed. L. Duchesne, ii (Paris, 1892), 293.

can, however, be disregarded, since the Milanese chronicler Landulf of St. Paul provides information about his election which is at once credible and wholly different.[1] Following older writers, and especially the eighteenth-century Milanese antiquary Giulini, most historians, including some of the most recent, have supposed that it relates to Anselm's predecessor, Arnulf III. If so, the king who invested him was the young King Conrad, who had lately revolted against his father, Henry IV, and whom Anselm III had crowned king of Italy at Monza and Milan.[2] On the other hand, an important minority of historians, including Duchesne, the editor of the *Liber Pontificalis*, has preferred Anselm III,[3] with the consequence that the king was Henry IV himself; although the case for doing so has never been fully presented. In fact, it is decisive, on the following grounds. First, if the account in the *Liber Pontificalis* be compared with the story of Arnulf's succession as recorded by the Swabian annalist Bernold, the conflict of evidence makes it very hard to accept that both sources can refer to the same archbishop. In the *Liber Pontificalis,* an archbishop was irregularly consecrated by a single catholic bishop, supported by the presence, although not by the laying on of hands, of other but schismatic bishops; having been deposed by a papal legate, he withdrew to a monastery, but, in return for an oath of loyalty to the pope and the Roman church, Urban II reinstated him. According to Bernold, Arnulf's consecration occurred in very different circumstances: at the council of Piacenza (1095), Urban II charged three German bishops of his own party, Archbishop Thiemo of Salzburg, Bishop Ulrich of Passau, and Bishop Gebhard of Constance, to go to Milan and consecrate Arnulf, whom Bernold described as 'diu quidem electum sed nondum consecratum'.[4] Attempts to reconcile these accounts have been based on one or other of two difficult hypotheses. Either the ceremony at Milan of which Bernold spoke was not (as he twice explicitly stated) a consecration but merely the reconciliation to the catholic

1. Landulf of St. Paul, *Historia Mediolanensis*, 2, ed. L. Bethmann and P. Jaffé, *M.G.H., Scr.* xx. 21. For details, see below, p. 292.

2. *E.g.* G. Giulini, *Memorie spettanti alla storia, al governo, ed alla descrizione della citta e della campagna di Milano ne'secoli bassi,* iv (Milan, n.d.), 309–10; W. von Giesebrecht, *Geschichte der deutschen Kaiserzeit,* iii (3rd edn., Brunswick, 1869), 651–2; G. Meyer von Knonau, *Jahrbücher des deutschen Reiches unter Heinrich IV und Heinrich V,* iv (Leipzig, 1903), 398 (although he used the evidence of the *Lib. Pont.* over again in his account of Anselm III: *ibid.* p. 201, n. 12); F. Savio, *Gli antichi vescovi d'Italia: la Lombardia, pte 1, Milano* (Florence, 1913), p. 449; F. Bonnard, 'Arnulfe III', *Dictionnaire d'histoire et de géographie ecclésiastiques,* ed. A. Baudrillart *et al.* iv (Paris, 1925), col. 643; *Storia di Milano,* ed. G. Treccani degli Alfieri, iii (Milan, 1954), 225–6; C. D. Fonsega, 'Arnolfo', *Diz[ion-ario] biog[rafico degli] Ital[iani],* iv (Rome, 1962), 284–5.

3. Duchesne, *op. cit.* ii. 294, n. 6; Schwartz, *op. cit.* p. 84, n. 1; P. F. Kehr, *Italia Pontificia,* vi, pt. 1, *Lombardia* (Berlin, 1913), p. 52; A. Becker, *Papst Urban II,* i (Stuttgart, 1964), 136, n. 481.

4. Bernold, *Chronicon, s.a.* 1095, *M.G.H., Scr.* v, pp. 462–3. For Bernold's account of Anselm III, see *op. cit., s.a.* 1093, pp. 456–7.

church of an archbishop who had already been consecrated, however irregularly; or else (as it is more commonly suggested) Urban caused Arnulf to be re-ordained by the canonically-requisite three catholic bishops – a procedure which, for all the current uncertainty about the doctrine of orders, would have gone far beyond Urban II's known principles and rulings in cases of bishops and priests.[1] The conflict of evidence suggests the simpler explanation, that the sources relate to different archbishops: Bernold to Arnulf III, but the *Liber Pontificalis* to his predecessor, Anselm III. Secondly, the material relating to Urban II which is preserved in the early twelfth-century canonical collection known as the *Britannica*[2] confirms that the *Liber Pontificalis* provides evidence for Anselm, not Arnulf. It includes a historical notice of Urban's dealings with Milan which is verbally almost identical with the account in the *Liber Pontificalis* (for which it was almost certainly the source), save that, in place of the final quotation from Urban's letter, there is a statement that the pallium was presented to the archbishop by Cardinal Hermann, whom the people of Milan met at the gates of the city. An inspection of the manuscript confirms that the name 'Anselm' is spelt out in full.[3] There follow extracts from Urban's letters which support the details of the historical notice: the irregular consecration by only one bishop[4]; the investiture by the king after a canonical election[5]; the archbishop's retirement to a monastery and his recall by Urban 'pro utilitate ecclesiae'[6]; the relaxation of the usual rule that the pallium must be conferred at Rome.[7] From the evidence of the *Britannica*, it is clear that the account in the *Liber Pontificalis* was ultimately based upon Urban's letters to Anselm III, and that he was the archbishop whose name its author abbreviated. Thirdly, Urban's complaint to the archbishop in a fragment in the *Britannica* that

... regem, ab sede apostolica excommunicatum et beati Petri gratia penitus alienum adisti, sacramento te ipsius astrinxisti, investituram ab eo accepisti quod omnino in Romana ecclesia prohibitum ipse non nescis,[8]

is intelligible if it refers to Henry IV's second excommunication in 1080 and to the investiture decree of 1075. It bears no relation to the

---

1. For Urban and re-ordinations, see L. Saltet, *Les réordinations* (Paris, 1907), pp. 218–57 and A. Schebler, *Die Reordinationen in der 'altkatholischen' Kirche* (Bonn, 1936), pp. 268–81.

2. B[ritish] M[useum], Addit[ional] MS. 8873; see P. Ewald, 'Die Papstbriefe der Brittischen Sammlung', nos 11–12, 33, *Neues Archiv der Gesellschaft für ältere deutsche Geschichtskunde*, v (1879), 355–6, 362, for the principal relevant material.

3. B.M. Addit. MS. 8873, fo. 143ᵛ, Ewald, no. 11; *cf.* fo. 148ʳ, Ewald, no. 33.

4. Ewald, *ubi supra*, no. 33a.

5. *Ibid.*; Urban II expressly accepted Anselm's consecration in spite of its irregularity ('prospectu utilitatis ecclesiae toleravimus').

6. *Ibid.* nos 12a,b; 33a,b.   7. *Ibid.* no. 12b.

8. *Ibid.* no. 33a. Landulf of St. Paul also states that Anselm III was invested by Henry IV: *Hist. Med.*, 13, *M.G.H., Scr.* xx. 26.

position of King Conrad after his adherence to the papal cause. The king in the *Liber Pontificalis,* for which this letter was ultimately a source, was, therefore, Henry IV and the archbishop was Anselm III. Fourthly, the reforming council which Archbishop Anselm IV held at Milan in 1098 made detailed provision about the clerks whom Anselm III had ordained before and after the monastic conversion to which the *Liber Pontificalis* and Urban II's letters also refer:

Ordinationes autem illorum, qui se a Thealdo iussi sunt execrari, decrevimus omnino irritas fieri; quae vero factae sunt ab Anselmo eius successore ante monasticam conversionem, sub domni papae examine illas ordinationes commisimus iudicandas. Eas tamen ordinationes, vel reconciliationes, quas post eius a monasterio reversionem, vel susceptum a Romana ecclesia pallium idem Anselmus fecit, ratas esse iudicamus . . .[1]

The council saw no need to legislate for any clerks whom Arnulf might have ordained during a period of canonical irregularity.

Thus, the references to Anselm III in the *Britannica* and in the acts of the council of Milan of 1098 clearly refer to the same figure as the archbishop of the *Liber Pontificalis* and place his identity beyond question. The *Liber Pontificalis* provides a reliable, if summary, account of the succession of Anselm III.

This conclusion gives rise to a second problem: what evidence is now left for the succession of Arnulf III? Most of what is usually said about it must be dismissed, because it depends on what the *Liber Pontificalis* in fact records of his predecessor: there is no direct evidence that Arnulf was irregularly consecrated, or that he received investiture at the hands of King Conrad, or that he was deposed by a papal legate and retired to a monastery from which Urban recalled him. The only assured facts are that, on the evidence of the *Catalogus,* Arnulf succeeded as archbishop on the day after the death of his predecessor in December 1093; and that, on the evidence of Bernold, he was not consecrated until Urban II had made special arrangements at the council of Piacenza in 1095. The delay calls for an explanation. Two possibilities remain. First, quite apart from the *Liber Pontificalis,* there is some indirect evidence that Arnulf may, indeed, have been invested by King Conrad. In 1097, Anselm IV was invested with the pastoral staff by the staunch Gregorian, Countess Matilda of Tuscany.[2] It is likely that, if his predecessor and successor received lay investiture, so, too, did Arnulf III; Conrad was the most likely person to have conferred it. Again, early in the reign of Anselm IV when Conrad no longer enjoyed the support of the papal party in Lombardy, he querulously asked the Patarene leader, Liutprand:

1. The acts of this council were first printed by N. Sormani, *La gloria de' santi Milanesi* (Milan, 1761), pp. 206–10, and thence by Giulini, *op. cit.* iv. 539–42.
2. Landulf of St. Paul, *Hist. Med.,* 2, *M.G.H., Scr.* xx. 21.

Cum sis magister patarinorum, quid sentis de pontificibus et sacerdotibus
regia iura possidentibus et regi nulla alimenta presentatibus ?[1]

The question would have had added point if Conrad had himself
invested churchmen like Arnulf III with *regia iura,* and it is noteworthy for the clear separation of these rights from the spiritual
aspect of ecclesiastical offices. It is, however, pertinent to ask
whether such an investiture would, indeed, serve to account for the
long delay which occurred before Arnulf's consecration. Urban II's
objections to the investiture of Anselm III, as they are preserved in
the *Britannica,* were not necessarily to investiture as such, but only
to the specific circumstances that Henry IV was under sentence of
excommunication; that Anselm had taken an oath to the king; and
that, in his case, the investiture was contrary to Gregory VII's
prohibition of the investiture of bishops by Henry IV, with its
strongly *ad hominem* purpose.[2] It is by no means clear that Urban II
thought inadmissible in principle an investiture with *regia iura,*
when it was not accompanied by the doing of homage and when it
was conferred by a ruler who was obedient to the papacy.[3] Nor is
there any reason why, if it occurred, it should have presented in
practice an obstacle to the prompt consecration of Arnulf III which
did not arise in the case of Anselm IV. Secondly, however, there
survives a further and somewhat neglected piece of evidence which
establishes that, in certain circles at Milan, Arnulf's succession at
first provoked bitter hostility, and that an urgent appeal against him
was addressed to Urban II which may well account for the long
delay before he was consecrated. It is a letter which was written to the
pope by five clerks whom Anselm III had ordained in circumstances
which left their own canonical position open to challenge.[4] This can
only refer to the first months of Anselm's reign, before he was
deposed and reinstated; the clerks had, therefore, followed his
example by being reconciled to the pope. But, when Anselm died,
they feared the consequences of Arnulf's accession and appealed to
the pope to confirm and protect them in their canonical position as
priests[5]:

1. *Op. cit.,* 3, p. 22.

2. Ewald, *ubi supra,* no. 33a. For Gregory VII and investiture, see esp. A. Nitschke,
'Die Wirksamkeit Gottes in der Welt Gregors VII', *Studi Gregoriani,* ed. G. B. Borino,
v (Rome, 1956), 194–201.

3. See A. Scharnagl, *Der Begriff der Investitur in den Quellen und der Literatur des Investi-
turstreites (Kirchenrechtliche Abhandlungen,* ed. U. Stutz, heft 56, Stuttgart, 1908), esp.
pp. 57–62.

4. Sormani, *op. cit.* pp. 62–64; Giulini, *op. cit.* iv. 537–8. Sormani copied the letter
from a MS. which he found in the library of the canons regular of St. Ambrose; Giulini
reprinted it with minor corrections. I have quoted Giulini's version.

5. In spite of Urban II's leniency towards Milanese clerks whose ordinations were
open to objection (Ewald, *ubi supra,* no. 33a; *Ep.* lxxiv [J. P. Migne,] P[atrologia] L[atina],
cli, col. 358), the position of those who were ordained by Anselm III before his monastic
conversion was still uncertain at the council of Milan in 1098: see the quotation from
the acts of the council, above, p. 288.

Domno H[urbano] Petri beati apostoli vicario, universalis ecclesiae culmine sublimato, Andreas, Oto, Arnaldus, Oldradus, necnon et Arnulphus,[1] debitae et voluntariae servitutis obsequium, vitae praesentis bravium, atque aeternae calculum. Universa ecclesia psallat odas Creatori, coronata tanto diademate Hurbani pontificis, cuius lampas nimis clara rutilat in tenebris. Ipse est flos clerorum, electus ex liliis, et verus apostolicus, manans fonte Patris, qui rigat spiritales imbres tempore famis credentibus populis, ut saginati referant laudes Omnipotenti. Ecclesia namque Romana est velut cardo, a quo etsi plures procedant radii, tamen unus uti Titan inter stellas lucet fulgidus, qui veraciter constat Sanctus Ambrosius; cuius sedes nunc viduata clarissimo praesule Anselmo, de quo moeret universa contio, heu, proh dolor! tristes reliquit nos orfanos consortio, sed utinam laetetur in palatio caelesti. Huius lacte nos eius filii karissimi educati, nunc aridi et sitibundi documento suae fidei, circumquaque pervagantes, nescimus quem sequamur, nisi te pastorem verum fontem vivi fluminis. Ergo sancte pater patrum Hurbane piissime, filios tui fidelis benigne suscipe, et protege more patris sub umbra alarum tuarum, ne Petri fides praedetur sub avaro accipitre. Nam sicuti decet fideles et obedientes sumus parati tibi sponso et sponsae Christi sanctae Romanae ecclesiae in omnibus obedire, salvo statu Mediolanensis ecclesiae sanctae. Taliter nobis permanentibus decet paternitatem vestram amicabiliter, fiducialiter, perpetualiter nos servos tuos benedicere. Dignitatem denique ipse pius praesul et pervigil sacerdotii nobis contulit indignis, quam rogamus ut confirmes litteris beatorum apostolorum Petri et Pauli sigillo signatis, benedicas et collaudes hanc perceptam gratiam, ut libere possimus authoritate canonica appellare sedem apostolicam. Quod ut facilius tua benignitas nobis concedat immeritis, exemplar antecessorum tuorum domni Alexandri et Gregorii papae tibi transmittimus, quod fideliter dedere magistris sanctis nostris Rodulpho, Arialdo, Petro, Nazario. . . .[2]

The reference to Arnulf as an 'avarus accipiter' who preyed upon the faith of St. Peter is a metaphor which suggests that the writers of the letter based their objection to him upon grounds of simony rather than of investiture. Simony was the charge which was most commonly brought by the extreme reforming factions at Milan against archbishops of whom they disapproved. A fragment which

1. Of these five clerks, only the first, Andrew, reappears by name. In 1103, he was *primicerius* of the Milanese clergy, and was deposed from his office, together with other clerks who had been ordained by Archbishop Anselm III, by Archbishop Grosolanus; they were reinstated by Pope Paschal II: Landulf of St. Paul, *Hist. Med.* 13, *M.G.H.*, *Scr.* xx. 26; for other references to Andrew, see chs. 6, p. 23; 20, p. 29; 31, p. 33; 37, p. 35; 40, p. 38. For the office of *primicerius*, see Landulf Senior, *Historia Mediolanensis*, ii. 35, ed. Bethmann and Wattenbach, *M.G.H., Scr.* viii. 71.

2. The series of names, which is cut short at this point, is of leaders of the Patarene movement between 1056 and 1075. For Rudolf and Ariald, see Peter Damiani, *Epistolae*, viii, nos. 14, 15, *P.L.* cxliv, cols. 367–9, and, for Ariald, Andrew of Strumi, *Vita sancti Arialdi*, ed. F. Baethgen, *M.G.H., Scr.* xxx. 1049–75. Nazarius is probably the *Nazarius clericus* of ch. 15, p. 1060, or, possibly, the *monetarius* of the same name: ch. 6, p. 1053. Peter is not otherwise known. For the use of *magister* as a Patarene title, see King Conrad's question to Liutprand, above, p. 289.

is preserved in the *Britannica,* and which was not used for the account of Urban II's dealings with Anselm III in the *Liber Pontificalis,* shows that, as early as the time when Urban was making every concession to Anselm in order to secure his loyalty, he had encountered hastily-brought allegations, probably from shocked survivors of the old Patarene movement, that Anselm had come by the see of Milan simoniacally:

Preterea quamvis te ignaro pecuniam regi frater tuus dicitur obtulisse, licet hoc nunc tandem et rarius asseratur, et nulla veracium virorum assercione subnixum sit, nos tamen necessitatem vehementissimam ecclesiae perpendentes et maximo te eius usui futurum, annuente Domino, confidentes, rigorem iusticiae canonicae auctoritate apostolica temperavimus.[1]

Later, in 1103, charges of simony were brought by the Patarenes against Anselm IV's successor and former co-adjutor, Archbishop Grosolanus.[2] In the light of the letter of the five priests, the delay before Arnulf III was consecrated is most probably to be accounted for if he, too, met with allegations of simony from factions at Milan which were under Patarene influence. If so, Urban only dismissed the allegations which were made when he was elected after a personal investigation; this had to await Urban's coming to Piacenza, where, as Bernold indicates, he was much concerned with the situation at Milan. Only afterwards was Arnulf consecrated 'ex concessione domni papae',[3] and in the most exceptional circumstances, by the three German bishops.

If this account of the succession of Arnulf III be correct, the dispute which arose in 1097 over that of Anselm IV in its turn becomes intelligible. The only detailed evidence for it is provided by Landulf of St. Paul, the nephew and apologist of the Patarene leader, Liutprand.[4] He located its origins in the latter part of Arnulf III's reign. When Pope Urban II made his return journey from Clermont, he visited Milan.[5] With the evident intention of pleasing Patarene ears and of rallying Patarene support for himself and for the archbishop whom he had so lately vindicated, he delivered an allocution

1. Ewald, *ubi supra*, no. 33a.
2. In the light of the Patarene campaign in 1103 against Archbishop Grosolanus (Landulf of St. Paul, *Hist. Med.,* 17, *M.G.H., Scr.* xx. 27) it is possible that, if Arnulf had been invested by King Conrad, this may have contributed to a charge of simony *ab obsequio.* The investiture of Anselm IV shows, however, that Urban II would not have allowed such a charge.
3. Bernold, *Chron. s.a.* 1095, *M.G.H., Scr.* v. 463.
4. During the Patarene campaign of Pope Gregory VII's days, Liutprand had emerged as the ecclesiastical aide of the lay leader, Erlembald: Landulf Senior, *Hist. Med.* iii. 18, *M.G.H., Scr.* viii. 86–87; Arnulf, *Gesta archiepiscoporum Mediolanensium,* iv. 9–10, ed. Bethmann and Wattenbach, *M.G.H., Scr.* viii. 28.
5. It was, in fact, Urban's second visit to Milan to rally Patarene support; he had visited the city after Piacenza and had been associated with Arnulf III at the solemn reburial of Erlembald's remains: see the inscription preserved in Sormani, *op. cit.* p. 64; Giulini, *op. cit.* iv. 319.

on the theme 'quod minimus clericulus de ecclesia Dei est maior quolibet rege mortali', and also inveighed against simony. He stimulated a brisk campaign against clerical vices; but he also provoked a schism amongst the Patarenes. Some of them followed a certain Nazarius in enthusiastic and unqualified obedience to him, while the remainder, led by Liutprand, did not. When Arnulf III died, it was Nazarius's faction which promoted the candidature of Anselm IV, and it remained a much-favoured party during his reign.[1] Liutprand's followers, on the other hand, tried to secure the election of Landulf da Baggio, who was the provost of the canons regular of St Ambrose.[2] That Anselm's cause prevailed was principally owing to the outside help which he received from the supporters in Lombardy of Urban II's political measures against the emperor. Landulf of St. Paul described how Cardinal Hermann, the bishop-elect of Brescia and ecclesiastical agent of Countess Matilda of Tuscany, hurried to Milan. Supported by a crowd which, he declared, was looking for the gratitude of the Roman church and for the favour of the bishop-elect of Brescia and of Countess Matilda, he procured the election of Anselm. Then, like his predecessor, Anselm was consecrated 'ab extraneis episcopis'; he received his pastoral staff from the countess and his pallium from the pope. Landulf of St. Paul complained that, with Anselm's election under these auspices, there began the dissensions that were to vex Milan for thirty years and that were the subject of his chronicle. In his opinion, Cardinal Hermann was, before anyone else, their cause.[3]

Such is the evidence for the circumstances of Anselm IV's accession. It helps to exclude such a recent explanation of the dispute as that Hermann intervened to oppose Landulf da Baggio because he saw in him the instrument of the feudal classes who were traditionally hostile to Roman interference at Milan.[4] The da Baggio family did, indeed, belong to the *capitanei*, the uppermost stratum of feudal society in Milan; but, before all families, it had consistently been prominent in reforming circles there during the second half of the eleventh century.[5] As part of his efforts to rally to his cause all reforming elements at Milan, Urban II had himself taken Landulf da Baggio and his canons under papal protection.[6] Above all, Landulf of St. Paul made it absolutely clear that Landulf da Baggio's candidature for the see of Milan had the strong support of Liutprand and his party in the Patarene schism of 1096; the

---

1. *Hist. Med.* 40, *M.G.H., Scr.* xx. 37.   2. *Op. cit.* 1–2, p. 21.   3. *Ibid.*
4. M. L. Marzorati, 'Anselmo di Bovisio', *Diz. biog. Ital.* iii (1961), 409.
5. Its members included Bishop Anselm I of Lucca, who became pope as Alexander II (1061–73), and Bishop Anselm II of Lucca, the canonist and Gregory VII's trusted papal vicar in Lombardy (1081–6).
6. Giulini, *op. cit.* iv. 538–9; he also took Liutprand and his church under papal protection: Landulf of St. Paul, *Hist. Med.* 11, *M.G.H., Scr.* xx. 25.

chronicler himself applauded him as a 'virum religionis'.[1] Thus, far from being a recrudescence of the hostility of unreformed Milan to Rome and to new ways, support for Landulf da Baggio came from a diametrically opposite direction: from extremist reformers like Liutprand. They yielded to none in their zeal against simony; instead, they were distinguished by a rigour which led them to resist the blandishments of Urban II as he eased the way for Milan to identify itself with his alliance against the emperor. As Landulf of St. Paul exhibited it, the disputed election of 1097 takes its place in the history of the factional differences among the champions of reform which had threatened the unity of Milan ever since Urban II had begun to wean it from its old allegiance to the emperor.[2] The first sign of disquiet had been the charge of simony which outraged reformers brought against the sometime imperialist Anselm III when Urban showed himself ready to come to terms with him.[3] A similar charge was probably brought against the hastily-elected Arnulf III when he was stigmatized as an 'avarus accipiter'; when he came to Milan after Clermont, Urban II patently failed to quieten the scruples of many of the Patarenes or to rally them to his support. Anselm IV came to office on the crest of the wave of anti-simoniac enthusiasm represented by Nazarius and his faction, and so was, perhaps, an implausible target for renewed charges of simony. Instead, he was resisted by Liutprand and the rival faction in the recent schism among the Patarenes on the issue of Milanese support for Urban II's alliance in Lombardy. For it is before all else clear from the evidence of Landulf of St. Paul that Anselm owed his succession to the agents of this alliance, and especially to Cardinal Hermann. It also emerges from the same source that, during and after Anselm's election, Liutprand's Patarenes consistently showed hostility to the archbishop, to Cardinal Hermann and to the Matildine party: when King Conrad lost Matilda's support, he naturally gravitated into close touch with Liutprand; and Liutprand's Patarenes crowned their resistance to the involvement of Milan in the wider purposes of Urban II by bitterly opposing Anselm IV's departure to the crusade of 1101 at the head of a Milanese contingent.[4] There thus ran through the whole history of Anselm IV's reign an implacable opposition between those supporters of reform who gave overall co-operation to Urban II on the one hand, and those who only approved of his steps against simony on the other. It is clear from the alignment of forces before, during and after the disputed

---

1. *Op. cit.* 2, p. 21.
2. For a fuller discussion of this change of front on the part of the Milanese, see my forthcoming article, 'The Papacy, the Patarenes and the Church of Milan', *Trans. R. Hist. Soc.* 5th ser. vol. xviii (1968). Above, Chapter V.
3. Ewald, *ubi supra*, no. 33a; for the text, see above, p. 291.
4. *Hist. Med.* 3–4, M.G.H., *Scr.* xx. 21–22. It emerges that Liutprand still kept in touch with Urban II despite his resistance to many of the pope's policies.

succession of 1097 that it was an episode in this opposition;
Landulf of St. Paul underlined it as being the decisive episode which
brought the opposition into the open.

A final consideration corroborates this. Landulf of St. Paul leaves
no room for doubting that, to the Patarenes who followed Liutprand,
Cardinal Hermann was peculiarly an object of hostility. His chronicle
also suggests that Anselm III and Arnulf III had both shown a
prudent reserve in their dealings with Hermann; they had been at
pains not to pursue their support of the Matildine party, valuable
as it was, to the point of provoking an open breach with those of
their subjects who disliked it. Hermann had been active at Milan as
early as Urban II's restoration of Anselm III; for, according to the
Liber Pontificalis and the *Britannica,* it was he who brought Anselm
the pallium. At about the same time, prompted by Countess Matilda,
the Gregorian party at Brescia had elected Hermann to be bishop of
their city; but, as Landulf of St. Paul noted with satisfaction, neither
Anselm III nor Arnulf III had ever performed his office as metropolitan by proceeding to consecrate him.[1] This decisive step was
reserved for Anselm IV after the council of Milan (1098).[2] Taken
together, the consecrations of Anselm IV under Hermann's super-
vision at the end of 1097 and of Hermann at the hands of Anselm in
1098 were a new stage in the commitment of the see of Milan to the
Matildine party. It was marked by an abandoning of all reserve
towards Hermann, and it led to the final and irrevocable alienation
from the archbishop of such reforming factions as the rump of the
Patarenes under Liutprand. Beginning with the disputed election of
1097, the majority of the Milanese, which, under the archbishop,
continued to give overall support to Urban II, was clearly divided
from the vocal and extremist minority which was prepared to support
him only in his resistance to simony and to similar gross ecclesiastical
abuses.

VII

THE PEACE AND TRUCE OF GOD IN THE ELEVENTH CENTURY

DURING THE LAST HUNDRED YEARS OR SO, HISTORIANS HAVE DEVOTED much study to the attempts to promote the Peace of God which was first proclaimed in Burgundy and Aquitaine during the final quarter of the tenth century, and the Truce of God which made its appearance there a generation or so later.   To begin with, it was largely from the point of view of the legal historian that this subject was approached.[1] More recently, its ideological, social and economic aspects have been well to the fore.[2]   The purpose of this article is to consider, in the light of modern discussion, the nature of the Peace and the Truce, and to suggest what they may have contributed to the structures of ecclesiastical and secular authority which began to be renewed in the eleventh century.

I

The purpose of the Peace of God, in its original form, was to place under special ecclesiastical protection certain categories of persons, such as monks, the clergy, and the poor; and certain categories of material things, like church buildings, church property, and poor people's means of livelihood.   It was no new thing for those in authority to offer their peace and protection to those who faced the violence of powerful and lawless men.   In the heyday of Carolingian rule and for far into its decline, this duty had been pre-eminently the king's.   When, for example, in 857 a *missus* of King Charles the Bald sought on his behalf to protect clergy and church lands, together with

---

[1] E.g., L. Huberti, *Studien zur Rechtsgeschichte der Gottesfrieden und Landfrieden*, i, *Die Friedensordnungen in Frankreich* (Ansbach, 1892), which remains the most useful compendium of sources.

[2] Particular mention may be made of the following works: R. Bonnaud-Delamare, "Fondement des institutions de paix au xie siècle", *Mélanges d'histoire du moyen âge dédiés à la mémoire de Louis Halphen* (Paris, 1951), pp. 19-26, and "Les Institutions de paix en Aquitaine au xie siècle", *Recueils de la société Jean Bodin*, xiv (1961), pp. 415-87; G. Duby, "Les Laïcs et la paix de Dieu", *I laici nella "societas christiana" dei secoli xi e xii* (Miscellanea del centro di studi medioevali, v, Milan, 1968), pp. 448-69; H. Hoffmann, *Gottesfriede und Treuga Dei* (Schriften der Monumenta Germaniae Historica [hereafter *M.G.H.*], xx, Stuttgart, 1964); B. Töpfer, *Volk und Kirche zur Zeit der beginnenden Gottesfriedensbewegung im Frankreich* (Berlin, 1957) — a particularly stimulating and valuable Marxist interpretation; E. I. Strubbe, "La Paix de Dieu dans le nord da la France", *Recueils . . . Jean Bodin*, xiv (1961), pp. 489-501.

nuns, widows, orphans and the poor, he provided for just such needs as did the later Peace of God.[3]   The Peace differed only because its sanctions were the bishops', not the king's; even in this it followed a still older usage whereby church councils excommunicated the invaders of church lands and property.[4]   This tradition was resumed with the enfeeblement of royal authority in western Francia.   The early tenth-century dialogue *De statu sanctae ecclesiae* looked to the ecclesiastical hierarchy, from bishops upwards through metropolitans and primates to the pope himself, for the excommunication of those who sacrilegiously seized church endowments.[5]   In practice, at various councils the bishops began to try to protect the lands of the church and of the poor.[6]   A familiar example is the Burgundian council of Anse (994), when two archbishops and nine bishops forbade lay magnates to violate the lands or churches of the monastery of Cluny, to build castles or fortifications that might threaten it, or to plunder its livestock.[7]

Such measures as this can scarcely be regarded as proclaiming the Peace of God, for they embodied no general peace for whole classes of society or categories of thing.   But during the last quarter of the tenth century such peaces were already appearing.   The councils of Le Puy (975) and Charroux (989 or 990) provide the first clear examples of which evidence survives.   At Le Puy Bishop Guy assembled an open-air meeting of the knights and peasants of his diocese in the field of Saint-Germain, "to hear from them what advice they had to give about keeping peace".   He sought to enforce an oath to respect the goods of the church and of the *pauperes,* and he overcame the resistance that he encountered by calling upon the armed support of his kinsmen the counts of Brioude and Gévandan.   The council of Charroux was attended by Archbishop Gumbald of Bordeaux and his suffragans.   Although the word *pax* does not occur in the record of its dealings, its three canons anathematized those who broke into

---

[3] *Allocutio missi cuiusdam Divionensis, M.G.H., Capitularia regum Francorum,* ed. A. Boretius and V. Krause, ii, pt. 1 (Hanover, 1890), no. 267, *caps.* 1-2, pp. 291-2.

[4] E.g. Orleans (538), *cap.* xxv, *M.G.H., Concilia,* i, pp. 80-1; Paris (556-73), *cap.* i, *ibid.,* pp. 142-3.

[5] E. Dümmler, "Über den Dialog *De statu sanctae ecclesiae*", *Sitzungs-berichte der königlich preussischen Akademie der Wissenschaften zu Berlin, ph.-hist. Classe,* xvii (1901), pp. 362-86, esp. pp. 381-2.

[6] E.g. Fîmes (881), *cap.* v, J. D. Mansi, *Sacrorum conciliorum nova et amplissima collectio* [hereafter Mansi], xvii, cc. 541-5; Vienne (892), *cap.* i, Mansi, xviii, c. 121; Trosly (909), *caps.* v, vii, *ibid.,* cc. 275-86. For the significance of such councils, see H. Maisonneuve, "La Morale d'après les conciles du xe et xie siècles", *Mélanges de science religieuse,* xviii (1961), pp. 1-46.

[7] Mansi, xix, cc. 99-102.

and robbed churches, those who made off with the beasts of law-abiding peasants and poor men, and those who attacked unarmed clerks.[8]   There followed many similar councils in or near Aquitaine: notably at Narbonne (990), Le Puy (*c.* 990-3), Limoges (994), Poitiers (*c.* 1011-14), Charroux (1027-8), Limoges (1028), Poitiers (1029-31), and Bourges (1031); also in Burgundy, as at Verdun-sur-le-Doubs (1019-21) and Anse (1025); and so forth.   With remarkable speed, the work of these councils in protecting vulnerable categories of persons and goods was taken up in most parts of France, including the royal demesne.

The Truce was a further stage in these developments.   Whereas the Peace sought to protect certain classes and their goods at all times, the Truce was an attempt to stop all violence at certain times.   Its first appearance was at the council of Toulouges (1027), in the county of Roussillon.   A *pactum vel treuga* was sworn that, "in order to enable every man to show proper respect for the Lord's Day", no one should attack his enemy between Saturday evening and Monday morning.   During the 1030s and 1040s, the Truce as an attempt to forbid violence on an ever longer list of days and seasons was rapidly disseminated as part of churchmen's endeavours to propagate peace. The canons of the council of Narbonne (1054) well illustrate the full development of legislation regarding the Peace and the Truce in the first half of the eleventh century.[9]

II

Such, to the modern observer, were the Peace and the Truce during their formative periods.   A contemporary would have wanted to set them in a fuller and less legal context.   The chronicler Ralph Glaber, for example, gave a chronologically telescoped account of the Peace when he was describing the time of peace and plenty which the year 1033 ushered in, however transiently, with the millennium of Christ's passion.   He told how the tempests, famines and plagues of recent years — notoriously years of general dearth throughout western Europe — were at last abated.   Therefore the bishops of Aquitaine and Burgundy assembled councils at which they associated with themselves abbots and laymen of all social classes.   To the councils were brought innumerable relics of saints, and rulings were made

---

[8] For Le Puy, see *Chronique du monastère de Saint-Pierre du Puy,* in C. Devic and J. Vaissete, *Histoire générale de Languedoc,* v (Toulouse, 1875), c. 15; for Charroux, Mansi, xix, cc. 89-90.

[9] For the council of Toulouges (or Elne), see Mansi, xix, cc. 483-4; for the council of Narbonne, *ibid.,* cc. 827-32.

"concerning the renewal of peace and the establishment of our holy faith". There were numerous miracles of healing. Led by the bishops, all present cried in unison to God, "Pax, pax, pax", for an everlasting sign of the promises that had been made between themselves and God.[10]

Ralph Glaber's picture of general enthusiasm and the background of deliverance from natural disasters against which he set Peace legislation, indicate that the Peace of God was a more complex matter than conciliar canons by themselves suggest. This is borne out by other evidence, such as hagiography, chronicles, sermons, and similar literature; and, indirectly, by archaeological investigations of churches and monasteries. Of outstanding importance are the writings of Adhemar of Chabannes, who not only wrote an important chronicle but also left a corpus of other material about such councils as Ralph Glaber summarily describes.[11] A complete picture of the sponsorship and nature of the Peace of God must be drawn from all such evidence.

The literary sources confirm Ralph Glaber's testimony that it was the bishops upon whom the Peace councils chiefly turned. This is to be expected, for, as Carolingian authority crumbled away, the episcopal order remained intact in its structure and functions. It was the bishops who convened the tenth-century gatherings which led up to the Peace councils. Above all it was the bishops, as distinct even from the monks, who exclusively disposed of the old judicial sanction of excommunication and the new judicial sanction of interdict by which the Peace was imposed: it was, after all, to the apostles whose successors the bishops were, not to the monks and still less to lay rulers, that Christ had left the power to bind and to loose upon earth. Nevertheless, as Ralph Glaber again suggests, the monks were prominent at the Peace assemblies. There emerged no Peace

[10] *Historiarum*, iv.5.14-16: Raoul Glaber, *Les Cinq Livres de ses histoires (900-1044)*, ed. M. Prou (Paris, 1886), pp. 103-5.

[11] Adhemar was born *c.* 988 near Limoges, where he entered the monastery of Saint-Martial. Although he soon migrated to Saint-Cybard, Angoulême, of which he remained a monk until his death on pilgrimage to Jerusalem in 1034, he was a lifelong zealot for Saint-Martial and its interests. For his chronicle, completed *c.* 1028, see Adémar de Chabannes, *Chronique*, ed. J. Chavanon (Paris, 1897). The principal collection of his other writings is L. Delisle, "Notices sur les manuscrits originaux d'Adémar de Chabannes", *Notices et extraits des manuscrits de la Bibliothèque nationale et des autres bibliothèques*, xxxv (1896), pp. 241-358. See also J. P. Migne, *Patrologia Latina* [hereafter *P.L.*], cxli, cc. 79-124; E. Sackur, *Die Cluniacenser in ihrer kirchlichen und allgemeingeschichtlichen Wirksamkeit* (Halle, 1892-4), ii, pp. 479-87, cf. i, pp. 392-6; C. de Lasteyrie, *L'Abbaye de Saint-Martial de Limoges* (Paris, 1901), pp. 422-6; Hoffmann, *Gottesfriede und Treuga Dei*, pp. 257-9.

propagandist more zealous than the monk Adhemar of Chabannes. It was the monks who brought the relics that drew the crowds and performed the miracles, and the ever-mounting renown of the monasteries as places of pilgrimage was harnessed to the cause of peace.[12]   The councils were enthusiastically resorted to by laity of all classes.   In Aquitaine, the dukes were prominent at them. Ralph Glaber's testimony to their eclectic social composition is supported by Adhemar of Chabannes.   According to him, the Peace gatherings at Limoges were attended by the *principes,* the *nobiles* and the *vulgaris plebs.*[13]   The councils made a further impact upon the laity because their canons were published locally by the bishops of the various dioceses.

The principal concern of the councils was for the protection of churchmen, unarmed laymen, and their goods.   From this angle it was no accident that the later decades of the tenth century witnessed the new departure of the Peace.   The juncture was determined by the progressive deterioration of public authority in France.   Whereas the ninth century saw the collapse of royal authority and of the central organs of secular government, the local unit of Carolingian administration, the *pagus,* remained largely intact until the second half of the tenth century.   Then over wide areas it, too, began more or less completely to disintegrate.   It was replaced by a multiplicity of local lords who built castles and who vied with each other for the control of their neighbourhoods, while they knew the restraining hand of no superior lay authority.   The problems to which the disintegration of the *pagus* gave rise were particularly acute in France south of the Loire, where the advent of the Capetians in 987 marked the final end of royal control.[14]   The Peace councils were the churchmen's self-defence, so far as any was possible.

Three specific problems were particularly pressing.   First, the churches, both secular and monastic, were the victims of depredations by local lords who ignored all human laws.   The author of the *De statu sanctae ecclesiae* already appreciated the threat which they presented to the possessions and the jurisidiction of churchmen.[15] By the end of the tenth century, his fears were evidently well

[12] Relics and miracles were important as early as Charroux: *Delatio corporis sancti Juniani in synodum Karrofensem, P.L.,* cxxxvii, cc. 823-6.   For monasteries and pilgrimage, see, besides Töpfer, *Volk und Kirche,* pp. 38-57, the work of J. Hubert, esp. "La Place faite aux laïcs dans les églises monastiques et dans les cathédrales aux xie et xiie siècles", *I laici nella "societas christiana",* pp. 470-87.

[13] Delisle, *art. cit.,* p. 291.

[14] For an analysis of these developments, see G. Duby, *La Société aux xie et xiie siècles dans la région mâconnaise* (Paris, 1953), esp. pp. 150-71.

[15] Dümmler, *art. cit.,* pp. 382, 384.

grounded. Cluny's troubles in 994 illustrate the predicament of many churchmen less influential than Abbot Odilo who found themselves face to face with new castles and their lords.[16] As the foundation and endowment of such monasteries as Cluny often reveals, such lords were sometimes in terror of spiritual sanctions. Charroux and later councils sought to constrain them to respect the peace of the church and of the poor by bringing to bear the threats of excommunication and interdict.

Secondly, the vacuum left by the creeping disintegration of public authority gave a new vitality to the feud as a kind of "wild justice" whereby the lay classes, and especially the lords of castles, might defend their own interests and set a limit to the worst consequences of lawlessness.[17] Such a means of self-vindication and self-defence was not so readily available to churchmen as it was to laymen, and they needed to contrive a remedy of their own. Moreover, in a society where fighting was the pastime of the upper classes, the legitimate feud all too readily spilled over into mere disorderly violence, which caused general devastation, not least upon church lands. As the Peace councils gathered momentum, a principal concern of the bishops was at least to restrict the feud to its acceptable function of upholding justice, and so to impose a limit upon unbridled violence and disorder. The *sacramentum pacis* which, as the councils spread northwards, Bishop Warin of Beauvais proposed in 1023 to King Robert the Pious, well illustrates this concern.[18] So, too, does the abortive attempt in *c.* 1033 by Archbishop Aimo of Bourges to declare a kind of "war upon war", by mobilizing the whole adult male population to coerce aristocratic peace-breakers.[19]

Thirdly, the mounting disorder of society fell with particular severity upon the peasantry. It did so the more as time went on, because the military and social upgrading of the knight in the burgeoning feudal society of France — itself in part the result of the church's increasing willingness to bless his profession of arms — was rapidly widening the gap between the *milites* and the *pauperes*. This significant early eleventh-century distinction made ever more serious the defencelessness of the poor.[20] Furthermore, in the south of

---

[16] The churchmen's outlook is well illustrated by Fulbert of Chartres, *Hymni et carmina ecclesiastica,* no. xx, *P.L.,* cxli, c. 349.

[17] For the feud in medieval society, see O. Brunner, *Land und Herrschaft,* 4th edn. (Vienna and Wiesbaden, 1959), pp. 1-110.

[18] C. Pfister, *Études sur le règne de Robert le Pieux (996-1031)* (Paris, 1885), Diplomes inédits de Robert, no. xii, pp. lx-lxi.

[19] Andrew of Fleury, *Miracula sancti Benedicti,* ii-iv, *Les Miracles de saint Benoît,* ed. E. de Certain (Société de l'histoire de France, Paris, 1858), pp. 192-8.

[20] See Duby's remarks, *art. cit., I laici nella "societas christiana",* pp. 453-5.

France, with its multiplicity of allodial holdings of all sizes and with its vineyards and horticulture, the poor were more vulnerable than in the feudally better-organized north where lay and ecclesiastical lords had a greater interest in the defence of a more dependent peasantry. Like the other unprotected classes, such as women, merchants and pilgrims, peasants had similar needs of protection to those of the clergy who, in obedience to their profession, went about unarmed. Such protection the councils aspired to ensure for them. The reasons were partly religious: the duty of protecting the poor had for long been insisted upon by such influential writers as Abbot Odo of Cluny.[21] They were also partly self-interested, for attacks upon the peasants as upon the other unprotected classes were bad for the ecclesiastical income that came from them both in cash and by way of services. And the more that churches themselves amassed lands and wealth, the greater their own problems became.

Therefore the Peace councils legislated to bring security to certain classes of persons and their goods. But if the evidence about them is considered as a whole, they were by no means only concerned with the violence and disorder of a disintegrated society. They also took account of other scourges which, while they were not so appropriate for positive legislation, were closely bound up in men's minds with the problem of peace. Ralph Glaber introduced the Peace councils in a context of deliverance from such recurrent famines as were caused by storm and flood in the early 1030s. Worse still were the epidemics that followed such crop failure. The sources for the early Peace councils are full of references to the dreaded visitation known by such names as the *ignis sacer*. It is now known to have been a gangrenous form of ergotism, the result of eating bread made from tainted rye-flour.[22] According to the prevalence upon damp corn of the mould known as ergot, its mental and bodily torments came and went with a suddenness for which eleventh-century men knew neither natural explanation nor human remedy. In their eyes, like the storm and famine which went before it, it fractured the order of human life much as did warfare and plunder. Lacking the means alike to prop

[21] E.g. in his portrait of a pattern lay lord, *Vita sancti Geraldi Auriliacensis comitis, P.L.,* cxxxiii, cc. 639-702.

[22] For a medical and historical account of this epidemic, see H. Chaumartin, *Le Mal des ardents et le feu Saint-Antoine* (Vienne-la-Romaine, 1946); also J. Rauch, "Der Antoniterorden", *Archiv für mittelrheinische Kirchengeschichte,* ix (1959), pp. 33-50. The modern drug L.S.D. is a derivative of ergot, and the taking of these substances has many effects in common, particularly psychologically. For a possible modern outbreak of ergotism in France, see J. G. Fuller, *The Day of St. Anthony's Fire* (London, 1969).

up a crumbling social order and to mitigate overwhelming natural disaster, they looked for a peace which was a deliverance from all manner of scourges that destroyed their welfare — human violence, storm, famine and epidemic.[23]   Hence the prominence of the cultus of the saints and the bringing of relics to the Peace councils.   To borrow some words of Professor Southern:

> When the machinery of government was simple or non-existent, these tangible agents of spiritual power [i.e. relics] had an importance in public life which they lost in a more complicated age.   The deficiencies in human resources were supplied by the power of the saints.   They were the great power-houses in the fight against evil; they filled the gaps left in the structure of human justice.[24]

The Peace councils looked to the saints and assembled their relics in order both to secure deliverance from natural disaster and to provide guarantors of men's own pledges of mutual peace and justice. Animated by their presence, the councils were times of religious enthusiasm and of exhortation to a repentance and conversion of life which would turn away God's wrath and show gratitude for his healing.

Thanks to Adhemar of Chabannes, it is at Limoges that the whole pattern of the quest for peace can be most fully seen.   Adhemar's writings repeatedly refer to the Peace council of 994.   According to his Chronicle, it was convened because the *ignis sacer* was everywhere raging.   Abbot Geoffrey of Saint-Martial, Limoges, called for a three-day fast, and afterwards a great open-air assembly met upon a hill outside the city:

> All the bishops of Aquitaine assembled together at Limoges.   The bodies and relics of the saints were solemnly conveyed there from all parts, while the body of St. Martial, the patron of Gaul, was borne from its sepulchre, so that everyone was filled with immeasurable joy.   All sickness everywhere ceased, and the duke [of Aquitaine] and the *principes* concluded a mutual pact of peace and justice.[25]

Adhemar's sermons of later years repeatedly drew out the moral of these events.   The *ignis sacer* was God's punishment for men's sins, and especially for the violence of powerful laymen.   The fiery punishment did, it was true, fall upon the poor, not the rich.   But "the righteous often dies for the ungodly": it was God's vicarious warning to the unrighteous rich that they should repent.   At St. Martial's intercession, God had mercifully stayed his anger from his

[23] Adhemar of Chabannes could claim that, at Limoges in 994, not only had an outbreak of the *ignis sacer* just miraculously ceased, but "within a short time warfare was turned into peace, disaster into safety, barrenness of the land into fertility, and famine into sufficiency": Delisle, *art. cit.*, p. 270.

[24] R. W. Southern, *The Making of the Middle Ages* (London, 1953), p. 137.

[25] *Chronique*, iii. 35, p. 158; cf. *Commemoratio abbatum Lemovicensium, P.L.*, cxli, cc. 82-3.

people.   In return it behoved the *principes* to answer by obeying the bishops', or rather God's, call to promise peace and justice.[26]   The concluding of peace under episcopal sanctions was thus part of a pattern of events which began with the sign of God's wrath, continued with healing by the intervention of the saints, and ended with men's answering contract of peace and justice.

Adhemar's writings leave little room for doubting that, at least in the minds of churchmen, the search for peace took the form of a religious movement which sought much more than the integrity of church property or even a respite from social disorder.   It came to embody something approaching their total view of Christianity. Adhemar described how the clergy of Aquitaine, at their regular twice-yearly councils at Limoges, made quasi-liturgical commemorations of peace, as a means of propagating it throughout society:

> The principal bishop arises; then, kneeling with all the clergy, he prays for the king and all set in authority, and for the peace and salvation of the whole church, beginning the seven penitential psalms.   Next he says appropriate prayers, and prayers for the absolution of sinners.   Then all, kneeling down, bow in silence.   Afterwards they stand up and the bishop begins to give the peace, and they all offer the kiss of peace to one another as at mass, so that they may remain in the peace of Christ and harmonious concord, and that peace may be upon them all and upon all the people.[27]

In much of the Peace propaganda, the Peace of God was thus represented as a renewal of the peace which Christ himself bequeathed to the church and of the pristine customs of apostolic Christianity. Adhemar, for example, rejoiced that, when it obeyed the bishops' call to refrain from violence, the *gens Aquitaniae* had been made the *filia pacis*.   For the peace of the bishops was the same peace that Christ himself committed to his apostles.   It was renewed whenever the bishops fulfilled his word to the seventy, "Say, 'Peace be to this house!'   And if a son of peace is there, your peace shall rest upon him".[28]

Upon the basis of the need to provide for physical peace and security there was thus erected a superstructure of the preaching and liturgical commemoration of peace in an ideal sense as the planting upon earth of the order that God willed to prevail.   The means to

[26] Delisle, *art. cit.,* p. 290; cf. pp. 293-6.
[27] Delisle, *art. cit.,* p. 271; cf. Sackur, *Die Cluniacenser,* i, pp. 392-6.   Such passages should be read in the light of the prayers concerning peace following the canon of the Latin mass, the frequent repetition of which was clearly crucial in shaping the outlook of eleventh-century clergy.
[28] Luke x. 5-6.   For the sermon, see *P.L.,* cxli, c. 115.   This and the following sermons are often regarded as apocryphal, but the matter deserves a fresh examination.   Their probable date is *c.* 1031.   See Bonnaud-Delamare, *art. cit., Recueils . . . Jean Bodin,* xiv (1961), pp. 433-7.

this was the renewal of the peace that Christ committed to the apostles at the beginning of the church — the peace of the church which, for centuries, churchmen had taught was broken by grave sin and restored when transgressors returned to it by way of penance. Such an understanding of peace linked it with all the associations of the word *pax* in Augustinian and later thought.[29] From its more limited connotation of freedom from human violence, peace gained, or recovered, a positive meaning in terms of divinely-sustained order, healing, and righteousness.

Adhemar's writings also provide evidence of another and related development to which the quest for peace at Limoges contributed. His power to secure deliverance from the *ignis sacer* won St. Martial great fame as the protector of Aquitaine, and his tomb at Limoges became a much-sought centre of pilgrimage.[30] He became the patron *par excellence* of peace in all its aspects. Now, in the light of the developing ideology of peace, the nearer in history he could be represented as standing to Christ the giver of peace, and to St. Peter as the head of the apostles to whom Christ committed it, the more impressive his patronage would be. So, with Adhemar as their tireless protagonist, the monks of Saint-Martial put forward the claims that their patron had been Christ's companion in his Ministry, at the Last Supper, and at the Ascension; that he was one of the seventy whom Christ had sent out with the gift of peace; that, as such, he was an apostle; and that, after the Ascension, St. Peter himself had sent him to evangelize Aquitaine.[31] The bishops and secular clergy of Limoges at first resisted this monastic legend-building; but Bishop Jordan at length conceded St. Martial's apostolicity, for it at once added lustre to his see and, especially in Adhemar's annual com-memorative sermons, gave new credibility to St. Martial's especial power to mediate the peace which Christ left behind him upon earth.[32]

This vintage example of eleventh-century legend-building about a patron saint marks out Limoges as something of a special case. But its prestige as a pilgrimage centre caused the ideas that were current there to be widely disseminated. Moreover, the Peace propaganda of Limoges was only an especially elaborate example of what was being put about throughout France and beyond in places which had no

[29] H.-X. Arquillière, *L'Augustinisme politique* (Paris, 1934), pp. 9-17, 144-50.
[30] *Chron.*, iii. 49, pp. 171-2.
[31] The legends figure in Adhemar's works, *passim*, the most elaborate statement being his *Epistola de apostolatu Martialis, P.L.*, cxli, cc. 89-112.
[32] The apostolicity was affirmed by various councils: e.g., Bourges (1031), canon i, Mansi, xix, c. 503.

prophet so eloquent as Adhemar of Chabannes. His characteristic pattern of ideas, which linked epidemics of the *ignis sacer,* the miraculous intervention of saints and their relics, and the concluding in response of pacts of peace and justice, seems to have been particularly widespread.[33] So, too, was his conviction that the purpose of Peace legislation was to renew the peace that Christ left with his apostles. For instance, at Poitiers (*c.* 1011-14) the preamble to the canons ran:

> How fair is the name of the peace and how beautiful is the repute of the unity which Christ left to his disciples when he ascended into heaven.

The council saw its task as being to restore this peace and unity: it met "for the renewing of the church", and it concluded a "renewal of peace and justice".[34] It was because the Peace councils proclaimed such a peace as this that, according to Ralph Glaber, those who attended them answered the bishops with their cries of "Pax, pax, pax". Peace among men was but one aspect of a wider Peace of God.

Such were the ideas that were developed in connection with the Peace of God. Both by reason of the safeguards which it promised against natural and human disasters, and of the religious enthusiasm which it generated and canalized, it has every title to be regarded as a coherent movement, and as one which involved all grades of society.[35] The Truce of God, which developed within it, was more strictly aristocratic. Its primary purpose was to restrain the military classes from the exercise of arms at certain times. The word *treuga* was in no way calculated to attract to itself such a wealth of religious meaning as almost inevitably gathered about the word *pax,* with its biblical, theological and liturgical overtones. Nevertheless, religious ideas centring upon the Peace had their effect upon the Truce, quickly making it more than just a negative ban upon certain activities. The simple prohibition of Toulouges, which, for the better keeping of the Lord's Day, forbade the shedding of blood on Sunday, was soon extended to Thursday, Friday and Saturday, for these days were reminders of the Last Supper, the Crucifixion, and the Entombment of Christ. The Truce was also proclaimed upon the

[33] *Miracula sancti Adalhardi abbatis Corbiensis, Recueil des historiens des Gaules et de la France,* x (Paris, 1760), pp. 378-9; Hugh of Flavigny, *Chronicon,* ii, *M.G.H., Scriptorum,* viii, p. 403; Landulf Senior, *Historia Mediolanensis,* ii. 30, *ibid.,* p. 67.

[34] Mansi, xix, c. 267. A similar understanding of peace is clear in Adhemar's account of the suppression of the Manichaean heresy at Charroux (1027-8): *Chron.,* iii. 69, p. 194.

[35] Töpfer's insistence upon this point was partly anticipated by L. C. MacKinney, "The People and Public Opinion in the Eleventh-Century Peace Movement", *Speculum,* v (1930), pp. 181-206.

greater saints' days and during such solemn seasons as Advent and Lent.[36] As it was right for all lay Christians to abstain at certain times from food, or from servile labour, or from sexual intercourse, so too it was a reasonable ascetic precept that the military classes should sometimes abstain from their favourite pastime of arms.

But this was a logic that demanded to be carried farther. If, in the name of Christian observance, men should keep themselves from shedding Christian blood at some times, ought they not to do so at all times? It did not take the proponents of the Truce very long to draw such a conclusion. In 1054, at the council of Narbonne, it was laid down that "no Christian should kill another Christian, for whoever kills a Christian undoubtedly sheds the blood of Christ".[37] At least in theory, the Truce had brought the Peace movement to the point where it should logically require complete internal peace to be maintained in the whole of Christian society. It was a critical point in more ways than one. The churchmen who were calling upon the knights to practise internal peace had also set their blessing upon the weapons of their warfare. The Peace movement could scarcely develop further unless a voice with sufficient authority complemented the precept of internal peace by finding an appropriate external outlet for those whose vocation was Christian warfare. Moreover, the internal peace towards which the Truce was pointing was the vainest of hopes unless it were reinforced by the active vigilance of temporal rulers — unless, that is to say, it became their peace.

By 1054, the Peace movement was hardly capable of further development unless it had an authoritative lead from popes and lay rulers, and unless it exchanged its original autonomy under the bishops for a place in more solid structures of ecclesiastical and temporal government.

III

If it be judged by its legislation and the ideas to which it gave currency, the movement for the Peace and the Truce of God up to the council of Narbonne was a remarkable one; but in face of the endemic lawlessness of French society, its practical effectiveness was less impressive. Under the shadow of famine or of the *ignis sacer,* such preaching as that of Adhemar of Chabannes commanded attention, and men promised to uphold peace and justice; when such disasters seemed remote they no doubt slipped back into their former ways.

[36] The extension of the Truce and its aspect as a religious discipline are evident in a council probably at Arles (*c.* 1042): Mansi, xix, cc. 593-6.
[37] Canon i, *ibid.,* c. 827.

After Narbonne, the Peace movement seems in general to have lost some of its impetus and coherence. The structures of the church and of lay society were not yet ready to take up the opportunities with which it presented them, and so to give it new life. The pattern of epidemic, healing, and the concluding of agreements of peace and justice, seems to have disintegrated. In particular, the close connection between the *ignis sacer* and endeavours to ensure peace was relaxed. This was especially so after *c.* 1070, when Count Jocelin II of Dauphiné brought home from Byzantium the body of one of the most famous of miracle-working saints, Antony of Egypt. St. Antony replaced St. Martial as the healer of the fire which henceforth bore his name, but he did not become a patron of peace. Nor did the Peace of God again find so eloquent a spokesman as Adhemar of Chabannes. The records of the Peace, which become fewer after Narbonne, come increasingly from the north of France, with its more thoroughly feudalized social structure. There, the emphasis fell, not upon the Peace as such with its lavish ideological overtones, but upon the more legal and disciplinary Truce. With this shift of emphasis, however, the letters and canon-law compilations of Ivo of Chartres testify to the continuing vitality of the Peace and the Truce as an institution of French life up to and beyond the end of the century.[38] If they had their beginnings in the *morcellement* and disorder of the Carolingian decline, they survived to make an ever-increasing contribution to the building up of ecclesiastical and temporal structures. They did so, not only in France, but also outside it in lands which were in various ways open to French influences. It is possible to follow at least some of the threads which ran from the institutions of the Peace and the Truce to the growing structures of the high Middle Ages.

The church

The Peace and the Truce did not contribute directly to the reassertion of papal authority in the head and members of the church which took place in the Gregorian age. But they played a vital part by creating in France a milieu within which the reformed papacy came to be, on the whole, quietly accepted by the French church, and within which Urban II in 1095 could demonstrate papal ascendency over French feudal society in the successful preaching of the First Crusade.

They prepared the ground for the papacy of Gregory VII, with its

[38] Yves de Chartres, *Correspondance*, ed. J. Leclercq, i (Paris, 1949), nos. 28, 44, 62, pp. 118-20, 174-84, 258; *Panormia, lib.* viii, *cap.* cxlvii, *P.L.,* cxli, c. 1343.

insistence upon the universal jurisdiction of St. Peter and his vicar, and upon the apostolic see as the apex of an ecclesiastical hierarchy. With the influential ideas of the Forged Decretals behind it, even the tenth-century *De statu sanctae ecclesiae* spoke with remarkable clearness, in dealing with the problems to which the Peace movement was to attempt an answer, of the clerical hierarchy of bishops, metropolitans and primates, with its supreme authority at Rome.[39] Early in the eleventh century, the papacy could occasionally figure as the ultimate guarantor of the Peace which the councils made.[40]   But in the long term it was more important that the widespread reliance upon spiritual sanctions as imposed by the bishops organized in their provinces, was already accustoming men to such an exercise of spiritual jurisdiction as the papacy was soon to claim for itself.   The episcopal order was consciously and with much accompanying propaganda attempting to renew the peace of the apostolic church as Christ had left it in the hands of St. Peter.   By its activities and by its ideas, it was establishing a milieu within which, as the apostolic see became stronger, the vicar of St. Peter could look with confidence for attention to his claims and for an understanding of his functions.

Furthermore, as events at Limoges reveal, the supernatural powers of the saints were of greater significance than the judicial activities of the bishops.   The higher the status of a saint, the greater was the advantage to a locality of his patronage.   Hence, St. Martial affords a classic example of the process — widely exemplified in the eleventh century — whereby lesser saints tended to be overshadowed by greater saints, lavish claims were advanced for patrons and prodigies of legend-building were performed to back them up, until at last lesser and greater saints alike were set in due subordination to St. Peter, the prince of the apostles and patron of the see of Rome.   At Limoges, St. Martial's reputation as a deliverer from epidemic and as an upholder of peace led to his meteoric rise from local saint to — at least in the eyes of the Limousin — the *patronus Galliae*.   Then there arose the question of his apostleship.   While the monks and the seculars of Limoges were locked in controversy about it, Adhemar of Chabannes insisted year in, year out upon St. Martial's nearness to St. Peter, both through their common apostleship in Christ's days upon earth, and also now as they together watched over Aquitaine.[41] St. Peter was made to matter to the Limousin; and even in Adhemar's day his vicar began to matter, too.   On the issue of St. Martial's

[39] Dümmler, *art. cit.*, pp. 381-2.   For the Forged Decretals, esp. Pseudo-Isidore, see W. Ullmann, *The Growth of Papal Government in the Middle Ages* (London, 1955), pp. 180-4.
[40] Adhemar of Chabannes, Sermon i, *P.L.*, cxli, cc. 117-8.
[41] Delisle, *art. cit., passim*, esp. pp. 254-5, 294.

apostolicity, both sides in turn appealed to Rome — the reluctant bishop abortively to Pope Benedict VIII, but the enthusiastic monks successfully to his successor John XIX.[42]   As the Peace movement grew and with it the legend of St. Martial, St. Peter and the apostolic see thus both impressed themselves on the consciousness of the Limousin.   It was the first step in a process which next saw the incorporation of Saint-Martial in St. Peter's family at Cluny.   With the legatine visit of Cardinal Peter Damiani (1063), this in its turn brought papal authority still more effectively to bear on Limoges, at the threshold of the Gregorian era.[43]

The Peace movement thus brought St. Peter near to the Limousin and in general it emphasized the activities of the episcopal hierarchy of which his vicar was always the head and was soon to be the very active head.   It also helped to create a favourable milieu for Urban II's French journey of 1095-6.   There can be little doubt that, in the genesis of the First Crusade, such institutions as the holy war and pilgrimage counted for more than did the Peace of God.   But Urban's preaching found its overwhelming response in the south of France, where the original Peace of God had accustomed men to hear the preaching of the renewal of Christian life.   As a French aristocrat by birth and as a former grand prior of Cluny, Urban was well placed to appreciate the use to the papacy of the Peace of God; through him the papacy for the first time effectively proclaimed it for its own purposes.[44]

A comparison between Clermont and the earlier Peace councils shows how considerably they set the stage for him.   At Clermont, there was a similar background of famines and epidemics, including the *ignis sacer,* which created anxiety and made men take thought for their sins and for the needs of the times.[45]   When Urban made his

[42] For an appeal to Benedict VIII to rule that, while St. Martial was one of the seventy, he was still only a confessor, see Bishop Jordan of Limoges's letter, *Ep.* iv, *P.L.,* cxli, cc. 1158-60; Benedict died before it arrived.   For John XIX's affirmation of St. Martial's apostolicity, which he emphasized by assigning him an altar in St. Peter's basilica, see *Ep.* xv, *ibid.,* cc. 1149-50.   Adhemar laid weight upon papal authority: Delisle, *art. cit.,* p. 299; Hoffmann, *Gottesfriede und Treuga Dei,* pp. 258-9.

[43] I discuss these developments at Saint-Martial in my forthcoming book, *The Cluniacs and the Gregorian Reform.*

[44] The principal peace legislation of the early reformed papacy was Nicholas II's (1059): *Ep.* viii, Mansi, xix, c. 873; canons xv-xvi, *ibid.,* c. 915.   But it was exceptional.

[45] Sigebert of Gembloux, *Chronica, s.a.* 1089-95, *P.L.,* clx, cc. 224-5; Orderic Vitalis, *Hist.,* ix. 2, ed. le Prévost, iii (Paris, 1845), p. 463.   According to the earliest historian of the Hospitallers of St. Antony, Urban II on his French journey and at Clermont was much concerned with the founding of his order, which devoted itself to the victims of the *ignis sacer,* and with reforming the cult of St. Antony: A. Falco, *Antonianae historiae compendium* (Lyons, 1534), fols. xliiiv- xlivv, xlviir-v.

summons to the Crusade, the circumstances were familiar. He addressed a great concourse of both clergy and laity. As at so many Peace councils from Le Puy (975) and Limoges (994) onwards, they assembled in the open. Their answering cries of "Deus le volt" recall the earlier cries of "Pax, pax, pax".

Urban almost certainly spoke at length about peace. There is no authentic record of what he actually said, but Fulcher of Chartres describes him as having been deeply moved by the internal turmoil of Christendom:

> He saw how the Christian faith was trampled under foot by all, both clergy and people, and how the warfare and strife of the princes of the world endlessly brought about the destruction of peace.

According to Fulcher, he revived the theme of the Peace movement as it was preached in earlier times, by calling upon Christians to renew the peace of the Church in its pristine quality.[46] The versions of Urban's speech agree that he urged an end to men's strife against their Christian neighbours, and the dedication of their arms to a salutary warfare against the heathen.[47] As the canons of Clermont were preserved by Bishop Lambert of Arras, they accordingly prescribe, for the first time in the history of the Peace of God, a perpetual peace within the whole of Christendom.[48] The Crusading propaganda that followed Clermont seems to have taken up this call.[49]

In all this, the Crusade in effect resumed the Peace movement where it was left by the canons of Narbonne (1054). Narbonne enunciated the principle that Christians ought not to shed Christian blood; Urban drew the conclusion of proclaiming a general peace within Christendom. The church had increasingly given its blessing to the warfare of knights and had begun to use them to keep peace; Urban directed them to a new field of battle in the holy war against the pagans of the east. The Truce of God was as it were an ascetic discipline; Urban associated with the keeping of peace at home and the journey to liberate Jerusalem the spiritual benefits that had previously been reserved for pilgrims.[50] His Crusade was the

---

[46] *Historia Iherosolymitana*, i. 1, *Recueil des historiens des croisades, historiens occidentaux*, iii (Paris, 1866), p. 321; cf. i. 4, p. 325.

[47] The best study of the chroniclers' record of Urban's speech is D. C. Munro, "The Speech of Pope Urban II at Clermont, 1095", *Amer. Hist. Rev.*, xi (1906), pp. 231-42; esp. p. 239.

[48] Canon i, Mansi, xx, c. 816.

[49] A. Gieysztor, "The Genesis of the Crusades; the Encyclical of Sergius IV (1009-12)", *Medievalia et Humanistica*, v (1948), pp. 3-23; vi (1950), pp. 3-34; esp. lines 26-31 of the text of the "Encyclical".

[50] C. Erdmann, *Die Entstehung des Kreuzzugsgedankens* (Weimar, 1935), is still the best analysis of the origins of the First Crusade.

complement of the Peace movement. He did not thereby succeed in bringing peace to France, but by making himself the proponent of peace he claimed the church and society of France for the papacy more fully than ever before.

Lay government

The Peace of God also made its contribution to building up the structures of lay society. But whereas in the case of the church it provided a milieu in which the popes could assert their headship of an existing hierarchy and effectively summon French chivalry to the Crusade, in the case of lay government its contribution was a more direct one. As in the early days of the Peace churchmen drew upon the expedients of Carolingian government and adapted them to meet their own needs in protecting clerks, church property and church dependents, so in the course of the eleventh century lay rulers began to claim from churchmen the Peace and the Truce in order to use them to build up their own authority once more.

It became the easier for lay rulers to claim them, because from the end of the eleventh century, in many countries of Europe, the forms of criminal justice began to change. Murderers, robbers and the like, whatever their social condition, increasingly suffered punishment in their bodies, while financial compositions for serious crimes became unusual. Popular justice tended to give place to the justice of lords and their officials, and lords accordingly made themselves the source of peace in their own lands. The traditions of the Peace and the Truce of God contributed to such developments, for when lay lords punished serious crimes in the name of their own peace they often drew upon these traditions in order to justify themselves and to provide a sanction for what they were doing.

In such ways as this the Peace and the Truce increasingly assisted the process, sometimes epitomized as "concentric concentration",[51] by which temporal authority was slowly rehabilitated in western Europe. Thus in France, the homeland of the Peace movement, the disintegration of the *pagus* round about the year 1000 represents the low-water mark of temporal authority. From this condition of weakness its political structures began to be renewed when growth points of authority and jurisdiction gradually appeared in the lesser and greater fiefs, whose lords used the resources that they found to hand. The kings in due course followed suit and so moved towards

[51] See H. Mitteis, *Lehnrecht und Staatsgewalt* (Weimar, 1933), pp. 282-3, 300-9; *Der Staat des hohen Mittelalters*, 5th edn. (Weimar, 1955), pp. 136, 208-9, 240-1.

the balanced feudal polity of the thirteenth century. In the light of such developments as this the contribution of the Peace and the Truce was made at gradually higher levels of society — first in a great fief like Aquitaine but afterwards in the monarchies not only of France but also of Germany and elsewhere. At the same time there was a movement away from the south of France to regions, especially to the north and north-east of the Loire, where there was a firmer institutional basis for the maintenance of justice and public order.

In the duchy of Aquitaine, the secular ruler began to use the Peace movement at a very early date, during the rule of Duke William V *Le Grand* (990-1029). William was a zealous sponsor of the Peace councils, and it was his intention by their means to win for the ducal authority some of the prestige that peace activities were securing for prelates like Archbishop Gumbald of Bordeaux.[52] It was the duke who summoned the council of Poitiers (*c.* 1011-14). Its canons, designed to secure the "renewal of peace and justice", were not only sanctioned by threats of excommunication, but peace-breakers were to appear before the lord of their region or the *iudex* of their *pagus*.[53] Early eleventh-century secular justice was thus linked with the Peace movement, and it gained in strength by being exercised in so timely a cause. A further hint of the duke's methods is provided by a charter of the Poitevin monastery of Saint-Maixent. It shows how he presided at further councils where the measures of Poitiers were renewed. As a consequence of his zeal, there in due course came before his son, Duke William VI *Le Gras* (1029-38), certain complaints from the monks of Saint-Maixent and of Saint-Léger that his local *iudices* had invaded their lands and wrongfully oppressed poor men. The duke, therefore, took steps to set matters right by taking sworn evidence about the rightful jurisdiction of the *iudices* from "the elders of the region and those who knew its ancient customs". Their findings were written down in a formal *descriptio* of the respective rights of the monks and the duke's officers, which was sworn to by the *principes* and *nobiles* who were present.[54]

This attempt in pursuance of the Peace of God to rehabilitate and rectify ducal authority did not long survive Duke William V. But in the second half of the century it was imitated with greater effect and permanence to the north in the duchy of Normandy. There ducal power had left no foothold for the Peace in its early days, when it was

[52] See Bonnaud-Delamare, *art. cit., Recueils . . . Jean Bodin*, xiv (1961), pp. 415-87.
[53] Mansi, xix, c. 267.
[54] *Chartes et documents pour servir à l'histoire de Saint-Maixent*, ed. A. Richard (Archives historiques du Poitou, xvi, 1886), no. cxi, pp. 109-11.

an episcopal remedy for near anarchy. It first appeared, almost certainly upon ducal initiative, in the time of Duke William the Bastard (1035-87) at the council of Caen (1047) which marked the revival of his fortunes following the battle of Val-ès-Dunes. The Norman measures seem to have drawn but little upon the older Peace movement with its dependence upon episcopal guidance and authority. They imposed a Truce as an instrument of discipline upon fighting men, but in the special sense of a prohibition of fighting on certain days which forbade all warfare save the duke's own. In Norman usage the words *pax* and *treuga* were synonyms for such a Truce, which was enforced by the duke's authority as well as by the sanctions of a church which was loyal to him. Thus from the start the Truce served to build up ducal power over the church and over the Norman aristocracy.[55]

After 1066, the Truce as thus first established in the continental part of the Anglo-Norman kingdom was the basis of important developments there. While evidence is scanty, it is enough to suggest that the Truce was the means by which ducal control was built up over criminal justice, and the lever by which ducal authority was raised high above that of all other lords. A major step forward was taken at the council of Lillebonne (1080), when, as Orderic Vitalis expressed it,

> counsel was taken to the common advantage by the king's wisdom, with the advice of his barons, for the good order of God's church and of the whole realm.

The first canon of Lillebonne dealt with the "Peace of God, commonly called the Truce". In it William reaffirmed his earlier legislation and added a new machinery for enforcing it:

> If anyone should be disobedient to the bishop, let the bishop show the matter to the lord in whose land he dwells, and let the lord deliver him to episcopal justice. If the lord should neglect to do so, let the king's *vicomte* be called in by the bishop and let him act without making any excuse.[56]

Never before in the history of the Peace of God had the temporal ruler provided so strong and automatic a sanction for its observance. Much, indeed, was still left in the hands of the bishops. Moreover, with the weaker rule of Duke Robert Curthose (1087-1106), the council of Rouen (1096) imposed the Peace and the Truce in pursuance of the decrees of Clermont with a clear affirmation of episcopal jurisdiction.[57] But the prevailing tendency was for the duke to take

[55] M. de Bouard, "Sur les origines de la trêve de Dieu en Normandie", *Annales de Normandie*, ix (1959), pp. 169-89.
[56] *Hist.*, v. 5, ed. le Prévost, ii (1840), pp. 315-6.
[57] Mansi, xx, cc. 921-6. Norman bishops held *placita treugae* into the thirteenth century.

over the keeping of public peace. The Norman *Consuetudines* of 1091, which set in writing the *consuetudines et iustitiae* of the duchy as they were in William I's day, show how the duke himself assumed the right to vindicate crimes that the Truce legislation from 1047 onwards had sought to put down.[58] After King Henry I of England had secured the duchy in 1106, he resumed his father's work. The main evidence for this is provided by the *Très ancien coutumier,* and in it particularly by Henry's ordinance of 1135 which summed up the developments of his reign.[59] From this it seems clear that the trend set by the *Consuetudines* had continued. The duke's courts were trying many cases of breaches of the Truce and merely paying certain of the incidents of justice to the bishops. In effect the Truce was providing the material from which the duke's peace was being built, and criminal jurisdiction was being concentrated upon the duke in a way that raised him above all other sources of justice.[60] Such, on the continent, was the Norman legacy to later Angevin rule.

In the Norman lands of the south, the Peace of God and its consequences for the structure of temporal government show considerable similarities with Normandy itself.[61] It was not until after the death in 1085 of the strong ruler Robert Guiscard that there is clear evidence for it. In Sicily, where a fairly rapid and thorough conquest favoured the establishment of a strong central authority, Count Roger I may, perhaps, have proclaimed a general peace of his own under lay authority as early as *c.* 1091-4,[62] although if he did, no details of it survive. In Apulia and Calabria, the Normans had penetrated piecemeal, and the problems of peace and order were therefore more intractable. The Truce of God seems to have been

---

[58] C. H. Haskins, *Norman Institutions* (Cambridge, Mass., 1918), pp. 277-84; cf. pp. 30-9.

[59] E.-J. Tardif, *Coutumiers de Normandie,* i, *Le très ancien coutumier de Normandie* (Rouen, 1881), no. lxxi, pp. 65-8.

[60] The subject of Normandy is discussed by J. Goebel, *Felony and Misdemeanour,* i (New York, 1937), pp. 280-335. The increasing concern of the counts of Flanders with Peace measures which were in many ways similar to the earlier Norman ones is outlined by Bonnaud-Delamare, "La Paix en Flandre pendant la première croisade", *Revue du Nord,* xxxix (1957), pp. 147-52.

[61] See esp. E. Jamison, "The Norman Administration of Apulia and Calabria", *Papers of the British School at Rome,* vi, no. 6 (London, 1913), pp. 239-43; C. Cahen, *Le Régime féodal de l'Italie normande* (Paris, 1940), pp. 107-10.

[62] Such an inference is commonly drawn from the words "I have established a lasting peace through all Sicily" in a charter of Roger's to the church of Patti: R. Pirro, *Sicilia sacra,* in *Thesaurus antiquitatum et historiarum Siciliae,* ed. J. G. Graevius, iii (Leyden, 1723), c. 840. But comparison with the language of similar charters suggests that they might simply refer to the expulsion of the Saracens.

introduced and developed there by the direct action of the papacy. Urban II established it at the councils of Melfi (1089) and Troia (1093);[63] and Paschal II renewed it at the council of Troia (1115).[64] So far as the evidence goes, these Truces depended upon episcopal sanctions. Their scope was gradually extended, so that the Truce of 1115 not only protected certain seasons, but also sought to introduce a continuous peace for three years.

But in due course Roger II used the Truce which was thus introduced to build up his own authority. Just before he assumed the Sicilian crown in 1130, he established a peace of his own which was very similar to that developed in Normandy by William I and Henry I. At an assembly of magnates at Melfi in 1129 he issued an edict prohibiting private war among his vassals. At the same time he compelled them to swear peace amongst themselves. They were to co-operate in maintaining peace and justice by bringing malefactors to his courts, and they were charged to protect the clergy and the non-military lay classes.[65] Roger thus established, and as king was to maintain, a general peace which made his own justice the basis of the public order for which the earlier Truce had striven.

The appropriation of the Peace of God by a territorial ruler of comital or ducal standing, of which the Norman lands provide the best examples, was also a feature of the region of Spain which had once formed part of the Carolingian Empire — the Spanish March of Catalonia. Its continuing links with the south of France had ensured that it quickly came within the ambit of the French Peace movement. After the council of Toulouges (1027), numerous councils there proclaimed the Peace and the Truce.[66] Both the papacy and the counts of Barcelona sought to gain advantage from their introduction. At the council of Gerona (1068), Cardinal Hugh Candidus as papal legate confirmed them and extended the scope of the Truce.[67] In 1079 Gregory VII instructed Bishop Berengar of Gerona to assemble clergy and laymen, and to establish under papal

[63] Mansi, xx, cc. 724-5, 790. Gregory VII, *Ep.* ix. 4, *Registrum*, ed. E. Caspar, *M.G.H., Epistolae selectae*, ii (Berlin, 1920-3), pp. 577-9, may provide evidence for the Truce at an earlier date.

[64] Mansi, xxi, cc. 139-40.

[65] Alexander of Telesia, *De rebus gestis Rogerii Siciliae regis*, i. 21, *Rerum Italicarum scriptores*, ed. L. A. Muratori, v (Milan, 1724), c. 620. Roger's detailed prohibition, at this time, of private war and brigandage may be inferred from *cap.* xxxi of the Assize of Ariano (1140): F. Brandileone, *Il diritto romano nelle leggi normanne e sueve nel regno di Sicilia* (Turin, 1884), p. 113.

[66] For a fine example of a Catalan Peace, see Hoffmann, *Gottesfriede und Treuga Dei*, pp. 260-2.

[67] Mansi, xix, c. 1072; cf. the council of Vich, *ibid.* c. 1076.

sanction a peace between the sons of Count Raymond Berengar I of Barcelona.[68]

If the Peace thus occasionally served to increase the authority of the papacy, it contributed with more lasting effect to the structure of lay government by feeding the authority of the counts of Barcelona. There is evidence for this in the *Usatici* of Barcelona, a collection of laws for the county, parts of which go back to the 1060s. Even in the earliest material the count took a considerable part in upholding peace and justice, especially in the region of Barcelona itself. As in Normandy so in the Spanish March, the temporal ruler early began to draw upon the Peace of God in order to build up his own peace in the land.[69]

In the long run kings were able to imitate the example which counts and dukes had set. The Peace first became a significant factor for the building up of Capetian authority when from the middle of the eleventh century peace arrangements upon the royal demesne had in common with early Norman legislation some of the features which favoured the ruler's authority.[70] It was in the next century, when papal endeavours were also directed towards building up peace in France,[71] that Kings Louis VI (1108-37) and Louis VII (1137-80) followed more resolutely the path of the dukes of Normandy. In the royal demesne they used the Truce to establish a peace which was essentially that of the king. As Capetian power grew, this peace became stronger and more widely diffused.[72]

The Emperor, too, in the long run drew upon the legacy of the Peace movement to his own considerable advantage. This was, it is true, a fairly late development. If the Peace of God as it was at first proclaimed in Aquitaine and the duchy of Burgundy had quickly spread into the kingdoms of Burgundy and Italy, it had no appreciable consequences there for the structure of temporal authority.[73] In Germany the strength of the Saxon and early Salian monarchy and its institutions, and the place of the bishops in the imperial church

[68] *Register*, vi.17, ed. Caspar, pp. 423-4.

[69] E. Wohlhaupter, *Studien zur Rechtsgeschichte der Gottes- und Landfrieden in Spanien* (Heidelberg, 1933), pp. 351-9. I have not been able to see a text of the *Usatici*.

[70] Bouard, *art. cit.*, *Annales de Normandie*, ix (1959), pp. 176-89.

[71] At the councils of Rheims (1119): Mansi, xxi, cc. 236-7; Clermont (1130), canon viii: *ibid.*, c. 439; and Rheims (1148), canon xi: *ibid.*, c. 716.

[72] Twelfth-century developments are traced by A. Grabois, "De la trève de Dieu à la paix du roi. Étude sur les transformations du mouvement de la paix au xiie siècle", *Mélanges offerts à René Crozet*, ed. P. Gallais and Y.-J. Riou (Poitiers, 1966), i, pp. 585-96.

[73] *M.G.H., Constitutiones*, i, nos. 419-21, 423, pp. 596-7, 602.

system, were so much in contrast with conditions in the south of France that the Peace movement could scarcely have found a place there. So far as the integrity of church lands was concerned, even in the tenth century the *De statu sanctae ecclesiae*, if somewhat idealistically, contrasted France with the happy state of affairs in Germany: there, far from rushing to despoil a vacant see, episcopal tenants dutifully placed their lands at the feet of a new bishop and humbly awaited his will.[74] In *c.* 1024, when a group of northern French bishops tried to commend the Peace of God to Bishop Gerard of Cambrai, whose diocese lay within the Empire, he for long argued against them. The keeping of the peace, he said, was the king's function, not a bishop's:

> The bishop's task is to pray; it is for the king to fight. Thus, kings should curb strife by force, end wars, and promote the concerns of peace. Bishops should exhort them to fight manfully for the public safety and should pray for them to be victorious.[75]

Further to the east and especially in *Germania* the embedding of the church and its jurisdiction in the imperial structure at once gave ecclesiastical justice firm backing and enabled the king to use it in reinforcement of his own. Thus the objects of the western Peace movement as regards public order were pursued under imperial authority: of this his biographer's striking account of the future Bishop Benno II of Osnabrück, wielding authority under Henry III at Goslar as both archpriest and *vicedominus* of the royal palace, provides a vivid if perhaps an extreme example.[76]

But with the minority of Henry IV (1056-65) the bonds of order and stability in the Empire began to be seriously relaxed. The Saxon rising of 1073 and Henry's struggle with Pope Gregory VII, and the feuds which they stimulated, made matters worse. The example of the French Peace became highly relevant: men asked for the kinds of relief that it afforded and it began to find serious imitators.[77] It was the bishops who first sought to use it in order to mitigate disorder. They proclaimed the Peace of God in councils at Liège (1082),

---

[74] Dümmler, *art. cit.*, pp. 385-6.
[75] *Gesta episcoporum Cameracensium*, iii. 27, *M.G.H., Scriptorum*, vii, p. 474.
[76] *Vita Bennonis II episcopi Osnabrugensis*, 6-8, ed. H. Bresslau (*Scriptores rerum Germanicarum*, Hanover, 1902), pp. 6-10.
[77] Henry III's own somewhat idiosyncratic zeal for peace, which may have been partly inspired by French models, had made no real imprint upon Germany: G. B. Ladner, *Theologie und Politik vor dem Investiturstreit*, 2nd edn. (Darmstadt, 1968), pp. 70-8.

Cologne (1083) and Mainz (1085).[78] At the last of them the king himself was present, and the Peace that it announced was intended to be observed in the whole Empire.

This introduction of the Peace of God was quickly followed by local assemblies at which general peaces (*Landfrieden*) were promulgated by lay authorities. Their purpose was to combat and limit knightly feuds, and to put down robberies and other offences that infringed public security. The whole populace was brought into them and, without respect for the distinctions of free and unfree condition that were still observed in the first German Peaces of God, punishments of life and limb were imposed upon all who offended against them. A lost Swabian *Landfriede* of 1083 was followed by one for Bavaria (1094) and by an undated Peace for Alsace; Bernold's Chronicle provides further evidence of endeavours to establish peace by the anti-imperial side.[79]

The king himself was quick to follow suit. Henry IV's imperial *Landfriede* of Mainz (1103) had the same general scope as the Peace of God of 1085, but, in content, it put forward the characteristic measures of the *Landfrieden* under imperial authority.[80] The author of the *Vita Heinrici IV* was well justified in regarding the *Reichslandfriede* of 1103 as the culminating point of Henry's reign.[81] For it embodied a coherent plan to extend royal protection to all classes of society, to check the lawlessness of the aristocracy and to bind it more closely to the crown, and to subject all classes to a criminal law whose basis was the peace of the Empire. In this way Henry IV's measures began the great series of *Reichslandfrieden* which was continued by Henry V, Frederick Barbarossa and Frederick II.[82] If other circumstances in their times had been favourable, it might well have been the beginning

---

[78] The text of the Liège Peace has not survived, but an account of it which may be basically reliable is given by Giles of Orval, *Gesta episcoporum Leodiensium*, iii. 13, *M.G.H., Scriptorum*, xxv, pp. 89-90; but cf. A. Joris, "Observations sur la proclamation de la trève de Dieu à Liège à la fin du xie siècle", *Recueils* . . . *Jean Bodin*, xiv (1961), pp. 505-45. Peace measures may have been introduced at Liège from as early as *c.* 1066. For Cologne and Mainz, see *M.G.H., Constitutiones*, i, nos. 424-5, pp. 602-8. The Mainz text closely follows that of Cologne.

[79] *M.G.H., Constitutiones*, i, nos. 427, 429, pp. 609-10; Bernold, *Chronicon*, *s.a.* 1093, *M.G.H., Scriptorum*, v, p. 457.

[80] *M.G.H., Constitutiones*, i, no. 74, pp. 125-6.

[81] *Cap.* 8, ed. W. Eberhard, *Quellen zur Geschichte Kaiser Heinrichs IV*, ed. F.-J. Schmale (Berlin, 1963), pp. 438-40.

[82] I follow here the judgements of H. Hirsch, *Die hohe Gerichtsbarkeit im deutschen Mittelalter*, 2nd edn. (Graz and Cologne, 1958), pp. 232-5; and K. Hampe, *Deutsche Kaisergeschichte in der Zeit der Salier und Staufer*, 10th edn., ed. F. Baethgen (Heidelberg, 1949), pp. 81-2. The Peace institutions of Germany are comprehensively studied by J. Gernhuber, *Die Landfriedensbewegung in Deutschland bis zum Mainzer Reichslandfrieden von 1235* (Bonner Rechtswissenschaftliche Abhandlungen, xliv, Bonn, 1952).

of such a strong monarchical power, based upon judicial and administrative superiority, as grew up in France and in the Norman lands.

This brief survey of lay government suggests that, so far as the distribution of the Peace of God and of its effects is concerned, it was proclaimed by churchmen and increasingly adapted by lay rulers for their own purposes, to their considerable advantage. The Peace and its consequences spread primarily within the boundaries of the former Carolingian Empire. There were good reasons why this should be so. It was in this Empire that the general maintenance of peace had become the duty of the lay ruler, while churchmen had filled out the idea of peace with Augustinian conceptions of divinely willed and sustained order and righteousness. There too, and (as the measures of its dukes illustrate) especially in Aquitaine, such Carolingian devices as the sworn inquest were remembered and were available to lay rulers in the service of peace and justice.

The Carolingian boundaries of the Peace developments of the eleventh century are especially clear in Spain: there, the Peace was of importance in the former Spanish March, but not as yet in the Christian kingdoms further to the west. The major exception is Norman Italy. There the Normans — "supremely the men who made things work, the assimilators who took over existing institutions and gave them a new efficiency unattainable by their originators"[83] — found it expedient, at the prompting of a French pope, to deal with the disorders of Apulia and Sicily after the death of Robert Guiscard by employing the means with which they had become familiar in Neustria. The Normans in Italy are the exception proving the rule which is so well illustrated by their kinsmen who conquered England. In this land which was never under the Carolingian sway and by contrast with Normandy, there was no real trace of the Peace or the Truce of God before 1066.[84] By the standard of the French church with its firm structure of bishops and archdeacons, its regular and busy councils, and its well-defined jurisdiction, the English church was no ready-made instrument for promoting peace even had the Normans wished so to use it. Instead, the remarkable strength of Anglo-Saxon royal administration and of the local organization of shires and hundreds put admirable alternative means of peace-keeping into the Normans' hands. If, as Richard FitzNigel wrote that the Conqueror's nephew Bishop Henry of Blois had told him, William I had added to native English laws "those Norman laws from overseas

[83] H. R. Loyn, *The Norman Conquest* (London, 1965), p. 30.
[84] Hoffmann, *Gottesfriede und Treuga Dei*, pp. 254-6. Domesday Book contains a reference to a *treuva regis* at Dover in Edward the Confessor's day from 29 Sept. to 30 Nov. (the word *pax* is interlined over *treuva*): i, f. 1ʳ.

which seemed to him most effective in preserving the peace (*ad regni pacem tuendam*)",[85] the Peace and the Truce of God were not among them.[86]   They were and remained as unimportant upon the soil of England as they were vital upon the soil of Neustria.[87]

But there were differences among the regions of the sometime Carolingian Empire itself: the Peace began in the west and only later did it penetrate into the east.   This reflected the long-term fortunes of the different regions.   The east, even before the imperial church system of the Ottos and Salians was established there, had undergone an *Entfrankungsprozess* — a discarding of many of the ideas and institutions of the Carolingian heyday — which was energetically pursued by Louis "the German" (843-76) and his successors.   Roughly following the divisions of the treaty of Verdun, the Carolingian lands split into three as regards their attitudes to Carolingian traditions of government.[88]   Only in Aquitaine and Neustria did the bishops transmit them in a fairly straight line to eleventh-century lay rulers, as by their proclamation of the Peace of God.   So when the crisis of royal authority broke in later eleventh-century Germany it was expedient to look westwards for models in devising new peace institutions.   Yet the burgeoning cultus of Charlemagne in high medieval Germany is a reminder that this borrowing was facilitated by the common Carolingian heritage of east and west.   Regarded in this light, the Peace movement of the eleventh century is evidence of the potency of this heritage in shaping much of continental Europe at its medieval apogee, and especially the institutions which promoted peace, justice and social order.

[85] *Dialogus de Scaccario*, xvi, ed. C. Johnson (London, 1950), p. 63.
[86] But the procedure of inquiry which the duke of Aquitaine used at Saint-Maixent in the 1030s may well have been used in France on other occasions and could have been known to those who planned the vaster *descriptio* of England, Domesday Book, of which Henry of Blois went on to speak.
[87] The only significant English evidence is that of the so-called *Leges Edwardi Confessoris* (c. 1135), which Maitland stigmatized as "private work of a bad and untrustworthy kind".   It speaks of a *pax Dei et sanctae ecclesiae* granted to clerks and their possessions, and to the whole kingdom at certain seasons: 1.1-2.8a, *Die Gesetze der Angelsachsen*, ed. F. Liebermann, i (Halle, 1903), pp. 628-9.   It is perhaps the result of an individual's revision in the light of continental practice of Anglo-Saxon legislation which prescribed a special royal peace at "holy tides" (e.g., v Ethelred 19, vi Ethelred 25, 1 Canute 17: Liebermann, *op. cit.*, i, pp. 243, 253-5, 296-7).
[88] E. Ewig, in the course of a valuable discussion, has epitomized the situation as " 'Entfrankung' im Osten, Fortbildung des hochkarolingischen Staatsgedankens im Westen, Stagnation in der Mitte": *Die mittelalterliche Kirche*, i, *Vom kirchliche Frümittelalter zur gregorianischen Reform* (*Handbuch der Kirchengeschichte*, ed. H. Jedin, iii/1, Freiburg, 1966), p. 146.

VIII

THE ANGLO-NORMAN *LAUDES REGIAE*

Liturgical sources do not always receive from historians the attention that is their due. Despite the monographs of E. H. Kantorowicz and B. Opfermann, this remains the case with the litany-like acclamations of rulers which modern writers usually designate the *Laudes regiae*. Only a small number of the texts that are in print are critically satisfactory, and much remains to be learned about their role in the public presentation of rulership in a religious context from Carolingian times up to the Fascist regime of Benito Mussolini. The purpose of the present study is to examine the use of the *Laudes regiae* in Normandy and England both before and after the Norman Conquest of 1066. Appendix I below comprises such texts as are known to survive from these lands and seem probably to belong to the reign of William I, duke of Normandy from 1035 to 1087 and king of England from 1066 to 1087; there is also a poetic form of *Laudes* having certain features in common with them. Appendix II contains two texts of the *Laudes regiae* from France, hitherto unpublished in their entirety, which serve to illustrate nearly contemporary usage there; and Appendix III comprises a somewhat later, almost certainly post-Conquest and perhaps twelfth-century, version from the duchy of Normandy. The discussion attempts a commentary upon and a comparison of these texts, in order to indicate their significance for the study of Anglo-Norman history.[1]

© 1981 by The Regents of the University of California 0083-5897/81/010037+43$00.50

[1] The following abbreviations are used:

AB: *Analecta Bollandiana* (1882-   ).

ASC: *The Anglo-Saxon Chronicle*, ed. D. Whitelock with D. C. Douglas and S. I. Tucker (London 1961).

AUF: *Archiv für Urkundenforschung* (1908-1942).

BN: Bibliothèque nationale, Paris.

DACL: *Dictionnaire d'archéologie chrétienne et de liturgie*, ed. F. Cabrol, 15 vols. (Paris 1907-1953).

HBS: Henry Bradshaw Society (London 1890-   ).

Kantorowicz: E. H. Kantorowicz, *Laudes regiae: A Study in Liturgical Acclamations and Mediaeval Ruler Worship* (Berkeley 1946; repr. 1958).

MGH Const.: *Constitutiones et acta publica imperatorum et regum* (Hanover 1883-   ).

_____ Libelli: *Libelli de lite imperatorum et pontificum* (Hanover 1891-1897).

_____ Script. rer. Germ.: *Scriptores rerum Germanicarum* (Hanover 1839-   ).

_____ Schriften: *Schriften der MGH* (Leipzig 1938-   ).

_____ SS: *Scriptores* (Hanover, etc. 1826-   ).

So far as the texts themselves are concerned, the first item in Appendix I below is the *Laudes regiae* as sung in Normandy at about the time of the Conquest of England. It occurs in two manuscripts which seem to be closely related to each other by reason of their place of origin. As often in versions of the *Laudes regiae* that were copied before about 1100, both examples appear on blank folios of manuscripts which are themselves not of a liturgical character. One is in Rouen, Bibliothèque municipale MS 489 (A.254) (hereafter F), fol. 71.[2] This manuscript is a copy of Boethius written at the abbey of Fécamp in the late eleventh or early twelfth century.[3] The other is in Salisbury Cathedral Library MS 89 (hereafter S), on the recto of the first, or title, folio.[4] This is a manuscript of Rufinus's Latin version of eight orations by Saint Gregory of Nazianzus; Bishop Osmund of Salisbury (1078-1099) may have brought it to England from Normandy for his cathedral library.[5] In the late Professor Wormald's judgment, both manuscripts — F and S — have the appearance of coming from the same scriptorium, that of Fécamp.[6] The texts of the *Laudes*

Opfermann: B. Opfermann, *Die liturgischen Herrscherakklamationen im Sacrum Imperium des Mittelalters* (Weimar 1953).

RS: Rolls Series, or *Rerum britannicarum medii aevi scriptores*, 99 vols. (London 1858-1896).

SS: Surtees Society (London, etc. 1835-   ).

ZRG kan. Abt.: *Zeitschrift der Savigny-Stiftung für Rechtsgeschichte, kanonistische Abteilung.*

I am grateful to the Bibliothèque nationale, Paris, to the Bibliothèque municipale, Rouen, to the Dean and Chapter of Salisbury Cathedral, to the Master and Fellows of Corpus Christi College, Cambridge, to the Trustees of the British Library, and to Durham University Library, for their kind permission to publish the material in the Appendixes. I am grateful for help with musical matters to Dr. J. Caldwell; for advice and information to Miss E. M. Rainey and Dr. W. Urry; and to Dr. M. Brett, Mr. C. E. Hohler, and Professor R. H. C. Davis for reading drafts of this study. All these scholars have been extremely generous with criticism and information. Responsibility for errors of fact and judgment remains entirely mine.

[2] Printed, with a facsimile of the text, in *Le graduel de l'église cathédrale de Rouen au XIIIe siècle*, ed. H. Loriquet et al. (Rouen 1907) 1.65-73 and pl. 1; Kantorowicz 167-168; Opfermann no. IV.2, 155-156.

[3] Described by H. Omont in *Catalogue générale des manuscrits des bibliothèques publiques de France, Départements* 1: *Rouen* (Paris 1886) 106-107. The invocation of St. Fromund (line 39) tends to confirm the Fécamp origin of the text. A late seventh-century bishop of Coutances, he was a patron of Fécamp where a chapel was dedicated to him: Orderic Vitalis, *Historia ecclesiastica* 11.30, ed. M. Chibnall, 6 vols. (Oxford 1969-   ) 6.138. He was venerated as a martyr by the twelfth century, perhaps in part through confusion with the English martyr Fremundus (died ca. 886). There were relics of Fromund at the monastery of Cerisy (dioc. Bayeux), which had a priory dedicated to him at Saint-Fromond (dioc. Coutances), and at Saint-Lô, Rouen. See AS Oct. 10 (Brussels 1861) 24 Oct. 842-849; G. Mathon, "Fromondo," *Bibliotheca sanctorum* 5 (1964) 1285-1286; V. Leroquais, *Les sacramentaires et les missels manuscrits des bibliothèques publiques de France*, 4 vols. (Paris 1924) 1.196, and *Les psautiers manuscrits des bibliothèques publiques de France*, 3 vols. (Mâcon 1940-1941) 2.243.

[4] F. Wormald, "An Eleventh-Century Copy of the Norman *Laudes regiae*," *Bulletin of the Institute of Historical Research* 37 (1964) 73-76. The MS is, however, not discussed by N. R. Ker, "The Beginnings of Salisbury Cathedral Library", *Medieval Learning and Literature: Essays Presented to Richard William Hunt*, ed. J. J. G. Alexander and M. T. Gibson (Oxford 1976) 23-49.

[5] Described by E. Maunde Thompson, in S. M. Lakin, *A Catalogue of the Library of the Cathedral Church of Salisbury* (London 1880) 18-19.

[6] Wormald (n. 4 above) 74.

regiae are almost identical, and they were probably copied into the manuscripts in Normandy at an early date by the same scribe. The lack of reference in line 28 to a particular bishop tends to confirm their monastic origin; it comes as no surprise in an abbey like Fécamp which was exempt from episcopal jurisdiction. The texts in F and S have similar musical notation in the form of unheighted neumes. Whereas the text in F is well preserved, that in S has suffered severe damage from damp and a considerable part has been lost through a tear.

The other texts in Appendix I originated in England. The second and third survive in London, British Library MS Cotton Vitellius E. XII (hereafter V), a late eleventh- or early twelfth-century manuscript which suffered severe damage in the Cottonian fire of 1731. The latter part of it, from fol. 116, mainly comprises a text of the Romano-Germanic pontifical. However, the final eight folios contain a miscellany of liturgical and similar items, and for the most part they remain readily legible. So far as can be judged in view of the damage by fire, the size, ruling, and lay-out of these folios indicate that they were from the first a part of the pontifical. Until the late nineteenth century, however, the eight folios were themselves arranged in an incorrect order, with results that have misled historians.[7] As the folios are now correctly arranged, they contain the following:

1. A form for the blessing of images of Saint Peter and Saint Swithun (fols. 153-154v); since they were patrons of the Old Minster of Winchester, this item suggests a Winchester provenance for the manuscript.
2. A form of episcopal benediction (fol. 155, formerly 160).[8]
3. A poetic form of *Laudes*, on the same folio. Items 2 and 3 form Appendix I.C below.
4. A form for the blessing of pilgrims' scrips and staffs (fols. 155v-157r, formerly 160v, 155r-156r).[9]

[7] The *Laudes regiae* from V were twice printed in the last century: *Liber pontificalis Chr. Bainbridge archiepiscopi Eboracensis*, ed. W. G. Henderson, SS 61 (1875) 279-283, whence Opfermann no. IV.3, 157-159 (correctly terminated); W. Maskell, *Monumenta ritualia ecclesiae anglicanae*, 3 vols., ed. 2 (Oxford 1882) 2.85-88. An independent but rather inaccurate version of the poetic *Laudes* from V appears in *Analecta hymnica medii aevi*, ed. G. M. Dreves and C. Blume, 51 (Leipzig 1908) no. 82, 87. For a description of the relevant part of V before its final folios were rearranged, see Henderson xxiv-xxvii, and the notice by W. H. Frere, *Pontifical Services Illustrated from Miniatures of the XVth and XVIth Centuries*, Alcuin Club Collections 3.1 (1901) 11, 97. The MS has been recently described by J. Brückmann, "Latin Manuscript Pontificals and Benedictionals in England and Wales", *Traditio* 29 (1973) 391-458, at 437-438. For English sources in general, see P. E. Schramm, "Ordines-Studien, III: Die Krönung in England," AUF 15 (1937-1938) 305-391; and for the Romano-Germanic pontifical, M. Andrieu, *Les Ordines romani du haut moyen âge* 1, Spicilegium Lovaniense 11 (Louvain 1931) 494-511. (Andrieu does not refer to V.)

[8] The form of benediction as a whole has no known close parallel, but for Appendix I.C, lines 2-3, cf. Berlin, Deutsche Staatsbibliothek MS Lat. 105 (Phillipps 1667), fol. 108v, eighth-ninth cent., and other texts as indicated in *Corpus benedictionum pontificalium*, ed. E. Moeller, Corpus Christianorum, ser. lat. 162 (Turnhout 1971) 141-142, no. 341.

[9] Referred to and partly printed, following the old foliation, in *Manuale et processionale ad usum insignis ecclesiae Eboracensis*, ed. W. G. Henderson, SS 63 (1875) nos. i-ii, 207*-208*.

5. A sermon of Saint Augustine of Hippo: *Sermo* 173, PL 38.937-939 (fols. 157v-159v, formerly 156v-158v).

6. A form of office for the dead (fols. 159v-160, formerly 158v-159).

7. The version of the *Laudes regiae* printed below as Appendix I.B (fol. 160v, formerly 159v).

The seven items are copied in at least two late eleventh- or early twelfth-century hands. Although these hands are similar to those in the body of the pontifical, there is no certainty that any of these items was added by a scribe who worked upon it. Items 2, 3, 6, and 7 have unheighted neumes which seem probably to have been copied with the texts and by the same scribes.

All these items except the *Laudes regiae* appear, once more following a text of the Romano-Germanic pontifical, in Cambridge, Corpus Christi College MS 163, pp. 283-296 (that is, again on the final folios), late eleventh or early twelfth century (hereafter W): this is another manuscript of probably Winchester origin.[10] Items appear as follows: 1 on pp. 283-286, 2 and 3 on pp. 286-287, 4 on pp. 287-290, 5 on pp. 290-294, and 6 on pp. 294-296. All are written in the same hand as that which occurs from p. 145 of the manuscript; but items 2 and 3 are written smaller in a space that had been left for them, while item 6 is similarly written at the end. There is room on the final folio for the *Laudes regiae* to have been copied. The relation of W to V is difficult to determine; it calls for a full comparative study of the two manuscripts. However, the appended texts are closely similar, although in W they are somewhat less carefully copied than in V. Some features, such as the less frequent use of ẹ, suggest that W may be of later date, as does the continuity of handwriting in W. It is likely that W was copied directly from V, and that items 2, 3, and 6 are written smaller because it was intended subsequently to add neumes. But the insertion of 2 and 3 into a space specially left raises the possibility that V and W are independent copies from two exemplars, one containing items 1, 4, and 5, and the other 2, 3, and 6. As it stands W lacks neumes, save that a single neume is written over the word *vos* in line 2 of the episcopal benediction, and there are hastily written neumes over three phrases in item 6. They are broadly similar to the neumes in V.

The final text of the *Laudes regiae* apparently from William I's reign which has so far come to light is in Durham University Library MS Cosin V.V.6 (hereafter C), fols. 19v-21. This manuscript is a gradual, the greater part of which is written in a single, late eleventh- or early twelfth-century hand. The *Laudes regiae* follow three texts of the *Gloria in excelsis Deo*, two of them troped; but they were themselves copied as an independent item. The chant is indicated by unheighted neumes, apparently written in the same hand as the Latin text. There are marginal doodles of sixteenth-century date, which include the decoration of the initial X of *Christus* in line 1 with a grotesque face. There can be no doubt that the text of the *Laudes regiae*

---

[10] See M. R. James, *A Descriptive Catalogue of the Manuscripts of Corpus Christi College, Cambridge* 1 (Cambridge 1912) 368-369; Andrieu (n. 7 above) 1.96-99; Brückmann (n. 7 above) 406-407.

was composed in the southern province, and probably at Christ Church, Canterbury. The saints invoked include the archbishops of Canterbury Augustine, Dunstan, and Alphege, Dunstan's name being in capital letters. The acclamation of the archbishop and the lack of reference to bishops and abbots point to the cathedral monastery of Christ Church, in which the archbishop took the place of an abbot. How and when C came to Durham — which was also a cathedral monastery — is less certain. A contemporary list of the gifts to the cathedral of Bishop William of Saint Carilef (1080-1096) includes a *gradale* which may have been C. If so, C was perhaps among the books that Christ Church, Canterbury, is known to have sent to the bishop. But a twelfth-century library list of 366 titles includes *unum gradale* among the *libri Thomae prioris* (?1161/2-1163), and Bishop Hugh du Puiset (1153-1195) gave four *gradalia* to the cathedral. Thus, while C is likely to have come to Durham in William of Saint Carilef's time, it may have been given to the cathedral at a later date.[11]

Appendix II below contains two texts of the *Laudes regiae* from France. The first is from a troper of Autun in the duchy of Burgundy, now Paris, Bibliothèque de l'Arsenal MS 1169 (637 TL) (hereafter A), fols. 22v-23; the manuscript is of eleventh-century date. The text names the Capetian king Robert the Pious (996-1031) and Bishop Walter of Autun (975/8-1024); the range of possible dates is therefore from 996 to 1024. Nazarius (line 13), with Celsus, was the principal patron saint of Autun. The *Laudes regiae* are followed by a separate form of episcopal *Laudes*. Both have unheighted neumes.[12] The second French *Laudes regiae* is from Nevers, also in the duchy of Burgundy. It occurs in the troper and proser Paris, Bibliothèque Nationale MS lat. 9449 (hereafter N), fols. 36v-37, of eleventh-century date. It is the nearest in date to the Norman Conquest of England among all the French versions that are known to survive. As kings of France it names both Henry I who acceded to the throne in 1031 and died on 4 August 1060, and his son Philip I who became coregent on 23 May 1059 and died in 1108. In its present form, therefore, it cannot date from before 23 May 1059 or from after 4 August 1060. The bishop referred to is Hugh of Champallemont, who succeeded in 1013 and who was present at Reims when Philip was crowned; he died on 7 May 1066.[13] Cyricus

---

[11] C is most fully described and discussed by K. D. Hartzell, "An Unknown English Benedictine Gradual of the Eleventh Century", *Anglo-Saxon England*, ed. P. Clemoes et al. 4 (Cambridge 1975) 131-144. For the Durham lists and catalogs, see *Wills and Inventories Illustrative of the History, Manners, Language, Statistics, &c., of the Northern Counties of England* 1, ed. J. Raine, SS 2 (1835) 1-4; *Catalogues of the Library of Durham Cathedral*, ed. B. Botfield, SS 7 (1838) 1-10 at 9, 117-119; C. H. Turner, "The Earliest List of Durham MSS," *Journal of Theological Studies* 19 (1918) 121-132. For the Canterbury gifts, see R. A. B. Mynors, *Durham Cathedral Manuscripts* (Oxford 1939) 32-45.

[12] For the Autun troper, see H. Martin, *Catalogue des manuscrits de la Bibliothèque de l'Arsenal* 2 (Paris 1886) 320-321, and L. Gauthier, *Histoire de la poésie liturgique au moyen âge* 1: *Les tropes* (Paris 1886) 126-127, no. 27; parts of the *Laudes regiae* are printed at 88 n. 1, and 150-151, also in A. Gastoué, *La musique de l'église* (Lyons 1911) 197 (I have not seen the latter work). For episcopal *Laudes*, see Kantorowicz 112-125.

[13] For the MS, see Gauthier (n. 12 above) 1.123-124, no. 21, and for the *Laudes regiae*, the discussion, with excerpts, 1.87-88. For the bishop, see *Recueil des historiens des Gaules et de la*

(line 9) was the patron saint of the cathedral of Nevers. The final section of this text has the character of an episcopal *Laudes* which is presented as an integral part of it. Except for the first section, the whole text is noted with neumes.

The text printed in Appendix III below is a later Norman *Laudes regiae* from Rouen, Bibliothèque municipale MS 537 (A.438) (hereafter O), fol. 90r-v. It appears on the end folio of a twelfth-century manuscript of the works of Paschasius Radbertus, Hilary of Poitiers, and others. The manuscript is either from the monastery of Saint-Ouen, Rouen, or from that of Lyre (dioc. Évreux).[14] The text of the *Laudes regiae* itself could be considerably older than the manuscript. There is no indication of when it was compiled; the reigns of William I and of his sons Robert Curthose (1087-1106) and Henry I (1106-1135) are all possibilities. However, if a specific victory were in mind, the acclamation of the duke as *invictissimus* (line 16) points to a date after the Norman Conquest of England in 1066, although it might allude to a later victory like Tinchebrai (1106). The invocation of Saint Romanus (line 34) points to compilation at Rouen, of which city he was bishop from 631 to 639. The *Laudes regiae* in O have no musical notation. As is indicated in the Appendix, spaces were left for a large number of capital letters which were not subsequently supplied. It was probably also intended that the chant should be inserted in the ample spaces between the lines.

Such are the texts with which this study is mainly concerned. The title *Laudes regiae* itself next calls for comment. It should be emphasized that it very seldom appears in medieval sources, but owes its currency to modern scholars. Ninth- and tenth-century texts do indeed often have at their head titles beginning with the noun *Laudes*, but it is followed by references to Christian festivals or devotional forms: *Laudes [in] festis diebus, Laudes de nativitate Domini sive in [festis] sanctorum, Laudes paschales, Laudes in pascha sive in pentecosten, Laudes cum laetania, Laudes sive rogationes.* In the tenth and eleventh centuries there appear the titles *Laetania ad missam in die sancto paschae, Rogatio*, and *Rogationes in dominica pascha.* From the twelfth century onward texts are sometimes entitled *Laus*, or *Laudes*, without addition. The designation *Laudes regiae*, as such, is known to occur only in twelfth-century and later titles from Chartres, and perhaps from Beauvais, although an eleventh-century text bears the title *Regale carmen*, and a twelfth-century text *Triumphus*.[15] In sources other than those which give texts, such as chronicles,

---

France, ed. M. Bouquet 11 (Paris 1781) 32. For the *Laudes regiae*, see also the discussion in Kantorowicz 116, n. 16. The text in N has little in common with the litanies in Bishop Hugh's sacramentary: *Sacramentarium ad usum æcclesiæ Nivernensis*, ed. J. Crosnier (Nevers 1873) 62-63, 119-120.

    [14] For a text and facsimile of the *Laudes regiae*, see Loriquet (n. 2 above) 1.69-73 and planche 2. The MS is described by Omont (n. 3 above) 123-124, who assigns it to Saint-Ouen; but it is ascribed to Lyre by G. Nortier, *Les bibliothèques médiévales des abbayes bénédictines de Normandie* (Caen 1966) [142].

    [15] These titles are listed, with details of the sources of most, in Opfermann 74-75, supplemented by H. Leclercq, "*Laudes gallicanae*," DACL 8.1898-1910, and by the Saint-Martial, Limoges, troper: BN MS lat. 1240, fol. 65v. The title *Laudes regiae* occurs in the sixteenth-century transcriptions by J. de Voisin of the twelfth-century Chartres sources: BN MSS lat. 9497, fol. 172v (as part of the rubric "In diebus solemnibus immediate post Kyrie eleison

letters, and official records, the terms *Laudes regales* and *Laudes imperiales*, but never *Laudes regiae*, occur as early as the ninth century.[16] In the eleventh and twelfth centuries the usual designations seem to have been *Laudes* or, from the opening words of the text, the *Christus vincit*; the last title seems to have been habitual in the Anglo-Norman lands.[17] This summary of medieval usage regarding nomenclature serves as a reminder that, while what modern scholars call the *Laudes regiae* no doubt served to display and augment the prestige of earthly rulers, they were always set in a solemn liturgical and Christocentric framework. They were related to such festivals as Christmas and, above all, Easter. They more often survive in tropers and similar books than in coronation orders. Their focus was upon the triumphant attributes of Christ himself. Although they had political and propagandist significance, they also had a religious basis the authenticity of which should not be mistaken or denied.

Considered as a liturgical form, the *Laudes regiae* drew upon elements which, when taken separately, went back to classical times and often to an origin in the city of Rome itself.[18] A full investigation of their history, which is much to be desired, would have to include the churches of both East and West. However, it was in the Gallo-Frankish church that the *Laudes regiae* took their distinctive shape. They appear in Frankish, rather than Roman, circles during the early Carolingian period, in the third quarter of the eighth century. The oldest text to survive is in an eighth-century psalter from Soissons, now Montpellier, Bibliothèque de l'École de médecine MS 409, fols. 343v-344, to be dated 783-787.[19] Other, more characteristically Gallo-Frankish examples occur in another psalter, Paris, Bibliothèque Nationale

---

incipiunt Laudes regiae") and 9508, fols. 92v-93; it further occurs in thirteenth- and fourteenth-century Chartres sources. *Triumphus* occurs in the Paris pontifical, BN MS lat. 9505, fol. 82, as transcribed by Voisin; the full title is: "Sequitur Triumphus qui nunquam nisi celebranti episcopo cantatur." It follows the collect of the Mass of Easter Day.

[16] *Thegani Vita Hludowici imperatoris* 16, MGH SS 2.594; *Le Liber pontificalis*, ed. L. Duchesne, 2 vols. (Paris 1884-1892) 2.88.

[17] *Laudes*: Bonizo of Sutri, *Liber de vita christiana* 2.51, ed. E. Perels (Berlin 1930) 59; *Christus vincit*: letter of William Giffard, bishop of Winchester (1100-1129), sometime chancellor of King William II of England (1087-1100), written between 1101 and 1103, in L. Valin, *Le Duc de Normandie et son cour (912-1204)* (Paris 1910) 258, no. 3, cited by Kantorowicz 169, n. 53; William FitzStephen, *Vita sancti Thomae* 78, in *Materials for the History of Thomas Becket, Archbishop of Canterbury* 3, ed. J. C. Robertson, RS (1877) 83; *The Great Roll of the Pipe for 34 Henry II (1187-8)*, Pipe Roll Society 38 (1925) 19; Gervase of Canterbury, *Chronica, a.* 1194, ed. W. Stubbs, RS (1879) 1.526-527, referring to Stephen's crown-wearing at Canterbury in 1141 and to Richard I's at Winchester in 1194.

[18] For their history, see, besides the works of Leclercq, Kantorowicz and Opfermann referred to in nn. 1, 15 above, A. Prost, "Charactère et signification de quatre pièces liturgiques composées à Metz en latin et en grec au IXe siècle," *Mémoires de la Société nationale des antiquaires de France*, ser. 4, 7 (Paris 1876) 149-320; R. Elze, "Die Herrscherlaudes in Mittelalter," ZRG 71, kan. Abt. 40 (1954) 201-223; and, in England, I. Bent, "The English Royal Chapel before 1300," *Proceedings of the Royal Musical Association* 90 (1963-1964) 74-95. I have been unable to see J. M. Hanssens, "De laudibus carolinis," *Periodica de re morali canonica liturgica* 30 (1941) 280-302, 31 (1942) 31-53.

[19] Printed in J. Mabillon, *Vetera analecta*, new ed. (Paris 1723) 171, whence PL 138.887-888; Leroquais, *Psautiers* (n. 3 above) 1.273-277, no. 231, esp. 275-276; Opfermann, no. I.1, 101; H. Coens, "Anciennes litanies des saints," AB 62 (1944) 132-136.

MS lat. 13159, fol. 163, of 796-800,[20] and Saint Gall, Stiftsbibliothek MS 397, pp. 1-3, of about 850, revised 858-867.[21] As the Montpellier text illustrates, the *Laudes regiae* began their history as a section of the Litany of the Saints.[22] But by the early ninth century they became detached from it as a separate liturgical form.

As such they were a unique form of litany which referred neither to Christ's humanity nor to man's weakness and need to express penitence. They were addressed solely and triumphantly to the victorious Christ in his divinity as the eternal king of heaven and earth, and as the exemplar and guarantor of power and prosperity to all the *potentes* who upheld the fabric of a unitary Christian society — pope, king, royal family, clergy, lay magnates, and warriors. The framework of the Gallo-Frankish *Laudes regiae* was as follows (the numbered sections of the analysis correspond to those in the left-hand margin of the texts in the Appendixes):

i. Their theme and tone were announced by the opening and usually repeated tricolon *Christus vincit, Christus regnat, Christus imperat*.

ii. Then they besought heavenly aid for the powerful upon earth in hierarchical order from the pope downwards. Each intercession was introduced by a call to Christ, *Exaudi Christe*; after the acclamation of each social rank the choir invoked a group of saints in its aid. At first the groups of saints tended to be fairly large; by the eleventh century they were often limited to three names. The sense of hierarchy was heightened since the saints were selected having in mind, at least in the background, their heavenly order, according to which the Blessed Virgin at their head was followed by archangels, John the Baptist, apostles, martyrs, confessors, and virgins.[23] Christ himself was usually called upon as *Salvator mundi* to aid the pope and as *Redemptor mundi* to aid the king, but occasionally the titles were reversed. Thus, at least in principle, the ranks of heaven and earth were exhibited in their graded and complementary powers and ministries as part of a single divine scheme. But in practice the order of the saints was habitually varied the more appropriately to match each grade of the earthly hierarchy: for the pope, there were invoked apostles, especially Saint Peter and Saint Paul, and saintly popes; for kings, the Virgin as chief of saints and archangels as next in rank to her; for the queen, virgins as became her sex; for the clergy, confessors; and for the warriors, soldier saints like the martyr Maurice

[20] Leclercq (n. 15 above) 1902-1903; Kantorowicz 14-15; Opfermann no. I.2, 102-103.

[21] Elze (n. 18 above) 218-220; see also R. E. Reynolds, "The Pseudo-Augustinian *Sermo de conscientia* and the Related Canonical *Dicta sancti Gregorii papae*," *Revue bénédictine* 81 (1971) 313, n. 5.

[22] For the Litany of the Saints, see esp. C. Kammer, *Die Litaneï von Allen Heiligen; die Namen-Jesu-Litanei; die Josefs-Litanei* (Innsbruck 1962); also E. Bishop, "The Litany of the Saints in the Stowe Missal," *Liturgica historica* (Oxford 1918) 137-164; H. Coens, AB 54 (1936) 5-37, 55 (1937) 49-69, 59 (1941) 272-298, 62 (1944) 126-168. Material similar to the *Laudes regiae* appears in at least one later version of the Litany of the Saints: see the late tenth-century *Laetania italica* in Coens, AB 55 (1937) 58-59.

[23] For the order of precedence, see Kammer (n. 22 above) 9-13. Kantorowicz 48-52 draws attention to the visual evidence of Byzantine ivory diptychs.

and the confessor Martin. In the age of Charlemagne with its emphasis upon royal and imperial authority, there was a strong tendency for kings to attract as their intercessors saints of higher heavenly rank than did popes, despite the priority in the earthly hierarchy that popes were unfailingly accorded.[24]

iii. There followed a further chanting of the tricolon.

iv. This marked a transition from the acclamations of men in their earthly ranks to a celebration of the victorious Christ himself, in a series of biblical, or biblically based, ascriptions such as *Rex regum*, *Victoria nostra*, or *Redemptio et liberatio nostra*, each of which had an answering *Christus vincit*. Earthly rulership was thus set against the archetype of Christ's redemptive majesty. The ascriptions varied in number, but were commonly in multiples of three.

v. Next came further ascriptions of praise to Christ, having a doxological character. They, too, were usually three in number, but by the late eleventh century there were sometimes fewer.

vi. The litany commonly ended with the *Kyrie eleison* and such cries expressing the prosperity of the Christian people under Christ and its earthly rulers as *Feliciter*, *Tempora bona maneant*, or *Multos annos*.

As the texts in Appendixes I.A and II illustrate, Gallo-Frankish *Laudes regiae* having this general character continued to be widely sung after Carolingian times, especially in France.[25] But other, and markedly different, groups of texts took their places beside them. Thus, early in the ninth century there appeared a distinct Frankish group, usually designated the Franco-Roman. This form of the *Laudes regiae* showed greater fixity than the Gallo-Frankish, and it concentrated upon the imperial family. The tricolon was sung once, not at the beginning but after the series of acclamations of earthly rulers; to each grade of these rulers it was usual to assign but one heavenly intercessor. As became the age of popes Nicholas I and John VIII, the pope's superiority was upheld by the customary allocation to him as his intercessor of Christ himself under the title *Salvator mundi*, while for the emperor the Virgin continued to be invoked.

[24] Kantorowicz 44-50; Opfermann 47-8; but cf. Elze's comments (n. 18 above) 204-205.

[25] There is no such comprehensive study as Opfermann of French acclamations, but there are helpful lists of MSS in Kantorowicz 191-192, 263-266. Apart from texts elsewhere referred to in this study, the following which date from before 1200 may be noted:

i. Texts from an ivory diptych of ca. 900 from Autun, now in the BN, in Kantorowicz plate VII (*Laudes regiae*), and 117 and plate XII (episcopal *Laudes*).

ii. From Limoges, troper, ca. 935, BN MS lat. 1240, fols. 65v-66v.

iii. From Limoges, troper, ca. 990, BN MS lat. 1118, fols. 38v-40, printed in *The Winchester Troper*, ed. W. H. Frere, HBS 8 (1894) 174-175.

iv. From Arles, tenth century, printed in Leclercq (n. 15 above) 1904-1905.

v. From Beauvais, early eleventh century, BN MSS lat. 9497 fols. 182v-183, 9508 fol. 390r-v, printed in Leclercq 1905.

vi. From Besançon, eleventh century, printed in PL 80.411-412.

vii. From Narbonne, troper, twelfth century, BN MS lat. 778, fols. 217v-218.

viii. From Soissons, *rituale*, late twelfth century, BN MS lat. 8898, fols. 30v-32, printed in Kantorowicz 215-216.

A third group of texts of the *Laudes regiae* emerged from the Gallo-Frankish between 950 and 1050 in Ottonian and early Salian Germany. It is especially well attested in manuscripts from South German monasteries like Saint Gall, Reichenau, Saint Emmeram at Regensberg, and Seeon. The principal distinguishing features of the German texts are that the *Christus vincit* tricolon was repeated more often — commonly in all some thirteen to sixteen times. An early tendency to prolong the list of saints who were invoked in favor of each grade of human society tended from the 1020s to give way to a limitation to three in each case. Section vi of the Gallo-Frankish form was curtailed or eliminated by the omission of the cries of well-being and, less frequently, of the *Kyrie eleison*. There was also a distinctive vocabulary, notably evident in the acclaiming of the army as the *exercitus Christianorum*, a phrase less often to be found in other groups.

With certain small exceptions, these older groups of texts of the *Laudes regiae* ceased to be copied in the Empire after the outbreak of its conflict with the papacy which began in earnest under Pope Gregory VII (1073-1085),[26] although such forms continued to be sung in England, France, Normandy, Sicily, and Dalmatia. In the twelfth century and after, emperor and pope in turn developed their own, much simplified *Laudes*. *Laudes imperiales*, at first acclaiming both pope and emperor but later only the emperor, appear in the imperial coronation *ordines* which were used at Rome. They were followed by *Laudes papales*, hailing the pope alone. Like the Franco-Roman *Laudes regiae* they did not open with the *Christus vincit* tricolon; indeed, later texts dispensed with it altogether. By their exclusive concentration upon either pope or emperor, these high-medieval *Laudes* illustrate the post-Gregorian tension between the *sacerdotium* and the *regnum* as the constituent elements of Christian society. No such duality marked the Carolingian and Ottonian ages in which the three earliest groups of the *Laudes regiae* — the Gallo-Frankish, the Franco-Roman, and the German — had taken shape.[27] It is to their world that all of the texts in the Appendixes to this study by tradition still belonged.

Such, in summary, were the character and the dissemination of the medieval *Laudes regiae* and their derivatives upon the continent of Europe. It remains, by way of introduction to Anglo-Norman practice, to indicate how and when the *Laudes regiae* were used liturgically. In their earliest, late eighth-century days, they took shape within longer litanies which were sung in procession.[28] But their separation from these litanies, which took place by the early ninth century, opened the way for them to be used upon the great festivals of the church's year, when the litanies themselves were not usually chanted. Their normal liturgical place came to be the introductory section of the Mass, usually between the collect and epistle but

[26] The sole example from the reign of Henry IV (1056-1106) is the, significantly, Wibertine text from Ivrea of 1089-1093, Opfermann no. III.15, 148-150.

[27] Opfermann gives full but not always textually satisfactory examples of the main groups; unfortunately he does not indicate the character of the MSS from which they are taken.

[28] See above; also E. Bishop, "Angilbert's Ritual Order for Saint-Riquier" (n. 22 above) 314-332, esp. 325, 331-332.

sometimes between the *Gloria in excelsis Deo* and the collect.[29] They thus assumed a festal character for which their celebration of the victorious Christ admirably adapted them; their special appropriateness at Eastertide is self-evident.[30] In view of their festal character, their chanting did not require the presence of the ruler,[31] fitting though his presence might be when circumstances permitted.

Moreover, the greater festivals of Christmas, Easter, and Pentecost in particular were of great significance for emperors and kings. They were times for coronations. In Carolingian times the *Laudes regiae* won a firm place in the imperial coronation Mass.[32] At least in the tenth and eleventh centuries, evidence for their chanting at coronations is otherwise very sparse; they are not, for example, a feature of German royal coronation orders. Where they occurred following coronation ceremonies, they served to recapitulate and complement the *collaudatio* of the new ruler together with his anointing and coronation. They declared the church's agreement with the ruler-making that had happened.[33] For this reason, they also frequently appear in connection with the periodic crown-wearings which kings from Carolingian times held at the greater festivals. Such crown-wearings increasingly assumed religious characteristics. Kings became accustomed to fast before them,[34] and it became a rule that an archbishop or bishop must set the crown upon the head of the emperor or king.[35] The king afterwards proceeded to a banquet at which he continued to wear his crown.[36] While crown-wearings gave the king no new status, they displayed him

[29] See Kantorowicz passim, esp. 80-91; J. A. Jungmann, *Missarum sollemnia* ed. 4, 2 vols. (Freiburg 1958) 1.497-499. The position is made clear in many sources, e.g. Opfermann, nos. I.6, 108; II.4-9, 116-122; III.8, 134; and in the heading of the twelfth-century Narbonne *Laudes regiae* in BN MS lat. 778, fol. 217v: "In die sancto pasche inter collectam et epistolam ante domnum archiepiscopum hec letania decantetur." Cf. *Gesta episcoporum Cameracensium* 3.55, ed. L. C. Bethmann, MGH SS 7.487; Benzo of Alba, *Liber ad Heinricum* 6.praef., ed. K. Pertz, MGH SS 11.656-657. For English usage, see Gervase of Canterbury (n. 17 above).

[30] At the end of the eleventh century, Bonizo of Sutri alluded to their use on ten occasions: Christmas, Epiphany, Easter, Ascension, Pentecost, a church's dedication festival, St. Peter and St. Paul, the Assumption, All Saints', and upon a bishop's anniversary day: Bonizo 2.51 (n. 17 above) 58-59.

[31] See the citation from BN MS lat. 778, n. 29 above.

[32] For coronations and crown-wearings, see esp. P. E. Schramm, *A History of the English Coronation* (Oxford 1937) 31-32; Kantorowicz 76-101; (for Germany) H.-W. Klewitz, "Die Festkrönungen der deutschen Könige," ZRG 59, kan. Abt. 28 (1939) (separate repr. Darmstadt 1964) 48-96; K.-U. Jäschke, "Frühmittelalterliche Festkrönungen? Überlegungen zu Terminologie und Methode," *Historische Zeitschrift* 211 (1970) 556-588.

[33] But for Charlemagne's imperial coronation of 800, see Kantorowicz 83-84, and Opfermann 64-65.

[34] Widukind of Corvey, *Res gestae saxonicae* 2.36, ed. H. E. Lohmann and P. Hirsch, *Quellen zur Geschichte der sächsischen Kaiserzeit*, ed. A. Bauer and R. Rau (Darmstadt 1971) 120.

[35] *Monachi Sazavensis continuatio Cosmae*, ed. R. Köpke, MGH SS 9.153; Cosmas of Prague, *Chronicae Bohemorum* 2.41, ibid. 95; Frederick I's privilege of 1158 for the duke of Bohemia, MGH Const. 1.236-237, no. 170. According to Bishop Gilbert of Limerick, writing early in the twelfth century with English circumstances in mind, at coronations and crown-wearings the right to crown belonged to a primate: *Liber de statu ecclesiae*, PL 159.1003; cf. Eadmer, *Historia novorum in Anglia* 6, ed. M. Rule, RS (1884) 292-293.

[36] For the banquet, see Milo Crispin, *Vita Lanfranci* 33, PL 150.53-54; also n. 46 below.

publicly in the regality that he had acquired in his first coronation, sometimes with the added glory of a public procession.[37] He appeared as the manifest ruler of his subjects both ecclesiastical and lay, within a single, divinely-ordered pattern of heavenly and earthly dominion. As thus presented, crown-wearings were the occasion of a solemn renewal of loyalty and solidarity between the ruler and his subjects.[38]

In Ottonian and early Salian Germany, where monarchy was relatively strong, it is probable that the *Laudes regiae* became firmly impressed upon the public mind in relation to coronations and crown-wearings, especially since, in the early eleventh century, the royal itinerary increasingly took the kings to the German cathedral cities.[39] In Capetian France royal power was less strong, and the kings were largely confined to their small demesne. Thus, as the *Laudes regiae* spread in France, they usually appeared as festal *Laudes*, associated with the observance of the church's greater festivals rather than with the glorification of earthly kingship. In some texts, local bishops were acclaimed before the Capetian king, and the felicitations of the sixth section might be transferred to them.[40] In Normandy at least, the *rex Francorum* was referred to without the honorific epithets, like *serenissimus* and *a Deo coronatus*, which were regularly attached to kings of Germany and Roman emperors.[41] The texts of the *Laudes regiae* and the setting in which they were chanted thus serve as a barometer of royal power and its effectiveness.

Such is the general background to the use of the *Laudes regiae* in the Anglo-Norman lands. The Normans took them up both in the duchy and in their eleventh-century conquests in northern and southern Europe.[42] It is a reasonable supposition, though nothing more, that the Fécamp text as copied into F and S is testimony to their use in Normandy before the Norman Conquest of England in 1066.[43] The absence from it of any reference to William as *rex* has no significance for the date, since the text of the *Laudes regiae* in O (Appendix III below), which is almost certainly post-Conquest, indicates that the Norman king-dukes were never acclaimed as *rex* in texts that were sung within the *regnum Francorum*. But the Fécamp text must have been current in Normandy before S came to Salisbury. It is far from clear where the Fécamp *Laudes regiae* may have been sung. The absence of reference to the archbishop of Rouen perhaps renders it unlikely that, at least as it

---

[37] Benzo 6.praef. (n. 29 above) 9.656-657; cf. Klewitz (n. 32 above) 71, 73-74.

[38] See, e.g., Widukind 2.31 (n. 34 above) 114. Thus, too, Hugh Capet solemnly wore his crown at Christmas 987: Richer, *Historiarum libri iiii* 4.13, ed. G. Waitz, MGH Script. rer. Germ. 134.

[39] See J. Fleckenstein, *Die Hofkapelle der deutschen Könige*, 2 vols., MGH Schriften 16 (Stuttgart 1959-1966) 2.199-208, 276-281.

[40] See items iv and v in n. 25 above, and App. II.B.

[41] See App. I.A, line 12, and App. III, line 11.

[42] See esp. Kantorowicz 157-179 and Opfermann 30-31.

[43] See, e.g., Schramm (n. 32 above) 234, and (n. 7 above) 316; D. C. Douglas, *William the Conqueror* (London 1964) 154, 249; J. Le Patourel, *The Norman Empire* (Oxford 1976) 239. H. Hoffmann's unsupported statement to the contrary should, however, be noted: "Langobarden, Normannen, Päpste," *Quellen und Forschungen aus italienischen Archiven und Bibliotheken* 58 (1978) 137-180, at 151.

stands, it was ever sung publicly in Rouen itself; the absence is, however, consistent with its use by the monks of the exempt abbey of Fécamp. But there is no rubrical evidence from Normandy or elsewhere that the *Laudes regiae* were sung as part of any monastic service; they are likely to have been sung publicly, whether at monasteries or elsewhere. All that can be said with safety is that the Fécamp text must have been known in Normandy, but was probably not chanted at Rouen, before S came to Salisbury. A letter of Bishop William Giffard of Winchester conclusively establishes that some text of the *Laudes regiae* was used in Rouen itself before the end of the eleventh century. But given the surviving Norman texts it is likely to have been nearer to that in O than to that in FS.[44]

In form the texts in FS and O are Gallo-Frankish. But there are modifications to suit the circumstances of early Capetian France and the claims of the Norman dukes. In line with the Normans' habitual insistence (at least when it suited them) upon authority and deference within the earthly order, in both texts the acclamation of the pope is immediately followed by that of the *rex Francorum*. His acclamation in texts of the *Laudes regiae* from Normandy, as well as from other parts of France both north and south of the river Loire, is a reminder of the support that even the earlier Capetian kings derived from the church and its ceremonies. But by a usage virtually unknown outside Normandy, the acclamation of the king is followed by that of a lay vassal, the Norman duke.[45] When it was introduced, the Normans may have adapted to a lay territorial ruler the practice, manifest in the Nevers text (Appendix II.B), whereby powerful bishops so reshaped the *Laudes regiae* as to emphasize their own public office. However, whether to avoid any suggestion of military autonomy and thus of challenge to Capetian authority, or simply because Normandy provided the French crown with no military service, the Fécamp text — by contrast with those in Appendixes II and III below — makes no reference to the army but only to the bishops, *principes*, and *iudices*. In Norman ducal texts, therefore, while hierarchy was respected, there was, with this sole qualification, an unparalleled blazoning of ducal power. The impression of rulership and triumph was accentuated by a lavish repetition of the tricolon, reminiscent of German texts; it is repeated by the Fécamp text in FS at least eighteen and perhaps twenty-four times.

---

[44] For the letter, see n. 17 above. Early in the eighteenth century, le Sieur de Moleon recorded the use of Rouen Cathedral, on solemn festivals when the archbishop celebrated Mass pontifically, of a text of the *Laudes regiae* which was a much modified version of that in O: *Voyages liturgiques de France* (Paris 1718) 323-324.

[45] See App. I.A, lines 20-21; cf. App. III, lines 16-17. The only other nearly contemporary references to individual laymen of nonroyal rank are in a Dalmatian text from Zara of ca. 1114: "Cledin inclito nostro comiti vita et victoria": Kantorowicz 152, and R. J. Hesbert, "L'Evangelium de Zara (1114)," *Scriptorium* 8 (1954) 177-204, esp. 178, 182-184, and pl. 20; and in the Bamberg *Laudes regiae* of the emperor Henry II: "N. ductori pacifico salus et vita": PL 140.54; Opfermann no. III.8, 134-136. William I's view of earthly precedence so far as the duchy is concerned is made clear in the canons of Lillebonne as printed by P. Chaplais, "Henry II's Reissue of the Canons of the Council of Lillebonne of Whitsun 1080 (? 25 February 1162)," *Journal of the Society of Archivists* 4 (1970-1973), 627-632, at 629; cited by Le Patourel (n. 43 above) 239 n. 2.

This text is thus a striking adaptation of current practice in Capetian France, as illustrated by the texts in Appendix II, to the circumstances of ducal Normandy as a fief of the French crown in which ducal authority was exceptionally strong and resolutely exercised.

So far as England is concerned, if the text of the *Laudes regiae* in C and its derivative versions are left for later consideration, there is no conclusive evidence that a form of *Laudes regiae* was used there before the Norman Conquest; nor is it demonstrable that formal crown-wearings comparable to those of the Norman kings were held, at which they might have been chanted.[46] Furthermore, whatever assessment may be made of the probabilities, there is no certainty that they had a place in William I's coronation at Westminster by Archbishop Aldred of York on Christmas Day 1066.[47] The text in V is the earliest testimony to their use in

[46] The arguments of H. G. Richardson and G. O. Sayles for pre-Conquest crown-wearings depend upon evidence which is of too late a date to establish their existence without contemporary corroboration: *The Governance of Mediaeval England from the Conquest to Magna Carta* (Edinburgh 1963) 32, 68, 142, 405-406, 409-412. Other evidence is equally inconclusive. Thus, (i) according to the *Carmen de Hastingae proelio* William I in 1066 wisely chose to occupy the palace of Westminster, "Nam veluti patrum testantur gesta priorum,/ Ex solito reges hic diadema ferunt": lines 671-672, *The Carmen de Hastingae proelio of Guy Bishop of Amiens*, ed. C. Morton and H. Muntz (Oxford 1972) 42. The editors believe that the poem was written soon after the battle: xxi-xxix; but it has been powerfully argued by R. H. C. Davis that it probably dates from the second quarter of the twelfth century and has little value as evidence: "The *Carmen de Hastingae proelio*," *English Historical Review* (EHR) 93 (1978) 246-261. (The allusion, anachronistic in 1066, to customary [*ex solito*] crown-wearings at Westminster reinforces this view.) (ii) An intrusive chapter (18) in the *Life of King Edward the Confessor*, which seems a later addition, opens with a lively picture of a crown-wearing by Edward at Mass and a subsequent banquet at Westminster: *The Life of King Edward the Confessor Attributed to a Monk of Saint-Bertin*, ed. F. Barlow (London 1962) 66-67, cf. 72-73, also xxxviii-xli. But, like the *Carmen*, this source may reflect post-Conquest ideas and customs. (iii) William of Malmesbury at one point referred to Edward the Confessor's coronation at Westminster (*coronatus est*) at Christmas 1065: *Gesta regum Anglorum*, ed. W. Stubbs, 2 vols., RS (1887-1889) 1.280. But in his *Vita Wulfstani*, based on an English Life by the monk Coleman, William expressly stated that the Conqueror introduced crown-wearings: *The Vita Wulfstani of William of Malmesbury* 2.12, ed. R. R. Darlington, London: Camden Third Series 40 (1928) 34. (iv) It is possible that the suffrages for pope and church, king and *principes*, and the local bishop and abbot, in the New Minster Litany of the Saints are an assimilation to a pre-Conquest text of the *Laudes regiae*, but the parallels are not sufficiently close to be conclusive: *Liber vitae: Register and Martyrology of New Minster and Hyde Abbey*, ed. W. de Gray Birch, Hampshire Record Society 1892, 266. (v) Some significance might be attached to the "imperial crown" that the Confessor commissioned in 1050 from his goldsmith, Abbot Spearhafoc of Abingdon; it may have been a more impressive object than that already in use, and intended for crown-wearings which the king unsuccessfully planned to introduce: *Chronicon monasterii de Abingdon*, ed. J. Stevenson, RS (1858) 1.462.463. But kings wore crowns on occasions other than formal crown-wearings.

[47] The sole evidence is that of the *Carmen de Hastingae proelio*, according to which William I was brought to Westminster Abbey for his coronation to the chanting of *laudes*: lines 805-808, 50, cf. lvi. Apart from the question of the reliability of this source, it is doubtful whether the *Laudes regiae* were intended. (i) The usual name of England and northern France was the *Christus vincit*; there is no Norman or English attestation of the term *Laudes* as a title of them: see p. 43 above. (ii) In the eleventh century the *Laudes regiae* were not usually sung processionally but in the Mass: see p. 46 above; cf. Prince Richard of Capua's reception *comme*

England. It is appropriate to the months between Queen Matilda's coronation in Westminster Abbey at Pentecost (11 May) 1068, again by Aldred, and Aldred's death on 11 September 1069; for both Matilda and Aldred are named in it. It is likely, but not demonstrable, that once the *Laudes regiae* had been naturalized in England, a version was sung at later Norman coronations.[48] It is also likely that, under William I, the *Laudes regiae* were chanted at the principal Mass on the days of his crown-wearings; and they were certainly in use from the time of his sons, who maintained tight control over the chanting of the *Laudes regiae* and paid the singers' fees at crown-wearings.[49] To the magnificence of the Conqueror's own crown-wearings the Anglo-Saxon Chronicle bore witness:

> Also, he was very dignified: three times a year he wore his crown, as often as he was in England. At Easter he wore it in Winchester, at Whitsuntide at Westminster, and at Christmas atGloucester, and then there were with him all the powerful men over all England, archbishops and bishops, abbots and earls, thegns and knights.[50]

---

roy in 1058 at Montecassino, which took place with a procession before the singing of *laudes* in a church adorned as for Easter, so that the courtyard outside rang with the chant: *Storia de'Normanni di Amato di Montecassino* 4.15, ed. V. de Bartholomaeis, Fonti per la storia d'Italia 76 (Rome 1935) 191. (iii) The word *laudes* had a range of meanings, including chants or hymns in a general sense: e.g., *Gerhardi Vita sancti Oudalrici episcopi* 15, ed. G. Waitz, MGH SS 4.405. In the *Carmen* it could refer to the chanting of the antiphon *Firmetur manus tua* which occurs at this point in the second English coronation order probably used at William's coronation: L. G. Wickham Legg, *English Coronation Records* (Westminster 1901) 15. Or, more likely, the author of the *Carmen* had in mind, for historical or antiquarian reasons, the *laudes hymnidicae* of Carolingian and later times, which were chanted at a ruler's *adventus*, e.g., *Ekkehardi Casuum sancti Galli continuatio*, MGH SS 2.84, 146-147; cf. Kantorowicz 32, 72-73. (iv) It is unlikely that a version of the *Laudes regiae* acclaiming the king as *a Deo coronatus*, as most did, would have been chanted before William's coronation and anointing; although it is not impossible that a modified form of the Fécamp text should have been used.

[48] An indication that they were familiar is provided by Geoffrey of Monmouth who, writing ca. 1140, echoed them in his anachronistic account of the king-making of Constantine of Brittany: *Historia regum Britanniae* 92, ed. E. Faral, in *La légende arthurienne: Études et documents*, Bibliothèque de l'École des hautes études 257 (Paris 1919) 3.169. Geoffrey's apparent citations of the *Laudes regiae*, "Ecce defensio nostra. Ecce spes nostra et gaudium," do not exactly correspond to any known text and may have been freely invented.

[49] See Bishop William Giffard's letter (n. 17 above); it stated that no chancellor or chaplain had powers in Rouen Cathedral regarding the choral service and in particular the *Christus vincit*. I take this to mean that royal officals did have power elsewhere, whether in Normandy or (more probably) in England; but cf. Kantorowicz 169-170. For the king's payment of an ounce of gold to the *cantores* at crown-wearings in England, but without reference to the *Christus vincit*, see Henry I's precept to Eudo Dapifer and Herbert the Chamberlain in J. Armitage Robinson, *Gilbert Crispin, Abbot of Westminster* (Cambridge 1911) 141 no. 18, Richardson and Sayles (n. 46 above) 217 n. 2; cf. Pipe Roll 34 Henry II (n. 17 above).

[50] E Version, *a.* 1087, 164. The story of the *Carmen de Hastingae proelio* that the king had new regalia — crown, scepter, and rod — made for his coronation (lines 753-786, 45-50) is improbable, given the time available. For the unreliability of this account of the coronation when compared with contemporary *ordines*, which the editors partly recognize (liv-lix), see F. Barlow, "The *Carmen de Hastingae proelio*," in *Studies in International History Presented to W. Norton Medlicott* (London 1967) 66, and Davis (n. 46 above) 251. But Harold's regalia as depicted in the

These were the powerful men whom the *Laudes regiae* acclaimed. William's own impressiveness at crown-wearings is pointed by Milo Crispin's anecdote of how, while the king sat at the banquet crowned and arrayed, a jester (*scurra*) cried out, "Behold! I see God! Behold! I see God!" (*Ecce Deum video, ecce Deum video*).[51]

The Pentecost court of 1068, which was the occasion of the queen's coronation, was well attended. Two diplomas reveal that, besides Archbishop Aldred of York who crowned her, Archbishop Stigand of Canterbury was present; indeed, despite his eclipse at the coronation service he took precedence over Aldred in the attestation of the diplomas. These attestations establish the presence of numerous Norman and English bishops, lay magnates, household officials, and royal chaplains.[52] The assembly was an occasion for William to impress his leading subjects and servants, both Norman and English; such liturgical forms at the coronation as the *Laudes regiae* provided him with the means of so doing.

Since coronations and crown-wearings were of so great consequence in the eyes of the Norman kings of England, it comes as no surprise that for the queen's coronation William I was not content merely to import the Fécamp *Laudes regiae* in a form adapted from Capetian France to the novel circumstances of Norman England; he made what seems to have been an absolutely fresh beginning. To the festal *Laudes regiae* for which the duke's presence, like the Capetian king's, was immaterial, he preferred a version that concentrated attention upon the king and queen in the glory of a regality that more amply reflected Christ's heavenly reign. When the Fécamp text in FS is compared with the text of 1068 in V, a number of differences strike the eye. The tricolon, although still emphasized by ninefold repetition, occurs in V less frequently. The chant is differently distributed between *cantores* and *chorus*; thus, in Normandy the former, but in England the latter, sang the acclamations. In view of the simple, litany-like character of the chant, the purpose of this difference may have

---

Bayeux Tapestry were scarcely impressive enough for the Conqueror's long-term purposes: pl. 33, in *The Bayeux Tapestry*, ed. F. M. Stenton, ed. 2 (London 1965) 255; it is likely that they were replaced at an early date in his reign. William's new crown appears to have had a German model: P. E. Schramm, *Herrschaftszeichen und Staatssymbolik*, 3 vols., MGH Schriften 13 (Stuttgart 1954-1956) 2.393-395, 570, 601, 633; 3.756.

[51] See n. 36 above. For the meaning of *scurra*, see J. D. A. Ogilvy, "*Mimi, scurrae, histriones:* Entertainers of the Early Middle Ages," *Speculum* 38 (1963) 603-619; J. Leclercq, " 'Joculator et saltator': S. Bernard et l'image du jongleur dans les manuscrits," *Translatio studii: Manuscript and Library Studies Honouring Oliver L. Kapsner OSB*, ed. J. G. Plante (Collegeville 1973) 126-129; M. Gibson, *Lanfranc of Bec* (Oxford 1978) 140.

[52] For the diplomas, see W. B. Stevenson, "An Old-English Charter of William the Conqueror in Favour of St. Martin's-le-Grand, London, AD 1068," EHR 11 (1896) 731-744; J. Earle, *A Handlist to the Land-Charters and Other Saxonic Documents* (Oxford 1888) 431-434; cf. *Regesta regum Anglo-Normannorum, 1066-1154*, ed. H. W. C. Davis 1 (Oxford 1913) 6-7, nos. 22-23. The *Carmen de Hastingae proelio* may imply that Stigand was also present at the king's own coronation: lines 803-804, 50-51; but the coronation *ordines* refer only to *duo episcopi* at the point of the service in question. For Stigand's canonical position which made it inexpedient that he should crown William, see F. Barlow, *The English Church, 1000-1066: A Constitutional History* (London 1963) 302-310; Gibson (n. 51 above) 113-115, 118, 151-154.

been to draw the assembled *populus* at Westminster into the eulogy of its rulers. As for the chant itself, the Fécamp notation employed only the virga, punctum, and pes, whereas in 1068 there were also used the clivis, clivis cephalicus, scandicus, and oriscus. While the fuller notation did not necessarily alter the basic structure of the melody, it serves to underline the difference of this version from the sole surviving Norman chant. As regards the Latin text, the version of 1068 remains broadly within the Gallo-Frankish tradition. Yet in every section there are differences from the Norman usage at Fécamp. The acclamations in the second section include the queen and the archbishop; the acclamation of the king is much more amply phrased; and a very different sequence of saints appears. Sections four and five, in which victorious attributes and a doxology are ascribed to Christ, have few common features in the Norman and English versions. In England, the sixth section, of cries expressing prosperity and good wishes, is wholly absent, an omission which tends to enhance the text's dramatic force.

But the uniqueness and skill of the *Laudes regiae* of 1068 emerge most clearly in respect of their structure. They exhibit a balance, order, and relationship between the hierarchies of heaven and earth which have no parallel in other texts of the *Laudes regiae* of whatever time and place. Not only was the earthly hierarchy, as usual, presented beneath the pope — Alexander II (1061-1073) — in the rightful national precedence of king, queen, archbishop, bishops and abbots, *principes* and army; but the hierarchy of heaven was related to it without variation of its own right order of the Blessed Virgin, archangels, John the Baptist, apostles, martyrs, confessors, and virgins. This ideal presentation and correlation of both hierarchies was achieved by the device, otherwise absolutely unexampled, of invoking as the pope's intercessors not Christ alone but — as at the opening of the Litany of the Saints — of all three Persons of the Trinity. Christ was by consequence not named, as he was in most Gallo-Frankish texts, on the king's behalf; there were assigned to him the very highest figures in the hierarchy of heaven — the Blessed Virgin and two archangels. The reasons for this lay-out can only be conjectured. It seems to have been designed to represent both pope and king as supreme in their respective spheres. The pope was linked with the Trinity, so that his spiritual supremacy was secured. But the king was linked with the head of the heavenly hierarchy. Within a single order of heaven and earth he was spiritually the pope's subject; yet otherwise he knew no superior. On the eve of Gregory VII's pontificate it was, no doubt, an over-simple presentation which begged the question whether there really was a single earthly hierarchy comprising both clerks and laymen in a harmonious relationship, or whether it comprised two distinguishable but interwoven parts whose respective claims were open to dispute. But it was well suited to William's purposes in the immediate aftermath of the conquest of England.

In effect, then, the *Laudes regiae* of 1068 expressed to perfection the "political theory" of the Norman Conquest. They exhibited with compelling force how William the Bastard, duke of Normandy, was now also William the Conqueror, king of

England, and how, as such, he both claimed and knew his place in the divinely appointed order of earth and heaven. With pope and king each supreme after his own fashion, the ground was already prepared for the Conqueror's refusal of fealty to Gregory VII in 1080; and yet there was no hint of the later Anglo-Norman thesis which disproportionately exalted royal power by making the king exhibit the image of God the Father but the episcopate that of God the Son.[53] In addition, there was a clear purpose to exhibit the new Norman regime in England as a coherent polity with a native coloring. The lay magnates, both Norman and English, were acclaimed as the *principes Anglorum.*[54] The acclamation of the archbishop of York *et omni clero sibi commisso* can have referred, in so far as it was more than a traditional phrase, only to the clergy of his own church of York and not to the national clergy.[55] But thereafter unity was underlined by the blessings called down, more insistently than in the Fécamp text, upon "*omnibus* episcopis et abbatibus . . . *cunctis* congregationibus . . .

[53] The immediately post-Conquest Norman view of the papacy, with the pope's primacy as "praesulum orbis terrae caput . . . et magister" is expressed by William of Poitiers: *Guillaume de Poitiers, Histoire de Guillaume le Conquérant* 2.3, ed. R. Foreville (Paris 1952) 152-155; cf. H. E. J. Cowdrey, "Pope Gregory VII and the Anglo-Norman Church and Kingdom," *Studi Gregoriani* 9 (1972) 79-114, esp. 83-85. For William's kingship, see C. W. Hollister, "Normandy, France and the Anglo-Norman *Regnum*", *Speculum* 51 (1976) 202-242, esp. 204-210. The later Anglo-Norman view referred to is illustrated by Hugh of Fleury, *Tractatus de regia potestate et sacerdotali dignitate* 1.3, ed. E. Sackur, MGH Libelli 2.466; and *Tractatus Eboracenses* 4, ed. H. Boehmer, MGH Libelli 3.665-666.

[54] In all early groups of *Laudes regiae* texts the usual word for the powerful, nonroyal laity is *iudices*, referring originally to the higher officials of the royal palace and government: Opfermann 43. But the Fécamp text has the acclamation *Omnibus Christianae legis principibus ac iudicibus* (lines 35-36); this is the first known occurrence of *principes* in this context except in the unparalleled Autun acclamation *Omnibus iudicibus regibus et principibus* (App. II.A, line 15). Before 1066 both English and Norman sources frequently used the term *principes*. In England it is common in charters, and the New Minster Litany of the Saints includes a suffrage "Ut regi nostro et principibus nostris pacem et victoriam nobis dones": Birch (n. 46 above) 266. In Norman usage *principes* described ducal vassals as well as the dukes: see M. Fauroux, *Recueil des actes des ducs de Normandie (911-1066)* (Caen 1961) 82, 90, 142, 262, 291, 337, 340, 434 – nos. 10, 14, 37, 104, 122, 153, 156, 225. In post-Conquest England it was used broadly of the military classes, e.g., in the diplomas of 1068 referred to in n. 52 above; and the *Acta Lanfranci*, in *Two of the Saxon Chronicles Parallel*, ed. C. Plümmer and J. Earle (Oxford 1892) 287. There can be no presumption that the phrase *principes Anglorum* in the *Laudes regiae* of 1068 was borrowed from a lost pre-Conquest text of the *Laudes regiae*.

[55] Two considerations enforce this view. (i) Comparison with later English texts of the *Laudes regiae* establishes that their acclamations of the archbishop of Canterbury referred only to his diocesan clergy: see the Cambridge and Worcester MSS cited below, pp. 65-66. (ii) Owing to the canonically irregular position of Stigand, Archbishop Aldred of York crowned both William and Matilda. But Stigand's position was not an inactive one. Not only was he present at Westminster at Pentecost 1068 (see above at n. 52), but in 1067 he had consecrated Bishop Remigius of Dorchester: see the latter's profession to Lanfranc in *Canterbury Professions*, ed. M. Richter, Canterbury and York Society 140 (1972-1973) 27, no. 32. His precedence was also respected in royal charters of 1069 in favor of Bishop Leofric of Exeter: *Regesta Anglo-Norman-norum* 1.8-9, no. 28, photograph in *Facsimiles of Anglo-Saxon Manuscripts*, ed. W. B. Sanders, 2 (Southampton 1881) xii and pl. 16; and of Saint-Denis: *Facsimiles of English Royal Writs to AD 1100 Presented to Vivian Hunter Galbraith*, ed. T. A. M. Bishop and P. Chaplais (Oxford 1957) pl. 28.

omnibus principibus . . . *cuncto* exercitui." The *Laudes regiae* of 1068 were drafted with skill and discretion to express William I's view of divine and human affairs as he at that time wished to communicate it to his subjects both French and English, as well as to the world at large.

There is no direct evidence from which to establish when, where, and by whom the *Laudes regiae* of 1068 were compiled. In the first place, however, although the use of another, lost Norman model cannot be excluded, comparison with the Fécamp and Saint-Ouen texts suggests that the indebtedness to Normandy was small. Nor are they significantly similar to the French texts printed in Appendix II or to other French examples. But they seem to have owed at least one major debt to the English devotional tradition. The selection of twenty-one invocations which they embody was almost certainly made from a form of the Litany of the Saints which was used in England by the time of the Norman Conquest. Although a foreign source for the litany is possible, none has so far come to light; but versions of it survive as follows in English sources close in time to V:[56]

1. Oxford, Bodleian Library MS Laud lat. 81 (768), fols. 144v-147, s. XI, a psalter connected with St. Augustine's, Canterbury. It contains all the invocations of the *Laudes regiae* of 1068 except Nicholas; Martin and Benedict, and Mary Magdalen and Perpetua, are by contrast with it transposed;

2. Rouen, Bibliothèque municipale MS 274 (Y.6), fols. 207v-208v, a sacramentary of 1016-1051 but of uncertain though English provenance; printed in *The Missal of Robert of Jumièges*, ed. H. A. Wilson, HBS 11 (1896) 287-289. It contains all except Nicholas and Mary Magdalen; Martin and Benedict are transposed;

3. Oxford, Bodleian Library MS Douce 296 (21870), fols. 117-119v, s. XI med., a psalter written for Peterborough. It contains all except Nicholas; Martin and Benedict are transposed;

4. Paris, Bibliothèque Nationale MS lat. 8824, fols. 183v-185, s. XI²/₄, a psalter of unknown provenance; printed in L. Delisle, *Bibliothèque de l'École des chartes*, ser. 4, 2 (1856) 148-151. It contains all except Nicholas; Martin and Benedict, and Mary Magdalen and Perpetua, are transposed;

5. London, British Library MS Cotton Titus D.XXVI, fols. 51v-56v, 1023-1035, a prayer-book from the New Minster; printed in *Liber vitae of the New Minster* (n. 46 above) 261-268. It contains all except Nicholas;[57] Martin and Benedict, and Mary Magdalen and Perpetua, are transposed;

[56] The list which follows does not claim to be exhaustive. For help with it I am greatly indebted to Mr. Hohler. In addition, a twelfth-century text having all the saints of the *Laudes regiae* of 1068, but in a less similar order, is in Oxford, Bodleian Library MS Auct. D.2.6 (3636), fols. 150v-152; and there is a text written ca. 1300 in Bodleian Library MS Gough Liturg. 8 (18338), fols. G.66-67v, printed in *The Monastic Breviary of Hyde Abbey, Winchester*, ed. J. B. L. Tolhurst 5, HBS 71 (1934 for 1932), not paginated.

[57] But for the addition on fols. 76v-79v of prayers to St. Nicholas, see Birch (n. 46 above) 268, no. 23.

6. Cambridge, Corpus Christi College MS 411, fol. 140r-v, s. XI in., an English, perhaps Christ Church, Canterbury, addition to a psalter from Tours. It contains all except Nicholas; Martin and Benedict, and Mary Magdalen and Perpetua, are transposed (a second litany, on fols. 137v-138, is more considerably different);

7. Cambridge, Corpus Christi College MS 422, "The Red Book of Darley", a porto of ca. 1061, provenance uncertain, perhaps written for Sherborne, Dorset. It contains two litanies, on pp. 378-379, 402-405. Both omit Nicholas while Martin and Benedict, and Mary Magdalen and Perpetua, are transposed; in the second, Agatha and Lucy are also transposed;

8. London, British Library MS Cotton Vitellius A.VII, fols. 17v-18v, a pontifical, probably from Ramsey Abbey, s. XI in. The text of the litany is very severely damaged by fire (other litanies, on fols. 20r-v, 113-114v, and 209v-210v, are, where legible, markedly different);

9. London, British Library MS Add. 28188, fols. 2-4v, s. XI ex., a pontifical of uncertain origin, but probably East Anglian and adapted for use at Exeter, printed in *The Leofric Collectar* 2, ed. E. S. Dewick and W. H. Frere, HBS 56 (1921 for 1918) 614-17. The litany is probably connected with no. 8; the invocations of the Trinity are lacking, and Benedict and Gregory are transposed (another litany, on fol. 7r-v, is considerably different);

10. Vatican Library MS Reg. lat. 12, "The Bury Psalter," fols. 159-160v, s.XI²/₄ , printed by A. Wilmart, "The Prayers of the Bury School", *Downside Review* 48 (1930) 198-216, at 200-1. The invocations of Nicholas and Mary Magdalen are missing, and Martin and Benedict are transposed.

These texts are closely related to each other and differ mainly by omissions. In addition, broadly similar litanies appear in the following:

11. Worcester, Cathedral Library MS F.173, fols. 8-9v, s. XI med., a sacramentary almost certainly from the Old Minster.[58] The invocation of Nicholas is lacking, Perpetua and Lucy are lost by damage to the manuscript, Martin and Benedict are transposed;

12. Cambridge, University Library MS Ff.1.23; fols. 274v-276v, s. XI²/₄ , a psalter perhaps from Winchcomb Abbey. It contains all the invocations except Nicholas; Martin and Benedict are transposed;

13. London, British Library MS Arundel 60, fols. 130-132v, s. XI med., a psalter from the New Minster, printed by F. Wormald, "The English Saints in the Liturgy in Arundel MS 60", AB 64 (1946) 72-86; cf. Wormald, *English Drawings*

---

[58] See J. K. Floyer, *Catalogue of Manuscripts Preserved in the Chapter Library of Worcester Cathedral*, rev. ed. S. G. Hamilton (Oxford 1906) 98-100, and the letter of C. H. Turner, dated 2 June 1915, bound into the Worcester Cathedral Library copy; N. R. Ker, *Catalogue of Manuscripts Containing Anglo-Saxon* (Oxford 1957) 465-466, no. 397; C. Hohler, "Some Service-Books of the Later Saxon Church," *Tenth-Century Studies*, ed. D. Parsons (London 1975) 73, 224.

of the Tenth and Eleventh Centuries (London 1952) 50, 66. All the invocations are present, with the transposition of Martin and Benedict and with the order Perpetua, Lucy, Agatha, Mary Magdalen.

These litanies are lengthy; but they include all, or almost all, of the invocations in the *Laudes regiae* of 1068, and they do so in a nearly identical order. The naming of Martin before Benedict in the *Laudes regiae* is highly unusual (although it is a feature of 9); it may be an idiosyncrasy of the compiler or copyist. When this possibility is allowed for, the correlation of names and order is too close to be a coincidence. It points to a source of the invocations in the *Laudes regiae* of 1068 in an English litany that was closely related to those which have been listed.

The litanies are attested from many localities. But at least three examples — 5, 11, and 13 — come from Winchester, while another — 10 — is from an abbey that was liturgically dependent upon it. The Winchester provenance of the manuscript V points to an exemplar from that city. Moreover, the surprising inclusion of Mary Magdalen in the *Laudes regiae* of 1068 also tends to confirm the use of a source connected with Winchester. Until the fifteenth century her name occurs in no other text whatsoever of the *Laudes regiae*.[59] But in the middle decades of the eleventh century her cultus began to spread in England as on the Continent, and it had a strong center at Winchester.[60] The direct borrowing of a New Minster text is unlikely, in view of that Minster's resistance to the Norman Conquest;[61] but later interlined changes in MS Cotton Titus D.XXVI show that the versions of it were copied and circulated. A derivative text, or a corresponding Old Minster litany, appears to be the source from which the selection of saints in the *Laudes regiae* of 1068 was made. A probable view about their origin, therefore, is that they were compiled in England, by a Winchester monk or clerk, between the king's stay in Winchester at Easter 1068 just before the queen joined him from Normandy and her Westminster coronation at Pentecost.[62]

But there are also some similarities in detail between the *Laudes regiae* of 1068 and German texts. They are, first, the application to William I of the imperial epithet

[59] See Elze (n. 18 above) 211, correcting Opfermann no. V.5, 169-170 (Caeremoniale romanum, 1488).

[60] For its spread, see V. Saxer, *Le culte de Marie Madeleine en occident des origines à la fin du moyen âge* (Paris 1959) esp. 44-45, 60-88, 153-182, pls. 1 and 2; "Maria Maddalena," *Bibliotheca sanctorum* 8 (Rome 1967) 1078-1104. The growing observance of her feast (22 July) is traceable in *English Kalendars before AD 1100*, ed. F. Wormald, HBS 72 (1934) 22, 78, 92, 106, 148, 162, 190, 204, 218, 260. It was established at Winchester by ca. 1060. The placing of the penitent, Mary Magdalen, before the virgins is explicable in the light of legends of her post-Resurrection years as a solitary and contemplative: see Kammer (n. 22 above) 66-67; J. E. Cross, "Mary Magdalen in the *Old English Martyrology*: The Earliest Extant 'Narrat Josephus' Variant of the Legend," *Speculum* 53 (1978) 16-25. For the Anglo-Saxon version, see *An Old English Martyrology*, ed. G. Herzfeld, Early English Text Society 116 (1900) 126-127.

[61] Its abbot, Aelfwig, fell with Harold at Hastings: Birch (n. 46 above) 35.

[62] ASC, D Version, *a*. 1067(8), 148.

serenissimus (line 8), which has many parallels in German texts while it is less usual in Gallo-Frankish texts of tenth- to twelfth-century date.[63] Secondly, the acclamations of the army as the *exercitus Christianorum* (lines 34-35) is normal in German texts but less usual in Gallo-Frankish texts.[64] Thirdly, a striking feature of the text of 1068 by contrast with all earlier texts in the Appendixes is the parallel terms, apart from the phrase *magno et pacifico*, in which the king and queen are acclaimed (lines 8-9, 14-15). Such a parity of description is to be found in four German texts from the time of the emperor Henry III and the empress Kunigunde and after; but it does not occur in any Gallo-Frankish text.[65] These similarities are hardly conclusive; but they raise the further possibility of German influence, and of an attempt on William's part to display his newly-won regality upon a German, rather than a Capetian model.

German influence might have come through Lotharingians who occupied English sees, notably Leofric of Crediton/Exeter (1046-1072) and Giso of Wells (1060-1088); or it might have followed such a visit as Archbishop Aldred of York's to Cologne and the German court in 1054. But there is no evidence of it. There is another channel that deserves examination: William's visit to Normandy in 1067 may have brought both German and papal ideas to bear upon the shaping of the *Laudes regiae* of 1068. William crossed from England in the spring, taking with him ecclesiastical and lay notables both Norman and English, including Stigand who held the sees of Canterbury and Winchester. William made a triumphal entry into Rouen and then held a solemn court at Fécamp which was attended, according to William of Poitiers, by a *frequentia venerabilium et praesulum et abbatum*. The king will have been reminded of the Norman *Laudes regiae* if, as is likely, they were already being sung in the duchy. He returned to England at the beginning of December 1067.[66]

During his stay in Normandy he had to decide the succession to the see of Rouen

---

[63] For German texts, see Opfermann nos. III.5, 6, 12, 14, 16; pp. 129, 131, 142, 147, 150; and for Gallo-Frankish examples of relevant date, see nos. ii, iii, and v in n. 25 above, and the Nevers text in Appendix II.B.

[64] For Gallo-Frankish examples, see nos. iii, v-vii in n. 25 above; and the Nevers text in Appendix II.B.

[65] For German texts, see Opfermann nos. III.9-11, 15, 17, pp. 136-151. In England Schramm pointed out the novel status of the queen as a sharer in the royal power: (n. 32 above) 23, 29-30; cf. Richardson and Sayles (n. 46 above) 152-153. For the evidence of coronation orders, see *Three Coronation Orders*, ed. J. Wickham Legg, HBS 19 (1900) 54-64 at 62-63; and *The Claudius Pontificals*, ed. D. H. Turner, HBS 97 (1971 for 1964) 115-122, at 121. (For the editor's opinion that the latter *ordo* was Lanfranc's work and for its indebtedness to imperial usage, see xli-xlii.) For Queen Matilda's quasi-royal position in Normandy immediately after the Conquest, see William of Poitiers 2.43 (n. 53 above) 260. For her later status in England, see the bond of association formed ca. 1077 between Bishop Wulfstan of Worcester and the heads of seven religious houses, in B. Thorpe, *Diplomatarium anglicum ævi saxonici* (London 1864) 615-617. For examples of the queen's status under Henry I, see *Quadripartitus, Augmentum* 25, and II.1, praefatio 14, in *Quadripartitus: ein englisches Rechtsbuch von 1114*, ed. F. Liebermann (Halle 1892) 88, 149; whence *Leges Henrici Primi* prooemium 2, ed. L. Downer (Oxford 1972) 80.

[66] ASC, D Version, *a*.1066-1067, 145-146; William of Poitiers 2.38-45, pp. 245-262.

following the death on 9 August of Archbishop Maurilius (1035-1067). When Lanfranc, then abbot of Saint Stephen's, Caen, declined it, William decided upon the translation of Bishop John of Avranches (1060-1067). A translation demanded papal sanction; to procure it William punctiliously dispatched Lanfranc to Rome. This canonical propriety is evidence that, at this time, relations between the apostolic see and the king-duke were based upon mutual favor and goodwill. Lanfranc presented his case to the pope in concert with Bishop Ermenfrid of Sion (Sitten), in the Valais, who between 1054/5 and 1070 paid a series of legatine visits to Normandy and England. Ermenfrid's part in securing the translation indicates that he had recently been in Normandy. Pope Alexander's consent was expressed in a surviving letter to John of Avranches, which was brought by unnamed *legati* who may, again, have included Ermenfrid.[67]

The precise nature of Ermenfrid's dealings with regard to Normandy at this time does not emerge. But it may have included his confirmation by papal authority of the Norman bishops' penitential ordinance following the battle of Hastings. Although not an ecclesiastical council, the Fécamp assembly at Easter with its large attendance of bishops is one possible occasion of the promulgation of the ordinance. The assembly of Norman bishops, which, later in the year, elected John of Avranches to the see of Rouen is a second.[68] Especially if it were associated with the Fécamp

---

[67] For Ermenfrid, see T. Schieffer, *Die päpstlichen Legaten in Frankreich vom Vertrage von Meersen (870) bis zum Schisma von 1130*, Historische Studien 263 (Berlin 1935) 53-55, 79-80; and H. E. J. Cowdrey, "Bishop Ermenfrid of Sion and the Penitential Ordinance following the Battle of Hastings," *Journal of Ecclesiastical History* 20 (1969) 225-242. For Alexander's letter, see the *Acta archiepiscoporum Rothomagensium*, Mabillon, *Vetera analecta* 224, whence PL 147.279-280; and ep. 56, PL 146.1339. The dates of the archbishops of Rouen and the bishops of Avranches present difficulties; see *Gallia Christiana* 11 (Paris 1759) 31-34. That John of Avranches was translated to Rouen at about the time of the Conqueror's return to England is suggested by Orderic Vitalis's statement that he was bishop of Avranches for seven years and three months: Orderic 4 (n. 3 above) 2.200; John was consecrated in Sept. 1060. William's good relations with the papacy at this time have been doubted by C. Morton, "Pope Alexander II and the Norman Conquest," *Latomus* 34 (1975) 362-382; but for criticism see Davis (n. 46 above) esp. 247 n. 4. In fact Alexander at this time warmly praised William in his letter to John of Avranches ("ex electione principis tui dilectissimi filii nostri Guillelmi regis Anglorum") and in his privilege for St. Stephen's, Caen ("a glorioso Willelmo principe Normannorum, ac victoriosissimo rege Anglorum"): epp. 55-56, PL 146.1339-1341.

[68] The ordinance begins: "Hec est penitentie institutio secundum decreta Normannorum presulum, auctoritate summi pontificis confirmata per legatum suum Ermenfridum episcopum Sedunensem": see now the text in Morton (n. 67 above) 381-382. I remain unconvinced by the defense of the date 1070, rather than 1067, for the drawing up of the ordinance offered by Morton, and also by C. N. L. Brooke, "Archbishop Lanfranc, the English Bishops, and the Council of London," *Studia Gratiana* 12 (1967) 39-60, esp. 58-59. Brooke points out the link in the MS sources with the councils of Winchester and Windsor in 1070. But there is no evidence that the ordinance originated then. The identical lacunae in the extant MSS point to a single, damaged exemplar of older and perhaps oversea origin which was then published in England. Against Morton's case, (i) the date 1070 imposes a very long delay between the sins and the penances; and (ii) the initial imposition of penances *secundum decreta Normannorum presulum* for sins committed in England is understandable in 1067 and in Normandy, during the confused

assembly, this ordinance, the circumstances of which it is difficult satisfactorily to explain, prompts the question how far William I's actions in 1066-1067 may have been in part modeled upon the emperor Henry III's towards the Hungarians in 1043-1044. In 1043 Henry secured from Pope Benedict IX a *vexillum ex beati Petri parte* before his campaign. In 1044, after his victory, he prostrated himself with his whole army before a relic of the Cross and declared a general amnesty. It is true that no penitential ordinance was involved. But Henry's example may have moved William to make a politic gesture of reconciliation and piety after a bloodier battle. It may also have influenced his decision in 1067 to found Battle Abbey as his own act of reparation.[69] It may underlie the acclamation of William in the *Laudes regiae* of 1068 as *rex pacificus* (line 9). There were certainly contacts between Normandy and the Empire, and as king of England William appears to have had both his crown and a draft coronation *ordo* constructed upon German models.[70] Bishop Ermenfrid of Sion was a prelate of the imperial church, whose familiarity with German versions of the *Laudes regiae* and with their use at coronations and crown-wearings is likely. In 1067, when he was concerned with Norman affairs, he may have advised William about his ecclesiastical plans in England, including the queen's coronation. His advice in this connection regarding a text of the *Laudes regiae* for use at Pentecost 1068 would explain both its studied but cautious deference to papal authority and its possible borrowings in detail from German models. If Ermenfrid were involved in laying down the lines of the *Laudes regiae* of 1068, the relatively late date of his activity in Normandy during the previous year points to his having perhaps given general advice which was implemented in England.

Whether (as is probable) they were wholly Anglo-Norman in origin or whether (as is, however, possible) they were eclectic and included German borrowings, the *Laudes regiae* of 1068 are unlikely to have remained for long in use. As they stand in V, they could have been sung only until at latest Archbishop Aldred's death. In V there is no trace of revision; they were not copied into W; and there is no evidence of

---

aftermath of the Conquest. The publication of an older Norman measure in England early in 1070, when some English bishops were about to be deposed and others were in exile or dead, is also plausible; the motive may have been to promote, by way of commutation, the building and endowment of churches. An entirely new measure at a time when the authority of a reconstituted English episcopate under Lanfranc must soon be established is not likely.

[69] For Henry III, see Bonizo of Sutri, *Liber ad amicum* 5, ed. E. Dümmler, MGH Libelli 1.583-584 (where Conrad II and Henry III are confused); *Annales Altahenses maiores, a.* 1044, ed. E. von Oefele, ed. 2, MGH Script. rer. Germ. 35-37; E. Strehlke, "Brief Abt Berno's von Reichenau an König Heinrich III," *Archiv für Kunde österreichischer Geschichtsquellen* 20 (1858) 197-206, esp. 200-201. Henry IV's sponsoring of *pax et reconciliatio* at Goslar in 1068 shows that his father's outlook persisted: see the annals for 1068 in Berthold, *Chronicon*, and Bernold, *Annales*, MGH SS 5.274, 429. For William's own concern in 1067 to establish peace in Normandy and in 1068 in England, see Orderic 4 (n. 3 above) 2.208-215; cf. the record of William's gift of the vill of Cullaclife to Bishop Wulfstan for the monks of Worcester in *Hemingi Chartularium ecclesiae Wigorniensis*, ed. T. Hearne, 2 vols. (Oxford 1723) 2.413-414.

[70] William of Poitiers 2.3, 42 (n. 53 above) 154, 258 spoke of Duke William's *amicitia* with Henry IV, and of the presence of German craftsmen in the duchy. For the crown and the coronation *ordo* see nn. 50 and 65 above.

other copies. They look like a *pièce d'occasion* for the queen's coronation alone. For, despite the virtuosity of their drafting, in the long term they were open to some obvious objections. Some people may have felt that the unprecedented invocation of the Trinity destroyed the Christocentric character of the text. Others may have demurred to the acclamation of the archbishop of York. As a form to be used, they were excessively determined by considerations of symmetry and conceptual neatness. If the saints invoked were arranged with unique consistency in their proper hierarchy, they were not appropriately assigned to the several orders of human society. John the Baptist and the apostles did not in themselves match the queen, nor did martyrs (rather than confessors) fit the archbishop. Above all, Mary Magdalen and three virgins were oddly matched with the *principes Anglorum* and the army. [71] It is not surprising that, probably even during the Conqueror's reign, chants were sung in Norman England which were markedly different from the *Laudes regiae* of 1068.

Thus, the triumphant and propagandist aspect of the *Laudes regiae* of 1068 is continued in the novel poetic *Laudes* in V and W which form the second part of Appendix I.C below. As a literary or quasi-liturgical genre they have no close precedent or parallel. However, their paschal theme is in a general sense reminiscent of the Easter chants, with neumes, in London, British Library MS Cotton Caligula A.XIV, fols. 13-17; and a trope in the Winchester Troper on the words *Deus sabaoth* — "Gloria, victoria, et salus aeterna sit Deo nostro in excelsis" — is close enough to have perhaps been an immediate inspiration. [72] Taken as a whole, they are clearly for use on public occasions: they are in two-line stanzas written in Leonine hexameters, the two lines of the first being used alternately as refrains for the remaining seven; and in V they have neumes similar to but slightly more complex than those of the *Laudes regiae* of 1068. They follow the outline of the first two sections of the *Laudes regiae* but make no reference to the tricolon. Lines 7-15 celebrate the redemptive work of the victorious Christ. Then a general plea that prayers may be heard (lines 16-18) leads up to prayers for the English king (lines 19-21) and his queen (lines 22-24), the bishops and their subjects with the English armies (lines 25-27), and the bishop of the diocese (lines 28-30). No proper names are given, and there is no indication of the date or circumstances of composition. Conclusions about them must of necessity be tentative. However, the text fits William I's reign. In view of the similarly expressed references to the king and queen (lines 19-20, 22-23) it is not likely to be of pre-Conquest date. [73] The imperial title in

[71] Although the invocation of virgins is not without parallel in German texts: Opfermann nos. III.9, 14, 137, 147.

[72] Frere (n. 25 above) 65. Similar verses survive from Saint-Martial, Limoges, in the tenth and eleventh centuries: *Analecta hymnica medii aevi*, ed. Blume and Dreves 49 (Leipzig 1906) 271-273, nos. 517, 520; cf. A. E. Planchart, *The Repertory of Tropes at Winchester*, 2 vols. (Princeton 1977) 1.280.

[73] See above at nn. 64-65. Richardson and Sayles (n. 46 above) 408-409 drew attention to the perhaps tenth-century panegyric of King Athelstan in which, at the coronation banquet, "Ille strepit cithara, decertat plausibus iste,/ In commune sonat, 'Tibi laus, tibi gloria, Christe' ":

these lines, *basileus/basilea*, may also be significant. Its use may have been in part determined by problems of scansion, since *regem* would not fit in line 20; or it could be the work of a consciously archaizing poet at any time in the Norman period. But William himself was several times elsewhere given the title *basileus*, which his Anglo-Saxon predecessors had used lavishly but by which his sons and the Angevin kings were not distinguished in any surviving source.[74] The text could scarcely come from the reign of William II, who had no queen. So it probably dates from William I's, and from his earlier years, for Queen Matilda died on 2 November 1083; and when it was copied into V and W it had been long enough used for the variant *dogmate plenum* to have arisen in line 19 for *fonte repletum*. It is best regarded as a very early Norman text, intended for a more popular and perhaps outdoor setting than the *Laudes regiae* with their firm anchorage in the Mass. It may have been a hymn for the reception (*susceptaculum*) of the bishop, perhaps sometimes together with the king and queen, in a city of Norman England. In view of the probable Winchester connections of V and W, the city is likely to be Winchester, from which it may have spread elsewhere.[75] If connected with Winchester, it must have been prepared after Stigand's deprivation from the see in 1070 and the succession of the royal chaplain Walkelin (1070-1098).

The last text in Appendix I below is of the *Laudes regiae* in a festal version which seems to have superseded in England the text of 1068. It is of more traditional Gallo-Frankish form. Occurring in manuscript C, it seems to represent the *Laudes regiae* as sung at Christ Church, Canterbury, in the later eleventh century, perhaps beginning in the Conqueror's own lifetime. It is a very different text indeed from that of 1068, as well as from the Norman text from Fécamp in F and S. The contrast with 1068 is the greater. In the first and third sections the tricolon is similarly sung. But in the second section, the powerful upon earth are acclaimed in the different, and highly unusual, order: pope, king, archbishop and his clergy, queen, *principes* and army, without reference to bishops and abbots. As in 1068 the acclamations are

---

William of Malmesbury 2.133 (n. 46 above) 1.146. But misled by the nineteenth-century printed editions they regarded the *Laudes regiae* and the poetic *Laudes* in V as parts of a single text. If the Athelstan panegyric is a source of either it is the poetic *Laudes*. But these are not related to a coronation; if they have some such pre-Conquest model as the citation in the panegyric, the debt cannot be close or significant.

[74] William is called *victoriosus Anglorum basileus* in the Leofric charter: see n. 55 above; he is called *basileus* in a charter of 1068 (Stevenson [n. 52 above] 740); and a Jumièges charter of ca. 1075 runs, "Ego Wuillelmus Normannie dominus, iure hereditario Anglorum patrie effectus sum basileus": *Chartes de l'abbaye de Jumièges*, ed. J. J. Vernier, 2 vols. (Rouen 1916) 1.82, no. 29.

[75] See W. Bulst, "*Susceptacula regis*: Zur Kunde deutscher Reichsaltertümer," in *Corona quernea: Festgabe Karl Strecker*, MGH Schriften 6 (Leipzig 1941) 97-135; also as possible models, Ratpertus and Hartmannus, *Versus ad processionem diebus dominicis*, i.e. the *Versus* from St. Gall beginning *Ardua spes mundi* and *Humili prece et sincera devotione*, in *Analecta hymnica medii aevi*, ed. Blume and Dreves 50 (Leipzig 1907) 237-239, 253-256, nos. 179, 191. In the final stanza the second of these uses the word *basileus* of God. (I am obliged to Mr. Hohler for drawing these items to my attention.) William I himself was received in London in 1068 "tam honorificientia monasteriali quam saecularibus officiis": Orderic 4 (n. 3 above) 2.210. (Orderic is probably here following the lost portion of William of Poitiers: ibid. 208 n. 1.)

sung by the *chorus*, not the *cantores*. But they are punctuated by further singing of the tricolon, whereas the more striking phrases in the acclamations of 1068 have no parallel. Thus, the king is acclaimed only as *a Deo coronato*, which, despite its Carolingian overtones, is the most colorless and routine of royal designations in *Laudes regiae* texts, while the queen has no honorific epithet whatsoever. The Canterbury text departs altogether from the model of an earthly hierarchy matched with a strictly graded presentation of the heavenly. It does not call upon the three Persons of the Trinity. Instead, after each of the five acclamations it invokes Christ as alternately *Salvator mundi* and *Redemptor mundi*. Then three saints are selected, with little regard for their heavenly rank, in order to match each human grade. Thus, the pope is supported by his predecessors Peter, Clement, and Sixtus; for the king there are invoked the royal martyrs King Edmund of East Anglia, the Catholic Herminigild, son of the Arian Visigothic King Leovigild (569-586),[76] and King Oswald of Northumbria; for the archbishop, the archbishops of Canterbury Augustine, Dunstan, and Alphege; for the queen the Blessed Virgin, Felicitas, and Perpetua (that is, the queen of heaven and two other female saints); and for the *principes* and the army, the soldier saints Maurice, George, and Sebastian. In this section, then, the Canterbury *Laudes regiae* has very few of the characteristics which made the version of 1068 so striking a manifesto of the "political theory" of the Norman Conquest. In the fourth and fifth sections it likewise shows few similarities with this text.

It also differs from the Fécamp *Laudes regiae* in most material aspects, save for the twentyfold repetition of the tricolon which is similar to its lavish use at Fécamp. Otherwise, in the second section, the material is differently distributed between *cantores* and *chorus*; the acclamations themselves differ in order and in substance; the choice and distribution of saints are different; there are no significant points of similarity between the fourth and fifth sections, while at Fécamp the doxology in the fifth section is twofold but at Canterbury threefold; and the Canterbury text, like that of 1068, omits any such sixth section as was added at Fécamp. There can be no doubt that the Canterbury text has an origin which is independent of the other Anglo-Norman, and indeed French, versions.

At first sight there is nothing to exclude a pre-Conquest date; indeed, this might seem to be indicated by the invocation in the king's support of the two Anglo-Saxon royal saints, who bore no relation to William I. The absolute *terminus a quo* of the text as it stands is the death of Alphege in 1012. However, it can also be argued that the royal saints, none of whom was a West Saxon and who died respectively in 870, 585, and in 641, bore little, and in one case no, relation to William's immediate Old English predecessors, either. The most probable hypothesis for the selection of saints

---

[76] It is impossible to account for the choice of Herminigild; perhaps it seemed desirable to avoid choosing all the royal martyrs from English examples. Herminigild is referred to by Bede, *De temporum ratione* 66, ed. C. W. Jones, *Bedae venerabilis opera* 1: *Opera didascalia*, Corpus Christianorum, ser. lat. 123B (Turnhout 1977) 522; this is a possible source. For his life, see B. Cignitti, "Ermenegildo, re, santo, martire," *Bibliotheca sanctorum* 5 (1964) 33-47.

in the Canterbury *Laudes regiae* is that, as apparently in the text of 1068, it was made from an existing Litany of the Saints. Unfortunately, except in the context of a form for the profession of a monk, no such Canterbury text of the late eleventh or early twelfth century is known to survive, although all the saints in the *Laudes regiae* except Sixtus and Herminigild appear in the Christ Church, Canterbury, calendar of 1012-1023 in London, British Library MS Arundel 155, fols. 2-7v.[77] If a selection were made from a litany, a likely occasion would be a demand for new liturgical texts following the change of dynasty in 1066.

There are, moreover, certain pointers to a post-Conquest date, and to Norman influence upon the compilation of the Canterbury text. Although the handwriting of C could be that of either an English or a Norman scribe, the neumes and the chant itself differ from those in the versions of Fécamp and of 1068; but the neumes are of Norman rather than English formation.[78] The text itself has an air of tentativeness and experiment which tells against the taking over in Norman times of an established Old English tradition. Thus, the order of precedence in the acclamations – king, archbishop, queen – can hardly have been permitted by any dynasty, whether English, Danish, or Norman, while there was a reigning queen; the archbishop's acclamation is out-of-line by reason of having a suffrage relating to him in the accusative not the dative case, followed by the words *Deus conservet* (lines 19-21), a usage reminiscent of episcopal *Laudes*, for example Appendix II.A, 36-41; and in the fourth section, the readings *Rex noster* (line 46) following *Rex regum*, and *Victoria nostra invictissima* (line 51) are clumsy and tautologous, when *Spes nostra* and *Arma nostra invictissima* would have been more usual and appropriate. These features suggest a compiler who was unfortunate in his sources and did not quite know his business. He may even have lacked enthusiasm, as the compiler of the *Laudes regiae* of 1068 evidently did not, for the task in hand. Finally, the acclamation of the lay magnates as *principes* probably follows Norman usage, in view of the unusual occurrence of this word at Fécamp.[79] Such considerations suggest a fresh compilation after 1066, not the perpetuation of an Old English text.

There are three further points which suggest a range of post-Conquest dates. First, the invocation of Alphege (line 25) fits more easily into a chant for use at Christ Church, Canterbury, after 1079, when Archbishop Lanfranc was persuaded by his visitor Anselm, then abbot of Bec, that Alphege might properly be venerated as a martyr-saint.[80] Secondly, an order of acclamations in which the queen follows the archbishop suggests a date of compilation when there was no reigning queen, so that in performance her acclamation would have been omitted. There was no queen between Matilda's death on 2 November 1083 and Henry I's first marriage on 11 November 1100. Thirdly, whereas the Canterbury *Laudes regiae* provide for the

[77] Wormald (n. 60 above) 169-181. For the monastic profession, see Turner (n. 65 above) xxxiii-xxxiv, 97-98.

[78] The neumes employed are the virga, punctum, pes, pes flexus, pes liquescens, clivis, clivis cephalicus, scandicus, and oriscus.

[79] See n. 54 above.

[80] Milo Crispin 37 (n. 36 above) PL 150.56-57.

acclaiming by name of the king, archbishop, and queen, they make no such provision for the pope (line 3, cf. lines 11, 19, and 28). Such an omission is not unexampled, for it is a feature of the Nevers text in Appendix II.B, line 3, cf. lines 8 and 13, as of the Saint-Ouen text in Appendix III, line 4, cf. lines 11, 16, and 23. But in an Anglo-Norman context the omission is explicable in the light of the Wibertine schism following the antipope Clement III's consecration at Rome on 24 March 1084 in opposition to Pope Gregory VII. As archbishop, Lanfranc showed a prudent reserve during his latter years as between pope and antipope; and it was not until May 1095, during the Whitsuntide court at Windsor, that King William II publicly recognized Clement's then rival, Urban II, as the rightful pope.[81] A likely, though not a proven, date for the Canterbury *Laudes regiae* would thus be in the years of uncertainty between 1084 and 1095. If C were among the books sent from Canterbury to Bishop William of Saint Carilef, such a date fits well.

From the time when the Norman and Anglo-Norman versions of the *Laudes regiae* in Appendix I were compiled, the history of such texts in the duchy and in the kingdom seems to have developed upon largely independent courses. The post-Conquest development in Normandy is illustrated by the Saint-Ouen text in Appendix III. Like all examples from the Norman lands it is characterized by a lavish repetition of the tricolon, which was repeated at least sixteen times. Otherwise it differs greatly from the Fécamp text in F and S. The earthly hierarchy is more fully set out, and includes the archbishop and the army. Although in both texts the saints were selected with at least a general regard for their suitability to those who were acclaimed, the choice and distribution of those invoked differ markedly. While both follow the sixfold formal division of the Gallo-Frankish tradition, the Saint-Ouen text makes a unique departure by placing the felicitations of the sixth section before the doxologies of the fifth. In view of the somewhat bombastic tone of lines 53-57, the purpose was perhaps to reproduce the greater dramatic force of the ending of the *Laudes regiae* of 1068. Nevertheless, overall the Saint-Ouen text has as little in common with this version as it has with that of Fécamp. Again, it shows no significant similarities to the Canterbury *Laudes regiae* in C. So far as the available evidence goes, it must be concluded that the singing of the *Laudes regiae* in Normandy and in Norman England developed upon entirely different lines.

There is no evidence whatsoever to show what text of the *Laudes regiae*, if any, was sung in England between 1068 and the emergence of the Canterbury text. In the twelfth and thirteenth centuries, however, their history in England, so far as texts are known to survive, follows closely from the Canterbury version and not at all from the text of 1068.[82] The sole twelfth-century example occurs in the pontifical,

---

[81] For William I, Lanfranc, and the schism, see Cowdrey (n. 53 above) 109-114; for William II, Eadmer 1 (n. 35 above) 52-69, and William of Malmesbury, *Gesta pontificum* 1, ed. N. E. S. A. Hamilton, RS (1870) 85-87.

[82] It is clear that in the 1160s the clerks of the royal chapel acclaimed the archbishop, using the nominative case: Wm. FitzStephen (n. 17 above). This is to be expected in the royal chapel, and there is no way of knowing whether they used an amended form of the text in C or another text of the *Laudes regiae* altogether.

Cambridge, Trinity College MS B.11.10, fols. 108v-109,[83] where it appears in a most unusual manuscript context — the third English coronation order.[84] It is copied integrally into the *ordo*, following the king's coronation with its final prayer *Sta et retine amodo locum*, and preceding the prayer *Deus qui solus habes immortalitatem*. Although some of the peculiarities remain, the text has been adapted from its tentative festal form in C to meet the needs of a coronation service. In the second section the acclamations are sixfold, following the usual order of pope, king, queen, archbishop, bishops and abbots, *principes* and army. Although the pope remains unnamed, his acclamation is filled out with the words *et salus perpetua*, while in the king's the word *pax* is added between *coronato* and *salus* (cf. lines 4 and 12 of Appendix I.D). The same saints as in C are invoked, though in a slightly different order; but only Benedict is invoked for the bishops and abbots. The first, third, fourth, and fifth sections are identical, save for the omission of *laus et* (cf. line 57) and of the final tricolon. The date of the text, as distinct from that of the manuscript, is uncertain. A connection with Henry II's coronation in 1154 has been suggested but is improbable, for it is far from certain that Queen Eleanor of Aquitaine was crowned with Henry in that year.[85] A date at any time up to that of the manuscript is possible, that is, to about the end of Henry II's reign (1154-1189). But in view of the manifest need for the *Laudes regiae* in C to undergo an early revision, it is likely that changes on the lines of those in the coronation version were made as soon as there was once more a queen, that is, in the reign of Henry I (1100-1135).

The appearance of the *Laudes regiae* in the context of a coronation order was, however, exceptional; their natural place continued to be in a troper or similar book, and for festal use. It is not surprising that they should twice figure in the mid-thirteenth-century Worcester antiphonary, Worcester, Cathedral Library MS F.160, fols. 100v-101 and 351-352.[86] Like the version in the Cambridge pontifical, both Worcester texts have sixfold, appropriately rearranged acclamations in the second section; but since the wording of the pope's and the king's acclamations, and the doxologies in section iv, remain as in C, they do not depend directly upon the

---

[83] Printed in *The Pontifical of Magdalen College*, ed. H. A. Wilson, HBS 39 (1910) 252-254, cf. 295-296; see Brückmann (n. 7 above) 411-412. The earlier parts of this MS were written ca. 1150-1175, but the later parts, including the *Laudes regiae*, perhaps a little later. The text of the *Laudes regiae* has no musical notation.

[84] See Turner (n. 65 above) 115-122 at 120-121, cf. xl-xli.

[85] This is stated only by the later writer Gervase of Canterbury (n. 17 above) 1.159-160. See Schramm (n. 32 above) 57, 252-253; but cf. W. L. Warren, *Henry II* (London 1973) 53.

[86] For the MS see Floyer (n. 58 above) 90-93, 186; and Frere (n. 25 above) xxx n. 2. For a text of the first occurrence of the *Laudes regiae*, with facsimiles, see "Antiphonaire monastique de Worcester," *Paléographie musicale* 12 (Tournay 1922-1925) 72-75, 201-202; cf. Kantorowicz 217-219. Frere 130-131 gave a composite edition of the two occurrences; but in line 2, for *Christus* read *Christe*; in lines 8 and 14 the earlier occurrence has *Angelorum*, but the words *regi Angelorum* and *regine Angelorum* are almost wholly erased; and in lines 49 and 51, for *immortalia* read *infinita*. In the MS neither occurrence is preceded by a title. The chant gives the impression of being a fourth-mode adaptation of what must originally have been modally and musically disparate elements.

text in the Cambridge manuscript. They have certain distinctive features in common: Etheldreda replaces Perpetua among the queen's intercessors; among the archbishop's, Thomas of Canterbury (died 1170) replaces Augustine; while the acclamation of bishops and abbots is replaced by the suffrage, modeled upon the archbishop's, *Episcopum et omnem clerum sibi commissum Deus conservet*; the Worcester saints Oswald, Wulfstan, and Egwin, together with Dunstan for a second time, are their intercessors. But the second Worcester text also has some peculiarities: Edward the Confessor (canonized in 1161) is added to the king's intercessors; the names of the archbishop and bishop are indicated as to be sung by the letter N; a concluding chant of the tricolon, present in the first text, is omitted in the second; and there are small alterations to and embellishments of the chant. The second text seems to be a slightly later revision of the first; it is in a different hand.

It thus emerges from a review of the twelfth- and thirteenth-century English texts of the *Laudes regiae* that, subject to a continuing process of modification to suit different times, places, and circumstances, the Canterbury *Laudes regiae* in C, or some very similar text, provided an important, if not the sole, pattern of later usage, both festal and in the coronation service.[87]

In conclusion, the surviving evidence for the text and for the use of the *Laudes regiae* in the Anglo-Norman realms, as also in England during the later Middle Ages, is meager. It is, however, clear that the English texts of the chant as sung in Norman England owed no major debt to the Norman versions as preserved at Fécamp and Saint-Ouen. There is no special relationship to French texts in general, and German influence is possible, especially upon the *Laudes regiae* of 1068. There is no evidence to indicate that the *Laudes regiae* had a history in England before the Norman Conquest. Rather, the Norman church in England produced its own, remarkable and contrasting forms. The highly original and propagandist version of 1068 was aptly compiled, perhaps with some guidance from a papal legate such as Bishop Ermenfrid of Sion, to express upon a particular occasion the Norman sense of triumph following the Conquest and the elevation of the Conqueror's status from the ducal to the royal. But, in the course of its revisions, the lower-key Canterbury *Laudes regiae* grew into a sensible, versatile, and generally acceptable text. Unlike its predecessor of 1068, it was not straitly tied to any such historical juncture as the Norman Conquest; but perhaps for that very reason it proved to have long-term serviceability.

APPENDIXES

In the manuscripts all the texts of the Appendixes are written as single paragraphs with their parts running on from each other; they are here so set out as to show the divisions between *cantores* and *chorus*. The spelling of the manuscripts is strictly adhered to except as indicated in the textual notes, but the use of capital letters, and

---

[87] For the very little that is known about the *Laudes regiae* in England after the Worcester occurrences, see Kantorowicz 173-177, and Bent (n. 18 above) 88-95. No later text has come to light.

in Appendix I.C the punctuation, are modernized. In the remaining items punctuation is omitted.

I

A. The Fécamp *Laudes regiae*

MSS: Rouen, Bibliothèque municipale MS 489 (A.254), fol. 71, late eleventh or early twelfth century (F); Salisbury, Cathedral Library MS 89, recto of title page, late eleventh or early twelfth century (S).

[i]	*Cantores*	Christus vincit	Christus regnat	⟨Christus imperat	*iii*
	Chorus	Christus vincit	Christus regnat	Christus imperat	*iii*
[ii]	*Cantores*	·Exaudi Christe		*Chorus⟩*	Exaudi Christe
	Cantores	Illi ⟨summo pontifici et universali papę	*Chorus*	Exaudi Christe	
5		vita			
	Cantores	Sancte Petre⟩		*Chorus*	tu illum adiuva
	Cantores	Sancte ⟨Paule		*Chorus*	tu illum adiuva
	Cantores	Sancte Iohannes		*Chorus*	tu illum adiuva
	Cantores	Christus⟩ vincit	Christus regnat	Christus imperat	*i*
10	*Chorus*	Christus vincit	Christus regnat	Christus imperat	*i*
	Cantores	Ex⟨audi Christe		*Chorus*	Exaudi Christe
	Cantores	Illi Francorum regi in⟩ Christi pace vita et	*Chorus*	Ex⟨audi Christe	
		victoria			
	Cantores	Sancte Michael		*Chorus*	tu illum adiuva˙
15	*Cantores*	Sancte Gabriel⟩		[*Chorus*]	tu illum adiuva
	[*Cantores*]	Sancte Raphael		[*Chorus*]	tu i⟨llum adiuva
	Cantores	Christus vincit	Christus regnat	Christus imperat	*i*
	Chorus	Christus vincit	Christus regnat	Christus imperat	*i*
	Cantores⟩	Exaudi Christe		*Chorus*	Exaudi Christe
20	*Cantores*	Gu⟨illelmo Normannorum duci salus et	*Chorus*	Exaudi Christe	
		pax continua⟩			
	Cantores	Sancte Maurici		*Chorus*	⟨tu illum adiuva
	Cantores	Sancte Sebastiane		[*Chorus*]	tu illum adiuva
	[*Cantores*]⟩	Sancte Adriane		*Chorus*	tu illum adiuva

The text of S *is severely damaged by the loss of much of the right-hand side of the folio and by damp; words lost or illegible in it are placed in angle brackets* ⟨ ⟩. *It is not clear from either MS, except in lines 1 and 9, when the tricolon was chanted in full and when only the first two words; I have followed the most usual practice in Gallo-Frankish texts. In lines 10, 19, 27, 32, 34, 52, and 55,* S *gives the direction* Item chorus *where* F *has* Chorus. *Where the directions* Cantores *and* Chorus *are in square brackets* [ ] *they are omitted in* F *but given in* S. *In* F *the unexplained reading* Sanctę *instead of* Sancte *occurs in lines 14-16, 22, 30, 31, 37, 38, and 39.*
4, 12 Illi: Illo FS
20 S *appears to have the initial* W *for the duke's name.*
23 *Add* Sancte *in the margin* F

25	*Cantores*	Christus vincit	⟨Christus regnat	Christus imperat	*i*	
	Chorus	Christus vincit	Christus regnat	Christus imperat	*i*	
	Cantores	Exaudi Christe⟩		*Chorus*		Exaudi Christe
	Cantores	Omnibus pontificali hono⟨re sublimatis		*Chorus*⟩		Exaudi Christe
		salutaris vitę gloria				
30	*Cantores*	Sancte Ambrosi		[*Chorus*]		tu illos adiuva
	Cantores	⟨Sancte Martine		[*Chorus*]		tu illos adiuva
	[*Cantores*]⟩	Sancte Benedicte		[*Chorus*]		tu illos adiuva

	Cantores	Christus vincit	Christus regnat	Christus imperat	*i*	
	Chorus	⟨Christus vincit	Christus regnat	Christus imperat	*i*	
35	*Cantores*	Omnibus Christiane⟩ legis principibus ac		*Chorus*		Exaudi Christe
		iudicibus salus ęterna				
	⟨*Cantores*	Sancte Georgi		[*Chorus*]		tu illos adiuva
	[*Cantores*]⟩	Sancte Tiburci		[*Chorus*]		tu illos adiuva
	Cantores	Sancte Frodmunde		[*Chorus*]		⟨tu illos adiuva

40 [iii]	*Cantores*	Christus vincit	Christus regnat	Christus imperat	
	Chorus⟩	Christus vincit	Christus regnat	Christus imperat	

[iv]	*Cantores*	Rex regum et dominus dominorum	*Chorus*	⟨Christus vincit
	Cantores	Gloria et spes⟩ nostra	*Chorus*	Christus vincit
	Cantores	Misericordia et auxilium ⟨nostrum	*Chorus*	Christus vincĭt
45	*Cantores*⟩	Fortitudo et victoria nostra	*Chorus*	Christus vincit
	Cantores	Arma nostra invictissima	⟨*Chorus*	Christus⟩ vincit
	Cantores	Lux via et vita nostra	*Chorus*	Christus vincit

[v]	*Cantores*	Ipsi soli regnum ⟨et imperium⟩ per immortalia secula seculorum Amen		
	Chorus	Christus vincit Christus regnat Christus imperat		
50	*Cantores*	Ipsi soli ⟨laus et gloria per omnia⟩ secula seculorum Amen		
	Chorus	Christus vincit Christus regnat Christus imperat		

[vi]	*Cantores*	Christe audi nos	*Chorus*	Christe ⟨audi nos
	Cantores⟩	Kẏrrieleẏson	*Chorus*	Kẏrrieleẏson
	Cantores	Christe eleẏson	*Chorus*	Christe eleẏson
55	⟨*Cantores*	Kẏrrieleẏson⟩	*Chorus*	Kẏrrieleẏson
	Cantores	Feliciter *iii*	*Chorus*	Feliciter *iii*
	⟨*Cantores*	Tempora bona maneant *iii*⟩	*Chorus*	Redempti sanguine Christi
	Cantores	Feliciter *iii*	*Chorus*	Feliciter *iii*
60	⟨*Cantores*	Regnum Christi⟩ veniat *iii*	*Chorus*	Deo gratias Amen

---

34 *This line should probably be followed by another reading* Cantores Exaudi Christe Chorus Exaudi Christe.

40-1 FS *do not indicate whether the tricolon is single or threefold.*

B.   The Anglo-Norman *Laudes regiae* of 1068

MS: London, B.L. MS Cotton Vitellius E.XII, fol. 160v, late eleventh or early twelfth century (V).

[i]	Christus vincit Christus regnat	Christus imperat *iii*	

[ii]   Exaudi Christe   Alexandro s[ummo pon]tifici et universali papę vita

      Pater de cęlis Deus   tu illum adiuva
5   Fili r[edemptor] mundi Deus   tu illum adiuva
      Spiritus sancte Deus   tu illum adiuva

      Christus vincit   Christus regnat   Christus imperat
      Exaudi Christe   Wilhelmo serenissimo a Deo coronato magno et pacifico regi vita et victoria
10   Sancta Maria   tu illum adiuva
      Sancte Michael   tu illum adiuva
      Sancte Raphael   tu illum adiuva

      Christus vincit   Christus regnat   Christus imperat
      Exaudi Christe   Mahthýldę serenissimę a Deo coronatę reginę
15   salus et vita
      Sancte Iohannes   tu illam adiuva
      Sancte Petre   tu illam adiuva
      Sancte Paule   tu illam adiuva
      Sancte Andrea   tu illam adiuva

20   Christus vincit   Christus regnat   Christus imperat
      Exaudi Christe   Aldrado Eboracensi archiepiscopo et omni clero sibi commisso salus et vita
      Sancte Stephane   tu illum adiuva
      Sancte Laurenti   tu illum adiuva
25   Sancte Vincenti   tu illum adiuva

      Christus vincit   Christus regnat   Christus imperat
      Exaudi Christe   Omnibus episcopis et abbatibus et cunctis congregationibus illis commissis salus et vita
      Sancte Martine   tu illos adiuva
30   Sancte Benedicte   tu illos adiuva
      Sancte Gregori   tu illos adiuva
      Sancte Nicholae   tu illos adiuva

      Christus vincit   Christus regnat   Christus imperat
      Exaudi Christe   Omnibus principibus Anglorum et cuncto ex-
35   ercitui Christianorum vita et victoria
      Sancta Maria Magdalena   tu illos adiuva
      Sancta Perpetua   tu illos adiuva

Square brackets [   ] *in the text indicate that it is illegible or deficient through damage to the borders of the folio; words within them are conjectural.*

Sancta Agatha   tu illos adiuva
Sancta Lucia   tu illos adiuva

40 [iii]   Christus vincit   Christus regnat   Christus imperat

[iv]   Redemptio et liberatio nostra   Christus vincit
        Victoria nostra   Christus vincit
        Misericordia nostra   Christus vincit
        Prudentia et iustitia nostra   Christus vincit
45   Fortitudo et temperantia nostra   Christus vincit
        Auxilium nostrum   Christus vincit
        Defensio nostra   Christus vincit
        [L]etitia et gloriatio nostra   Christus vincit
        Vita et salus nostra   Christus vincit

50 [v]   Ipsi soli honor [   ] per infinita secula seculorum Amen
        Chorus ita
        Ipsi soli decus potestas et imperium [per infinita secula seculorum Amen]
        Chorus ita
        Ipsi soli gloria laus et iubilatio per infinita secula [seculorum Amen
55   *Chorus ita*]

---

50 *Two nouns appear to be lost.*

C.   A form of episcopal benediction followed by a poetic *Laudes*

MSS: London, B. L. MS Cotton Vitellius E.XII, fol. 155, late eleventh or early twelfth century (V); Cambridge, Corpus Christi College MS 163, pp. 286-287, late eleventh or early twelfth century (W).

Benedicat vos divina maiestas Domini.
Benedicat vos Spiritus sanctus qui in specie columbę in Iordane fluvio super Christum requievit.
Ille vos benedicat qui de cęlo dignatus est descendere in terram et de suo sancto
5   sanguine nos redemit.
Benedicat Dominus sacerdotium vestrum et introitum vestrum. Alleluia.

Gloria victori sit Christo laude perhenni,
Qui super astra manet, cuius victoria pollet.
    Gloria victori sit Christo laude perhenni.
10   Pro mundi vita persolvitur hostia viva,
Quam mors dum mordet necis in se tela retorquet.

---

1 vos: nos W
2 columbę: columbe W

4 cęlo: celo W

    Gloria victori sit Christo laude perhenni.
Per mortis praetium Pharaonem vicit iniquum,
Et spolians herebum nobis dedit astra polorum.
15   Qui super astra manet, cuius victoria pollet.
Ecce preces nostras quas fundimus audiat istas,
Cunctos qui proprii nos sanguinis abluit undis.
    Gloria victori sit Christo laude perhenni.
               vel dogmate plenum
Moribus ornatum Salomonis fonte repletum
20 Poscimus Anglorum nostrum salvet basileum.
      Qui super astra manet, cuius victoria pollet.
Poscimus et nostram salvet Christus basileam
Nobilem atque piam gestantem dogmatis ẏdram.
    Gloria victori sit Christo laude perhenni.
25 Prẹsulibus nostris subiectis cum sibi totis,
Angligenis turmis concedat dona salutis.
      Qui super astra manet, cuius victora pollet.
Nostro pontifici cuius sumus in diocesi
Det regnum vitẹ qua scandit et ipse supernẹ.
30   Gloria victori sit Christo laude perhenni.

---

13 praetium: pretium W
19 Salamonis *corrected to* Salomonis W
19 *vel* dogmate plenum *interlined, apparently in the same hand* V; *certainly so* W
20 nostrum: nostrorum W
29 vitẹ: vite W

D.   The Canterbury *Laudes regiae*

MS: Durham, University Library MS Cosin V.V.6, fols. 19v-21, late eleventh century (C).

[i]	Christus vincit	Christus regnat	Christus imperat	*Hoc ter*	
	Et chorus respondeat iii				

[ii]	*Cantores*	Exaudi Christe	*Chorus*	Summo pontifici et universali pape vita
5	*Cantores*	Salvator mundi	*Chorus*	tu illum adiuva
	Cantores	Sancte Petre	*Chorus*	tu illum adiuva
	Cantores	Sancte Clemens	*Chorus*	tu illum adiuva
	Cantores	Sancte Sixte	*Chorus*	tu illum adiuva
	Cantores	Christus vincit Christus regnat Christus imperat		
10	*Chorus idem*			
	Cantores	Exaudi Christe	*Chorus*	N. regi Anglorum a Deo coronato salus et victoria
	Cantores	Redemptor mundi	*Chorus*	tu illum adiuva
	Cantores	Sancte Eadmunde	*Chorus*	tu illum adiuva
15	*Cantores*	Sancte Erminigelde	*Chorus*	tu illum adiuva
	Cantores	Sancte Osuualde	*Chorus*	tu illum adiuva

	Cantores	Christus vincit Christus regnat Christus imperat		
	Chorus idem			
20	*Cantores*	Exaudi Christe	*Chorus*	N. archiepiscopum et omnem clerum sibi commissum Deus conservet
	Cantores	Salvator mundi [fol. 20]	*Chorus*	tu illum adiuva
	Cantores	Sancte Augustine	*Chorus*	tu illum adiuva
	Cantores	Sancte DUNSTANE	*Chorus*	tu illum adiuva
25	*Cantores*	Sancte Ælphege	*Chorus*	tu illum adiuva
	Cantores	Christus vincit Christus regnat Christus imperat		
	Chorus idem			
	Cantores	Exaudi Christe	*Chorus*	N. regine Anglorum salus et vita
30	*Cantores*	Redemptor mundi	*Chorus*	tu illam adiuva
	Cantores	Sancta Maria	*Chorus*	tu illam adiuva
	Cantores	Sancta Felicitas	*Chorus*	tu illam adiuva
	Cantores	Sancta Perpetua	*Chorus*	tu illam adiuva
	Cantores	Christus vincit Christus regnat Christus imperat		
35	*Chorus idem*			
	Cantores	Exaudi Christe	*Chorus*	Omnibus principibus et cuncto exercitui Anglorum salus et victoria
	Cantores	Salvator mundi	*Chorus*	tu illos adiuva
40	*Cantores*	Sancte Maurici	*Chorus*	tu illos adiuva
	Cantores	Sancte Georgi	*Chorus*	tu illos adiuva
	Cantores	Sancte Sebastiane	*Chorus*	tu illos adiuva

[iii]   *Cantores*   Christus [fol. 20v] vincit   Christus regnat   Christus imperat
        Chorus [*idem*]

45 [iv]	*Cantores*	Rex regum	*Chorus*	Christus vincit
	Cantores	Rex noster	*Chorus*	Christus regnat
	Cantores	Gloria nostra	*Chorus*	Christus imperat
	Cantores	Auxilium nostrum	*Chorus*	Christus vincit
	Cantores	Fortitudo nostra	*Chorus*	Christus regnat
50	*Cantores*	Liberatio et redemptio nostra	*Chorus*	Christus imperat
	Cantores	Victoria nostra invictissima	*Chorus*	Christus vincit
	Cantores	Murus noster inexpugnabilis	*Chorus*	Christus regnat
	Cantores	Defensio et exultatio nostra	*Chorus*	Christus imperat

[v]	*Cantores*	Ipsi soli laus et iubilatio et benedictio per infinita secula seculorum
55		Amen
	Chorus	Christus vincit Christus regnat Christus imperat
	Cantores	Ipsi soli laus et iubilatio et benedictio per infinita secula seculorum Amen
	Chorus	Christus vincit Christus regnat Christus imperat
	Cantores	Ipsi soli honor et claritas et sapientia per infinita secula seculorum
60		Amen [fol. 21]
	Chorus	Christus vincit Christus regnat Christus imperat

---

44 C *omits* idem

II

A. An Autun *Laudes regiae* of 996-1024, followed by an episcopal *Laudes*

MS: Paris, Bibliothèque de l'Arsenal MS 1169 (637 TL), fols. 22v-23, eleventh century (A).

[i] Christus vincit   Christus regnat   Christus imperat
R. in choro similiter iii

[ii] Exaudi Christe   Illi summo pontifici et universali pape vita *Ter*
      Sancte Petre   *R*. tu illum adiuva
5   Sancte Paule   *R*. tu illum adiuva
      Sancte Gregorii   *R*. tu illum adiuva

      Exaudi Christe   *R*. Rodberto magno et pacifico regi vita et victoria
      Sancte Dionisii   tu illum adiuva
      Sancte Cornelii   tu illum adiuva
10   Sancte Medarde   tu illum adiuva

      Exaudi Christe   Vualterio huius aecclesiae pontifici et omni clero et
                          ·populo sibi commisso salus et vita *Ter*
      Sancte Nazarii   tu illos ad[

          ]vasii   tu illos adiuva

15   Exaudi Christe   *R. scola* Omnibus iudicibus regibus et principibus et
                          cuncto exercitui Christianorum vita et victoria
      Sancte Mauricii   tu illos adiuva
      Sancte Martine   tu illos adiuva
      Sancte Sebastiane   tu illos adiuva

20 [iv] Rex regum   Christus vincit   Christus regnat   *ut supra*
      Gloria nostra   Christus [fol. 23] vincit   Christus regnat
      Misericordia nostra   Christus vincit   Christus regnat
      Spes nostra   Christus vincit
      Auxilium nostrum   Christus vincit   Christus regnat
25   Fortitudo et victoria nostra   Christus vincit
      Lux et vita nostra   Christus vincit   Christus regnat
      Liberacio et redemcio nostra   Christus vincit
      Arma nostra invictissima   Christus vincit
      Murus noster inexpugnabilis   Christus vincit
30   Defensio et exultacio nostra   Christus vincit

[v] Ipsi soli gloria et potestas per immortalia secula seculorum Amen
     Ipsi soli virtus et victoria per omnia secula seculorum Amen
     Ipsi soli laus et iubilacio per infinita secula seculorum Amen

---

7 regi: rege A
13-14 *A single line of the text left blank* A
20-30 *Thus* A; *it is probable, in view of the direction* ut supra, *that the complete tricolon was sung throughout.*

Lectio epistole

35 *In fine misse post finitam collectam antequam dicatur* Amen

Hunc diem	*R*. Multos annos
Deus conservet *Ter*	Feliciter Feliciter Feliciter
Tempora bona habeas *Ter*	*R*.
Te pastorem	*R*. Deus elegit
40 In istam sedem	Deus conservet
Annos vite	*R*. Deus multiplicet Amen
Ite missa est	Deo gratias

---

34 Lectio: Leccio A
35 misse: missa A

B.   A Nevers *Laudes regiae* of 1059-1060

MS: Paris, B.N. MS lat. 9449, fols. 36v-37, late eleventh century (N).

[i] CHRISTUS VINCIT   CHRISTUS REGNAT   CHRISTUS IMPERAT   *TRIBUS VICIBUS*

[ii] Exaudi Christe *iii*	Summo pontifici et universali pape vita
Salvator mundi	tu illum adiuva
5 Sancte Petre	tu illum adiuva
Sancte Paule	tu illum adiuva
Sancte Andrea	tu illum adiuva
Exaudi Christe [*iii*]	Hugoni pontifici nostro salus et vita
Sancte Cyrice	tu illum adiuva
10 Sancte Nazari	tu illum adiuva
Sancte Genesii	tu illum adiuva
Sancte Simphoriane	tu illum adiuva
Exaudi Christe *iii*	Heinrico regi Filippo regi serenissimo a Deo coronato magno et pacifico vita et victoria
15 Redemptor mundi	tu illum adiuva
Sancta Maria	tu illum adiuva
Sancte Michael	tu illum adiuva
Sancte Gabriel	tu illum adiuva
Sancte Raphael	tu illum adiuva
20 Exaudi Christe *iii*	Omnibus iudicibus et cuncto exercitui Christianorum vita et victoria
Sancte Dionisii	tu illos adiuva
Sancte Martine	tu illos adiuva
Sancte Remigi	tu illos adiuva

25 [iii] Christus vincit   Christus regnat   Christus imperat   *iii*

---

13 regi ... regi: rege ... rege N

[iv]	Lux via et vita nostra	Christus vincit
	Rex regum et Deus deorum	Christus vincit
	Gloria et iubilacio nostra	Christus vincit
	Misericordia et redempcio nostra	Christus vincit
30	Spes semper et fiducia nostra	Christus vincit [fol. 37]
	Auxilium et refugium nostrum	Christus vincit
	Fortitudo et iusticia nostra	Christus vincit
	Prudencia et temperancia nostra	[Christus vincit]
	Liberacio et redempcio nostra	Christus vincit
35	Arma nostra invictissima	Christus vincit
	Murus noster inexpugnabilis	Christus vincit
	Victoria nostra	[Christus vincit]
	Defensio et exaltacio nostra	Christus vincit

[v] Ipsi soli honor imperium gloria et potestas per immortalia secula seculorum Amen
40   Christus vincit   Christus regnat   Christus imperat

[vi]	Christe audi nos	Kyrrieleyson
	Christe leyson	Kyrrieleyson
	Te pastorem *iii*	Deus elegit
	Ista sede *iii*	Te conservet
45	Annos vite *iii*	Deus multiplicet
	Felicter Feliciter Feliciter *iii*	
	Tempora bona habeas	
	Tempora bona habeas	
	Tempora bona habeas	
50	Multos annos Amen	

---

39 immortalia: *reading uncertain* N

III

A text of the *Laudes regiae* from Saint-Ouen

MS: Rouen, Bibliothèque municipale MS 537 (A.438), fol. 90r-v, early twelfth century (O).

[i] [*Cantores*] [Ch]ristus vincit   Christus regnat   Christus imperat
     Chorus R.   Christus vincit   Christus regnat   Christus imperat   *iii*

[ii]	*Cantores*	[E]xaudi Christe	*Chorus*	Christus vincit
	Cantores	[S]ummo pontifici et universali pape	*Chorus*	Christus vincit
5		vita et salus perpetua		
	Cantores	[S]alvator mundi	*Chorus*	[t]u illum adiuva
	Cantores	[S]ancte Petre	*Chorus*	tu illum adiuva

As in Appendix I.A, it is not clear except in line 1 when the tricolon was chanted in full and when only the first two words; I have followed the most usual practice in Gallo-Frankish texts. Words and letters in square brackets [ ] are lacking in the MS.

	Cantores	Christus vincit	Christus regnat	Christus imperat		
	Chorus	Christus vincit	Christus regnat	Christus imperat		
10	*Cantores*	[E]xaudi Christe			*Chorus*	Christus vincit
	Cantores	[R]egi Francorum N. pax salus et victoria			*Chorus*	Christus vincit
	Cantores	[R]edemptor mundi			*Chorus*	tu illum adiuva
	Cantores	[S]ancte Dionisi			*Chorus*	tu illum adiuva
	Cantores	Christus vincit	Christus regnat	Christus imperat		
15	*Chorus*	Christus vincit	Christus regnat	Christus imperat		
	Cantores	N. Normannorum duci invictissimo pax salus et victoria			*Chorus*	Christus vincit
	Cantores	[S]ancte Stephane			*Chorus*	tu illum adiuva
	Cantores	[S]ancte Vincenti			*Chorus*	tu illum adiuva
20	*Cantores*	Christus vincit	Christus regnat	Christus imperat		
	Chorus	Christus vincit	Christus regnat	Christus imperat		
	Cantores	[E]xaudi Christe			*Chorus*	Christus vincit
	Cantores	N. archiepiscopo et omni clero sibi commisso pax vita et salus continua			*Chorus*	Christus vincit
25	*Cantores*	[S]ancta Maria			*Chorus*	tu illum adiuva
	Cantores	[S]ancte Andrea			*Chorus*	tu illum adiuva
	Cantores	[S]ancte Iohannes			*Chorus*	tu illum adiuva
	Cantores	Christus vincit	Christus regnat	Christus imperat		
	Chorus	Christus vincit	Christus regnat	Christus imperat		
30	*Cantores*	[E]xaudi Christe			*Chorus*	Christus vincit
	Cantores	[E]piscopis et abbatibus et omnibus sibi commissis pax salus et vera concordia			*Chorus*	Christus vincit
	Cantores	[S]ancte Martine			*Chorus*	tu illos adiuva
	Cantores	[S]ancte [fol. 90v] Romane			*Chorus*	tu illos adiuva
35	*Cantores*	[S]ancte Benedicte			*Chorus*	tu illos adiuva
	Cantores	Christus vincit	Christus regnat	Christus imperat		
	Chorus	Christus vincit	Christus regnat	Christus imperat		
	Cantores	[E]xaudi Christe			*Chorus*	Christus vincit
	Cantores	[C]unctis principibus et omni exercitui Christianorum pax salus et victoria			*Chorus*	Christus vincit
40						
	Cantores	[S]ancte Maurici			*Chorus*	tu illos adiuva
	Cantores	[S]ancte Sebastiane			*Chorus*	tu illos adiuva
	Cantores	[S]ancte Georgi			*Chorus*	tu illos adiuva
[iii]	*Cantores*	Christus vincit	Christus regnat	Christus imperat		
45	*Chorus*	Christus vincit	Christus regnat	Christus imperat		
[iv]	*Cantores*	[R]ex regum [R]ex noster [S]pes nostra			*Chorus*	Christus vincit
	Cantores	[M]isericordia nostra [L]iberatio nostra et redemptio nostra			*Chorus*	Christus vincit

---

12 [R]edemptor mundi: [R]edemptor O
15 *It is probable that this line should be followed by a reading like lines 10, 22, 30, and 38.*

[vi]	*Cantores*	[T]empora bona veniant *iii*	*Chorus*	Christus vincit
50	*Cantores*	[P]ax Christi veniat *iii*	*Chorus*	Christus vincit
	Cantores	[R]egnum Christi veniat *iii*	*Chorus*	Christus vincit
	Cantores	[F]eliciter *iii*	*Chorus*	Christus vincit

[v]   *Cantores*   [I]psi soli laus et imperium gloria et potestas per immortalia secula seculorum Amen

55   *Chorus*   Ipsi soli laus et imperium gloria et potestas per immortalia secula
       similiter   seculorum Amen

                   [I]psi soli laus et iubilatio per infinita secula seculorum Amen

---

49-57   *For the order of sections v and vi see above.*

POPE GREGORY VII AND THE ANGLO-NORMAN CHURCH AND KINGDOM

A survey of Gregory VII's relations with the Anglo-Norman lands which King William I (1066-87) ruled, with Archbishop Lanfranc of Canterbury (1070-89) as his principal ecclesiastical adviser in England, falls readily into three periods. First, between 1066 and 1073 Gregory, as Archdeacon Hildebrand of the papal *palatium*, was much concerned with the Norman conquest of England and with events before and after Lanfranc left his abbey of St. Stephen's, Caen, for the see of Canterbury. Secondly, during the next nine years or so relations between Gregory and William were kept basically stable and amicable, despite many tensions, by the need of these two strong-willed but politically vulnerable rulers to preserve each other's good will and support. Thirdly, from about 1082 special problems were raised by the deterioration of Gregory's position in Rome until he died in exile, and by the weakness of Gregory and of his successors Victor III (1086-7) and at first Urban II (1088-99), in face of the imperialist antipope Clement III (1080-1100). But before the course of events in these periods can be discussed it is necessary to consider the underlying bonds of conviction and interest which drew the papacy and the Anglo-Norman kingdom together, in spite of all the factors which tended to prejudice their good relations. For the strength of these bonds is often insufficiently appreciated.

I

From Gregory's standpoint William's lands, and especially the English kingdom which he conquered by the sword in 1066, constituted one of the peripheral kingdoms and principalities of Latin Christendom which it was his urgent concern as pope to bring into the closest possible association with the apostolic see. The reasons for this concern were partly political. Even before Gregory became pope in 1073 the questions of who should succeed to the see of Milan and of how its new archbishop should be appointed, started the conflict with King Henry IV of Germany which was to overshadow Gregory's pontificate. Moreover from 1073 Gregory was deeply and repeatedly at odds with King Philip I of France on account of his simony and of his exploitation of the church. Inside Germany and France Gregory sought to appeal directly to the princes and to the lower feudal classes. Outside them he endeavoured to counterbalance their two kings' resistance to the apostolic see by drawing the peripheral regions of Latin Christendom as closely to it as possible. Thus the obedience and service of the newer kingdoms might redress the resistance and hostility of the older (1).

Underlying Gregory's political motive for being concerned with the peripheral lands of Europe was a religious one. As Gregory understood his apostolic office it committed him as the vicar of St. Peter to announce to all peoples, and especially to their rulers, the requirements of Christian righteousness (*iustitia*), and to demand their obedience. He felt himself no less obliged to secure that in every part of Christendom such abuses as simony and the non-observance of clerical celibacy were banished from the church, and that the church itself was everywhere open to the authority of the apostolic see. Local bishops and clergy should allow neither hindrance by others nor their own procrastination to prevent them from promptly attending the Lenten and November councils of the Roman church when they were summoned to do so; while papal legates must be free to enter and to circulate wherever Gregory sent them. By such means he was resolved to ensure that the demands of righteousness were heard and implemented in the farther, no less than in the nearer, parts of the Christian world.

In pursuit of this concern for the peripheral lands, Gregory set out the broad lines of his attitude towards William in letters, all of them bearing the characteristic marks of his own dictation, which he wrote at various dates between 1073 and 1083, but which are remarkably consistent in their high estimate of William's kingly office and in their firm insistence upon his kingly duties. Above all, Gregory found in William's strong and prospe-

---

(1) Cf. G. LADNER, *Theologie und Politik vor dem Investiturstreit*, 2nd edn., Darmstadt, 1968, pp. 78-84.

rous rule a sure indication of God's favour (2). He was a *potentissimus rex*, raised up by the grace of God, who should in return
acknowledge Jesus Christ as the source of honour, protection,
and almighty help (3). Because of this high appraisal of his
kingship William was the only lay ruler of his day whom Gregory
addressed in terms of Pope Gelasius I's famous pronouncement
regarding the spiritual and temporal government of the world (4).
(Elsewhere in his letters Gregory cited Gelasius only during an
abstract consideration of the imperial power in his second letter
to Bishop Hermann of Metz) (5). Following Gelasius he explained how God had divided the governance of this world between two dignities, the papal and the royal, which were to preserve mankind from error and mortal danger by ruling it according
to their diverse offices. Gregory's reference to Gelasius was
more than a reminder of William's duty of obedience: it was a
signal recognition of his standing as a king. Gregory in effect
invested William's prosperous kingship with the honour which
Gelasius had ascribed to the very highest temporal office — the
Empire. Only when he had thus exalted the kingship and,
therefore, William's own standing as a king, did Gregory go on
to distinguish the greater from the less: the royal dignity must
be governed by the care and disposition of the papal, for popes
must render account to God even for kings.

Gregory indicated to William at an early date the nature
of the obedience which a king should show to the pope. In essence
it was the duty of a good son to his mother, the holy Roman
church. It consisted of three things: first, an unremitting zeal
for righteousness in all things, as opportunity arose to exhibit
it; secondly, a due care for the churches which were committed
to the king's protection; and thirdly, a warfare against sin and
a cultivating of the Christian virtues (6). In his last surviving
letter to William Gregory spoke in similar terms, which show

---

(2) *Reg.*, V, 19, 4 Apr. 1078, p. 382. (References to the Register of Gregory VII are
to *Gregorii VII Registrum*, ed. E. CASPAR, *MGH, Epistolae selectae*, ii, Berlin, 1920-3).

(3) *Reg.*, VII, 23, 24 Apr. 1080, p. 501.

(4) *Reg.*, VII, 25, 8 May 1080, pp. 505-7.

(5) *Reg.*, VIII, 21, 15 Mar. 1081, p. 553. The Gelasian text was made familiar by its
inclusion in the Pseudo-Isidorian Decrees.

(6) *Reg.*, I, 70, 4 Apr. 1074, p. 101.

how lasting was his undertone of official confidence in William, despite their many differences. He rejoiced in the friendship in which a common love of St. Peter had for so long joined them. and he encouraged William to continue in works which were congruous with this friendship (7).

Gregory's letters of course set forth a standard to which he wished William's rule to conform, not a practice which William fully exhibited and maintained. In fact he exercised with a masterful authority the protection which Gregory, when setting out his duty, allowed to be his function over the churches which were committed to him. Not only was William thereby following a strong tradition of early eleventh-century kingship which had its best example in the Emperor Henry III, but he had good political reasons for so doing. Before 1066 as duke of Normandy, he had in part built up his ducal authority by means of an ecclesiastical revival in its bishoprics and monasteries. In England after 1066 a reformed, reorganized, and revitalized church was similarly an indispensable instrument of his kingly rule (8). Early in the twelfth century the chronicler Eadmer described the king's invincible determination to transplant to England the laws and customs of which he and his fathers had enjoyed the advantage in Normandy, so that all matters whether spiritual or temporal might depend upon his will (9). In this last phrase of the chronicler there is a note of exaggeration. But Eadmer went on to illustrate specifically the rules of church government which the Conqueror introduced. No one in his realms might recognize a bishop of Rome as pope save by his order, nor might anyone receive letters from a pope unless they were first shown to the king (10). At ecclesiastical councils summoned by the archbishop of Canterbury as primate, no canons might be passed save such

---

(7) *Reg.*, IX, 37, 1082-3, p. 630.

(8) Cf. D.C. Douglas, *William the Conqueror*, London, 1964, pp. 105-32, 317-45.

(9) Eadmer, *Historia novorum in Anglia*, i, ed. M. Rule, London: Rolls Series, 1884, pp. 9-10.

(10) It is unlikely that this rule applied to all papal letters, for such a rule was neither practicable nor expedient. It probably had in view letters whose reception implied the recognition of a new or doubtfully legitimate pope. Eadmer was recording only such rules as mattered for his later narrative: the issue of receiving papal letters arose in connexion with King William II's attitude to Anselm's recognition of Pope Urban II: *Hist. nov.*, ed. Rule, pp. 52-3.

as the king had approved and already seen. William was resolved
to be master in his own kingdom, and by insisting upon such
rules of church government he was certain to run into some degree
of conflict with Gregory's view of his obedience.

But when all this has been said from the viewpoint of after-
times, William during his life was deeply beholden to Gregory
for exalting his kingship and for his generous recognition of its
Christian quality. William was a bastard by birth and familiar
nickname, who lacked royal blood, and who alike owed the subjection of a rebellious duchy and the winning of an alien kingdom
to the power of his sword. He would not lightly forfeit the good
will of a pope who applauded him as a *potentissimus rex* blessed
by God, and who admonished him in terms which, as everyone
schooled in canon law knew, a famous pope of Christian antiquity
had addressed to an emperor. Moreover, to the lustre which
Gregory's words added to his kingship there must be added the
more tangible, and critically important, help which William received from the apostolic see, when Gregory was already prominent at Rome as Archdeacon Hildebrand, in connexion with
the invasion of England and the initial reordering of the English
church.

II

At the time of the conquest of England, the official Norman
attitude to the reformed papacy was a remarkably positive and
favourable one. It was made clear by the Conqueror's admirer
and partisan, the chronicler William of Poitiers, who wrote *c.*
1073-4. He declared that the pope presided as head and master
of all the bishops of the world, and he applauded Pope Alexander
II (1061-73) for his unwavering pursuit of the way of truth:
wherever he could he corrected iniquity, yielding place to no
one (11). Such a view of the papacy, based partly upon conviction and partly upon expediency, admirably suited the Norman
book in connexion with the conquest of England, and Duke William prepared the way for his expedition by sending to Rome

---

(11) Guillaume de Poitiers, *Histoire de Guillaume le Conquérant*, ii. 3, ed. R. Foreville, Paris, 1952, pp. 152-4.

Archdeacon Gilbert of Lisieux (12). While the case which Gilbert presented there is not directly known, it probably turned upon King Harold of England's alleged perjury following his oath to support the duke's succession to the English crown upon the death of King Edward the Confessor (13). A further pretext was no doubt the schismatic character of Archbishop Stigand of Canterbury. Stigand had been given the see in 1052 after the expulsion of Archbishop Robert of Jumièges; he had received the *pallium* from the antipope Benedict X, and had probably been condemned by subsequent popes. Presented with such arguments the pope ruled that William's claim to the English crown was a just one, while Harold's usurpation was an iniquity to be avenged. As a mark of his own favour and of St. Peter's protection during the expedition he sent William the *vexillum sancti Petri* to fly at the head of his host (14).

As Duke William undertook the conquest of England with the validating sanction of papal blessing, so, in 1070, when he felt ready to proceed with the reordering of the English church, his own hand was usefully strengthened by papal authority. The king had the help of legates whom, in Orderic Vitalis' words, he welcomed, ' hearing and honouring them as angels of God ' (15). Thus legates approved his decisions during the Easter and Whitsun councils at Winchester and Windsor. They were party to the deposing of Stigand from his sees of Canterbury and Winchester, as of his brother Ethelmar from Elmham. It is clear that William had for long intended that Lanfranc should be archbishop of Canterbury and had approached Alexander II to bring his purpose to effect. On Lanfranc's own testimony it was Alexander's legates Bishop Ermenfrid of Sion and Hubert, cardinal of the Roman church, who, at a council in Normandy, commanded him by virtue of the authority of the apostolic see to obey the

---

(12) ORDERIC VITALIS, *Historia ecclesiastica*, iii, *The Ecclesiastical History of Orderic Vitalis*, ed. M. CHIBNALL, ii, Oxford, 1969, p. 142.

(13) For the prominence given to Harold's alleged perjury in the Norman justification of the Conquest, see STENTON's contribution to *The Bayeux Tapestry: a Commemorative Survey*, ed. F.M. STENTON, 2nd edn., London, 1965, pp. 9-24.

(14) Both WILLIAM of Poitiers and ORDERIC VITALIS, *ubi supra*, recorded the giving of the papal banner. For a discussion of such banners, see C. ERDMANN, *Die Entstehung des Kreuzzugsgedankens*, Stuttgart, 1935, esp. pp. 139-40, 172-3, 181-3.

(15) *Hist. eccles.*, iv, ed. CHIBNALL, ii. 236.

king's wishes (16); while Gregory later reminded Lanfranc that he owed his promotion to Canterbury to the apostolic see (17).

Archdeacon Hildebrand's leading part in the events of 1066 and 1070 cannot be doubted. In 1080, as pope, he reminded William of his debt to his zeal at the outset of his reign. At Rome Gregory had suffered great calumny from those — he probably had Cardinal Peter Damiani in mind (18) — who upbraided him for sponsoring the conquest, with its inevitable burden of homicides (19). More immediately, Norman gratitude to Gregory was registered in the cordial messages of congratulation and loyalty which both William and Lanfranc sent to him soon after he became pope, and to which he replied in like manner (20).

Papal help in his early days as king must be added to the lasting value of Gregory's commending of his kingship as a factor which always disposed William to set a high value upon papal good will and assistance.

III

The nature and the limitations of Lanfranc's obligation to the apostolic see must be separately considered, for he was, especially in the long run, less beholden to Gregory than was his royal master, and correspondingly less concerned to retain his favour. Lanfranc's much qualified indebtedness to the papacy arose partly

---

(16) LANFRANC, *Ep.* 3, to Pope Alexander II, pp. 19-20. (References to Lanfranc's letters, or to other letters printed with them, are to *Beati Lanfranci archiepiscopi Cantuariensis opera quae supersunt omnia*, i, ed. J.A. GILES, Oxford and Paris, 1844). For a fuller discussion of these events, see COWDREY, *Bishop Ermenfrid of Sion and the Penitential Ordinance following the Battle of Hastings* in: *Journal of Ecclesiastical History*, xx (1969), 225-42.

(17) Cf. LANFRANC, *Ep.* 11, to Pope Gregory VII, p. 32.

(18) For the views about war of Peter Damiani and others at Rome, see ERDMANN, *Die Entstehung des Kreuzzugsgedankens*, pp. 130-3.

(19) *Reg.*, VII, 23, 24 Apr. 1080, pp. 499-500. The bloodshed at Hastings was remembered in later anti-Gregorian polemic: *Wenrici scolastici Trevirensis epistola*, 6, ed. K. FRANCKE, *MGH, Libelli de lite*, i. 294. The reference to Bishop Ermenfrid of Sion in ALEXANDER II, *Ep.* lvi, MIGNE, *PL*, CXLVI, 1339, increases the likelihood that the Norman penitential ordinance to atone for the bloodshed was issued, under papal authority, in 1067 rather than 1070: cf. COWDREY, *art. cit.* in: *Journ. Eccles. Hist.*, xx (1969), 233, n. 6.

(20) *Reg.*, I, 70, 4 Apr. 1074, p. 101, to King William, cf. *Reg.*, I, 71, 4 Apr. 1074, pp. 102-3, to Queen Matilda; *Ep. vag.* 1, 1073, to Lanfranc (References to Gregory VII's *extravagantes* are to *The Epistolae vagantes of Pope Gregory VII*, ed. COWDREY, Oxford, 1972).

from the events of 1070 which brought him to Canterbury, but
also because as archbishop he was concerned to establish a primacy in his church which was analogous to those traditionally
associated with Sens in France or Toledo in Spain. He needed
papal co-operation in order to succeed, and within strict limits
he received it. His ambition for Canterbury had two parts,
for both of which he had to take account of Pope Gregory I's
instructions to St. Augustine of Canterbury, made generally
familiar by their inclusion in Bede's *Ecclesiastical History* (21):
papal instructions called for papal sanction if they were to be
affirmed or modified. First, Lanfranc wished to vindicate a
primatial authority over the whole of the British Isles. To such
a claim Gregory I's instructions were not unfavourable, for they
gave Augustine authority over ' all the bishops of Britain ', and
the papacy at first gave useful countenance to Lanfranc's aspiration. Alexander II described the church of Canterbury as
' metropolis totius Britanniae ' (22), while in a letter of 1073 to
Lanfranc Gregory urged him to correct certain moral offences
amongst the ' Scotti ' (i.e. Christians of either Ireland or Scotland)
in terms which implied recognition of Lanfranc's rights over
Celtic lands (23). Thus far, the papacy was serviceable to him.

Secondly, however, Lanfranc was determined to assert the
superiority of the church of Canterbury over that of York. Gregory I's instructions provided for no such superiority. They
envisaged two equipollent provinces of London and York: while
Augustine lived he should have authority over the whole British
church; but after his death the seniority of the bishops of London
and York was to be determined solely by the dates of their personal consecration. This arrangement was never effective. While
the historical circumstances of the Anglo-Saxon period left the
southern metropolis, established at Canterbury, with an im-
measurably greater prestige than that of York, their relative
standing and jurisdiction remained ill defined. Thus Lanfranc's
claim to a superiority of Canterbury over York stood out as a
novelty, for which there was insufficient historical warrant.

---

(21) BEDE's *Ecclesiastical History of the English People*, i, 29, ed. B. COLGRAVE and R.
A.B. MYNORS, Oxford, 1969, pp. 104-6.
(22) LANFRANC, *Ep.* 6, ALEXANDER II to Lanfranc, p. 27.
(23) *Ep. vag.* 1.

Nevertheless, King William intended that in England as in Normandy the ecclesiastical unity of his lands should reinforce their political unity. Lanfranc therefore sought so to assert Canterbury's authority over the whole English church that he might be able to assist the king by bringing about its thoroughgoing reform and reorganization. To the same end, although William appointed Thomas of Bayeux to be archbishop of York before Lanfranc accepted the church of Canterbury, Thomas's consecration was delayed so that Lanfranc might perform it. His consecration at Canterbury was compatible with Gregory I's instructions, but in their light it is understandable that Thomas should have demurred to giving Lanfranc the definitive profession of obedience that he demanded.

Lanfranc's later behaviour strongly suggests that, since his claim to authority over York was so weakly supported by canonical and historical precedent, he would have preferred it to be settled politically by his royal master in England before he had recourse to the papacy for the confirmation of a *fait accompli*. The difficulty was that as archbishop he must quickly receive the *pallium* from Rome. Ominously for future relations between Lanfranc and Gregory VII, there survives a letter from Archdeacon Hildebrand to Lanfranc firmly overruling his request to be excused from coming for the *pallium* in person *ad limina apostolorum* (24). So, in the event, Lanfranc of Canterbury and Thomas of York in 1071 travelled to Rome in company. Up to a point the journey was to Lanfranc's advantage. He was accorded the signal honour of receiving not only the customary *pallium* from the high altar of St. Peter's but also, from the pope's own hands, a second, personal *pallium*, such was given but seldom, and only to metropolitans of outstanding personal distinction. If it had no implications for the dispute with York it was a considerable mark of favour, and in a subsequent letter Lanfranc begged Alexander to think of him ' quod de fideli ac servo beati Petri, ac vestro sanctaeque Romanae ecclesiae ' (25). But when it came to settling the nature of his authority over York Lanfranc received less comfort from the pope: he lost nothing but neither did he gain. Thomas of York raised two issues at Rome:

---

(24) LANFRANC, *Ep.* 8, pp. 29-30.
(25) LANFRANC, *Ep.* 5, pp. 26-7.

he claimed the allegiance to York of the bishops of Lincoln, Lich-
field, and Worcester; and he asserted York's independence of
Canterbury. Alexander made no decision but remitted both
issues for settlement by an English council. They were discussed
by the king's Easter court at Winchester in 1072. Here, at
home, in large measure Lanfranc had his way.   The three disputed
dioceses were left to his authority, and the general rule was established that the archbishop of York should make a profession
of obedience to the archbishop of Canterbury — to Lanfranc
unconditionally but to his successors conditionally. At the next
assembly of the king's court, the Whitsun assembly at Windsor,
these decisions were confirmed in the presence of the papal legate
Hubert.

    After the meeting at Windsor Lanfranc applied to the papacy
for a final and permanent guarantee of his rights, of which Thomas
of York's profession, still qualified as to the future, left him in
need. He sent Alexander II a long account of the proceedings
and of his case for claiming a primacy, together with a copy of
the decisions taken, which he asked should without delay be
embodied in a papal privilege (26). To Archdeacon Hildebrand
he sent a further cordially worded covering letter asking that
his rights and those of his church should receive papal confirmation (27). Whether because of the weakness of Lanfranc's
case in particular or of his distaste for primatial claims in general, Hildebrand answered with caution, saying that in such a matter as this the apostolic see could not act unless Lanfranc once
more came to Rome in person. Hildebrand invited him to come,
so that the claims of Canterbury and other weighty matters might
be discussed and decided (28). In fact Lanfranc did not come,
and the papacy gave no decision in the matter of the primacy.
Thanks to Hildebrand's hesitation the case of York was brought
no nearer to being resolved (29).

    Thus what Lanfranc gained in the course of 1072 he secured
not from the papacy but from meetings of the Anglo-Norman

---

(26) LANFRANC, *Ep.* 5, pp. 23-7.

(27) LANFRANC, *Ep.* 7, p. 29.

(28) LANFRANC, *Ep.* 8, pp. 29-30.

(29) Although Alexander did confirm the status of Christ Church, Canterbury, as a
monastic community: LANFRANC, *Ep.* 6, pp. 27-8. For Lanfranc's dealings in 1072, see R.W.
SOUTHERN, *The Canterbury Forgeries* in: *English Historical Review*, lxxiii (1958), 193-226.

magnates and churchmen acting at the king's court and mainly under the king's authority. He could, indeed, never neglect the need to secure papal sanction for the vindication of his claims in the long term. But from 1072 his contact with the papacy became distant and cool, while his commitment to the king remained absolute. Letters from Rome suggest that there was a corresponding cooling off in papal regard for Lanfranc. When writing to the Conqueror Alexander II praised Lanfranc as ' carissimum membrum et unum ex primis Romanae ecclesiae filiis ', and in 1073 Gregory could write to him as to a close confidant (30). But thereafter all evidences of warmth disappeared from papal letters to and about him. He identified himself ever more closely with William, to whom he principally owed such primatial rights as he enjoyed. Consequently, it was upon the mutual respect, interest, and usefulness of Gregory and William, not upon any sympathy or warmth of feeling between Gregory and Lanfranc, that the maintenance of good relations between the papacy and the Anglo-Norman lands increasingly depended.

IV

Until the gathering storm of Gregory's last years his relations with William settled down to a sometimes uneasy, yet at root sufficiently well founded, balance of respect and reserve. As seen from William's point of view the character of this balance is made clear by his reaction to the requests that Gregory made of him, in respect of his English kingdom, for the performance of fealty to the pope and for the regular payment of Peter's Pence. The two requests came to a head together, in all probability during the early summer of 1080 (31). Gregory then

---

(30) LANFRANC, *Ep.* 9, p. 31: Alexander's next phrase about Lanfranc, *lateri nostro assidue non adiunctum esse dolemus*, is probably of regret that Lanfranc had not become a member of the papal *palatium*, not of rebuke because he had come too seldom to Rome; *Ep. vag.* 1.

(31) The date of Gregory's request for fealty cannot be established with certainty, but, in general, Z.N. BROOKE's arguments for the early summer of 1080, immediately after William's return from Normandy, remain highly probable despite subsequent criticism: *Pope Gregory VII's Demand for Fealty from William the Conqueror* in: *Eng. Hist. Rev.* xxvi (1911), 225-38; *The English Church and the Papacy from the Conquest to the Reign of John*, Cambridge, 1931, pp. 140-4. The date 1075-6 was unconvincingly suggested by H. TILLMANN, *Die päpstlichen Legaten in England bis zur Beendigung der Legation Gualas (1218)*, Bonn, 1926, p. 16,

dispatched as his legate to William his emissary Cardinal-sub-deacon Hubert. Hubert brought three letters to members of the royal family, all of them couched in terms of praise and solicitude for William. Following hard upon another important letter to the king of only a fortnight before, they indicate by their number and cordiality the quite exceptional importance which Gregory attached to Hubert's visit (32). He wrote to the king, giving his flattering exposition of the duties of Christian kingship in Gelasian terms (33); to Queen Matilda, praising her for her virtues; and to their eldest son, Count Robert of Normandy, rebuking him for his late rising against his father (34), and exhorting him to show him proper obedience for the future. Gregory made no reference whatsoever in writing to the purpose of Hubert's coming. His requests, brought verbally, must be inferred from William's answer to him and from a letter of Lanfranc which accompanied it (35).

The first request, which William firmly disallowed, and in favour of which Lanfranc thought it prudent to inform Gregory that he had vainly advocated before the king (36), was that William should do fealty to Gregory and to his successors. The precise terms upon which Gregory sought William's fealty do not emerge from the sources, and it is not possible with certainty to infer them by comparison with that done to the pope by other lay rulers. The means by which Gregory bound to the apostolic see those whom he attracted to its temporal obedience and service were many and various. His relations with each temporal ruler must be studied as a special case (37). Thus Gregory's

---

n. 25, and 1079 by A. FLICHE, *La Réforme grégorienne*, ii, Paris and Louvain, 1926, pp. 346-9.

(32) *Reg.*, VII, 25-7, 8 May 1080, pp. 505-8; cf. *Reg.*, VII, 23, 24 Apr. 1080, pp. 499-502.

(33) Despite BROOKE's arguments *ubi supra*, it is unnecessary to find feudal overtones in this letter. As regards the pope's duty to answer for kings before God's judgement Gregory followed Gelasius. The phrase *viventium possidere terram* was a common synonym for ' to inherit eternal life ': cf. Pss. 26.13, 51.7, 141.6. There is similarly no allusion to fealty in *Reg.*, VII, 23.

(34) Cf. ORDERIC VITALIS, *Hist. eccles.*, v, ed. A. LE PRÉVOST, ii, Paris, 1840, pp. 294-5, 377-90.

(35) LANFRANC, *Epp.* 10-11, pp. 32-3. I follow BROOKE, *ubi supra*, in holding that, in all probability, these letters belong together and relate to the request for fealty. The last two sentences of *Ep.* 11 are best taken to refer to the king's refusal of fealty in *Ep.* 10.

(36) LANFRANC, *Ep.* 11, p. 33. It was in this letter that Lanfranc so strongly resisted Gregory's summons to Rome: see below, p. 94-95.

(37) Cf. ERDMANN, *Die Entstehung des Kreuzzugsgedankens*, pp. 199-206.

request to William may have been for nothing more than the
personal fealty which he obtained a year later from Count Ber-
trand II of Provence (38).   Or it may have been for such a fealty
in respect of his lands, with the corollary that they were a papal
fief, as he received in June 1080 from the Norman Duke Robert
Guiscard for his south-Italian possessions (39).   William's firm
tone in reply perhaps suggests the second alternative; though the
verbal nature of Gregory's approach may indicate that Hubert
was sent to sound out by negotiation upon what terms, if any,
William might do fealty.   But beyond the bare fact that fealty
was requested it is impossible to penetrate.   Nor does it clearly
emerge upon what grounds Gregory based his claim.   If, as is
possible, Gregory invoked the ' Donation of Constantine ' the
sources give no hint of it.   The simultaneous request for Peter's
Pence may indicate that he deemed it to imply a debt of fealty,
but the history of Peter's Pence provides scant warrant for this (40).
It is most probable that he invoked the circumstances of the
conquest of England in 1066.   The conferring of the *vexillum
sancti Petri* need not of itself have implied a claim to the Conqueror's personal fealty, still less to superiority over his English
kingdom as a papal fief (41).   But William of Malmesbury spoke
of his receiving the papal banner ' in omen regni ' (42); the
chronicler may thus have regarded it not only as a promise of
blessing and victory but also as a symbol of investiture (43).
The poet Wace suggested in even stronger terms that papal
sponsorship of the Conquest constituted England a papal fief (44).

---

(38) *Reg.*, ix, 12*a*, 25 Aug. 1081, p. 590.

(39) *Reg.*, VIII, 1*a-c*, 6 June 1080, pp. 515-7.   But these texts must be read in the
light of the treaty of Melfi (1059).

(40) The strongest evidence is ALEXANDER II's fragmentary *Ep.* cxxxix, MIGNE, *PL*,
CXLVI, 1413.   But despite the argument of BROOKE, *The English Church and the Papacy*,
p. 141, the term *fidelis* and the phrase *sub apostolorum principis manu et tutela* cannot be ascribed
feudal overtones unless there is explicit reason.

(41) Cf. ERDMANN, *Die Entstehung des Kreuzzugsgedankens*, pp. 166-84.

(42) *De gestis regum Anglorum*, iii. 238, ed. W. STUBBS, ii, London: Rolls Series, 1889,
p. 299.

(43) For banners as symbols of investiture, see ERDMANN, *Kaiserfahne und Blutfahne*
in: *Sitzungsberichte der preussischen Akademie der Wissenschaften*, ph.-hist. Kl., xxviii, Berlin,
1932, pp. 885-9.

(44) Wace wrote that William was to hold England of God and St. Peter, and that
he received from the pope a ring as well as a banner to show his dependence: *Roman de Rou*,
11446-59, *Le Roman de Rou et des ducs de Normandie*, ed. F. PLUQUET, Rouen, 1827, ii. 140.

Yet these twelfth-century sources are not confirmed in this matter by their eleventh-century predecessors, and their evidence
is insufficient to support more than the most tentative suggestion.
That Gregory requested fealty and that William firmly refused
it are facts beyond question.   But the terms of Gregory's request
and his grounds for advancing it are altogether uncertain.

The conciliatory tone of Gregory's letters during the early
1080s shows that he accepted with a good grace William's firm,
diplomatic, and dignified refusal. This is readily explicable.
Gregory had a high regard for William as a reforming king (45).
In Spain at about the same time he was ready to drop his much
more strongly stated claims to feudal superiority over the Spanish
kingdoms when another strong ruler, King Alphonso VI of León-
Castile, vigorously championed reform (46).   Again Gregory would
not lightly have risked damaging his concurrent negotiations
with the Normans of southern Italy by quarrelling over fealty
with the Norman king of England. Above all, William fully
and with a good grace met Gregory's second request, for the
due and regular payment of Peter's Pence.

By the eleventh century Peter's Pence was an ancient custom
whose origins were, and remain, obscure (47).   But the pope
regarded it as an annual tribute from the English king to which
he had a right: part of it he should retain, and part should be
appropriated to the Roman church of Santa Maria *in schola Anglorum* (48).   The mid-eleventh-century papacy was much concerned
to assert its claim to such tributes.   Thus, Alexander II called
upon the king of Denmark to pay a *census* which was broadly
similar to the English tribute (49); while Gregory VII tried to
revive the many *census* which were owed to the papacy by French
monasteries enjoying its protection (50), and an annual payment
of at least a penny from each household which he believed to
have been sanctioned by Charlemagne (51).   Gregory's concern

---

(45) E.g. *Reg.*, IX, 5, to Bishops Hugh of Die and Amatus of Oléron, 1081, pp. 579-60.

(46) See COWDREY, *The Cluniacs and the Gregorian Reform*, Oxford, 1970, pp. 221-44.

(47) The fullest study is P. FABRE, *Étude sur le Liber censuum de l'Église romaine*, Paris, 1892, pp. 129-46.

(48) ALEXANDER II, *Ep.* cxxxix, MIGNE, *PL*, CXLVI, 1413.

(49) *Ep.* vi, MIGNE, *PL*, CXLVI, 1283.

(50) *Ep. vag.* 12, 1075.

(51) *Reg.*, VIII, 23, 1081-4, pp. 566-7.

for all St. Peter's dues from England was evident as early as 1074, when he asked King William to oversee St. Peter's rights and revenues in England no less carefully than he did his own (52). In 1080 the king replied to Gregory's verbal request about Peter's Pence by apologizing that the money which his predecessors had been wont to send to the Roman church had been negligently collected during his three years' absence in Normandy; what had already been collected he was sending by Hubert, while the remainder would be dispatched as soon as possible by Lanfranc's messengers (53).

William thus admitted his liability to pay Peter's Pence, and he also declared himself to be well disposed towards the apostolic see: 'Pray for us', his letter to Gregory ended, 'and for the state of our kingdom, for we loved your predecessors, and we are disposed to love you sincerely and to honour you obediently before all men'. The greeting with which the letter began expressed William's amity in a no less remarkable way: 'salutem cum amicitia'. In the light of the letter as a whole and of the refusal of fealty the word *amicitia* has the appearance of being carefully chosen. It carried diplomatic overtones, which went back to classical Roman times, of mutually respected sovereignty, of a common commitment to peace and protection, and of friendly political collaboration. William was skilfully conveying to Gregory that in his eyes the temporal relation of the pope and the English king was not that of lord and vassal, however defined, but that of an *amicitia* which joined two great and feudally independent rulers. In fact he used a word which was Gregory's own: it was not of common occurrence in his letters, but he had himself used it of his relationship with William (54); and in his last letter to William he would again speak of the *amicitia* which had for so long retained them in mutual affection and service (55).

In the light of such a use of the word by both sides the relation which was established between pope and king may best

---

(52) *Reg.*, I, 70, 4 Apr. 1074, p. 102.

(53) LANFRANC, *Ep.* 10, p. 32. Lanfranc duly saw to the collection of Peter's Pence in his own diocese: see *The Domesday Monachorum of Christ Church, Canterbury*, London, 1944, p. 80.

(54) *Reg.*, VII, 1, to Cardinal-subdeacon Hubert, 23 Sept. 1079, p. 459.

(55) *Reg.*, IX, 37, 1083, p. 630.

be understood as an *amicitia* which, from William's side, had
its willing pledge in the payment of Peter's Pence, but which
did not admit of fealty with its implication that the king was
not in the fullest sense lord in his own land. It was upon such
a basis that the balance of relations between Gregory and William was for long maintained.

V

Now that the balance of the political relationship between
Gregory and the Anglo-Norman kingdom has been thus determined, it is possible to place in perspective the respects in which
it was most obviously threatened. They arose from Gregory's
claims to the active obedience of the archbishops of Canterbury
and Rouen, and to the paying of regular visits to Rome by the
other English and Norman bishops.

Archbishop Lanfranc of Canterbury became, in this connexion, particularly recalcitrant. It is a measure of his dedication
to the king's interests in England, both ecclesiastical and secular,
that, after his visit to Rome in 1071 to receive the *pallium* and
apart from a journey to Normandy in 1077 to attend the consecration of his former abbey of St. Stephen's, Caen, and other
Norman churches, he seems never after he became archbishop
to have left English shores; even in 1071 he had gone to Rome
with reluctance and only upon Archdeacon Hildebrand's pressing
insistence (56). Again, Lanfranc's canonical collection was based
upon the False Decretals and so contained many texts which
emphasized papal authority. But it is well known that in his
use of it he drew attention to the rights rather than to the duties
of metropolitans, and set little store by the active authority of
the pope (57). He therefore needed no restraint by the king
upon the several occasions when Gregory called on him to visit
Rome. Gregory's first summons of which record survives was
in a letter of March 1079 (58). Gregory rebuked him for his
negligence in not visiting Rome since he became pope. He put
it down partly to Lanfranc's fear of William, but still more to

---

(56) LANFRANC, *Ep.* 8, pp. 29-30.

(57) See BROOKE, *The English Church and the Papacy*, pp. 57-73, esp. 71-2.

(58) *Reg.*, VI, 30, 25 Mar. 1079, pp. 443-4.

his own fault. Gregory made clear the possibility of a crisis: if the king were indeed hindering the bishops from coming to Rome he might well provoke sanctions against himself. Lanfranc could forestall these sanctions by urging the king to behave with justice towards the church and by himself obeying Gregory's wishes and reiterated commands that he should visit Rome.

Gregory's demand that Lanfranc should pay a visit *ad limina* was evidently renewed in a further letter, now lost, which he sent by his legate Hubert when he came to England in 1080 to seek the king's fealty. The year of the second excommunication of Henry IV was not a juncture at which Gregory could with prudence have revived his threat to the Norman king. Lanfranc's own answer survives (59), and in it he seized his opportunity, while Gregory was urgently seeking the favour of the English kingdom, to deprecate the pope's insistence upon the regular visits of archbishops to Rome. In terms which verged upon the contumacious Lanfranc declared that he could not understand what such facts as his prolonged absence or distance from Rome, or even an argument based upon the duties of his high office, had to do with the question of an archbishop's reverence for the apostolic see. So far as the canons required it of him Lanfranc protested that he showed obedience to Gregory's commands. If he should ever come to Rome he would certainly show Gregory, by deeds rather than by words, that his own early love for Gregory had increased: it was Gregory's love for him which had grown cooler.

Gregory does not seem to have replied immediately. But probably in the early summer of 1082 he once more approached Lanfranc in the most peremptory terms (60). He reminded him how often he had called upon him to prove his loyalty and Christian duty by coming to Rome. Whether from his own pride or from his negligence (significantly, Gregory no longer blamed the king) Lanfranc had so far abused Gregory's patience by failing to do so. Excuses based on the labour and difficulty of the journey were inadmissible; Lanfrance must prove his obedience by coming to Rome before the next All Saints' Tide. Should he fail to appear he would be suspended from all his episcopal functions.

---

(59) Lanfranc, *Ep.* 11, pp. 32-3.

(60) *Reg.*, IX, 20, May-June 1082, pp. 600-1.

The upshot of this letter is not known, but there is no reason to think that Lanfranc ever set out for Rome. Equally there is no indication that Gregory implemented his threat. In view of his need for King William's favour and aid in face of Henry IV's ever increasing hostility it is more than unlikely that he ventured to do so. When it came to the issue the balance of their good relations was too important for it to be put in jeopardy.

With the archbishops of Rouen Gregory's dealings were more stringent, but they were less continuous; and it is impossible to detect positive signs that they at any time seriously threatened his understanding with the king: the archbishops of Normandy had neither Lanfranc's personal stature nor his key political position, and therefore Gregory's dealings with them were of less consequence for William. During the early years of Gregory's pontificate the archbishop of Rouen was John II, an able and reforming if a conservative prelate. In 1067 he had been translated from Avranches, a proceeding for which William I with canonical propriety sought papal approval through Bishop Ermenfrid of Sion and Abbot Lanfranc of Caen (61). Nothing emerges about Gregory's dealings with him up to 1078. Then Gregory wrote to King William about a chronic paralysis which Gregory understood to have incapacitated him for his duties (62). Gregory spoke to the king of the care which the pope owed to churches which were widowed of their pastors. He sent his legate Hubert to investigate the gravity of John's sickness: if he were incapable of ruling but lucid in mind he should be pressed to resign; if he were not lucid a competent successor should be canonically elected.

When mentioning a canonical election Gregory made no reference to the king's interest in it, whether by recognizing or by excluding his rights; and he cannot have expected that William would brook any infringement of them, when all the sees of Normandy and of England had been for so long at his disposal. But he stimulated William to act, and Norman tradition remembered that papal intervention had been important (63). Thus,

---

(61) ALEXANDER II, *Ep.* lvi, MIGNE, *PL*, CXLVI, 1339.

(62) *Reg.*, V, 19, 4 Apr. 1078, pp. 382-3.

(63) William was enthroned *cum apostolica auctoritate, tum regio munere, tum denique communi electione*: *Acta Rotomagensium archiepiscopum*, MIGNE, *PL*, CXLVI, 280.

before John died on 9 September 1079, William appointed as his successor William Bona Anima, a son of Bishop Radbod of Séez (64) who had replaced Lanfranc as abbot of St. Stephen's, Caen. Gregory made no objection of which there is record to the fact of royal nomination; but he found William Bona Anima to be personally of questionable suitability. He wrote to his legate Hubert that he had heard him to be the son of a priest: if this were true he would never assent to his promotion (65). Possibly the messengers whom the king sent to Rome early in 1080 quietened Gregory's anxieties on this score (66), for no crisis between king and pope ensued. But so far as the archbishop himself was concerned Gregory quickly raised the issue of his visiting Rome. Probably in 1081 Gregory rebuked him because, although he had written a letter professing his love for Gregory, he had failed to come to Rome or receive his *pallium*. Gregory forthwith imposed upon him the sanction with which he was later to threaten Lanfranc: he suspended him from his episcopal functions until he had obtained his *pallium* at Rome (67). There is no evidence about King William's reaction, but there is no reason to suppose that it was a strong one, or that good relations with Rome were jeopardized.

In two other ways the years following 1079 saw Gregory putting pressure upon the Anglo-Norman lands to secure the greater obedience of the bishops to Rome and to the pope's local agents. First, Gregory was concerned to secure the bishops' attendance at his councils and upon less formal visits. In the late 1070s he believed that King William was deliberately obstructing the coming to Rome of English bishops (68). In September 1079 he went so far as to instruct his legate Hubert to summon at least two bishops from each of the three Anglo-Norman provinces to attend his Lent council of 1080, or at least to come to the apostolic see by the following Easter (69). It is clear that no Norman bishop, at least, came. For Gregory's letter of cen-

---

(64) Orderic Vitalis, *Hist. Eccles.*, iv, ed. Chibnall, ii. 254.

(65) *Reg.*, VII, 1, 23 Sept. 1079, p. 459.

(66) *Reg.*, VII, 23, 24 Apr. 1080, p. 501. Bishop Radbod is said to have been a widower when he was ordained.

(67) *Reg.*, IX, 1, 1081, pp. 568-9.

(68) *Reg.*, VI, 30, 25 Mar. 1079, p. 443.

(69) *Reg.*, VII, 1, 23 Sept. 1079, p. 460.

sure in 1081 to Archbishop William Bona Anima of Rouen condemned his suffragans, as well as himself, for their failure to
visit Rome. Since becoming pope Gregory could not recall having seen any of them. He insisted that the archbishop's suffragans, too, must look to their duty, unless they wished to be
visited with the severest censures (70).

Secondly, Gregory put into effect a more thoroughgoing
plan to draw the province of Rouen more decisively into the
orbit of the reformed papacy. In 1079 he established in favour
of Archbishop Gebuin of Lyons a primacy over the four provinces
of Lyons, Rouen, Tours, and Sens, which made up the ancient
Roman imperial province of Gallia Lugdunensis (71). There is
no evidence that Gregory consulted William I, as duke of Normandy, before he initiated so sweeping a change in the ecclesiastical position of his Norman lands. Nor is it known whether William in any way reacted to the *fait accompli*. But as
events developed Gregory's plan had little effect. Gebuin, who
later in 1079 fell deeply into disgrace with Gregory for his measures
against the liberty of Cluny (72), for his part seems seldom to
have interfered in affairs outside the province of Lyons. Gregory's standing legates, Bishops Hugh of Die and Amatus of
Oléron, remained his normal agents. When, in 1082, Hugh of
Die succeeded Gebuin as archbishop of Lyons, the primacy of
Lyons became swallowed up in his office as standing legate (73).
Thus the primacy never became, in itself, a grave issue so far
as William was concerned.

It is furthermore of the utmost significance for understanding
William's patience in face of Gregory's demands upon the Anglo-
Norman clergy that, upon the one occasion when Gebuin as primate did trench upon William's Norman interests, Gregory made
a decisive intervention against him upon the king's behalf. One
of the most sensitive regions in William's lands was the county
of Maine, which, lying between Normandy and the hostile county

---

(70) *Reg.*, IX, 1, pp. 568-9.

(71) *Reg.*, VI, 34-5, 20 Apr. 1079, pp. 447-52. Gregory was careful to assert and reserve the rights of the apostolic see.

(72) See COWDREY, *The Cluniacs and the Gregorian Reform*, pp. 51-5.

(73) See the discussion by FLICHE, *La Réforme grégorienne*, ii. 229-31, and the documents in *Recueil des historiens des Gaules et de la France*, ed. M. BOUQUET (= *RHF*), xiv.
667-74.

of Anjou, had been in his hands since 1063. In 1073 there was a revolt in Maine and William was forced to reconquer it. As early as the spring of that year, according to Orderic Vitalis ' quidam Romanae ecclesiae cardinalis presbyter ' to William's advantage helped to compose peace in Maine (74). Thereafter two of William's principal supporters in the county were Bishop Arnald of le Mans and Abbot Juhel of Saint-Pierre de la Couture. The king gave la Couture to Juhel after expelling his predecessor, Reginald, on account of his Angevin sympathies. In spite of allegations by Reginald's partisans that the king thereby openly defied Gregory's prohibition of lay investiture, Bishop Arnald supported William and performed Juhel's consecration as abbot (75). Soon after Archbishop Gebuin of Lyons received his primacy he made it clear in a letter which he wrote to the bishops of the province of Tours that the Angevin bishops had sent Reginald to him, and that Gebuin had strongly condemned King William's high-handed intervention at la Couture. Gebuin described Reginald as ' a rege Anglorum quinquennio cruciatum ', adding that he had taken him to Rome where Gregory had favoured his case. Gebuin therefore now laid down that Juhel should be expelled from la Couture ' sicut maledictus adulter ' and his supporters excommunicated; that la Couture should be placed under interdict until Reginald was restored; and that Bishop Arnald, as Juhel's consecrator, should be suspended from his episcopal office (76). Bishop Amatus of Oléron in all likelihood afterwards confirmed Gebuin's proceedings (77). The turn which events had taken posed a threat to William's whole position in Maine. His reaction was to make a direct approach to Gregory, for the situation at le Mans was a principal concern of an embassy which William sent to him early in 1080. With surprising

---

(74) ORDERIC VITALIS, *Hist. eccles.*, iv, ed. CHIBNALL, ii. 309-10.

(75) Letter of Archbishop RALPH of Tours to Bishop Arnald of le Mans, *RHF*, xiv. 667-8, no. 1. Ralph's anxiety to persuade Arnald to do justice quickly and quietly on behalf of Abbot Reginald and to forestall his recourse to Rome is significant: Ralph perhaps anticipated that Gregory might take the Norman side. As regards the investiture decree, it was consistent with Gregory's moderation towards William that he neither pressed it upon Normandy nor promulgated it in England.

(76) *RHF*, xiv. 668-9, no. 3.

(77) *Reg.*, VII, 22, to Bishop Arnald of le Mans, 24 Apr. 1080, p. 499; cf. *RHF*, xiv. 671-2, no. 9. Gregory did not name the legate, but the fact that in 1081 Amatus still refused to have dealings with Juhel suggests that he had suspended him: *Reg.*, IX, 5, pp. 579-80.

completeness in view of William's high-handed actions at le Mans in 1074 Gregory at once vindicated his interests. In the name of righteousness (*iustitia dictante*) he restored William's partisan, Bishop Arnald, to the exercise of his office, expelled Reginald from la Couture as an intruder and a perjurer, and instructed Arnald to restore Juhel to his abbacy (78). Gregory for long persisted in his solicitude for William: in 1082, following Arnald's death in November 1081, he wrote to Archbishop Ralph of Tours asking him to carry out the consecration of a successor, Hoel, whom Arnald had favoured but whom Count Fulk of Anjou was strenuously resisting (79).

There is no mistaking the care with which Gregory safeguarded William's political interests. Gregory's restraint over the affairs of le Mans and his support for the king's interests in Maine do much to explain why William did not more actively resist his demands upon Lanfranc and the Anglo-Norman episcopate at large, and why his refusal of fealty to the pope should have been tempered by a profession of friendship. For William political considerations were paramount. To secure them he would go far in tolerating even Gregory's direct threats against the episcopate, so long as the pope did not actually proceed to ultimate sanctions. Gregory, for his part, was unlikely to do so, if the cost were that of alienating a ruler whose friendship he had good reasons, of both an ecclesiastical and a political character, especially to cherish.

VI

Such an understanding and tendency towards collaboration between pope and king are apparent in Gregory's other dealings with William's lands.

It is perhaps surprising to find that this is first of all true of matters which involved papal legates. For it might be anticipated that Gregory's innovation of standing legates would lead to friction over Norman affairs, when from 1076 onwards the zealous and extreme Gregorians Bishops Hugh of Die and Amatus of Oléron began to have a place in Norman history.

---

(78) *Reg.*, VII, 22-3, 24 Apr. 1080, pp. 499-502.
(79) *Ep. vag.* 48.

It was perhaps amongst the bishops that they encountered the greatest hostility, for when rebuking Archbishop William Bona Anima, Gregory suggested that he had gone out of his way to avoid them (80). But Hugh of Die, at least, found a friend in the duchy who was also in touch with the king. In letters which may well date from before Gregory's death Anselm of Bec already began the warm and confidential correspondence with Hugh which was to be so important to them both in later years (81).

Gregory for his part showed conspicuous concern to use his standing legates in such a way as to preserve his understanding with William. This clearly emerges in their dealings with the church of Dol, in the north-eastern corner of Brittany. Like Maine, it was politically a critical area for William, who had for long guarded against dangers which might arise from a turbulent region so near to his duchy; and he found a principal ally in Archbishop Juhel of Dol.

In 1076 one of William's Breton followers, Ralph de Gael, whom he had made earl of Norfolk but who had lately rebelled against him, established himself at Dol, to which William therefore laid siege. Ralph de Gael's supporters sent to Rome asking for a new archbishop to be appointed. It was strongly in their favour that Archbishop Juhel was a man of utterly scandalous life. Gregory prudently disallowed the Bretons' own nominee, but he himself chose and consecrated a politically neutral figure who might have been acceptable to William, Ivo (Evenus), abbot of Saint-Melaine, Rennes, to replace Juhel (82). Gregory sought to use King William's presence at Dol to secure his aid in getting rid of a married and simoniac prelate of whom he, too, might be expected at heart to disapprove (83). Before the king can have received Gregory's letter he suffered a severe defeat at the hand of King Philip of France, and was compelled to abandon his siege of Dol. But Gregory persisted in his attempts at reform. Still seeking at once to get rid of Juhel and to conciliate

---

(80) *Reg.*, IX, 1, 1081, pp. 568-9. The legates were not named, but Hugh and Amatus were in northern France.

(81) *Epp.* 100, 109, iii. 231-2, 241-2. (References to St. Anselm's letters are to *S. Anselmi Cantuariensis archiepiscopi opera omnia*, ed. F.S. Schmitt, iii-v, Edinburgh, 1946-51).

(82) *Reg.*, IV, 4-5, 27 Sept. 1076, pp. 300-3.

(83) *Ep. vag.* 16.

William, he employed his legates to further both objectives. In March 1077, replying to a lost letter from William, he held fast to his nomination of Ivo as archbishop. But he also undertook to send Hugh of Die to Dol: together with the legate Hubert and a monk called Teuzo, Hugh was to conduct an inquiry locally and satisfy William of the justice of what Gregory had done (84). Next year Gregory wrote to Hubert and Teuzo, relating how Juhel's continuing contumacy had brought Hugh of Die and Ivo of Dol to Rome. He remitted the whole problem of the church of Dol for Hugh to settle at the council of Lyons (1080), to which the king of England was to be invited to send envoys in order to be satisfied about the justice of the proceedings (85). Juhel's death in 1081 fairly soon afterwards relieved the matter. Until it occurred the significant point is that Gregory should have sought so to use Hugh of Die as to satisfy William of the justice of his proceedings, although William had for political reasons supported a grossly unsatisfactory archbishop, and although he had lost the military power in the region which would have enabled him to interfere.

In other connexions involving the standing legates Gregory was consistently yet more deferential to William. If Amatus of Oléron indeed injudiciously confirmed Gebuin of Lyon's sentence against William's partisans in Maine, Gregory was swift to reverse it (86). Again, probably in 1081, Gregory wrote a most revealing letter to Hugh of Die and Amatus of Oléron concerning their hasty action in reportedly suspending almost all the upper clergy of Normandy for failure to attend a council, probably the council which the legates held at Saintes on 8 January 1081 (87). Gregory was at great pains to exculpate the Norman bishops, saying that, as he had heard, their absence was not from disobedience but from fear of King Philip of France. (The bishops would have had to cross Poitou in order to obey a summons to the Saintogne). Gregory cautioned his two legates to proceed with proper moderation whenever William's interests

---

(84) *Reg.*, IV, 17, 31 Mar. 1077, pp. 322-3.

(85) *Reg.*, V, 22-3, 22 May 1078, pp. 385-8.

(86) *Reg.*, VII, 22, 24 Apr. 1080, p. 499.

(87) *Reg.*, IX, 5, pp. 579-80. The exceptions were Archbishop William of Rouen and Abbot Juhel of la Couture. Probably William was bound by Gregory's sentence in *Reg.*, IX, 1, while Amatus deemed his sentence against Juhel to be still in force.

were involved. If the king did not always behave as Gregory would have wished, he was a reforming monarch who showed himself more worthy of honour and approval than other kings. The legates were accordingly instructed to use Gregory's messenger at once to carry letters revoking their over-hasty suspension of the Norman churchmen, including the abbot of la Couture. They were not again without Gregory's own approval to offer any such provocation to the king.

The keynote of Gregory's dealings with his standing legates in relation to William was thus conciliation. His employment of temporary legates also tended, on balance, to keep communications between the apostolic see and the Norman lands open and based upon mutual understanding. Heinrich Böhmer wrote that between 1073 and 1080 it is probable that no papal legate entered England (88). As a bare statement of fact this can hardly be denied. But an exaggerated interpretation should not be placed upon it. There is no reason to suppose that William resisted the coming of legates so long as their activities did not challenge his own authority, and his own debt to papal legates during the four years following the conquest of England has already been noticed. Moreover the king was often in Normandy, and there, after 1073, the coming of papal legates was by no means unknown, and it served the king's ends as well as the pope's. This was the case in regard to Maine, and in 1074 Gregory sent two legates, named Peter and John Minutus, in connexion with William's arrangements to complete the foundation of the abbey of St. Stephen's, Caen (89). Later on, Gregory's principal contact with Anglo-Norman affairs was through the Roman cardinal Hubert, who had already come to William's lands in 1070 and 1072. Hubert's activities, so far as they concerned William, included three further visits. In 1077, when Gregory commissioned him with regard to the church of Dol, he also gave him important verbal instructions: 'Because we have sent Hubert to you', Gregory wrote to the king, 'there are many matters about which we have no need to write, for in all matters which he transmits to you upon our behalf he is

---

(88) *Kirche und Staat in England und in der Normandie im XI. und XII. Jahrhundert*, Leipzig, 1899, p. 131.

(89) *Reg.*, I, 70, 4 Apr. 1074, p. 102.

himself as it were an authentic letter of ours which faithfully embodies our words ' (90). There is no means of knowing what this business was, but in the spring of 1078 Gregory sent Hubert upon a second visit to investigate the sickness of Archbishop John II of Rouen (91), and further, with the monk Teuzo, to take part in composing the affairs of Dol (92). Hubert in the event remained in north-western France until the autumn of 1079, when Gregory rebuked him for staying so long. He may have used the pretext of collecting Peter's Pence in England (93). But it is more likely that, exceeding Gregory's instructions, he had concerned himself overmuch with Flemish affairs and had delegated his dealings with William to Teuzo, who in his turn had dealt more sharply with the king than Gregory approved (94). Hubert duly returned to Rome and thirdly, in the spring of 1080 he was sent back to England, probably bearing the verbal requests for an oath of fealty and for the regular payment of Peter's Pence (95), as well as messages for the queen (96). Hubert duly collected a sum of money by way of Peter's Pence, but he died at Bec before he could return to Rome (97).

Gregory supplemented his legatine contacts with the Anglo-Norman kingdom by the sending of letters. The number of them to survive is small, but it is sufficient to suggest that in practice Gregory was able to approach churchmen directly about matters which came to his notice, and that his letters did not incite the king to anger. Some of these letters have already

---

(90) *Reg.*, IV, 17, 31 Mar. 1077, p. 323.

(91) *Reg.*, V, 19, 4 Apr. 1078, pp. 382-3.

(92) *Reg.*, V, 22, 22 May 1078, p. 386.

(93) *Reg.*, VII, 1, 23 Sept. 1079, p. 459: ' Nam pecunias sine honore tributas, quanti pretii habeam, tu ipse optime potuisti dudum perpendere '. ERDMANN here saw a reference to Peter's Pence: *Die Entstehung des Kreuzzugsgedankens*, p. 142, n. 38. But he also referred to a pseudo-Augustinian canon preserved in ANSELM of Lucca's *Collectio canonum*. Gregory probably used it metaphorically, not literally, for his letters suggest that Hubert had been in Flanders, not England, and that he had incurred his disapproval there: *Reg.*, VI, 7, to Bishop Hugh of Die, 25 Nov. 1078, pp. 407-8; *Reg.*, VII, 1, pp. 459-60.

(94) *Reg.*, VII, 1.

(95) *Reg.*, VII, 23, 24 Apr. 1080, pp. 499-502; *Reg.*, VII, 25, 8 May 1080, pp. 505-7; LANFRANC, *Epp.* 10-11, pp. 32-3.

(96) *Reg.*, VII, 26, 8 May 1080, p. 507.

(97) ANSELM, *Ep.* 125, iii. 265-6; for Hubert's earlier acquaintance with Anselm, cf. *Ep. vag.* 34.

been discussed. In addition, Gregory wrote to Lanfranc in November 1073, urging him to restrain Bishop Herfast of Elmham from violating the rights of Abbot Baldwin of Bury St. Edmunds, whose abbey Pope Alexander II had taken into papal protection. Lanfranc was to seek the king's good will for the abbot's case; if the bishop were recalcitrant he and the abbot should visit Rome together for Gregory to settle their dispute (98). A month later Gregory wrote a letter of advice to Bishop Remigius of Lincoln about his future dealings with a priest who had committed homicide, and whom Remigius had referred to Gregory at Rome (99). Amongst Gregory's *extravagantes* there is also a letter of *c.* 1079 to Anselm of Bec in which Gregory sought his prayers and called upon him to remedy a complaint which a pilgrim had laid at Rome against one of his monks (100). Lanfranc's letters yield a case of a woman securing from Rome a papal letter to Lanfranc ordering him to hear a dispute which she had with Bishop Stigand of Chichester (101). The decrees of Gregory's Lent and November councils may also have found some currency in England. Apart from the decrees of the Lent council of 1079 concerning Berengar of Tours, in which Lanfranc had a particular interest, certain decrees of the November council of the same year survive, in late eleventh-century hands, having been copied into a tenth-century MS. of Penitentials which has strong connexions with Exeter (102). All this evidence suggests that Gregory in practice enjoyed a reasonable freedom to communicate with Anglo-Norman churchmen.

Upon at least one occasion King William was himself not unwilling to seek Gregory's help in a matter concerning the English church. After he had been appointed bishop of Durham in 1080, William of St. Carilef wished to institute a monastic chapter

---

(98) *Reg.*, I, 31, 20 Nov. 1073, pp. 51-2. LANFRANC in a letter reproved Herfast for his lax ways, but did not allude in it to Gregory's letter: *Ep.* 26, pp. 47-8.

(99) *Reg.*, I, 34, 2 Dec. 1073, p. 55.

(100) *Ep. vag.* 34.

(101) *Ep.* 31, p. 51. Since Stigand's dates as bishop were 1070-87 the letter might date from the last years of Alexander II.

(102) Oxford, Bodleian Library, MS. Bodley 718 (2632). The decrees, which are accompanied by a small amount of other canonical material, are as follows: fo. vi^v: *Reg.*, VI, 5b, nos. (11), (7), (8), on pp. 404-5; fo. vii^v: *ibid.*, nos. (1), (3), (9), on pp. 402-5; fo. 180^r (in a different hand): *ibid.*, no. (10), on p. 405.

in his cathedral, thereby reviving the usage of St. Cuthbert's time. At the king's bidding he went to Rome and informed Gregory of the past and present state of the church of Durham. He returned from Rome bearing Gregory's command and authority to restore the monastic life in his cathedral, and in 1083 he successfully did so (103).

In the light of the strong and mutual current of collaboration which prevailed between pope and king in all the matters which have been reviewed, the most satisfactory appreciation of Gregory's attitude to William is the one which he himself made in 1081, not to the king nor to any of his family or supporters, but to his own standing legates Hugh of Die and Amatus of Oléron (104). Gregory granted that in some respects William did not conduct himself with such scrupulous obedience (*ita religiose*) as he himself would have wished. But in several ways he showed himself more worthy of honour and approval than other kings (*ceteris regibus se satis probabiliorem et magis honorandum ostendit*). He neither destroyed nor sold the churches of God (105). He strove to provide peace and righteousness for his subjects. When ' certain enemies of the cross of Christ ' had incited him against the apostolic see he had had no dealings with them (106). Moreover he had caused priests to abandon their wives, and

---

(103) *De iniusta vexatione Willelmi episcopi primi*, 1, in *The Historical Works of Simeon of Durham*, i, ed. T. ARNOLD, London: Rolls Series, 1882, pp. 170-1. For the text and history of a later, spurious privilege of Gregory for the church of Durham, see *Quellen und Forschungen zum Urkunden- und Kanzleiwesen Papst Gregors VII.*, 1 Teil, Quellen: Urkunden. Regesten. *Facsimilia* , ed. L. SANTIFALLER, Vatican City: Studi e Testi, 190, 1957, no. +210, pp. 247-50.

(104) *Reg.*, IX, 5, pp. 579-80. Such an estimate of William was current elsewhere in Gregorian circles on the continent: cf. BERNOLD, *Chronicon, a.* 1084, *MGH, Scr.*, v. 439.

(105) Cf. ALEXANDER II, *Ep.* lxxxiii, MIGNE, *PL*, CXLVI, 1365-6; *Reg.*, V, 19, 4 Apr. 1078, p. 382.

(106) The precise matter referred to is not clear. Before the Norman Conquest of 1066 William had made a pact of *amicitia* with the young Henry IV: WILLIAM of Poitiers, *Hist. de Guillaume le Conq.*, ii. 3, ed. FOREVILLE, p. 154. But the Saxon chronicler BRUNO recorded that William made the excuse that his newly conquered kingdom was too insecure for him to leave when Henry sought his help against the Saxons in the rising of 1073-5: *Saxonicum bellum*, 36, ed. E. LOHMANN and F.-J. SCHMALE, *Ausgewählte Quellen zur deutschen Geschichte des Mittelalters*, ed. R. BUCHNER, xii, Berlin, 1963, p. 242. LAMPERT of Hersfeld spoke of a rumour in 1074 that William might come to the help of Archbishop Anno of Cologne against the German king: *Annales, a.* 1074, ed. O. HOLDER-EGGER and W.D. FRITZ, *Ausgewählte Quellen*, ed. BUCHNER, xiii, Berlin, n.d., p. 252. Gregory may have remembered such reports of William's attitude to Henry, or there may have been later approaches by Henry's party.

laymen to give up tithes that they unjustly held (107).   Towards
a ruler who was thus far a conscientious reformer — and, it might
have been added, who was of exemplary marital chastity —
Gregory counselled compromise and forbearance:

> It should not be deemed improper that his authority
> should be somewhat mildly dealt with and that, hav-
> ing regard to his own worthiness, the faults of his
> subjects and those whom he loves should be in some
> measure tolerated. ... It seems to us that he can much
> better and more easily be won for God and attracted
> to an unwavering love of St. Peter by amicable mild-
> ness and a show of reason than by the severity and
> rigour of righteousness.

This letter is an epitome of Gregory's dealings with the Anglo-
Norman kingdom.   What is notable about them is not so much
the very real strains and stresses which were never far below
the surface, as the deeper undercurrents of collaboration and
mutual understanding, though not the identity of purpose, which
held pope and king together.   As William appreciated the value
of papal sanction for his kingship, so Gregory appreciated the
worth of the strongest and most reforming of the peripheral
states of Latin Christendom as a counterweight to the hostile
ruler of the Empire and the intractable French king.   To drive
William into alliance with either of them would have been a
grave setback; to have his friendship was politically an incal-
culable asset, and by its means the reform of the Anglo-Norman
church was being effectively promoted, albeit in something less
than a fully Gregorian way.

VII

During the troubles that increasingly beset Gregory in the
1080s, he for his part was more than ever concerned to secure
whatever aid was possible from the Norman lands of the north,

---

(107) As is well known Lanfranc's policy fell short of Gregory's requirements regarding
clerical celibacy in that, while enforcing the celibacy of the newly ordained, he did not require
parochial clergy who were already married to put away their wives.   But the legislation
of the ecclesiastical councils which William held in Normandy was more strictly Gregorian,
as was some English practice: see DOUGLAS, *William the Conqueror*, pp. 332-3.

just as from those of the south. King William and Archbishop Lanfranc, on the other hand, were presented with the problem of how great a commitment it was prudent to retain towards the Gregorian cause as Henry IV ever more seriously menaced it. Thus, the relations of the papacy and the Anglo-Norman kingdom at this time gave rise to a number of new problems.

There is no clear evidence as to whether or not the urgent appeals for help which Gregory addressed to France at this time came to Normandy or to England, although it is likely that they did (108). But as early as 1082 the king's half-brother Odo, bishop of Bayeux and earl of Kent, sought to intervene at Rome, ostensibly in Gregory's interest. According to William of Malmesbury and Orderic Vitalis, Odo disbursed large sums of money to the Roman citizens and recruited in England a large retinue of knights who would follow him to Rome. William, who was apprehensive lest such an exodus of knights should weaken the defences of his English kingdom, hastily crossed the sea, seized Odo, and with Lanfranc's concurrence imprisoned him in Normandy for the remainder of his reign (109). When Gregory heard of Odo's arrest he reacted with energy. To the king he wrote a conciliatory letter, first recalling the friendship which had for long united them and urging William to persist in his devotion to the church and in his zeal for righteousness. He then said that one thing alone cast a shadow upon his mind: William had put worldly caution and consideration before divine law by imprisoning his brother despite his episcopal office (110). Gregory's tone in this letter suggests that he may have hoped to overcome William's fears for his kingdom and to secure Odo's release for his Roman expedition. But it stands in sharp contrast to a brief surviving fragment of a letter which Gregory addressed

---

(108) *Reg.*, IX, 21, 1082, pp. 601-3; *Epp. vag.* 51, 54, 55. That Anselm may have read *Ep. vag.* 54 is suggested by the opening of his own *Ep.* 271, iv. 186, *Clamavimus et iterum clamavimus et adhuc clamamus ad deum et ad vos et ad totam ecclesiam Normanniae...*, which is surely a recollection of Gregory's phrase, *Clamo, clamo, et iterum clamo.*

(109) WILLIAM of Malmesbury, *De gestis reg. Angl.*, iii. 277, ed. STUBBS, ii. 334; ORDERIC VITALIS, *Hist. eccles.*, vii, ed. LE PRÉVOST, iii. 188-92. William implied and Orderic stated that Odo hoped to become pope. The E version of the Anglo-Saxon Chronicle supports the date 1082 for Odo's imprisonment. For Lanfranc, see the *De iniusta vexatione Willelmi episcopi primi*, 13, *The Historical Works of Simeon of Durham*, ed. ARNOLD, i. 184.

(110) *Reg.*, IX, 37, pp. 630-1. This letter, the last in the Register, is incompletely preserved.

to Archbishop Hugh of Lyons. Its tone was one of outrage that the king should have dared to lay hands upon a bishop and to hold him captive in despite of the respect which was due to the priesthood (111). The fragment does not reveal what Hugh was instructed to do. But Gregory's reaction may have had its repercussions in the pleas against Odo's captivity which his brother Count Robert of Mortain and others continued to make to the king right up to the time of his death (112).

Whatever may have been William's response to this *démarche* about Odo, there is no doubt that up to Gregory's death and beyond it he maintained touch with at least one of Gregory's closest followers. This is established by a letter which Gregory's devoted standing legate in Lombardy, Bishop Anselm II of Lucca, wrote to William *c.* 1085 (113). Anselm not only praised William for his victories in war and for his just, merciful, and religious rule in time of peace, but he also thanked him for services (*beneficia*) of a direct and tangible, if unspecified, kind which he had received from him. In a postscript written in his own hand Anselm urged William to succour the Roman church: the church counted upon him above all other princes because of his many actions on its behalf and of his own excellency of life; he should rally to it as to its head and mother, and speedily do all in his power to deliver it from its adversaries' hands. Gregory's principal supporter in northern Italy was evidently persuaded of William's continuing and active attachment to the Gregorian cause.

Nevertheless since 1080 there had been an antipope in the person of Archbishop Wibert of Ravenna, who had assumed the name of Clement III. With Henry IV's backing he so far prospered that in 1084 he was enthroned at Rome and there performed Henry's imperial coronation. Nothing is known of William I's attitude to him, but Archbishop Lanfranc, who had for long been more distant in his attitude to Gregory than had

---

(111) *Ep. vag.* 53.

(112) ORDERIC VITALIS, *Hist. eccles.*, vii, ed. LE PRÉVOST, iii. 245-7.

(113) *Die Hannoversche Briefsammlung*, i, *Die Hildesheimer Briefe*, 1, *Briefsammlungen der Zeit Heinrichs IV.*, ed. C. ERDMANN and N. FICKERMANN, *MGH, Die Briefe der deutschen Kaiserzeit*, v (Weimar, 1950), pp. 15-17. I accept ERDMANN's arguments regarding its date in his *Studien zur Briefliteratur Deutschlands im elften Jahrhundert: Schriften der MGH*, i, Stuttgart, 1938, pp. 169-70.

the king, certainly had contacts with his party. The earliest
evidence for them is a letter which Lanfranc wrote to a certain
Hugh, before Gregory's death but after he was expelled from
Rome (114). In all probability his correspondent was Cardinal
Hugh Candidus, Clement's ardent supporter and Gregory's embittered opponent since the council of Worms (1076). Lanfranc
answered a letter from Hugh which had not been sent to him
unsolicited, for it was brought by a messenger who had taken
a yet earlier letter from Lanfranc to Hugh. In reply to it Hugh
had sent Lanfranc a full presentation of the Wibertine case. Of
this case Lanfranc now offered a shrewd and measured critique.
There were some things about it which displeased him. He
did not approve of the verbal abuse of Pope Gregory, nor of
calling him Hildebrand (115), nor of stigmatizing his legates
as ' thorns in the flesh (*spinosulos*) '. Lanfranc also declared
that Hugh's commending of Clement — Lanfranc was, significantly, prepared to concede Wibert's papal name — with so many
and such great praises, was premature: it was wrong to praise
or blame men during their lifetime, or to anticipate God's final
judgement upon them. However Lanfranc conceded two points
to Hugh: he did not believe that Henry IV (to whom he referred
as *gloriosus imperator*) would have taken so grave a step, i.e. as
to supersede Gregory by Clement, without good reason; nor would
he have obtained such a victory, i.e. as to expel Gregory from
Rome, without great help from God. Lanfranc then turned to
more practical matters, and was cautious. He did not approve
that Hugh should himself come to England unless he first secured
license to do so from the king (116). This island, he said in
conclusion, had not yet rejected Gregory, nor had it decided
whether to obey Clement. When the arguments on both sides
had been heard, if that were possible, then England would be
able to see more clearly what ought to be done.

  Lanfranc's circumspect and non-committal letter leaves no
room for doubt that, if William was sedulously keeping in touch
with the Gregorians, and if the English church as guided by Lan-

(114) LANFRANC, *Ep.* 65, pp. 79-80.

(115) For an example of Hugh Candidus' abuse of Gregory VII, see the decrees of the
council of Brixen (1080): ed. ERDMANN, Anhang C, *Quellen zur Geschichte Kaiser Heinrichs
IV.*, *Ausgewählte Quellen*, ed. BUCHNER, xii, pp. 477-80.

(116) From the summer of 1084 until the late autumn of 1085 William was in Normandy.

franc did not renounce its obedience to Gregory, Lanfranc was nevertheless in prudent communication with the Wibertines. If he took care not to reject Gregory his estimate of the chances of a Wibertine victory was high enough for him to prepare the way for a possible future recognition of Clement III.

It was a natural sequel that, when Gregory's death left matters in further suspense, Clement should have been at pains to win Lanfranc over. Three letters of Clement to him survive, although they lack dates (117). In the first, of *c*. 1085-6, Clement invited Lanfranc to Rome and asked for his help in the church's troubles. In the second, of *c*. 1086-9, he again invited Lanfranc to Rome, asked him to send Peter's Pence, and besought him to stir up the king and the bishops to help the church. In the third, which appears to date from between early 1088 and mid-1089, he commended Lanfranc in extravagant terms as a scholar and theologian. He again asked him for Peter's Pence, and he requested him to counsel King William II (1087-1100) to reseize the nuns of Wilton of some land which they had lost in his father's days.

These letters call for a careful assessment. P.F. Kehr, in particular, saw in them evidence of a close approach by Lanfranc and the English church to the Wibertine party after Gregory VII had died. Kehr argued that Clement wrote about Peter's Pence as though he had positive reason to anticipate its payment. Moreover he must have had a direct approach from the Wilton nuns about their lost land; such an approach was hardly feasible unless there were a background of official communication between England and the Wibertines. It was therefore likely that, when Clement sent his third letter to Lanfranc if not before, the English court recognized Clement as at least *de facto* the rightful pope (118). Again, it may be argued that not only was such a recognition a natural development following Lanfranc's letter to Hugh, but Clement's three letters have survived because they were copied into the end of Lanfranc's own collection of canons. It is likely that the entry

---

(117) Discussed and edited by F. LIEBERMANN, *Lanfranc and the Antipope* in: *Eng. Hist. Rev.*, xvi (1901), 328-32.

(118) P.F. KEHR, *Zur Geschichte Wiberts von Ravenna (Clemens III.)* in: *Sitzungsberichte der preussischen Akademie der Wissenschaften*, Berlin, 1921, pp. 356-60.

was made with Lanfranc's knowledge (119). If it were, Lanfranc must surely have ascribed to them a canonical value based upon Clement's authority at Rome.

It would, however, be hazardous to conclude that after Gregory died the English kingdom gave Clement even a much qualified recognition, or that Lanfranc was in favour of giving it. It is impossible to know whether Clement heard of the plea from Wilton because the nuns sent expressly to him, or because his partisans prevailed upon a pilgrim to the tombs of the apostles who was already in Rome to seek his assistance rather than his rival's. As regards the requests to Lanfranc for a visit to Rome and for Peter's Pence, Urban II's comparable letter of 1088 shows that they were a likely, indeed almost an automatic, adjunct of a letter announcing a new pope's accession (120). There is moreover no evidence that Lanfranc sought, or at any time sent an answer to, Clement's letters. They may well have been dispatched upon an unsought Wibertine initiative, in order to take advantage of the opening which Lanfranc's correspondence with Hugh had already made. Above all Clement's three letters were not so drafted as to impress such an experienced statesman as Lanfranc. Kehr himself noticed the lack of confidence in his own person and office with which Clement wrote, and the exaggerated terms of adulation and flattery in which he addressed Lanfranc. Clement's letters also contain the misconception that the archbishop, not the king, paid Peter's Pence. Thus, in many respects they struck an altogether false note when compared with those of Gregory VII and Urban II. When he observed the undertones of self-distrust, misconception, and lack of authority which characterized their drafting, Lanfranc is more likely to have been confirmed in his hesitation about Clement than moved to espouse his cause.

Several pieces of evidence drawn from the last three years of Lanfranc's life tend to confirm that his own position, and that of the English church, did not move significantly beyond that to which, before Gregory's death, he gave expression in his letter to Hugh. First, there is the evidence of a letter which he wrote to Abbot Rodolf of Saint-Vanne, Verdun, who was

---

(119) Cf. Brooke, *The English Church and the Papacy*, p. 145.
(120) *Ep.* iii, Migne, *PL*, CLI, 286-7.

a high Gregorian. In 1085 Thierry, the Henrican bishop of Verdun, expelled the abbot and a group of his monks, who found refuge at Saint-Bénigne, Dijon. Its abbot, Jarento, another high Gregorian, would receive permanently into his monastery only those monks who promised stability there. Rodolf scrupled to make such a promise, on the ground that he had already vowed stability at Verdun (121). In his predicament Rodolf sought Lanfranc's counsel, and he received a wise and sympathetic answer that he should take a new vow of stability at Dijon (122). Lanfranc's letter proves that, whatever contact he, found it prudent to maintain with the Wibertines, he was also in touch with the Gregorians of Dijon, and it suggests that their dealings with him were amicable and approving. Secondly, not long before Lanfranc died Anselm wrote from Bec a most cordial letter to him. He prayed for Lanfranc's health as needful both for himself and for the church, and he praised him for a sanctity which was pleasing to God. It is hard to believe that Anselm would have written in such terms if he knew Lanfranc to be personally inclined towards the Wibertine party, or to have done anything which might commit the English church to it (123). Thirdly, on 10 April 1088, more than a year before Lanfranc died, Urban announced to him his election as pope. Like Anselm he wrote with warm cordiality, making no suggestion that Lanfranc's loyalty was in question, and he sent to him Roger, a cardinal-deacon of the Roman church (124).

Such well disposed letters render it difficult to resist the conclusion that, whatever hardening may have occurred in William II's attitude to the papacy by the time of Anselm's appointment to the see of Canterbury in 1093 (125), during Lanfranc's lifetime the English church and kingdom did nothing whether *de iure* or *de facto* to cast public doubt upon its willingness to obey the Gregorian papacy. The habit of deference to Gregory and his supporters and of ultimate loyalty to his cause which

---

(121) HUGH of Flavigny, *Chronicon*, ii, *MGH, Scr.*, viii. 472-3.

(122) *Ep.* 66, pp. 80-1.

(123) *Ep.* 124, iii. 264-5. If, as is possible, Anselm composed the epitaph to Lanfranc in *PL*, CLVIII, 1049-50, the point is reinforced.

(124) *Ep.* iii, *ubi supra.*

(125) EADMER, *Hist. nov.*, i, ed. RULE, pp. 52-3.

had been formed under the Conqueror persisted until Urban II was securely established upon the papal throne.

VIII

It would fall beyond the scope of this study to inquire into the hold of Gregorianism upon the Anglo-Norman church under the Conqueror's sons. In their highly feudalized lands, where the apparatus of the secular power grew rapidly, where the Conqueror's masterful authority over the church was maintained without his reforming zeal, and where the ' Norman Anonymous ' wrote treatises which have prompted their latest editor to describe him as ' the sharpest, and in many respects also the profoundest, dogmatic opponent of Gregory VII in his own age ' (126), the reception of Gregorianism was in general a qualified one. Moreover few Anglo-Norman chroniclers wrote of Gregory VII, and those who did so were brief in their remarks. William of Malmesbury was not uncritical of him: Gregory was ' a man of blessed favour with God and perhaps of excessive sternness towards men ' (127). However Eadmer of Canterbury wrote of him summarily but favourably in terms which may reflect Anselm's judgement: he was ' of honourable memory ' (128), while at Saint-Évroul Orderic Vitalis summed up his life with sympathy and penetration:

> A monk from boyhood he was well instructed in the law of the Lord, and being of great zeal for righteousness he suffered many persecutions. He sent papal edicts throughout the world, and sparing no man he solemnly proclaimed the judgements of heaven, inviting all men by threats and by entreaties to the wedding-feast of the Lord of Hosts (129).

In these few words a monk of English birth, living in a Norman monastery, showed that at least one Anglo-Norman churchman was able to form an authentic impression of Gregory's character and pontificate.

---

(126) K. PELLENS, *Die Texte des normannischen Anonymus*, Wiesbaden, 1966, p. xxxi.

(127) WILLIAM of Malmesbury, *De gestis reg. Angl.*, iii. 266, ed. STUBBS, ii. 325.

(128) *Hist. nov.*, i, ed. RULE, p. 52.

(129) *Hist. eccles.*, iv, ed. CHIBNALL, ii. 298.

X

POPE GREGORY VII'S 'CRUSADING'
PLANS OF 1074

Professor Prawer has observed that Pope Gregory VII's plans of 1074 to bring
military help to the Byzantine Empire are not without a bearing upon the
development of the crusading idea.[1] The plans are familiar and have often been
discussed; it is, indeed, doubtful whether anything new can be said about them
unless further information comes to light. It may nevertheless be useful to
bring together more completely than has hitherto been done the relevant evidence from papal, Italian, and Byzantine sources, and to review its significance
in the current state of scholarly opinion.

Gregory's plans had a twofold background—in his burgeoning hope for the
reunion of the Eastern and Western Churches, and in his troubled dealings
with Robert Guiscard, the Norman duke of Apulia and Calabria. The reunion
of the Churches was an especial concern of Gregory's earliest years as pope,[2]
and his concern was intensified by his impression of the plight of Eastern
Christians following the Seljuq victory at Manzikert in 1071. He alluded to
reunion in a letter of 9 July 1073 to the Eastern Emperor Michael VII Dukas
(1071-8), in which he cordially acknowledged the emperor's written and verbal

---

1 Prawer, *Histoire,* 1:159-161; cf. Carl Erdmann, *Die Entstehung des Kreuzzugsgedankens*
(1935; repr., Stuttgart, 1955), pp. 145-153, trans. Marshall W. Baldwin and Walter Goffart,
The Origin of the Idea of Crusade (Princeton, 1977), pp. 160-169 [hereafter cited, from the
trans., as Erdmann, *Origin*].

2 See esp. Richard Koebner, "Der Dictatus Papae," in *Kritische Beiträge zur Geschichte des
Mittelalters. Festschrift für Robert Holtzmann zum sechzigsten Geburtstag* (Berlin, 1933), pp.
64-92; Julia Gauss, *Ost und West in der Kirchen- und Papstgeschichte des 11. Jahrhunderts*
(Zürich, 1967), pp. 41-68.

messages brought by two eastern monks, Thomas and Nicholas. He affirmed his wish to renew the ancient concord of the Roman church and its daughter of Constantinople, and he expressed his intention of sending Patriarch Dominicus of Grado to discuss more fully the matters that he had raised. In the meantime his own messenger would convey and bring back messages.[3] However, nothing is known of consequent negotiations; although Dominicus was in Venice during September 1074, having presumably by then completed any journey that he made.[4]

Gregory's policy towards Byzantium was thus based upon good will; but his attitude to Robert Guiscard was one of gathering disenchantment. As Archdeacon Hildebrand he had helped to negotiate the treaty of Melfi (1059) and the alliance by which the Norman leaders Robert Guiscard and Prince Richard of Capua were together to become protectors of the apostolic see.[5] But by the late 1060s Norman expansion towards the papal lands in Central Italy was causing Pope Alexander II (1061-73) such anxiety that the papacy sought to control the Normans by playing upon their divisions.[6] When Gregory became pope in April 1073 he at first sought to negotiate with Robert Guiscard.[7] But by autumn he, too, was concerned to counter Robert Guiscard's expansiveness by seeking to divide him from Richard of Capua. On 14 September Richard took an oath of fealty to Gregory, who was at Capua from 1 September to 15 November. Writing on 27 September to Erlembald, the Patarene leader at Milan, Gregory rejoiced that the Normans, who had conspired together to the peril of the Roman church, would now make peace with each other only when he so willed.[8] Gregory clearly intended that his separate understanding with

---

3   Gregory VII, *Registrum* 1.18, ed. Erich Caspar, MGH Epp. sel. 1-2 [hereafter cited as *Reg.*], pp. 29-30. For Gregory's eastern policy, see esp. Walther Holtzmann, "Studien zur Orientpolitik des Papsttums und zur Entstehung des ersten Kreuzzuges," *Historische Vierteljahrschrift* 22 (1924), 167-199, repr. in *Beiträge zur Reichs- und Papstgeschichte des hohen Mittelalters. Ausgewählte Aufsätze von Walther Holtzmann,* Bonner historische Forschungen 8 (Bonn, 1957) [hereafter cited, from the reprint, as Holtzmann], pp. 51-78; and Georg Hofmann, "Papst Gregor VII. und der christliche Osten," *Studi Gregoriani* 1 (1947), 169-181.

4   See the charter in L.A. Muratori, ed., *Antiquitates italicae medii aevi,* 1 (1738), 243-246; also *Reg.* 2.39, 31 December 1074, pp. 175-176.

5   For papal relations with the Normans, see esp. Ferdinand Chalandon, *Histoire de la domination normande en Italie et Sicile,* 1 (1907; repr. New York, 1960); Josef Déer, *Papsttum und Normannen. Untersuchungen zu ihren lehnsrechtlichen und kirchenpolitischen Beziehungen,* Studien und Quellen zur Welt Kaiser Friedrichs II. 1 (Cologne, 1972); and David Whitton, "Papal Policy in Rome, 1012-1124" (Univ. of Oxford D. Phil. thesis, 1979).

6   Chalandon, *Domination normande,* 1:222.

7   Vincenzo de Bartholomaeis, ed., *Storia de' Normanni di Amato di Montecassino,* 7. 7-9, Fonti per la storia d'Italia 76 (Rome, 1935) [hereafter cited as Amatus], pp. 297-299. Amatus' work survives only in an early fourteenth-century French version.

8   Amatus, 7.10, 12, pp. 300, 303; *Reg.* 1. 21a, 25, pp. 35-36, 41-42.

Richard of Capua would set a curb upon Robert Guiscard. But at the end of 1073 Robert Guiscard's capture of Amalfi was a reminder of his power, and also a blow to Gregory's ally Prince Gisulf of Salerno.[9] In February 1074 Robert Guiscard attacked Benevento and Pandulf, the son and heir of Prince Landulf VI whom Gregory favoured, was killed.[10] The duke of Apulia was clearly an increasing danger to the papacy and its South Italian friends, which it was in Gregory's interest yet more strongly to counter.

Gregory's freedom of action with regard both to Byzantium and to South Italy appeared to be the greater because King Henry IV of Germany was preoccupied by the Saxon rising which had begun in 1073 and which he did not master until his victory at the Unstrut in June 1075. His situation had prompted Henry in the autumn of 1073 to send Gregory a submissive letter which convinced the pope of his good will and obedience.[11] Thus, by early 1074 Gregory saw the way open to embark upon wide-ranging plans which would advance his ends both in the Byzantine Empire and in South Italy.[12]

The earliest testimony to what he had in mind is a letter of 2 February 1074, which he sent to Count William of Upper Burgundy.[13] He recalled a solemn promise which the count had made at Rome in the days of Alexander II that, if he were summoned, he would return there to fight for the *res sancti Petri*. He urged William now to prepare a force of knights to uphold the liberty of the Roman church by coming with his army to Rome in St. Peter's service should that prove necessary. He was also to transmit the summons to Count Raymond of Saint-Gilles, the future leader of the First Crusade whom Gregory here described as Prince Richard of Capua's father-in-law, Count Amadeus II of Savoy who was the son of Marchioness Adelaide of Turin, and other *fideles sancti Petri* who had likewise made promises at St. Peter's tomb. If his own reply were positive, William was further to charge the messenger by whom he sent it to enlist the support of Countess Beatrice of Tuscany together with her

---

9   *Chronici Amalphitani fragmenta,* 22, in Muratori, *Antiq. ital.* 1:211; cf. Chalandon, *Domination normande,* 1:233-234. For Gregory's favour towards Gisulf, see *Reg.* 1.2, 23 April 1073, p. 4.

10 *Chronica sancti Benedicti,* MGH SS 3:203; *Annales Beneventani a.*1073, MGH SS 3:181; cf. Gerold Meyer von Knonau, *Jahrbücher des Deutschen Reiches unter Heinrich IV. und Heinrich V.,* 2 (1894; repr., Berlin, 1964), 340. For Gregory's treaty of 12 August 1073 with Landulf, see *Reg.* 1.18a, pp. 30-31.

11 *Reg.* 1.29a, pp. 47-49, cf. 1.25.

12 The most detailed modern analysis of the evidence is in Meyer von Knonau, *Jahrbücher,* 2:341-344, 441-442; see also Augustin Fliche, *La Réforme grégorienne,* 2 (Paris, 1926), 169-172.

13 *Reg.* 1.46, pp. 69-71; cf. Amatus, 7.12, p. 303.

daughter Matilda and Matilda's husband Duke Godfrey of Lorraine.[14] Gregory declared that, in seeking to recruit so considerable a force, he had a twofold purpose. First, it would serve to pacify the Normans, who would thereby be intimidated, without any shedding of Christian blood, into obedience to righteousness (*iustitia*). Secondly, Gregory planned to cross to Constantinople and help Christians who, being greatly vexed by the Saracens, eagerly besought his aid. His use of the first person plural confirms that he purposed himself to travel to the East. He underlined the centrality of Constantinople in his plan by adding—rather artificially after summoning the *fideles sancti Petri* for the defence of St. Peter's property in Italy—that the knights who were already with him would suffice to deal with the rebellious Normans. On 1 March 1074, Gregory followed up this letter with a general summons to all Christians who were prepared to defend their faith.[15] He described its bearer as a Western Christian recently returned from the East with an eye-witness account, similar to others that he had received, of Seljuq campaigns almost to the very walls of Constantinople and of the slaughter of Christians in their thousands. He urged his hearers to the defence of the Eastern Empire and its Christian subjects; they were to report back to him what divine mercy prompted them to do. In this summons Gregory made no reference to the Normans, nor did he say anything about the leadership or organization of his expedition.

Historians have often regarded Gregory's initiative in thus summoning an expedition to the East as a direct and deliberate response to the Emperor Michael VII's approach of 1073.[16] But Walther Holtzmann was undoubtedly correct to see in this approach nothing more than a background factor. At no time did Gregory refer to it, while in his summons of 1 March he declared that his information was from reports of western travellers. In 1073-4 the situation of the Byzantine Empire seems, in fact, to have given rise to no pressing and immediate need for western military help. There is no evidence that Michael VII asked for it in any way analogous to Alexius Comnenus' appeal read to the council of Piacenza (1095), and there is no reason to presume an appeal.[17] Gregory at this stage made no express reference to the reunion of the Churches

14   On 3 January 1074 Gregory had already invited Matilda to accompany her mother on a visit to Rome and referred to other correspondence: *Reg.* 1.40, pp. 62-63.
15   *Reg.* 1.49, pp. 75-76. This letter, like *Reg.* 1.46, bears the marks of Gregory's own dictation.
16   Paul Riant, "Inventaire critique des lettres historiques des croisades," *AOL* 1 (1881), 62-64; Meyer von Knonau, *Jahrbücher,* 2:340-341 (but cf. 2:274-275); *Reg.* 1.18, p. 29, n. 2; Peter Charanis, "Byzantium, the West and the Origins of the First Crusade," *Byzantion* 19 (1947), 17-36, at pp. 20-21.
17   Holtzmann, pp. 56-57. For the situation in the Byzantine Empire, see Riant, "Inventaire," pp. 61-65.

which might suggest that he was actively negotiating about it. Everything points to the plan being Gregory's own, devised at his own time and in his own way, and taking its cue from travellers' reports rather than diplomacy with the Byzantine authorities.

It was against the dissident Normans that Gregory in the first instance directed it. Erdmann went so far as to argue that he deliberately took as his model Pope Leo IX's ill-fated expedition against the Normans in 1053. Admittedly there are similarities: not only did Gregory seek Lotharingian help as Leo had sought German,[18] but his assertion to Count William of Burgundy that he intended to restrain the Normans by intimidation rather than by shedding Christian blood echoes Leo's own design.[19] Yet it is hardly likely that Gregory would take as his model a campaign that led to the *débâcle* at Civitate, while the similarity of tactics can be explained by the prevailing war ethic of the reform papacy. Gregory acted as seemed best in face of the depredations of Robert Guiscard's Normans. At his Lent council in March 1074 he prepared the ground by excommunicating the duke and his accomplices, as a means to bringing about their repentance for infringing papal interests.[20]

At some time after 9 May Gregory felt ready to begin his expedition.[21] He could hope to gather together a fairly impressive host. Amongst lay figures, Countess Matilda of Tuscany, Marquis Azzo II of Este, and Robert Guiscard's brother-in-law and implacable enemy Prince Gisulf of Salerno had attended his Lent council; Matilda and Gisulf, at least, appear to have stayed on at Rome. Archbishop Guibert of Ravenna, too, had stayed, having promised Gregory that after Easter (20 April) he would give great military help against the Normans and also against the counts of Bagnorea, which lay to the east of Lake Bolsena, and would personally join his expedition. Gregory counted upon the aid of Prince Richard of Capua, whom the Montecassino chronicler Amatus described as being at this time his friend and ally. But Amatus makes it clear that it was upon Countess Matilda of Tuscany that Gregory mainly relied for forces.[22] Robert Guiscard was Amatus' hero and Gisulf of Salerno his *bête noire.* He poured scorn upon Gregory's plan to intimidate the duke by weight of numbers, saying that, since Gregory could not find men to aid him, he

---

18   Although as early as 7 April Gregory chided Duke Godfrey of Lorraine for his failure to fulfil his promise to aid St. Peter and send knights for his warfare: *Reg.* 1.72, pp. 103-104.
19   Erdmann, *Origin,* pp. 123, 160-161, 169; see Leo IX, Ep. 103, PL 143: 777-781, at col. 779AB.
20   *Reg.* 1.85a, p. 123.
21   9 May is the date of Gregory's last letter before he left Rome: *Reg.* 1.83, pp. 118-119.
22   Bonizo of Sutri, *Liber ad amicum,* 7, ed. Ernst Dümmler, MGH LdeL 1: 602-604; Amatus, 7.12, pp. 303-304. Gregory also referred to his debt to Countesses Beatrice and Matilda in his letter to Empress Agnes of 15 June: *Reg.* 1.85, pp. 121-123.

sought the help of women. When Beatrice and Matilda of Tuscany promised to
bring 30,000 knights who, to make victory quite sure, would include a stiffen-
ing of 500 Germans, Gregory replied that, with Prince Richard's help, 20,000
would suffice to vanquish the paltry Norman rabble. But the countesses
insisted upon overwhelming forces, and Gregory deferred to their judgement
and determination.[23]

Thus far Amatus; the facts of the campaign were more prosaic. Gregory at
first travelled northwards from Rome to meet the Tuscan forces. (It is not clear
that Archbishop Guibert of Ravenna had any part in determining the direction
of the march, or even that he was still present.) In the week after Pentecost two
of his letters, with the remarkable dating *Data in expeditione,* show him to have
been, on 12 June, at Monte Cimino between Sutri and Viterbo and, on 15 June,
at San Flaviano which is to the south-east of Lake Bolsena and on the road
northwards from Viterbo.[24] Amatus named Monte Cimino as the assembly
point of the army, but Bonizo of Sutri San Flaviano.[25] The expedition speedily
ended in fiasco. Three reasons were given. First, according to Amatus, Prince
Gisulf of Salerno failed in his role of paymaster; willing though he was to
compass the destruction of Robert Guiscard he distributed only contemptible
rewards—"Indian girdles and bands and cheap cloths, fit only for girding
women and equipping servants or for adorning walls." Secondly, again according to Amatus, the Pisan contingent of the Tuscan army recalled old grievances
against Gisulf; for his safety Gregory had to send him away secretly to a refuge
in Rome. Thirdly, according to Bonizo of Sutri, a sudden insurrection stirred
up by Gregory's Lombard enemies called Countesses Beatrice and Matilda
back to Tuscany. With his objectives wholly unfulfilled Gregory had perforce
to return to Rome, where he fell seriously ill.[26] He sought abortively to deal
with Robert Guiscard by way of negotiation: the duke obeyed his summons to
a meeting at Benevento bringing a strong retinue, but Gregory was unable to
attend.[27] During the summer Robert Guiscard allied himself with Duke Sergius
of Naples against the principality of Capua. This prompted the mediation of
Abbot Desiderius of Montecassino and led to a reconciliation, albeit short-

---

23   Amatus, 7.12, pp. 303-304.
24   *Reg.* 1.84-85, pp. 119-123. De Bartholomaeis' identification of Gregory's *ad Sanctum Flabia-
     num* (Amatus 7.13, p. 305, n. 1), seems preferable to the more usual Fiano, to the east of
     Viterbo near the River Tiber, e.g. *Reg.* 1.85, p. 123, n. 1.
25   Amatus, 7.13, pp. 305-306; Bonizo of Sutri, 7, p. 604.
26   Amatus, 7.13-14, pp. 305-307 and (for Pisan grievances against Gisulf) 8.4, pp. 346-347;
     Bonizo of Sutri, 7, p. 604.
27   Amatus, 7.14, pp. 306-307.

lived, between Robert Guiscard and Richard of Capua.[28] Gregory's expedition had come to nothing, and the political situation in South Italy which followed was evidently beyond his control.

An inevitable consequence was that his wider plan to help the Byzantine Empire could not as yet be pursued. It was further hindered in the autumn of 1074 because Gregory was engaged in a conflict with King Philip I of France, against whom he sought to enlist the French bishops and lay magnates.[29] Yet the Byzantine plan was not without an echo, for on 10 September Gregory wrote to Duke William of Aquitaine a letter praising his readiness for St. Peter's service, but stating that it was not convenient then to write further about his expedition to the East, "since rumour has it that the Christians across the sea have repelled the fierceness of their pagan adversaries, and [Gregory] was still awaiting the counsel of Providence as to his future course of action." [30]

Gregory again relied upon hearsay; there is no hint that he had received an official communication from Byzantium, nor is there evidence that a major victory had been won there. In fact, whether directly or indirectly, Gregory's uncertainty is likely to have been the result of Byzantine diplomacy, of which it is impossible to discern how far if at all he was ever aware.[31] For the Emperor Michael VII's assessment of his need for standing, rather than merely occasional, western help against the Turks had led him to look for a possible ally in Gregory's adversary Robert Guiscard.[32] Michael was prepared to pay the price of abandoning Byzantine claims to sovereignty over the South Italian themes of Longobardia and Calabria. It was, therefore, with Robert Guiscard rather than with Gregory that he maintained communication.[33] He continued the attempts of his predecessor Romanus IV Diogenes (1067-71) to conclude a marriage alliance. He at first sought the hand of one of Robert Guiscard's daughters for his brother Constantine.[34] He was undeterred by the duke's

28   Amatus, 7.15-17, pp. 307-309. For Gregory's hesitant attitude to Robert Guiscard, see his letter to Countesses Beatrice and Matilda, *Reg.* 2.9, 16 Oct. 1074, pp. 138-140, which also reflects his dismay that his earlier plan had come to nothing.

29   *Reg.* 2.5, to the French archbishops and bishops, 10 September, pp. 129-133; *Reg.* 2.18, to Duke William of Aquitaine, 13 November, pp. 150-151. See Erdmann, *Origin,* pp. 162-166.

30   *Reg.* 2.3, pp. 126-128; cf. the language of *Reg.* 2.9.

31   For Byzantine diplomacy at this time, see Chalandon, *Domination normande,* 1:235-236, 258-264; Charanis (as n. 16).

32   John Scylitzes, Continuation of George Cedrenus, *Synopsis historiarum,* ed. Immanuel Bekker, CSHB, 2 (Bonn, 1839), 724.

33   There is no evidence that Gregory induced Robert Guiscard to make peace with Byzantium in 1074: Steven Runciman, *The Eastern Schism* (Oxford, 1955), p. 59.

34   For his letters see Konstantinos N. Sathas, *Bibliotheca graeca medii aevi,* 5 (Paris, 1876), 385-392, nos. 143-144; they are listed by Franz Dölger, *Regesten der Kaiserurkunden des oströmischen Reiches von 565-1453,* 2 (Munich, 1925), 18, nos. 989-990.

reluctance, and after the birth in 1074 of his own son Constantine he proposed that this child should be betrothed. Robert Guiscard now agreed, in due course dispatching a daughter to be brought up at Constantinople where she was given the name Helen.[35] The text survives of a marriage treaty, dated August 1074, in which the betrothed couple were accorded the title *basileis*, while Robert Guiscard himself was given the Byzantine rank of *nobilissimus* and many other gifts; he bound himself and his successors to friendship with Byzantium. Dölger has pointed out that the genuineness of the chrysobull is questionable on diplomatic grounds. But, with due caution, its date and purport are a guide to the probable course of events in the late summer of 1074.[36]

In the light of these events it would be surprising if the Byzantine emperor in 1074 renewed contact with the pope, and in the absence of evidence it may be presumed that he did not. Gregory, however, continued to hope for the obedient collaboration of Henry IV of Germany in the affairs of both Empires. On 7 December 1074 he sent the king two letters of admonition about them.[37] The second, which is one of five items in Gregory's Register inscribed *Dictatus pape*,[38] again canvassed an expedition to the East. Gregory said that he was prompted by pleas of Eastern Christians *(christiani ex partibus ultramarinis)*, most of whose number were daily suffering destruction and slaughter at the hands of the heathen. They had therefore asked him to send whatever help he could, lest the Christian religion perish in their time. Gregory's words suggest

---

35   Scylitzes, in George Cedrenus, 2:720, 724; Anne Comnène, *Alexiade,* 1.10.3, 12.2, ed. Bernard Leib, 1, rev. ed. (Paris, 1967) [hereafter cited as Anna Comnena], 37, 43, 171; John Zonaras, *Epitomae historiarum,* 18.17.7, ed. Theodore Büttner-Wobst, CSHB, 3 (Bonn, 1897), 714; Amatus, 7.26, pp. 318-320; Guillaume de Pouille, *La Geste de Robert Guiscard,* 3.501-502, ed. Marguerite Mathieu, Istituto siciliano di studi bizantini e neoellenici, Testi 4 (Palermo, 1961), pp. 190, 306.

36   The Greek text of the treaty is printed by P. Bezobrazov, "Chrisovul imperatora Michaila VII Duki," *Vizantiiskii Vremennik* 6 (1899), 140-143, with corrections by Eduard Kurtz in *Byzantinische Zeitschrift* 9 (1900), 280. For summaries and comment, Dölger, *Regesten,* 2:19, no. 1003, and Bernard Leib, *Rome, Kiev et Byzance à la fin du XIe siècle* (Paris, 1924), pp. 172-174. Anna Comnena's statement that when Nicephorus III Botaniates was deposed in late March 1081 Constantine "had not yet reached his seventh year" is consistent with the date August 1074. Some Italian chronicles assigned Helen's dispatch to Constantinople to 1076: Lupus Protospatarius, *Chronicon a.* 1076, MGH SS 5:60; Romuald of Salerno, *Chronicon,* ed. Carlo A. Garufi, RIS² (Città di Castello, 1909-1935), p. 189.

37   *Reg.* 2.30-31, pp. 163-168; see Christian Schneider, *Prophetisches Sacerdotium und heilsgeschichtliches Regnum im Dialog, 1073-1077,* Münstersche Mittelalter-Schriften 9 (Munich, 1972), esp. pp. 85-91.

38   The five are *Reg.* 1.47, to Countess Matilda of Tuscany, 16 February 1074, pp. 71-73; *Reg.* 2.31 and 2.37 which concern Gregory's "crusading" plans, p. 165 and pp. 172-173; *Reg.* 2.43, to Bishop Hugh of Die, 5 January 1075, pp. 179-180; *Reg.* 2.55a, Gregory's twenty-seven theses on papal power entered between letters of 3 and 4 March 1075, pp. 201-208.

that he was responding, not to any official approach from the Byzantine emperor or court, but to "grass-roots" appeals of humbler, provincial Christians. He went on to say that he would himself endeavour, and would encourage other Christians, to bring help, to the point of laying down their lives for the brethren. He claimed that many both in Italy and beyond the Alps, to the number of more than 50,000, were already willing to follow him as general and pontiff *(dux et pontifex)* upon a campaign *(expeditio)* which should proceed in arms against the enemies of God and, under the pope's guidance, should reach the Lord's sepulchre at Jerusalem. Besides the military predicament of Eastern Christians, Gregory said that a second consideration moved him greatly *(permaxime)* to contemplate such a task. The church of Constantinople, which differed from the apostolic see as regards the procession of the Holy Spirit, was looking for agreement with it; the Armenians—dissident since the council of Chalcedon (451)—were almost all estranged from the Catholic faith; and almost all Eastern Christians were awaiting what the faith of the apostle Peter might determine about their different beliefs.[39] Therefore it was time for Gregory to fulfil Christ's charge to St. Peter: *tu aliquando conversus confirma fratres tuos.*[40] Like his predecessors who had travelled eastwards to establish the Catholic faith—although, in fact, none had so travelled since Pope Constantine I (709-711)—Gregory must follow any way that Christ might open up to the twofold goal of confirming the faith and of defending Christian peoples *(pro eadem fide et christianorum defensione).* Gregory finally stated the role that he proposed for Henry, should an expedition take place. He sought Henry's counsel and, so far as the king was willing, his aid *(a te quero consilium et, ut tibi placet, auxilium)*; and he would leave Henry as protector of the Roman church during his absence. In face of all human doubts and conflicts Gregory trusted in the Holy Spirit to make clear to Henry what his plans and objectives were.

By 16 December Gregory was ready to issue a general summons—also inscribed in his Register as *Dictatus pape* — to all the *fideles sancti Petri,* especially those beyond the Alps.[41] Gregory presumed his hearers' familiarity with his purpose of bringing military aid to Christians beyond the sea in the Byzantine Empire, whom the devil was by his own devices striving to turn from the Catholic faith, and by his members the heathen was daily slaughtering like

---

39 For the Byzantine Church, see Runciman, pp. 1-78; the history of the Armenians is summarized by Arnold J. Toynbee, *Constantine Porphyrogenitus and his World* (Oxford, 1973), pp. 384-406.

40 Luke 22.32.

41 *Reg.* 2.37, pp. 172-173.

cattle. His plan had now matured beyond the hypothetical terms of his letter to Henry IV, for he called on some of his hearers to come to him as instructed by the bearer of his letter. He and they together would prepare the way for all who would journey beyond the sea. Gregory named no assembly date, but his dispatch on the same day of letters assuming his presence in Rome at the Lent council of 22-28 February 1075 shows that he did not plan to go before the spring.[42] On or soon after 16 December he revealed more of his plan to Countess Matilda of Tuscany in a letter bearing the marks of his own dictation.[43] He confessed that there were some whom he blushed to tell, lest he seem to be led by a mere fancy, how he was determined to cross the sea in aid of Christians who were being slaughtered like cattle. He made no mention of Henry IV, but he set out the part to be played by the group of pious women whose close spiritual association he had cultivated earlier in the year.[44] Henry's mother, the Empress Agnes, wished to accompany the expedition with Gregory and to bring Matilda with her; Gregory anticipated much strength from their prayers. Countess Beatrice was to stay in Italy and safeguard the interests there of the pope and of Countess Matilda.

Unlike Gregory's earlier plan, his winter preparations left no direct trace in sources other than his letters. From them it appears that he concentrated upon what were now more clearly defined than before as his twin objectives in the East: his military objective of freeing Eastern Christians from Muslim attacks, and his pastoral objective of bringing all Eastern Christians to unity in the faith of St. Peter. He made no express mention of the Normans; and his purpose as expressed in his general summons, that he and his retinue would prepare the way for a journey beyond the sea, will hardly bear Erdmann's interpretation that it was directed against Robert Guiscard.[45] The natural interpretation of his letter is not that a fully assembled host would first overawe the Normans and then proceed to the East according to his earlier plan; it is that an advance party to the East would be the forerunner of a larger company soon to follow. Gregory perhaps wished in December to exclude any such division of aims between South Italy and the East as had marked his first plan, and also any such feuds as had developed between the Pisans and the Salernitans.

42   *Reg.* 2.35-36, pp. 171-172.
43   *Briefsammlungen der Zeit Heinrichs IV.*, ed. Carl Erdmann and Norbert Fickermann, MGH
     Briefe 5 (1950), 86-87, Die Hannoversche Briefsammlung (1. Hildesheimer Briefe), no. 43;
     The Epistolae vagantes of Pope Gregory VII, ed. Herbert E.J. Cowdrey (Oxford, 1972), pp.
     10-13, no. 5.
44   *Reg.* 1.85, pp. 121-123.
45   Erdmann, *Origin*, p. 167, n. 74.

There is, however, no evidence that this time forces ever assembled; indeed, Gregory's letter of 22 January 1075 to Abbot Hugh of Cluny already expressed his anguish of mind that his endeavours on the Church's behalf had been without avail. The Eastern Church had fallen away from the Catholic faith, and Satan was everywhere killing Christians by means of his members. In the West, there were no earthly princes who preferred God's honour and right-eousness to temporal gain; while his Italian neighbours, whether Romans, Lombards, or Normans, were worse than Jews and pagans.[46] Gregory clearly regarded his plans of 1074 as in total ruins. It was, indeed, the case that the plans and counter-plans of that year achieved nothing, whether for better or for worse. They did not improve matters in South Italy, for at his Lent council of 1075 Gregory again excommunicated Robert Guiscard, together with his nephew Robert of Loritello, as *invasores bonorum sancti Petri*.[47] The West brought no help to the East, nor were relations between the Churches improved. But they did not make matters worse. Despite the Emperor Michael VII's dealings with Gregory's adversary Robert Guiscard, about which Gregory may or may not have known, Gregory in 1078 excommunicated his supplanter, Nicephorus III Botaniates (1078-81); and in 1080, after Gregory renewed at Ceprano his alliance with Robert Guiscard, he praised Michael VII as *gloriosissimus imperator*.[48]

In the political world Gregory's plans came to nothing, but they may have had repercussions and interactions in the world of ideas. The first evidence for this is two odes written by Archbishop Alfanus I of Salerno to Prince Gisulf and his brother Guy.[49] Alfanus incited them to achievements whose scope matched Gregory's intentions. He urged the prince to continue his warfare against the Normans and to extend it against both Greeks and Turks.[50] Before Guy he opened up a yet more glorious prospect. He praised him for his past victories over the Normans—the *gens Gallorum* who had settled in Lombard Italy *velut una lues pecorum*. These victories were but an earnest of those to come, not only against the Normans but to win the Byzantine throne: *Evigilet studium Graeca trophaea tuum*.[51] The odes date from before Gisulf's quarrel

46 *Reg.* 2.49, pp. 188-190.
47 *Reg.* 2.52a, pp. 196-197.
48 *Reg.* 6.5b, p. 400; 8.6, 25 July 1080, pp. 523-524. For the latter letter and its circumstances, see Chalandon, *Domination normande*, 1:265-266, and Holtzmann, pp. 57-58.
49 *I carmi di Alfano I arcivescovo di Salerno*, ed. Anselmo Lentini and Faustino Avagliano, Miscellanea cassinese 38 (Montecassino, 1974), pp. 143-144, 150-152, carmi 17, 20; also PL 147:1256-1258, nos. 34-35.
50 Carme 17; see Anselmo Lentini, "Le odi di Alfano ai principi Gisulfo e Guido di Salerno," *Aevum* 31 (1957) [hereafter cited as Lentini, "Le odi"], 230-240, at p. 233.
51 Carme 20, line 100; see Lentini, "Le odi," pp. 234-236.

with Guy at an unknown date in 1075, before the end of which year Guy was in any case killed by the Normans.[52] No date before 1074 suggests itself, although Gregory's plans of that year provide a probable model. Despite attempts by Schipa and Lentini to date the odes precisely—in early 1074 and summer/ autumn 1075 respectively[53]—it is not likely that they relate to any particular historical juncture in those years. They read like a talented court prelate's encomia of his political patrons. They play on such local Salernitan themes as hatred of the Normans whom Alfanus represents as flooding the land after the murder of Prince Guaimar V in 1052, and on a tradition of hostility to Byzantium. Indeed, Alfanus' call to Guy to seek the Byzantine throne fits uneasily with Gregory's continuing good will towards the Emperor Michael VII. Nevertheless, given the general similarity of purport, the odes probably took their inspiration from Gregory's call for an expedition having military aims in both South Italy and Byzantium, and illustrate its power to kindle the imagination of those towards whom it was directed.

Secondly, Gregory's plans call for comparison with Sibylline prophecies of the last emperor and comparable literature which were current in the eleventh century. Before 1074, Latin texts of the Tiburtine Sibyl had already coloured, in ways foreshadowing Gregory's plans, the ultra-imperialist Bishop Benzo of Alba's representation of Henry IV at the time of the Cadalan schism of 1061-3. Benzo then concocted a letter purporting to be from the Byzantine Emperor Constantine X Dukas (1059-67) to the antipope Honorius II. Constantine proposed that he and the antipope should form a league with the boy-king Henry, in which Constantine would pay soldiers who, under papal leadership *(te praevio)* would go *usque ad sepulchrum Domini,* destroying the Normans and restoring Christian *libertas* for all time.[54] These objectives were manifestly

---

52   Amatus, 8.12, pp. 352-353. For the date of Guy's death, see Michelangelo Schipa,"Storia del principato longobardo di Salerno," 10-12, *Archivio storico per le province napolitane* 12 (1887), 513-588 [hereafter cited as Schipa, "Storia"], at p. 572; Lentini, "Le odi," p. 238.

53   Michelangelo Schipa, *Alfano I, arcivescovo di Salerno. Studio storico-literario* (Salerno, 1880), pp. 17, 37-42; "Storia," p. 569; Lentini, "Le odi," pp. 232, 233, 238. Lentini's argument for 1075 fails because of his unsupported presumption that Michael VII's treaty with Robert Guiscard was made in 1075, and that Gregory knew of and reacted to it.

54   Benzo of Alba, *Ad Henricum IV imperatorem libri VII,* 2.12, ed. Karl Pertz, MGH SS 11:617. For the Tiburtine Sibyl, see Ernst Sackur, *Sibyllinische Texte und Forschungen* (Halle-an-der-Saale, 1898), pp. 177-187, at pp. 185-186). See also the texts and comment in Adso Dervensis, *De ortu et tempore Antechristi, necnon et tractatus qui ab eo dependunt,* ed. D. Verhelst, CC cont. med. 45 (Turnhout, 1976), pp. 26, 46-47, 53, 72, 101-102, 106-110, 123, 135, 140, 149 The indispensable discussion of the older material is Carl Erdmann, "Endkaiserglaube und Kreuzzugsgedanke im11. Jahrhundert," *Zeitschrift für Kirchengeschichte* 11 (1932), 384-414, also Prawer, *Histoire,* 1:172-173. The date and content of Constantine's supposed letter are discussed by Hugo M. Lehmgrübner, *Benzo von Alba, ein Verfechter der kaiserlichen Staatsidee unter Heinrich IV.* (Berlin, 1887), pp. 93-94, 99-111.

similar to Gregory's in 1074. If such ideas formed something of the background of his plans, they in their turn foreshadowed the programme which Benzo was to set before the grown-up Henry in 1085/6. Benzo recalled Charlemagne's legendary connection with Jerusalem and identified Henry as the future *signifer christianae religionis.* The whole world looked to him as a redeemer. Alluding to the mid-eleventh-century prophecy of the Cuman Sibyl, for which Erdmann suggested an origin in the circle of Gregory's ally Countess Matilda of Tuscany, Benzo set out how Henry would restore Apulia and Calabria to their pristine state before the Norman incursion, how he would wear his crown in Byzantium, and finally how he would proceed to Jerusalem where, having reverenced the Holy Sepulchre, he would also be crowned.[55] The similarities between Benzo's writings and Gregory's plans of 1074 are remarkable, and Erdmann raised the question whether Gregory knew at least the Tiburtine Sibyl's prophecy and sought to claim for himself something of the last emperor's role. In other words, by leading an army to the Holy Sepulchre, did Gregory seek to claim for the papacy a world role which the Sibylline literature associated with the emperor, while he relegated Henry, as emperor-to-be, to an ancillary role as protector of the Roman church? And was Gregory's bid to vindicate the faith of St. Peter among Eastern Christians a pre-empting of such an idea as Benzo's, that the whole world would look to Henry as a redeemer? Erdmann's own cautious answer should be decisive: the hypothesis of an influence upon Gregory is attractive — so attractive that historians would be wise to refrain from adopting it in default of positive evidence in the sources.[56]

Together with Gregory's plans of 1074, such flights of fancy as those in Alfanus' odes and in the Sibylline prophecies with their echoes in Benzo of Alba are mainly of interest as showing how, even before the First Crusade, men were beginning to envisage political and military actions on an international scale having the Holy Sepulchre in some way among their objects. As regards the direct bearing of Gregory's plans upon the crusade, at least one writer, with hindsight, declared that they inspired Pope Urban II's preaching of it. Urban's *Vita* in the *Liber pontificalis* records that Urban had heard how Gregory had called upon the *ultramontani* to go to Jerusalem for the defence of the Christian faith and to free the Lord's sepulchre from its enemies' hands; he successfully preached an expedition which Henry IV's hostility had frustrated.[57] But in 1074

---

55   Benzo of Alba, *Ad Heinricum.* 1.14-15, 17, cf. 19, pp. 604-607, for the date, see Lehmgrübner, *Benzo von Alba.* pp. 28-29. Erdmann edited the text of the Cuman Sibyl: "Endkaiserglaube," pp. 396-398, with comment on pp. 400, 406-408.

56   Erdmann, "Endkaiserglaube," p. 408.

57   *Le Liber pontificalis,* ed. Louis Duchesne, 2 (Paris, 1892), 293.

Urban was still a monk at Cluny, and the *Vita* seems to depend upon a reading of Gregory's letters, not upon a living tradition at Rome about what really happened. While it is likely that Urban became acquainted with Gregory's plans at least after becoming cardinal-bishop of Ostia in 1080, it is impossible not to agree with Professor Riley-Smith that they fell short of the armed pilgrimage that Urban's preaching called forth, and therefore of a crusade as a modern historian may reasonably define it: "Gregory's letters contain no clear link between the planned expedition and pilgrimages, no Indulgence and, again, no sign of the vow and resulting protection for crusaders." [58] Yet many ingredients of crusading preaching and motives were already discernible. Gregory repeatedly emphasized the martyrdom for the sake of Christian brethren and in the name of Christ, which was a main inspiration of crusading zeal. If he did not promise an indulgence even to the extent that Alexander II had fore-shadowed it in 1063 to French knights before the Barbastro campaign,[59] he laid stress on the eternal reward which his warfare would convey: *per momentaneum laborem aeternam potestis acquirere mercedem.* [60] Above all, in 1074 Gregory twice issued general summonses, appealing to the military classes on both sides of the Alps to wage religiously motivated warfare for the liberation of Eastern Christians and for the promotion of Christian unity. Such plans for a papally directed campaign which enlisted the international military classes of Western Europe, which promised the crown of martyrdom and other spiritual rewards, and which encompassed worship at the Holy Sepulchre within its objectives, marked a significant stage in the development of the idea of crusade. It is more likely than not that Gregory's plans were powerfully present in Urban's mind when he preached his sermon at Clermont in 1095.[61]

---

58   Jonathan Riley-Smith, *What Were the Crusades?* (London, 1978), p. 75; cf. Paul Rousset, *Les Origines et les charactères de la première croisade* (1945; repr., New York, 1978), pp. 50-53.
59   *Epistolae pontificum Romanorum ineditae,* ed. Samuel Loewenfeld (1885; repr., Graz, 1959), p. 43, no. 82.
60   *Reg.* 2.37, p. 173.
61   Cf. Hans E. Mayer, *The Crusades,* trans. John Gillingham (Oxford, 1972), p. 22.

CARDINAL PETER OF ALBANO'S
LEGATINE JOURNEY TO CLUNY (1080)

T H E purpose of this study is to provide a more satisfactory printed text than has hitherto been available of the so-called *Carta Petri Albanensis episcopi et cardinalis Romani de immunitate Cluniaci.* The *Carta* is important for understanding the conflict which was sporadically waged during and after the eleventh century by the monks of Cluny on the one hand, and the bishops of Mâcon in whose diocese Cluny lay, backed by their metropolitans the archbishops of Lyons, on the other. The central issue in this conflict was the exemption from the spiritual authority and jurisdiction of the bishops which, despite recurrent episcopal hostility, the popes had conferred upon Cluny. Moreover, the papacy had for long actively reinforced the immunity from the temporal claims of all outside lordship, whether ecclesiastical or lay, which Cluny received in its Foundation Charter. Thus, the Cluniacs looked to Rome for the defence of their abbey and many of its monastic dependencies against the claims of the bishops to exercise jurisdiction over them, and for the defence of their lands and men against all manner of inroads by outside powers, but especially the lawless violence of neighbouring lords. As the eleventh-century papacy grew in strength, Cluny enjoyed papal support partly by the issuing of papal privileges in its favour, and partly by the dispatch of legates to vindicate it locally. The *Carta* records the activities of a legate who in 1080 came to its aid in respect of both its exemption and its immunity.

It is a measure of the importance which the Cluniacs later attached to the *Carta* that, although the original has not survived, there are copies of it in four of the Cluniac manuscripts of the eleventh to thirteenth centuries which are now in the Bibliothèque nationale at Paris. They are as follows:[1]

A: Bibl. nat. nouv. acq. lat. 2262, late eleventh–early twelfth cent. This manuscript, known as Cartulary C of Cluny, is listed in Stein, no. 987, and described by Delisle, no. 136, and Bruel, i, pp. xxviii–xxxi. The *Carta* is on pp. 8–10, no. 9. There is slight damage to the text of lines

---

[1] References to the lists and descriptions of the manuscripts are as follows: H. Stein, *Bibliographie générale des cartulaires français ou relatifs à l'histoire de France* (Paris, 1907); L. Delisle, *Inventaire des manuscrits de la Bibliothèque nationale, Fonds de Cluni* (Paris, 1884); *Recueil des chartes de l'abbaye de Cluny*, edd. A. Bernard and A. Bruel, 6 vols. (Collection des documents inédits sur l'histoire de France, Paris, 1876–1904).

25–8 and 61–4 of the present edition, owing to a tear in the corner of the parchment.'

B: Bibl. nat. lat. 17716, late twelfth cent. This manuscript is described by Delisle, no. 129. The *Carta* is on fols. 88ᵛ–90ᵛ. The text of lines 25–6, 75–6, 89–91, and 136–7 is partly lost owing to tears in the parchment.

C: Bibl. nat. nouv. acq. lat. 766, thirteenth cent. This manuscript, known as Cartulary D of Cluny, is listed in Stein, no. 988, and described by Delisle, no. 137, and Bruel, i, pp. xxxi–xxxiv and vi, pp. v–viii. The *Carta* is on fols. 68ʳ–69ʳ.

D: Bibl. nat. lat. 5458, late thirteenth cent. This manuscript, known as Cartulary E of Cluny, is listed in Stein, no. 989, and described by Delisle, no. 140, and Bruel, i, pp. xxxiv–xxxvii. The *Carta* is on fols. 121ʳ–123ᵛ.

So far as the text of the *Carta* is concerned, there is no clear overall pattern of relationship amongst the four versions. In general B agrees with A and almost certainly depends directly upon it. Besides being of considerably later date than A and B, C and D represent a different textual tradition; although there is very occasionally an agreement between B and C, but not between B and D, against the other versions. C and D appear to have a common source. Where they differ, C is almost invariably to be preferred; indeed, as the textual apparatus will make abundantly clear, D contains a number of very unsatisfactory readings which are peculiar to it. There is no doubt that, with the single major qualification which will be noticed in the next paragraph, A is the best of the four versions and D the worst. Thus, A forms the basis of the text which follows in the Appendix.

The *Carta* was printed by M. Marrier in his *Bibliotheca Cluniacensis* (Paris, 1614),[1] basing his text upon D. In one respect his choice was not unfortunate, for the exception to the inferiority of D is that the textual tradition of C and D preserves an important passage in lines 29–35 of the text as printed below, which had dropped out of the tradition of A and B; D offers slightly the better form of it. That the passage belongs to the original text of the *Carta* can scarcely be doubted. The Latin of A and B, which lack it, cannot be satisfactorily construed. The last forty words of the passage omitted in A and B introduce the first of two decisions (lines 31–56, cf. 110–39), which the legate issued in the course of his activities at Cluny, and they are clearly an integral part of a verbatim citation in the *Carta*. The omission is readily accounted for by the passing of a copyist's eye from the words *infra terminos* in line 29 to the

---

[1] Cols. 511–14. Marrier's text was reprinted in *Recueil des historiens des Gaules et de la France*, xiv, ed. M.-J.-J. Brial (Paris, 1806), 47–9. The *Carta* is listed, with some textual notes, in *Recueil des chartes de l'abbaye de Cluny*, ed. Bruel, no. 3549 (vol. iv, p. 677).

same words in line 35—the more readily if in the original the syllable *in-* came at the end of a line.

However, if Marrier's printing of D was in this one respect fortunate, in all others it was not fortunate. For among the erroneous and unsatis- factory readings which are characteristic of D, there are some which are very misleading. The following are the most noteworthy of these. In line 14, D originally gave the name of the grand prior of Cluny as *Hugonem*, not *Oddonem*. Although in D the error is crudely corrected to *Hoddnem*, Marrier adopted the reading *Hugonem*. He thereby obscured the fact that the prior in question was Odo I (*c.* 1070–1079/80), later cardinal-bishop of Ostia (1080–8) and then Pope Urban II (1088–99).[1] In line 57, the text of D makes nonsense of the name of the place where Peter of Albano met the Burgundian bishops, by reading *an set* instead of *Ans(a)e* (Anse-sur-Saône). Marrier extended *an set* to *anno sequenti*, thus adding a confusion to the chronology of events. In line 62, he compounded the difficulty by following D in wrongly giving the date of Peter of Albano's meetings with the bishops as *MLXXVIII*, whereas the three earlier texts agree in reading *MLXXVIIII*.[2] Thus, Marrier's text is in important respects unsatisfactory and misleading, and a new, critical edition of the *Carta* may be useful.

So far as its subject-matter is concerned, I have discussed elsewhere the background to the dispute which brought Cardinal Peter of Albano (*c.* 1072–89) to Cluny.[3] Shortage of evidence makes the course of the immediate crisis of 1079–80 in many respects obscure, but a probable reconstruction of it is as follows.

[1] For Urban as grand prior of Cluny and for the chronology, see A. Becker, *Papst Urban II.* (Schriften der Monumenta Germaniae historica, 19/i, Stuttgart, 1964), i. 41–51. The copyist of D seems to have made a simple mistake by at first confusing the names of Abbot Hugh and Prior Odo. But he has misled some scholars into identifying the prior with Abbot Hugh's nephew of the same name, Hugh of Montaigu. Also, the true date of Odo's becoming cardinal-bishop of Ostia is 1080, not, as has widely been concluded, 1078.

[2] i.e. the council took place in 1080, reckoning the beginning of the year from 1 Jan. For the *stylus Florentinus* and its use at Cluny, see R. L. Poole, *Studies in Chronology and History* (Oxford, 1934), pp. 13–20.

[3] *The Cluniacs and the Gregorian Reform* (Oxford, 1970), esp. pp. 53–6. For earlier studies of this matter, and of Peter of Albano, see A. Hessel, 'Cluny und Mâcon. Ein Beitrag zur Geschichte der päpstlichen Exemtionprivilegien', *Zeitschrift für Kirchengeschichte*, xxi (1901), pp. 516–24; G. Letonnellier, *L'Abbaye exempte de Cluny et le Saint-Siège* (Archives de la France monastique, 22, Paris and Ligugé, 1923); — Rony, 'Un procès canonique entre S. Jubin, archevêque de Lyon, et S. Hugues, abbé de Cluny', *Revue Mabillon*, xviii (1928), pp. 177–85; T. Schieffer, *Die päpstlichen Legaten in Frankreich vom Vertrage von Meersen (870) bis zum Schisma von 1130* (Historische Studien, 263, Berlin, 1935), pp. 119–21; G. Miccoli, *Pietro Igneo. Studi sull'età gregoriana* (Rome, 1960).

It seems to have begun early in 1079 at the prompting of the canons of the cathedral of Saint-Vincent, Mâcon, whose actions throughout it were consistently aggressive and turbulent. They levelled some charges of a purely temporal kind against Cluny, and prevailed upon the bishop of Mâcon, the less resolute and essentially peaceable Landeric of Berzé (1074–96), to travel to Rome and plead his church's cause before Pope Gregory VII (1073–85). Landeric had the support of his metropolitan, Archbishop Gebuin of Lyons (1077–82). However, Gregory reacted to his complaints with caution, and sought to negotiate a reconciliation between the bishops and Abbot Hugh of Cluny (1049–1109). Cluny's Burgundian opponents appear to have reacted against Gregory's caution by impatiently taking the law into their own hands. The *Carta* indicates that Archbishop Gebuin placed an interdict upon certain churches on Cluny's lands,[1] and that he was a party to the expulsion of Cluniac monks from Pouilly-lès-Feurs, a priory which Cluny had possessed since 966 and which lay within his diocese.[2] Bishop Landeric also became directly involved by excommunicating certain of Cluny's chapels and their chaplains.[3] These actions by the bishops were doubly offensive to Gregory. He deplored the strife between Archbishop Gebuin and Abbot Hugh, to both of whom he looked for collaboration in the work of reform; and he laid down that whichever of them resisted a settlement of their dispute would incur his grave anger.[4] More offensive still, the bishops' actions radically challenged a series of papal privileges which exempted Cluny and its possessions from episcopal jurisdiction and interference, and especially his own privilege of 1075.[5] The bishops were throwing down the glove to papal authority in a way which Gregory was the last pope to disregard. Abbot Hugh seized the initiative which now lay open to him by sending his grand prior, Odo, to Rome.

Gregory's immediate response was to dispatch Peter of Albano to Cluny as his legate. The *Carta* is the legate's final account of his dealings in Burgundy which he wrote before his departure,[6] and it provides the only connected narrative of events which has survived. It describes how, after his arrival, Peter took some initial steps on the feast of the Purifica-

---

[1] ll. 110–23.   [2] ll. 123–30.   [3] ll. 23–4.

[4] See his letter to Bishop Hugh of Die in *The Epistolae Vagantes of Pope Gregory VII*, ed. Cowdrey (Oxford, 1972), no. 30 (Apr.–May, 1079), pp. 76–8.

[5] For Gregory's privilege, see L. Santifaller, *Quellen und Forschungen zum Urkunden- und Kanzleiwesen Papst Gregors VII., Teil i, Quellen: Urkunden, Regesten, Facsimilia* (Studi e Testi, 190, Vatican City, 1957), no. 107 (9 Dec. 1075), pp. 95–100. For earlier papal documents in Cluny's favour, and for the history of episcopal resistance to its position, see Cowdrey, *The Cluniacs and the Gregorian Reform*, pp. 15–22, 32–57.   [6] l. 8.

tion (2 February 1080) in the Lady Chapel and in the monastery of Cluny. He confirmed the papal privileges which had been issued on Cluny's behalf, freed from excommunication the chapels and chaplains which the bishop of Mâcon had placed under sentence, and forbad the bishop to impose such illicit sanctions for the future. But the most important of his actions on 2 February was to reinforce Cluny's immunity from any kind of lay interference by securing its lands and their inhabitants from all kinds of violence and assault. This was the purpose of the first of the two formal pronouncements which Peter incorporated in the *Carta*.[1] After prohibiting homicide, plunder, and robbery in Cluny's vicinity, it defined for the first time of which there is record the precise topographical limits of Cluny's immediate *banleuca*. They were to begin from a stream called the Saunat to the south-west of Cluny; thence they ran by way of the church of Saint-Germain, Ruffey, to the cross at Lournand and so to a mill on the River Grosne at Tornsac; next they passed through the vill of Varennes and thence by another, unidentified landmark (*Ios*) to the starting-point on the Saunat. Next, Peter's pronouncement restrained the knights of six neighbouring castles, Brancion, Berzé-le-Châtel, Saint-Jean-de-la-Bussière, Suin, Sigy-le-Châtel, and Uxelles, from plundering the peasantry of Cluny's vills and from subjecting them to unjust exactions. Finally, it placed a special responsibility upon the knights of the town of Cluny itself to avoid complicity in such abuses. All breaches of this ordinance were to incur the penalty of excommunication.[2]

Having thus dealt with Cluny's local and temporal interests, Peter of Albano proceeded to convene an ecclesiastical council to meet at the traditional place, the church of Saint-Bernard, Anse, some sixty-five kilometres distant from Cluny. His purpose was to settle, in accordance with the pope's instructions to him, the issues in dispute between Cluny and the Burgundian bishops who resisted its exemption. In the *Carta* Peter of Albano carefully specified the date of the council—6 February 1080. At it, Abbot Hugh was supported, amongst others, by the Cluniac Warmund, archbishop of Vienne (1077–81)[3] and Bishop Agano of Autun (1055–98).

According to the legate's account, he first called upon Bishop Landeric of Mâcon, who expressed his readiness to be subject to the

[1] ll. 31–56.

[2] There is a topographical description of Cluny's *banleuca* in T. Chavot, *Le Mâconnais. Géographie historique* (Paris and Mâcon, 1884), p. 110. For a useful map, see N. Hunt, *Cluny under Saint Hugh (1049–1109)* (London, 1967), plate x.

[3] For Warmund, see N. Huyghebaert, 'Un légat de Grégoire VII en Flandre, Warmond de Vienne', *Revue d'histoire ecclésiastique*, xl (1944–5), pp. 187–200.

judgement of the pope and his legate. Archbishop Warmund thereupon came forward with some new allegations against him. Warmund had lately returned from Rome, bearing instructions from Gregory to visit Cluny and communicate some unspecified messages to Abbot Hugh. Since he was at Cluny during an Embertide—perhaps that of Michaelmas or December 1079—Abbot Hugh called on him to ordain some monks in accordance with Cluny's privileges of exemption.[1] This last action called forth the militancy of the canons of Mâcon. As Warmund was leaving Cluny, they and their henchmen set upon him; they so insulted and assaulted him that he had to flee back to Cluny for refuge. Bishop Landeric was absent at the time, so not directly to blame. But when Warmund complained to him in writing, he did nothing to avenge the crime. So, on his own behalf and on the monks', Warmund now sought redress from the papal legate. Peter thereupon read out Gregory's privilege for Cluny of 1075, and declared Landeric to be excommunicated for his failure to uphold it. He then raised the matter of the excommunication of Cluny's chapels and chaplains. This led to a prolonged debate, in which the bishop weakly denied knowledge of Cluny's papal privileges, while Abbot Hugh insisted that he had given him warning about them. The legate therefore suspended him from his office and reserved his case for the pope's own decision. The canons of Mâcon gave an angry and threatening response to the suspension. Peter replied by excommunicating them for their violence against Archbishop Warmund of Vienne, and according to a form which the pope had provided he freed all whom Bishop Landeric had unjustly excommunicated.

Finally, the legate called upon Archbishop Gebuin of Lyons to obey papal precepts and accede to the form of submission which the pope had provided for him to make. When he proved obdurate, Peter proceeded against him according to Gregory's instructions. His sentence forms the second of the decisions which appear verbatim in the *Carta*.[2] He freed from interdict all Cluny's churches which the archbishop had wrongfully banned and declared invalid any similar sentences in the future. He restored to Cluny the priory of Pouilly, ordered that the nuns who had been intruded with Gebuin's connivance should leave by the first Sunday in Lent (1 March 1080), and guaranteed to the Cluniacs an undisturbed possession of it for the future.

Peter of Albano thus upheld Cluny's immunity against the temporal depredations of its neighbours, and its exemption against the claims of the local episcopate to exercise spiritual jurisdiction over both it and its

---

[1] It is clear from the manuscript versions that Abbot Hugh, not Gregory, initiated the ordinations; I correct my statement in *The Cluniacs and the Gregorian Reform*, p. 54.   [2] ll. 110–39.

churches. The *Carta* is his own record of this twofold vindication. Gregory quickly confirmed and completed his legate's work by his allocution in praise and defence of Cluny at his Lateran council of March 1080.[1] As regards the new departure which Peter of Albano made when he defined the topographical limits of Cluny's *banleuca*, Pope Urban II continued his work by making a solemn and similarly detailed definition of its limits in October 1095, when he visited his former monastery to consecrate the high altar of Abbot Hugh's third church.[2] Peter's legatine journey thus met with the full approval of Rome, and it is a landmark in the close relationship of sympathy and interest which bound Cluny to the reformed papacy of the later eleventh century.

APPENDIX[3]

Carta Petri Albanensis Episcopi et Cardinalis Romani de Immunitate Cluniaci

Qualiter domnus Petrus Albanensis episcopus et cardinalis auctoritate beatorum apostolorum et domni Gregorii papae loca circumiacentia Cluniaco monasterio infra terminos inferius adnotatos muniuit, et quam uiriliter restitit Lugdunensi archiepiscopo in his que male innodauerat, quam prudenter absoluit, et Matiscensem episcopum qualiter a 5 liminibus sanctae ecclesiae disiunxit.

Ego Petrus Dei gratia Albanensis episcopus et cardinalis Romane ecclesiae, quod in his partibus Burgundiae, preceptis et informatione domni mei VII Gregorii papae, anno intronizationis eius septimo egi, scripto et annotatione ad posteritatis memoriam transmittendum ratum 10 duximus. Domnus Hugo Cluniacensis abbas, propter infestationes que inferebantur ab episcopis Lugdunensi et Matiscensi, Gebuino uidelicet et Landrico, suo principali loco et cellis et adiacentiis, misit domnum

1–6 *This paragraph is lacking in* CD   11 duximus: duxi CD
12 Matiscensi: Matisconensi C

[1] *The Epistolae Vagantes of Pope Gregory VII*, ed. Cowdrey, no. 39, pp. 96–8; cf. no. 38, pp. 94–6.
[2] *Sermo* i, J. P. Migne, *Patrologia Latina*, 151. 561–4; cf. *De aduentu Vrbani papae II ad monasterium Cluniacense*, in S. Baluze, *Miscellanea*, vi (Paris, 1713), p. 475.
[3] In the text which follows, punctuation and the use of capital letters are modernized. ę is printed as ae. The apparatus records only significant variant readings, not minor differences of spelling and transpositions of words.
I am grateful to the authorities of the Bibliothèque nationale for supplying photographs of the manuscripts, and for permission to publish the text.

Oddonem priorem ipsius Cluniaci ad limina beatorum apostolorum
15 Petri et Pauli, et ad uiscera paternae pietatis domni mei supradicti
beatissimi domni Gregorii papae; qui tandem post multiplicem
diuersorum uerborum trutinationem, tanti loci calamitati et inqui-
etudini compassus, me tantillum ad illas dirimendas ac determinan-
das delegauit. Quique ueniens post multos labores et sudores in iam
20 dictum locum in die purificationis beate Mariae, tam in capella
eiusdem gloriose Virginis quam in monasterio, sermone perorato,
auctoritate pontificum Romanorum per priuilegia huic loco attributa
publice corroborans manifestaui; capellas et capellanos quos contra
Romana priuilegia Matiscensis episcopus excommunicauerat absolui;
25 et si deinceps aliqua presumptione excommunicauerit cum facere
nullomodo possit, ne quisquam obseruet uel inde curet omnes astantes
commonefeci, et insuper ut nulla persona cuiusque dignitatis uel
potestatis rapinas, predas, siue aliquas infestationes loco isti, habi-
tatoribus, atque confugientibus infra terminos subnotatas inferre
30 presumat, apostolica mihi auctoritate concessa tali modo statui et
determinaui: Ego P[etrus] Dei gratia Albanensis episcopus et legatus
apostolicae sedis interdico ex parte omnipotentis Dei et beati P[etri]
apostolorum principis, necnon etiam ex parte domni mei Gregorii papae,
ut nullus omnino homo cuiuslibet potentiae uel dignitatis huic Cluni-
35 acensi loco infra terminos inferius annotatos, homicidia, predas, siue
rapinas uel aliquas inuasiones, facere presumat. Hii sunt autem termini:
a riuo de Salnai, et ab aecclesia Rufiacensis uillae et cruce de Lornant,
a termino quoque molini de Tornasac, per uillam quae dicitur Varenna,
per terminum qui dirigitur per Ios ad riuum de Salnane. Si quis autem
40 huius nostri interdicti seu interminationis inuentus fuerit uiolator siue
infractor, ab hodierna die et deinceps nouerit se uinculo anathematis
innodandum quousque digna satisfactione peniteat. Ammoneo etiam
omnes milites qui in his proximis nobis castellis habitant, uidelicet
Branciduno, Berziaco, Buxeria, Seduno, Setgiaco, et Oscella, ut ruricolis
45 nostris seu rusticis qui in circumiacentibus huic loco habitant uillis
nullam lesionem uel torturam inferre presumant. Malas quoque consuetudines quas actenus ab eis requisierunt, siue de conducto siue de

14 Oddonem: Hugonem *altered to* Hoddnem (*sic*) *by the original scribe* D
apostolorum *om.* D   16 domni: *om.* CD   22 auctoritate: auctoritatem CD   per: qui B   attributa: attributam CD   23 contra: eadem
add. CD   26 quisquam: *text lost owing to a tear in the parchment* A; quis
quod, *then* absoluet *deleted* D   27 cuiusque: eiusque D   29–35 infra
terminos . . . loco infra: *this passage is lacking in* AB, *which read only in*
31 P[etrus]: *om.* C   37 Salnai: Salna D   38 Tornasac: Tornesac D
39 per terminum: a termino etiam CD   Ios: *thus in* ABCD   Salnane: Salnac
BC; Salnat D   44 Setgiaco: Segiaco C

substantia eorum, ulterius ab eis non repetant neque inde eos aliquo
modo apprehendere aut ledere presumant. Sed et his qui necdum has
malas consuetudines requisierunt ne in posterum eas requirant inter- 50
dicimus ex parte Dei et contradicimus. Precipue uero milites qui in hac
Cluniacensi uilla habitant hoc cauere monemus, ne huius mali conci-
tatores fiant; quia quanto uicinius commanent, tanto eos oportet a
seruorum Dei iniuriis abstinere. Quod si quispiam huius precepti
tenorem infregerit, supradicte excommunicationis ultione feriatur 55
donec satisfactione puniatur. Hoc peracto, colloquium cum episcopis
propter quorum molestationem missus fueram Ansae apud sanctum
Bernardum habendum statui, in quo tante discordie malum secundum
informationem quam a domno meo papa Gregorio acceperam deter-
minare ualerem adiutorio omnipotentis Dei. Tandem post festum 60
beatae Agathae VIII Id. Februarii, illucescente feria V, anno ab incarnatione Domini MLXXVIIII, indictione II, ad supradictum locum
uenientes, presentibus domno Warmundo Viennensi archiepiscopo et
domno Hugone Cluniensi abbate et domno Aganone Eduensi episcopo
et aliquibus abbatibus cum prudentibus uiris plurimis, conuenimus 65
domnum Landricum Matiscensem episcopum, si uellet acquiescere et
subdi preceptis apostolicis ac nostre paruitati qui uice apostolica
fungebamur. Qui cum libenter se uelle acquiescere respondisset,
domnus archiepiscopus Viennensis querimoniam tam suam quam
Cluniensis monasterii his uerbis fecit: 'Dudum, domne cardinalis et 70
legate apostolice sedis, rediens Roma, precepto domni Gregorii papae
ueni Cluniacum nonnulla ex parte ipsius domno abbati intimaturus.
Tum quia tempus oportunum instabat faciendis sacris ordinibus, iussus
et rogatus a domno abbate et fratribus, aliquos fratrum secundum
auctoritatem priuilegiorum pontificum Romanorum ab olim ipsi loco 75
datam ordinaui. His peractis, dum redirem, Matiscenses canonici,
insidiis mihi paratis, derepente fulti armata manu et pedestri super me
ac nostra irruerunt, baculum pastoralem cum propria tunica et sagmario
tulerunt, seruientes nobis cedentes ualde dehonestauerunt, lanceam
gutturi proprio admouentes, "Ne uiuat uiolator et adulterator sponsae 80
sanctae Vincentii" clamabant, et cum magno dedecore ad Cluniacum
uellem nollem reuersus sum. Inde a domno Matiscensi qui tunc aberat
iustitiam per litteras quesiui, sed huc minime impetraui; quam a uobis

49 modo: uel *add.* CD   53 quanto: canto C   55 infregerit: non *erased,*
then fregerit D   56 donec: digna *add.* CD   puniatur: peniteat CD
57 fueram: fuerat A; fuerat *corrected to* fueram B   Ansae: an set D   62
MLXXVIIII: MLXXVIII D   65 cum: aliquibus *add.* D   68 fungebamur: fungebamus D   respondisset: respondisse D   70 his uerbis:
hisumbis (*sic*) B   fecit: fecisset C   79 cedentes: cedente D   82
Matiscensi: episcopo *add.* C   83 huc: usque *add.* CD

qui estis apostolice sedis legatus mihi et dominis Cluniensibus supplico
85 fieri.' Post haec, lecto beatissimi papae Gregorii VII priuilegio, eundem
Matiscensem anathematis iaculo perfossum comperimus, quoniam
contra Romanorum decreta pontificum et precipue domni Gregorii
fecisse didicimus. Tunc eundem interrogauimus utrum priusquam
capellas et capellanos Cluniacenses excommunicasset hoc in priuilegio
90 sibi interdictum fuisse cognouisset. Ille uero cum se priuilegium
minime legisse fateretur, domnus abbas Cluniensis respondit: 'Nonne
ego dixi uobis, uos priuilegiorum auctoritati obuiare si uel capellas uel
capellanos nostri monasterii interdiceretis?' Tandem cum nonnulla
negaret et plurima negare nequiret, dixi ei ut aut culpam suam inde
95 faceret aut condigna satisfactione se purgaret. Quod super hoc diu
multumque conuentus, cum neutrum facere uellet, obstinatia sua
exigente a pontificali et sacerdotali officio usque ante presentiam domni
nostri Gregorii papae, cuius auctoritatem spernebat, eum suspendimus.
Tunc supradicti Matiscenses canonici, audita sui pontificis suspensione
100 ultra modum efferati, addentes peiora prioribus, conuitia multa
intorserunt in nos cum minis. Postea dehonestatores domni archiepiscopi clericos et laicos ab introitu omnium aecclesiarum et a corpore
et a sanguine Domini Ihesu Christi, donec peniteant et condigne
satisfaciant, separauimus, et queque iniuste episcopus excommuni-
105 cauerat secundum datam nobis formam absoluimus. Ad ultimum
domnum Lugdunensem allocuti sumus, ut sicut sapiens obediret
preceptis apostolicis et formae qua nos informauerat domnus noster
Gregorius papa. Qui cum sepe inuitatus et ammonitus nequaquam
uellet oboedire, eius faciente inoboedientia subnotatam secundum
110 quod nobis erat preceptum protulimus promulgationem: Quoniam
frater noster Gebuinus Lugdunensis archiepiscopus nec fraternae
karitatis consilio nec aequitatis rationi nec apostolicis domni mei
beatissimi papae Gregorii, cuius uice indigni fungimur, decretis et
preceptis uult acquiescere et obedire, ut ecclesias Cluniensis cenobii,
115 quas iniuste excommunicasse uidetur, secundum tenorem imposite
legationis uelit absoluere, illas uidelicet quas ante cognitum predictum
domni nostri Gregorii papae decretum siue per apostolicorum con-
cessionem priuilegiorum siue aliter adquisisse et tenuisse probatur.

84–5 et dominis . . . supplico fieri: *erased but supplied in the margin by a later
hand* D   90 fuisse cognouisset: fuisset AB   93 nonnulla: nulla
AB   94 nequiret: non posset C   inde: suam inde *add.* A; suam *add.*,
then inde *deleted* B   95 condigna: cum digna D   Quod: Qui CD
100 conuitia: *reading uncertain in* A; cum uicia B   103 a: *om.* CD
105 formam: forma A   106 domnum: *om.* D   107 formae:
forte D   115 imposite: nobis *add.* CD   116 predictum:
predicti CD

Ideo nos, necessitate coacti, auctoritate beatorum apostolorum P[etri] et P[auli], sicut nobis iniunctum est, supradictas aecclesias absoluimus. 120 Si uero idem archiepiscopus easdem aecclesias siue capellanos earum iniuste interdicere presumpserit, talem interdictionem et excommunicationem irritam esse decernimus. Poliacum autem, quia sine canonico iudicio, uiolenter eiectis monachis, a Cluniensi monasterio per iniustam expoliationem ablatum et abstractum est, apostolicae aequitatis con- 125 cessione Cluniensi cenobio reddimus et ut libere possideat omnino precipimus. Sanctimonialibus quae predictum Poliacum inuaserunt ex parte beatorum apostolorum P[etri] et P[auli] precipimus, ut usque ad primam dominicam proxime quadragesimae eundem locum dimittant eumque monachis quos eiecerunt ex integro restituant. Quod si facere 130 noluerint, ab introitu aecclesie corporis dominici et sanguinis post predictum terminum eas omnino separamus; et ne in eadem Poliaci aecclesia quandiu ipse sanctimoniales ibidem remanere presumpserint diuinum officium celebretur, apostolica interdictione prohibemus. Si quis autem clericorum aut laicorum predictas sanctimoniales contra 135 interdictum nostrum ad obtinendum eundem locum aliquo malo ingenio uel uiolentia adiuuare ac defendere ausus fuerit, sciat se ab omnium aecclesiarum introitu et a communione corporis et sanguinis Domini esse separatum, donec resipiscat.

119 apostolorum: *om.* D   121 archiepiscopus: ira commotus *add.* CD
129 proxime: *om.* C

XII

THE MAHDIA CAMPAIGN OF 1087

IN 1087 a sea-borne force comprising mainly Pisans and Genoese, but augmented by men from Rome and Amalfi, attacked and plundered the Moslem town of Mahdia and its suburb Zawīla. Mahdia (al-Mahdīya) is situated on the North African coast, between Sousse and Sfax, in what is today Tunisia. The principal account of the Mahdia campaign is the Latin rhythm usually known as the *Carmen in victoriam Pisanorum*. Pertz long ago drew attention to its value for historians of the eleventh century[1]; and Erdmann regarded the expedition as a forerunner of the First Crusade. In his judgment it was 'ganz als Kreuzzug ausgeführt'.[2] The *Carmen* has been several times printed, but in editions which are inadequate and difficult to obtain. The purpose of this study is to present the most accurate text possible, together with comment on it and a discussion of the historical circumstances of the victory that the *Carmen* celebrates. Since the events of 1087 left their mark upon the memory of the western Moslem world, they will be considered from the Moslem as well as from the Christian angle.[3]

1. G. H. Pertz, *Archiv der Gesellschaft für ältere deutsche Geschichtskunde*, vii (1839), 539.
2. C. Erdmann, *Die Entstehung des Kreuzzugsgedankens* (Stuttgart, 1935), pp. 180, 272–4, 284–5, 291.
3. The following abbreviations are used:
Amari: M. Amari, *Biblioteca arabo-sicula*, 2 vols. (Turin and Rome, 1880–1). (Italian translations of Arabic sources.)
E.I.: *Encyclopaedia of Islam*, eds. M. T. Houtsma *et al.*, 4 vols. (London and Leyden, 1908–36).
E.I.²: *Encyclopaedia of Islam*, 2nd edn., eds. B. Lewis *et al.*, 3 vols (London and Leyden, 1960–).
Fonti: Fonti per la storia d'Italia, 94 vols. (Rome, 1887–).
G.F.: *Gesta Francorum et aliorum Hierosolimitanorum*, ed. R. Hill (London, *etc.*, 1962).
M.G.H.: *Monumenta Germaniae historica.*
  Briefe: Die Briefe der deutschen Kaiserzeit, 5 vols. (Weimar, 1949–).
  DD HIV: Diplomata regum et imperatorum Germaniae, vi: *Die Urkunde Heinrichs IV.*, ed. D. von Gladiss, 2 vols. (Berlin and Weimar, 1941–59).
  Epist. sel.: Epistolae selectae, 5 vols. (Berlin, 1916–).
  Schriften: Schriften der M.G.H., 24 vols. (Leipzig and Stuttgart, 1938–).
  SS.: *Scriptores*, 32 vols. (Hanover, *etc.*, 1826–1934).
Migne, P.L.: J. P. Migne, *Patrologiae cursus completus, Series Latina*, 221 vols. (Paris, 1841–64).
Muratori, *Antiq.*: L. A. Muratori, *Antiquitates Italicae medii aevi*, 6 vols. (Milan, 1738–42).
Muratori, *R.I.S.*: L. A. Muratori, *Rerum Italicarum scriptores*, 25 vols. (Milan, 1723–51).
R.I.S.²: *Rerum Italicarum scriptores*, new edn., 34 vols. (Città di Castello, Bologna, 1900–).

The text of the *Carmen* has survived through only a single copy, in Brussels, Bibliothèque royale Albert Ier, MS. 3879–919, fos. 63^r–65^v. This twelfth-century manuscript of 174 folios is of Italian origin.[1] It opens with the words: 'Incipit prologus libri Guidonis compositi de variis historiis pro diversis utilitatibus lectori proventuris.' It includes a geographical compendium by the same Guido of Pisa, but there is no suggestion that he was the author of the *Carmen*. The Brussels manuscript as a whole is the work of a somewhat careless copyist, who made many slips in transcribing an already existing version of the *Liber Guidonis*.[2] The text of the *Carmen* which it includes is thus at very least at two removes, and perhaps more, from the original.

In the manuscript the *Carmen* has no title or introductory rubric. It consists of seventy-three stanzas, each intended to have four divisions of fifteen syllables. It is written in the 'Lombardic' measure traditionally used for historical poems and dirges, comprising rhythmic trochaic tetrameters.[3] But, at least as the *Carmen* stands in this copy, the metrical composition is far from faultless and the rhyme sometimes fails. The scribe indicated the divisions within each stanza by means of the punctuation. For this purpose he used the symbol ? which, apart from the full point at the end of almost every stanza, is the only mark used. I have punctuated as he does, but with the substitution for the ? of a comma, semi-colon, colon or exclamation mark as the sense suggests. Thus, except where the rhythm breaks down badly, punctuation indicates the division into tetrameters; where serious breakdown occurs I have adhered to the punctuation of the manuscript. In a far from satisfactory text I have been as sparing as possible with major emendation; where it appeared essential it is recorded in the textual notes. I have corrected without comment a number of minor mis-spellings, and for ease of reference I have numbered the stanzas of the *Carmen*. Thus, reference is made to the number of the stanza, with the letters *a*, *b*, *c*, *d* added as appropriate to indicate divisions. Capital letters follow modern conventions.

For the date and authorship of the *Carmen* there is no direct evidence whatsoever, either internal or external. The fervid tone of urban patriotism indicates a Pisan author. The drawing of so many comparisons with the military heroes and warlike events of the Old Testament points to a clerk rather than a layman; indeed, to a

---

1. For a fuller description of the manuscript, see J. van den Gheyn, *Catalogue des manuscrits de la Bibliothèque royale de Belgique*, v (Brussels, 1905), pp. 27–30, no. 3095; also C. P. Bock, 'Lettres à Monsieur L. Bethmann sur un manuscrit de la Bibliothèque de Bourgogne', *Annuaire de la Bibliothèque royale de Belgique*, xii (1851), 41–213.

2. Bock, pp. 44, 69–71.

3. F. J. E. Raby, *A History of Secular Latin Poetry in the Middle Ages*, 2 vols. (2nd edn., Oxford, 1957), ii. 153–4.

clerk familiar with the propaganda of Christian warfare emanating from the circle of Bishop Anselm II of Lucca.[1] It has generally, and probably rightly, been supposed that the *Carmen* was composed very soon after the victory at Mahdia.[2] The statement that the Pisans consecrated a church to St Sixtus[3] does not necessarily point to a late date: it may express an intention rather than its fulfilment; if not, consecration may not have been long delayed, for the great third church at Cluny, begun in 1088, was sufficiently advanced in building for Pope Urban II to consecrate its high altar in 1095. Furthermore, three comparable poems appear to have been written soon after the victories which they celebrated. The *Carmen de Hastingae proelio* may have been composed within months of the battle of Hastings in 1066. The *Carmen de bello Saxonico* appears to date from the winter following King Henry IV of Germany's victory on the Unstrut in 1075. At Pisa itself, the *Liber Maiolichinus*, which applauded the victorious Balearic campaign of 1114–15 against the Moslems, was nearly contemporary with it.[4] The *Carmen* concerning the victory at Mahdia has a similar ring of triumphant immediacy. On the other hand, it shows no awareness of either the summoning or the success of the First Crusade, in which the Pisans under Archbishop Daimbert took part. Still less does it read like one of the *excitatoria* written to encourage recruiting for the Crusade. There is every reason to see it as a pre-Crusading composition, dating from or immediately after the late summer of 1087.

A wide variety of further sources, both Christian and Moslem, refer to the Mahdia campaign. So far as the Latin sources are concerned, they may be listed according to their provenance. The earliest record at Pisa comes in the *Chronicon Pisanum*. It gave a brief notice which may itself depend on the *Carmen*, for it added only local detail regarding the church of St Sixtus.[5] In his *Annales Pisani*, of late twelfth-century date, Bernardo Maragone incorporated the notice of the *Chronicon* with only verbal alterations.[6] The fourteenth-century vernacular compilation which begins the *Cronaca di Pisa* of Ranieri Sardo included a similar account, adding some independent if legendary details.[7] The late *Breviarium Pisanae*

1. *Infra*, pp. 16–17.

2. *e.g.* by Erdmann, p. 273; and the *Repertorium fontium historiae medii aevi*, ed. A. Potthast, new edn., iii (Rome, 1970), p. 136.   3. 70c.

4. *The Carmen de Hastingae Proelio of Guy Bishop of Amiens*, eds. C. Morton and H. Muntz (Oxford, 1972), pp. xv–xxix; *Carmen de bello Saxonico*, in *Quellen zur Geschichte Kaiser Heinrichs IV.*, ed. F. J. Schmale (*Ausgewählte Quellen zur deutschen Geschichte des Mittelalters*, xii, Berlin, 1963), pp. 22–23; *Liber Maiolichinus de gestis Pisanorum illustribus*, ed. C. Calisse, *Fonti*, xxix (1904), p. ix.

5. *Chronicon Pisanum seu Fragmentum auctoris incerti*, *s.a.* 1088, *Gli Annales Pisani di Bernardo Maragone*, ed. M. Lupo Gentile, *R.I.S.*², vi, pt. 2, pp. 101–2.

6. *s.a.* 1088, as in the last note, pp. 6–7.

7. *Cronaca di Pisa di Ranieri Sardo*, *s.a.* 1076 or 1085 in different MSS., ed. O. Banti, *Fonti*, xcix (1963), 19–20.

historiae also added some legendary details to Bernardo Maragone.[1] At Genoa, in the middle of the twelfth century, Caffaro merely noted an expedition to Africa in 1088. But a footnote to his original codex placed it in the reign of Pope Victor III, that is, in 1087, giving brief details.[2]

The expedition was recorded in Swabia soon after it occurred by the leading Gregorian chronicler, Bernold of St Blasien. He told of an Italian attack on the lands of a pagan African king, and of their devastation.[3]

In South Italy it was the chroniclers of Montecassino who provided the leading testimony. The *Chronica monasterii Cassinensis* ascribed the initiative in the Mahdia campaign to the abbot of Montecassino, Desiderius, who on 9 May 1087 was consecrated pope as Victor III.[4] Both the older recensions of the *Annales Cassinenses* simply recorded the Pisan attack on and victory over the Saracens in Africa.[5] The *Annales Beneventani* similarly recorded the Pisan and Genoese raid upon them.[6] Amongst the Norman chroniclers, only Gaufredus Malaterra, who completed his work by 1101, referred to the Mahdia campaign.[7] One papal letter made a retrospective, if indirect, allusion. In 1092, when Pope Urban II raised the see of Pisa to an archbishopric and subjected the churches of Corsica to it, he gave among his reasons the renown of Pisa through its triumphs over the Saracens.[8]

On the Moslem side, a variety of writers referred to the Mahdia campaign with its, for them, disastrous results. First, the Pisan *Carmen* had its counterpart in a long elegiac *ḳaṣīda*,[9] by a writer named Abu al-Ḥasan ibn Muḥammad al-Ḥaddād who seems to have been an eye-witness of events at Mahdia. Only the opening lines of the poem survive, and these in a mutilated state[10]; but they communicate the dismay felt in the defeated and sacked cities at the scale and ferocity of the assault. The fragment of the *ḳaṣīda* was transmitted by another writer, Abu 'l-Ṣalt Ummaya.[11] An Andalusian

---

1. *s.a.* 1075, 1088, as printed in Muratori, *R.I.S.* vi. 168; see O. Banti, 'Studio sulla genesi dei testi cronistici pisani del secolo xiv', *Bulletino dell'Istituto storico italiano per il medio evo e Archivio Muratoriano*, lxxv (1963), 264, 267–8.

2. *Annali Genovesi di Caffaro e de'suoi continuatori*, ed. L. T. Belgrano, *Fonti*, xi (1890), p. 13 and n. 4.

3. Bernold, *Chronicon, s.a.* 1088, ed. G. Waitz, *M.G.H., SS.* v. 447.

4. iii. 71, ed. W. Wattenbach, *M.G.H., SS.* vii. 751.

5. *Annales Cassinenses ex annalibus Montis Cassini antiquis et continuatis excerpti, s.a.* 1087, ed. G. Smidt, *M.G.H., SS.* xxx, pt. 2, p. 1424. So, too, the *Annales Ceccanenses*, edited as the *Chronica Fossaenovae*, Muratori, *R.I.S.* vii. 866.

6. *s.a.* 1089, *M.G.H., SS.* iii. 182.

7. *De rebus gestis Rogerii Calabriae et Siciliae comitis et Roberti Guiscardi ducis fratris eius, auctore Gaufredo Malaterra*, iv. 3, ed. E. Pontieri, *R.I.S.*² v, pt. 1, pp. 86–87.

8. *Ep.* 63, Migne, *P.L.* cli. 345.

9. For a discussion of this poetic form, see F. Krenkow, 'Ḳaṣīda', *E.I.* ii. 796–7.

10. Amari, ii. 64–65; English version in W. Heywood, *A History of Pisa* (Cambridge, 1921), pp. 38–39.

11. S. M. Stern, 'Abu 'l-Ṣalt Ummaya', *E.I.*² i. 148–9.

by birth, he came to Mahdia in A.H. 505/A.D. 1111–12 as an exile from Alexandria. He became the panegyrist of three of Mahdia's early twelfth-century emirs, for one of whom, al-Ḥasan (515/1121–563/1167), he composed a lost historical work. Material for the history of Mahdia which is derived from him is, therefore, of good authority. The *Riḥla* (*Travels*) of al-Tidjānī incorporated from Abu 'l-Ṣalt the fragment of the *ḳaṣīda*. The *Riḥla* is an account of its author's extensive journey in North Africa during 706/1307 and the three following years[1]; in it he also made use of Abu 'l-Ṣalt's record of the events of 1087.[2]

Within the medieval period five further Moslem historians referred to them: the Mosul author Ibn al-Athīr, who completed his *al-Kāmil* (*Collection of Histories*) some two years before his death in 630/1233[3]; the Egyptian al-Nuwairī (677/1279–732/1332), in his *Nihāyat al-'Arab* (*The Ultimate Aim*)[4]; the *al-Bayān al-Mughrib* (*Admirable Exposition*), written in 706/1306–7 by Ibn ʿIdhārī of Morocco[5]; Ibn al-Khaṭīb (713/1313–776/1375), who wrote his *Aʿmāl al-Aʿlām* (*Deeds of Famous Men*) at Granada towards the of his life[6]; and Ibn Khaldūn (732/1332–808/1406), most of whose work was done in the Maghreb and Egypt, in his *Kitāb al-ʿIbar* (*Universal History*).[7]

Historians usually give 1087 as the date of the Mahdia campaign. The month of the attack on the Moslem cities is settled by the testimony of the *Carmen* that Zawīla was won on the feast-day of the Pisan patron St Sixtus (6 August).[8] But, leaving aside manifest impossibilities, the more reliable sources vary as to the year between 1087 and 1088; and some modern authorities prefer the latter.

1087 is pre-eminently the date of the Montecassino sources – both the *Annales Cassinenses* and the *Chronica monasterii Cassinensis*; it also appears in the *Annales Ceccanenses* and the footnote to Caffaro. But in the Brussels manuscript of the *Carmen*, a concluding note,

---

1. M. Plessner, 'Al-Tidjānī', *E.I.* iv. 744–5.

2. Amari, ii. 62–65; French trans. by A. Rousseau, 'Voyage du Scheikh et-Tidjani dans la régence de Tunis', *Journal Asiatique*, vᵉ sér., i (1853), 374–5.

3. Amari, i. 440–2; French trans. Ibn el-Athir, *Annales du Maghreb et de l'Espagne*, tr. E. Fagnan (Algiers, 1898), pp. 487–8. For the author, F. Rosenthal, 'Ibn al-Athīr', *E.I.*² iii. 723–5.

4. Amari, ii. 153–4. For the author, I. Kratschkowsky, 'Al-Nuwairī', *E.I.* iii. 968–9.

5. Amari, ii. 32–33; French trans. *Histoire de l'Afrique et de l'Espagne intitulée Al-Bayano'l Moghrib*, tr. E. Fagnan, i (Algiers, 1901), 448–50. For the author, J. Bosch-Vilá, 'Ibn ʿIdhārī', *E.I.*² iii. 805–6. The *al-Bayān* also preserved the fragment of the *ḳaṣīda*.

6. Spanish trans. by R. Castillo-Marquez, *El Africa del Norte en el 'Aʿmal al-Aʿlām' de Ibn al-Jatib* (Madrid, 1958), p. 84. For the author, see also J. Bosch-Vilá, 'Ibn al-Khaṭīb', *E.I.*² iii. 835–7.

7. French trans. Ibn Khaldoun, *Histoire des Berbères et des dynasties musulmanes de l'Afrique septentrionale*, tr. Baron de Slane, new edn. by P. Casanova, ii (Paris, 1927), 24. For the author, M. Talbi, 'Ibn Khaldūn', *E.I.*² iii. 825–31.

8. 23a.

which seems to refer to the date of the campaign rather than to that of composition, runs: 'ANNI [*sic*] DOMINI MILLESIMO OCTUAGESIMO OCTAVO'. The date 1088 is also that of the other leading Pisan sources – the *Chronicon Pisanum* and Bernardo Maragone. It may originate in the use of the *calculus Pisanus*, which reckoned dates as from the 25 March of the preceding year.[1] If this were all, there would be no conflict of evidence, and the date 1087 would be confirmed. But the non-Pisans Bernold of St Blasien and Caffaro of Genoa also gave 1088. Moreover, the Moslem sources show a similar ambiguity: the *al-Bayān*, al-Tidjānī, Ibn al-Khaṭīb and Ibn Khaldūn gave A.H. 480 (8 April 1087–26 March 1088), but Ibn al-Athīr and al-Nuwairī 481 (27 March 1088–15 March 1089). There have also been suspicions that the date 1087 was introduced tendentiously at Montecassino, in order to invest its sometime abbot, Pope Victor III, who died on 16 September 1087, with a consequence that he did not merit.[2]

For three reasons, however, the earlier year can be accepted with confidence. First, and most important, from the Moslem side the testimony of Abu 'l-Ṣalt, and also of the *al-Bayān*, associates the Moslem misfortune with a solar eclipse. Such an eclipse, visible (as Abu 'l-Ṣalt said) in near-totality along virtually the whole of the North African coast, did, indeed, occur on 1 August 1087[3]; while there was no eclipse in 1088. Secondly, the chapter of the *Chronica monasterii Cassinensis* which represents Pope Victor III as a sponsor of the Mahdia campaign probably contains a kernel of truth. His connection with the campaign is, indeed, not positively demonstrable; but the principal argument advanced against it is worthless. It confronts the admittedly biased Montecassino evidence with the silence of the twelfth-century Pisan chronicles about papal involvement, and claims that this silence is conclusive against his complicity. But such an argument disregards the assertions of the *Carmen* that Rome gave powerful help to the Pisans and Genoese; that the participants figured as pilgrims of St Peter; and that the Moslem emir of Mahdia eventually agreed to hold his lands of St Peter and, as Bernold corroborates, to pay a tribute to Rome.[4] By thus connecting the campaign with Rome, the *Carmen* makes papal sponsorship more than likely. It must have been provided by either Victor III or Urban II. It is hard to place the campaign in Urban's first year as pope, for so far as his movements are known

1. See R. L. Poole, *Studies in Chronology and History* (Oxford, 1934), pp. 11–13.

2. Based on the estimate of A. Fliche, *e.g.* in his article 'Le pontificat de Victor III', *Revue d'histoire ecclésiastique*, xx (1924), 409–10. I hope to examine the Montecassino evidence, and the political activity of Victor III, in a study of Montecassino and the reformed papacy.

3. T. H. von Oppolzer, *Canon of Eclipses*, tr. O. Gingerick (New York, 1962), p. 218, no. 5449; also Chart 109.

4. 12*a*, 34, 60.

he spent the spring and summer of 1088 away from Rome in South Italy and Sicily amongst the Normans who were not involved.[1] But Victor III was active, both politically and militarily, in or near Rome from May to July 1087, when the Pisan expedition is likely to have been *en route*.[2] In the light of these activities the Montecassino writers, whatever their exaggerations, have probability on their side in associating it with Victor's active months between March and September 1087. Thirdly, another figure behind the Mahdia campaign was Countess Matilda of Tuscany, in which marquisate Pisa was situated.[3] Although the evidence for her dealings is scanty in the extreme, in 1085–7 she was in touch with Desiderius-Victor about papal affairs. Only seven days after Gregory VII's death on 25 May 1085 he urged her to promote a papal election.[4] Early in 1087 she was concerned with events turning upon his own final acceptance of the papal office[5]; and in the following summer she was at Rome with an army: with Victor's co-operation she sought to free it from the imperialist antipope Clement III (Archbishop Wibert of Ravenna).[6] Thus, she had a part in the despatch of two military expeditions – to Rome and to Mahdia. They fit together well as concurrent enterprises of 1087, each favoured by Victor III, to restore the prestige and fortunes of the Gregorian papacy[7]; whereas the countess is not known to have taken any like part in the events of 1088.

On all grounds, therefore, 1087 stands as the true date of the Mahdia campaign. By that year the state of the towns of Moslem Ifrīķiya invited such an attack as that mounted by the Pisans and Genoese.[8] The Fatimid caliphate of Cairo had been established in 969 as a rival to the Abbasid caliphate of Baghdad, and it extended its authority widely in North Africa. But throughout the eleventh century it suffered a decline which left all too much room for the local rivalries of such emirs as the Zīrids who ruled Mahdia in 1087, as well as for the attacks of their Arab enemies. The Zīrids were a Berber dynasty who, in the later tenth century, supported the Fatimids in opposition to the largely nomadic Zenāta of the

1. *Regesta pontificum Romanorum*, ed. P. Jaffé, 2nd edn. by W. Wattenbach, i (Leipzig, 1885), 658–9; A. Becker, *Papst Urban II.*, i (*M.G.H., Schriften*, 19, pt. 1, Stuttgart, 1964), pp. 116–18.

2. *Chron. mon. Cass.* iii. 68–69, pp. 749–50, 751; Jaffé, *Regesta*, i. 656.

3. *Infra*, pp. 11–12.   4. *Chron. mon. Cass.* iii. 65, p. 748.

5. See Archbishop Hugh of Lyons' letter to her in Hugh of Flavigny, *Chronicon*, ii, *M.G.H., SS.* viii. 466–8.

6. *Chron. mon. Cass.* iii. 69, p. 750.

7. See Erdmann's remarks, pp. 284–5.

8. For the African background, G. Marçais, *Les Arabes en Berbérie du xie au xive siècle* (Paris, 1913); Marçais, 'Zīrids', *E.I.* iv. 1229–30; C. Courtois, 'Grégoire VII et l'Afrique du Nord', *Revue historique*, cxcv (1945), 97–122, 193–226, esp. 213–15; H. R. Idris, *La Berbérie orientale sous les Zīrides, x^e–xiie siècles*, 2 vols. (Paris, 1962); R. Le Tourneau, 'Nouvelles orientations des Berbères d'Afrique du Nord, 950–1150', *Islamic Civilisation, 950–1150*, ed. D. S. Richards (Oxford, 1973), pp. 127–53.

Maghreb, themselves partisans of the Umayyad caliphs of Cordova. Early in the eleventh century the Sanhādja, the confederation of mainly settled peoples to which the Zīrids belonged, split into two. The Ḥammādids with their capital (until 1090) at al-Ḳal'a became the fierce rivals of the Zīrids to the east, with their capital at Kairouan. In the early years of their emir al-Mu'izz (406/1016–454/1062), the Zīrids of Kairouan achieved power and wealth. But in 442/1050 al-Mu'izz rashly withdrew his allegiance from the Fatimid Caliph al-Mustanṣir and recognized the Abbasids. To punish this apostasy the Fatimids directed against Ifrīḳiya the nomad Arab tribes known as the Banū Hilāl and the Banū Sulaim. Nomad attacks upon the Zīrid lands were the more devastating because the Ḥammādids, who so long as the Zīrids had served the Fatimids were loyal to the Abbasids, now changed sides and joined forces with the Banū Hilāl. They laid waste the open country of the Zīrids, and in 449/1057 al-Mu'izz was compelled to abandon Kairouan for Mahdia, of which his heir presumptive, Tamīn, had been governor since 445/1053. Despite some campaigning, al-Mu'izz was unable, when he died, to hand on to Tamīn the possession of more than Mahdia and its immediate surroundings.

Tamīn – the *Timinus* of the *Carmen* – ruled at Mahdia from 454/1062 until 501/1108. He was a vigorous ruler, who sought to revive the fortunes of the Zīrid dynasty in three ways that are material for an understanding of the *Carmen*; for each of them increased his vulnerability to oversea attack. First, he tried (but despite his taking of Tunis in 460/1067 and 491/1097–8 without lasting success) to recapture lands in Ifrīḳiya which the Zīrids had lost to their local enemies. Several Moslem sources – al-Tidjānī, Ibn al-Athīr, al-Nuwairī and the *al-Bayān* – stated that he was absent on such an expedition when the Pisans and Genoese arrived, so that they caught him at a disadvantage.[1]

Secondly, Tamīn encouraged corvettes from Mahdia to make forays into the Mediterranean against Christian shipping and Christian lands. Ibn al-Athīr expressly referred to Tamīn's frequent raids on the Italians (*Rūm*), in which he laid waste their country and harassed the people. Such raids were the basis of the extravagant assertions of the *Carmen* about Tamīn's depredations and the number of Christian prisoners in his gaols.[2] If Tamīn's piracy was a nuisance which invited retaliation, it also exposed his weakness. A successful raid in 466/1074 on Nicotera in Calabria was followed in 468/1075 by a further assault upon Mazzara. The Normans inflicted an

---

1. The very late history of Tunisia by Ibn abī Dīnār (al Ḳayrawānī), written either in 1092/1681 or in 1110/1698, says that he was besieging Gabès and Sfax: E. Pellissier and G. Rémusat, *Histoire de l'Afrique de Mohammed-ben-abi-el-Raini-el-Kairouani* (Paris, 1845), p. 146; *cf.* Amari, ii. 283. But this is a confusion with an expedition earlier in the year: Idris, i. 292–3.   2. 4*cd*, 7–9.

overwhelming defeat on this second attack and put a stop to Zīrid raids on South Italy.[1] The menace of Moslem raids on Italy and elsewhere was underlined in the *Carmen*[2]; and an awareness that the tables could be turned, as well as the memory of the attacks, prepared the way for such a campaign as that of 1087.

Thirdly, in his early years Tamīn sought to recover power through warfare against the Normans in Sicily. Sicily had once been subject to Zīrid authority; but by the early 1060s, when the Norman conquest began, it was disputed amongst rival emirs who had become virtually independent of Mahdia. In 1062, however, under Norman pressure some of the Sicilian Moslems turned thither for help. Tamīn sent his sons Ayyūb and 'Alī with an army. 'Alī was quickly killed, but Ayyūb endeavoured to set up a lordship of his own, until in 1068/9 the Norman Count Roger I inflicted upon him a defeat which led to his withdrawal. Zīrid intervention in Sicily almost certainly had the consequences of slowing down the Norman conquest and of increasing Christian hostility to the Zīrids.[3] Tamīn's resistance to the Normans had longer consequences, as well. In 1076 Pope Gregory VII was anxious to further his struggle against Henry IV of Germany by rehabilitating the papal alliance with the Normans of South Italy which had been inaugurated by the treaty of Melfi (1059).[4] In the same year· he also solicited the good will of the prospering Ḥammādid enemies of the Zīrids: he wrote to their emir, al-Nāṣir (454/1062–481/1088), thanking him for his release of Christian captives and sending two envoys from the papal household.[5] In 1076, Gregory thus cultivated the Zīrids' enemies on both sides of the Sicilian Channel. Tamīn's intervention in Sicily had led to his alienation from the papacy as the enemy of its would-be friends. This alienation was, it is true, ambivalent. The Normans were never reliable papal allies, and Count Roger I of Sicily concluded a treaty with Tamīn which, according to Gaufredus Malaterra, in 1087 led to his refusing an offer of Mahdia when the Pisans found that they could not permanently hold it.[6] The *entente* between Tamīn and Roger held good at the time of the First Crusade.[7] On the other hand, the alienation of the Zīrids from the Gregorian papacy set the stage for a papally sponsored campaign against them in 1087; while on the Norman side the Sicilian intervention began an underlying tradition of

1. Gaufredus Malaterra, iii. 8, 9, p. 61.
2. 7; this stanza, of course, contains gross hyperbole.
3. F. Chalandon, *Histoire de la domination normande en Italie et en Sicile*, 2 vols. (Paris, 1907), i. 201–5; Idris, i. 283–6.
4. *Gregorii VII Registrum*, iii. 11, 15, ed. E. Caspar, *M.G.H.*, *Epist. sel*. ii. 1–2, pp. 271–2, 276–7; see Chalandon, i. 243–4.
5. *Greg. VII Reg.* iii. 21, pp. 287–8; see Courtois, *ubi supra*, p. 7, n. 8.
6. iv. 3, pp. 86–87.
7. Ibn al-Athīr, in Amari, ii. 450–2; English trans. in F. Gabrieli, *Arab Historians of the Crusades* (London, 1969), pp. 3–4.

hostility which culminated in the sack of Mahdia in 1148 by Admiral George of Antioch.[1]

The political and military endeavours of al-Mu'izz and Tamīn thus undermined Zīrid security and invited external attack. They may also have led to some weakening of the urban defences of Mahdia itself. Both al-Tidjānī and the *al-Bayān* cited the citizens' lack of weapons and munitions, and the insufficiency and dilapidation of the city walls, amongst their reasons for the ease of the Pisan victory. But these sources probably painted an exaggerated picture of Mahdia's impoverishment in order to excuse the defeat.

For Mahdia was without question a strong, rich and well-built city. It was founded and strongly fortified in 308/921 by the Shī'i Mahdī 'Ubaid Allāh (died 322/934), founder of the Fatimid dynasty, after whom it was named. It stood on a narrow peninsula which extends eastward for a kilometre and a half; and on the mainland to the south-west lay its prosperous merchant suburb of Zawīla, the *Sibilia* of the *Carmen*.[2] Zawīla was virtually a second city in size and defences; it was so regarded not only by the *Carmen*, but also by the Moslem chroniclers of its misfortune and by the geographer al-Idrīsī. His work, completed in 548/1154, shows how rich Mahdia still was at the end of the Zīrid period.[3]

For its wealth was firmly established upon the trade-routes of the western Moslem world.[4] These routes grew with the exploitation, since the ninth century, of the immense gold deposits of the western Sudan (that is, of the regions to the south of the River Niger). Caravan routes from the cities of Gāna and Gao led across the Sahara Desert to al-Garīd and thence to the cities of Ifrīkiya. Planted to take advantage of these routes, Mahdia became a centre for craftsmanship in and for the export of gold. Its hinterland yielded iron ore (its city gates were constructed of solid iron) and timber; it was thus a centre of shipbuilding. It was a notable producer of cloth and silk. In the later eleventh century the attacks of the Banū Hilāl and the Banū Sulaim did serious harm to its trade and industry. Such disturbances tended to inhibit the flow of gold from the Sudan towards Egypt and Syria, and to hinder the supply of timber for the construction of ships. They helped to open the Eastern Mediterranean to the Italian merchants and to the Crusaders. But if these developments weakened a city like Mahdia, and hindered its trade and industry, they did not destroy

1. Chalandon, ii. 157–66, esp. 164.

2. For Mahdia and Zawīla, see esp. G. Marçais, 'Al-Mahdīya', *E.I.* iii. 121–2, and Idris, ii. 449–52. For their archaeology, Marçais, *L'Architecture musulmane d'occident* (Paris, 1954), pp. 78–79, 89–92. In 444/1052–3 al-Mu'izz gave Zawīla a wall.

3. Edrîsî, *Description de l'Afrique et de l'Espagne*, edd. and tr. R. Dozy and M. J. de Goeje (Leyden, 1866), pp. 126–8. Al-Idrīsī wrote at the behest of Roger II of Sicily.

4. See esp. the maps at the end of M. Lombard, *Les Métaux dans l'ancien monde du vᵉ au xiᵉ siècle* (Paris and The Hague, 1974).

its wealth. If Mahdia in 1087 had become vulnerable to Italian attack, it remained a rich city, well worth plundering.[1]

From the ninth century onwards, the circulation of gold in the Moslem economy had increasing effects in reviving the economy of western Europe. For there were certain commodities – notably slaves, furs, timber and tin – in great demand amongst the urban populations of the highly sophisticated Moslem world, which its domestic resources could not supply. In part, the demand was met by imports from Europe. The principal trade routes which carried them ran, in the north, from the North Sea, by way of the Baltic or Poland, the rivers of Russia and the Caspian Sea, to Iran, Mesopotamia and Armenia; and, in the south, through France and Spain to Sicily and North Africa, and so to Egypt and Syria. Europe imported few commodities in return; payment was largely in gold, of which the Moslems had virtually inexhaustible supplies but in which the West was deficient. Much of this gold did not remain in western Europe, but facilitated a revival of trade with Byzantium. From there, the West was able increasingly to import silk, ivory, spices, dyestuffs and other luxury commodities, and – no less valued – relics. By the late eleventh century, the results of this revival of trade were manifest in the burgeoning of towns and the institutions of urban life, not least in Italy. The most precocious developments were in the southern seaports of Amalfi, Naples and Gaeta, but above all at Venice in the Adriatic. Especially with the growth of Pavia as a market centre, north Italian cities like Pisa and Genoa followed. All explored trading contacts, not only with Byzantium, but also with the Levant and North Africa. There were also openings for contraband to the Moslem powers, especially the timber and naval supplies that Byzantium was so anxious to keep from them. It was this economic vitality, ultimately generated by the demand of the Moslem world, which so quickened Pisa and Genoa that a campaign like the Mahdia expedition of 1087 became conceivable. When Moslem North Africa was showing signs of political and economic malaise, they were finding the will and the means to venture boldly across the sea.

Not only the *Carmen* but also the consensus of the Christian and Moslem sources reveal Pisa as taking the leading role in the Mahdia campaign. It is not easy to determine the state of Pisa's urban development in 1087.[2] As a *placitum* of 1067 illustrates,[3] it was

1. For the developments summarized in this and the next paragraphs, see Lombard, *Espaces et réseaux du haut moyen âge* (Paris and The Hague, 1972), esp. pp. 23–29, 66–69, 138–9, 172–3; and *Les Métaux dans l'ancien monde*, esp. pp. 159–62, 195–235.

2. See esp. W. Heyd, *Histoire du commerce du Levant au moyen âge*, i (Leipzig, 1885), 120–2; Heywood, *A History of Pisa*, pp. 5–14; Y. Renouard, *Les Villes d'Italie de la fin du xe siècle au début du xive siècle*, ed. P. Braustein, 2 vols. (Paris, 1969), i. 167–72; J. K. Hyde, *Society and Politics in Medieval Italy* (London, 1973), pp. 29–32, 49–51.

3. Muratori, *Antiq.* iii. 1091–2.

traditionally subject to the marquess of Tuscany. In following decades, the rulers of Tuscany sometimes acted in person at Pisa, as when at Easter 1074 Countess Matilda and her mother Beatrice held their court there[1]; but sometimes, as in 1077, they delegated their authority to the viscount.[2] The office of viscount was becoming hereditary in a family which was to assume the name Visconti. A *Ugo vicecomes* witnessed the *placitum* of 1067, and to this family belonged the *Ugo vicecomes* who was the hero and martyr of the Mahdia campaign of 1087.[3] The name recurs in the *Liber Maiolichinus* amongst the leaders of the Pisan expedition of 1114–15 to the Balearic Islands.[4] Countess Matilda's continuing authority at Pisa was indicated in 1091 when, at her request, Pope Urban II made Corsica ecclesiastically subject to Bishop Daimbert of Pisa, and in 1092 when, once more at her request, Urban raised the see to an archbishopric.[5]

But the late eleventh century also saw the beginning of the Italian city communes with their officials the consuls, drawn from the urban aristocracy. At Pisa, the earliest mention of consuls appears in the *Carta Sarda*, a document in which the judge of Torres, in Sardinia, gave certain privileges to the Pisans. It can be dated to the episcopate of Bishop Gerard (1080–5), and was drawn up 'pro honore xu piscopum Gelardu, et de Ocu biscomte et de omnes consoles de Pisas'.[6] *Ocu biscomte* is without doubt the *Ugo vicecomes* of the *Carmen*; and the *Carmen* further referred to the presence on the Mahdia campaign of two Pisan *principales consules*, themselves distinct from two *cives nobiles*.[7] Renouard was probably correct to regard the consuls as 'peut-être seulement les chefs de l'association des commerçants-a[r]mateurs',[8] for in 1090 Bishop Daimbert's *concordia* with the citizens referred simply to a council of *boni homines* elected by a general assembly of the city.[9] Only in a further *concordia* of 1094 did consuls appear as city officials.[10] In 1087 the voluntary mercantile association which was to burgeon into the commune was still at an early stage of its development in relation to the older sources of authority in the city. It was not in conflict with them. But it had become a force to be reckoned with,

1. *Chronicon sancti Huberti Andaginensis, cap.* 25, eds. L. C. Bethmann and W. Wattenbach, *M.G.H., SS.* viii. 583–4.

2. Muratori, *Antiq.* iii. 1095–6.

3. 42–49.

4. *Liber Maiolichinus*, ll. 760–7, 1403, 2827, 2836, 3315–16, pp. 34–35, 58, 107, 108, 124; *cf.* F. Patetta, 'Il preteso epitaffio di Ugo Visconte morte nella spedizione dell'anno 1087 contro i pirati saraceni di Mehdia', *Atti della Reale academia delle scienze di Torino*, xlvi (1911), 570–84.

5. *Epp.* 51, 63, Migne, *P.L.* cli. 330–1, 344–6.

6. P. Brezzi, *I comuni cittadini Italiani* (Milan, 1940), pp. 102–3. Bishop Gerard's commitment to reform is established by Urban II, *Ep.* 51.

7. 21*ab.*   8. i. 169.

9. *Statuti inediti della città di Pisa dal xii al xiv secolo*, ed. F. Bonaini, 3 vols. (Florence, 1854–7), i. 16–18.   10. *Ibid.* iii. 890–1.

and the *Carmen* shows how vigorously it could flex its muscles in the Mahdia campaign.

At Genoa matters took a broadly similar course, but more slowly and with greater domestic stresses and strains; though the evidence is more sparse than for Pisa.[1] During the first half of the eleventh century Genoa (which was outside the marquisate of Tuscany) formed part of the march of the Obertenghi, who had their principal castle at Luni. But in 1056 the bishop succeeded in finally ending their power over the city.[2] Thereafter its rulers were the bishops, recruited from three vicecomital families which had a stake there. Power thus devolved upon a narrow aristocracy of landed proprietors who systematically appropriated church revenues and lands; while the bishops lost prestige because they were clients of this aristocracy.[3] By *c.* 1080 the citizens had grown sufficiently in numbers and determination to organize themselves against the bishops and the aristocracy. They grouped themselves in three city regions – the *castra*, the *civitas* and the *burgum*. The Genoese chronicler Caffaro testifies that in 1098, during the First Crusade, the citizens formed a *compagna* for three years with six consuls.[4] He said that there was also a period of a year and a half before when there was no consulate.[5] The inference is that the *compagna*, which formed the basis of the Genoese commune, was in existence by the middle 1090s, at latest. The little that can be seen of its emergence indicates that at Genoa, as well as at Pisa, a rising citizen body which could participate in the First Crusade was already well placed in 1087 to venture upon such an expedition as that to Mahdia.

There was a history, if not a very recent one, of both joint and separate maritime operations involving the two cities. In 1015 and 1016, responding to attacks by the Saracens of the Balearic Islands, they mounted an attack on Sardinia and expelled the Emir Mudjāhid.[6] In 1034 the Pisans, acting alone, attacked the North African coast, seizing Bône and defeating Tamīn's father, al-Mu'izz.[7] In 1063, when Tamīn's sons were fighting in Sicily, the Pisans sent a fleet to help the Norman leader Robert Guiscard with his conquest. For reasons which are not clear, the Normans did not accept

---

1. See esp. U. Formentini, *Genova nel basso impero e nell'alto medioevo* (*Storia di Genova delle origine al tempo nostro*, ii, Milan, 1941), pp. 215–78; V. Vitale, *Breviario della storia di Genova*, 2 vols. (Genoa, 1955), i. 10–18; Renouard, i. 231–3.

2. *Codice diplomatico della repubblica di Genova*, ed. C. Imperiale, i, *Fonti*, lxxvii (1936), pp. 6–9, no. 3; see also F. Niccolai, *Contributo allo studio dei più antichi brevi della compagna Genovese* (Milan, 1939), pp. 15–17, and pp. 99–101, docs. ii–iii.

3. For papal concern as early as 1074, *Gregorii VII Reg.* i. 48, p. 74.

4. *Annales Ianuenses, Annali Genovesi di Caffaro e de' suoi continuatori*, ed. L. T. Belgrano, *Fonti*, xi (1890), p. 5.

5. *De liberatione civitatum orientis, ibid.* p. 111.

6. Bernardo Maragone, *s.a.* 1016, 1017, pp. 4–5; for the memory of these events, see *Liber Maiolichinus*, ll. 921–74, pp. 40–43.

7. Maragone, *s.a.* 1035, p. 5.

Pisan help in attacking Palermo. But the Pisans were able to sack the city and carry off great booty, some of which they applied to begin the building of their new cathedral dedicated to the Virgin Mary.[1] The next two decades saw no similar expedition, and the Pisans and Genoese engaged in local warfare against each other.[2] But the Mahdia campaign was within the older tradition[3]; and it pointed the way to further joint enterprises at Valencia in 1092[4] and at Tortosa in 1093,[5] as well as to Pisan and Genoese participation in the First Crusade.

If the economic development and internal politics of Pisa and Genoa thus called into being communes of the citizens which sought to try out their strength by such oversea adventures as the Mahdia campaign, each city also experienced a contest for its external loyalty in which the nascent communes proved susceptible to the ideas of the reformed papacy and looked to it as an ally.[6] Pisa lay within the dominions of the staunch and militant Gregorian partisan, Countess Matilda of Tuscany. This led Henry IV to bid for its loyalty. In 1081, during a stay at Pisa, he issued an imperial diploma in its favour, limiting his rights of taxation and jurisdiction[7]; and his largesse to Pisa appears to have continued by gifts to its church in 1084 and 1089.[8] When the papalist Bishop Gerard died in 1085, his successor, Daimbert, received deacon's orders at the hands of the Wibertine and excommunicate Archbishop Wezilo of Mainz (1084–8).[9] Once again, Henry IV seems to have been seeking to control Pisa, now by imposing a bishop as his vicegerent there. Henry does not seem to have found much support amongst the citizens. It has been well observed that his diploma of 1081 is significant for what it did not say.[10] It made no reference to

---

1. *Ibid. s.a.* 1063, pp. 5–6, where the inscription set up in the cathedral is cited; Gaufredus Malaterra, ii. 34, p. 45.

2. Maragone, *s.a.* 1066, 1072, 1078, p. 6; Ranieri Sardo, *s.a.* 1075, pp. 18–19.

3. P. Tronchi was certainly mistaken when he asserted that in 1087 the Mahdia campaign was preceded by a successful joint expedition 'alle Spiagge di Damiata' (Damietta); he was perhaps misled by later Pisan sources such as Ranieri Sardo, who wrote of the 1087 campaign as attacking *Darmaria.* But Tronchi appears to have seen a text of the Pisan treaty with the Genoese before the campaign: *Memorie istoriche della città di Pisa* (Leghorn, 1682), pp. 29–30.

4. Latin sources do not refer to this expedition; for the Arabic sources see R. Dozy, *Recherches sur l'histoire et la litérature de l'Espagne pendant le moyen âge,* 2 vols. (3rd edn., Leyden, 1881), ii. 140 and Appendix xv, pp. lv–lvi.

5. *Annales Ianuenses,* p. 13.

6. For the reformed papacy and the communes, see G. Fasoli, 'Gouvernants et gouvernés dans les communes italiennes du xiᵉ au xiiiᵉ siècle', *Recueils de la Société Jean Bodin pour l'histoire comparative des institutions,* xxv (1965), 47–86, esp. 60–71.

7. *M.G.H., DD HIV,* ii. 442–3, no. 336.

8. By whatever underlies the corrupt diplomas in *ibid.* ii. 477–9, 534–5, nos. 359, 404.

9. Urban II, *Ep.* 11, Migne, *P.L.* cli. 294–5. For Wezilo and Italian affairs, see also the obscure passage in Benzo of Alba, *Liber ad Heinricum,* vii. 8, ed. K. Pertz, *M.G.H., SS.* xi. 681; *cf.* H. Lehmgrübner, *Benzo von Alba, ein Verfechter der kaiserlichen Staatsidee unter Heinrich IV.* (Berlin, 1887), pp. 90–91.

10. Hyde, pp. 49–50.

institutionalized leaders – bishop or viscount or consuls. Yet the *Carta Sarda*, which must be dated to within four years of it at most, referred to all three; it is, therefore, highly likely that these local leaders were hostile to Henry. Their loyalty was to the countess, and so to the Gregorian papacy.

It was no less natural for the Genoese to look in a similar direction. In 1087 the bishop of Genoa was Conrad II. He was so committed an imperialist as to have subscribed to the decrees of the synod of Brixen (1080), which nominated Archbishop Wibert of Ravenna to be antipope.[1] Conrad himself belonged to the Genoese aristocratic family named Manganelli.[2] He was, therefore, objectionable to the populace as a member of the old order, and to the reformed papacy because identified with lay control over the church. The citizens and the papacy had a common interest. There is a little evidence for popular resistance, similar to that of the Patarenes of Milan, against the clerical establishment.[3] It tends to confirm that, like the Pisans, the Genoese were open to embrace the loyalties and ideology of reform.

It was, therefore, appropriate that although, as all the sources show, the Pisans and the Genoese formed the bulk of the Mahdia expedition, they should have recruited further elements from circles nearer the reformed papacy. The *Carmen* spoke of powerful military aid from Rome itself,[4] and also of the presence of a leading figure, Pantaleone, from Amalfi.[5] Pantaleone was a member of a prominent merchant family. His grandfather, of like name, had a house at Constantinople, where in the 1060s he negotiated with the Emperor Constantine X Ducas in the interests of Henry IV of Germany and the antipope Cadalus.[6] However, his son Maurus was a devotee of Montecassino: in 1066 he gave a set of bronze doors for its church, and in 1071 he entered it as a monk.[7] Pantaleone the younger was the eldest of Maurus's six sons. Besides other munificent acts he founded hospitals in Antioch and Jerusalem.[8] Pantaleone the elder

1. *Dekret der Brixener Synode*, in *Quellen zur Geschichte Heinrichs IV.*, ed. Schmale, p. 482. For Conrad and the episcopal succession at Genoa, see G. Schwartz, *Die Besetzung des Bistums Reichsitaliens unter den sächsischen und salischen Kaisern mit den Listen der Bischöfe 951–1122* (Leipzig and Berlin, 1913), p. 148.

2. So referred to in 1134 by Pope Innocent II: L. T. Belgrano, 'Registrum curiae archiepiscopalis Januae', *Atti della Società Ligure di storia patria*, ii, pt. 2 (1867), 449, no. 27.

3. *Ibid.* p. 448.

4. 12; the reference to Scipio shows that the aid was military.

5. 13*ab*. For Amalfi, see A. O. Citarella, 'The Relations of Amalfi with the Arab World before the Crusades', *Speculum*, xlii (1967), 299–312, and 'Patterns in Medieval Trade: the Commerce of Amalfi before the Crusades', *Journal of Economic History*, xxviii (1968), 531–55.

6. Benzo of Alba, *Liber ad Heinricum*, ii. 7, iii. 2, 11. *M.G.H.*, *SS*. xi. 615, 623, 626–7.

7. *Storia de'Normanni di Amato di Montecassino*, viii. 3, ed. V. de Bartholomaeis, *Fonti*, lxxvi (1935), 343, 345; *Chron. mon. Cass.* iii. 18, p. 711.

8. The sons are named in the inscription of an ivory casket, perhaps first given by Maurus to Montecassino, but later in the possession of Farfa: A. Hofmeister, 'Maurus von Amalfi und die Elfbeinkassette von Farfa aus dem 11. Jahrhundert', *Quellen und*

was referred to by the exalted title *patricius*; in the *Carmen* his grandson is called *sipantus* – a Latinization of the Byzantine title *hypatos*, the equivalent dignity to consul.[1] It is not clear from the *Carmen* whether he led an Amalfitan contingent, or whether he was personally the captain of the Roman force.

Military leadership of the Mahdia campaign rested with the Pisans, whose viscount, Hugh, was described in the *Carmen* as *dux* and *princeps*.[2] But there were more powerful sponsoring figures in the background. The most significant is Countess Matilda of Tuscany. She had been made familiar with the idea of a military expedition against the Saracens when Gregory VII sought to recruit her for his abortive eastern campaign against the Seldjuk Turks in 1074.[3] She was also a close associate of Gregory's standing legate in Lombardy, Bishop Anselm II of Lucca. Anselm had been the leading propagandist of Gregorian thought about the admissibility of warfare in pursuit of Christian aims,[4] and in 1085 he strove to mobilize the rulers of western Christendom in defence of the Gregorian papacy.[5] Matilda's connections, as well as her lordship of Pisa, disposed her to favour the campaign of 1087, and her complicity may be inferred from the bishop, *Benedictus presul*, who, in the *Carmen*, unmasked Tamīn's duplicity and harangued the Christian army before Zawīla.[6]

The only Italian bishop of that name to hold office in 1087 was Benedict of Modena.[7] Possibly a sometime member of the cathedral chapter of Lucca, he was appointed bishop of Modena in 1085 at Matilda's instance.[8] On 18 March 1086 he was in Mantua with the countess and other bishops, at the death-bed of Anselm II of Lucca.[9] In 1087 the see of Pisa was (from the Gregorian point of view) vacant following the death of Bishop Gerard, while at

Forschungen aus italienischen Archiven und Bibliotheken, xxiv (1933), 341–3; H. Bloch, 'Monte Cassino, Byzantium and the West in the Earlier Middle Ages', *Dumbarton Oaks Papers*, iii (Cambridge, Mass., 1946), pp. 207–12. See also Amato, viii. 3, pp. 341–3.

1. Benzo of Alba, *ubi supra*, p. 15, n. 6. For the dignity of patrician at Byzantium, see J. B. Bury, *The Imperial Administrative System in the Ninth Century* (London, 1911), pp. 26–27. For *hypatos*, see pp. 25–26. A Latinization of the rarer and higher *dishypatos* (p. 27) is also possible.   2. 45a.

3. *The Epistolae vagantes of Pope Gregory VII*, ed. and tr. H. E. J. Cowdrey (Oxford, 1972), pp. 10–13, no. 5.

4. Erdmann, pp. 223–9; I. S. Robinson, 'Gregory VII and the Soldiers of Christ', *History*, lviii (1973), 169–92, esp. 183–8, 191.

5. See his letter to King William I of England, *Die Hannoversche Briefsammlung: i, Die Hildesheimer Briefe*, no. 1, *Briefsammlungen der Zeit Heinrichs IV.*, eds. C. Erdmann and N. Fickermann, *M.G.H., Briefe*, v. 15–17.

6. 20–21, 23–29.

7. Schwartz, p. 184.

8. Bernold, *Chron.*, *s.a.* 1085, p. 443.

9. *Vita Anselmi episcopi Lucensis auctore Bardone presbytero*, cap. 41, ed. R. Wilmans, *M.G.H., SS.* xii. 25; *Vita Anselmi Lucensis episcopi auctore Rangerio*, ll. 6965–6, eds. E. Sackur, G. Schwartz and B. Schmeidler, *M.G.H., SS.* xxx, pt. 2, 1301. Rangerius wrote: 'A Mutina Benedictus adest, facundia cuius/utilis aecclesiae per loca multa fuit'; which is in keeping with his role in the *Carmen*.

Genoa Bishop Conrad was an imperialist. It was natural for Matilda to sponsor as spiritual overseer of the expedition to Mahdia a bishop like Benedict of Modena, who belonged to her own lands and who was an associate of so zealous a propagandist of the *militia sancti Petri* as Anselm II of Lucca.

Modern historians sometimes describe Benedict of Modena as a papal legate. There is no proof that he was so; although there is a similarity between his role in 1087 and those of the legates Bishop Adhemar of le Puy on the First Crusade and Cardinal Boso on the Pisan expedition to Majorca in 1114–15.[1] But whatever Benedict's status, it is beyond reasonable question that the papacy itself had an active interest in the Mahdia campaign. The *Chronica monasterii Cassinensis*, indeed, presented it in exaggerated terms: the campaign originated in papal counsels; Pope Victor III himself gathered a Christian army 'from almost all the peoples of Italy'; and he directed the warriors to Africa under the *vexillum sancti Petri* with a promise of the remission of all their sins.[2] Other sources, including the *Carmen*, do not corroborate any of these statements. Written perhaps some fifty years after the event, they are certainly coloured by memories of the First Crusade as well as by the local patriotism of the Montecassino chronicler. But despite the scantiness of the evidence, there is a circumstantial likelihood that the campaign enjoyed Victor's approval and backing. Countess Matilda herself had a long-standing attachment to Montecassino and its abbot which she proved *c.* 1080 by protecting them against Pisan tolls.[3] Matilda and Victor were in touch, probably regularly, when the campaign must have been in transit. For if the *Carmen* be approximately correct in assigning three months to the preparation of ships[4] and if a month or so be allowed for the favourable voyage from Pisa to Mahdia,[5] preparations must have been afoot when, following the council of Capua in March 1087, Victor finally decided to accept election as pope.[6] Archbishop Hugh of Lyons made it clear, in his querulous letter to Matilda following this acceptance, that Matilda was accessible to papal circles: she had two cardinals with her, and letters could pass to her by pilgrims and other messengers.[7] And it is almost certain that many of the

1. For Boso, see the *Liber Maiolichinus*, ll. 1151–3, 1198–1205, 2208–51, pp. 49, 51, 86–87.   2. iii. 71, p. 751.

3. *Registrum Petri Diaconi*, no. 450, printed in Muratori, *Antiq.* i. 957–8; cf. *Chron. mon. Cass.* iii. 61, p. 745. For a discussion of Matilda's relations with Montecassino, see T. Leccisotti, 'Riflessi Matildici sull'arce Cassinese', *Atti e memorie della Deputazione di storia patria per le antiche provincie Modenesi*, 9th ser., iii (1963), 233–43; text of Matilda's grant on p. 237.

4. 10c.   5. 14.
6. *Chron. mon. Cass.* iii. 68, p. 749.

7. Letter in Hugh of Flavigny, *Chronicon*, ii, *M.G.H.*, *SS.* viii. 466–8. Archbishop Hugh specified the two cardinals as *He. et B.* The former was probably Bishop Hermann of Brescia. Matilda's conduct in the following months proves that she disregarded the letter.

Mahdia campaigners on their outward voyage made a pilgrimage to St Peter at Rome[1]; for the *Carmen* declares that, before Zawīla, St Peter recognized amongst them his own badge – the purses (*scarsellae*) of pilgrims.[2] Since Mahdia had no significance as a goal of pilgrimage to St Peter, the natural explanation is that participants had gone to Rome, and had thereafter retained the badge of their completed pilgrimage. As they arrived at Zawīla very early in August, they are likely to have come to Rome in the high summer of 1087 when, following what must have been careful diplomatic preparations, Victor and Matilda were fighting, with some success, for the city.[3] In these circumstances, such a pilgrim visit could hardly have failed to secure the blessing of the vicar of St Peter; and it would help to explain the recruitment of Roman forces for the campaign. Finally, according to the *Carmen* the papacy benefited from Tamīn's peace terms so remarkably that its author can hardly have failed to have envisaged papal sponsorship.[4] The evidence is too slight to allow a definition of this sponsorship; but it seems certain to have been more than nominal.

The Mahdia campaign, then, took place primarily owing to the initiative of Pisan and Genoese mercantile circles, ready by 1087 to advance more boldly than before into a Moslem world showing signs of political and economic vulnerability. But it was also sponsored by Countess Matilda of Tuscany and Pope Victor III. Its outcome, therefore, had a bearing on the continuing struggle of the Gregorian papacy with Henry IV of Germany. The Mahdia campaign brought long-term benefits both to the burgeoning communes at Pisa and Genoa and to the papacy. In the two cities, the lavish booty was a timely endowment of the citizens' cause against their rivals and a sign of their power. In Pisa the victory at Mahdia was commemorated by a church to St Sixtus (himself a pope martyred in the Decian persecution of 258), and by the embellishment and endowment of the cathedral.[5] The *Carmen* itself has a propagandist undertone in its eulogy of *Ugo vicecomes*, when it incites the Pisans to remain faithful to his house and family[6]:

1. There is nothing in the *Carmen* which supports the view that the expedition assembled at Pantelleria. The only statement to this effect is in the Moslem chronicler Ibn al-Athīr who added the improbable detail that the expedition took four years to prepare. Al-Nuwairī, on the other hand, spoke of all the Christian forces going to Pantelleria. For evidence that the Pisans and Genoese returned home direct, see stanza 69 and n.

2. 34. For the pilgrim's staff as a *signaculum sancti Petri*, see the examples from eleventh-century liturgical texts cited in A. Franz, *Die kirchlichen Benediktionen im Mittelalter*, ii (Freiburg-im-Breisgau, 1909), pp. 271–89, esp. 275, n. 6.

3. *Chron. mon. Cass.* iii. 69, p. 750.

4. 60; see *supra*, p. 6. There is no proof that tribute or spoils reached Rome. But they may have helped Urban II to enter the city in June 1089, as he said, 'sine omni Nortmannorum ope': P. F. Kehr, 'Due documenti pontifici illustranti la storia di Roma negli ultimi anni del secolo xi', *Archivio della Reale società Romana di storia patria*, xxiii (1900), 277–8.   5. 70–72.   6. Esp. 48.

henceforth the martyr and his memory were to be pledges of loyalty to the commune and to the countess. The Genoese, too, built a church of St Sixtus as a memorial of victory.[1]

There were likewise benefits for the Gregorian papacy. In drawing them, it was probably mindful of the exploit of those merchants of Bari who, earlier in 1087, had seized the body of St Nicholas at Myra in Lycia from its Byzantine custodians. On the pretext that the vacuum of power following the Seldjuk attacks left it vulnerable to Moslem raids, they brought it home to their native city. So far as can be ascertained, despite Barese claims to the contrary the papacy had no part in planning this *coup de main*. But the arrival at Bari of what speedily became one of the most famous relics in western Christendom strengthened the citizens, who were Gregorian in sympathy, against the cathedral clergy and the aristocracy who were Wibertine. In 1085 Archbishop Urso had acceded to the Wibertine cause; following the arrival of the relics, the Gregorians under Archbishop Elia quickly turned the tables.[2] The *Chronica monasterii Cassinensis* did not overlook the coincidence that the relics of St Nicholas arrived in Bari on 9 May 1087, the day of Victor III's consecration in St Peter's, Rome.[3] Such a favourable event may have encouraged his sponsorship of the Mahdia expedition. For it was an object-lesson in the way a mercantile enterprise could redound to the papal advantage by securing the loyalty of an Italian city.

It was Pope Urban II (elected and consecrated on 12 March 1088) who gathered in the benefits made available by the events of Victor's brief reign. Nothing is known of his activities during it, save that, as Cardinal Odo of Ostia, he rallied to Victor in March 1087 and in May consecrated him pope.[4] He was, however, present at the death-bed of Victor, who commended him to the cardinals

1. Caffaro, p. 13, n. 4. According to Formentini (p. 277, n. 80), the church was kept from Bishop Conrad's control by being given to the Benedictine abbey of San Michele della Chiusa. Urban II's bull of 11 March 1095 records its possession of a church in Genoa: J. von Pflugk-Harttung, *Acta pontificum Romanorum inedita*, ii (Stuttgart, 1884), p. 158, no. 191; but I am unable to verify that it was St Sixtus. Nor can I verify Formentini's statement that an inscribed Arabic stone discovered in 1858 was formerly at the door of the church; though it may have been a trophy of the Mahdia campaign: M. Amari, 'Nuovi ricordi arabici su la storia di Genova', *Atti della Società Ligure di storia patria*, v (1867), 632–3 and *Tavola* 1. Amari says that the stone was found in the church of Santa Maria di Castello.

2. F. Nitti di Vito, 'La traslazione delle reliquie di San Nicola', *Iapigia*, viii (1937), 295–411, and *La ripresa gregoriana di Bari (1087–1105) e i suoi riflessi nel mondo contemporaneo e religioso* (Trani, 1942); A. Gambacorta, 'Culto e pellegrinaggi a San Nicola di Bari fino alla prima Crociata', *Pellegrinaggi e culto dei santi in Europa fino alla prima Crociata* (*Convegni del Centro di studi sulla spiritualità medievale*, iv, Todi, 1963), 485–502, esp. 497–500. For the claim that the pope sent the expedition, see the *Leggenda del monaco Niceforo*, ll. 99–102, and the *Translatio s. Nicholai episcopi ex Myra . . . scripta ab Iohanne archidiacono Barensi*, ll. 131–2, Nitti di Vito, *Iapigia*, viii. 338, 361.

3. iii. 68, p. 750. Also recorded in a marginal note to the *Annales Cavenses*, s.a. 1087, *M.G.H., SS.* iii. 190; see Nitti di Vito, *Iapigia*, viii. 303.

4. *Ubi supra*, p. 4, n. 4.

as his successor[1]; and, in his early years as pope, he referred to himself
as following Victor no less than Gregory VII.[2] This suggests that
he stood near to Victor during his lifetime and, therefore, that he
cannot have been unaware of the Mahdia campaign, nor of the
coup at Bari. Both were signs that the tide was turning in favour of
the Gregorian papacy, and that it had an alternative means of
revival to the dreaded Normans who, at best unreliable as allies,
had devastated Rome in 1084 and had thereby brought about
Gregory VII's withdrawal to Salerno. Bari and Mahdia help to
make comprehensible both Odo's rallying to Victor III in the
spring of 1087, and Victor's own belated willingness to assume an
active role as pope. They also help to explain Urban II's actions as
pope. Urban himself visited Bari in 1089; he bound it firmly to the
papacy by personally consecrating Archbishop Elia as well as the
confessio, or shrine, of St Nicholas, and also by confirming Elia's
rights as metropolitan and by conferring the *pallium*.[3] In Lombardy,
Urban was even quicker to reveal at Milan his willingness to make
all possible accommodations in order to harness to the papal cause
the forces of Italian city life, and at the same time to secure the
loyalty of the episcopate.[4] At both Pisa and Genoa the situation
created by the Mahdia campaign enabled him to pursue a like
course to those at Milan and Bari. At Pisa, the imperialist bishop-
elect, Daimbert, saw it as his advantage to turn to the Gregorian cause.
In a letter to Bishop Peter of Pistoia and Abbot Rusticus of
Vallombrosa – whose shock at his own flexibility he sought to
relieve – Urban shows that he had reordained Daimbert deacon and
raised him to the episcopate.[5] Reconciled to Urban, Daimbert
enjoyed Countess Matilda's favour; he was able to achieve a *modus
vivendi* with the commune; and in 1099 he led the Pisans on the
Crusade.[6] At Genoa, likewise, Urban was quickly in correspondence
with Bishop Cyriacus in terms which suggest that he won the
bishop's loyalty[7]; Bishop Airaldus (1097–1116) was certainly
papalist[8]; and the Genoese, like the Pisans, came to support the
First Crusade.

The re-orientation at Pisa and Genoa was the outcome of a

1. *Chron. mon. Cass.* iii. 73, p. 753.
2. *Epp.* 1, 2, 4, Migne, *P.L.* cli. 283–5, 286–8; Pflugk-Harttung, *Acta pont. Rom.
ined.*, ii, no. 175, pp. 141–2.
3. *Anonymi Barensis . . . chronicon, s.a.* 1090, Muratori, *R.I.S.* v. 154; Urban II, *Ep.*
26, Migne, *P.L.* cli. 307–9.
4. H. E. J. Cowdrey, 'The Papacy, the Patarenes and the Church of Milan', *Transactions of the Royal Historical Society*, 5th ser., xviii (1968), 25–48, esp. 43–48; and 'The
Succession of the Archbishops of Milan in the time of Pope Urban II', *ante*, lxxxiii
(1968), 285–94. *See above*, Chapters V & VI.
5. *Ep.* 11, Migne, *P.L.* cli. 294–5. Bishop Peter was himself a sometime monk of
Vallombrosa; Urban's letter demonstrates the active concern of the Tuscan reforming
monastery for Pisa in the mid-1080s.
6. *Ubi supra*, p. 12, nn. 9–10.
7. *Ep.* 123, Migne, *P.L.* cli. 394; Schwartz, p. 148.   8. *Ibid.*

communal development and of the formation of a Gregorian-minded clergy and laity, both of which the Mahdia campaign accelerated. The *Carmen* bears witness to this by its propaganda for local patriotism and for warfare with a strongly religious undertone, undertaken with papal sponsorship.

The *Carmen* also shows how closely the mental outlook and the modes of warfare of the Pisans and Genoese eight years earlier antici-pated the Crusade. When all allowance is made for a common debt to the tradition of holy war which had gained ground in western Europe since the conversion of the Germanic peoples to Christianity, the *Carmen* shows impressive similarities with the anonymous *Gesta Francorum*, written by a fighting knight from Norman South Italy who fought his way to Antioch and Jerusalem.

The warfare about which their authors wrote was, in identical terms, a holy warfare: Christ himself was the true leader and champion of the fighting host[1]; swift and complete victory in battle was the gift of God[2]; and the spoils of war were Christ's gift.[3] Similar supernatural forces contended on the Christian side: just as before Zawīla the Pisans experienced the help of St Michael and St Peter, so at Antioch Christ sent the Crusaders the help of a numberless heavenly host led by St George, St Mercurius and St Demetrius.[4] Especially in Bishop Benedict's harangue, the *Carmen* makes lavish reference to the military exploits of the Old Testament – to the fall of Jericho, David's slaying of Goliath, the victories of Judas Maccabeus, the deliverance of Israel from Pharaoh in the Exodus, the destruction of Sennacherib's host by the hand of an angel.[5] The lay author of the *Gesta Francorum* did not draw such comparisons, although they are characteristic of the circle of Countess Matilda of Tuscany, and especially of its image of Anselm II of Lucca.[6] But Benedict's harangue anticipated clerical preaching and ministrations before Antioch and Jerusalem[7]; and just as the Pisans made confession and took communion at Zawīla, so did the Crusaders at Antioch.[8] Both sources saw the Christian fallen as glorious martyrs for the Christian faith.[9]

Their Moslem adversaries were similarly represented. In Tamīn the Pisans affected to see the incarnation of all that is evil: he was like Antichrist, a cruel dragon, godless, foolish, proud, infamous, accursed, perfidious.[10] No such single Moslem leader faced the First Crusade, though Emir Kerbogha of Mosul was 'filled with pride'[11]; but the Byzantine Emperor Alexius Comnenus was pilloried in the same vein as unjust, wretched, and full of vain and evil

1. 14*a*, 30*cd*, 72*cd*; *cf*. *G.F.*, p. 37.
2. 1–3; *cf*. *G.F.*, pp. 20–1, 41, 70.
3. 67*cd*; *cf*. *G.F.*, pp. 19–20.
4. 33–34, *cf*. *G.F.*, p. 69.
5. 25–28, 36, 68; *cf*. Erdmann, p. 273.
6. Erdmann, pp. 223–4.
7. 23–29; *cf*. *G.F.*, pp. 68, 90.
8. 29*cd*; *cf*. *G.F.*, 67–68.
9. 46; *cf*. *G.F.*, pp. 4, 17, 40.
10. 5*ab*, 6*c*, 12*b*, 13*d*, 21*cd*.
11. *G.F.*, p. 66.

thoughts.[1] In Pisan eyes the Moslems collectively were the enemies of the Creator, just as the author of the *Gesta Francorum* regarded the Turks as 'enemies of God and holy Christendom'.[2] For the one, the Moslems were like beasts; and for the other, barbarians.[3] The two sources travestied the religion of Islam. Most exceptionally in a pre-Crusading source, the *Carmen* knew the name of Mahomet[4]; but he was misrepresented as a Trinitarian heretic, worse than the Alexandrian heresiarch Arius (*c.* 250–*c.* 336),[5] and he was condemned for his denial of Christ's divinity.[6] In the *Gesta Francorum*, too, the Moslems denied both the Trinity and the divinity of Christ; and they were polytheists.[7] It is no surprise that both authors rejoiced to tell of the savage slaughter of defeated Moslems – on the one hand at Pantelleria, Zawīla, Mahdia, and in the subsequent cutting down of the Arab nomads; and on the other at Antioch, Marra, Tripoli and, above all, in Jerusalem itself.[8]

But the most significant detail by far of the *Carmen* in relation to the First Crusade is the wearing by the Pisans and Genoese, as they prepared to attack Zawīla, of the pilgrim badge of a purse.[9] It has been argued that Urban II's decisive step at Clermont was to associate the hitherto separate institutions of holy war and pilgrimage in the novel combination of an armed pilgrimage. Thus, it was as a *peregrinatio*, or pilgrimage, that the *Gesta Francorum* understood the expedition of 1096–9 to liberate the Holy Sepulchre at Jerusalem.[10] But in 1087 (though for the first time of which there is record) the Pisans already wore pilgrim insignia as they prepared themselves to fight. Pilgrimage and holy war were evidently drawing together. Yet the incident does not disclose the full scenario of the Crusade. The Pisans probably wore the purse because of a pilgrimage to Rome which was already completed,[11] not because they saw their expedition as itself a *peregrinatio*. Nor does the *Carmen* indicate that the campaign as such was, like the Crusade, undertaken by a vow, or that it carried in itself the spiritual benefits appropriate to a pilgrimage. The Crusade was foreshadowed, but a critical step had yet to be taken.

The foreshadowing of the Crusade during his predecessor's reign may, however, have contributed to Urban II's own mental preparation for his achievement at Clermont in calling it forth. As a scion of a French aristocratic family and a former grand prior of Cluny, he already had a deep insight into the forces which were

---

1. *G.F.*, pp. 6, 10, 17.   2. 26*a*; *cf. G.F.*, 22, 32.
3. 47*b*; *cf. G.F.*, p. 31.   4. 32*a*, 52; *cf. G.F.*, pp. 52, 96.
5. 32, 52.   6. 32*d*.
7. *G.F.*, pp. 21, 52, 96.
8. 17, 37–39, 50–54, 65; *cf. G.F.*, pp. 48, 80, 85, 91–92.   9. 34*d*.
10. See H. E. J. Cowdrey, 'Cluny and the First Crusade', *Revue bénédictine*, lxxxiii (1973), 285–311, esp. 291–4; and 'The Genesis of the Crusades', *The Holy War*, ed. T. P. Murphy (Columbus, Ohio, 1976); *See below*, Chapter XV.
11. *Ubi supra*, p. 18, nn. 1–2.

impelling western chivalry to such an enterprise as the Crusade, and he was able to mobilize them for it. By its blend of maritime adventure with a religious fervour rooted in the idea of a *militia Christi*, the Mahdia campaign showed that the Italian cities, as well, had a potential which might be guided and directed. This potential is not to be defined in terms of the frustration of a trade with the eastern Mediterranean in which Pisa and Genoa as yet had only a small part; if only because these cities were not prompt to respond to Urban's call. It was, rather, due to the internal revival of the western economy following the long-term stimuli of Moslem gold and economic demand. By the late 1080s, this revival had brought cities like Pisa and Genoa to the point of readiness to venture regularly into the eastern Mediterranean. Such events as the bringing of St Nicholas's relics to Bari and the victorious Mahdia campaign gave evidence of this readiness. Before the Crusade, Urban strongly approved of Pisa's forays against the Saracens in 1087 and 1092; and he took full note of its growing material prosperity.[1] So shrewd an observer as he is not likely to have missed the lesson of Mahdia, that this vitality might well respond to a religious appeal directing it to papal ends. At Rome, the double character of the Mahdia expedition, as pilgrimage and as holy war, can scarcely have escaped him. It was a natural development for these aspects, discrete in 1087, to coalesce in 1095, and for Urban himself to establish the connection. Erdmann went too far in commenting that the Mahdia campaign was 'ganz als Kreuzzug ausgeführt'. But the *Carmen* indicates that it had its place in the formation of the Crusading idea. It may well have done so at the most critical point of all – in the mind of the future pope Urban II himself.[2]

TEXT[3]

MSS.: Original: none. Copy: Brussels, Bibliothèque royale Albert Ier, MS. 3897–919, fos. 63r–65v, twelfth cent.

Printed: F. de Reiffenberg, *Bulletin de l'Académie de Bruxelles*, x, pt. 1 (1843), 524–45; also *Annuaire de la Bibliothèque royale de Belgique*, v (1844), 112–35. E. du Méril, *Poésies populaires latines du moyen âge* (Paris, 1847), pp. 239–51. L. T. Belgrano, *Atti della Società Ligure di storia patria*, iv (1866), pp. ccxvi–ccxxvii. P. Pecchiai,

1. *Ep.* 63, Migne, *P.L.* cli. 345.
2. Among those who have helped me with particular points I especially thank Rear-Admiral G. C. Leslie, Mr M. Maclagan, Dr J. D. North, and Dr P. C. H. Wernberg-Møller.
3. Copyright Bibliothèque royale Albert Ier, Brussels. I am most grateful to the authorities of the Library for photographs and for permission to publish.

Gloriosa Pisa (Rome, 1907), pp. 73–92. F. Schneider, *Fünfundzwanzig lateinische weltliche Rhythmen aus der Frühzeit (Texte zur Kulturgeschichte des Mittelalters,* 1, Rome, 1925), pp. 34–42.[1]

Summary. 1–3: Introduction. 4–9: The enemy – Mahdia and its ruler Tamīn. 10–14: Preparations and the assembly of the expedition. 15–18: The sacking of Pantelleria. 19–39: The capture and sack of Zawīla, with Bishop Benedict's harangue (24–30). 40–57: The attack on Mahdia, including a eulogy of the fallen *Ugo vicecomes*. 58–60: Tamīn's terms of surrender. 61–65: Arab nomads intervene at Zawīla and in the Christian camp. 66–69: The return journey. 70–72: Pious uses to which the Pisans devoted their spoils. 73: Ascription of praise.

1. Inclitorum Pisanorum scripturus istoriam, antiquorum Romanorum renovo memoriam; nam extendit modo Pisa laudem admirabilem, quam olim recepit Roma vincendo Cartaginem.
2. Manum primo redemptoris collaudo fortissimam, qua destruxit gens Pisana gentem impiissimam; fit hoc totum Gedeonis simile miraculo, quod perfecit sub unius Deus noctis spatio.
3. Hic cum tubis et lanternis processit ad prelium; nil armorum vel scutorum protendit in medium; sola virtus Creatoris pugnat terribiliter, inter se Madianitis cesis mirabiliter.
4. Sunt et Madianite signati ex nomine, hos in malo nam Madia nutriebat homine; sita pulchro loco maris civitas hec impia, que captivos constringebat plus centena milia.
5. Hic Timinus presidebat Saracenus impius, similatus Antichristo draco crudelissimus; habens portum iuxta urbem factum artificio, circumseptum muris magnis et plenum navigio.
6. Hic tenebat duas urbes opibus ditissimas, et Saracenorum multas gentes robustissimas; stultus et superbus nimis elatus in gloria, qua de causa Pisanorum fit clara victoria.
7. Hic cum suis Saracenis devastabat Galliam, captivabat omnes gentes que tenent Ispaniam, et in tota ripa maris turbabat Italiam; predabatur Romaniam usque Alexandriam.
8. Non est locus toto mundo neque maris insula, quam Timini non turbaret orrenda perfidia; Rodus Ciprus Creta simul et Sardinia, vexabatur et cum illis nobilis Sicilia.
9. Hinc captivi redemptorem clamabant altissime, et per orbem universum flebant amarissime; reclamant ad Pisanos planctu fo. 63ᵛ miserabili; concitabant Genuenses fletu lacrimabili.
10. Hoc permotus terremotu hic uterque populus, iniecerunt manus suas ad hoc opus protinus, et component mille naves solis tribus mensibus, quibus bene preparatus stolus lucet inclitus.

1. I have been unable to see Pecchiai's edition. V. Biagi, *Laude votiva dei Pisani per la vittoria riportata nel 1087 su Timino re dei Saraceni* (Pisa, 1930), is a propagandist translation without scholarly value.

5*d.* circumseptum: circum septis.
9*c.* reclamant; *the metre demands* reclamabant.

11. Convenerunt Genuenses virtute mirabili, et adiungunt se Pisanis amore amabili; non curant de vita mundi nec de suis filiis; pro amore redemptoris se donant periculis.

12. His accessit Roma potens potenti auxilio, suscitatum pro Timini infami martirio; renovatur hinc in illa antiqua memoria, quam illustris Scipionis olim dat victoria.

13. Et refulsit inter istos cum parte exercitus, Pantaleo Malfitanus inter Grecos sipantus; cum forte et astuta potenti astutia est confusa, maledicti Timini versutia.

14. Hos conduxit Ihesus Christus quem necabat Africa, et construxit omnes ventos preter solum Iapiga; Cherubin emittit illum cum aperit hostia, qui custodit paradisum discreta custodia.

15. Pervenerunt navigando quandam maris insulam, quam Pantalaream dicunt cum arce fortissimam; huius incole palumbos emittunt cum litteris, qui renuntient Timino de viris fortissimis.

16. Hic est castrum ex natura et arce mirabile, nulli umquam in hoc mundo castrum comparabile; duo milia virorum hoc tenebant oppidum, qui nec Deum verebantur nec virtutem hominum.

17. Accesserunt huc econtra mirandi artifices, et de lignis nimis altis facti sunt turrifices; destruxerunt occiderunt sicut Deus voluit, et fecerunt quod a mundo numquam credi potuit.

18. Sex ut puto soli viri qui exisse viserant; alios mandant palumbos qui factum edisserant; quo audito rex Timinus desperat de viribus, et hoc factum perturbatus tractat cum principibus.

19. Inter hec regalis stolus discedit et navigat, et iam videt illas urbes quas Timinus habitat; mare terra muri pleni paganis teterrimis, quos conduxerat superbus ab extremis terminis.

20. Hic incepit adulando demulcere populum, et captivos promittendo protrahebat otium; set hoc sprevit Benedictus astutus, Dei nutu illuminatu, luce Sancti Spiritus.

21. Vocat ad se Petrum et Sismundum principales consules, Lambertum et Glandulfum cives cari nobiles; revelat quod hoc Timinus facit ex insidia, hoc totum ex tradimento et mira perfidia.

22. Hinc conscendunt parvas naves tracti ad concilium; decreverunt solam pugnam tracti ad prelium, ut hoc solum iudicaret divinum iudicium. fo. 64^r

23. Hoc fuit antiquum festum sancti Sisti nobile, qui sunt semper Pisanorum de celo victorie; in hoc Benedictus presul populum alloquitur, et silentio indicto murmur omne moritur.

24. Preparate vos ad pugnam milites fortissimi, et pro Christo omnis mundi vos obliviscimini; maris iter restat longum non potestis fugere; terram tenent quos debetis vos hostes confundere.

25. Non expavescatis de eorum numero, nam sunt turpiter defuncti timentes in heremo; neque vos conturbent domus altis hedificiis; Hierico namque prostrata cum muris altissimis.

13cd. *The text is corrupt.*
14a. necabat: *perhaps* negabat.
20cd. *The text is corrupt.*
22. *The stanza lacks a fourth part.*
23b. *Thus in the MS.;* qui *should perhaps read* quo *or* cui.
25a. *The text is corrupt;* expavescatis *is corrected in the MS. from* expavescantis.

26. Inimici sunt factoris qui creavit omnia, et captivant Christianos per inani gloria; mementote vos Golie gigantis eximii, quem prostravit unus lapis David parvi pueri.

27. Machabeus ille clarus confidens in Domino, non expavit ad occursum plurimorum hominum; nec confidens in virtute cuiusquam fortissimi, sed in maiestate sola Dei potentissimi.

28. Vos videtis Pharaonis fastum et superbiam, qui contempnit Deum celi regnantem in secula; Dei populum affligit et tenet in carcere; vos coniuro propter Deum iam nolite parcere.

29. Hinc incitamentis claris multis similibus, inardescunt omnes corde irritantur viribus; offerunt corde devote Deo penitentiam, et communicant vicissim Cristi eucharistiam.

30. Universi creatorem laudant unanimiter; habent vitam atque mortem utrumque similiter; invocabant nomen tuum Ihesu bone celitus, ut turbares paganorum triplices exercitus.

31. Iam armati petunt terram cum parvis naviculis, et temptabant maris fundum cum astis longissimis; se demergunt ut leones postquam terram sentiunt; aquilis velociores super ostes irruunt.

32. Et excelsi Agareni invocant Machumata, quod conturbavit orbem terre de sua perfidia; inimicus trinitatis atque sancte fidei, negat Ihesum Nazarenum verbum Dei fieri.

33. Sed fit clamor Pisanorum altus et nobilior, nam intonuit de celo sonus terribilior: Michael cecinit tuba ad horum presidium, sicut fecit pro dracone cum commisit prelium.

34. Altera ex parte Petrus cum cruce et gladio, Genuenses et Pisanos confortabat animo, et conduxerat huc princeps cetum apostolicum; nam videbat signum sui cum scarsellis populum.

35. Et econtra Agareni concurrunt similiter; telis spatis et sagittis hos petunt ostiliter; fit hic pugna dura nimis sed in parvo tempore, nam ceperunt Agareni statim terga vertere.

36. Misit namque Deus celi angelum fortissimum, qui Senacherib percussit fo. 64ᵛ in nocte exercitum; quod cum vident hi qui stabant intra muros fieri, obserarunt portas illis qui fugebant miseri.

37. Occiduntur et truncantur omnes quasi pecudes; non est illis fortitudo qua possint resistere; perimuntur in momento paganorum milia, antequam intrarent portas et tenerent menia.

38. Postquam desuper et subter intrarunt fortissime, pervagantur totam urbem absque ulla requie; occiduntur mulieres virgines et vidue, et infantes alliduntur ut non possint vivere.

39. Non est domus neque via in tota Sibilia, que non esset rubicunda et sanie livida; tot Saracenorum erant cadavera misera, que exalant iam fetorem per centena milia.

40. Urbs est una desolata festinant ad aliam, et contendunt transilire ad alta palatia; ubi stabat rex Timinus satis miserabilis, qui despiciebat Deum ut insuperabilis.

41. Iussit portas aperire et leones solvere, ut turbarent Christianos pugnantes inprovide; set conversi sunt leones ad honorem glorie, nam vorarunt Saracenos in laude victorie.

29c. devote: vote; *the reading should perhaps be* devoto.

42. Hic evenit tibi Pisa magnum infortunium, nam hic perdis capud urbis et coronam iuvenum; cadit Ugo vicecomes omnium pulcherrimus; dolor magnus Pisanorum et planctus miserrimus.

43. Nam cum omnes Saraceni erupissent subito, sustinet hic mille viros cum asta et clippeo; cum nescit cessare loco et recusat fugere, mille cesis Saracenis cadit ante iuvenes.

44. Hic inponunt illum scuto et ad naves deferunt; plangunt omnes super illum quasi unigenitum; O decus et dolor magnus Pisanorum omnium! O confusio triumphi et magnum incommodum!

45. O dux noster atque princeps cum corde fortissimo! similatus rex Grecorum regi nobilissimo, qui sic fecit ut audivit responsum Apollinis; nam ut sui triumpharent sponte mortem subiit.

46. Sic infernus spoliatur et Sathan destruitur, cum Ihesus redemptor mundi sponte sua moritur; pro cuius amore care et cuius servitio, martẏr pulcher rutilabis venturo iudicio.

47. Non iacebis tu sepultus ha in terra pessima, nec te tractent Saraceni qui sunt quasi bestia; Pisani nobiles te ponent in sepulchrum patrium; te Italia plorabit legens epitaphium.

48. Erimus in domo tua fideles et placidi, et vivemus apud tuos tutores et baiuli; nullus umquam contra tuos levabit audaciam, quia tu care pro Pisa posuisti animam.

49. Non est mora corpus findunt et eiectant viscera; balsamum infundunt multum et cuncta aromata, et componunt quadam fo. 65^r capsa de ligno composito, ut mater et coniux eum videant quoquo modo.

50. Hinc exarsit ira tanta his et Genuensibus, quod non homo neque murus neque quicquam penitus, valet horum sustinere furores et fremitus; unde fit Saracenorum maximus interitus.

51. Sic irrumpunt omnes portas et Madiam penetrant, et accurrunt illuc prope quo stat fera pessima, que turbabat omnes gentes de sua perfidia; modo latet circumclusa in muris altissima.

52. Alii petunt meschitam pretiosam scemate; mille truncant sacerdotes qui erant Machumate, qui fuit heresiarcha potentior Arrio, cuius error iam permansit longo mundi spatio.

53. Alii confundunt portum factum mirabiliter; darsanas et omnes turres perfundunt similiter; mille naves traunt inde que cremantur litore, quarum incendium Troie fuit vere simile.

54. Alii irrumpunt castrum atque turres diruunt; equos regios et mulas omnes interficiunt; aurea vexilla mille traunt et argentea, que in Pisa gloriosa sunt triumphẏ premia.

55. Concurrentes pervenerunt ad illud palatium, mille passuum ut credo quod tenebat spatium; quinquaginta cubitorum murus latitudine, erat idem quater tanta murus altitudine.

56. Super hunc procere turres ad nubes altissime, ubi vix mortalis homo iam possit aspicere; scale facte circumflexe faciles contendere, ubi nullus neque valet neque scit ascendere.

57. Multitudo paganorum hoc tenebant cassarum, nam Cassandi sic appellant hoc tale palatium, quod Pisani circumfusi contendunt destruere; set lassati iam non audent hoc tale confundere.

45b. rex *is perhaps an error for* est.

58. Et iam isti fatigati pausabant in requie; ipse rex misellus nimis pacem cepit petere; donat auri et argenti infinitum pretium; ditat populum Pisanum atque Genuensium.

59. Iuravit per Deum celi suas legens litteras, iam ammodo Christianis non ponet insidias, et non tollet tulineum his utrisque populis, serviturus in eternum eis quasi dominis.

60. Terram iurat sancti Petri esse sine dubio, et ab eo tenet eam iam absque conludio; unde semper mittet Romam tributa et premia; auri puri et argenti nunc mandat insignia.

61. Et cum starent ad videndam donorum potentiam, ecce gentes Arrabites intrarunt Sibiliam; leves multum supra modum cum discurrunt pedites, euro vento leviores cum bellantur equites.

62. Docti retro et astuti fugando respicere, valent melius in fuga hostes interficere; leviores super omnes gentes in giro volubiles, macris equis insidentes corporibus ductiles. fo. 65^v

63. Et istorum tam valentium iam centena milia, urbs relicta a Pisanis tenebant Subilia; ripa maris insistentes et implentes litora, turbant reliquos Pisanos servantes navilia.

64. Quod cum audiunt qui stabant in Madia nobiles, plus quam leopardi currunt ordinati mobiles; ipse rex Timinus spectat altis edificiis, letaturus utriusque populi periculis.

65. Sed nec armis nec virtute confiderunt Arabes, fuga nimium veloces fugientes agiles; nam quicumque remanserunt depugnantes manibus, Pisanorum figit telum et detruncant gladiis.

66. Sic Madia superata recepta Sibilia, iam Pisani gloriosi intrarunt navilia; destruxerunt pretiosa passim edificia, cuncta simul reportantes cum parvis eximia.

67. Captivorum persolverunt plus ad centum milia, quos recepit Romania iam ex longo misera; Saracenos et captivos ducunt sine numero, quod est totum tuum donum Ihesu sine dubio.

68. Ecce iterum Ebrei Egyptum expoliant, et confuso Pharaone iterum coniubilant; transeunt in mari magno ut terra siccissima; Moÿses educit aquas de petra durissima.

69. Nam ut veniunt ad Curras quasdam maris insulas, ubi nullus vidit aquas ad potandum limpidas; fit hoc visu et auditu nimis admirabile, terra parum circumfossa potant aquas largiter.

70. Sunt reversi gloriosi virtute mirabili, et quo durat iste mundus honore laudabili; sancto Xisto consecrarunt perpulchram ecclesiam, et per orbem universum sanctis mandant premia.

71. Set tibi regina celi stella maris inclita, donant cuncta pretiosa et cuncta eximia, unde tua in eternum splendebit ecclesia, auro gemmis margaritis et palliis splendida.

72. Clericis qui remanserunt pro tuo servitio, donaverunt partes duas communi consilio; sic volebas tu regina sic rogasti filium, cuius illis prebuisti in cunctis auxilium.

63*c*. *The MS. adds* si *after* implentes.
65*d*. detruncant gladiis: *thus in the MS.; perhaps* detruncat gladius.
71*d*. *The MS. adds* et *after* gemmis.

73. Sit laus tibi trine Deus unus et altissime, super omnes gloriose in cunctis fortissime, qui timere et amare debes super omnia, cuius manet sine fine sempiterna gloria. AMEN.

ANNO DOMINI MILLESIMO OCTUAGESIMO OCTAVO.

Date. ANNO: ANNI

NOTES TO TEXT

1–4. Mahdia is some 170 km from the site of Carthage, which Scipio Africanus Major (236–184 B.C.) defeated in 202. The Pisan victory at Mahdia is also likened to Gideon's over the Midianites (Judg. vi–viii); the play upon words depends on the Vulgate terms for Midianites (*Madianitae*) and Midian (*Madian*).

10c. The figure of 1,000 ships, like the more than 100,000 captives of stanza 4*d*, is grotesquely exaggerated. Even the Moslem sources, concerned to magnify the number of the victors, said only 400 vessels (Ibn al-Athīr, al-Nuwairī), or 300 warships and 30,000 warriors (al-Tidjānī and the *al-Bayān*).

14d. Gen. iii. 24.

15–18. The sacking of Pantelleria was described by Ibn al-Athīr, who also recorded the sending of messages to Tamīn by pigeon; al-Nuwairī referred briefly to the sacking.

23ab. St Sixtus' Day (6 Aug.) was traditionally favourable for Pisan warfare. Maragone recorded a victory over the Saracens in 1005: *s.a.* 1006, p. 4; and Ranieri Sardo another over the Genoese on the Arno in 1075: pp. 18–19.

25b. Num. xiv. 26–37.

25d. Josh. vi. 20.

26cd. I Reg. (I Sam.) xvii.

27. I Macc. iii–ix.

28. Exod. i–ii.

33cd. Rev. xi. 15, xii. 7.

36ab. IV Reg. (II Kgs.) xix. 35.

45bc. Codrus, king of Athens: Lycurgus, *Against Leocrates, caps.* 84–88.

53b. darsanas: the inner harbour or arsenal.

53d. *Cf.* Aeneas' description in Virgil, *Aeneid*, ii.

57a. cassarum: castle, derived from the Arabic *ḳaṣr*.

57b. Cassandi: Abu 'l-Salt named Tamīn's principal palace as the Ḳaṣr 'al-Mahdī.

58cd. The Moslem sources acknowledged a vast payment of gold and silver to the Pisans and Genoese. Al-Tidjānī mentioned 1,000 dinars, Ibn al-Athīr 30,000, al-Nuwairī 80,000, and Ibn al-Khatīb and Ibn Khaldūn 100,000.

59c. tulineum: toll.

61b. The *gentes Arrabites* were probably Banū Hilāl, as much concerned to discomfit Tamīn as to plunder the Christian camp.

67. The number of Saracen captives – 100,000 – is the same as that given for Christian captives in stanza 4*d*. One captive may have been a son of Tamīn, referred to as public herald in a Pisan treaty with Amalfi of 1126; F. Bonaini, 'Due carte pisano-amalfitane dei secoli xii e xiv', *Archivio storico italiano*, 3rd ser., viii (1868), 6. He was presumably a son of the harem.

68a. Exod. xii. 36.

68c. Exod. xiv. 21–22.

68d. Exod. xvii. 6.

69a. ad Curras: Quirra, a rocky mass off south-eastern Sardinia rising to some twelve metres above sea level, with surrounding reefs. It is named as *Quira* in a maritime chart edited by C. Desimoni and L. T. Belgrano, 'Atlante idrografico del medio evo posseduto del Prof. Tammar Luxoro', *Atti della Società Ligure di storia patria*, v (1867), 55, and *Tavola* iii. It is clear that the Pisans and Genoese returned home by a direct route.

70c. The Pisan chroniclers recorded the building of the church of St Sixtus in the Cortevecchia.

XIII

THE GENESIS OF THE CRUSADES:
THE SPRINGS OF THE HOLY WAR

Our subject in this volume is how men thought about war in the medieval and early modern periods, and how their thinking has contributed to contemporary outlooks upon warfare and violence. A convenient starting point for our deliberations is a comment upon changes in the Western estimate of warfare over the centuries, which William Stubbs made in the third volume of his *Constitutional History of England,* originally published in 1878. "The kings of the middle ages," he wrote, "went to war for rights, not for interests, still less for ideas."[1] For rights . . . for interests . . . for ideas. Implicit in those three phrases is a downhill progression from bad to worse in the pretexts upon which wars have been waged; and Stubbs was not without a remarkably prophetic concern that, with the French Revolution, the Europe he studied and lived in might not have embarked upon its final stage. He made his comment with King Henry V of England in mind. Henry went to war for rights. He had, or at least he professed to have, a rightful claim to the crown of France, which he was denied; his warfare was, therefore, the continuation of a judicial process by other means. If he gloried in war as the highest and noblest work of kings, his aggressive designs were, nevertheless, subject to a measure of legal justification. Such legal justification itself implied principles that, however imperfectly kings themselves may have attended to them, reinforced the doctrines of limited warfare that, at least since the early twelfth century, canonists and schoolmen had been seeking to formulate.

We move on from the fifteenth century to the seventeenth and eighteenth centuries. By then, kings such as Louis XIV and Frederick II fought for interests—like the Spanish Succession, or control of Silesia. That was a rather worse sort of warfare, Stubbs thought, than warfare for rights. No cloak of justice now hid naked selfishness. Kings advanced excuses, rather than legal justifications, for their aggressions. And yet, warfare for interests was still not too bad: it remained limited; few people were killed, and those were mostly soldiers. As regards thought about war, the centuries of warfare for interests consolidated and continued the doctrines of limited war that had gained increasing currency in the Middle Ages.

With the French Revolutionary period, however, there moved toward the center of the picture a far more destructive and fearful warfare—warfare for ideas. Stubbs was not confident that what he saw as having been the formative and stabilizing principles of European history—dynasty, nationalities, and freedom, all of them having deep roots in the Christian tradition—were in his day any longer secure.[2] In particular, the principle of nationalities, in its current form, had been "mostly unlucky in its prophet" (that is, Napoleon I); and Stubbs was also alarmed by "the first attempts at a propaganda of liberty, and the first attempts at a propaganda of nationality" in the French Revolution. He seems to have been anxious lest such unlimited warfare for ideas as had ominously marked the Revolutionary epoch and had been resurgent under Napoleon III, might become the order of the day.[3]

There were grounds for such anxiety, quite apart from those that we, with our experience of the total wars of the present century, can recognize with the benefit of hindsight. For Europe inherited from the Middle Ages another tradition about warfare, besides that of limited war. The eleventh and following centuries had witnessed the vast upsurges of the Crusades, in whose inception Stubbs had rightly seen a "war of idea." In the name of God the participants sought to extirpate those whom they saw as aliens, both inside and outside Christian society. "Scarcely a single movement now visible in the current of modern affairs," wrote Stubbs, again, "but can be traced back with some distinctness to its origin in the early middle ages."[4] The Crusades were such a point of origin; they were effectively the starting point of a view of total warfare that stands in contrast to limited hostilities for rights or interests. They left an indelible mark upon the Western consciousness, which goes far to justify Stubbs's half-articulated fear lest warfare for ideas—secularized, now, but waged with quasi-religious fervor—might again become prevalent.[5]

My concern today is with this last kind of warfare—total, ideological warfare, and the springs of its compulsion upon men. I shall try to set out what seem to me to emerge from modern scholarly inquiry as the reasons why, in the late eleventh century, men came, in the Crusade, to wage it so extensively against what seemed alien to them, and why what they then did has shaped Western ideas so profoundly. I shall then try to suggest some lessons that might today be drawn from the rise and decline of crusading ideas, and from the alternative tradition of limited warfare, which is also a medieval legacy.

When we study the First Crusade, preached at Clermont in 1095 by Pope Urban II, we are fortunate in having, in the Chronicle known as the *Gesta Francorum,* an anonymous account of it, composed by a fighting knight while it was still taking place. He was a highly sophisticated and articulate man—a skilled, professional warrior with a developed sense of feudal loyalty and social obligation. The opening words of the *Gesta* set forth the origin of the Crusade in these words:

> When that time had already come, of which the Lord Jesus warns his faithful people every day, especially in the Gospel where he says, "If any man will come after me, let him deny himself, and take up his cross, and follow me," there was a great stirring of heart throughout all the Frankish lands, so that if any man, with all his heart and all his mind, really wanted to follow God and faithfully to bear the cross after him, he could make no delay in taking the road to the Holy Sepulchre as quickly as possible.[6]

Besides the strongly religious motivation, you will notice that the knight did not focus attention upon events in the East as having been decisive for the "great stirring of heart" that led to the Crusade. We can, I think, put on one side as not of key importance a whole group of factors that historians once thought were critical—I mean factors arising in the Muslim or Byzantine East. The anonymous knight fought with and for high ideals: to suffer for the Name of Christ and to set free the road to the Holy Sepulchre.[7] But he had little real knowledge of his Muslim enemies or of what was going on in their lands: he just thought of them as heathens, who denied the faith of Christ and holy Christendom for which he had taken arms. In the mid-1090s not much was happening in the East to concentrate his mind. If there was some atrocity propaganda in the air, Western piety was not being affronted by serious Muslim attacks upon Christians. Nor, so far as we can see, did Eastern Christians themselves particularly wish to be liberated from the Muslim yoke. Such events as the burning of the Church of the Holy Sepulchre in 1009 by the mad Caliph Hakim were few and far between, and there was no major recent outrage that stirred men to the heart. Islam was by and large a tolerant religion; while subject Christians kept themselves duly humble and paid their taxes, they were not badly off. Nor was it unduly hard for Christians from the West to make their pilgrimages to Jerusalem and the other Holy Places. Pilgrims, after all, are profitable and best not deterred. The Muslims did well from their tolls, from their lodging, and from providing them with supplies. So they let them journey.

Again, in the circumstances of 1095, the Byzantine emperor, Alexius Comnenus, wanted anything but the vast and unmanageable crusading hordes that were soon to come his way. The threat of the Seldjuk Turks, so deadly when they routed the Byzantines at Manzikert in 1071, had receded by 1092, with the death of the last great sultan, Malik Shah. Thereafter, Alexius could do with— indeed he actively sought—a limited supply of mercenaries who would make his diplomacy more credible. Crusaders by the thousands, under independent command, spoiling for war, and whom he could not control, were not what the circumstances of Byzantium in 1095 called for.

Nor was frustrated trade with the East really a factor in causing the Crusade. Up to 1095, the Amalfitans—the most active in the East of the Italian merchants—traded much as they wished. During the First Crusade, the Genoese, the Pisans, and the Venetians were cautious about joining in until they saw that there was money to be made. It was not a desire for trade that stimulated the Crusade, but vice versa.

All things considered, historians would, I think, now be pretty generally agreed that the First Crusade, the "great stirring of heart" in the West, was not, at root, caused by any pull of events in the East. On the contrary, knights like the author of the *Gesta* were impelled to go by constraints and shifts within Western society itself—its social classes, its institutions, and its ideas. I shall discuss four of these constraints and shifts, taking first what I think was perhaps the least important of them in bringing about the Crusade.

First, there was the rise in the population of western Europe during the eleventh century, combined with progressively more sophisticated standards of law and order. This combination tended to produce a surplus population whose aristocracy had every incentive to seek new, external outlets for its martial ardor and its desire for land. Conditions of landownership and inheritance were especially important. They were commonly not based on anything like primogeniture, or impartible descent from father to eldest son. Especially in southern France, there was often some kind of shared possession, such as the so-called *fraternitia,* or *frérêche,* by which inheritance passed to all brothers in common, or to a more extended family circle. Some brothers could be accommodated on the family land. But younger brothers were under pressure, and they also had an interest, to seek their sustenance elsewhere—in a monastery, perhaps, or in holy orders; but, if these choices were not attractive to them, in some lay outlet compatible with their birth.

Rising standards of public order tended to restrict such outlets near home. In France, the post-Carolingian breakdown of authority, and the gravest manifestations of feudal anarchy, seem to have reached their nadir in the generation following the year 1000.

Thereafter, such expedients as the Peace and the Truce of God—by which the Church, first by itself and then with the collaboration of lay authorities, gave its peace to certain classes of society and to certain seasons of the year—curbed opportunities of brigandage and of the fortunes of the sword. Peace-breakers were stigmatized as aliens within society, to be persecuted by a kind of "war upon war" having strong religious sanctions. By 1054, at the Council of Narbonne, it was even asserted that "no Christian should kill another Christian, for whoever kills another Christian undoubtedly sheds the blood of Christ."[8]

As such limitations upon domestic warfare increased, the surplus male offspring of the military classes came under pressure to seek new outlets for their martial and predatory energies at a distance from the places of their birth.

Contemporaries were not unaware that such pressures made men ready to be stirred by the summons to the Crusade. Yet I believe that their power, though considerable, can easily be exaggerated. The internal colonization of Europe could, and did, provide for much of the rising population. So did the increasing use of mercenary knights and the expansion of aristocratic households. Above all, we should mark how few Crusaders settled permanently in Outremer. The initial military establishment of the Kingdom of Jerusalem after 1100 seems to have been only some 300 knights and 1,200 footsoldiers. In the long run, the kingdom suffered from the endemic weakness that, although men came in plenty from the West to conquer the Holy Land, there were never enough who would stay to colonize it effectively. Pressure of population in the West was evidently not serious enough to displace sufficient men who would take up the land available in the East. Demographic or economic factors go only a small way toward explaining the popularity in the eleventh century of the holy war and of the Crusade.

More important—and this is my second factor—was the rise of the knights in social status, and the enhanced sophistication that attended this rise. South Italian Norman though he was, the author of the *Gesta Francorum* typified where many knights of the West had got to by about 1100. He was decidedly a *gentleman*—a man of substance and standing, who rode on horseback and fought with expensive weapons and equipment. He was proud of his knighthood, and he had a strong professional ethic, based upon loyalty to his feudal lord, Bohemond—*bellipotens Boamundus*. Yet he was not blindly loyal. He approved of Bohemond when, in real or politic deference to the law of the land, he did not plunder townships in the Byzantine Balkans. But he parted company at Antioch, when Bohemond turned aside from the Crusade to establish a principality for himself. And there is no mistaking the genuinely religious conviction of our knight, as expressed, for example, in the passage that I earlier cited. Knights had not always been as highly motivated, as sophisticated, as professional, as "gentlemanly," as he. Not long since, they had often been little better than predatory toughs, without *esprit de corps* as a social group. *Knecht* in German still means servant: that indicates the level of many eleventh-century knights before, as the century went on, the elite of their class rose in the world by acquiring land and gentility, and by entering more honorable service and companionship.

This rise in the knights' standing followed changes in military technique—the development of castles, for instance, and the growth of fighting on horseback—which enhanced the standing and prestige of those who fought. But for our purpose today, it is important that the Church—the clergy—also had much to do with the upgrading and dignification of knighthood. The clergy had little choice but to assist the process. In the Carolingian heyday of strong kingship, emperors and kings had seen to the security of the Christian people and defended them from their foes. "Look favorably, O God," the Carolingian clergy had prayed, "upon the Roman empire, that the peoples [that is, its enemies] who trust in their own fierceness may be restrained by the right hand of your power." When the Roman empire—as upheld by emperors and kings—became but a shadow, the defense of the Christian people necessarily tended to devolve upon the knights. To perform their new role, they must be raised from their low estate and given something of the dignity of kings. So, from about 950, we find formulas for the liturgical blessing of the banners under which knights fought. Where the clergy once prayed for kings, they now prayed for knights, as in this *Oratio super militantes:*

> Bless, O Lord, your servants who bend their heads before you. Pour on them your stablishing grace. In the warfare in which they are to be tested, preserve them in health and good fortune. Wherever and whyever they ask for your help, be speedily present to protect and defend them.[9]

In the eleventh century, we also find formulas for the blessing of swords and weapons. There emerged a religious ceremony of knightly investiture; in France after 1070, the dubbing of knights appears widely in the sources. As kings were crowned, so knights were invested. Knighthood now was, or could be, a vocation. The Church was in direct touch with the profession of arms, without the king as an intermediary. The warfare of knights was securing a new sanction and a new prestige. It was becoming holy war.

Since the knights were becoming so important, the clergy were also concerned to effect what German historians, in a good but untranslatable word, call their *Versittlichung*—that is, the raising of their social, ethical, and religious outlook through the determination of the objectives and limits of their warfare. They supplied them with an ideology. Hence the importance of such a work as Abbot Odo of Cluny's *Life of Gerald of Aurillac,* a paradigm Christian knight who drew the sword only in defense of the poor and of righteousness. Hence, too, the Peace and the Truce of God, the "war upon war" that churchmen tried to sponsor. Churchmen sanctioned warfare, but within strict limits and with a minimum of violence. (According to his panegyrist, Gerald of Aurillac, to avoid bloodshed, fought only with the *flat* of his sword![10]) Peace should be the quality of the Christian society itself. Yet fighting was the knights' way of life, and the Church was blessing their weapons. It was difficult to accomplish the *Versittlichung* of the knights, or to enable them to fulfill their social and professional role, within Christian society. If domestic peace were to be secured, it was requisite to find outlets for knightly war outside it. So, in the eleventh century, the Church encouraged knights to take part in the Reconquest in Spain by holy wars against the Muslims there. The ethics of the *Chanson de Roland* took shape in French chivalric society. The knights had come of age. Enhanced in social status, with a novel religious sanction for their carrying of arms, and habituated to the assigning of Christian objectives for their warfare, they were being well prepared to experience a "great stirring of heart" when the call came to the Eastern Crusade.

By thus insisting upon the Church's patronage of the military classes, I have already begun to touch upon a third *sine qua non* of the Crusade within the Western world. It was a radical change in Christian thought and practice in relation to the waging of war, so that warfare for ends of which the Church approved might be proclaimed as without reservation right and meritorious. To the very eve of the First Crusade, it is astonishing how ambiguous Western Christians were in their attitude toward warfare. The clergy were blessing swords and—understandably enough in the circumstances of the time—were praying ever more earnestly for the knights' success in warfare. They were, in effect, sanctioning "holy war." And, over the centuries, one can point to various "holy wars": like the upholding of the Peace and the Truce of God, or the Spanish campaigns, which we have noticed; or like the forays against the Muslims of the Mediterranean to whose participants the ninth-century popes Leo IV and John VIII held out a martyr's crown; or tenth-century Ottonian wars against the Magyars; or Pope Leo IX's ill-starred campaign of 1053 against the Normans of South Italy, which we have not noticed; and others.

Yet right into the second half of the eleventh century, and therefore on the very eve of the First Crusade, the Christian West was also teaching that killing or wounding in warfare, however legitimate the cause, was gravely sinful and merited severe penance. From this point of view, warfare was far from having the Church's blessing and approval: it stood under its condemnation. Far from being a legitimate service in the name of Christ, the profession of arms was not really fitting for a Christian man. This ambiguity of attitude—this "double-think," as it must seem to us—on the Church's part, is nowhere better illustrated than by the Battle of Hastings in 1066. The Norman host fought under a papal banner, in what was deemed to be a just cause, at the command of the legitimate prince. And yet, soon after Hastings, the Norman bishops, with a papal legate at their elbow, imposed penances upon the warriors for their transgressions upon the field of battle: for killing a man, a year's penance; for wounding, forty days; and so forth. This was fully in line with the principal canon-law collection of the early eleventh century, the *Decretum* of Burchard of Worms.[11]

If we turn from practice to ideas, it was also in line with the dominant official view of Western Christianity during its first eleven centuries. For the West had never given a full and unqualified blessing to the waging of war, not even of "just war," or war waged with a greater or lesser degree of ecclesiastical backing. True, St. Augustine of Hippo, though only in a few brief passages, had, for the first time in Christian history, put forward a theory of the "just war."[12] He had also come to approve of the coercion of the Donatists as stiff-necked resisters of Catholic authority, setting all too much emphasis upon Christ's words in a parable, *Compelle intrare,* "Compel them to come in"; as developed by Pope Gregory I, this justification for warfare became very influential in the Middle Ages. Moreover, the conversion of the Franks and other Germanic peoples had long since begun to incorporate war in the popular substructure of Christian thought, including thought about kingship. Christianity did not extinguish Germanic warrior ideals, so it had to accommodate what it could not destroy. For example, a feature of the post-Carolingian period was the growing cult of the Archangel Michael. Scholars have rightly seen in it the Christian substitute for Woden, and it is no surprise that Michael had no more ardent devotees than the recently converted Normans. His sanctuary at Monte Gargano, in North Apulia, where he had appeared in battle late in the fifth century, became a favorite center of Norman pilgrimage. His cult was calculated to foster a warrior ethic within Christianity. He was captain of the hosts of heaven: if God accepted the military service of angels, why should he not also accept the military service of men?[13] But this was a "grass-roots" reaction, rather than (with a few exceptions in Carolingian times) the official view of responsible spokesmen. Far into the eleventh century, not only canonists like Burchard of Worms but also the ablest and most reform-minded propagandists at the papal court set their faces against the acceptance of war. They found no place (if they knew of it) for Saint Augustine's teaching about a "just war," and they had reservations about coercion. "In no circumstances," insisted Cardinal Peter Damiani, "is it licit to take up arms in defence of the faith of the universal church; still less should men rage in battle for its earthly and transitory goods."[14] Even the fiery Cardinal Humbert deprecated the persecution of heretics by force of arms; he argued that Christians who took the sword against them themselves became hardened in ways of violence and rapine.[15]

Until those who spoke officially for Christianity took a different view, anything like a Crusade—as a war promoted and blessed by the Church, and which won only benefits for those who fought— was unthinkable. The change of mind that occurred in the late eleventh century was largely owing to one man, who, as Hilde-brand, was archdeacon of Rome from 1059 to 1073, and who, as Gregory VII, was pope from 1073 to 1085. (It was he who was behind the giving of a papal banner in 1066 to William of Nor-mandy.) Historians have often stressed the epoch-making charac-ter of his work. Caspar called him "the great innovator who stands alone."[16] Tellenbach has written that "Gregory stands at the greatest—from the spiritual point of view perhaps the only— turning-point in the history of Catholic Christendom; . . . the world was drawn into the church, and leading spirits of the new age made it their aim to establish the 'right order' in [a] united Christian world."[17] No aspect of this change of front in the so-called Grego-rian Reform is more significant than the transformation of the Church's official attitude to warfare, so that, from being inherently sinful, it was, or at least might be, meritorious to engage in it, and so to promote "right order" in human society by force of arms.

Let me illustrate in two ways the change that Gregory brought about. First, he very often used in his letters the phrase *militia Christi*—the warfare of Christ. That, to be sure, was a traditional phrase. It harked back to Saint Paul's words about a Christian warfare that was not against flesh and blood, and for which the Christian must be shod with the preparation of the gospel of peace. Later generations had, accordingly, thought of the *militia Christi* as the *spiritual* combat of the martyr and the monk; it stood in the sharpest antithesis to the (wrongful) warfare of earthly arms—to *militia secularis*. Gregory took the critical step of proclaiming that earthly warfare could, after all, be an authentic part of the *militia Christi*. During his struggle with Henry IV of Germany, he called, in an altogether novel way, upon the knights of all lands to dedicate their swords to the service of Christ and of Saint Peter, and to realize their Christian vocation by so doing. Second, and consistent with this, Gregory's reign saw the proclaiming of a new kind of soldier-saint. There had been soldier-saints before, like, for example, Saint Maurice, Saint Sebastian, Saint George, or Saint Martin. But if you read their legends, you will notice that, by and large, they had gained recognition as saints *despite* being soldiers. Saint Maurice, for example, was a member of the Theban legion in Gaul, who, according to the widely read legends about him, disobeyed military orders—there are different versions—either to offer heathen sacrifices, or to punish Christians. Saint Martin even sought discharge from the Roman army, declaring, "I am Christ's soldier; I am not allowed to fight."[18] Gregory began to recognize among his contemporaries soldier-saints who were saints *because* they were soldiers; like Erlembald of Milan, the fierce Patarene leader who perished in 1075 during the savage communal violence that he had provoked. In Gregory's eyes, he was a true *miles Christi*—a soldier of Christ; in 1078 he made it clear that he regarded him as virtually a saint.[19]

It was only after Gregory had so drastically revised the official attitude of the West to warfare, and after his ideas had been disseminated by such publicists as Bishop Anselm II of Lucca—only, therefore, at the very end of the eleventh century—that the preaching of a Crusade became feasible. Only then could a man like the author of the *Gesta Francorum* have heard and answered a papal summons to go eastward, traveling with words from the Gospel upon his lips, and fortified by the assurance that, far from being sinful, his warfare would avail for the remission of sins and the winning of salvation.

The factors that we have so far noticed as contributing toward the Crusade have all concerned the knights, and the secular and religious status of their warfare. Fourth, I turn to something rather different, which historians are increasingly judging to have been of cardinal importance for understanding how the First Crusade came about. It is the state of the Church's penitential discipline at the end of the eleventh century.

No reader of eleventh-century sources, especially those relating to the Crusade, can fail to be struck by men's insistent preoccupation to secure the remission of sins—*remissio peccatorum*. Now, one might well ask whether this has not always been a key matter of Christian concern. Does not the Creed say, "I acknowledge one baptism for the remission of sins (*in remissionem peccatorum*)"? Indeed. But there are historical junctures when a particular matter of Christian dogma or concern, like justification in the Lutheran Reformation or personal conversion in the teachings of John Wesley, strikes home to men with exceptional force. When the First Crusade was being prepared, it seems to have been so with the remission of sins.

One reason for this was that the penitential system of the West was in disorder and confusion. During the twelfth and thirteenth centuries, this would be put right. As a result, an instructed Christian would know pretty clearly how the remission of sins was available to him. If he fell into mortal sin, say by homicide, he would suppose that he had incurred both guilt and punishment. He must confess his sin to a priest and be absolved; that would take away his guilt and free him from eternal punishment. Left with a burden of temporal punishment both in this life and after death (that is, in purgatory), he could, by availing himself of the indulgences that the Church now offered, draw upon the boundless mercy of God and the merits of the saints to lighten this, as well. In the eleventh century, all was not so clear and simple. Penance was still being imposed under an older system that had its heyday in Carolingian times. It knew little of the clear-cut and reassuring distinctions of the later order—between guilt and punishment, eternal and temporal punishment, penance and indulgence. Originally, the Christian had done a penance that, once performed, restored him as he had been before he had sinned. There were already grounds for anxiety in this: could a man be *sure* that his penance was equal to his sin? Before long, penances were being commuted for money: still more urgently, was not more than money needed for the remission of sins? And, by the eleventh century, penitents were often restored to communion before—not, as originally, after—they completed their penance. There was now certainly much left to be done before they could be fully assured that their sins were remitted. For one reason or another, they increasingly took thought for what they might do over and above the penitential system.

For members of the upper classes, there were two courses of action in particular, either or both of which they felt pressed to consider. Best of all, a man could become a monk, and so give himself to a life that was altogether one of penance. As a less effective variant on this course, which was therefore more fraught with anxiety, he could found or endow a monastery; then, his goods and the monks' prayers these goods endowed would avail for the remission of sins at the Day of Judgement. The alternative course of action was to go on pilgrimage. The popularity of pilgrimage to places like Monte Gargano, Compostela, Rome, and Jerusalem, shows how widely the feudal classes sought by this means to gain the remission of their sins. Like the monk, the pilgrim gave up his knightly status and activities; for it was demanded of a pilgrim that he travel unarmed. He carried only his purse and his staff, so that he abandoned himself to the mercy and protection of God. But unlike the monk's, the pilgrim's change of status was only temporary. Once back from Monte Gargano or wherever it was, he reverted to his secular way of life. If many became monks, more became pilgrims. We need only recall Count Fulk Nerra of Anjou with his three journeys to Jerusalem, or Duke Robert the Devil of Normandy, to remember how the most ruthless of men were wont, in moods of penitence, to seek relief of their sins through pilgrimage. The build-up of pilgrimages, like the vast amount of monastic conversion, foundation, and endowment, shows how insistent the desire for the remission of sins became.

When the call to the Crusade was made, it fulfilled this desire more acceptably than anything that had gone before. The choices hitherto available of becoming a monk or a pilgrim required a fighting man to abandon altogether, whether for good or only for a time, his chosen way of life. He had to "drop out" of knightly activities. But now, following the change made by Gregory VII in the Church's attitude toward warfare, the Crusade offered the knight the remission of sins *in and through* the exercise of his martial skills. "If any man," ran the crusading canon of Clermont, "sets out from pure devotion . . . to liberate the church of God at Jerusalem, his journey shall be reckoned to him in place of all penance."[20] At Clermont in 1095, the Crusade emerged, quite suddenly and with the maximum of dramatic appeal, as the knight's own way of gaining remission of sins by waging the warfare that was his life, in the service of Christ and in vindication of Christ's name against the Muslims. The point was well taken by a chronicler of the First Crusade, Guibert of Nogent:

> In our own time, God has instituted a holy manner of warfare, so that knights and the common people who, after the ancient manner of paganism, were aforetime immersed in internecine slaughter, have found a new way of winning salvation. They no longer need, as they did formerly, entirely to abandon the world by entering a monastery or by some other like commitment. They can obtain God's grace in their accustomed manner and dress, and by their accustomed way of life.[21]

No wonder that knights flocked to the Crusade in their hundreds, or that its ideals could soon find expression in Saint Bernard's "praise of the new warfare"—his *De laude novae militiae;* when, as the final stage of the development, monks and knights were fused together in that hitherto unthinkable form of Christian society, the military religious order of the Templars:

> Advance in confidence, you knights, and boldly drive out the enemies of the cross of Christ; be sure that neither death nor life can separate you from the love of God, which is in Christ Jesus. . . . How famously do

such victors return from battle! How blessed are such martyrs when they die in battle! . . . For if they are blessed who die in the Lord, how much more are they blessed who die for the Lord?[22]

This was a far cry, indeed, from the reluctance to sanction warfare by Cardinals Peter Damiani and Humbert less than a hundred years before. A Christian warfare for ideas had now indelibly registered itself in the consciousness of the Catholic West, and had done so because of the internal changes in that consciousness, which we have considered.

To summarize, then: I have identified four factors that, as recent inquiry suggests, so shaped Western society that it was not only ready to rally to the Crusade, but also was subject to those pressures within itself that (rather than external causes) were principally responsible for bringing the Crusade into being. They were: pressure of population and growth of internal order; the increasing social and religious sophistication of the knightly class; a radical change in the official Christian ethic of war; and the strains and stresses set up within society by the Church's penitential system. Severally and together, they reached their full potency at the end of the eleventh century, and only then. Thus, the last decade of the century could witness the critical step in beginning the Crusades. But what, exactly, was this critical step? What was it that enabled these pressures to break forth and so produced the Crusade?

The Swabian chronicler Bernold had no doubt. "The lord pope," he wrote, "was the prime author of that expedition";[23] the critical step was his preaching. Bernold was probably right. Pope Urban II was the very man to bring to a head the developments we have examined. As Odo de Lagery, he sprang from a noble family in Champagne, and thus understood, from within, the aspirations, ethics, and institutions of French military society. As prior of the great Burgundian monastery of Cluny, he could appreciate men's quest for the remission of sins and their readiness to undertake penitential exercises in order to secure it. As cardinal-bishop of Ostia under Gregory VII, he knew that pope's work at first hand, and he declared himself the inheritor of its essential aims.[24] I cannot myself doubt that, since Urban was such a man, the Crusade became what he intended it to become, and that his preaching was critical in shaping it.

The eleventh century had, of course, seen some actual or planned campaigns that in some ways anticipated the First Crusade; but these serve only to emphasize the novelty of Urban's initiative. Apart from the Norman Conquest of England, French knights had crossed the Pyrenees to take part in the Christian Reconquest. To one campaign, Pope Alexander II had attached a promise of spiritual benefits not unlike those associated with the First Crusade. Such holy wars against the infidel undoubtedly prepared the way for the Crusade. Yet, when compared with it, they were on a smaller scale; there was nothing equivalent to the Crusader's vow; and they wholly lacked the characteristics of pilgrimage that (as I shall suggest in a minute) were of the essence of the Crusade as Urban preached it.

Gregory VII, too, had in 1074 tried to organize a kind of Crusade to the East, which looks still more like the First Crusade. He proposed himself to lead a military expedition, primarily to help Byzantium against the Turks. He hoped thereby to reconcile the Roman and the Byzantine churches, and also the Armenians who had been dissident from Rome since the fifth century. He hoped, as well, that his host might worship at the Holy Sepulchre. As protector of the Roman Church while he was away, he proposed to leave Henry IV of Germany, who for the moment seemed to be obedient because of his preoccupation with the Saxon rising. Gregory planned to travel in the company of pious ladies—the Empress Mother Agnes and Countess Beatrice of Tuscany. Not surprisingly, the knights of western Europe made no response to so bizarre a summons. Its unrealistic conception illustrates the weakness of all Gregory's plans to enlist knights in the *militia Christi,* as a warfare with the sword waged directly for papal ends. Strong as were the tendencies that favored a Crusade, they could not be straightly harnessed, as Gregory hoped, to the hierarchical ends of the papacy. Far from preparing the way for the Crusade of 1095, Gregory went far to alienate the military classes by adopting too direct and hierarchical an approach.

Urban II was more understanding and diplomatic. Whereas Gregory imposed his own view of obedience to the vicar of Saint Peter, Urban played upon the constraint that men felt to perform works that would bring remission of sins. Whereas Gregory asserted his own political and military leadership, Urban saw that his expedition must be commanded by the natural leaders of French chivalry—men like Raymond of Saint-Gilles, count of Toulouse. Gregory worked across the grain of lay society; Urban worked with it.

Our problem in determining just how he provoked the "great stirring of the heart" is difficult, because we have no authentic record of what he said and little evidence of what he may have said. Historians are not agreed as to the probabilities. But our evidence strongly suggests that, from the start, the Crusaders thought that they were taking part in a *peregrinatio,* or pilgrimage, and, less certainly, that they were going to Jerusalem to worship, and to free the churches of the East from Jerusalem to Constantinople. The author of the *Gesta Francorum,* for instance, regarded his companions as *peregrini.* (For up to the thirteenth century, neither Latin nor the vernacular languages had words for "crusade" or "crusader.") But Urban's Crusade was quite unlike earlier *peregrinationes.* In the past, the many who had become pilgrims could expect spiritual benefits only if they went *unarmed.* The First Crusade was an *armed* pilgrimage. Its members looked for remission of sins because they went not only to pray but also to fight. It seems likely that Urban's critical step was to announce his expedition as, in effect, a pilgrimage whose members could claim spiritual benefits although they went armed—or, rather, *because* they went armed. He thereby linked together two things that hitherto had been incompatible—pilgrimage and holy war. A pilgrimage to Jerusalem, with appropriate spiritual benefits, provided a framework into which a holy war against the Muslims was now fitted.

Whatever the precise content of Urban's preaching, it struck the right note. Its spark lit the fire that the deeper trends within western Europe during the previous decades had been preparing. For those experiencing the pressure of population and the constraints of public order, it offered an overseas expedition with new lands to conquer or new booty to win. To knights with an enhanced social standing and a new religious sanction, it presented a worthy opportunity for a fight. Since Gregory VII had dispelled qualms about the licitness of warfare even in a Christian cause, it provided a call to arms that promised spiritual benefits. Those who felt the need for the remission of sins could now find it in and through the activities of their own order of society; they need not abandon them for the cloister or an unarmed pilgrimage. Seldom in human history has one man's initiative satisfied so many and such various aspirations. When Urban spoke at Clermont, it was indeed true, in Gibbon's words, that "a nerve was touched of exquisite feeling; and the sensation vibrated to the heart of Europe."[25]

As we look back across nine hundred years to the age of Gregory VII and Urban II, we cannot fail to recognize it as one of the most powerfully formative periods in our common culture, outlook, and institutions. It saw the reversal of a thousand years of Christian tradition, when the Gregorian papacy accepted warfare without reservation as a meritorious activity, and the profession of arms as a Christian vocation so long as it was directed toward the extirpation of what is alien to Christianity both inside and outside Christian society. It is because of this reversal that the Crusade could mold Western ideas so profoundly, and modern views about war could take shape. The Crusade itself, as a kind of war aimed at propagating one set of ideas and habits of life, the Christian, as against another set, such as the Muslim, has exercised an especial influence in this century. Did not Eisenhower describe his part in the Second World War in terms of a "Crusade in Europe"?

Yet the real lessons to be drawn from the Crusade are deeper and more complex. I revert to Stubbs's dictum with which I began: "The kings of the middle ages went to war for rights, not for interests, still less for ideas." As the words "still less for ideas" remind us, long before the Middle Ages were over, such total warfare as the Crusades, fought for ideas, tended to give place to limited warfare for rights or interests, which has itself yielded only

in quite recent times to renewed warfare for ideas. It seems fair to
suggest that, however deeply warfare for ideas may have penetrated
the Western consciousness and shaped Western attitudes, it tends,
when it becomes a danger, to be so as the result of such sets of
domestic circumstances as provoked the Crusades. The Crusades
began at a time of uncertainty and unsettlement in the institutions
and ideas of a society undergoing rapid change, which prompted a
search for alien elements within and outside it to serve as targets of
ideological and physical aggression. (We may recall how the
People's Crusade of 1096, which I have left outside the scope of
this paper, directed itself not only against the Muslims in the East
but also, in the first major outbreak of the anti-Semitism that found
its high-water mark in Nazi Germany, against the Jews of the
Rhineland.) Men seem in all ages to engage in the aggressive
warfare of ideas less for external gains than to relieve the internal
tensions and problems of their own society.

Such reflections are calculated to make us sceptical of the
credentials of warfare for ideas. With our experience of twentieth-
century ideological war, few of us, perhaps, would dissent from the
verdict that stands at the end of Runciman's *History of the
Crusades:*

> The triumphs of the Crusade were the triumphs of faith. But faith
> without wisdom is a dangerous thing. By the inexorable laws of history
> the whole world pays for the crimes and follies of each of its citizens. In
> the long sequence of interaction and fusion between Orient and Occi-
> dent out of which our civilization has grown, the Crusades were a tragic
> and destructive episode. The historian as he gazes back across the
> centuries at their gallant story must find his admiration overcast by
> sorrow at the witness that it bears to the limitations of human nature.
> There was so much courage and so little honour, so much devotion and
> so little understanding. High ideals were besmirched by cruelty and
> greed, enterprise and endurance by a blind and narrow self-
> righteousness; and the Holy War itself was nothing more than a long act
> of intolerance in the name of God, which is the sin against the Holy
> Spirit.[26]

That is a severe judgement, but I think it is a just one. A conclusion
that we may well draw from the study of the Crusades is that

societies, like individuals, should strive for the self-knowledge that lays bare and relieves the internal pressures that generate wars of ideas and "holy wars," and so render them powerless to issue in aggression, whether psychological or physical.

Are we, then, committed to an antiwar ideology? We should probably hesitate. Counterideologies often tend toward the very evils that they profess to oppose. And, given the limitations of human nature, it is hard to envisage an order of things in which force, exercised under due authority, is not called for as the sanction of justice, both within and among states. Perhaps we would do well to look again at the view of war that emerged during the centuries when (as Stubbs reminds us) wars were, on the whole, not total but were limited to the pursuit of rights and interests. This view itself looked back behind the Crusades to the teaching of Saint Augustine about the "just war," which spokesmen in the eleventh century ignored. It was discussed by the canonists and schoolmen of the twelfth and thirteenth centuries, but more fully worked out in early modern times, notably by Spanish Dominicans like Vitoria and De Soto, and Jesuits like Suarez and Molina. "It is the acme of barbarity," wrote Vitoria, "to look for and take pleasure in reasons for killing and destroying men whom God has created and for whom Christ died."[27] As against wars of ideas that arise from the internal strains of individuals and societies, this view sanctions only limited wars that can be shown to arise from the facts of a given situation. Wars may be fought only for causes and reasons that are clearly defined and just, and at the command of a legitimate ruler. There must be no other feasible means of gaining the objectives that are envisaged, and the ruler must be under an overwhelming obligation to secure them. The damage that may be foreseen must not be disproportionate to the attainable objectives, and a ruler may apply only the minimum force that is necessary to gain them.

I do not suggest that this historical tradition about war can simply be adopted by our generation without further thought or modification. But it indicates a historical approach to the problem of war, which deserves to be considered as an alternative both to the holy war tradition and to radically antiwar ideologies. I venture the opinion that the conscious adopting of such an approach, and the general recognition of its validity, are among the conditions of survival for liberal and democratic societies, and for mankind.

Bibliographical Note. Modern discussion of the origin of the Crusades centers upon Carl Erdmann, *Die Entstehung des Kreuzzugsgedankens,* Forschungen zur Kirchen- und Geistesgeschichte 6 (Stuttgart: W. Kohlhammer, 1935). This work has found no translator, and no apology is needed for drawing heavily upon its argument in this paper. The second chapter of H. E. Mayer, *The Crusades,* trans. J. Gillingham (Oxford: Oxford University Press, 1972) is also fundamental. See, too, E. O. Blake, "The Formation of the 'Crusade Idea,'" *Journal of Ecclesiastical History* 21 (1970): 11–31. For the status of eleventh-century knights see P. van Luyn, "Les *milites* dans la France du XIe siècle," *Le Moyen Âge* 77 (1971): 5–51, 194–238. Gregory VII's attitude toward war is examined by I. S. Robinson, "Gregory VII and the Soldiers of Christ," *History* 58 (1973): 169–92. Urban II's preaching at Clermont is discussed by Dana C. Munro, "The Speech of Pope Urban II at Clermont, 1095," *American Historical Review* 11 (1906): 231–42, and H. E. J. Cowdrey, "Pope Urban II's Preaching of the First Crusade," *History* 55 (1970): 177–88. For the Peace and Truce of God in relation to the Crusade, see Cowdrey, "The Peace and the Truce of God in the Eleventh Century," *Past and Present,* no. 46 (February 1970), pp. 42–67. Saint Augustine's attitude toward coercion is discussed by Peter Brown, *Religion and Society in the Age of St. Augustine* (London: Faber & Faber, 1972), especially pp. 260–78, 301–31; and medieval developments are reviewed in Helmut Beumann, ed., *Heidenmission und Kreuzzugsgedanke in der deutschen Ostpolitik des Mittelalters,* Wege der Forschung 7 (Darmstadt: Wissenschaftliche Buchgesellschaft, 1963), especially the papers by Beumann and Hans-Dietrich Kahl. There are useful references to the canonists and schoolmen in Gaines Post, *Studies in Medieval Legal Thought: Public Law and the State, 1100–1322* (Princeton: Princeton University Press, 1964). Joshua Prawer, *The World of the Crusaders* (London and Jerusalem: Weidenfeld and Nicholson, 1972), pp. 147–52, includes comments on the vitality of crusading ideas into the fifteenth century. For the Spanish Dominicans and Jesuits, see Bernice Hamilton, *Political Thought in Sixteenth-Century Spain* (Oxford: Clarendon Press, 1963), especially pp. 135–57, 169–70; and for the whole development, G. Combès, *La Doctrine politique de Saint Augustin* (Paris: Les Petits-fils de Plon et Nourrit, 1927), pp. 417–26.

I am grateful to the Cambridge University Press for allowing me to quote the concluding paragraph of Sir Steven Runciman's *History of the Crusades.* I also thank Dr. Henry Mayr-Harting, who read and commented upon a draft of this paper; I owe a number of valuable points to him, and he has improved it in many ways.

1. William Stubbs, *The Constitutional History of England,* Clarendon Press Series, 5th ed., 3 vols. (Oxford, 1891–1903), 3:75.

2. See Stubbs's "Inaugural" of 1867, as Regius Professor of Modern History at Oxford, in his *Seventeen Lectures on the Study of Medieval and Modern History* (Oxford: Clarendon Press, 1887), p. 17.

3. Stubbs developed his views in two lectures delivered in 1880, "On the Characteristic Differences between Medieval and Modern History," printed in his *Seventeen Lectures,* pp. 238–76; see especially pp. 272–73.

4. Stubbs, *The Constitutional History of England,* 3:75.

5. Stubbs, however, regarded the Crusades with too great approval for him fully to establish the connection. For his judgment of them, see especially *Seventeen Lectures*, pp. 180–81, 253–54.

6. *Gesta Francorum et aliorum Hierosolymitanorum: The Deeds of the Franks and other Pilgrims to Jerusalem,* ed. and trans. Rosalind Hill, Medieval Classics (London and New York: T. Nelson, 1962), p. 1.

7. Ibid., p. 62.

8. Canon 1, Joannes Dominicus Mansi, *Sacrorum conciliorum nova et amplissima collectio,* vol. 19 (Venice: Anthony Zatta, 1774), column 827.

9. On liturgical prayers see Erdmann, *Die Entstehung*, pp. 24–26, 40, 72–78, 326–35. For those cited, see pp. 25 n. 71 and 327–28.

10. The Latin text of the *Life of Gerald of Aurillac* is in J. -P. Migne, ed., *Patrologiae cursus completus . . . series Latina,* 221 vols. (Paris: J. -P. Migne, 1844–64), 133: 639–704 (hereafter cited as *PL*); there is an English translation in *St. Odo of Cluny,* ed. and trans. Gerard Sitwell (London and New York: Sheed and Ward, 1958), pp. 90–180. For Gerald's manner of fighting see *PL*, 133:646–47; for English translation see *St. Odo,* ed. Sitwell, p. 100.

11. See H. E. J. Cowdrey, "Bishop Ermenfrid of Sion and the Norman Penitential Ordinance following the Battle of Hastings," *Journal of Ecclesiastical History* 20 (1969): 225–42.

12. See especially his *Quaestiones in Heptateuchum* 6.10, ed. I. Fraipont and Dona-tien de Bruyne, Corpus Christianorum, Series Latina 33 (Turnhout: Brépols, 1958), pp. 318–19 and *De civitate Dei* 1.21, ed. B. Dombart and A. Kolb, Corpus Christianorum, Series Latina 47 (Turnhout: Brépols, 1955), p. 23.

13. For the new emphasis that was placed upon the militant aspects of Saint Michael in Carolingian and Ottonian times, see J. J. G. Alexander, *Norman Illumination at Mont St. Michel, 996–1100* (Oxford: Oxford University Press, 1972), pp. 85–100.

14. *Ep.* 4.9 (*PL*, 144:316). Peter's idea of the proper, i.e., spiritual, warfare of a Christian is well illustrated by his *Vita sancti Romualdi,* cap. 7 (*PL*, 144:962). For a severe judgment upon a smith who took to making weapons of war, see *Opusculum* 43, cap. 3 (*PL*, 145:681–82).

15. *Adversus simoniacos* 2.18, ed. F. Thaner, *Monumenta Germaniae Historica* (hereafter *MGH*): *Libelli de lite,* 3 vols. (Hanover: Hahn, 1891–97), 1:159–60.

16. E. Caspar, "Gregor VII. in seinen Briefen," *Historische Zeitschrift* 130 (1924): 30.

17. Gerd Tellenbach, *Church, State and Christian Society at the Time of the Investiture Contest,* trans. R. F. Bennett, Studies in Mediaeval History, no. 3 (Oxford: Basil Blackwell, 1940), p. 164.

18. For Saint Maurice, see especially the *Passio Acaunensium martyrum,* ed. Bruno Krusch, *MGH: Scriptores rerum Merovingicarum,* 7 vols. (1885–1920), 3:32–39; for Saint Martin, see Sulpicius Severus, *Vita Sancti Martini,* cap. 4, ed. C. Halm, Corpus Scriptorum Ecclesiasticorum Latinorum, vol. 1 (Vienna: G. Geroldi, 1866), p. 114.

19. Berthold, *Annales, a.* 1077, ed. George H. Pertz, *MGH Scriptores,* 32 vols. (Hanover: Hahn, 1826–1934), 5:305–6. Gregory's change of view was to some extent anticipated in the Ottonian Empire, when, for example, Saint Maurice, a soldier-saint *from a long-distant past,* began to be venerated as an active patron of tenth-century warfare and politics. See especially Albert Brackmann, "Die politische Bedeutung der Mauritius-Verehrung im frühen Mittelalter," *Gesammelte Aufsätze,* 2nd ed. (Darmstadt: Wissenschaftliche Buchgesellschaft, 1967), pp. 211–41, and Helmut Beumann, "Das Kaiser-tum Ottos des Grossen: ein Rückblick nach tausend Jahren," *Wissenschaft vom Mittelal-*

ter (Cologne and Vienna: Böhlau, 1972), pp. 411–58, especially pp. 435–43. Other saints of Christian antiquity came to be similarly regarded, but no *contemporary* warrior was venerated as a saint.

20. *The Councils of Urban II,* ed. Robert Somerville, Annuarium historiae conciliorum, Supplementum, vol. 1 (Amsterdam: Hakkert, 1972–), vol. 1, *Decreta Claromontensia,* p. 74.

21. *Historia quae dicitur Gesta Dei per Francos,* cap. 1, in *Recueil des historiens des Croisades: Historiens occidentaux,* 5 vols. (Paris: Imprimerie nationale, 1844–95), 4:124.

22. *De laude novae militiae,* cap. 1. (*PL*, 182:922).

23. *Chronicon, a.* 1096 (*MGH: Scriptores,* 5:464).

24. *Ep.* 1 (*PL*, 151:283–84).

25. Edward Gibbon, *A History of the Decline and Fall of the Roman Empire,* ed. J. B. Bury, 7 vols. (London: Methuen, 1909–14), 6:268.

26. Sir Steven Runciman, *A History of the Crusades,* 3 vols. (Cambridge: Cambridge University Press, 1951–54), 3:480.

27. Cited by Hamilton, *Political Thought,* p. 157.

NOTE

At the time this Chapter was written there was no translation of Carl Erdmann's book *Die Entstehung des Kreuzzugsgedankens*. This has now been rectified: *see below*, Chapter XIV.

XIV

'THE ORIGIN OF THE IDEA OF CRUSADE'

CARL ERDMANN. *The Origin of the Idea of Crusade*. Translated by Marshall W. Baldwin and Walter Goffart. Princeton: Princeton University Press 1977. Pp. xxxvi, 446.

There must indeed be a large number of medieval historians who can say, with the present reviewer, that few books have opened more windows for them than Carl Erdmann's study of the origin of the idea of crusade. First published in 1935, it has at long last appeared in English translation. This version reads extremely well, and it is furnished with a foreword and an abundance of additional footnotes which together indicate the directions of scholarly advance during the forty-two years that separate the translation from the original. Old though it now is, generations of English-language historians will henceforth be grateful that so fundamental a work has become more readily available.

In such circumstances the reviewer's most useful service may well be to place and assess it in the development of the modern study of crusading origins. It is important to recognize what Erdmann sought to achieve. He did not set out to write a comprehensive account of the origins of the crusading movement for he confined himself to the idea of crusade as it developed up to Pope Urban II's preaching at Clermont in 1095. Even so, he worked upon a vast canvas. Two of the new perspectives from which he viewed the crusading idea deserve special emphasis. First, he believed that its origin was not mainly to be inferred from the sequel to Urban's preaching: the capture of Jerusalem in 1099 and the freeing of the Holy Sepulchre; the establishment of the Latin kingdom of Jerusalem; and the vision of Jerusalem as the goal of a pilgrimage which, though now pursued by force of arms, nevertheless won the benefits of pilgrimage. Urban's crusade was not in any such sense a fresh beginning. It was, instead, the culmination of a centuries-long development based upon holy war and Christian knighthood; and, in bringing this culmination about, Urban's predecessor but one as pope, Gregory VII (1073–85), had a scarcely less critical role than Urban himself. Seen from such an angle Jerusalem was for Urban no more than the immediate objective of a campaign (*Marschziel*); his true war aim (*Kriegsziel*) was the liberation of the entire eastern Church by a holy war whose makings were written ever larger upon western Christianity from the days of St Augustine of Hippo and Pope Gregory I. Second, therefore, for Erdmann the idea of crusade was not a response to major happenings in the Moslem-dominated East such as an especially severe harassing of Christians by the Seldjuk Turks, nor were Byzantine campaigns in the East like those of the tenth-century Emperor Nicephorus Phocas relevant to it. Rather, its origin lay fairly and squarely in the West, where it was bound up with the struggles of Latin-Christian peoples as they defended themselves against the external and internal enemies of their peace. It became fully manifest in the eleventh century, when they eventually equipped themselves with an honourable knightly class, and with a sophisticated ethic of war and of the profession of arms.

Despite a spirited attempt by S. Kindlimann in 1969 to revive the argument that Nicephorus Phocas's campaigns were 'genuine Crusades,' in its essentials the second of Erdmann's perspectives has stood the test of time; and one may doubt whether it could ever be radically challenged. In detail the largest modification to be called for is probably that Erdmann regarded the shaping of the crusading idea somewhat too largely in terms of the institutions of French feudal society. He was by no means unaware of Italian factors, like the Patarenes of Milan; and he did full justice to the theoretical contributions of bishops Anselm II of Lucca and Bonizo of Sutri. However, Italian sources deserve more prominence than he gave them. The anonymous author of so cardinal a source for the First Crusade as the author of the *Gesta Francorum*, to which Erdmann made remarkably little reference even when allowance is made for his deliberate cut-off with the preaching of the crusade in 1095, was after all a Norman knight from south Italy. Moreover, the *Carmen in victoriam Pisanorum*, whose significance Erdmann greatly undervalued, indicates how strongly the emerging Italian merchant cities of Pisa and Genoa by 1087 had anticipated the holy war ideas of the *Gesta Francorum*. They combined them with zeal for the papacy and contact with its Tuscan allies in the circle of Countess Matilda. By birth and early career, Urban, as the Pope who proclaimed the crusade, was shaped by French society; but as cardinal-bishop of Ostia and as pope he was also aware of such Italian developments. It is likely that Italy as well as France made major contributions to the idea of crusade, both in its long-term evolution and as it crystallized in Urban's own mind.

So far as its essential point is concerned, that the crusade was the outcome of a prior historical development of holy war and Christian knighthood in which Gregory VII was crucial, Erdmann's first perspective, too, has been generally adopted by subsequent scholars. G. Tellenbach's conclusion that 'Gregory stands at the greatest – from the spiritual point of view perhaps the only – turning-point in the history of Catholic Christendom; in his time the policy of converting the world gained once and for all the upper hand over the policy of withdrawing from it,' has been seen to have one of its most convincing demonstrations in Erdmann's masterly exposition of how Gregory's pontificate saw a wholesale change in the Church's attitude to *militia Christi* – to warfare in Christ's name. But Erdmann's preoccupation with knights and holy war has seemed altogether too large and constricting, especially in relation to prilgrimage as a source of the idea of crusade. He did, indeed, see the First Crusade as a unification of holy war with pilgrimage; and as such it was a novelty that Urban first brought about. But his conception of pilgrimage was oddly and misleadingly narrow: it concentrated exclusively upon pilgrimage to the sites of primitive Christianity and particularly to Jerusalem itself. These sites, of course, lay outside western Christendom. So, precisely because Erdmann was justifiably so concerned to establish the idea of crusade as a western phenomenon, his narrow definition of pilgrimage compelled him as early as his author's preface to push it aside as a hitherto exaggerated influence. Subsequent scholarship, of which the East German B. Töpfer is perhaps here the outstanding representative, has, however, shown how very important domestic pilgrimage had become by the eleventh century within Western Christendom itself. It took the form, not only of long-distance but internal journeys to great centres like Rome, Compostela, or Monte Gargano, but also – and particularly in France – of shorter ones to local centres like Saint-Martial at Limoges, St Mary Magdalen at Vézelay, St John the Baptist at Angély, and a host of lesser places. Few men, even if poor, can have lived outside fairly easy range of a pilgrimage centre. Pilgrimage entered the everyday framework of medieval religion and life. As such, it can be accorded its due place as a source of the idea of crusade without contradicting the crusade's Western origins. At the same time, since there was a gradation in pilgrimages from local centres to Jerusalem as the culmination, there is no need to follow Erdmann in his denial that Jerusalem can have been the principal war aim of Urban's crusade as preached at Clermont. In fact there is considerable evidence to suggest that it was.

Historians have therefore tended to rescue pilgrimage from where Erdmann left it in the margin of the idea of crusade, and to restore it to the centre of the picture. This restoration has been mightily helped by their fresh understanding of the eleventh-century concern to secure by every available means the *remissio peccatorum*. Today it seems remarkable that Erdmann should have paid this phrase so little attention, for it is writ large in all the eleventh-century sources for the idea of crusade and for the ambiance within which the crusade came to maturity. It was seminally and fundamentally studied by H.E. Mayer in the second chapter of his history of the crusades, first published in 1965; this chapter undoubtedly represents the most important single contribution to the understanding of crusading origins since Erdmann's book appeared. The concentration of historians upon the *remissio peccatorum* has led to an accentuation of religious factors in the origin of the crusade, but in full awareness of their political, social, and economic context. A long-established search for remission either through association with the monastic order or through unarmed pilgrimage made men sensitive to the promise of remission through a crusade which Urban represented as itself a *peregrinatio* – but also as what contemporaries called a *novum salutis promerendae genus*: an *armed* pilgrimage. Pilgrimage as a domestic, Western institution made the crusade particularly suited to the knights whose development Erdmann himself so brilliantly described.

He recognized that 'the idea of the armed pilgrimage was proclaimed for the first time at Clermont.' But his undervaluing of pilgrimage caused him to underestimate how great a novelty it was. At this point the Italian evidence of the *Carmen in victoriam Pisanorum* is decisive. For it shows how, so late as 1087, the concepts of holy war and pilgrimage remained as distinct as Erdmann shows that they had earlier been. It is now widely appreciated that our use of the word crusade is somewhat arbitrary and even anachronistic, because the Latin and vernacular languages of the eleventh and twelfth centuries had no corresponding term. But, given the novelty of Urban's fusion of holy war and pilgrimage, few present-day historians would follow Erdmann in his ready use of the word, without even the safeguard of inverted commas, in such connections as the Spanish campaign of 1064 or Gregory VII's investiture in 1080 of Duke Robert Guiscard of Apulia. They would see in the emergence of the armed pilgrimage at Clermont in 1095 a turning point before which the word crusade is best completely avoided, and in Urban an even more decisive figure than Erdmann allowed.

It is not surprising that, in the work of such historians as J. Brundage and J. Riley-Smith, who emphasize the subsequent history of papal pronouncements and of canon law, there is a renewed tendency to consider even the origins of the idea of crusade in the light of developments after 1095. This may be seen as another necessary correction of Erdmann, when he leaned so heavily upon the evidence of earlier centuries.

Nevertheless he was basically right when he directed attention to these centuries, and to western institutions and events. While modifications of his work have been considerable, all subsequent inquiry has in the last analysis sprung from it. For the understanding of the idea of crusade it remains, and will for long remain, fundamental.

Erdmann's book is also of fundamental interest in a quite different context. It was first published in a year, 1935, when the National Socialist regime was well established in Germany; and it is dedicated 'with un-shaken faith in the future of the German spirit.' The translators refer to Erdmann's unconcealed distaste for the regime, to the consequent set-backs to his academic career, and to his premature death in 1945 as a conscript interpreter in the Balkans. Erdmann's book itself, with its calm but relentless unveiling of the springs of holy war in the Middle Ages, may be regarded as a protest of the human spirit against fanaticism and aggression in any age. The dedication affirmed his confidence that such things are aberrations, which can and will be overcome by men who recognize them for what they are, albeit by a sacrifice worth more than martyrdom in holy war. Erdmann gave noble expression to this confi-dence in a farewell letter written to his sister from Tirana only some five months before he died:

For my part I have settled my account, and for what is left of my life I already stand beyond fear and hope. I no longer count upon returning to Germany. ... But, at the same time, I can affirm that this awareness has served only to exalt me and to set me free. More than I used to be, I am ready to take life as it comes and to be thankful for what each day brings. And surely, as a true humanist one must be able even to welcome life's end and know how to die *en philosophe*. ... Because my lot has enabled me to achieve things that I can look back upon with satisfaction, I have nothing to say against such a conclusion. Ultimately it is death alone that proves whether or not a man really holds fast to his own ideal. And so I shall take my departure without hatred and in all serenity, accepting destiny at least for my own self.

Erdmann here indicates a highly individual and personal solution to a universal human problem. But it will not escape notice that Tirana, from which he wrote, is by the *Via Egnatia*, along which Urban called so many crusaders who passed from Durazzo to seek Constantinople and Jerusalem. Written in such circumstances by the historian of the origin of the idea of crusade, Erdmann's letter highlights the significance of his best-known book. Like all great historical writing, it is not merely an investigation of the past but also an address to the present and to posterity.

CLUNY AND THE FIRST CRUSADE

Historians have for long disputed what part Abbot Hugh of Cluny (1049-1109) and the Cluniac monastic family under his rule may have played in preparing the way for, and in actually promoting, the First Crusade ; but the question remains, and perhaps always will remain, fraught with uncertainty. For this as for many other topics of Cluniac history in the eleventh century, only a modicum of direct evidence has survived. The difficulties which arise from this dearth of information are compounded because Cluny's response to the preaching of the Crusade in 1095 by Pope Urban II (1088-1099) is but one aspect of the wider problems of its attitude to the world outside the cloister and to the aims and programme of the reformed papacy. About these problems there is fundamental disagreement amongst historians. It is held by those who would minimize Cluny's external concern that, as a body, the Cluniacs maintained a position of detachment from the Gregorian papacy and its initiatives. If certain individual monks, of whom Abbot Hugh was not a good example, often promoted these initiatives, they no more committed Cluny as an institution than the firm political stance of a few individual members of a present-day university can be held to involve the university itself. I have stated my own conclusions in this matter at length elsewhere, arguing that it is improper to brush aside the corporate indebtedness to the papacy which Cluny acquired and acknowledged during the first two centuries of its history, and the services which its abbot and monks performed in return.

According to this argument, Cluny became indebted to the papacy by the late eleventh century because it shared with the apostolic see of Rome a dedication to the princes of the apostles, St. Peter and St. Paul. Building upon this dedication, the energetic defence which the papacy on several occasions made of Cluny's immunity and exemption against its local assailants made it, in papal eyes, a paradigm of the liberty of the church which the Gregorians were seeking to vindicate. Because Cluny was so deeply indebted to the papacy for the defence of its rights, especially under Abbot Hugh its spiritual and its external activities tended increasingly to be biased towards papal interests. Such a tendency was already manifest, if with some important qualifications, under Pope Gregory VII (1073-1085) ; it was confirmed when, in 1088, there ascended the chair of St. Peter, in the person of Pope Urban II, a sometime grand prior of Cluny who was at once a most loyal son of Abbot Hugh and a professed upholder of strict Gregorian principles. The consistent praise of successive eleventh-century popes for Cluny and for the services of its abbots and monks bears eloquent witness to the recognition at Rome of this pattern of things, while such evidence as is available from Cluny and the church at large tends to confirm that the praise was not undeserved. [1]

Such an appreciation of Cluny's position in relation to the reformed papacy represents an endeavour to follow a middle course between the extremes of claiming that there was either a radical antithesis or a wholesale identity between the Cluniac and the papal reforms in the days of Abbot Hugh ; although the latter is by far the lesser error. The reforms were different but compatible, and what drew them together was far more important than what held them apart. An attempt to appraise Cluny's contribution to the papal initiative of the First Crusade should keep this general background in mind. In developing my earlier, very briefly stated conclusions on this problem, [2] I shall first draw attention to the characteristics of Cluniac monasticism — most of them made sufficiently familiar by earlier discussions of the subject — which render it unlikely that Cluny should in the long term have directly and positively anticipated the ideas and practice of Crusading. Secondly, I shall notice some important, but less often discussed, respects in which Cluny nevertheless did much indirectly to prepare the ground for the preaching of the Crusade as it stemmed from Urban II's initiative. Finally, in the light of these discussions, I shall re-examine the very scanty evidence which has survived for Cluny's attitude to the Crusade after 1095 and compare it with certain other reforming attitudes ; it may thus be possible to see whether, once the Crusade had begun, Abbot Hugh and his monks are likely to have viewed Urban II's initiative with approval and to have been active in sponsoring it.

---

1. See H. E. J. Cowdrey, *The Cluniacs and the Gregorian Reform*, Oxford, 1970, p. 3-63.
2. *Ibid.*, p. 180-187.

I

There is fairly general agreement amongst recent inquirers into Cluniac history that, at least until well into the last third of the eleventh century, the characteristic features of Cluniac monasticism and the leading themes of Cluniac writing render it unlikely that Cluny should have made a major positive contribution to the genesis of the Crusading idea. The cardinal concern of the Cluniacs was with the prayers, alms, and discipline of the monastic life. They fully shared the general contemporary estimate of the monastery as the one really safe haven from the storms and shoals of a radically hostile and sinful world. For the monks themselves, it was the *asylum penitentium* — the sure refuge of salvation ; their overriding concern for the laity was to draw them into the closest association possible with monastic prayers and alms, and so to secure for them the remission of their sins. It was ever active to enrich and endow its corporate monastic life. But at all times its zeal to win money and land went hand in hand with a pressing and overriding concern to win spiritual benefits for those, as well outside as inside the cloister, who in any way adhered to its monastic order. [1] The familiar picture of Cluny as exhibiting a disproportionate concern for external liturgical observance has recently been corrected by a more adequate appreciation of the interior spirituality of the Cluniacs. [2] Its spirituality was based upon an aspiration to renew the simplicity of the pentecostal church and to realize something of the peace and silence of eternity. If such were the characteristics of Cluniac religion, Cluny is not likely to have done much to promote the idea of a 'holy war', as a joint enterprise in which knights were directed towards the winning of spiritual benefits by warfare against the heathen according to ends determined by ecclesiastical authorities. [3] Still less is it likely to have done much in the long term to prepare directly for the Crusade which lay beyond the holy war.

There is clear evidence to suggest that the Cluniacs on the whole showed little alacrity to accommodate themselves to novel

---

1. *Ibid.*, p. 128-135.

2. K. HALLINGER, *Zur geistigen Welt der Anfänge Klunys*, in *Deutsches Archiv für Erforschung des Mittelalters* 10 (1954), p. 417-445 ; Eng. trans. in *Cluniac Monasticism in the Central Middle Ages*, ed. N. HUNT, London, 1971, p. 29-55.

3. See esp. C. ERDMANN, *Die Entstehung des Kreuzzugsgedankens*, Stuttgart, 1935, particularly, p. 60-64.

ideas in such matters.   In his preaching Abbot Odilo (994-1049)
insisted that it was by men of prayer and preaching, not by wiel-
ders of earthly arms, that the heathen should be encountered
and overcome. [1]   In an important letter written *c.* 1035 to Abbot
Paternus of the Spanish monastery of San Juan de la Peña,
Odilo declared that his monks were praying for the welfare of
the kingdom of Aragon and for its deliverance from pagan attack.
He appointed that psalms should be recited daily at Cluny for
King Ramiro I of Aragon (1035-1063), in view of his perils at
the hands of his own brothers and of the heathen.   The psalm
Deus, quid multiplicati sunt was recited after Matins *pro eius pace
et salute corporis et mentis,* and the psalm *Levavi oculos meos* after
all other offices. Odilo's letter makes it clear that his intention
was to intercede for the king personally in his predicament,
leaving the issue in the hand of God.   He gave no hint that
prayer was offered for the victory of Spanish armies. [2]   Cluny
for long made an impression upon the world which corresponded
to this aloofness from military involvement.   Thus, when, in
1050, the Emperor Henry III asked Abbot Hugh to be the godfather of his son, he declared that the excellence of Cluniac religion and its acceptability to God lay in the very fact of its distance from the everyday affairs of this world. [3]

One aspect of Cluny's concern for all men's salvation was that
it did, indeed, unite a zeal for monastic reform with a desire to
raise the religious standards of those outside the cloister, and
especially of kings and members of the military classes.   But
its desire was pre-eminently for their spiritual and moral well-
being and for the establishment of social peace.   Thus, Abbot
Odo (927-942) was remembered for his desire to foster concord
amongst kings and princes. [4]   So far as the aristocracy is concerned, historians have rightly devoted much attention to Abbot
Odo of Cluny's *Life of Gerald of Aurillac.* [5]   In due course it
will be suggested that in one important respect this work may

---

1. See esp. the evidence discussed by É. DELARUELLE, *L'idée de croisade
dans la littérature clunisienne du XIᵉ siècle et l'abbaye de Moissac,* in *Annales
du Midi* 75 (1963), p. 419-439 ; Eng. trans. in HUNT, *op. cit.,* p. 191-216.

2. Ep. 2, in *Patrologia Latina,* ed. J. P. MIGNE (= *PL*), 142. 941-942.
The psalms are 3 and 120 (121).

3. *Monumenta Germaniae Historica* (= *MGH*) *Diplomata,* 5, no. 263, p. 351 ;
Ep. 6, *PL* 159. 931-932.

4. JOHN OF SALERNO, *De vita sancti Odonis abbatis,* 1. 14, 2. 19, *PL* 133. 49,
71.

5. *PL* 133. 639-704 ; Eng. trans. in G. SITWELL, *St. Odo of Cluny,* London
and New York, 1958, p. 90-180.

have helped indirectly to prepare the ground for the reception of the Crusading idea. But in general Odo's depiction of the count as an exemplary Christian layman did not suggest that it was right or meritorious, or something to be sought after, that men should take up arms against other men, however wicked, and shed their blood. Gerald was, indeed, vigilant to put down violence and rapine ; but his prior concern was to promise his enemies peace and reconciliation. Only as a last resort and an unavoidable necessity did he resort to the sword, and then, according to Odo, he would order his men to fight with the flat of the sword and with their spears reversed. His victories were won, not by bloodshed and by force of arms, but by the invincible power of God. Odo boasted that, while his hero was always victorious, he never himself wounded anyone nor was he wounded by anyone. [1] If such was the general character of the most influential early Cluniac discussion of warfare, it is unlikely that Cluny played a considerable positive part in shaping the ideology of the holy war and of the Crusade which developed from it.

Equally, Cluny played no demonstrable part in sponsoring the holy war by encouraging particular individuals to take part. Historians have long since ceased to assign to Cluny the decisive part which it was formerly alleged to have played in the Spanish 'Crusades' of the eleventh century, both by promoting military expeditions from France and by directing their activities while in Spain. [2] I have argued elsewhere that, in any case, there has been much exaggeration of the scale of Cluniac activity in Spain up to the 1070s. [3] When the Spanish kings expressed their debt to Cluny for such help as they received, they spoke in terms of the spiritual and intercessory services of the monks themselves, rather than of the military service of soldiers whom they sent. [4]

Perhaps the most familiar evidence for monastic support of campaigns in Spain comes from the pages of the historian Ralph Glaber. He began his *Histories* at the monastery of Saint-Bénigne, Dijon, which the Cluniac William of Volpiano had reformed, and he concluded them at the Cluny of Abbot Odilo,

---

1. 1. 8, *PL* 133. 646-647 ; Eng. trans. p. 100. For an anecdote which illustrates this, see 1.40, *PL* 133. 666-667 ; Eng. trans., p. 128-129.
2. For older views, see DELARUELLE, *art. cit.*, p. 420-421 ; Eng. trans. in HUNT, *op. cit.*, p. 192-194.
3. *The Cluniacs and the Gregorian Reform*, p. 214-225.
4. See DELARUELLE, *art. cit.*, p. 422-424 ; Eng. trans., p. 195-197.

to whom he dedicated them ; they, therefore, at least reflect a viewpoint which is compatible with Cluny's.   When writing of the plight of Spanish Christians at the time of Almanzor's attacks, Ralph Glaber did, it is true, approvingly record the actions of monks — not, however, Cluniacs — who, because knights were lacking, took up arms and met martyrs' deaths for the Christian cause. [1]   But this is an exceptional incident which provides no evidence of a general Cluniac approval of such warfare.   Again, he wrote of how, *c.* 1033, men in 'Africa' (the reference is clearly to Christian Spain) sent the booty of warfare against the Moslems to Cluny in token of their devotion to it. [2]   But he did not suggest that their devotion sprang from anything more than a desire to have the protection of St. Peter and the prayers of his monks. The *Histories* give no hint that Abbot Odilo and his monks actively sponsored or directed warfare in Spain.

Nor did Cluny's very lively concern for the pilgrimages which were so pronounced a feature of eleventh-century religion in any way anticipate the mutation by which the traditional unarmed *peregrinatio* became the armed *peregrinatio* of the Crusade.   The pages of Ralph Glaber show that Cluny was well aware of the great expansion of pilgrimage to Jerusalem which followed the conversion to Christianity of King Stephen of Hungary (997-1038) and the consequent opening up of an overland route to the Holy Land. [3]   He approvingly recorded such pilgrimages to Jerusalem as those of Duke Robert I of Normandy (1027-1035) and Count Fulk Nerra of Anjou (987-1040). [4]   But while his pilgrims commonly had a pious desire to die at the Holy Places, he gave no hint that they desired to fight, or become martyrs, for their liberation. [5]   Even his notice of the destruction in 1009 of the Church of the Holy Sepulchre contained no hint of an urge to avenge it by force of arms or to free it from the pagans. [6]   More generally, it has been correctly observed that Abbot Odilo's preaching, like Cluniac spirituality in general, showed little interest in the earthly surroundings of Christ's life, but was centred upon the resurrection and upon the glorious aspect of the Christian mysteries. Genuine though Cluny's concern with pilgrimages undoubtedly

---

1. *Raoul Glaber. Les Cinq Livres de ses Histoires*, ed. M. PROU, Paris, 1886 ; see 2.19.18, p. 44.
2. *Ibid.*, 4.7.22, p. 109-110.
3. *Ibid.*, 3.1.2, p. 52.
4. *Ibid.*, 1.5.21, 2.4.5, 4.6.20-21, 4.9.26, p. 20, 32, 108-109, 113.
5. *Ibid.*, 4.6.18, p. 106-107.
6. *Ibid.*, 3.7.24-25, p. 71-74.

was, its spokesmen did not so present Christianity as to raise sharply in men's minds the predicament of the Holy Places or to stimulate a change in the peaceful nature of pilgrimage. [1]

Because Cluny's attitude to both holy war and pilgrimage was so conservative, it comes as no surprise that the sharpest tensions between Pope Gregory VII and Abbot Hugh arose from the abbot's prudent reserve when presented with Gregory's essentially novel desire to unite the chivalry of Christendom in a *militia Christi* which was to be not, as traditionally, the spiritual warfare of the ascetic, but warfare with the sword in the interests of religion and reform. The most familiar illustration is Gregory's sharp indignation when Hugh admitted to the cloister Duke Hugh I of Burgundy (1075-1078), upon whose military collaboration Gregory particularly counted. [2] Abbot Hugh's reception of the duke was characteristic of his practice. As his biographer Gilo wrote,

> He shrewdly took note of men who had the makings of monks and elicited from them monastic vows. ... As men come from a raging tempest into a haven, so, through him, the great of many ranks and walks of life were converted from their turbulent and restless ways into the calm of monastic peace. [3]

At this point Abbot Hugh's reluctance to move from the traditional Cluniac (and more general) aversion to warfare towards Gregory's novel summoning of knights to a *militia Christi* of the sword, sets him at a distance from the pope whom in other ways he served and followed. [4] It is a touchstone of the distance at which Cluny stood from the developments during the eleventh century which directly anticipated the Crusade.

II

Nevertheless, there were significant ways in which, before 1095, Cluny prepared both the world with which it was in contact

1. See DELARUELLE, *art. cit.*, p. 433-435 ; Eng. trans., p. 209-211.
2. *Register*, 6.17, 2 Jan. 1079, ed. E. CASPAR, *MGH Epistolae selectae*, 2, p. 423-424.
3. *Vita sancti Hugonis* [1.7], in A. L'HUILLIER, *Vie de Saint Hugues, abbé de Cluny*, Solesmes, 1888, p. 582. [References in square brackets to material by or about Abbot Hugh are to my forthcoming *Memorials of Abbot Hugh of Cluny*].
4. See COWDREY, *op. cit.*, p. 139-141.

and its own monks to respond favourably to the Crusade, once it was preached by the pope. It is convenient to begin with the more general of these ways and move towards the more particular.

In general, the ways in which Cluny met with exceptional fullness and effectiveness the religious needs and aspirations of eleventh-century laymen did much to make them receptive to the Crusade. The sources for eleventh-century history, and especially those relating to the Crusade, witness to the profound need which men felt so to dispose of their lives and their goods that they might gain the remission of their sins *(remissio peccatorum)*. The especial prominence of this need seems to have resulted from the current state of the penitential discipline of the western church. [1] In the course of the twelfth and thirteenth centuries, this discipline would be radically revised. If an instructed Christian fell into grave sin, it would henceforth be clear how the remission of sins was available to him. He would know that he had incurred both guilt and punishment. He must confess his sin, be absolved, and do a relatively moderate penance ; this would take away his guilt and free him from eternal punishment. He was left with a burden of temporal punishment, both in this life and in the next, that is, in purgatory ; to lighten it he could avail himself of the indulgences which the church now offered as a means of drawing upon the boundless mercy of God and the merits of the saints. In the eleventh century, all was not so clear and straightforward. Christian penance was still performed within the obsolescent framework of an older order which knew little of the clear and orderly distinctions of later times — guilt and punishment, penance and indulgence, eternal and temporal punishment. In the heyday of this older order, the Christian had simply done a penance which, when complete, restored him to grace as he has been before he had sinned. Before long, penances were often commuted for money. By the eleventh century, penitents were being restored to communion before, not as originally after, they had done the penance which they were assigned. Men's penances seemed increasingly to fall short of what was surely called for before they could be confident of the remission of their sins. So they took thought for what they must do over and above their penances. For the military classes

---

1. For discussions, see H. E. MAYER, *Geschichte der Kreuzzüge*, Stuttgart, 1965, p. 31-46, Eng. trans by J. GILLINGHAM, London, 1972, p. 25-40 ; COWDREY, *op. cit.*, p. 121-128.

there were two especial possibilities.   One was a close association with the monastic order.   At best, a man might become a monk and give himself over to a life of penitence.   Or he might at least found or endow a monastery, so that some part of his wealth was withdrawn from his use to endow the prayers and alms of the monks ; then, both his gifts and the monks' devotions would speak for him at the Day of Judgement.   A second possibility was to go on pilgrimage.   The popularity of pilgrimages to such places as Monte Gargano, Compostela, Rome, and Jerusalem shows how widely the military classes, in particular, sought by this means to secure the remission of their sins.

It is necessary only to turn over the pages of Cluny's charters and read the religious sentiments which the monks put into the minds of the donors, in order to appreciate how powerfully Cluny proclaimed and played upon men's need to find the remission of their sins, and sought by the forms of its monastic life to minister to it ; [1] and its concern to encourage pilgrimages is well known. Its propaganda was widespread in those regions of France from which the First Crusade largely drew its strength — first in Burgundy, Provence, and Aquitaine, and, by the 1090s, in northern France and Flanders as well.   Here, it prepared the ground for a widespread response to the Crusade by its unceasing insistence that men should be vigilant to undertake good works, and especially to enter upon ways of personal commitment like monastic vows or pilgrimage, in order to secure the remission of their sins.   It thereby conditioned them to respond to fresh calls to commitment when these were issued by due authority. With its assurance that 'if any man sets out from pure devotion... to liberate the Church of God at Jerusalem, his journey shall be reckoned in place of all penance,' [2] the summons to the Crusade gained so widespread a response in large measure because of such propaganda as that of the Cluniacs about the necessity for taking steps to secure the remission of sins.

The traditional monastic recommendations to the military classes who sought the remission of their sins, however, differed from the Crusade in a critically important way : they required the knight to seek remission by setting aside his secular status and activities.   If he became a monk, he did so permanently, and if he became a pilgrim he did so temporarily ; for it was

---

1. Cfr COWDREY, *op. cit.*, p. 128-134.
2. *Canon* 2, in *Sacrorum conciliorum nova et amplissima collectio*, ed. J. D. MANSI, Florence and Venice, 1759-1793 (= MANSI), 20. 816.

required of a pilgrim that he should travel unarmed, carrying
only his purse and staff, so that he cast himself entirely upon the
protection and providence of God.   It was a large part of the
secret of the success of the Crusade that it took the unprecedented
step of permitting the fighting man to secure the remission of
sins in and through his knightly vocation and skill.   As a historian of the First Crusade, Guibert of Nogent, succinctly put it,

> In our own time God has instituted a holy manner of warfare, so
> that knights and the common people who, after the ancient manner
> of paganism, were formerly immersed in internecine slaughter, have
> found a new way of winning salvation *(novum repperirent salutis
> promerendae genus)*. They no longer need, as formerly they did,
> entirely to abandon the world by entering a monastery or by some
> other similar commitment. They can obtain God's grace in their
> accustomed manner and dress, and by their ordinary way of life. [1]

Save in so far as the Crusade was proclaimed by a Cluniac
pope, Cluny directly contributed nothing to this 'new way of
winning salvation'.   But Guibert's words suggest that it may
have indirectly helped to prepare the ground in other ways than
by being to the fore in urging men to take appropriate actions
for the remission of their sins.   He said that the Crusade enabled
knights to 'obtain God's grace in their accustomed manner and
dress, and by their ordinary way of life.'   An important strand
of thought in Abbot Odo's *Life of Gerald of Aurillac*, which is
somewhat incongruously interwoven with the tendency towards
non-violence which has already been noticed, represents this
exemplary hero as, however reluctantly and with whatever avoi-
dance of bloodshed, devoting his sword to the putting down of
violence and oppression, and so to the service of God in armed
conflict.

> His household and dependants demanded that he should ... give
> himself to the service of others.   ... For his dependants pleaded
> querulously saying, ' Why should a great man suffer violence from
> persons of low degree who lay waste his property ? ', adding that,
> when these discovered that he did not wish to take vengeance they
> devoured the more greedily that which was rightfully his.   It would
> be more holy and honest that he should recognize the right of armed
> force, that he should unsheath the sword against his enemies, that he
> should restrain the boldness of the violent ; it would be better that
> the bold should be suppressed by force of arms than that the undefended

---

1. *Historia quae dicitur Gesta Dei per Francos*, I, in *Recueil des historiens des
Croisades. Historiens occidentaux*, Paris, 1841-1895 (= *RHF, hist. occ.*), 4. 124.

districts should be unjustly oppressed by them. When Gerald heard this he was moved, not by the attack made upon him but by reason, to have mercy and give help. ... He therefore extended himself to repress the insolence of the violent. ... For some of the Fathers, and of these the most holy and most patient, when the cause of justice demanded, valiantly took up arms against their enemies, as Abraham, who destroyed a great multitude of the enemy to rescue his nephew, and King David, who sent his forces even against his own son. Gerald did not fight invading the property of others, but defending his own, or rather his people's rights. ... It does not darken his glory, then, that he fought for the cause of God, for whom the whole world fights against the unwise. [1]

Odo did not attach positive religious merit to such warfare. But his mirror of a godly count was widely read in the tenth and eleventh centuries. In this portrait of Gerald of Aurillac, with which it is hard to find a parallel in contemporary hagiography, Odo helped to attune the knightly class to respond to such a call as that of the Crusade, when it came, and to dedicate its arms to purposes of which churchmen approved.

Guibert also wrote that, by the Crusade, those who 'were formerly immersed in internecine slaughter have found a new way of winning salvation.' Besides such literature aimed at the *Versittlichung* of the military classes as the *Life of Gerald of Aurillac*, an important eleventh-century means to the better ordering of French society was the movement for the Peace and Truce of God. [2] This movement was of considerable consequence for the First Crusade, which in an important sense was a continuation and development of it. To make the Crusade possible, the Council of Clermont decreed a general peace in the whole of Christendom ; [3] while all the versions of Urban II's speech at Clermont suggest that he made great play of the argument that Christian knights should maintain inviolable peace at home and dedicate their military energies to the freeing of the eastern Christians and Holy Places from pagan servitude. [4]

From the start, Cluny played a small though positive part in the Peace movement. It early benefited from the respite which

---

1. 1.6-8, *PL* 133. 646-647 ; Eng. trans., p. 99-101. I give SITWELL's translation.

2. For a discussion of the Peace and the Truce in relation to the Crusade, see COWDREY, *The Peace and the Truce of God in the Eleventh Century*, in *Past and Present* 46, Feb. 1970, p. 42-67. Above, Chapter VII.

3. *Canon* 1, MANSI 20.816.

4. See D. C. MUNRO, *The Speech of Pope Urban II at Clermont*, in *American Historical Review* 11 (1906), p. 231.

the Peace of God offered from lay incursions. [1] The *Lives* of
Abbot Hugh show him to have been for personal as well as for
public reasons an ardent supporter of it. Among his motives
for entering the monastic life was his revulsion at the way in
which his father, Dalmatius, lord of Semur-en-Brionnais, trained
his sons in the use of arms by sending them on forays to plunder
his poorer neighbours. [2] Accordingly, in the 1060s Hugh was
active against the depredations of Duke Robert of Burgundy
(1031-1075) against the bishop of Autun and others. At a council
in Autun, Hugh, at the instance of the archbishops of Lyons and
Besançon and the bishops of Chalon-sur-Saône and Mâcon,
preached the Peace of God and brought the duke to repent. [3]
Again, *c.* 1070-1072, Hugh proclaimed and vindicated the Peace
at the request of the bishops of Chalon and Mâcon. [4] These
incidents were of no great significance in themselves. But they
are recorded by a biographer who wrote some half a century
later, and they indicate that Hugh was well remembered as a
champion of the Peace movement which supplied an important
part of the background of the preaching of the Crusade. Hugh's
actions may well have impressed the significance of the Peace
upon the future Urban II when he was a monk of Cluny. They
may also have prepared the minds of Cluny's lay devotees to
respond to a call which was partly couched in its terms.

In the decade before 1095, certain other, and more specific,
developments may be observed at Cluny, which were not only
of possible importance in preparing outsiders to hear the call
to the Crusade, but which, still more, were calculated to influence
Abbot Hugh and his subjects themselves. It is likely to have
been of significance for its response to Urban's call that, through
its daughter monastery of Moissac, near Toulouse, Cluny was in
touch with the church of Jerusalem, and so made aware of its
vicissitudes. For many years before the Crusade, the church
of Jerusalem had received endowments in France and elsewhere.
One of these was the subject of a charter of 8 May 1088, in which
Sergius, abbot of Jerusalem, described how he had come to France
at the order of Patriarch Euthymius II (*c.* 1081-1094) and had

---

1. *Recueil des chartes de l'abbaye de Cluny*, ed. A. BRUEL, *Documents inédits
sur l'histoire de France*, Paris, 1876-1903 (= BRUEL), no. 2255.
2. GILO, *Vita sancti Hugonis* [1.2], in L'HUILLIER, *Vie de saint Hugues*,
p. 577.
3. HUGH THE MONK, *Vita sancti Hugonis* [4], in *Bibliotheca Cluniacensis*,
ed. M. MARRIER, Paris, 1614 (= BC), cols. 439-440.
4. *Ibid.*, [7], BC, col. 440.

given the lands of his church at La Salvetat de Montcorbeil *in manu et providentia abbatum et seniorum Cluniacensium seu Moisiacensium scilicet domni Hugonis abbatis et omnium successorum eius*, to hold of the patriarch on condition that an annual rent should be paid to collectors who would come annually from the patriarch. [1] At least from 1088, therefore, Jerusalem was of immediate concern to Abbot Hugh and to one of his principal subordinate houses, and its interests were exercising his mind.

Of far greater importance was the development of Cluny's relationship with King Alphonso VI (1065-1109) of León-Castile. Far too much attention has in the past been concentrated upon Cluny's supposed sponsoring of 'holy wars' in Spain, and upon a large Cluniac involvement in Spanish ecclesiastical and political life, as in some way a direct preparation for the First Crusade. More worthy of study are the bonds of intercession which grew up during the eleventh century between Cluny and the Spanish kings. As has been noticed, they began to exist in the time of Abbot Odilo ; but it was after 1072 that they began to assume major significance. [2] The date 1072 is important ; for in that year Alphonso VI was delivered from imprisonment at the hands of his brother, King Sancho II of Castile, as he believed by the intervention of St. Peter, who answered the intercessions of the Cluniacs. [3] Thereafter Alphonso rose quickly to the leading place among the rulers of Christian Spain, and he honoured his debt to Cluny by a profound and enduring commitment to it. In 1077, the year in which it is probable that Abbot Hugh paid his first visit to Spain, Alphonso doubled the annual *census*, or tribute, of a thousand gold pieces which his father, Ferdinand of Castile (1035-1065), had granted to Cluny, and appropriated it to the buying of wheat for the monks. [4]

This massive Spanish tribute was indispensable if Abbot Hugh was to proceed with the ambitious plan of rebuilding upon which he at this time embarked at Cluny. Between 1077 and 1085-1086 he undertook a major reconstruction of the monastic buildings, and in 1088 he began to build his third church, designed

---

1. PARIS *Bibliothèque nationale* MS. Doat, 128, fols. 216v-217v. The text is printed in the article by A. GIEYSZTOR as cited below, p. 302, n. 1, in *Medievalia et Humanistica* 6 (1950), p. 25, n. 102.

2. See C. J. BISHKO, *Liturgical Intercession at Cluny for the King-Emperors of Leon*, in *Studia Monastica* 3 (1961), p. 53-76.

3. See COWDREY, *The Cluniacs and the Gregorian Reform*, p. 226-227.

4. BRUEL, 3441, 3509. The dates of these and other charters cited have been corrected as necessary.

to . be the largest and most distinguished church in western
Europe. [1] His consequent concern for the well-being of the
kingdom of León-Castile as a source of tribute was increased by
the conversion to Cluniac Customs of the important Leónese
monastery of Sahagún (1080) and numerous other houses, by
Alphonso VI's marriage in 1079-1080 to his own niece Constance
of Burgundy, and by the appointment in 1086 as first archbishop
of the restored see of Toledo of a Cluniac monk, Abbot Bernard
of Sahagún.

It was, therefore, of the gravest concern to Abbot Hugh, and
seems profoundly to have influenced his attitude to warfare
against the Saracens, when Alphonso's realms were invaded by
the Almoravids, a fanatical Berber sect which the Moors of Spain
had called to their aid. In 1086 they inflicted a severe defeat
on Alphonso at the battle of Zallaca, and for a time the king was
unable to maintain his contributions to Cluny. Hugh's dismay
can be inferred from Alphonso's reply to his representations
about the tribute :

> You are well aware that for the present I am much preoccupied
> with bringing peace to the cities of Spain. When, as I hope will soon
> be the case, they are in my obedience I will supply help for the church
> which you are building and will respond fully to your need.

Even in these circumstances Alphonso sent Hugh ten thousand
talents towards the expenses of the third church. [2] In 1090,
when the Almoravid threat had subsided and when Abbot Hugh
visited him at Burgos, he renewed his annual tribute in perpetuity
at the level of 1077. [3]

Coming just when the third church must have been in process
of planning, the Almoravid invasion put in question Abbot
Hugh's ability to complete his most cherished design. It is not
surprising that, both from his longstanding duty of intercession
for Alphonso and from anxiety for his tribute, he should have
decided to increase the Cluniacs' intercessory support for
Alphonso, both in life and in death. His decree survives in a
text drawn up between 1090 and 1093. [4] The first of many

---

1. See K. J. CONANT, *Cluny. Les églises et la maison du chef d'ordre*, Mâcon,
1968, p. 69-98.
2. BRUEL, 3562.
3. BRUEL, 3638.
4. *Statuta sancti Hugonis abbatis Cluniacensis pro Alphonso rege Hispa-
niarum* [*Misc.* 1], *PL* 159. 945-946. For the date, see BISHKO, *art. cit.*, p. 72-74.

liturgical benefits which Hugh promised was that the psalm *Exaudiat te Dominus* [1] should regularly *(sine intermissione)* be chanted at Terce on the king's behalf. The significance of his choice is apparent when it is compared with the psalm *Domine, quid multiplicati sunt* which Abbot Odilo had chosen some sixty years before. The latter psalm was traditionally regarded as a personal plea for deliverance from his enemies made by David as he fled from Absalom. *Exaudiat te Dominus*, on the other hand, is a 'royal psalm' for a godly king as he set out to do battle, in which liturgical prayer was offered, with sacrifice, for the victory of his army. [2]

It opens with the corporate prayer that God will help the king to the victory in arms that the singers long for him to win :

> The Lord hear you in the day of trouble !
>   The name of the God of Jacob defend you !
> May he help you from the sanctuary,
>   and give you support from Zion !
> May he be mindful of all your sacrifice,
>   and favour your burnt offering !

The monks are not likely to have forgotten Alphonso's magnificent devotions to Cluny, and especially to the third church, when they thus sang of the king's sacrifice and burnt offering.

> May he grant you your heart's desire,
>   and fulfil all your mind !
> May we rejoice in your victory,
>   and in the name of the Lord our God may we be exalted.
> May the Lord fulfil all your petitions !

The psalm goes on to speak with confidence of the king's power to overcome his enemies in the name of God :

> Now know I that the Lord will save his anointed ;
>   he will answer him from his holy heaven,
>   and will save him by the power of his right hand.
> Some trust in chariots and some in horses ;
>   but we will call upon the name of the Lord our God.
> They will be bound and fall ;
>   but we shall arise and stand upright.

Finally there is a prayer for his victory in battle :

> O Lord, give victory to the king,
>   and hear us in the day when we call upon you.

---

1. *Psalm* 19 (20).
2. See E. PODECHARD, *Le Psautier*, Lyons, 1949, I, p. 97-100.

As a preparation of men's minds for the Crusade which was so soon to be preached, the significance of this psalm is clear. In the circumstances of crisis and anxiety created by the Almoravid attacks and the consequent threat to the building of the third church, Abbot Hugh decreed that the monks of Cluny and its dependencies wherever they were should pray in an altogether unprecedent way for the military victory of a Christian host in battle against the Moslems which, if not expressly meritorious, met with full divine favour and sanction. No biblical themes and texts etch themselves more deeply upon the mind than those which are made familiar by regular and solemn liturgical recitation. By 1095 Cluniac monks, and all who were present at their office of Terce, were being habituated to the idea of holy war and were promoting it by their devotions. One piece of evidence indicates how deeply this habituation entered Cluniac life. In 1093, on the death of Queen Constance, it is credibly recorded that Alphonso VI wished to enter Cluny as a monk ; but Abbot Hugh dissuaded him, saying that the times demanded that he should remain where he was, in the world. [1] It was indeed a far cry from the days when Gregory VII had rebuked Hugh for giving very different advice to the duke of Burgundy.

There is, of course, no suggestion that Abbot Hugh directed to the Crusade the same concern which, faced with the Almoravid attacks and the threat to the financial resources needed for the third church, his monks had recently shown for the prosperity of Christian warfare in Spain. There survives absolutely no liturgical evidence to indicate whether or not the Cluniacs interceded for the Crusade or individual Crusaders. But after the anxieties of the past decade and the change of attitude to warfare against the Saracens which the monks of Cluny had recently shown, it is hard to believe that many of them were not well disposed to help their former prior Pope Urban II upon his journey, to approve of his preaching, and to encourage the laymen who responded to his call. Such slight evidence as there is indicates that, once the call to Crusade had been made, the Cluniacs indeed responded as Urban would have wished.

III

First of all, an examination of Urban's itinerary in France discloses how prominently Cluny and its dependencies figured

---

1. BERNOLD, *Chronicon, s.a.* 1093, *MGH Scriptores,* 5. 457.

amongst the places at which he stayed. Before the Council of Clermont he visited Cluny itself (5582-3, 18-25 Oct. 1095) [1] and Souvigny (5584-5, Nov. 1095). Between the Council and his departure from France in July 1096 he stayed at Sauxillanges (3 Dec.), Saint-Flour (5603-4, 7 Dec.), Limoges (5607-13, 30 Dec. - 6 Jan. 1096), Poitiers (13-27 Jan.), Angély (5638, 7 Apr.), Saintes (5639-42, 12-20 Apr.), Layrac (5645, 7 May), and Moissac (5647, 13 May). [2] Furthermore, Urban's French journey was punctuated by the issue of a long series of privileges and other *acta* in favour of Cluny and its houses. At Piacenza he had already issued a privilege in Cluny's favour and had confirmed Abbot Hugh's personal right to wear the mitre and other episcopal insignia (5551, 16 Mar.). When he visited Cluny he consecrated the high altar of the third church and confirmed its immunity (5583, 18-25 Oct., cfr 5602, 5 Dec. 1095) ; at the council of Clermont he repeated this confirmation, [3] and settled a dispute between Cluny and la Chaise-Dieu (18-28 Nov.) ; he also there issued privileges for Nogent-le-Rotrou (5594) and Sahagún (5597). Before the Council he had issued a privilege for Souvigny (5586), and after it the list of his *acta* includes Marcigny (5603), Sauxillanges (5604), Angély (5606), Mornay (5613), Binson (5621), Montierneuf (5638), Limoges (5639), Montaut (5645), Saint-Orens (5647), Beaulieu (5648), Layrac (5649), Saint-Martin-des-Champs (5652), and Figeac (5654). That Urban's itinerary is known to have included stays at ten Cluniac houses suggests that the resources of the Cluniac monastic family were everywhere at his disposal, and that the Cluniacs played an active part in planning his itinerary. His support for Cluny and for sixteen other Cluniac houses may well register his appreciation for such help, as well as his long-term debt to Abbot Hugh and his sometime monastery. The Cluniacs of Moissac, at least, seem also to have helped in a positive way with recruiting for the Crusade. The document known as the 'Encyclical of Pope Sergius IV' has been shown to be, in all probability, a propaganda pamphlet designed

---

1. References in this paragraph are to the numbers and dates of items in P. Jaffé, *Regesta pontificum Romanorum*, 2nd. edn., Leipzig, 1885-1888, i. 681-689.

2. It should be remenbered that during Feb. and Mar., Urban was for the most part in Anjou and other regions where Cluny had few dependencies for him to stay.

3. *De adventu Urbani II ad monasterium Cluniacense*, in É. Baluze, *Miscellanea*, t. 6, Paris, 1713, p. 475 ; Urban II, *Sermo 1*, PL 151. 561-564.

to promote the Crusade, which was produced at Moissac soon after Urban's departure. [1]

Abbot Hugh's personal contribution to Urban's journey and to the propagation of the Crusade is extremely hard to estimate, on account of the lack of information about his itinerary and activities in the 1090s. [2] He may be presumed, but not strictly proved, to have been at Cluny when the pope consecrated the new high altar, and according to Pope Paschal II's privilege of 1100 for Cluny he was at the Council of Clermont. [3] Otherwise, there is no clear indication of his whereabouts until he is known to have been at Cluny on 12 April 1096. [4] It is not certain whether or not he accompanied the pope on any part of his journey after Clermont, or whether or not, if he remained at Cluny, he was at once active in propagating the Crusade. But there is some indication in Cluny's charters that in due course he encouraged knights to go to Jerusalem both in 1096 and in 1101.

When interpreting the charters, two points must be borne mind. First, since their purpose was to record transactions in land and money, they may too easily seem to indicate that the monks' concern was essentially economic, and that the Cluniacs probably saw in the Crusade only a pretext for adding to their wealth and revenues. Such a view is probably an over-simplification. Cluny was never neglectful of opportunities to increase its corporate wealth. But it would indeed be hard to account for its vast and continuing lay support, and for the striking ways in which its religious observances seem to have fulfilled lay aspirations, if it was not also genuinely sensitive to the spiritual currents of the day, of which the Crusading impulse must be counted as one, and if it was not recognized by contemporaries to have been so. Secondly, monastic charters were normally

---

1. A. GIEYSZTOR, *The Genesis of the Crusades : the Encyclical of Pope Sergius IV (1009-1012)*, in *Medievalia et Humanistica* 5 (1948), p. 3-23, and 6 (1950), p. 3-34. The text is printed on p. 33-34 of the second article.

2. For Hugh's itinerary, see H. DIENER, *Das Itinerar des Abtes Hugo von Cluny*, in *Neue Forschungen über Cluny und die Cluniacenser*, ed. G. TELLEN-BACH, Freiburg-im-Breisgau, 1959, p. 355-393. For the inconclusiveness of the evidence for possible Cluniac influence upon Count Raymond IV of Saint-Gilles at the time of the Crusade, see J. H. and L. L. HILL, *Raymond IV de Saint-Gilles*, Toulouse, 1959, p. 7-8. Similarly, the collaboration of Abbot Hugh with Clementia of Burgundy in reforming monasticism in Flanders while her husband, Count Robert II of Flanders, was absent on the Crusade, yields no evidence for Hugh's attitude towards Crusaders : see É. DE MOREAU, *Histoire de l'Église en Belgique*, 2, 2nd edn., Brussels, 1945, p. 183-185.

3. *Ep.* 31, *PL* 163. 52.

4. BRUEL, 3703.

drafted by the monks themselves, who expressed in their pream-
bles religious ideas which they themselves were propagating, or
of which they at least approved. Thus, the terms in which
Cluny's charters refer to Crusading reflect attitudes of mind
which were acceptable to the monks, and which were probably
encouraged by them.

Two charters of 1096 indicate that the monks at Cluny encouraged knights to go on the Crusade, and that they fully accepted
its military character and objectives. In one, a knight expressed
his wish to take part in 'the very numerous and great summons
and expedition of Christian people pressing to go to Jerusalem
and fight on God's behalf against the pagans and the Saracens,'
and made express reference to his desire to journey under arms.
He pledged his possessions to Cluny in return for financial support, and the charter refers to these arrangements as having been
made in Abbot Hugh's own presence. [1] In another charter of
the same year, two brothers pledged land to Cluny in return for
money, since 'for the remission of their sins they were going with
others upon the expedition to Jerusalem.' [2] There is further
evidence for Cluny's attitude to the Crusade in connection with
the expedition of 1101. A would-be Crusader expressed in a
charter his desire to go to Jerusalem and adore Christ where he
had once walked upon earth. He first made amends for the
depredations of his men upon the lands of St. Peter. He came
to Abbot Hugh and made certain donations to Cluny ; the abbot
then demonstrated his approval of the knight's intention of
going to Jerusalem by himself placing the cross on his shoulder
and a ring on his finger. [3] Another charter spoke of a knight as
going to Jerusalem because he was 'moved by the example of
those who purposed to save their souls.' [4] The formulas which
occur in these charters indicate that the Cluniacs from the first
understood and approved of the nature and purpose of the
Crusade.

While there is no conclusive evidence for the spread of Cluniac
monasticism to the East at any relevant date, [5] there are certain
sources which tend further to confirm that Abbot Hugh himself

---

1. *Ibid.*
2. BRUEL, 3712.
3. BRUEL, 3737. Hugh's conferring the cross on this knight invites comparison with his giving the tonsure to another knight in Bruel, 3873.
4. BRUEL, 3755.
5. See *The Letters of Peter the Venerable*, ed. G. CONSTABLE, 2, Cambridge
(Mass.), 1967, p. 291-292.

approved of those who journeyed to the Holy Land. When a Flemish clerk named Hugh, who later became the second Latin archbishop of Edessa (?-1144), passed through Cluny on his way to Jerusalem, Abbot Hugh admitted him to confraternity with his monks. In 1119, when three former Cluniac monks visited him at Edessa, he still valued this confraternity and remembered with gratitude the cordial welcome which the abbot had given him. [1] In 1102, when Henry IV of Germany was minded to end the schism and go to Jerusalem, he wrote to Abbot Hugh and informed him of his intention, seeking his prayers on his behalf. [2] Henry clearly expected that his godfather would approve of such a way of returning in penitence to the church. Finally, before Bishop Berard of Mâcon (1096-1121) temporarily departed for Jerusalem in 1109, Abbot Hugh is said to have settled all the issues which were outstanding between them. [3]

There seems to be no other evidence which bears directly upon the reaction of Abbot Hugh and the Cluniacs to the Crusade ; but, such as it is, the material which has been discussed indicates that, once Urban had launched the Crusade, they actively supported it and perhaps showed warmth in doing so. Some confirmation that this was probably so can be found if Abbot Hugh's outlook is placed in relationship with that of two other elder statesmen of ecclesiastical reform — Archbishop Hugh of Lyons (1082-1106) and Archbishop Anselm of Canterbury (1093-1109). From the middle 1090s the archbishops drew nearer to each other and to Abbot Hugh through personal contact and through the mutual seeking of advice and consolation ; and all three were in touch with Popes Urban II and Paschal II through meetings, by letters, and by messengers. It cannot be argued that this network of relationships led to the development of a full community of outlook amongst those concerned. But there is evidence of progress towards a common mind and sympathy, which merits fuller study than it has received. [4]

---

1. *Tractatus de reliquiis sancti Stephani Cluniacum delatis*, 2, in *BC*, cols. 565-568 ; *RHC, hist. occ.*, 5. 318. The date of the clerk's visit is not known.

2. *Epistolae Heinrici IV.*, no. 31, ed. C. ERDMANN, in *Quellen zur Geschichte Kaiser Heinrichs IV.*, ed. F.-J. SCHMALE, *Ausgewählte Quellen zur deutschen Geschichte des Mittelalters*, 12, Berlin, 1963, p. 100-102.

3. Paschal II, *Ep.* 308, *PL* 163. 281. The letter may be spurious, but, if so, it was written at Mâcon at an early date and is admissible as evidence for Abbot Hugh's attitude to the bishop's journey.

4. The starting point for a study is F. LIEBERMANN, *Anselm von Canterbury und Hugo von Lyon*, in *Historische Aufsätze dem Andenken an Georg Waitz gewidmet*, Hanover, 1886, p. 156-203.

Of the three men, Hugh of Lyons was unquestionably a consistent supporter of the Crusade.   In Gregory VII's days, when, as
bishop of Die and archbishop of Lyons, he had been a standing
legate in France, his ultra-Gregorianism had set him in some
contrast with the more moderate and politic Hugh of Cluny.
But after Archbishop Hugh's excommunication by Pope Victor III
and his restoration by Urban II he appears in a somewhat milder
light : Urban II used him in France less than Gregory had done,
and Urban's own influence was a diplomatic and conciliatory
one.   By 1095 Hugh of Lyons stood less in contrast with Hugh
of Cluny than had been the case under Gregory VII, and it is
significant that when the archbishop died it was Abbot Hugh
who informed Anselm of Canterbury of the event. [1]   Hugh of
Lyons was with Urban II on his French journey : he was at Cluny
when the pope consecrated the high altar, [2] and at Clermont he
played a part, together with Urban II, in bringing about agreement between Cluny and la Chaise-Dieu. [3]   The older view that
he at once took a Crusading vow has no foundation, although he
certainly encouraged one knight, Gaudemar of Carpinelle, to
fight in the East. [4]   His zeal for Jerusalem was principally manifest after 1100.   In that year, according to Hugh of Flavigny, he
held a council at Anse, near Lyons, together with three other
archbishops and nine bishops.   After proclaiming a domestic
peace, the council deliberated *de via Iherosolimitana* ; those who
had already vowed to go to Jerusalem and had not gone were
excommunicated.   Archbishop Hugh sent legates to Rome
informing Paschal II of his own wish to go eastward.   In granting his request, the pope appointed him papal legate in the
East, [5] and he departed during or after December 1100 ; he was
absent from Lyons until the spring of 1103. [6]   Nothing is known
of any legatine dealings by him, though his association with the
unfortunate Crusade of 1101 cannot have been a close one.   But
his approval of Crusading and his zeal to promote it are not in
doubt.

Anselm of Canterbury knew Hugh of Lyons well and held him

---

1. [*Ep.* 9] ; in *Sancti Anselmi Cantuariensis archiepiscopi opera omnia*,
ed. F. S. SCHMITT, 2nd ed., Stuttgart, 1968, t. II, *Ep.* 409.
2. URBAN II, *Sermo* 1, PL 151. 561-562.
3. BRUEL, 3693.
4. RAYMOND OF AGUILERS, *Historia Francorum* (*ex* PARIS *Arsenal* MS.
H. 103), RHC, *hist. occ.*, 3.307-308.
5. *Chronicon*, 2, *MGH Scriptores*, 8.487.
6. See W. LÜHE, *Hugo von Die und Lyon*, Leipzig, 1898, p. 163-169.

in the highest regard. Anselm's letters well illustrate their friendship, [1] and Eadmer emphasized how, in 1097, Anselm was particularly anxious to be advised by both Hugh of Lyons and Hugh of Cluny about his impasse with King William II of England. [2] Anselm's own attitude to the Crusade underwent a larger development than historians have appreciated. There is no question of his having desired, like Hugh of Lyons, himself to go to the East. But once the Crusading movement was under way, his wider relationships with the popes and the other reformers brought him, with whatever initial reluctance, to countenance and ultimately even to approve the Crusading activities of others. His progressive change of view may be traced as follows.

Some nine years before the First Crusade, while he was still abbot of Bec, Anselm showed himself to be as far as was Cluny from having sympathy with the military movements which led up to Crusading. He strongly counselled a Norman knight not to follow his elder brother into the military service of Byzantium but, instead, to become a monk :

> I warn, advise, beg, beseech, and command you as one most dear, to renounce the Jerusalem which is now not a vision of peace but of tribulation, and the treasures of Constantinople and of Babylon which must be seized with bloodstained hands. Embark rather upon the way to the heavenly Jerusalem, which is the vision of peace, where you will find real treasures which may be had only by those who despise the others. [3]

After 1095, however, Anselm's attitude to the Crusade was already determined by considerations somewhat different to those expressed in this letter. He was not present at Clermont, [4] but he quickly became aware that the pope had summoned Christendom to a Crusade when Urban himself sent to the Anglo-Norman lands Jarento, the high Gregorian abbot of Saint-Bénigne, Dijon ; and it was not Anselm's way to disregard papal utterances. Jarento came to England and discussed the Crusade

---

1. *Epp.* 100, 190, 260-261, 389-390 ; cfr 208, 210, 322, 409.

2. EADMER, *Historia novorum in Anglia*, 2, ed. M. RULE, London : Rolls Series, 1884, p. 91 ; cfr *The Life of St. Anselm*, 27, 39, 53, ed. R. W. SOUTHERN, London, etc., 1962, p. 103, 116, 130.

3. *Ep.* 117.

4. Urban had summoned him, and he was represented by a monk of Bec, named Boso : *Vita abbatum Beccensium : vita Bosonis*, 2, *Beati Lanfranci opera*, ed. J. A. GILES, 1, Oxford, 1844, p. 328-329.

with the king ; then, in Normandy, he negotiated the agreement between the king and his brother, Duke Robert, which enabled the latter to join the Crusade. [1] Against this background of negotiations, Eadmer says that Anselm was persuaded that it was right and proper *(et rationis esse et honestatis)* for him to contribute to the money which King William advanced to his brother for the Crusade ; though he pleaded lack of resources to excuse a contribution of only two hundred marks, which suggests that he as yet viewed the Crusade with acquiescence rather than with approval. [2] Nevertheless, his single surviving letter of 1096 regarding the Crusade sought to restrain only monks from going to Jerusalem, and did so in express harmony with the pope's own prohibition ; it contains no suggestion that laymen should also be discouraged. [3]

During his first exile Anselm seems to have moved towards a more positive acceptance of the Crusade. In 1098-1099 he was much in Urban II's company ; [4] he is likely to have heard more of it from the pope himself. From May 1099 to August 1100 he was with the Crusading supporter Hugh of Lyons, and he attended the Council of Anse at which Hugh legislated so strenuously for the Crusade. Hugh of Flavigny, indeed, placed Anselm second only to Hugh of Lyons himself amongst the prelates by whose authority the Council took place. This may well exaggerate Anselm's role at Anse, but it indicates that he approved of its proceedings. Certainly, in 1103, when Hugh of Lyons returned from the East, he exchanged cordial letters with Anselm : Hugh thanked Anselm for his prayers, and Anselm rejoiced that Hugh had fulfilled his desire to visit the place where man's salvation was won. [5]

Anselm's gratification with the military outcome of the First Crusade is a further landmark in his thought about it. It was expressed in his letters to King Baldwin I of Jerusalem (1100-1118), with whose family Anselm had old and cordial bonds.

---

1. HUGH OF FLAVIGNY, *Chron.* 2, *MGH Scriptores*, 8. 474-475. Jarento had been educated at Cluny : *ibid.*, 8.413.

2. EADMER, *Hist. nov.* 2, p. 74-75.

3. *Ep.* 195, written in the late summer of 1096. Anselm never relaxed his opposition to the departure of monks for Jerusalem : *Ep.* 410. For a fuller discussion of events referred to in this and the following paragraph, see COWDREY, *Pope Urban II's Preaching of the First Crusade* in *History* 55 (1970), p. 183-185.   Below, Chapter XVI.

4. EADMER, *Life of St. Anselm*, 33, p. 110-111.

5. *Epp.* 260-261.

After Baldwin became king, Anselm wrote to him, praising God

> who of his grace has raised you to the royal dignity in the land where
> Our Lord Jesus Christ himself ... has planted anew his church, which
> because of men's sins had by God's judgement there been for so long
> oppressed by the heathen ; but which by God's mercy has in our time
> so wonderfully been restored, that it might thence be propagated
> throughout the world. [1]

Anselm exhorted Baldwin to practise Christian kingship and
especially to respect the liberty of the church, and he followed
this letter with another in which he proclaimed the duty of the
king of the earthly Jerusalem to reign as another David and to
provide a pattern for all the kings of the earth. [2] Anselm's
praise of the Latin Kingdom shows that his conception of Jerusalem had, indeed, changed since the days when he was abbot
of Bec, and it is reasonable to suppose that his stays with Urban II
and Hugh of Lyons had assisted the change.

It was accompanied by a no less radical revision of his estimate
of the military service of knights against the Moslems. There
is, it is true, no direct evidence for his attitude to service in the
East. But in a letter to Bishop Diego Gelmírez of Compostela
he makes sufficiently clear the general principles of his thought
after his return in 1100 from his first exile :

> You ask me to summon our knights to your help against the Saracens:
> we will gladly call upon them when the time is convenient, and arouse
> them to aid the Christians. But you will know that the English
> kingdom is almost daily receiving tidings of wars which are being
> prepared against it on all hands. So I fear that we shall be unable to
> help you very much, from fear of the enemies who are assailing us.
> ... But with God's help we will strive to achieve by our prayers and
> devotions what we are in no position to do by the recruitment of
> knights. [3]

When taken as a whole, the evidence for Anselm's appraisal
of the Crusade leaves no room for doubt that he warmly accepted
the outcome of the First Crusade in setting up the kingdom of
Jerusalem, that he had come to terms with the military means
by which it had been achieved, that he now accordingly viewed
with approval the warfare of Christian knights against the Sara-

---

1. *Ep.* 235.
2. *Ep.* 324.
3. *Ep.* 263. Diego Gelmírez was elected bishop in 1100 and consecrated on
24 Apr. 1101. He received his *pallium* as first archbishop of Compostela at
Rome on 1 May 1102. This letter, therefore, probably dates from late 1101.
Diego Gelmírez died in 1139 or 1140.

cens, and that he prayed for the victory of Christian armies on
the field of battle.

That Anselm may have taken part in prayer for such victory
whenever the psalm *Exaudiat te Dominus* was chanted at Cluniac
offices which he attended during his exile was, perhaps, a factor
in determining his change of mind. At all events, whereas
Anselm had made little contact with Hugh of Cluny before he
first visited Cluny in 1097 during his first exile, the two men
henceforth became very close to each other indeed. Both Eadmer and the *Dicta Anselmi* testify to the friendship which they
established. [1] Abbot Hugh's biographer Gilo spoke of Anselm
as Hugh's *collega consimilis*, and he recorded a widely publicized
vision of Abbot Fulgentius of Afflighem, who saw both men,
after they had died within eight days of each other, being received into heaven as 'twin champions' of Christ. [2] Of Abbot
Hugh's nine surviving letters, three are addressed to Anselm,
his *tam gloriosus tamque spiritualis amicus* to whom he cleaved
as to part of his own self. 'Whoever', he asked, 'who has known
the sweetness of your conversation would not receive and vene-
rate you as an angel of God?' [3] There is no evidence that the two
men discussed the Crusade or related topics, but given their
importance it is unlikely that they failed to exchange views upon
them. It is probable that Hugh of Cluny's views regarding
warfare against the Saracens in both East and West grew in a
manner similar to Anselm's, and that he was not the odd man
out in the trio of senior reformers.

There is a final consideration which tends to support the view
that Abbot Hugh probably promoted the Crusade and approved
of its results. The slight evidence which remains for Cluniac
attitudes to Crusading after Abbot Hugh's death indicates that
those who claimed to be his disciples favoured it. This was the
case with Hugh's successor as abbot, Pontius (1109-1122), a
nephew of the Crusading leader Count Raymond IV of Saint-
Gilles, whom one of Hugh's biographers described as *eius patris
pii pius filius*. [4] A Cluniac narrative describes how, when three
of his monks wished to go to Jerusalem, Pontius encouraged

---

1. *Life of St. Anselm*, 46, p. 123 ; *Memorials of St. Anselm*, edd. R. W.
SOUTHERN and F. S. SCHMITT, London, 1969, p. 196. Anselm wished his
sister Richeza to enter the Cluniac house of Marcigny : *Ep.* 328.

2. GILO, *Vita sancti Hugonis* [1.15, 2.16], in L'HUILLIER, *Vie de saint
Hugues*, p. 588, 616-617.

3. [*Epp.* 6, 8, 9] ; St. ANSELM, *Epp.* 259, 409, 411.

4. HUGH THE MONK, *Vita sancti Hugonis* [12], *BC*, col. 441.

them. One of them, Gelduin du Puiset, became abbot of the Palestinian monastery of St. Mary in the Valley of Jehoshaphat ; it was he whose visit to Archbishop Hugh of Edessa revived the memory of Abbot Hugh's kindness to him. In the shadow of the Crusaders' defeat at the *Ager Sanguinis* in 1119, he sent for safety to Cluny, through Gelduin du Puiset, a relic of St. Stephen which, in 1120, Pontius placed over the high altar. The dispatch and reception of this relic, and the narrative in which they are recorded, are an indication of the links between Cluny and the first generation of the Crusading movement. [1] It is also significant that, when Pontius ceased to hold the abbacy in 1122, he went from Rome to the Holy Land, where he carried in battle the Holy Lance so rich in associations with Raymond of Saint-Gilles on the First Crusade. [2] Again, the Cluniac monk Gilo, whom Pontius admitted to Cluny and who wrote an admiring *Life* of Abbot Hugh, had himself written a Crusading epic on the history of Jerusalem just before he became a monk, [3] and as cardinal-bishop of Tusculum he, in 1128-1129, served as a papal legate in the crusader states of the East. [4] Such small pieces of evidence suggest that those who claimed to stand in the line of Abbot Hugh were supporters of Crusading.

In conclusion, then, the evidence for settling the problem of Cluny's attitude to the First Crusade is meagre in the extreme. But, especially if it is set against a background of a general tendency to collaboration between the Cluny of Abbot Hugh and the reformed papacy, there is a strong likelihood that its outlook and practice responded to changing circumstances. Following the crisis in its own affairs after the Almoravid attacks upon Christian Spain, it seems to have responded favourably when a Cluniac pope took the critical step of summoning the chivalry of western Europe to an armed campaign against the Saracens in the East as well as in the West. [5] Cluny had, indeed, done little

---

1. As above, p. 304, n. 1.

2. PETER THE VENERABLE, *De Miraculis*, 2.12, *PL* 189. 923 ; ORDERIC VITALIS, *Historia Ecclesiastica*, 12.30, ed. A. LE PRÉVOST, 4 (Paris, 1852), p. 424-425 ; *Anselmi Gembliacensis continuatio*, in *MGH Scriptores*, 6.379.

3. *Historia Gilonis cardinalis episcopi de via Hierosolymitana*, *RHC, hist. occ.*, 5, p. 721-800.

4. WILLIAM OF TYRE, *Historia rerum in partibus transmarinis gestarum*, 13.23, *RHC. hist. occ.*, 1, part 1, p. 591-593.

5. East and West were closely linked in Urban's mind ; see the sources cited in COWDREY, *art. cit.*, in *History* 55 (1970), p. 185-186. Below, Chapter XVI.

to sow the seed of the Crusade, but it had done much to prepare the ground for Urban II to sow it. Once the seed was sown, it seems on all counts far more likely than not that Abbot Hugh and the monks who were subject to him collaborated in bringing it to harvest. There is nothing positively to suggest that they helped on a wide scale or in a systematic manner. But it was no part of the papal intention to involve the monastic order deeply and directly in the Crusade. When Urban II wanted Cluniac help, particularly by facilitating his itinerary in France, by actively encouraging laymen and, where appropriate, clerks and monks to go to the East, and by speaking with approval of the deliverance of Jerusalem and the Eastern churches, he seems to have received all the help that he desired.

POPE URBAN II'S PREACHING
OF THE FIRST CRUSADE

IT IS DOUBTFUL whether the precise terms in which Urban II preached the First Crusade at the conclusion of the Council of Clermont, on 27 November 1095, will ever be known with certainty. Some altogether new evidence would have to be discovered regarding his actual words. In the chronicles of the Crusade, there are, it is true, five quite early versions of his preaching: in Fulbert of Chartres (written in 1101), Robert the Monk (1107), Baldric of Dol (c.1108–10), Guibert of Nogent (c.1109), and William of Malmesbury (who wrote some thirty years after the Crusade). Of these writers, the four earliest wrote as though they had been present at Clermont; Fulcher, and perhaps the other three, may well have been. Where they exhibit a measure of agreement regarding a theme of Urban's preaching, there is some likelihood of a genuine recollection or transmission of it. But Robert, Baldric, and Guibert all said that they gave the gist of Urban's words, not an accurate report of them; and there are considerable differences amongst the five versions. It is more than likely that the chroniclers availed themselves of the customary licence by which medieval writers put into the mouths of their characters such discourses as the writers themselves deemed to be appropriate. If they did so, their departures from Urban's own words may well have been considerable. There can be no doubt that the response to Urban's preaching greatly exceeded his expectations. The chroniclers' versions may have been to some extent influenced by the character of this response, so that they misrepresent what Urban said to elicit it. Historians have found no sure criteria for determining what were the Pope's original themes, in so far as they may have been preserved by the chroniclers; and they have differed in their attempts to reconstruct them or to define what they may have been.[1]

All of the chroniclers' accounts, with the exception of Fulcher's, represent the Pope as making much of the call to deliver the Holy City of Jerusalem from pagan domination. But it is an attractive hypothesis that, in November 1095, Urban was not primarily concerned with Jerusalem, if indeed he mentioned it at all. Ever since he had become Pope in 1088, he had been anxious to improve relations with the Byzantine Emperor, Alexius Comnenus, and to promote the union of the Eastern and Western Churches.[2] In March 1095, at

---

[1] For the most widely influential reconstruction, see D. C. Munro, 'The Speech of Pope Urban II at Clermont, 1095', *American Historical Review*, xi (1906), 231–42.

[2] W. Holtzmann, 'Studien zur Orientpolitik des Papsttums und zur Entstehung des ersten Kreuzzuges', *Beiträge zur Reichs- und Papstgeschichte des hohen Mittelalters* (Bonn, 1957), pp. 51–78, and 'Die Unionsverhandlungen zwischen Kaiser Alexios 1 und Papst Urban II im Jahre 1089', *ibid.* pp. 79–105; S. Runciman, *The Eastern Schism* (Oxford, 1955), pp. 61–2, 71–2, 76–9.

the Council of Piacenza, Alexius's envoys had moved Urban to call upon western warriors to go to Byzantium and help Alexius to defend the Church against the pagans.[3] May it not have been that, in France, Urban intended to publish a further and wider statement of this call? If so, his summons was to help the Eastern Christians in general. If Jerusalem came into the picture, it did so secondarily and not necessarily as a military objective. Perhaps, even, it did not come in at all, but was introduced later by an upsurge of popular enthusiasm and religious zeal.

In one form or another, such questions have been widely asked, especially since they were canvassed by C. Erdmann in a study of the origin of Crusading ideas, which has dominated discussion during the past generation.[4] Erdmann saw the First Crusade as the culmination of the long process by which there took shape, in Western Europe, the idea of a holy war against the heathen, sponsored by the Church. In Western Francia especially, after the waning of royal power under the later Carolingians, it was upon the knights that the task of defending Christian peoples by force of arms against their internal and external foes increasingly rested; in recognition of this, the Church began to bless their weapons of warfare. With the Spanish 'Crusades' of the eleventh century, the notion of the holy war against the infidel gained currency. In due course, Pope Gregory VII (1073–85) finally broke with the age-long reluctance of Christians fully to recognize the licitness of the profession of arms. He called upon the military classes to take part in a 'militia Christi', or 'militia sancti Petri', in which they placed themselves at the service of the vicar of St. Peter. His 'Crusading' plan of 1074 was an abortive attempt to mobilize them to help the Eastern Churches in face of Seldjuk attacks; and he expressed the hope that those who took part might, perhaps, also go on and reach the Holy Sepulchre.[5] Urban built upon Gregory's work; but he did not repeat the mistake that led to its frustration. He appreciated that a call which was too straitly tied to the hierarchical claims of the Apostolic See was likely to find but little response. So he took the novel step of associating his own summons to a military enterprise with the idea of a pilgrimage. Hitherto, it had normally been requisite for a pilgrim to travel unarmed; those who responded to Urban's summons at Clermont might make their journey armed, and yet still enjoy the spiritual benefits of a pilgrimage.

Erdmann believed that, when Urban first preached this unprecedented phenomenon, an armed pilgrimage, he referred to Jerusalem; but that he did so without emphasis. In line with what had happened at Piacenza, the overriding purpose of the Crusade, as Urban envisaged it, was the freeing of the Eastern Churches; there was no special reference to any one locality as being

---

[3] Bernold, *Chronicon, s.a.* 1095, *Monumenta Germaniae Historica* [= *M.G.H.*], *Scriptorum*, v. 462. The suggestion has been made that Alexius Comnenus himself used the pagan domination of the Holy Sepulchre as a pretext for seeking Urban's aid: P. Charanis, 'The Origin of the First Crusade', *Byzantion*, xix (1949), 17–36. But it rests upon the unsupported evidence of the thirteenth-century writer Theodore Skutariotes. This is insufficient to establish it as a possible influence upon the Pope.

[4] *Die Entstehung des Kreuzzugsgedankens* (Stuttgart, 1935).

[5] *Register*, i. 46, 49, ii. 31, 37, ed. E. Caspar, *M.G.H. Epistolae selectae*, ii. 69–71, 75–6, 165–8, 172–3; *Epistolae collectae*, no. 11, ed. P. Jaffé, *Monumenta Gregoriana* (Berlin, 1865), pp. 532–3. It is not certain whether Gregory's plan directly influenced Urban.

the primary military concern of the Crusaders. Urban mentioned Jerusalem briefly and almost incidentally, as a means of recruiting men for the Crusade. In Erdmann's terminology, the goal of the holy war (*Kriegsziel*) was the freeing from the Turkish yoke of the Eastern Churches in general. Jerusalem was merely the goal of the journey (*Marschziel*); it was a secondary, devotional destination, to be attained in strict subordination to the real business of the expedition. Urban believed that these two goals of the Crusade were compatible; and, in a sense, events proved him right. But as the Crusaders responded to his call, they themselves quickly distorted his intention, by making the liberation of the Holy Sepulchre itself the goal of the holy war. This distortion was the result of the Crusaders' enthusiasm. What Urban had intended to be a means of recruiting became, in the minds of the Crusaders, the military end of their journey.

Such is Erdmann's powerfully argued thesis. It has sometimes impressed itself so strongly upon the minds of his critics that, even when the logic of their own arguments has pointed towards the centrality of Jerusalem in Urban's preaching at Clermont, they have been markedly reluctant to follow it. Two of the most important discussions, since Erdmann's, of the origins of Crusading ideas may serve as examples of this.[6] M. Villey has convincingly criticized Erdmann for his too ready identification of the Crusade with the already existing phenomenon of the holy war.[7] In Villey's view, Crusade and holy war should not be used as near-synonyms. The holy war was a much broader conception than the Crusade: although the eleventh century showed various manifestations of the holy war, there was nothing before 1095, even in Spain, which should be called a Crusade. Historians should reserve this term for campaigns that broadly satisfied the juridical categories which later canonists were to devise: there should, that is to say, be a preaching of the cross; clear and express spiritual privileges should be attached to participation; and special obligations should be laid upon those who took part by reason of their having taken the cross.

Villey's criticism of Erdmann's view of Crusading would appear to carry further implications. Erdmann insisted upon Urban's having assigned a general goal to the Crusade—the liberation of the Eastern Churches—because he identified the Crusade with a holy war, which itself had the generalized end of defending Christian peoples against the heathen or of recovering the Christians' land that the heathen unjustly detained. But the more the Crusade is seen as (in Villey's phrase) a 'new synthesis', which carried the promise of specific spiritual benefits and which imposed upon the participants a number of special obligations, the more likely it becomes that the Pope should have laid emphasis upon a particular goal, whose attainment represented the discharge of the obligations and won the enjoyment of the

---

[6] It must be remembered that medieval Latin had no special noun for a Crusade up to the thirteenth century, when such words as *crux*, *crusata*, and *croseria* came gradually into use. Writers had hitherto used such nouns as *iter*, *expeditio*, and, above all, *peregrinatio*. The modern word *Crusade* is not, therefore, capable of precise definition in terms which were current in the formative period of the Crusades.

[7] *La Croisade: essai sur la formation d'une théorie juridique* (Paris, 1942), esp. pp. 9-14, 77-91.

benefits. Villey, however, pursued no such line of argument; partly, perhaps, because he gave but little attention to the Crusade in its aspect as a 'peregrinatio' or pilgrimage. He was content to express general agreement with Erdmann's distinction between the *Kriegsziel* and the *Marschziel* of the First Crusade. He also agreed with Erdmann that it was the hearers of Urban's preaching, not the Pope himself, who focused attention upon Jerusalem as the prime object of the journey, and who intended to capture it rather than merely to win spiritual benefits.

A similar hesitation in pursuing a critique of Erdmann is evident in H. E. Mayer's chapter on the origin of the Crusades in his excellent general survey of Crusading.[8] In certain respects, indeed, he revises Erdmann's conclusions quite drastically. With ample warrant in the sources, he regards the idea of the armed pilgrimage, which for Erdmann was a subordinate factor in the genesis of the Crusade, as in fact a decisive one. The Crusaders were armed pilgrims, whose warfare had the character of a holy war. Since pilgrimages were journeys to a particular place, like Monte Gargano, Compostela, or Jerusalem, it might be anticipated that such an emphasis upon pilgrimage would bring Jerusalem into the centre of the picture. But Mayer argues differently. He adheres to Erdmann's opinion that, at Clermont, Urban had a general aim of bringing help to the Christian Churches of the East. However, he goes further than Erdmann by altogether excluding Jerusalem from Urban's initial preaching. He rightly comments that Erdmann's distinction between the *Kriegsziel* and the *Marschziel* of the Crusade expressed 'perhaps a somewhat subtle interpretation' of events. The eleventh-century religious connotations of Jerusalem were too potent and attractive for it to have served merely as a recruiting device. If Urban indeed referred to it, it must have dominated the Crusade from the start. So, while adhering to Erdmann's view that Urban made the freeing of the Eastern Churches in general the goal of the Crusade, Mayer dissents from him by concluding that, because Jerusalem was too potent an idea to have been a subordinate one at Clermont, it must be supposed to have had no place at all. Pointing to the initial amorphousness of the Crusading organization, he suggests that it is most readily explicable if Urban did not mention Jerusalem, and if, in the succeeding months, public opinion threw it up as the goal of the Crusade with such force that Urban had to acknowledge it. But Mayer's emphasis upon Urban's part in determining the character of the Crusade as an armed pilgrimage makes this supposition paradoxical. It points to a more drastic revision of Erdmann and to the alternative supposition about Jerusalem—that, just because it was so powerful an idea, it is unlikely not to have been at the heart of Urban's preaching from the very start.

That it was has been proposed by another historian who has contributed to the debate that Erdmann started—P. Rousset.[9] In support of his case, Rousset drew attention to evidence which historians have too seldom pondered—the incidental references to the First Crusade which occur in sources

---

[8] *Geschichte der Kreuzzüge* (Stuttgart, 1965), pp. 15–46.
[9] *Les Origines et les caractères de la première croisade* (Neuchâtel, 1945), esp. pp. 57–73.

strictly contemporary with its summoning and assembly. He makes clear the value of this evidence. But his treatment of it is brief, and he did not sufficiently consider whether it genuinely harks back to the Pope's preaching. It is, therefore, worth while surveying more fully the available material. It falls into five categories: (i) chronicles providing contemporary evidence for 1096, (ii) charters of 1096, (iii) contemporary letters, (iv) the *excitatoria* by which men were urged to rally to the Crusade, and (v) the letters and other rulings of Urban himself. The first four categories come from sources which, in general, probably knew Urban's intentions well. They speak of the military liberation of Jerusalem as the purpose of the Crusade with a clearness that is no less apparent in Urban's own writings.

(i) So far as chronicles are concerned, the earliest source of information is the *Fragmentum historiae Andegavensis*. It was written in Anjou in 1096, and so within a few months of Urban's prolonged stay there to preach the Crusade. The author was almost certainly Count Fulk le Réchin (1060–1109) himself. This gives it particular value, for not only did Urban assiduously cultivate the Count as a possible recruit for the Crusade, as the *Fragmentum* bears witness, but Fulk resisted all his blandishments. Fulk's account is not likely to be coloured by enthusiasm for an enterprise in which he did not allow himself to become actively involved. It describes how, towards the beginning of Lent 1096, 'the Roman Pope came to Anjou and urged its people to go to Jerusalem and subdue the race of the heathen who had seized that city and all the land of the Christians up to Constantinople'.[10] Fulk provides clear and early testimony that Urban made Jerusalem the goal of the Crusade and that he called for its military deliverance. Other chronicles tend to confirm this. The chronicle of Saint-Maixent, a monastery where Urban is known from his letters to have been on 31 March after he left Anjou, records how 'by the Pope's order, many men, noble and base, rich and poor, from all lands, . . . went on the journey to the Holy Sepulchre'.[11] Again, Bernold of St. Blasien's account of Urban's French journey speaks of an *expeditio* of which the Pope was the true architect; Jerusalem was its goal and its purpose was to deliver the Christians from the pagans.[12]

These chronicles indicate that from as early as thirteen weeks after the Council of Clermont, Urban was certainly speaking of an expedition which had Jerusalem as its goal, and which was to liberate the Christians of the East from a pagan subjection which extended from Jerusalem up to Constantinople.

(ii) A similar picture emerges from a small number of charters that survive in which, before the Crusaders left, some of them gave lands to, or made other arrangements with, French monasteries. Such charters are of especial

[10] 'In fine cuius anni, appropinquante quadragesima, venit Andegavim papa Romanus Urbanus et ammonuit gentem nostram ut irent Jerusalem expugnaturi gentilem populum qui civitatem illam et totam terram christianorum usque Constantinopolim occupaverant': *Fragmentum historiae Andegavensis*, in *Chroniques des comtes d'Anjou et des seigneurs d'Amboise*, ed. L. Halphen and R. Poupardin (Paris, 1913), pp. 237–8. Lent began on 27 February.

[11] *Chronicon sancti Maxentii Pictavensis*, s.a. 1096, in *Chroniques des églises d'Anjou*, ed. P. Marchegay and É. Mabille (Paris, 1869), p. 412. Although compiled in the twelfth century, the *Chronicon* is made up from earlier material.

[12] Bernold, *Chron. s.a.* 1096, *M.G.H. Scriptorum*, v. 464.

value because they were usually drafted, not by the donors, but by the monks themselves. Thus, they express ideas which had the approval of monks who, if they obeyed Urban's directives, were not themselves involved in the Crusade. If the monks were thus somewhat detached from the Crusaders' enthusiasms, they were in an excellent position to know Urban's mind. His French journey of 1095-6 and his organization of the Crusade were largely undertaken with the assistance of the monasteries.[13] Thus, the language of the small number of monastic charters which refer to the Crusade, provides significant if indirect evidence of the Pope's intentions.

Some particularly early evidence occurs in the charters of Cluny, of which Urban was a sometime Grand Prior. He stayed there just before he went to Clermont, and Abbot Hugh of Cluny was himself present at the Council. Cluny's understanding of the Crusade was formed in the closest touch with Urban, and it emerges as early as a charter of 12 April 1096. In it, a prospective Crusader was said to be involved 'in this manifold and great awakening and campaign of Christian people who are contending to go to Jerusalem, to fight on God's behalf against the heathen and the Saracens'; he was further said to be going on the pilgrimage (*peregrinatio*) to Jerusalem. A further, but undated, charter of 1096 refers to the impending departure of two brothers for Jerusalem 'in expeditione'.[14] Cluny's intimate connections with Urban make it likely that its charters were faithful to his own intentions when they referred to Jerusalem in these terms.

Other monastic charters spoke of the Crusade in a similar way. After Urban turned south on leaving the Touraine and Poitou in the spring of 1096, he did not visit the great abbey of Saint-Victor, Marseilles; but he passed within its well-organized sphere of influence. A charter of Saint-Victor, dated 24 August 1096, defined the intention of two Crusader brothers much as the Cluniac charters had done. They were going to Jerusalem, and for two reasons: to undertake a pilgrimage, and to help with the deliverance of innumerable Christian peoples from the fury of their oppressors.[15] A similar combination of motives occurs in a charter of Saint-Père, Chartres, which, although undated, clearly looks forward to the First Crusade. It also illustrates how the Crusade served Urban's purpose as expressed in his speech at Clermont, by leading men to desist from violence at home in order to seek the deliverance of Jerusalem:

> Whenever the impulse of warlike fierceness roused me [a Crusader was made to explain] I would gather about myself a band of mounted men and a crowd of followers. I would descend upon the vill and freely give the goods of the men of St. Peter to my knights for food. Now, therefore, I am going as a pilgrim (*peregre*) to Jerusalem, which is still in bondage with her sons, to secure the divine pardon that I seek for my misdeeds.[16]

[13] R. Crozet, 'Le Voyage d'Urbain II et ses négotiations avec le clergé de France', *Revue historique*, clxxix (1937), 271-310.

[14] *Recueil des chartes de l'abbaye de Cluny*, ed. A. Bruel, v (Paris, 1894), nos. 3703, 3712, pp. 51-3, 59.

[15] *Cartulaire de l'abbaye de Saint-Victor de Marseille*, ed. M. Guérard, i (Paris, 1847), no. 143, pp. 167-8.

[16] *Cartulaire de l'abbaye de Saint-Père de Chartres*, ed. M. Guérard, ii (Paris, 1840), no. xxxvi, pp. 428-9.

This theme, once again with a naming of Jerusalem, recurs in December 1096, in the cartulary of Saint-Chaffre du Monastier, a monastery situated near Le Puy which had close associations with Bishop Adhemar, Urban's legate on the Crusade.[17]

Very occasionally, there are, indeed, references to the Crusade in contemporary charters without an express mention of Jerusalem. Thus, the record of a gift to the Cluniac priory of Marcigny was dated 'in the year when Urban came to Aquitaine and summoned a Christian army to repress the ferocity of the eastern pagans'.[18] Again, on his journey home from France in 1096, Urban negotiated about the Crusade with Count Humbert II of Savoy. While the matter was being discussed, Humbert gave Cluny the priory of Bourget, and, in his charter, he spoke only of his proposed journey beyond the sea.[19] But these charters do not deny that Jerusalem was the goal; they are best regarded as incomplete statements of why men went to the Crusade.

Taken together, the charters, which come from many localities, serve to confirm the chronicles, although they lay greater emphasis upon the character of the Crusade as a pilgrimage. They testify to the centrality of Jerusalem and its military liberation in the monastic understanding of the Crusade. It is probable that this understanding reflects Urban's own intentions.

(iii) Amongst strictly contemporary letters, especial interest attaches to the single letter of St. Anselm's which refers to the Crusade. It is addressed to Bishop Osmund of Salisbury and is probably to be dated in the late summer of 1096.[20] Anselm wrote to secure the correction of the Abbot of Cerne. Amongst the charges that he brought against him, the first was that, in spite of the Pope's prohibition, he had exhorted his monks to go on the Crusade (*ire in Hierusalem*), and that he had already sent one young monk off to join it. He was himself making ready to go to Jerusalem and, with some associates, he had already bought a ship in which to travel. Anselm insisted to Osmund that he be forbidden to go, or to send his monks, to Jerusalem. Osmund was also to issue orders to every monastery of his diocese that no monk should dare to venture upon the Crusade (*ut nullus monachus hoc iter Hierosolimitanum praesumat arripere*).

It is most remarkable that, in the course of a short letter written in England

---

[17] The Abbot of Saint-Chaffre referred to three knights, 'Jerosolimitanum iter ad expugnandos barbaros arripientes'. They had agreed to desist from unjust demands upon the monks and to seek absolution from the bishop: *Cartulaire de l'abbaye de St-Chaffre du Monastier*, ed. U. Chevalier (Paris, 1884), no. cccxcviii, pp. 139–41.

[18] *Le Cartulaire de Marcigny-sur-Loire (1045–1144)*, ed. J. Richard (Dijon, 1957), no. 119, pp. 87–8.

[19] S. Guichenon, *Histoire généalogique de la royale maison de Savoye*, iv (Lyons, 1660), 27.

[20] *Ep.* 195, *S. Anselmi Cantuariensis archiepiscopi opera omnia*, ed. F. S. Schmitt, iv (Edinburgh, 1949), 85–6. The date is uncertain. Schmitt's suggestion of 1095 is too early, since the Council of Clermont did not meet until late November 1095. Moreover, Anselm asked for his letter to be sent to the Bishops of Exeter, Bath, and Worcester. The see of Worcester was vacant from the death of Wulfstan II on 19–20 January 1095 until the succession of Samson, consecrated 8 June 1096; this date is the *terminus a quo*. The letter is likely to have been written very soon after it. Anselm twice said that he acted in consultation and agreement with King William II, who was however absent and beyond easy communication when he actually wrote. This points to a date immediately after William left for Normandy in the late summer of 1096. For the events of this summer, see Eadmer, *Historia novorum in Anglia*, ed. M. Rule (London, Rolls Series, 1884), pp. 74–6.

and at so early a date, Anselm should have three times referred to the Crusade in terms of an intention 'ire in Hierusalem' (or 'in Hierosolymam'), and once as an 'iter Hierosolimitanum'. There can be no doubt about the form in which it presented itself to him. This form is likely to have been determined by Urban's own intentions; for there was an intermediary between the Pope and the Archbishop who is likely to have made them authentically known to him. Early in 1096, the high Gregorian, Abbot Jarento of Saint-Bénigne, Dijon, was sent to the Anglo-Norman lands 'ex praecepto papae' in connection with the Crusade. He came to England and negotiated with William II; then, in Normandy, he brought about an agreement between the King and Duke Robert, and saw the latter off to the Crusade.[21] Jarento may well have influenced those who, according to Eadmer, persuaded Anselm that it was right and proper (*et rationis esse et honestatis*) for him to assist the King in raising the money which he advanced to his brother for the Crusade upon the security of the Duchy. At all events, Anselm seems to have considerably revised his own opinions. For his letter of 1096 and his attitude to the 'expeditio Ierosolimitana' as Eadmer recorded it, demand close comparison with an earlier letter written, probably in 1086, during a visit to England while he was still Abbot of Bec.[22] In it, he urged a young Norman layman not to follow his elder brother to the east in the military service of Byzantium. Anselm pleaded with him, instead, to become a monk at Bec:

> I warn, advise, beg, beseech, and command you as one most dear, to renounce the Jerusalem which is now not a vision of peace but of tribulation and the treasures of Constantinople and Babylon which must be seized with bloodstained hands. Embark instead upon the way to the heavenly Jerusalem, which is the vision of peace, where you will find real treasures which may only be had by those who despise the others.

Between 1086 and 1096, Anselm's attitude clearly changed. As abbot of Bec, he deprecated the departure of Norman laymen to fight for the Byzantine Emperor against his pagan enemies; but as Archbishop of Canterbury, he was prepared to concede, if perhaps reluctantly, that the Crusade was an enterprise which the English Kingdom might support. In 1096, he is only known to have forbidden the participation of monks, about whom he knew that Urban himself had legislated.[23] His change of attitude is most readily explicable if it were a response to a clear and specific papal approach about the Crusade, such as Abbot Jarento might have brought; for to such expressions of the papal will, Anselm felt a duty of obedience that overrode his personal opinions. This obedience would have been the more readily forthcoming if Urban had sought it, not merely for such help to Byzantium as Anselm had earlier so unfavourably regarded, but for an 'iter Hierosolimi-

[21] Hugh of Flavigny, *Chronicon*, ii, *M.G.H. Scriptorum*, viii. 474–5. Urban had summoned Anselm to Clermont, and Anselm had sent Boso, a monk of Bec, to represent him; but Boso's return was long delayed on account of illness: *Vita abbatum Beccensium, Vita Bosonis*, 2, *Beati Lanfranci opera*, ed. J. A. Giles, i (Oxford, 1844), 328–9.

[22] *Ep.* 117, *Opera omnia*, iii (Edinburgh, 1946), 252–5.

[23] Anselm always maintained his opposition to the departure of monks for Jerusalem: *Ep.* 410, *Opera omnia*, v (Edinburgh, 1951), 355.

tanum' which was different, and to which the Pope himself had assigned wider and more spiritual ends.

(iv) Amongst the *excitatoria* by which propagandists sought to recruit and encourage participants in the First Crusade, there is one that may come still nearer both in time and in place to Urban's own activity in summoning the Crusade. It is the so-called 'Encyclical of Pope Sergius IV'.[24] This document purports to be Sergius's summons to the Christians of North Italy and elsewhere to respond to the destruction of the Church of the Holy Sepulchre at Jerusalem in 1009 by the mad Fatimid Caliph Hakim: Sergius exhorted them to follow him to the Holy Land, to destroy its oppressors, and to restore Christ's burial-place. The genuineness of the 'Encyclical' was for long a matter of debate.[25] But A. Gieysztor has advanced strong arguments that it was fabricated as propaganda for the First Crusade at the Cluniac monastery of Moissac, near Toulouse; it originated in connection with Urban's stay there in May 1096, 'to create a respectable precedent so that all savor of the novel and the dangerous would be eliminated from the project of the expedition'.[26] A date just after Urban's departure is, perhaps, preferable to one during his stay: it would be hard to account for the execrable Latin if papal clerks had been at hand; and Urban's visit to Moissac was a brief one. But there is every likelihood that the 'Encyclical' originated at Moissac, or at some other monastery, in the wake of Urban's journey; that it was the work of monks who sought to encourage recruits for the Crusade; and that they acted from recent and intimate acquaintance with Urban and his intentions. The almost exclusive preoccupation of the 'Encyclical' with the liberation of Jerusalem indicates that Urban was well known to have had it prominently amongst his aims.

(v) Urban's own letters and rulings of 1095 and 1096 about the Crusade point to the same conclusion as does the evidence which has so far been examined. They do much to bridge the gap that still remains open between the early spring of 1096 and Clermont itself.

It is, indeed, the case that, during the last two years of his pontificate and in the context of Spanish affairs, Urban was twice to refer to the Crusade in terms of a general purpose of defeating the Saracens, with no reference whatsoever to Jerusalem. In 1098, his privilege for the see of Huesca expressed his gratitude that the distresses of Christian peoples were being relieved and that the Christian faith was being exalted in two continents—by Christian victories over the Turks in Asia as over the Moors in Spain.[27] Soon afterwards, he wrote to the Counts of Besalù, Empurias, and Roussillon, urging them, if they were minded to campaign in Asia, that they should instead campaign at Tarragona, nearer home. He said that it was for the knights of other provinces to help the Asian Christians: let them rather help their own

---

[24] A. Gieysztor, 'The Genesis of the Crusades: the Encyclical of Sergius IV (1009–12)', *Medievalia et Humanistica*, v (1948), 3–23; vi (1950), 3–34. The text is printed on pp. 33–4 of the second article.

[25] Amongst those who accepted it as genuine was Erdmann: *Die Entstehung des Kreuzzugsgedankens*, pp. 102–6.

[26] *Art. cit., Med. et Hum.*, vi (1950), 26, cp. p. 21.

[27] *Ep.* ccxxxvii, J. P. Migne. *Patrologia Latina* [=*P.L.*], cli. 504–6.

neighbours.[28] But a presentation of the Crusade in these general terms is to be expected in a Spanish context, which provides no parallel to make natural a mention of Jerusalem.[29]

The remaining, and much earlier, sources for Urban's own view of the Crusade indicate that, in intending to bring help to all the Eastern Churches, he had Jerusalem and its liberation particularly and constantly in mind. As early as 1089, he was beginning to think of Jerusalem in relation to Christian action on the frontiers with Islam. Once again, the context is a Spanish one. Urban wrote to encourage the ecclesiastical and lay magnates of Tarragona and Barcelona to help the material rehabilitation of the Church and city of Tarragona. He promised them the same spiritual benefits as would accrue from a pilgrimage to Jerusalem.[30] His letter foreshadows such an amalgamation of the ideas of pilgrimage to Jerusalem and of the vindication of Christendom against Islam, as the charter evidence points to in his preaching at Clermont and after.

His own pronouncements of 1095–6 tend to confirm that this was how his mind developed. They strongly suggest that he named Jerusalem as the goal of the Crusade; that he did so in terms of its military liberation; and that he also attached to the expedition the spiritual benefits of a pilgrimage. Thus, on 22 July 1096, when Urban received from Count Raymond of Provence the renewed subjection to the Roman Church of the monastery of Saint-Gilles, Urban's charter referred to the Count as 'in Hierosolimitanam expeditionem iturus'.[31] Again, the well-known letters which Urban wrote concerning the Crusade to all the faithful in Flanders and to the clergy and people of Bologna, testify, although with some difference of emphasis, to his concern to deliver the city of Jerusalem from the pagan yoke. The undated letter to the Flemings, usually assigned to late December 1095, first refers, in general, to the oppression of the Churches of God in eastern parts. But it was this oppression and that of the Holy City of Christ together that constituted the 'calamitas' which moved him to initiate the Crusade:

> We believe that you are already well informed about the barbaric fury which, by its attacks which move us to compassion, has laid waste the Churches of God in eastern parts and, moreover, what is shocking to mention, has delivered the Holy City of Christ, made illustrious by his passion and resurrection, together with its churches, into an intolerable servitude. Grieving as was due in face of such a calamity, we journeyed in France and in large measure stirred up the rulers and subjects of that land to seek the liberation of the Eastern Churches.[32]

[28] P. F. Kehr, *Papsturkunden in Spanien, i, Katalanien,* no. 23, *Abhandlungen der Gesellschaft der Wissenschaften zu Göttingen, ph.-hist. Klasse, N.F.,* xviii, pt. 2 (1926), pp. 287–8. For the date, see Erdmann, *Die Entstehung des Kreuzzugsgedankens,* p. 294.

[29] A further incident which has been interpreted as telling against Urban's concern with Jerusalem is his sending back of Archbishop Bernard of Toledo when, perhaps in 1099, he appeared in Rome on his way to join the Crusade in Syria: Roderic of Toledo, *De rebus Hispaniae,* vi. 27, *Hispaniae illustratae . . . scriptores,* ed. A. Schott, ii (Frankfurt, 1603), 107. But Roderic expressly says that Urban sent Bernard back because clerks should not desert their churches. He tends to confirm that Urban named Jerusalem at Clermont: Bernard, who had been at the Council, went towards Syria 'eius [Urban's] indulgentiis provocatus', while Urban preached the Crusade 'eo quod ab Agarenis Hierosolymitana civitas tenebatur'.

[30] *Ep.* xx, *P.L.* cli. 302–3.   [31] *Ep.* cciv, *P.L.* cli. 477–8.

[32] H. Hagenmæyer, *Die Kreuzzugsbriefe aus den Jahren 1088–1100* (Innsbruck, 1901),

Urban's letter to the Bolognese, written from Pavia on 19 September 1096, contains no such reference to the liberation of all the Eastern Churches. Jerusalem comes right to the fore, so that Urban was concerned only with it and its liberation:

> We have heard that some of you have formed a desire to journey to Jerusalem, and you are aware that this pleases us greatly. Know that we remit the whole penance due for their sins to all who set out, not from greed of this world's goods, but simply for the salvation of their souls and for the liberation of the Church (*ecclesiae liberatione*).[33]

His preoccupation with the Holy City is readily explicable, and does not point to a subsequent change in his thought. For he wrote to confirm the spiritual benefits of the Crusade, and to insist upon his rules about who might and who might not go on it; he had no need to refer to any wider objective than Jerusalem.

However, he reverted to the Eastern Christians as a whole as well as to Jerusalem in another, seldom noticed letter which he sent on 7 October 1096 from Cremona to the monks of Vallombrosa. He wrote to repeat his prohibition, of which he also reminded the Bolognese, of the departure to the Crusade of clerks and monks without the leave of their bishops and abbots. He also restated his intention for the Crusade. As he envisaged it, it was essentially the self-dedication (*oblatio*) of the knights who had set out for Jerusalem in order to liberate the enslaved part of Christendom. He had stirred up their hearts to take part in such an 'expeditio' with a view to restoring the former liberty of Christians.[34] This letter may well be taken as embodying the most balanced statement that survives of Urban's own view of the Crusade. Not only does it recapitulate the points made in his two earlier letters, but it tends to confirm the other evidence that he preached a Crusade having Jerusalem as its goal, by which he intended to effect the liberation of it as of all the Eastern Churches.

That Jerusalem and its liberation were central to Urban's plan for the Crusade from its very inception is, finally, suggested by a piece of evidence from the Council of Clermont itself. Its canons survive in a version preserved

---

no. ii, pp. 136–7. It is difficult to agree with Mayer's interpretation of the letter, that Urban spoke principally of the liberation of the Eastern Churches and only incidentally of Jerusalem: *Geschichte der Kreuzzüge*, p. 17. It would be truer to say that he saw the servitude of the Holy City as the most challenging aspect of the 'calamitas' of all the Eastern Churches.

[33] Hagenmeyer, *op. cit.* no. iii, pp. 137–8. The phrase 'ecclesiae liberatione' should probably be referred to the Church of Jerusalem, rather than to the Church at large, in the light of canon ii of Clermont, quoted below.

[34] W. Wiederhold, 'Papsturkunden in Florenz', no. 6, *Nachrichten von der Königl. Gesellschaft der Wissenschaften zu Göttingen, ph.-hist. Kl.* (1901), Heft 3, pp. 313–14. The relevant portion of this letter, which Hagenmayer did not print, is as follows: 'Audivimus quosdam vestrum cum militibus qui Ierusalem liberandae christianitatis gratia tendunt, velle proficisci. Recta quidem oblatio, sed non recta divisio; nos enim ad hanc expeditionem militum animos instigavimus, qui armis suis Saracenorum feritatem declinare et christianorum possint libertati pristinae restituere: eos autem qui de relicto seculo spirituali se militiae devoverunt, nos nec arma baiulare nec iter hoc inire volumus, immo etiam prohibemus. Porro religiosos clericos sive monachos in comitatu hoc proficisci sine episcoporum vel abbatum suorum licentia secundum disciplinam sanctorum canonum interdicimus. Videat ergo religionis vestrae prudentia, ne in negotio hoc aut sedis apostolicae contemptum aut animarum vestrarum periculum incurratis.'

by one of the participants, Bishop Lambert of Arras. Of his thirty-two canons, the second alone directly concerns the Crusade. It refers in the clearest terms to Jerusalem as being its goal, and the spiritual benefits to be gained from reaching Jerusalem are attached to an intention to liberate it, not merely to journey there: 'If any man sets out from pure devotion, not for reputation or monetary gain, to liberate the Church of God at Jerusalem, his journey shall be reckoned in place of all penance.' [35]

The evidence that has been reviewed all suggests that Urban had Jerusalem in mind from the very beginning of his plans for the Crusade. It may well never be possible to disprove a theory such as Erdmann's. But there is nothing stronger to support it than an interpretation of the letter to the Flemings which probably understates the place of Jerusalem in it. There is no early evidence that positively and unambiguously suggests that there was a major change in Urban's purpose for the Crusade as the months went by, or that he capitulated to public opinion as regards Jerusalem. The alternative view is not only more likely but also better documented. Urban at all times seems to have preached Jerusalem as the goal of the Crusade, and to have looked upon it as standing at the heart and centre of the Eastern Churches which he desired to free from pagan domination.

[35] J. D. Mansi, *Sacrorum conciliorum nova et amplissima collectio*, xx. 816.

XVII

THE LATIN KINGDOM OF JERUSALEM

DURING THE PAST TWENTY YEARS or so, students of the Crusades have become familiar with the many articles by Joshua Prawer, professor at the Hebrew University of Jerusalem. These articles have already set in motion a reappraisal of the history and institutions of the Crusader states of Syria and Palestine.[1] The appearance in a European language of his full-scale history of the Latin kingdom of Jerusalem, published in Hebrew in 1963, has, therefore, been eagerly awaited. It has now become available in an excellent French translation (*Histoire du royaume latin de Jérusalem*. Translated by G. Nahon. Paris: Éditions du Centre national de la recherche scientifique. i (1969), 686 pp.; ii (1970), 618 pp. £21·00 the set). These two volumes more than fulfil our expectations. They will serve for many years as a standard work not only upon the Latin Kingdom, but also on very many of the wider issues of Crusading history.

As the seventy pages of invaluable select bibliography which begin the first volume show, Prawer draws upon the whole range of modern Crusading scholarship. But—one is reminded of the late A. H. M. Jones's work on the later Roman Empire—the real value of his conclusions is that they stand four-square upon an immediate and unprejudiced familiarity with both Christian and Moslem sources, to which he adds a good deal of fresh and valuable material from Jewish writers. His acquaintance with Palestinian topography is such as only a resident can command, and he puts it to the fullest use; for example, he makes the campaign leading to the battle of Hattin (1187) intelligible as never before. The elements of similarity and, still more, of contrast between the medieval Crusader kingdom and the modern state of Israel, though seldom expressed, are always suggestive in the background; thus, the precariousness of the Crusader settlement and the importance of its relations with the wider world are thrown up in high relief.

So far as the Latin kingdom itself is concerned, the most influential special studies of recent years have been those of La Monte,[2] still valuable for its discussion of particular institutions but outdated in its understanding of feudal development, and of Richard,[3] a fine and comprehensive account of the kingdom in all its aspects, which itself represented a major step forward of lasting value. Prawer seeks to develop the subject in two general respects. First, he shows how fundamental to the history of the kingdom at every juncture from its inauguration in 1099 up to the fall of Acre in 1291 was the problem of insufficient Frankish population and, therefore, of deficient human and material resources. Earlier historians have, of course, been aware

[1] Aspects of Prawer's work have been made familiar by Sir Steven Runciman's Creighton Lecture, *The Families of Outremer: the Feudal Nobility of the Kingdom of Jerusalem, 1099–1291* (London, 1960), and by the useful chapters on Crusading history in general in J. Riley-Smith, *The Knights of St. John in Jerusalem and Cyprus, 1050–1310* (London, 1967). H. E. Mayer's *Geschichte der Kreuzzüge* (Stuttgart, 1965) is much influenced by Prawer's articles.
[2] J. La Monte, *Feudal Monarchy in the Latin Kingdom of Jerusalem* (Cambridge, Mass., 1932).
[3] J. Richard, *Le Royaume latin de Jérusalem* (Paris, 1953).

of the problem, but Prawer largely breaks new ground by showing how endemic and decisive it was. Palestine was conquered but never really colonized. The First Crusade left few settlers behind, and the Crusade of 1101, which might have made all the difference, in fact brought little help. The initial military establishment of the kingdom was probably only some 300 knights and 1,200 foot soldiers. Even by the 1180s, the Frankish population is not likely to have risen above 100–120,000, with a fighting strength of perhaps 1,500 knights and 20,000 foot soldiers.[4] The Franks of all social classes were almost entirely town-dwellers, and the countryside remained largely peopled by an indigenous and potentially hostile population, three or four times more numerous than the Frankish upper crust. If demographic weakness gives the history of the kingdom a depressing unity of theme, it also makes it a tale of shallow roots and ineffective institutions. Comparisons between the 'first' and 'second' kingdoms, or large generalizations about them, give place to the tracing of change and dislocation from reign to reign and from decade to decade. The 'first' kingdom under Fulk of Anjou and Baldwin III was very different from what it had been under Baldwin I and Baldwin II, and it was different again under Amalric I and his successors.

Secondly, Prawer consolidates the work which he has done in many articles by showing how considerably the structure of the first kingdom was altered.[5] Many historians, including La Monte, have regarded the kingdom as having changed little because it was from its inception the classic case of a feudal society in which rights and authority were denied to the king in the interests of the nobility. If the Norman kingdoms of Sicily and England stand at one extreme as centralized feudal states in which the king's rights were safeguarded, the kingdom of Jerusalem, even more than early Capetian France, stands at the other extreme as the home of a 'pure feudalism', based upon the barons' rights. After the success of the First Crusade, the feudal nobility established itself first; the king whom it set up had to accept its predominance and that of the law which the feudal High Court declared and upheld. Other historians besides Prawer have criticized such a static picture of feudalism in the kingdom, and have held that the king's power grew to be an effective one. Richard, in particular, associates the achieving of strong monarchical authority with the reign of Amalric I (1163–74). He draws an analogy with Capetian France. Rather as the twelfth- and thirteenth-century Capetians gradually built up their authority in the French state by accumulation as reign followed reign, so, up to Amalric, did the kings of Jerusalem. The principal evidence for this was Amalric's *Assise sur la ligece*. By it, the king claimed the liege homage of all rear-vassals, thus—according to some historians—outdoing even the Capetians by, in effect, repeating King William I of England's Oath of Salisbury in 1086.

Prawer regards the Capetian analogy as inadmissible and misleading. Amalric's *Assise* must stand at the centre of any discussion, and Prawer

---

[4] As a comparison, Saladin had some 12,000 horsemen at Hattin.

[5] Three of Prawer's most important articles, which it is helpful to read with his book, are: 'Les premiers temps de la féodalité dans le royaume latin de Jérusalem', *Tijdschrift voor rechtsgeschiednis* (= *Revue d'histoire du droit*) xxii (1954), 401–24; 'La noblesse et le régime féodal du royaume latin de Jérusalem', *Le Moyen Âge*, lxv (1959), 41–74; 'Estates, Communities and the Constitution of the Latin Kingdom', *Proceedings of the Israel Academy of Sciences and Humanities*, ii, no. 6 (Jerusalem, 1966), 1–27, 39–42. The last two articles are available, in English, in *Lordship and Community in Medieval Europe*, ed. F. L. Cheyette (New York, etc., 1968), pp. 156–79, 376–403.

contends that it promoted the nobility's interests far more than the king's. It did, indeed, do something for the king by reserving to him the liege homage of all rear-vassals. But this was not an altogether unprecedented step: particular cases of such liege homage can be found before the *Assise*. After it the increasing stratification of the Frankish nobility into a few great lords and a multitude of impoverished, town-dwelling knights left the rear-vassals wholly unfitted to assist the crown in the way that in England the knights of the shire assisted the Angevin kings. The most important consequence of the *Assise* was, therefore, one which did not favour the crown. At least in theory, all members of the noble classes, whether higher or lower, secured membership of the High Court. By this novel step, the *Assise* established the legal identity of the whole nobility. In the High Court, it became a separate estate with its own solidarity as against the crown. The vertical links in society created by liege homage were more than counteracted by the horizontal links which henceforth bound the barons to each other.

It had not always been so in the kingdom of Jerusalem. Prawer shows that, at least in relation to their own Frankish subjects, the kings were never stronger than in the earliest days of the kingdom. In number, these subjects were a mere handful. Many of them were relatively humble followers of Godfrey of Bouillon, who were used to the effective feudal lordship of Lower Lorraine. Their prospects of survival and prosperity alike depended upon strong kingship. The early kings were favourably placed to rule as well as to reign, and they did so. Even Amalric I's brother and predecessor Baldwin III (1143–63) could and did determine cases in which a lord risked forfeiture of his fief by a simple royal judgement passed without the intervention of any court. Under Amalric, the setback to royal power was partly caused by the (very un-Capetian) growth and consolidation, generation by generation, of the baronial lordships, at the king's expense. Up to about 1130 they were hardly a factor in the life of the kingdom, for the dearth of population and resources was such as to prevent their emergence. Between 1130 and 1160 an increasing number were established. Thereafter there were few new foundations, but those which existed grew in wealth, power and judicial identity, to the king's disadvantage. Lesser lords were too impoverished to take advantage of the enhanced legal standing which Amalric's *Assise* afforded them, whereas Reynald of Châtillon, as lord of Transjordan, could boast to King Guy (in 1186) that he was no less lord over his territory than Guy was over his own.

English historians have so far shown some signs of reluctance to accept Prawer's construction of the *Assise sur la ligece*. There has been a tendency to keep much nearer to Richard's view that monarchical authority was not seriously infringed up to the death of the leper-king Baldwin IV in 1185. It is therefore worth asking how plausible Prawer's view seems, now that it can be considered as part and parcel of his fuller account of the kingdom. To the present reviewer it makes better sense than the contrary one. The circumstances in which the *Assise* was drawn up will always be obscure, but they appear to have arisen from Amalric's campaign against Gerard of Sidon who had confiscated a vassal's fief without the judgement of a court. Amalric needed the barons' help against Gerard. It would therefore be paradoxical if an assise which originated in the king's need to purchase baronial support against one of their number should have been decisive in exalting monarchical authority. In the light of Prawer's account of how baronial power in the kingdom grew, it is reasonable to look for an analogy to the *Assise* not in Capetian France or Norman England, but in Hohenstaufen Germany. Amalric's situation with regard to his magnates was not unlike that of Frederick Barbarossa in 1180, when he had to make large concessions to the princes in order to secure their support against Henry the Lion. Seen in this way, the provisions of the *Assise* which mattered most, in the short term as well as in the long, are more than likely to have been the concessions to the barons which made Heinrich Mitteis long ago call the *Assise* 'the Magna Carta of the feudal vassals' corporate right to resist (*Widerstandsrecht*)'. Again, it is true that the anonymous law-book known as the *Livre au roi*, of *c*. 1198–1205, sought to uphold the early twelfth-century royal right to disseise in some cases without a judgement. But from Amalric's time we look in vain for such forfeitures as Baldwin III had been able to effect: the king might proceed against a baron only by strict process of feudal law. That is to say, from the time of the *Assise* the king was denied in practice anything like the exercise of *vis et voluntas* which was the standby of his Angevin contemporaries in England. Such a restriction is more likely to have brought about the atrophy of royal power than its increase.

Certainly the institutions of the later twelfth-century kingdom remained starved and stunted. It is symptomatic that at no time did the kings manage to supplement, let alone dispense with, the system of government by great household officers—steward, constable, marshal, chamberlain and chancellor—which the earliest Crusaders brought with them from eleventh-century Europe. By 1200 Capetian France had largely outgrown it; the kings of Jerusalem were quite unable to do likewise. Instead, in the generation before Hattin the kings associated the magnates who came from Europe with the court, thereby exacerbating the conflicts between 'native' and 'newcomer' barons which rent the kingdom. At the same time, the Military Orders came to the fore as élite and always mobilized fighting forces backed by human and material resources in many parts of Christendom; but their very indispensability made them, like the foreign merchant enclaves in the coastal towns, increasingly independent of the king. Familiar in themselves, such weaknesses assume their true significance when set against the harsh facts of the underpopulation of the kingdom and the arrested development of its political and feudal institutions. The full effects of the declining power of the monarchy may not have been fully apparent until after Hattin. But there are strong grounds for tracing its causes well back into the history of the 'first' kingdom, and for seeing the *Assise sur la ligece* as prominent among them.

A corollary of this conclusion is that the elements of disintegration which became open and effective in the thirteenth century were very strongly foreshadowed under the 'first' kingdom. The thirteenth-century kingdom has not been so much studied as the earlier one; in his second volume Prawer offers not so much a drastic reappraisal of established positions as an examination of all aspects of the kingdom with an altogether new range and depth. In general he penetrates more deeply the territory which Richard has well mapped out. Thus, he cites with approval Richard's suggestive phrase that the mid-thirteenth century saw the 'denationalization of the kingdom': a disintegration of the Frankish identity which had persisted for so long as the line of Lotharingian and Angevin kings remained. The time of the absentee

Hohenstaufen kings from 1225 to 1268, in particular, saw the movement towards 'a kingdom without a king, a republic without a president'. The *haute noblesse*, building upon the *Assise* of Amalric I, insisted upon the rights of their class by a punctilious legalism, enshrined in the works of such lawyer-barons as Philip of Novara and John of Ibelin, which became an end in itself. In Prawer's words, 'The Frankish nobility raised the institutions of the kingdom to the level of an ideal and sacrosanct constitution, to which they were prepared to sacrifice both themselves and the kingdom'. While the baronage was thus forced back upon itself, the kingdom was dissolved into a congeries of alien groups with enclaves in Palestine. The Military Orders, divided amongst themselves, regarded the kingdom as only a pretext for their activities elsewhere, while the Italian merchant cities, taking advantage of concessions made in the earliest days of the First kingdom, regarded the coastal towns only as enclaves to support their wider commercial concerns. As always, the demographic problems of the kingdom were fundamental: there were not the men in Palestine, nor was there the immigration to Palestine, for matters to be otherwise.

Prawer's concern with the demographic problems of a conquered but never satisfactorily colonized country justifies the generous attention which he gives to the European homeland of the Crusaders. It compels him to ask why the Crusaders came, and what factors affected from generation to generation their willingness to defend or colonize the conquests of the First Crusade. He has, therefore, a great deal to say about the changing forms of Crusading and anti-Crusading propaganda in the west, his work providing the fullest overall guide to these subjects which is available.

Prawer holds, almost certainly rightly, that economic explanations of the origins of Crusading, such as pressure of growing population in Western Europe, are insufficient to explain the movement to the East: expansion in the West could and did absorb most of the population. The main clues are to be found in the realm of religious ideas, and Prawer rightly lays stress upon the attractive power of Jerusalem in the eleventh-century West. The point is critical for our understanding of the fortunes of the Latin kingdom. For a kingdom founded upon a wave of enthusiasm for Jerusalem could survive only if the enthusiasm for Jerusalem were sustained. Prawer shows how, when the Second Crusade was preached, Jerusalem was already losing its centrality in men's minds. He analyses St. Bernard's preaching to show how the destination of the Crusade was coming to matter less than the state of mind in which the Crusaders set out. Spiritual preparation for the Crusade —the cleansing and sanctification of the individual soul—was assuming a larger significance than the defence of Jerusalem or of any particular Christian land. The chief criticism of Prawer at this point must be that he discusses the motivation of the early Crusades exclusively in terms of the biblical idea of Jerusalem. Other themes were being developed, and many of them helped to detach the Crusade from a necessary connection with Jerusalem. To give but one example, very much early crusading ideology may be regarded as a development of eleventh-century ideas about monasticism and penance. By the time of the Second Crusade, the monastic commonplace that monastic vows were a second baptism which cleansed men from sin as baptism does, became adapted to the Crusaders' vow: 'Verily, dear sons, reborn of a new baptism of repentance, you have put on Christ once more, you have received again the garment of innocence to keep it stainless.'[6] At Clermont in 1095, what counted in place of all penance had been the fulfilling of the Crusading vow by actually reaching Jerusalem; now, it was the first undertaking of the vow that won men grace. It was of less importance whether it was fulfilled in Jerusalem, or in Portugal, or amongst the Wends—or, in the long run, against the internal enemies of Western Christendom. The Crusade was becoming independent of Jerusalem.

The Holy Places would always draw pilgrims; such events as the loss of Edessa or Jerusalem itself would prick men's hearts; and popes would issue Crusading bulls. But if Jerusalem was to continue to attract men to defend and colonize the Holy Land, despite the turn taken by Western ideas about Crusading, it had to be seen to deserve their help. It rapidly ceased to do so. In Prawer's words, 'The Latin kingdom . . . quickly became a lay state, perhaps even more secular than the states of Europe.' Early experiments in theocracy failed, and three of the first four patriarchs were deposed for their unworthiness. The almost immediate failure of the kingdom to invest itself with a religious identity was compounded by its ultimate loss of a national identity. The kingdom of Jerusalem offered no real incentive for newcomers from the west to come as more than pilgrims and visitors. Starved of resources of its own, it failed to attract colonizers or defenders in sufficient numbers to make it permanently viable.

Prawer deals with the Moslem East no less trenchantly than with the Christian West. Each of the great Moslem enemies of the Crusaders, from Zengi to Baybars, is considered in a fresh and stimulating way. His reassessment of Saladin merits especial attention. It is a reaction against a recent tendency to idealize him. Historians have, it is true, recognized Saladin's great shortcomings as a strategist and administrator, and there is no gainsaying the impermanence of his rallying of the Moslem world. But he has been characterized as 'an utterly simple and transparently honest man', who showed single-minded and consistent dedication to the *Jihad* against the Christians and to the task of restoring the reign of law within the Islamic world.[7] While in no way denying Saladin's greatness, Prawer points the way towards a more critical view. For him, Saladin is a man who carefully built up his personal authority by the skilful and systematic use of diplomacy and propaganda. It was the task of followers like Imad ed-Din and al-Fadil so to establish Saladin's name by letters and dispatches to all parts of the Moslem world that he could overcome his rivals within it and emerge as the supreme champion of Islam. At the climax of Saladin's career after the capture of Jerusalem, Imad ed-Din was sending off over seventy letters a day! Saladin's biographies completed the process of image-building: their number is no 'fortunate conjunction' (Gibb), but evidence of his followers' mastery of propaganda media. Much of our evidence about Saladin tells us about him not as he was, but as he was at pains to appear.

Prawer sees him as a leader whose character and role both underwent development. At first, like Zengi before him and like many a young officer of his own generation, he was out to carve a career for himself. Then, after

---

[6] *De expugnatione Lyxbonensi*, ed. C. W. David (New York, 1936), p. 72, cf. p. 154.

[7] Cf. H. A. R. Gibb, 'The Achievement of Saladin', *Bulletin of the John Rylands Library*, xxxv (1952–3), 44–60. For another, more critical assessment, C. Cahen, 'Ayyubids', *The Encyclopaedia of Islam*, i (new edn., 1960), 797–8. A modern biography of Saladin is badly needed.

Nur ed-Din's death, he emerged as an autonomous prince. Unscrupulously using Nur ed-Din's son as a means, Saladin sought to take over all his lands; we recall Gibbon's censure that 'it was only for a kingdom that Saladin would deviate from the rule of equity': at a lower level, the keeping of a good name was too necessary to be put at risk. Again, the destruction of the kingdom of Jerusalem was not always his first concern; it became so only as the fruit of mature experience, and after he had acquired the lordship of Moslem Syria. Neither a Machiavellian nor an idealist, Saladin should be seen as a man of his time.

This estimate of Saladin, together with Prawer's insistence upon his defeats as well as his victories, is sufficiently critical to make him take second place as a Moslem leader, at least by implication, to Sultan Baybars of Egypt. In the light of his victories and of the long continuance of the Mameluke rule which he established, Prawer does not hesitate to call Baybars 'the greatest Moslem statesman of the Middle Ages'.[8] His treatment of the Crusading leaders is no less striking. He surprisingly, and on balance unconvincingly, blames Richard Cœur de Lion for not attacking Jerusalem: it is unlikely that Richard failed to appreciate, as did both the Military Orders and Saladin, that if Jerusalem could be taken it could not, given the resources of the kingdom, be effectively held; although it must be conceded that Prawer exposes the shortage of hard evidence that Richard did think in this way. His discussions and comparison of the Crusading achievements of the Emperor Frederick II and King Louis IX—who suffers by comparison with both Frederick and Baybars—are masterpieces of interpretation.

The scope of Prawer's volumes is such that they are far more than a history of the Latin kingdom of Jerusalem. They are, in effect, a new history of the whole Crusading movement written not from the viewpoint of the West which initiated it but of the Palestine which it sought to colonize. Whether or not Prawer's conclusions about it find acceptance in detail, and many of them will certainly generate controversy, they must be mastered by everyone who studies and teaches the Crusades.

AN EARLY RECORD AT DIJON OF THE EXPORT
OF BECKET'S RELICS

MS. 634 (379) OF THE BIBLIOTHÈQUE MUNICIPALE at Dijon is a Martyrology and Obituary of 165 folios which came from the abbey of Saint-Bénigne in the same city.[1] The Martyrology of Usuard is copied on fos. 7–61 in a twelfth-century hand. There follows a blank folio and then, on fos. 63–97, a somewhat mutilated text of the Rule of St. Benedict. The Obituary, in a twelfth-century hand with additions that reach into the early thirteenth century, occupies fos. 126v–161. The remaining contents are a miscellany which includes, in the lower half of fo. 61v following the Martyrology, a notice of a visit to Saint-Bénigne on Friday 27 April 1190 by two monks of Christ Church, Canterbury. They brought relics of Thomas Becket, and the record in the chapter book indicates that the community of Saint-Bénigne considered the gift to be of exceptional importance. The use of the word 'tunc' in the last two sentences shows that the entry was made after the monks' departure. However the handwriting is consistent with there having been no great lapse of time. The purpose of this note is to draw attention to the visit and its circumstances, and to publish a text of the notice.

The background is as follows. Thomas Becket had suffered martyrdom in Canterbury cathedral on 29 December 1170, and Pope Alexander III had canonized him in 1173. His cultus spread rapidly overseas as well as in England. The *Miracula* of William of Canterbury, who wrote between June 1172 and December 1174, referred to the circulation in France, Flanders and Italy not only of 'ampullae sancti Thomae' and such receptacles containing holy water from the scene of his death but also of other relics. On 28 July 1174 Bishop Reginald of Bath dedicated a church at Saint-Lô (dioc. Coutances) to Becket. French pilgrims came to his tomb at Canterbury; they included, in 1178, Archbishop William of Reims, and, in 1179, King Louis VII with a number of his magnates.[2] The notice in the Dijon manuscript shows that the Third Crusade provided an opportunity further to propagate Becket's cultus in Capetian France. The two monks whom it named travelled in the retinue of Archbishop Baldwin of Canterbury (1184–90), Becket's successor but one in the see. After taking the cross Baldwin went to Normandy on 6 March 1190 and joined the king, who had already crossed the Channel on 12 December. Richard left Rouen on 26 March and travelled to Marseilles by way of Vézelay and Lyons. On 30 March Baldwin was still with the king at Gisors, but thereafter he travelled separately. Nothing is known about his journey save that he joined the king at Marseilles by 1 August. Unlike the king he

[1] For a description of the manuscript, see *Catalogue générale des manuscrits des bibliothèques publiques de France*, v: *Dijon* (Paris, 1889), pp. 164–5. I should like to thank M. P. Gras, Conservateur of the Bibliothèque municipale, Dijon, for permission to publish the notice, and to the Institut de recherche et d'histoire des textes for a partial microfilm of the manuscript. I am also grateful to the late Dr. W. Urry for information and for several useful discussions, and to Dr. Henry Mayr-Harting for a stimulating conversation.

[2] *Materials for the History of Thomas Becket, Archbishop of Canterbury*, ed. J. C. Robertson and others (7 vols., Rolls Ser., 1875–85), i. 249–50, 438, 511–12, 518; *Calendar of Documents Preserved in France*, i. 323–4, no. 911; *Radulfi de Diceto Decani Lundoniensis Opera Historica*, ed. W. Stubbs (2 vols., Rolls Ser., 1876), i. 426, 432–4; ii. 285.

sailed straight to the Holy Land. He died there on 19 November during the siege of Acre.[3]

The two monks evidently visited Dijon on their way with Baldwin from Gisors to the Rhône valley and Marseilles. Nothing further is known about one called Aimery. But it comes as no surprise to find his companion, William 'Acelini', in the archbishop's entourage, although it is more remarkable that he should have been a bearer of Becket's relics. The archbishop had for long been in dispute with almost all the monks of Christ Church over his plan to set up a collegiate church at Hackington. William figures in two sources as one of the minority who supported him and so earned the bitter reproach of the remainder. First, he is named as 'Willelmus Azelinus' in three of the *Epistolae Cantuarienses* which were written soon after the crisis point of 6 October 1189, when Archbishop Baldwin sought to force Roger Norreys, another of the minority, upon the Christ Church monks as their prior. In a letter written soon after 6 October by the convent to its sub-prior, there is a reference to 'Robertum medicum et Willelmum Azelinum, qui proditores nostri diutius extiterunt': Baldwin had used them as his envoys to the monks but with no result. Another letter, written some six days later, alluded to their earlier secession: 'Discesserunt enim a nobis qui non erant ex nobis, R. medicus et Azelinus omnium pestium pessimus. Per hos duos revelata sunt abscondita nostra, et facti sunt in diabolum malum in Israel'. The 'duo apostatae', it was later remarked, became Roger Norreys's agents in ruthlessly wasting the convent's estates. On 24 November a further letter of the convent informed its sub-prior of the recent arrival at Dover of the papal legate John of Anagni. Messengers from Baldwin had travelled to inquire in what capacity he came; with them had gone Azelinus—again described as 'apostata'—and another clerk who represented Roger Norreys. According to the letter the two were not sober when they met the legate, and their mission was profitless.[4] These events marked the worst stage of the convent's relationship with Baldwin. Richard I, king since 3 September, stayed at Canterbury on his way to France from 25 November to 5 December and negotiated a compromise between them. He was followed at Canterbury on about 11 December by the papal legate. Gervase of Canterbury's account of his visit is a second source for William which confirms the picture presented by the letters. In the legate's discussion with the Christ Church monks about what should be done with their excommunicate enemies it emerges that an unnamed knight—evidently William Fitz Nigel who on 13 January 1188 had forcibly entered the convent on Archbishop Baldwin's behalf by breaking through a wall—had gained admittance by his agency: 'per manum monachi fugitivi Acelini scilicet, qui relicto conventu archiepiscopum sequebatur, omnia capituli denudans archana'.[5] The gravity of William's alienation from the convent in the later months of 1189 is plain. It is

[3] For the itineraries of Richard and Baldwin as relevant to this note, see *Chronicles and Memorials of the Reign of Richard I*, ed. W. Stubbs (2 vols., Rolls Ser., 1864–5), i. 142–53; *The Historical Works of Gervase of Canterbury*, ed. W. Stubbs (2 vols., Rolls Ser., 1879–80), i. 457–88, 523–4; *Radulfi de Diceto Opera Historica*, ii. 72, 84; *Gesta Regis Henrici secundi Benedicti abbatis*, ed. W. Stubbs (2 vols., Rolls Ser., 1867), ii. 97–8, 100, 142, 147. See also L. Landon, *The Itinerary of Richard I* (Pipe Roll Soc., li, 1935), pp. 17–39. Joseph Iscanus's brief account, in a letter to Abbot Martin of Florennes, of his meeting Baldwin in France and of his intention to travel with him to Jerusalem sheds no light on the archbishop's route (*Joseph Iscanus: Werke und Briefe*, ed. L. Gompf (Mittellateinische Studien und Texte, iv, Leiden and Cologne, 1970), p. 222, Ep. 3, cf. pp. 20–1, 71, 79, 210–11).

[4] *Chronicles and Memorials of Richard I*, ii. 311–13, 321–2, nos. 326–7, 334. Stubbs's Introduction remains the fullest account of the dispute.

[5] *Historical Works of Gervase of Canterbury*, i. 482, cf. p. 399; *Chronicles and Memorials of Richard I*, ii. 131–3, nos. 156–7, and Introduction, p. lx. For William Fitz Nigel's actions on the afternoon of Becket's death (29 Dec. 1170), see D. Knowles, *Thomas Becket* (1970), p. 141.

therefore surprising that in the following spring he should appear in the Dijon notice, not only as Baldwin's travelling companion to the Third Crusade, but also as a bearer of Becket's relics: for the store of relics was in the convent's custody. This may indicate that there had been a reconciliation between him and the convent; although it must be said that Gervase of Canterbury in no way tempers the hostility of his record. At all events, the very fact of Baldwin's journey with Canterbury monks bearing relics of Becket to a French monastery is a small indication of the success of king and legate in at least temporarily composing affairs at Canterbury.

The carrying of Becket's relics by members of Baldwin's entourage is one amongst several examples of Becket's significance for the Crusade itself. According to a late but probably reliable Canterbury tradition, during his stay at Canterbury Richard venerated Becket's tomb, and he did so again when he returned from captivity in March 1194.[6] In May 1190 Becket appeared, together with St. Edmund king and martyr and St. Nicholas, to deliver an English ship from the perils of the Bay of Biscay: as their spokesman, he declared that the three saints were 'custodes huius navigii regis Angliae'.[7] In the Holy Land the Third Crusade saw the founding at Acre of a *capella* dedicated to St. Thomas, and the establishment of the order of St. Thomas of Acre.[8] Before Acre itself Archbishop Baldwin's contingent of 200 knights and 300 other attendants fought under a 'vexillum, cui gloriosus martir Thomas inscriptus fuerat'.[9] On a false rumour reaching England of Richard I's return from captivity in Germany, Prior Geoffrey of Christ Church, Canterbury, travelled to Rouen to meet him, 'deferens secum de vestimentis beati martyris Thomae, et os quoddam de corona ipsius' as a gift to secure his favour.[10]

The Dijon notice therefore sheds a little more light on the spread of Becket's cultus, upon the sequel to Richard I's reconciliation of Archbishop Baldwin and the monks of Christ Church, and upon evidences of devotion to Becket amongst those from England who took part in the Third Crusade.

Dijon, Bibliothèque municipale, MS. 634 (379) fo. 61v

Anno ab incarnatione Domini M°C°lxxxx°, v° kl. Maii proxima vi feria ante ascensionem Domini, venerunt duo monachi Cantuarienses in ecclesia nostra et dederunt nobis de reliquiis beati Thome archiepiscopi et martýris, id est, de corio lecti ipsius, de lectisternio, de cuculla, de panno sanguine suo intincto, et de panno intincto liquore corporis sui liquefacti. Sunt autem eorum monachorum nomina Willelmus Acelini et Aýmericus, qui cum domno iam dicte Cantuarie archiepiscopo Iherosolimam tunc proficiscebantur. Erat tunc annus a passione ipsius beati Thome nonus decimus.

---

[6] See the Christ Church, Canterbury, Obituary, British Library, Arundel MS. 68 fo. 23, 6 Apr.; the Obituary is at this point of early 15th-century date, but it depends on earlier material. Cf. the 13th-century St. Albans tradition in *Rogeri de Wendover ... Flores Historiarum*, ed. H. G. Hewlett (3 vols., Rolls Ser., 1886–9), i. 46–7, and *Matthaei Parisiensis ... Historia Anglorum*, ed. F. Maddan (3 vols., Rolls Ser., 1866–9), ii. 13–14, 47.

[7] *Gesta Regis Henrici Secundi*, ii. 116–17.

[8] *Radulfi de Diceto Opera Historica*, ii. 80–1; cf. A. J. Forey, 'The military order of St. Thomas of Acre', *Eng. Hist. Rev.*, xcii (1977), 481–503, esp. 481–6.

[9] *Das Itinerarium peregrinorum*, ed. H. E. Mayer (Stuttgart, 1962), p. 349, cf. p. 82 n. 12; *Chronicles and Memorials of Richard I*, i. 116.

[10] *Materials for the History of Thomas Becket*, ii. 268–70. The chapter in question is part of a later addition (*ibid.*, p. xxiv).

INDEX

2

Ceolwulf, king of Northumbria III 505, 514, 516, 519
Chalcedon, council of (451) I 459, 461-2, 470-1, 476, 481; II 313; X 35
Charroux, council of (989/90) VII 43, 46-7; (1027/8) VII 44, 47, 52
Clement III, antipope IV 7; see also Guibert, archbishop of Ravenna
Clement II, pope IV 7
Clermont, council of (1095) V 47; VI 293; VII 56-8; X 40; XII 22; XIII 11, 23; XIV 121, 124; XV 295, 301-2, 305-6; XVI 177-82, 187-8; XVII 233
Cluny, Cluniacs V 42; VII 43, 47; IX 98; XII 3; XIII 24; XVI 182
Cologne, council of (1083) VII 64-5
Conrad II, bishop of Genoa XII 15-17, 19
Conrad II, emperor IV 2, 4-14; V 28
Conrad, king V 45; VI 286, 288-9, 293
Constantine X Ducas, emperor X 38; XII 15
Constantine I, pope X 35
Cyprian, St., bishop of Carthage I 449-50, 475-9

Daimbert, archbishop of Pisa XII 3, 12, 14, 20
Diego Gelmirez, bishop (archbishop) of Compostela XV 308
Dol, see of IX 101-4
Donatism I 450-3, 468

Ecgfrith, king of Northumbria III 517
Edwin, king of Northumbria III 505
Egbert, bishop (archbishop) of York III 516-17, 520
Egbert, monk III 512-13
Elia, archbishop of Bari IX 19-20
Erlembald of Milan IV 14; V 31-2, 34-9, 46-7; VI 291; X 28; XIII 20
Ermenfrid, bishop of Sion VIII 59-60, 67; IX 84-5, 96

Fécamp VIII 38-9, 52-3, 58-60
Felix III, pope I 456, 458-9, 462, 472-4; II 313
Ferdinand, king of Castile XV 297
Fulgentius, abbot of Afflighem XV 309

Gebuin, archbishop of Lyons IX 98-9, 102; XI 484, 486-7, 491
Gelasius I, pope I 458-9, 662-3, 472-5; II 313; IX 81, 90
Gerald of Aurillac XIII 16; XV 288-9, 294-5
Gerona, council of (1068) VII 62
Gilbert, archdeacon of Lisieux IX 84

Gildas III 506
Gisulf, prince of Salerno X 29, 31-2, 37-8
Godfrey, archbishop of Milan V 36, 39, 41
Godfrey of Bouillon, duke of Lower Lorraine XVII 230
Gratian I 448-9; II 311
Gregory I, pope I 479-80; III 503, 520, 523; IX 86-7; XIV 122
Gregory VII, pope (see also Hildebrand, archdeacon) IV 14-15; V 37, 39, 42-3; VI 289; VII 54-5, 62-4; VIII 46, 53-4; XIII 19-20, 23, 25, 27; XIV 122-4; XV 286, 291; XVI 178
Grosolanus, archbishop of Milan VI 291
Guibert, archbishop of Ravenna (see also Clement III, antipope) V 40; IX 109; X 31-2; XII 15
Guibert of Nogent XIII 23; XV 294-5; XVI 177
Guy, archbishop of Milan IV 1; V 26-9, 33, 36

Hakim, caliph XIII 12; XVI 185
Henry II, emperor IV 2, 4-6, 14; VIII 49
Henry III, emperor IV 2, 6, 13; V 25; VII 64; VIII 58, 60; IX 82; XV 288
Henry IV, emperor V 36-7, 40, 43, 45; VI 285-9; VII 64-5; VIII 60; IX 79-80, 95, 106, 108-10; X 29, 34-6, 39; XII 3, 9, 14-15, 18; XIII 20; XV 288, 304
Henry I, king of England VII 61-2; VIII 42, 66
Henry II, king of England VIII 66
Henry I, king of France VIII 41, 75
Herfast, bishop of Elmham IX 105
Hermann, bishop of Brescia VI 292-4
Hildebrand, archdeacon (see also Gregory VII, pope) V 31, 33, 36; IX 84, 87; XIII 19
Hubert, papal legate IX 84, 90, 95-7, 103-4
Hugh, abbot of Cluny X 37; XI 483-91; XV 285-6, 291, 296, 306, 309-11; XVI 182
Hugh, bishop of Die, archbishop of Lyons IX 98, 100-3, 106-7, 109; XII 17; XV 304-8
Hugh Candidus, cardinal VII 62; IX 110-11
Hugh of Chapallemont, bishop of Nevers VIII 41, 75
Hugh I, duke of Burgundy XV 291, 300
Hugh, Pisan viscount XII 12, 16, 18-19
Humbert, cardinal XIII 19, 24

ignis sacer VII 48-51, 53-4
Innocent I, pope I 455-8, 460-1, 464-8, 471, 475, 480-1; II 313